on

Equity Jurisprudence

Commentaries
on
Equity Jurisprudence
As Administered
In
England and America

By
JOSEPH STORY

One of the Justices of the Supreme Court of the United States,
and Dane Professor of Law in Harvard University

"Chancery is ordained to supply the Law, not subvert the Law"
- Lord Bacon

"His ergo ex partibus juris, quidquid aut ex ipsa re, aut ex simili, aut ex majore, minoreve, nasci videbitur, attendere, atque elicere, pertentando unamquamque partem juris, oportebit."
-Cic. De Invent. Lib. 2, cap 22.

THIRTEENTH EDITION
BY
MELVILLE M. BIGELOW, PH. D.

IN FOUR VOLUMES

Volume I

BeardBooks
Washington, D.C.

Copyright 1886 by William W. Story

Reprinted 2000 by Beard Books, Washington, D.C.

ISBN 1-58798-035-5

Printed in the United States of America

TO THE HONORABLE

WILLIAM PRESCOTT, LL.D.

Sir, — It affords me sincere gratification to be allowed to dedicate this work to you, upon your retirement from the Bar, of which you have been so long a distinguished ornament. More than one third of a century has elapsed since, upon my first admission to practice, I had the honor of forming an acquaintance with you, which has ripened into a degree of friendship of which I may be truly proud. It has been my good fortune, through the whole intermediate period, to have been a witness of your professional labors, — labors equally remarkable for the eminent ability, untiring research, profound learning, and unsullied dignity with which they were accompanied. They have brought with them the just reward due to a life of consistent principles and public spirit and private virtue, in the universal confidence and respect which have followed you in your retreat from the active scenes of business. This is a silent but expressive praise, whose true value is not easily overestimated. I trust that you may live many years to enjoy it, for the reason so finely touched by one of the great jurists of antiquity: Quia conscientia bene actæ vitæ, multorumque benefactorum recordatio jucundissima est.

JOSEPH STORY.

Cambridge, *December*, 1835.

PREFACE TO THE THIRTEENTH EDITION.

The present edition of this work is printed from the last one to receive the author's revision, the fourth, published in the year 1846. In later editions a practice had grown up of making changes in the original text and notes in one way or another, generally by bracketed interpolation. Now and then this has had the effect of interfering seriously with the continuity of a particular discussion, or with the connection of the parts of a whole statement of law. Then too in process of time the brackets had sometimes dropped out of place, or dropped out altogether, and the result was that the work of the author could not always be distinguished from that of his editors. This evil is now removed, and in the present edition the original text and notes reappear intact (save the correction of some misprints), entitled to speak again with all the weight of authority of Mr. Justice Story.

Further, the editor's notes (here printed in double columns) have been rewritten back to the same fourth edition. The editions since the fourth had generally been edited as so many distinct pieces of work, with the natural result of an accumulation of a mass of notes, sometimes discordant and always perplexing. This evil too has now been done away. For better or worse, each note of the present edition is a unit. Many of the annotations too on the more important subjects have taken the form, and the editor hopes may prove to have some of the merits, of monographs. These, it may be remarked, should be read through to be fully understood, at least by the student.

For valuable help the editor tenders his best thanks to Mr. George J. Tufts of the Boston Bar.

M. M. B.

BOSTON, *February* 1, 1886.

ADDENDA.

To the authorities cited, vol. i. p. 116, note, in the paragraph beginning 'Other cases,' add, 'Green Bay Canal Co. *v.* Hewitt, 62 Wis. 316, a case however of construction.'

Add to note (*b*), § 308, 'See Tate *v.* Williamson, L. R. 2 Ch. 55, in regard to what makes a relation of confidence.'

At the close of the note ending 'for minute examination,' vol. i. p. 316, add, 'With this compare, in regard to gifts to strangers, Cooke *v.* Lamotte, 15 Beav. 234; Hoghton *v.* Hoghton, Ib. 278, 298.'

After Dawson *v.* Collis, vol. ii. p. 19, add, 'See Behn *v.* Burness, 3 Best & S. 751, and note, Am. ed.'

After Hammersley *v.* De Biel, vol. ii. p. 290, add, 'Alderson *v.* Maddison, 5 Ex. D. 293, 298.'

ADVERTISEMENT

TO THE FOURTH EDITION.

The present edition of the Commentaries on Equity Jurisprudence was prepared for the press by the late author, and will be found to be considerably enlarged from the former editions, both in the text and notes. His thorough revision and correction of the whole work has left little else to be done than to add such illustrations and citations as have grown out of the very recent cases.

W. W. STORY.

Boston, *April*, 1846.

PREFACE.

THE present work embraces another portion of the labors devolved upon me by the founder of the Dane Professorship of Law in Harvard University. In submitting it to the profession, it is impossible for me not to feel great diffidence and solicitude as to its merits as well as to its reception by the public. The subject is one of such vast variety and extent that it would seem to require a long life of labor to do more than to bring together some of the more general elements of the system of Equity Jurisprudence as administered in England and America. In many branches of this most complicated system, composed, as it is, partly of the principles of natural law, and partly of artificial modifications of those principles, the ramifications are almost infinitely diversified, and the sources as well as the extent of these branches are often obscure and ill-defined, and sometimes incapable of any exact development. I have endeavored to collect together, as far as my own imperfect studies would admit, the more general principles belonging to the system in those branches which are of daily use and practical importance. My main object has been to trace out and define the various sources and limits of equity jurisdiction as far as they may be ascertained by a careful examination of the authorities, and a close analysis of each distinct ground of that jurisdiction as it has been practically expounded and applied in different ages. Another object has been to incorporate into the text some of the leading doctrines which guide and govern Courts of Equity in the exercise of their jurisdiction, and especially in those cases where the doctrines are peculiar to those courts or are applied in a manner unknown to the Courts of Common Law. In many cases I have endeavored to show the reasons upon which these doctrines are founded, and to illustrate them by principles drawn from foreign jurisprudence as well as from the Roman civil law. Of course the reader will not expect to find in these Commentaries a minute or even a general survey of all the doctrines belonging to any one branch of Equity Jurisprudence, but such expositions only as may most fully explain the nature and limits of equity jurisdiction. In order to accomplish even this task in any suitable manner it has become necessary to bestow a degree of labor in the examination and comparison of authorities from which many jurists would shrink, and which will scarcely be suspected by those who may consult the work only for occasional exigencies. It will be readily seen that the same train of remark and sometimes the same illustrations are repeated in different places. As the work is designed for elementary instruction, this course seemed indispensable to escape from the inconvenience of perpetual references to other passages where the same subject is treated under other aspects.

The work is divided into three great heads: First, the Concurrent Jurisdiction of Courts of Equity; secondly, the Exclusive Jurisdiction; and, thirdly, the Auxiliary or Assistant Jurisdiction. The Concurrent Jurisdiction is again subdivided into two branches: the one, where the subject-matter constitutes the principal (though rarely the sole) ground of the jurisdiction; the other, where the peculiar remedies administered in equity constitute the principal (though not always the sole) ground of jurisdiction. The present volume embraces the first only of these branches of Concurrent Jurisdiction. The remaining subjects will be fully discussed in the succeeding volume. I hope also to find leisure to present, as a fit conclusion of these Commentaries, a general review of the Doctrines of Equity Pleading, and of the Course of Practice in Equity Proceedings.

In dismissing the work to the indulgent consideration of the profession, I venture to hope that it will not be found that more has been promised than is performed; and that if much has been omitted, something will yet be found to lighten the labors of the inquisitive, if not to supply the wants of the learned.

CAMBRIDGE, MASS.,
December, 1835.

CONTENTS TO VOLS.

                                                               PAGE

INDEX TO CASES CITED xiii

CHAPTER I.

                                                             SECTION

THE TRUE NATURE AND CHARACTER OF EQUITY JURISPRUDENCE   1–37

CHAPTER II.

THE ORIGIN AND HISTORY OF EQUITY JURISPRUDENCE . .   38–58

CHAPTER III.

GENERAL VIEW OF EQUITY JURISDICTION   59–74

CHAPTER IV.

CONCURRENT JURISDICTION OF EQUITY. — ACCIDENT . . .   75–109

CHAPTER V.

MISTAKE 110–183

CHAPTER VI.

ACTUAL OR POSITIVE FRAUD 184–257

CHAPTER VII.

CONSTRUCTIVE FRAUD 258–440

CHAPTER VIII.

ACCOUNT 441–529

CHAPTER IX.

ADMINISTRATION 530–589

CHAPTER X.

LEGACIES 590–608

CHAPTER XI.

CONFUSION OF BOUNDARIES 609–623

CHAPTER XII.

DOWER 624–632

CHAPTER XIII.

MARSHALLING OF SECURITIES 633–645

CHAPTER XIV.

PARTITION 646–658

CHAPTER XV.

PARTNERSHIP 659–683

CHAPTER XVI.

MATTERS OF RENT 684–687

CHAPTER XVII.

PECULIAR REMEDIES IN EQUITY. — DISCOVERY. — CANCELLATION AND DELIVERY OF INSTRUMENTS 688–711

CHAPTER XVIII.

SPECIFIC PERFORMANCE OF AGREEMENTS AND OTHER DUTIES 712–793 *b*

CHAPTER XIX.

SECTION

COMPENSATION AND DAMAGES . . . . 794–799 *b*

CHAPTER XX.

INTERPLEADER 800–824

CHAPTER XXI.

BILLS QUIA TIMET 825–851

CHAPTER XXII.

BILLS OF PEACE 852–860

CHAPTER XXIII.

INJUNCTIONS . . . . 861–959 *b*

CHAPTER XXIV.

EXCLUSIVE JURISDICTION. — EXPRESS TRUSTS 960–982

CHAPTER XXV.

EXPRESS TRUSTS. — MARRIAGE SETTLEMENTS 983–997

CHAPTER XXVI.

EXPRESS TRUSTS. — TERMS FOR YEARS 998–1003

CHAPTER XXVII.

EXPRESS TRUSTS. — MORTGAGES . . . . 1004–1035 *c*

CHAPTER XXVIII.

EXPRESS TRUSTS. — ASSIGNMENTS . . . . 1036–1057 *b*

CHAPTER XXIX.

EXPRESS TRUSTS. — WILLS AND TESTAMENTS . . . . . 1058–1074 *a*

CHAPTER XXX.

EXPRESS TRUSTS. — ELECTION AND SATISFACTION . . . 1075–1123 *a*

CHAPTER XXXI.

Express Trusts. — Application of Purchase-money . 1124–1135

CHAPTER XXXII.

Express Trusts. — Charities 1136–1194

CHAPTER XXXIII.

Implied Trusts 1195–1300

CHAPTER XXXIV.

Penalties and Forfeitures 1301–1326

CHAPTER XXXV.

Infants 1327–1361

CHAPTER XXXVI.

Idiots and Lunatics . . . . 1362–1365 a

CHAPTER XXXVII.

Married Women 1366–1429

CHAPTER XXXVIII.

Set-off 1430–1444

CHAPTER XXXIX.

Establishing Wills 1445–1449

CHAPTER XL.

Awards 1450–1463

CHAPTER XLI.

Writs of Ne Exeat Regno and Supplicavit . . . . 1464–1479 a

CHAPTER XLII.

Bills of Discovery, and Bills to Preserve and Perpetuate Evidence 1480–1516

CHAPTER XLIII.

SECTION

PECULIAR DEFENCES AND PROOFS IN EQUITY 1517–1532

[Added by I. F. REDFIELD.]

CHAPTER XLIV.
ESTOPPELS IN EQUITY 1533–1556

CHAPTER XLV.
RAILWAYS AND OTHER COMPANIES 1557–1572

CHAPTER XLVI.
THE EFFECT OF JUDGMENTS AT LAW. — FOREIGN JUDGMENTS 1573–1587

INDEX . . . . pp. 877–947

CASES CITED.

A.

Abbott v. Dermott	i. 165
v. Keeson	ii. 341
v. L'Hommedieu	ii. 96
v. Winchester	ii. 700
Abeel v. Radcliff	ii. 81
Abell v. Howe	ii. 280, 828
Aberamen Iron Works v. Wicken	i. 682; ii. 104
Abergavenny v. Powell	ii. 839
Abernethy v. Hutchinson	ii. 253
Abraham v. Bubb	ii. 219, 220
Academy of Visitation v. Clemens	ii. 503
Acer v. Wescott	i. 402
Ackerman v. Emott	ii. 618
Ackroyd v. Smithson	ii. 113, 115
Ackworth v. Ackworth	ii. 459
Acton v. Acton	ii. 701
v. Pearce	i. 145; ii. 57
v. White	ii. 718, 721
v. Woodgate	ii. 117, 272, 344, 345, 364, 365
Adair v. Shaw	i. 472, 549, 591, 592; ii. 606, 628
Adam v. Briggs Iron Co.	i. 659
Adams v. Adams	i. 555, 590; ii. 273, 383, 757, 805
v. Angell	ii. 342
v. Barry	ii. 822
v. Blodgett	i. 378
v. Buchanan	ii. 576
v. Claxton	i. 422; ii. 338, 363, 615
v. Clifton	ii. 619
v. Curtis	ii. 701
v. Gay	i. 308
v. Lambert	ii. 500
v. Michael	ii. 229, 231
v. Popham	ii. 230
v. Scott	ii. 332
v. Stevens	i. 152, 179
Adams v. Whitcomb	ii. 801
Adamson v. Armitage	ii. 711, 712
Adderley v. Dixon	ii. 32, 35, 38, 41, 42, 43, 63, 125
Addington v. McDonnell	ii. 95
Addis v. Knight	ii. 773
Addison v. Cox	ii. 355
v. Dawson	i. 240, 241, 243
Adley v. Whitstable Co.	i. 71, 532; ii. 3
Adlington v. Cann	ii. 509
Adye v. Feuilleteau	ii. 617, 618, 619
Agar v. Blethyn	ii. 709
v. Fairfax	i. 658, 659, 665
v. Macklew	i. 676; ii. 794
v. Regent's Canal Co.	ii. 187
Agard v. Valencia	ii. 202
Agar-Ellis v. Lascelles	ii. 677, 680
Ager v. Peninsular Nav. Co.	ii. 242
Agra Bank, Ex parte	i. 335
v. Barry	i. 400
Aguilar v. Aguilar	ii. 707, 728, 729
Ahrend v. Odiorne	i. 78, 79; ii. 76, 560
Aiken v. Bruen	i. 431
v. Peay	i. 510
Aiman v. Stout	i. 249
Ainslie v. Medlycott	i. 166, 215
Ainsworth v. Walmsley	ii. 258
Aislabie v. Rice	i. 292
Aitchison v. Dixon	ii. 736
Akely v. Akely	ii. 795
Akerly v. Vilas	ii. 210
Alabama Ins. Co. v. Lott	ii. 14
Albany City Bank v. Schermerhorn	ii. 160, 161, 200
Albany Mining Co. v. Aud. Gen.	ii. 13
Albert v. Perry	ii. 674
Albert Ins. Co., In re	ii. 654
Albion Ins. Co., In re	i. 670
Albretch v. Wolf	ii. 847
Alcock v. Sparhawk	ii. 592
Aldborough v. Frye	i. 341, 342, 343, 346, 350, 353, 354, 355

CASES CITED.

Alden v. Truber	ii. 13
Alderson, Ex parte	ii. 303, 366
Aldrich v. Blake	ii. 342
v. Cooper	i. 517, 527, 570, 571, 572, 573, 574, 575, 576, 578, 637, 641, 643, 647; ii. 580, 707
v. Hapgood	i. 514
v. Thompson	ii. 139, 141
Aldridge v. Westbrook	i. 558
Aleworth v. Roberts	i. 633
Alexander v. Alexander	ii. 396
v. Coldwell	i. 153
v. Pendleton	i. 416; ii. 172, 173, 175, 176, 177
v. Wellington	ii. 357
Alger v. Parrott	ii. 399
Alison, In re	ii. 332, 851
Allan v. Allan	ii. 816, 834
v. Backhouse	i. 500; ii. 392
v. Bower	ii. 82
Allen, Ex parte	i. 246
v. Allen	i. 577; ii. 759, 851
v. Anderson	ii. 435, 436
v. Anthony	i. 406
v. Arne	i. 433
v. Atchison	i. 411
v. Brown	i. 158
v. Buffalo	ii. 12
v. Center Valley Co.	i. 684
v. Coster	ii. 687
v. Hammond	i. 161
v. Harding	ii. 44
v. Hearn	i. 298
v. Jackson	i. 279
v. Macpherson	i. 195, 198, 250, 441, 442; ii. 779
v. Merton	ii. 234
v. Morris	i. 411
v. Papworth	ii. 724
v. Poulton	ii. 436
v. Richardson	i. 217
v. Seckham	i. 406
v. Storer	i. 24; ii. 11
v. Talbot	ii. 869
v. Webb	ii. 81
v. Webster	ii. 397
v. Woodruff	ii. 58
v. Yeater	i. 154, 157
Allerton v. Allerton	i. 214
Alley v. Deschamps	ii. 27, 36, 57, 101
Allis v. Billings	i. 238
Allison v. Shilling	ii. 52
v. Sutherlin	i. 525
Allnut, In re	ii. 285
Allore v. Jewell	i. 242, 249, 256
Allsopp v. Whistcroft	i. 294
Almony v. Hicks	ii. 11, 13
Almy v. Reed	i. 87
Alnete v. Bettam	ii. 140
Alsager v. Rowley	i. 428, 592
Alsop v. Bowers	i. 580
Alsopp v. Patten	ii. 75
Alston, Ex parte	i. 638
Alter's Appeal	i. 190
Alton v. Harrison	i. 377
Ambler v. Choteau	i. 30
v. Whipple	i. 682
Ambrose v. Ambrose	ii. 535
Ambrose Tin Co., In re	i. 333
American Academy v. Harvard College	ii. 495
Ames v. Ames	i. 66
v. Clark	ii. 275
Amesbury v. Brown	i. 499, 501
Amherst Bank v. Root	i. 338
Amory v. Meredith	ii. 388
Amoskeag Mfg. Co. v. Spear	ii. 256, 258
Amsinck v. Barklay	ii. 803
Ancaster v. Mayor	i. 582, 584, 587
Anderson v. Anderson	i. 682; ii. 713
v. Armistead	i. 391
v. Dawson	ii. 722
v. Dwyer	i. 490
v. Elsworth	ii. 22
v. Gregg	ii. 620
v. McGowan	ii. 387
v. Pignet	i. 634
v. Roberts	i. 387, 436, 437
v. Talbot	ii. 13
v. Tydings	i. 187
Anding v. Davis	ii. 321
Andrew v. Bible Soc.	ii. 491
v. Clark	ii. 547
v. Spurr	i. 158
Andrews, In re	ii. 405
v. Bell	ii. 95
v. Berry	ii. 819
v. Bishop	i. 582
v. Brown	ii. 129
v. Brunefield	ii. 388
v. Essex F. & M. Ins. Co.	i. 168, 171
v. Pavis	i. 198
v. Salt	ii. 680
v. Sparhawk	ii. 474
v. Trinity Hall	ii. 431
v. Wrigley	i. 427, 590; ii. 470
Anewalt's Appeal	ii. 553
Angel v. Smith	ii. 159, 160, 161, 200
Angell v. Angell	ii. 812, 824, 831, 832, 835, 837
v. Hadden	ii. 138, 140, 142, 153, 734
v. Johnson	i. 391

CASES CITED.

Angier v. Angier ii. 758, 759, 803
Angus v. Angus ii. 635, 636
— v. Dalton ii. 235
— v. McLachlan ii. 570
Ann Berta Lodge v. Leverton ii. 75
Annis v. Bonar i. 362
Anon i. 91, 99, 541, 549, 553, 557, 558, 566, 568, 573, 601, 602, 605, 665, 673, 681; ii. 19, 40, 68, 82, 85, 155, 167, 187, 198, 227, 233, 259, 260, 337, 338, 431, 483, 484, 498, 504, 521, 602, 737, 794, 800, 802, 803, 820, 822, 834, 855
Ansdell v. Ansdell ii. 808
Anthony v. Valentine i. 28, 29, 31; ii. 13
Antrobus v. Davidson i. 648
— v. Smith i. 433, 434; ii. 23, 116, 120, 290
Aplyn v. Brewer ii. 623
Appleby v. Dodd i. 479
Applegate v. Mason i. 637
Appleton v. Rowley ii. 399, 713
Appleyard v. Seton i. 79
Archer's Case i. 449; ii. 293
Archer v. Hudson i. 311, 312
— v. Meadows i. 441
— v. Moss i. 194
— v. Preston ii. 61, 62, 209
Arden v. Patterson ii. 373, 374
Argiasse v. Muschamp ii. 62, 209, 634
Arkwright v. Newbold i. 110, 149, 206, 208, 209, 210
Arlin v. Brown ii. 560
Armitage v. Baldwin i. 519, 521
— v. Pulver i. 509, 510, 511
— v. Wadsworth i. 88, 96; ii. 17
Armstrong's Appeal i. 580
Armstrong v. Armstrong ii. 160
— v. Gilchrist i. 76, 454, 456
— v. Kosciusko i. 197
— v. Ross ii. 570
— v. Toler i. 59
Arnald v. Arnald i. 617
Arnett v. Bailey i. 659
Arnold v. Bright i. 204
— v. Chapman i. 575, 576; ii. 512
— v. Dixon ii. 554
— v. Garner ii. 612
— v. Kempstead ii. 428, 430
— v. Middletown ii. 14
— v. Richmond Iron Works i. 238
— v. Woodhams ii. 277
Arnot v. Alexander ii. 81
Arnott v. Bicoe i. 231; ii. 855
Arnsby v. Woodward ii. 657, 658
Arrington v. Liscomb ii. 12

Arthington v. Fawkes ii. 174
Arthur v. Bokenham ii. 349
— v. Case ii. 231
Artz v. Grove ii. 68
Arundel v. Phipps i. 380; ii. 25, 36
— v. Trevillian i. 268
Arundell v. Phipps ii. 699
Ashbrook v. Ryon i. 610, 611
Ashburton v. Ashburton ii. 689
Ashby v. Palmer ii. 113
Ashcomb's Case ii. 379
Ashcraft v. De Armond i. 238, 242
Ashley v. Baillie i. 552
Ashmore v. Evans ii. 99
Ashton v. Atlantic Bank i. 406, ii. 280
— v. Corrigan ii. 49
— v. Exeter i. 624
— v. McDougall ii. 714
Ashurst's Appeal ii. 629, 847
Ashworth v. Munn ii. 526
Asiatic Banking Co., Ex parte ii. 367
Astley v. Gurney ii. 768
— v. Reynolds i. 301
— v. Weldon ii. 645, 651
Aston v. Aston ii. 220
— v. Exeter i. 81; ii. 817
— v. Heron ii. 200
— v. Pye ii. 20
— v. Robinson ii. 59
— v. Wood ii. 282, 493, 531
Astor v. Miller i. 494
— v. Wells i. 410, 413
Atcheson v. Mallon i. 295
Athenæum Assur. Co. v. Pooley ii. 214
Atherford v. Beard i. 298
Atherton v. Crowther ii. 398
— v. Nowell ii. 758
Athill, In re i. 639
Athol v. Derby ii. 61
Atkins v. Chilson i. 158; ii. 646
— v. Farr i. 276
— v. Hatton i. 622, 624
— v. Hill i. 598, 599, 600
Atkins v. Rison i. 100; ii. 99
— v. Tredgold ii. 852
Atkinson v. Atkinson ii. 683
— v. Elliot ii. 768
— v. Leonard i. 70, 89, 90; ii. 801, 803
— v. Littlewood ii. 429, 441
— v. Manks ii. 137, 139, 140, 141, 146, 147, 152, 155
— v. Ritchie ii. 641
— v. Webb ii. 441
Atkinsons v. Allen ii. 876
Atkyns v. Kinnear ii. 651
Atlantic Bank v. Tavener ii. 702

CASES CITED.

Atlanta R. Co. v. Speer ii. 34
Attenborough v. London Dock Co. ii. 149
Attorney-Gen. v. Andrews i. 20
— v. Bains ii. 508, 509
— v. Balliol College ii. 583
— v. Barbour ii. 630
— v. Bay State Brick Co. ii. 224
— v. Berryman ii. 502
— v. Boucherett ii. 523
— v. Boultbee ii. 503, 510
— v. Bowyer ii. 482, 488, 492, 504, 507
— v. Brentwood School ii. 488, 489
— v. Brereton ii. 482, 483, 485, 499
— v. Bristol ii. 511
— v. Brown ii. 484
— v. Browne ii. 494
— v. Brunning i. 566
— v. Bunce ii. 525
— v. Burdet ii. 507, 508
— v. Caldwell ii. 512
— v. Carlisle ii. 494
— v. Chester ii. 493, 504, 518
— v. Christ Church i. 533
— v. Christ's Hospital ii. 526
— v. Clarendon ii. 498
— v. Clarke ii. 493, 523
— v. Cleaves ii. 202, 224, 227
— v. Cockermouth Board ii. 224
— v. Cohoes Co ii. 223, 224
— v. Colney Asylum ii. 230
— v. Combe ii. 494, 504, 509
— v. Continental Life Ins. Co. ii. 366
— v. Coopers' Co. ii. 502, 510, 511, 514, 631
— v. Cornthwaite i. 557
— v. Coventry i. 696; ii. 523
— v. Day ii. 57, 69, 74
— v. Dimond i. 593
— v. Dixie ii. 498, 511
— v. Doughty ii. 227
— v. Downing ii. 504, 523
— v. Drapers' Co. ii. 502, 510, 511, 514

Attorney-Gen. v. Dublin ii. 484, 488, 490, 494
— v. Duplessis ii. 815
— v. Dutch Church ii. 503
— v. Ely ii. 265
— v. Ely R. Co. ii. 224
— v. Fishmongers' Co. ii. 847
— v. Forbes ii. 223, 224, 226
— v. Foundling Hospital ii. 523
— v. Fullerton i. 624
— v. Galway i. 30
— v. Garrison ii. 630
— v. Gee ii. 230
— v. Gibson ii. 506
— v. Gladstone ii. 494
— v. Gleg ii. 510
— v. Goulding ii. 523
— v. Graves ii. 512
— v. Great Eastern Ry. Co. ii. 224
— v. Great Northern Ry. Co. i. 20
— v. Green ii. 503
— v. Guardians of Poor i. 20
— v. Guise ii. 502
— v. Hall ii. 412
— v. Hamilton i. 661
— v. Hankey ii. 511
— v. Harrow School ii. 500
— v. Heelis ii. 494
— v. Herrick ii. 522
— v. Hewer ii. 499
— v. Hickman ii. 501
— v. Hicks ii. 511
— v. Hubbuck i. 683
— v. Hurst i. 579; ii. 511, 512, 514
— v. Ironmongers' Co. ii. 502, 505, 510, 511, 517, 520
— v. Jackson ii. 89, 501, 789, 793
— v. Jeanes ii. 499
— v. Johnson ii. 223, 225, 226
— v. Kell ii. 494
— v. Kirk ii. 260
— v. Leeds ii. 230
— v. Lepine ii. 517, 519, 636
— v. Llandaff ii. 506
— v. London ii. 505, 517, 518, 523

CASES CITED.

Attorney-Gen. v. Lonsdale ii. 427, 494
   v. Manchester ii. 498
   v. Marchant ii. 511
   v. Marlborough ii. 220
   v. Matthews ii. 528
   v. Mayor i. 449
   v. Merrimac Mfg. Co. ii. 495
   v. Metropolitan R. Co. ii. 224
   v. Middleton ii. 485, 499, 521, 523
   v. Minshall ii. 510
   v. Moore ii. 523. 525
   v. Morgan ii. 11
   v. Newman ii. 483, 484
   v. Nichol ii. 227, 229, 232
   v. Norwick i. 20
   v. Oglander ii. 503, 505, 523
   v. Oxford ii. 523
   v. Painters' Co. ii. 522
   v. Parker ii. 500
   v. Parkhurst i. 241
   v. Parmenter i. 250
   v. Parnther i. 243
   v. Peacock ii. 504
   v. Pearce ii. 493
   v. Pearson ii. 517, 524, 525
   v. Plat ii. 504, 510
   v. Power ii. 493, 502
   v. Price ii. 398, 500, 522
   v. Pyle i. 601
   v. Ray ii. 834
   v. Reynolds i. 19
   v. Richards ii. 223
   v. Richmond ii. 230
   v. Rye ii. 487, 507, 508
   v. Shore ii. 524
   v. Shrewsbury Bridge Co. ii. 224
   v. Sitwell i. 168, 170, 172, 174, 176, 339; ii. 68, 69, 89, 91
   v. Skinners' Co. ii. 488, 489
   v. Smart ii. 499
   v. Smith i. 406
   v. Sothen i. 250, 251
   v. Soule ii. 495, 499
   v. South Sea Co. ii. 524
   v. St. John's Hospital ii. 505
   v. Stepney ii. 493, 510
   v. Stephens i. 408, 619, 621, 624; ii. 865

Attorney-Gen. v. Stewart ii. 226, 505, 526
   v. Sturge ii. 517
   v. Syderfin ii. 502, 504
   v. Tancred ii. 483, 486
   v. Tindall ii. 512
   v. Tompkins ii. 512
   v. Trinity Church ii. 511
   v. Trinity College ii. 514
   v. Tudor Ice Co. i. 19, 30; ii. 224
   v. Turner ii. 780, 782
   v. Tyndall i. 570, 573, 579, 637
   v. United Kingdom Tel. Co. ii. 224
   v. Utica Ins. Co. i. 19; ii. 523
   v. Wansay ii. 503, 522, 523
   v. Wax Chandler's Co. ii. 511
   v. Whitchurch ii. 510
   v. Whiteley ii. 500
   v. Whorwood ii. 740
   v. Wilson ii. 511, 514
   v. Winchelsea i. 579; ii. 511, 512, 514
   v. Windsor ii. 875
   v. Woolwich i. 141
Attridge v. Billings ii. 688
Atwell v. Atwell ii. 553
Atwood v. Fisk ii. 6
   v. Lamprey i. 122
   v. Vincent ii. 560
   v. Small i. 204, 207, 223, 225
Aubrey v. Middleton ii. 592
Auburn Plank Road Co. v. Douglass ii. 232
August v. Seskind i. 411
Ault v. Goodrich ii. 846
Auriol v. Smith ii. 790, 795
Aurora, The ii. 587
Austen v. Taylor ii. 273, 275
Austin v. Bell ii. 344
   v. Ewell ii. 104
   v. Halsey ii. 572
Auter v. Miller ii. 59, 71
Avent v. McCorkle ii. 576
Averall v. Wade i. 421, 482, 495, 497, 505, 516, 637, 641, 643, 614, 648; ii. 555, 580
Averill v. Loucks i. 683
Avery v. Holland i. 81
   v. Petten i. 506, 518
   v. Ware i. 458

CASES CITED.

Axmann v. Lund	ii. 238, 239
Axtel v. Chase	i. 156
Ayer v. Hawkins	i. 460
v. Stewart	ii. 842
Aylesford v. Morris	i. 352
Aylesford's Case	ii. 80, 84
Aylet v. Dodd	ii. 523
Aylett v. Ashton	ii. 725
Ayliffe v. Murray	i. 328
Aylward v. Kearney	i. 327
Aynsley v. Glover	ii. 182
v. Woodsworth	i. 487, 491
Ayre's Case	i. 211, 212
Ayres v. Adams	ii. 341
v. Husted	i. 639, 651, 653
v. Methodist Church	ii. 491
v. Waite	ii. 333

B.

Babcock v. Eckline	i. 369, 373
Baber, In re	ii. 364
Bach v. Symes	ii. 570
v. Andrew	ii. 541
v. Kett	ii. 435
v. Stacy	ii. 230, 232
Backus v. Murphy	i. 689
Bacon v. Bacon	ii. 626
v. Bonham	i. 343, 353; ii. 348
v. Bronson	i. 199, 227
v. Cottrell	ii. 130
v. Jones	ii. 238, 262
v. Markley	i. 216, 403
Badeau v. Rogers	ii. 137, 139
Badger v. Badger	i. 545; ii. 844
v. Boardman	ii. 55
v. McNamara	i. 309, 333, 455, 458, 469
Badgley v. Bruce	i. 627, 629
Baggott v. Meux	ii. 714
Bagnall v. Carlton	i. 332
Bagot v. Oughton	i. 586, 587
Bagott v. Mullen	i. 511
Bagshaw v. Eastern Ry Co.	ii. 868
v. Parker	i. 681
Bailey v. Bailey	ii. 594
v. Devereaux	ii. 200
v. Ekins	i. 566; ii. 394, 473
v. Hobson	i. 535; ii. 220
v. Lloyd	ii. 390
v. Sisson	i. 29, 668
v. Snelgrove	i. 611
v. Taylor	i. 78; ii. 237, 248
Baillie v. Baillie	ii. 199, 210
Bain v. Brown	i. 322
v. Fothergill	ii. 126
v. Sadler	i. 567, 569, 589
Bainbridge v. Smith	i. 185
Bainbrigge v. Browne	i. 311, 312
Baines v. Barnes	ii. 11
v. Dixon	ii. 391
v. Otley	ii. 398
Baird v. Torrey	ii. 677
Baker, Ex parte	ii. 695
Baker, In re	ii. 842
Baker v. Bayley	ii. 291
v. Biddle	i. 27; ii. 275
v. Bradley	i. 313
v. Gilman	i. 365
v. Gray	ii. 328
v. Johnston	ii. 863
v. Jordan	i. 273
v. Massey	i. 118
v. Mellish	ii. 212
v. Monk	i. 343
v. Morgan	ii. 874
v. Newton	ii. 712
v. Paine	i. 167, 168, 171, 172, 174, 175
v. Peck	i. 329
v. Pool	i. 122
v. Rogers	ii. 175
v. Sebright	i. 538
v. Shelbury	ii. 48
v. Sutton	ii. 496
v. Tucker	i. 311
v. White	i. 275
v. Whiting	ii. 372, 374
v. Williams	i. 307, 609
Baldwin v. Campfield	ii. 535
v. Cawthorne	i. 379
v. Rochfort	i. 340
v. Salter	ii. 95, 100
v. Society for Diffusing Useful Knowledge	ii. 263
v. Tucker	ii. 15
Baleman v. Boynton	ii. 790
Balfour v. Welland	ii. 466, 471, 476
v. Weston	i. 105
Ball v. Ball	ii. 677
v. Coggs	ii. 41
v. Coutts	ii. 692, 753, 754
v. Harris	ii. 393, 469, 471, 473
v. Mannin	i. 240, 248
v. Montgomery	i. 272; ii. 753, 756, 757, 761, 865
v. Smith	ii. 548
v. Storie	i. 167, 169, 174, 175
Ballard v. Shutt	i. 533
v. Tomlinson	ii. 230
Ballett v. Sprainger	i. 499
Balmain v. Shore	ii. 544
Baltimore Ins. Co. v. Dalrymple	ii. 335
Baltimore & O. Ry. Co. v. Wheeling	ii. 868

CASES CITED.

Bamfield v. Wyndham	i. 582
Bamford v. Turnley	ii. 233
Banbury v. Briscoe	ii. 18
Bancroft v. Consen	ii. 272
v. Dumas	i. 460
Banet v. Alton Ry.	ii. 868
Banfield v. Whipple	i. 377
Bangs v. Smith	ii. 388
Banister, In re	i. 217
Bank of Alexandria v. Lynn	ii. 65
Augusta v. Earle	ii. 869
Commerce v. Bogy	ii. 366
v. Owens	i. 636
Ireland v. Beresford	ii. 195, 213
Louisville v. Hall	i. 683
Ogdensburg v. Arnold	ii. 164
Pennsylvania v. Wise	i. 492
Scotland v. Christie	i. 459, 460, 465
United States v. Beverly	ii. 383
v. Biddle	i. 80
v. Daniel	i. 116, 147
v. Etting	i. 334
Westminster v. Whyte	ii. 321
Bankart v. Houghton	ii. 862
v. Tennant	ii. 861
Bankhead v. Alloway	i. 542
Banks v. Sutton	i. 634
Banner v. Berridge	ii. 283, 332
v. Lowe	i. 489
Bannerman v. Weaver	i. 278
Banta v. Moore	i. 594
Baptist Assoc. v. Hart	ii. 478, 483, 488, 492, 503, 517
v. Smith	ii. 477, 480, 503, 518, 523
Baptiste v. Peters	i. 157
Baptist Soc. v. Hail	ii. 493, 503
Barber v. Barber	ii. 846
v. Cary	ii. 332
Barbone v. Brent	ii. 203, 204
Bardwell v. Perry	i. 653, 684
Barfield v. Nicholson	ii. 261
Barford v. Street	ii. 721
Bargent v. Thompson	i. 86
Barham v. Thanet	i. 586
Bariantinski, In matter of	ii. 697
Baring v. Dix	i. 681
v. Nash	i. 656, 658, 661, 664, 668
Barker v. Dacie	i. 454, 455, 456, 537
v. Devonshire	ii. 592
v. Elkins	ii. 204, 205
Barker v. Goodair	i. 687, 689
v. Hodgson	ii. 641
v. Mar. Ins. Co.	i. 322
v. May	i. 553, 566
v. Ray	i. 194; ii. 779
Barkley v. Barkley	ii. 41
v. Lane	ii. 271
Barkworth v. Young	ii. 290
Barley v. Walford	i. 209
Barlow v. Bishop	ii. 715
v. Gaines	ii. 320
v. Grant	ii. 687
Barnard's Case	ii. 220
Barnard v. Davis	ii. 343
v. Jewett	ii. 534
v. Large	ii. 295
v. Lee	ii. 100
v. Wallis	ii. 264
Barnardiston v. Lingood	i. 342
Barned's Banking Co., In re	i. 411
Barnes v. Baker	ii. 224
v. Barnes	ii. 32, 35, 39
v. Boston R. Co.	ii. 75, 76, 79
v. Calhoun	ii. 231
v. Mayo	ii. 14
v. Patch	ii. 401, 411
v. Racster	i. 639, 640, 642, 644; ii. 580
v. Wood	ii. 53, 104
Barnett v. Nichols	ii. 649, 848
Barney v. Beak	i. 355
v. Myers	ii. 580
v. United Telephone Co.	ii. 239
Barnsdale v. Lowe	ii. 838, 839
Barnsley v. Powell	i. 180, 194, 196, 197, 198, 261, 313, 441, 442; ii. 48, 849
Baron v. Grillard	ii. 821
v. Husband	ii. 348, 363
Barr v. Lapsley	ii. 24, 44
v. Spier	i. 681
Barreli v. Joy	ii. 272, 614
v. Sabine	ii. 322
Barrett v. Beckford	ii. 441, 463
v. Hartley	ii. 612
v. Weston	i. 397, 423
Barrington v. Horne	ii. 49
Barrisford v. Done	i. 104
Barron v. Paulling	ii. 317
v. Porter	ii. 367
v. Robbins	ii. 11
Barrow v. Barrow	i. 393; ii. 437
v. Greenough	i. 264; ii. 106
v. Paxton	ii. 335
v. Rhinelander	i. 542
v. Richards	ii. 230
Barrs v. Fewkes	ii. 546

CASES CITED.

Barry v. Stevens	i. 309, 469
Barrymore v. Ellis	ii. 714, 722
Barstow v. Kilvington	i. 172
Bartholomew v. May	i. 582
v. McKinstry	i. 359, 379
Bartlett v. Bartlett	ii. 13, 532
v. Broderick	i. 180
v. Drew	i. 557
v. Hodgson	ii. 630
v. Johnson	ii. 336
v. Pickersgill	ii. 71, 537, 538
v. Varner	i. 402, 415
v. Wells	i. 252, 392
Bartlette v. Crittenden	ii. 253
Barton v. Barbour	ii. 197
Barwick v. English Joint-Stock Bank	i. 212, 213, 214
Bascom v. Albertson	ii. 491, 493
Baskcomb v. Beckwith	ii. 103
Baskerville v. Brown	ii. 776
Baskins v. Calhoun	i. 179
Bass v. Bass	i. 78
Bassett v. Brown	i. 26, 27; ii. 11
v. Daniels	i. 405
v. Granger	ii. 401
v. Percival	i. 584
v. Salisbury Co.	ii. 228
Batchelder v. Sargent	ii. 735
Bate v. Hooper	ii. 860
v. Scales	ii. 629
Bateman v. Bateman	ii. 391
v. Ross	ii. 764
v. Willoe	ii. 204, 205
Bates's Case	ii. 358
Bates v. Chester	i. 300
v. Dandy	ii. 743
v. Dewson	ii. 398
v. Graves	ii. 781
v. Kempton	i. 610, 614
v. Lilley	ii. 153
Bates & Henckill, Ex parte	i. 177
Batesville Institute v. Kauffman	i. 180
Bath & Montague's Case	i. 100, 101, 130, 163, 164, 202, 249, 259, 433
Bath v. Sherwin	i. 57, 60, 62, 82, 88; ii. 176
Bathurst v. Burden	ii. 40, 229
v. Murray	ii. 692
Batstone v. Salter	ii. 541
Batten v. Earnley	i. 604, 605; ii. 167
Battersbee v. Farringdon	i. 358, 362
Battersley v. Smith	i. 300
Battine, Ex parte	ii. 356
Battle v. Davis	ii. 159
Batty v. Chester	i. 59
Baugh v. Price	i. 312
v. Read	ii. 453
Bax, Ex parte	i. 448, 450
Baxter v. Conolly	ii. 41
v. Portsmouth	i. 240, 242
Bayard v. Hoffman	i. 361, 364, 375
Bayler v. Commonwealth	ii. 47
Bayley v. Edwards	i. 625
v. Greenleaf	ii. 560, 575, 576
v. Powell	ii. 547
v. Williams	i. 305
Baylies v. Payson	ii. 272
Bayliss v. Williams	i. 318
Bayly v. Tyrell	ii. 373
Baynard v. Norris	i. 405, 406
Baynum v. Baynum	ii. 804, 806
Beach v. Bestor	i. 377
v. Dyer	ii. 96
Beadel v. Perry	ii. 182
Beak, In re	i. 611
Beal v. Chase	i. 293, 294
v. Warren	i. 431
Beall v. Fox	ii. 491
Bean v. Farnham	ii. 789
v. Smith	i. 27, 310, 383, 387, 388, 408, 436, 437
Beard v. Beard	ii. 704
v. Nuthall	ii. 289
v. Travers	ii. 691
Beardmore v. Treadwell	ii. 229
Bearry v. Pitt	i. 339
Bear's Estate	i. 377
Beasley v. Arcy	ii. 771
v. Maggreth	i. 251
v. Watson	ii. 686
Beattie v. Ebury	i. 205, 207
v. Johnson	ii. 674
Beatty v. Dixon	i. 103, 621
v. Kurtz	ii. 233
Beauchamp v. Huntley	ii. 208
v. Winn	i. 112, 113, 118, 151, 154
Beaufort v. Berty	ii. 663, 672, 674, 675, 676
v. Patrick	ii. 865
v. Wellesley	ii. 682
Beauland v. Bradley	i. 311
Beaumont v. Bromley	i. 173
v. Boultbee	i. 236, 542
v. Oliveira	i. 579; ii. 495
v. Reeve	i. 299
v. Squire	i. 288
Bechinall v. Arnold	ii. 827
Beck v. Kantorowicz	i. 323
Becker v. Smith	ii. 99
v. Sweetser	ii. 358
Beckett v. Booth	i. 516
v. Cordley	i. 65, 392, 395, 396
Beckford v. Kemble	ii. 208, 210
v. Wade	ii. 844
Beckley v. Dorrington	i. 428, 592

CASES CITED.

Beckley v. Newland i. 269, 350; ii. 108, 353, 354
Beddow v. Beddow ii. 239, 790
Bedell v. Carll i. 610
— v. Hoffman ii. 138, 139, 154, 155
Bedford v. Backhouse i. 409
— v. British Museum ii. 54, 65, 230
— v. Coke i. 300
Bedford Ry. Co. v. Stanley ii. 86
Bedilian v. Seaton ii. 271
Beebe v. Knapp i. 210
— v. Robinson ii. 260
Beecher v. Beecher i. 85
Beecker v. Beecker i. 599
Beekman v. Bonsor ii. 503
Beemont v. Fell i. 191
Beeson v. Beeson i. 328
Beevor v. Luck i. 517; ii. 328
Begein v. Anderson ii. 229
Behn v. Kemble i. 209
Belcher, Ex parte ii. 615, 616
— v. Belcher i. 313
Belchier, Ex parte ii. 623
— v. Butler i. 421
— v. Parsons ii. 623
Belfast v. Chichester ii. 833, 834
Belford v. Crane i. 365
Belknap v. Belknap ii. 187, 612
— v. Sealey i. 156
— v. Trimble ii. 231
Bell's Appeal ii. 383
Bell's Case i. 211, 212; ii. 619
Bell v. Coleman ii. 463
— v. Cureton ii. 117
— v. Elliott i. 390
— v. Gardiner i. 85, 154, 162
— v. Hunt ii. 145
— v. Locke ii. 254
— v. McCawley i. 437
— v. Phyn i. 683; ii. 514
— v. Quinn i. 206
— v. Twilight i. 416
— v. Whitehead ii. 247
Bellage v. Souther i. 321
Bellamy v. Burrow i. 298
— v. Jones ii. 837
Bellasis, In re ii. 285
— v. Uthwatt ii. 410, 442, 447, 449
Bellew v. Russell i. 317, 318, 320, 321
Belvedere v. Rochfort i. 586
Belvidere's Case i. 587
Beman v. Rufford ii. 868
Bemis v. Call i. 392
Benbow v. Low ii. 822

Benbow v. Townsend ii. 272, 532, 533, 538
Bench v. Biles ii. 592
Bending v. Bending ii. 429
Benfield v. Solomons i. 306, 427, 428
Ben. Franklin Ins. Co. v. Gillett i. 121
Bengough v. Walker ii. 440, 441, 447, 459
Benham v. Keane i. 400
Benn v. Dixon i. 606
Bennet v. Bachelor ii. 546
— v. Bennet ii. 447, 539
— v. Davis ii. 710
— v. Mayhew ii. 548, 549
— v. Vade i. 194, 198, 199, 248; ii. 823
— v. Whitehead i. 533, 534
Bennett, Ex parte i. 329, 330
— v. Abrams ii. 12, 41
— v. Aburrow ii. 388, 389
— v. Batchelor i. 601
— v. Bedford Bank i. 367
— v. Hayter ii. 504
— v. Judson i. 209, 214
— v. Titherington i. 407
— v. Walker ii. 828
— v. Wyndham ii. 393
Bense v. Cox i. 572
Bensely v. Burden ii. 349
Benson v. Baldwin i. 95
— v. Baldwyn i. 694, 697, 698
— v. Benson ii. 713
— v. Gibson ii. 645
— v. Heathorn i. 322, 474
— v. Leroy i. 566; ii. 200
— v. Whittam ii. 408
Bent v. Cullen ii. 396
— v. Young i. 592
Bentley v. Craven i. 333
— v. Mackay ii. 23
Benwell v. Inns i. 294
Benyon v. Fitch i. 352
— v. Nettleford i. 79
Berdoe v. Dawson i. 311, 344
Beresford v. Hobson ii. 738, 755
Berg v. Radcliffe i. 179
Beringer v. Beringer i. 194
Berkeley v. Smith ii. 229
Berkley v. Bishop i. 355
Bermon v. Woodbridge i. 480
Bernal v. Donegal i. 343, 353
Bernard's Case i. 211
Bernard v. Bagshaw ii. 622
— v. Minshull ii. 406
Bernards v. Stebbins i. 102, 157, 186
Berney v. Pitt i. 339
— v. Sewell ii. 164
Berrington v. Evans i. 561; ii. 598, 601

CASES CITED.

Berrisford v. Milward	i. 395
Berry v. Mutual Ins. Co.	i. 65, 397, 422, 423; ii. 324
v. Planters' Bank	i. 301
v. Sowell	i. 153
v. Wade	ii. 49
Berthold v. Berthold	i. 515, 518
Bertie v. Abingdon	i. 501; ii. 164
v. Faulkland	i. 290; ii. 646
Besant, In re	ii. 680
v. Wood	ii. 95, 99, 761, 764
Besch v. Frolich	i. 681
Besley v. Besley	i. 217
Best v. Hamand	i. 217
v. Stanford	ii. 113, 299, 302
v. Stow	i. 157
Bettesworth v. St. Paul's	ii. 29, 46, 56
Betts v. Burch	ii. 651
v. Gillais	ii. 129
v. Gunn	i. 111, 158
v. Neilson	ii. 129
Beurmann v. Van Buren	i. 361
Beverley v. Beverley	i. 272, 394
Beverly's Case	i. 239, 240, 241, 243; ii. 663, 666, 669, 671, 693
Beverly v. Peter	ii. 551
v. Walden	i. 249
Bexwell v. Christie	i. 226, 295
Bibb v. Freeman	i. 359
Bickell's Appeal	ii. 842
Bicknell v. Field	ii. 211
Biddle v. Hussman	i. 495
v. Moore	i. 70
v. Ranney	i. 455
Bigelow v. Foss	ii. 866
v. Topliff	ii. 321
Biggs v. Peacock	i. 668
Bigland v. Huddleston	ii. 418, 424
Bilbie v. Lumley	i. 110, 118, 136; ii. 605
Bill v. Claxton	i. 429
v. Cureton	i. 378
v. Kinaston	i. 605
v. Price	i. 355
Billon v. Hyde	i. 455
Bingham v. Bingham	i. 118, 123, 134, 146, 159
Binkes v. Rokeby	ii. 103
Binney v. Annan	ii. 41
Binstead v. Coleman	ii. 80
Birch v. Blagrave	i. 300
v. Corbin	ii. 145
v. Ellames	i. 400; ii. 323, 324
v. Talbot	i. 461
v. Wade	ii. 385
v. Wright	ii. 311
Birchard v. Scott	ii. 495
Birchell, Ex parte	ii. 673
Birchett v. Bolling	i. 673; ii. 34, 40
Birch-Wolfe v. Birch	i. 537; ii. 220
Bird v. Harris	ii. 159, 161, 546
v. Lake	ii. 651
Birdsall v. Colie	i. 680
Birdsey v. Butterfield	i. 206
Birke v. Abbott	ii. 311
Birkett, In re	ii. 493, 494
Birmingham v. Kirwan	ii. 415, 417, 429
Birmingham Gas Co. v. Ratcliffe	i. 455
Birt v. Birt	i. 590
Biscoe v. Perkins	ii. 295, 296
Bishoff v. Wethered	ii. 875
Bishop v. Aldrich	ii. 19, 20
v. Church	i. 171, 177, 537; ii. 773
v. Day	i. 337
v. Rosenbaum	ii. 191
v. Schneider	i. 410
v. Webster	ii. 795
Bissell v. Axtell	i. 554
v. Kellogg	i. 306; ii. 12
v. Morgan	ii. 793
Bize v. Dickason	ii. 605
Black's Appeal	i. 684
Black's Case	ii. 769
Black v. Lamb	i. 76, 179
v. Philadelphia R. Co.	ii. 225
v. Thornton	i. 431
Blackborn v. Edgely	i. 311
Blackburn v. Bell	ii. 206
v. Staples	i. 172; ii. 287
Blackburne v. Gregson	ii. 562, 563, 564, 571, 575
Blackford v. Christian	i. 247, 248, 249
v. Preston	i. 299
Blackhall v. Combs	ii. 206
Blacklow v. Laws	ii. 711, 712
Blackwell's Case	i. 555
Blackwell v. Ball	ii. 398, 401, 402
Blackwood v. Jones	ii. 863
Blades v. Blades	i. 400
Blagden, Ex parte	ii. 766, 773
v. Bradbear	ii. 71
Blagge v. Miles	ii. 388
Blagrave v. Routh	i. 318, 319
Blaiklock v. Grindle	ii. 431
Blain v. Murphy	i. 627
Blair v. Browley	ii. 851
Blake v. Banbury	ii. 417, 427, 430
v. Blake	i. 554, 604; ii. 19, 165
v. Brooklyn	ii. 234
v. Dorgan	i. 682
v. Hungerford	i. 65
v. Langdon	ii. 773
v. Luxton	ii. 291
v. White	i. 335; ii. 195
Blake Crusher Co. v. New Haven	i. 390
Blakemore v. Blakemore	i. 118
Blanchard v. Blood	ii. 710

CASES CITED.

Blanchard v. Detroit R. Co.	ii. 34, 81
v. Doering	ii. 234
Blanchet v. Foster	i. 273, 275
Bland, Ex parte	ii. 556, 587
v. Middleton	ii. 647
Blandheir v. Moore	ii. 160
Blandy v. Kimber	i. 310
v. Widmore	ii. 441, 445, 446
Blasdel v. Fowle	i. 301
Blatch v. Wilder	ii. 384
Blatchford v. Ross	ii. 867
Blatchley v. Osborn	i. 416
Blaydes v. Calvert	ii. 802, 803, 804
Blenkinsopp v. Blenkinsopp	i. 273
Blennerhassett v. Day	ii. 793
Blewitt v. Roberts	ii. 396
Bligh, In re	ii. 693
v. Brent	i. 684
v. Darnley	i. 577
Blight v. Blight	i. 488
v. Page	ii. 641
Blinkhorn v. Feast	ii. 547
Bliss v. Bible Soc.	ii. 503
v. Hall	ii. 233
v. Prichard	ii. 844
Blisset v. Daniel	ii. 263
Blockley, In re	ii. 539
Blodget v. Blodget	ii. 13
Blodgett v. Hildreth	ii. 536
Bloomar, In re	i. 660
Bloomer v. Spittle	ii. 90
Blore v. Sutton	ii. 81, 122, 127
Blossom v. Van Amringe	ii. 8
Blount v. Blount	ii. 60
v. Burrow	i. 617
Bluck v. Capstick	i. 682
Blundell v. Brettargh	i. 105
Blunden v. Barker	i. 311
Blunt v. Gee	i. 627
v. Norris	ii. 315
v. Tomlin	ii. 80
Boal v. Morgner	ii. 711
Boaler v. Mayor	i. 336
Boardman v. Jackson	ii. 11
v. Meriden Co.	ii. 258
v. Mossman	ii. 629
v. Mostyn	ii. 82
v. Thompson	ii. 373
Boazman v. Johnson	i. 516, 571
Bobbitt v. Shryer	i. 391
Boden v. Willow	i. 81
Bodenham v. Purchase	i. 460, 465
Bodine v. Exchange Ins. Co.	ii. 654
Bodman v. Tract Soc.	ii. 504
Boehen v. Williamsburg Ins. Co.	ii. 654
Bogan v. Daughdrill	ii. 104, 125
Bogey v. Shute	ii. 222
Bogie v. Bogie	ii. 19, 20
Bogle v. Stewart	ii. 165
Bohannon v. Bohannon	ii. 80
Bohn v. Headley	i. 429
Boles v. Johnston	ii. 873
Bolling v. Doneghy	i. 525
Bolster v. Catterlin	ii. 234
Bolton v. Bolton	i. 659
v. Deane	i. 631, 697
v. De Peyster	ii. 388
v. Jacks	ii. 383
v. Prentice	ii. 756
v. Ward	i. 654
v. Williams	i. 189; ii. 140, 142, 728
Bomberger v. Turner	ii. 130
Bonaparte v. Camden & Amboy R. Co.	ii. 232, 233, 264
Bonar v. McDonald	i. 338
Bond v. Hays	i. 307
v. Hill	i. 664
v. Hopkins	i. 17, 62, 81, 546; ii. 212, 278, 844, 845, 818, 849
v. Kent	ii. 571, 572
v. Lockwood	i. 535
v. Simmons	ii. 739, 750
Bone v. Cooke	ii. 628, 629
v. Pollard	ii. 542
Bonesteel v. Bonesteel	ii. 801
Boney v. Hollingsworth	i. 311
Bonfield v. Hassell	ii. 23
Bonney v. Ridgard	i. 427, 428; ii. 469, 470
Bonser v. Cox	i. 335
v. Kinnear	ii. 406
Boome v. Mouck	ii. 417
Boon v. Barnes	ii. 575
Boone v. Chiles	ii. 278, 826, 843, 846
v. Hall	ii. 343
v. Hardie	i. 373
v. Missouri Iron Co.	ii. 96
Booten v. Scheffer	ii. 54, 99
Booth v. Carter	ii. 526
v. Leycester	ii. 199
v. Rich	ii. 330
v. Smith	i. 493
v. Vicars	ii. 399
v. Warrington	ii. 848
Boothby v. Boothby	i. 343
Bootle v. Blundell	i. 581, 582; ii. 392, 780, 781, 782, 783
Bor v. Bor	ii. 432, 435
Borell v. Dann	i. 255, 408
Borr v. Vandall	i. 468
Bos v. Helsham	i. 217
Bosanquet v. Dashwood	i. 251, 302, 305, 307, 308, 446

CASES CITED.

Bosanquet v. Wray i. 460, 464, 466, 690
Boschert v. Brown i. 334
Bostick v. Blades i. 279
Bostleman v. Bostleman ii. 537
Bostock v. Blakeney ii. 610
   v. Floyer ii. 614
Boston Diatite Co. v. Florence Mfg. Co. ii. 240
Boston Franklinite Co. v. Condit ii. 386
Boston Lead Co. v. McGuirk i. 87
Boston & M. R. Co. v. Bartlett ii. 95, 851
Boston Rolling Mills v. Cambridge ii. 233
Boston Water Power Co. v. Gray ii. 789, 791, 793
Bostwick v. Isbell ii. 159
   v. Stiles i. 96
Bosvil v. Brander ii. 740, 743, 744, 749
Boswell v. Coaks i. 321
Boteler v. Allington ii. 295
Botsford v. Burr ii. 71, 535, 536, 537, 538
Bottomley v. Brooke ii. 771
Boucicault v. Fox ii. 254
Bouck v. Wilber ii. 795
Boughton v. Boughton i. 433; ii. 417, 418, 436
Boulo v. New Orleans R. Co. ii. 234
Boultbee v. Stubbs i. 334, 335, 516; ii. 194
Bourdillon v. Adair ii. 752
Bourne v. Bourne ii. 113, 552
Boursot v. Savage ii. 280
Boutelle v. Smith i. 293
Boutillier v. Tick ii. 792
Boutts v. Ellis i. 610
Bouverie v. Prentice i. 625, 696
Bovey v. Smith i. 408; ii. 610
Bovill v. Hammond i. 672
Bowaman v. Reeve i. 575
Bowditch v. Andrew ii. 398
   v. Bannelos ii. 279
   v. Green i. 506, 514, 515
   v. Soltyk ii. 153
Bowen v. Beck ii. 341
   v. Chase i. 24
   v. Clark ii. 191
   v. Hoskins i. 524
   v. Matheson i. 293
Bowes v. Heaps i 339, 341, 342, 344
   v. Strathmore i. 272
   v. Toronto i. 296
Bowker v. Hunter ii. 547
Bowles v. Bowles ii. 401

Bowles v. Orr ii. 205, 208, 212
   v. Stewart i. 235, 260, 262; ii. 823
Bowling v. Bowling ii. 168
Bowmaker v. Moore ii. 213
Bowman v. Carruthers i. 209
   v. Wathen ii. 845
   v. Yeat i. 625, 693
Bowra v. Wright i. 660
Bowser v. Colby ii. 656, 657
Bowsher v. Watkins ii. 165
Bowtree v. Watson i. 345
Bowyer v. Bright ii. 103, 105
   v. Pritchard ii. 145
Box v. Barrett i. 191, 192; ii. 428
Boyce v. Grundy i. 27, 29; ii. 6
   v. Lorillard Ins. Co. i. 111, 150
Boyd v. Allen i. 668
   v. De la Montagnie i. 311
   v. Hunter i. 80, 629
   v. Lewis i. 458
   v. McLean ii. 535, 536, 538, 608
   v. Petrie ii. 331
Boyes v. Cook ii. 388
Boynton v. Boynton ii. 437
   v. Champlin ii. 569
   v. Hazelboom ii. 90, 102
   v. Hubbard i. 266, 267, 298, 350, 352
   v. Parkhurst ii. 707
Boyse v. Rossborough ii. 780, 784
Bozon v. Bolland ii. 370
Brace v. Marlborough i. 418, 419, 421, 423, 424, 438, 530; ii. 337, 554
   v. Wehnert ii. 45
Bracebridge v. Buckley ii. 653, 656
Bracken v. Bentley i. 605
   v. Miller i. 416
Brackenbury v. Brackenbury ii. 8
Bradbury v. Barding i. 204
Braddick v. Thompson ii. 789
Bradfield v. Dewell ii. 224
Bradford v. Brownjohn i. 495
Bradish v. Gibbs ii. 700, 702, 703, 710, 718, 724
Bradley v. Angel ii. 770
   v. Crackenthorp ii. 838
   v. George ii. 580
   v. Hughes ii. 713
   v. Hunt i. 611, 614, 616
   v. Norton ii. 255
   v. Westcott ii. 721
Bradshaw v. Bradshaw ii. 673, 687
Bradwin v. Harper i. 190, 191
Brady v. Waldron ii. 220, 320
Bragdon v. Appleton Ins. Co. ii. 654
Braithwaite, In re i. 605

Braithwaite v. Britain	i. 686; ii. 469
Bramley v. Alt	i. 226, 295
Bramwell v. Halcomb	ii. 238, 242, 245, 247, 262
Branch v. Mitchell	ii. 11
Brandreth v. Lance	ii. 252
Brandlyn v. Ord	i. 416, 423
Brandon, In re	ii. 693
v. Brandon	ii. 401
v. Brown	i. 158
v. Robinson	ii. 277, 720
Bransby v. Grantham	ii. 420
Branson v. Kinsie	ii. 331
Brant v. Brant	i. 580
Brasbridge v. Woodroffe	ii. 547
Brashear v. West	ii. 343, 344, 345
Brashier v. Gratz	ii. 90, 95, 99, 101
Breadalbane v. Chandos	ii. 204
Breathwit v. Rogers	i. 302, 303
Breck v. Smith	ii. 801
Brecknock Canal Co. v. Pritchard	i. 104; ii. 641
Brecon v. Seymour	i. 421
Breed v. Lynn	ii. 233
Breedon v. Breedon	ii. 475
Breknell v. Evans	1. 397
Brennan v. Bolton	ii. 79
Brent v. Brent	i. 502
Brest v. Offley	ii. 405
Brett v. Greenwell	ii. 755
Brewer v. Bain	ii. 789, 792
v. Boston Theatre	i. 218, 332; ii. 603
v. Brown	i. 205, 208
v. Herbert	i. 69, 105; ii. 55, 111
v. Jones	i. 158
v. Marshall	i. 294
v. Norcross	ii. 770
v. Wall	ii. 52
Brewster v. Hammet	i. 690
Briant v. Reed	ii. 152
Brice's Case	i. 685
Brice v. Brice	ii. 437
v. Stokes	ii. 626, 629
Brick v. Brick	ii. 321
Brickenden v. Williams	ii. 385
Bridge v. Abbot	ii. 398
v. Brown	ii. 685
v. Eggleston	i. 376
v. Hindall	ii. 804
Bridgeford v. Masonville Mfg. Co.	i. 87
Bridger's Case	ii. 861
Bridges v. Longman	ii. 654
v. McClendon	i. 110, 150
v. Mitchill	i. 546; ii. 846
Bridgewater v. Edwards	i. 95, 693
Bridgeworth v. Collins	ii. 398

Bridgford v. Riddell	ii. 708
Bridgman, In re	ii. 631
v. Dove	i. 582
v. Gill	ii. 847, 851
v. Green	i. 248, 263
Briggs, Ex parte	i. 227, 405
v. Davis	ii. 328
v. French	ii. 209
v. Jones	ii. 324
v. Oxford	ii. 220
v. Penny	ii. 406
v. Rice	i. 218, 405
v. Taylor	i. 405; ii. 614
v. Upton	ii. 398
Brigham v. Home Ins. Co.	ii. 24
Bright v. Boyd	i. 102, 189, 392, 394, 395; ii. 130, 131, 583, 586
v. Bright	ii. 80
v. Eynor	i. 195, 199
v. Legerton	ii. 847, 862
Brightman v. Hicks	ii. 76
Brighton Arcade Co. v. Dowling	ii. 769
Brinckerhoff v. Lansing	i. 394, 396; ii. 191
v. Lawrence	i. 607
v. Thalhimer	ii. 330
Brisbane v. Dacres	i. 98, 111
Brisben's Appeal	ii. 592
Briscoe v. Power	ii. 580
Bristol v. Cox	ii. 821
Bristow v. Skirrow	ii. 385
v. Ward	ii. 432
British Assurance Co. v. Great Western Ry. Co.	i. 27, 28
Brittlebank v. Goodwin	ii. 845
Britton v. Bathurst	i. 98
v. Miller	ii. 401
Broadbent v. Barlow	i. 638
v. Imperial Gas Co.	ii. 224, 228, 229
Broadhurst v. Balguy	ii. 615, 629
Brock v. Barnes	i. 314
Brockelhurst v. Jessop	ii. 316, 331
Brockwell's Case	i. 211
Broder v. Saillard	ii. 230
Broderick's Will	i. 198, 441, 548; ii. 779
Broderick v. Broderick	i. 203, 221, 227, 235
Brodie v. Barry	ii. 436, 706, 725
v. Howard	ii. 588
Brokaw v. Hudson	ii. 398
Bromage v. Genning	ii. 103
Bromfield, Ex parte	ii. 113
Bromeley v. Holland	i. 70, 89, 90, 94; ii. 4, 8, 9, 10, 13, 15
v. Smith	i. 301, 302, 344
Brook v. Gally	i. 355

	PAGE		PAGE
Brook v. Hertford	i. 661, 665	Brown v. Pring	i. 139
v. Skinner	i. 562	v. Ray	i. 525, 527
Brooke v. Enderby	i. 460, 466	v. Selwin	ii. 548
v. Haymes	ii. 863	v. Vandergrift	i. 84
Brookings v. White	ii. 321	v. Vermuden	ii. 174
Brookman, In re	ii. 285	v. Wales	i. 621; ii. 18
v. Rothschild	i. 329	v. Yeale	ii. 492
Brooks v. Brooks	ii. 700	Browne v. Like	ii. 722, 728
v. Curtis	ii. 861	Brownell v. Brownell	i. 543, 545, 546
v. Greathed	ii. 161	Browning v. Morris	i. 301, 302, 303, 305, 307
v. Howland	ii. 12		
v. Jennings	i. 98	v. Watkins	ii. 152
v. Reynolds	i. 558, 560, 562	Brownsmith v. Gilborne	ii. 109
v. Stotley	i. 80	Brownsword v. Edwards	ii. 815
v. Woods	i. 627	Brua's Appeal	i. 308
Brooksbank v. Smith	ii. 848, 850	Bruce v. Bonney	i. 158
Brophy v. Bellamy	ii. 680, 685	v. Delaware Canal Co.	ii. 229
Brotherhood's Case	ii. 862	Bruerton's Case	i. 493
Broughton v. Wimberley	i. 509	Bruin v. Knott	ii. 686, 687
Brown, In re	i. 407	Brunker, Ex parte	ii. 800, 801
v. Adams	i. 465; ii. 616	Bryan v. Hickson	i. 555
v. Amyot	i. 481, 490	v. Hixon	ii. 210
v. Armistead	i. 112	v. Hitchcock	i. 203
v. Bamford	ii. 714	v. Howland	ii. 272
v. Baptist Soc.	ii. 524	Bryant v. Carson	ii. 335
v. Brewerton	i. 331	v. Cormick	ii. 161, 164
v. Brown	i. 260, 568; ii. 17, 401, 437, 790, 791, 822	v. Cowart	ii. 321
		v. Isburgh	ii. 19
v. Buena Vista	ii. 202, 203, 814, 851	v. Stearns	i. 660
		Brydges v. Landen	ii. 592
v. Bulkley	i. 319	Bryson v. Whitehead	i. 295; ii. 41
v. Clark	ii. 711, 713	Bubb v. Yelverton	ii. 220
v. Collins	ii. 683	Buccle v. Atlee	i. 554, 555
v. Dewey	ii. 321	Buccleugh v. Metropolitan Board of Works	ii. 792
v. Dudbridge	ii. 48, 815		
v. Edsall	i. 81	Buchan's Case	ii. 619
v. Fagan	i. 154	Buchan v. Sumner	i. 683
v. French	ii. 618	Buchanan v. Hamilton	ii. 631
v. Gilman	ii. 574	v. Matlock	i. 198
v. Haff	ii. 43, 125	v. Rucker	ii. 874
v. Heathcote	ii. 347, 576	Buck v. Dowley	ii. 74, 89
v. Higgs	i. 103, 106, 181; ii. 384, 385, 405, 406, 410	v. Swasey	ii. 602
		Buckbee v. United States	ii. 654, 659
v. Joddrell	i. 240, 242	Buckeridge v. Glasse	ii. 549
v. Jones	i. 181	Buckland v. Papillon	ii. 40
v. Kennedy	i. 332	Buckle v. Mitchill	i. 358, 430; ii. 5, 59
v. Kenney	i. 156	Buckley v. Howell	i. 187
v. Lapham	ii. 341	v. Lavauze	i. 330
v. Leach	ii. 316	Buckmaster v. Harrop	ii. 71, 74, 75
v. Lee	i. 505, 510	Buckner v. Stewart	i. 509
v. Lynch	ii. 609	Buden v. Dore	ii. 815
v. Monmouthshire Ry. Co.	ii. 869	Budge v. Gammon	ii. 617
		Buffar v. Bradford	ii. 547
v. Moore	i. 611	Buffum v. Deane	i. 492
v. Newall	ii. 264	Bugden v. Bignold	ii. 580
v. Nichols	i. 556	Bulkeley v. Walch	ii. 335
v. Peck	i. 292	Bulkley v. Wilford	i. 236, 313, 328; ii. 609
v. Pocock	ii. 713		

CASES CITED.

Bull v. Church	ii. 427, 428
v. Harris	i. 545
v. Valley Falls Co.	ii. 231
Bullers v. Dickinson	ii. 230
Bullock v. Adams	ii. 99
v. Boyd	i. 80
v. Dommitt	i. 104; ii. 611
v. Menzies	ii. 758, 761
v. Narrott	i. 203
Bullpin v. Clarke	ii. 730, 732, 735
Bulmer v. Jay	ii. 399
Bulstrod v. Letchmere	ii. 821
Bulteel, Ex parte	i. 189
Bumpus v. Plattner	i. 416
Bunacleugh v. Poolman	ii. 335
Bunbury v. Bunbury	ii. 210
Bunce v. Gallagher	ii. 11
v. Reed	ii. 332
Bunn v. Markham	i. 609, 610
v. Winthrop	ii. 116, 119, 273, 289
Bunse v. Agee	i. 154
Burbank v. Whitney	ii. 491
Burdell v. Denig	ii. 237
Burden v. Sheridan	ii. 537
v. Stein	ii. 231
Burdett v. Clay	ii. 342
v. Willett	ii. 607
Burdick v. Garrick	ii. 283, 847
Burdon v. Dean	ii. 740, 744, 758
Burford v. Lenthall	ii. 498, 520, 521, 670
Burg's Case	i. 387
Burgess v. Burgess	ii. 257
v. Lamb	ii. 200, 222
v. Wheate	i. 12, 60, 68; ii. 530, 531, 550, 560
Burgh v. Burgh	i. 416
v. Francis	i. 567
Burhans v. Burhans	i. 29, 658
Burk's Appeal	ii. 52, 53
Burk v. Brown	i. 541
v. Chishman	i. 525
Burke v. Anderson	i. 179
v. Green	ii. 373
v. Jones	ii. 852
v. Parke	ii. 795
v. Speer	ii. 14
Burkholder v. Ludlan	ii. 80
Burlace v. Cooke	i. 416, 635
Burles v. Popplewell	i. 560
Burley v. Russell	i. 252, 392
Burn v. Burn	i. 175, 177, 178
v. Carvalho	ii. 366, 367, 368, 370
Burnet v. Burnet	ii. 687
Burnett v. Sanders	i. 79
Burnham v. Kempton	ii. 224, 225, 228
Burns v. Huntington Bank	i. 518
Burnside v. Wayman	i. 158
Burr v. Hutchinson	i. 150, 151, 152
v. Sim	ii. 112
v. Smith	ii. 491
Burrell v. Dodd	i. 654
Burrough v. Philcox	i. 181; ii. 385, 386
Burroughs v. Elton	i. 428
v. McNeil	i. 81
Burrow v. Debo	ii. 844
v. Scammell	ii. 125, 126
Burrows v. Jemino	ii. 212
v. Locke	i. 216
v. Walls	i. 331
Burrus v. Roulhac	ii. 569
Burt v. Barlow	i. 134
Burtenshaw v. Gilbert	i. 103
Burton v. Gleason	ii. 11
v. Pierpont	ii. 707, 709
v. Smith	ii. 555, 557
v. Wiley	ii. 873
Burwell v. Fauber	i. 591
Bury v. Oppenheim	i. 311
Busen v. Foster	ii. 872
Bush v. Western	ii. 177
Bushby v. Munday	ii. 208, 210
Bushnell v. Avery	ii. 13, 15
v. Bushnell	i. 400, 401
Bust v. Barlow	i. 167
Bustros v. White	ii. 821
Butcher, Ex parte	i. 686
v. Butcher	i. 263; ii. 75
v. Churchill	i. 506, 518, 519, 521
v. Staples	ii. 80
Bute v. Cunynghame	i. 497, 516, 571
Butler v. Baker	ii. 421
v. Butler	i. 587; ii. 596, 609, 702
v. Cumpston	ii. 734
v. Duncan	i. 342
v. Freeman	ii. 666, 667, 674, 682, 683, 691
v. Gray	ii. 385
v. Haskell	i. 256
v. Hicks	ii. 24
Butman v. Porter	ii. 288
Butterworth v. Walker	ii. 90
Butts v. Andrews	ii. 64
Buxton v. Broadway	ii. 15
v. Lister	i. 225, 673; ii. 24, 25, 33, 35, 38, 39, 40, 90
Byers v. Domley	i. 659
Byne v. Potter	ii. 8
v. Vivian	ii. 8, 11
Bynum v. Hill	ii. 591
Byrne v. Edmonds	i. 180
Byrchell v. Bradford	ii. 610

CASES CITED.

C.

Cadbury v. Duval	ii. 474
v. Smith	ii. 847
Cadman v. Cadman	ii. 554
v. Homer	i. 222
Cadogan v. Kennett	i. 358, 360, 364, 368, 376; ii. 259, 260
Cadwallader's Appeal	ii. 95
Cadwallader v. West	i. 237
Cafe v. Bent	i. 606
Caffey v. McMichael	ii. 688
Caffrey v. Darby	i. 472; ii. 629
Cage v. Cassidy	ii. 198
v. Russell	ii. 646, 653
Caillard v. Estwick	i. 375
Cain v. Gimon	ii. 327
v. Warford	i. 249
Caines v. Grant	ii. 542, 544
Cairncross v. Lorimer	ii. 864
Cairns v. Colburn	ii. 541
Cairo R. Co. v. Holbrook	ii. 197, 202
v. People	ii. 34
Calcraft v. Roebuck	ii. 102
Caldwall v. Baylis	ii. 221
Caldwell, Ex parte	i. 425; ii. 347
v. Ball	i. 63
v. Cresswell	i. 495
v. Dickinson	ii. 795
v. Renfrew	ii. 290
v. Wentworth	i. 460
Caledonian Ry. Co. v. Helmsburgh Trustees	i. 296
Calhoun v. Calhoun	ii. 688
Calisher v. Forbes	ii. 355
Callaghan v. Callaghan	ii. 22, 116, 120, 273, 354
Calmady v. Calmady	i. 658, 662
Calverley v. Williams	i. 159, 161, 166; ii. 102
Calvert v. Aldrich	i. 529; ii. 581
Calwell v. Warner	i. 180
Camberwell Building Soc. v. Holloway	i. 215, 216, 217
Camblos v. Philadelphia R. Co.	ii. 181
Cambridge Bank v. Delano	i. 218, 402, 405
Camden v. Murray	ii. 281, 688
Camden Ins. Assoc. v. Jones	ii. 429, 436
Camden R. R. Co. v. Stewart	ii. 81
Camp v. Bostwick	i. 335, 510
Campau v. Campau	i. 659
Campbell v. Brown	ii. 532, 535
v. Campbell	i. 66, 664; ii. 418
v. Dearborn	ii. 76, 321
Campbell v. Dent	i. 466
v. French	i. 190, 192; ii. 752
v. Hatchett	i. 153
v. Hicks	ii. 95
v. Hodgson	i. 460
v. Horne	i. 263
v. Houlditch	ii. 208
v. Ingilby	ii. 437
v. Ketcham	i. 244
v. Lowe	i. 659, 661
v. Macomb	i. 643, 649
v. Mesier	i. 477, 505
v. Moulton	i. 334
v. Mullett	i. 684, 685; ii. 604
v. Murphy	i. 627
v. Murray	i. 65
v. Radnor	ii. 518
v. Scott	ii. 242, 244
v. Shrum	ii. 596
v. Twemlow	ii. 793
v. Walker	i. 328, 329, 330
Campion v. Cotton	i. 380
Canal Bank v. Bank of Albany	i. 159
v. Hudson	i. 411; ii. 560, 583
Cane v. Allen	i. 316, 317, 318, 319, 329
Canedy v. Marcy	i. 115
Cann v. Cann	i. 123, 124, 129, 133, 137, 138, 139, 140, 142, 198, 217, 353; ii. 831
Cannel v. Buckle	i. 145; ii. 56, 57, 699, 701, 718
Cannock v. Colliery Co., In re	ii. 37
Cannon v. Copeland	ii. 130
v. Johnson	i. 668
v. McNab	i. 70
Canterbury v. House	i. 552
v. Wills	i. 551, 552
Capel v. Butler	i. 337
v. Girdler	ii. 302
Cappell v. Hall	i. 296
Capper v. Harris	ii. 43
Carder v. Fayette Co.	ii. 428
Cardiff v. Cardiff Waterworks Co.	ii. 224
Cardigan v. Curzon-Howe	ii. 291
Carew's Case	i. 234
Carew v. Rutherford	i. 293
Carey v. Askew	i. 604
v. Bertie	i. 533; ii. 482, 521, 640, 617, 652, 663, 667, 693
v. Faden	ii. 244, 247
v. Goodinge	ii. 547
Cargill v. Bower	i. 215
Carleton v. Leighton	ii. 353, 354
Carley v. Lewis	i. 129
v. Wilkins	i. 209

Carlisle v. Cooper	ii. 224, 229
v. Wilkins	ii. 322
v. Wilson	i. 73, 444, 450, 452, 453, 454, 456; ii. 174
Carlton v. Dorset	i. 272
v. Jackson	ii. 341
v. Leighton	ii. 325
v. Salem	i. 31
Carmichael v Hughes	ii. 686
Carmore v. Park	i. 423
Carnan v. Bowles	ii. 247
Carnes v. Nesbit	ii. 28, 648
Carny v. Palmer	i. 376
Caro v. Pensacola	ii. 173
Carpenter v. American Ins. Co.	i. 152, 211, 216
v. Bowen	i. 527
v. Carpenter	i. 373, 392; ii. 866
v. Cushman	ii. 847
v. Elliot	i. 251
v. Heriot	i. 311
v. Miller	ii. 406, 493
v. Mitchell	ii. 561, 729
v. Muren	i. 377
Carper v. Munger	i. 156
Carr, Ex parte	i. 216
In re	ii. 743
v. Duvall	ii. 87
v. Eastabrooke	ii. 433, 463, 753, 761
v. Hodge	i. 459
v. Lowe	i. 593
v. Passaic Land Co.	ii. 81
v. Rising	ii. 320
v. Silloway	i. 611
v. Taylor	ii. 749
v. Williams	i. 156
Carrell v. Potter	ii. 110
Carrick v. Ford	ii. 738
Carrier v. Sears	i. 238
Carriere v. De Calonne	ii. 801
Carrington v. Hollabaird	ii. 873
Carroll v. Brown	ii. 5, 12
v. McPike	i. 593
Carson v. Percy	ii. 90
v. Phelps	ii. 273
Carswell v. Spencer	i. 549
Carter, Ex parte	ii. 328
v. Balfour	ii. 491
v. Barnardiston	i. 581
v. Carter	i. 185; ii. 286, 789
v. Grimshaw	i. 365
v. Hampton	i. 556
v. Neal	ii. 580
v. Palman	i. 318; ii. 550
v. Sims	ii. 575
v. Taylor	i. 659, 661
Carter v. United Ins. Co. of N. Y.	ii. 379, 381
v. Wake	ii. 323
v. White	ii. 286
v. Williams	i. 405, 406; ii. 320
Carteret v. Paschal	ii. 349
v. Petty	ii. 61, 633, 635
Cartier v. Carlile	ii. 255, 256
Cartwright v. Green	ii. 821
v. Hateley	i. 79
v. Miller	ii. 41, 81
v. Pettus	ii. 633, 635
v. Pulteney	i. 661, 668
Carvalho v. Burn	ii. 347
Carver v. Bowles	ii. 431, 439, 452
v. Peck	ii. 60, 557
v. Pinto Leite	ii. 822
Carville v. Carville	ii. 384
Cary v. Abbot	ii. 502, 503
v. Askew	ii. 436
v. Cary	ii. 408
Casborne v. Scarfe	ii. 314, 315
Casburne v. Inglis	ii. 312
Case v. Beauregard	i. 359, 556, 557
v. Boughton	i. 209
v. Denison	i. 611
v. Phelps	i. 365
Casey, In re	ii. 679
v. Cavaroc	i. 68
Cash v. Earnshaw	i. 682
Caskell v. Lathrop	i. 64
Cassedy v. Jackson	ii. 370
Castle v. Bader	ii. 873
v. Palmer	i. 374
v. Wilkinson	ii. 53
Castleton v. Fanshaw	ii. 852
Castner's Appeal	ii. 397
Castrique v. Behrens	ii. 876
v. Imrie	ii. 876
Castro v. Murray	ii. 211
Catchside v. Ovington	i. 551, 552
Cathcart's Appeal	ii. 367
Cathcart v. Robinson	i. 358, 368, 433; ii. 29, 43, 65, 66, 91, 125
Catlin, In re	i. 378
v. Valentine	ii. 228
Caton v. Caton	ii. 77
v. Rideout	ii. 702
Cator v. Bolingbroke	ii. 575
v. Cooley	i. 409
Catt v. Tourle	i. 294; ii. 348
Cattell v. Lowry	ii. 14
Cavan v. Pulteney	ii. 423, 425
Cave v. Cave	i. 65, 413; ii. 826
Cavender v. Cavender	ii. 614, 631
Cavendish v. ——	ii. 791
Cawdor v. Lewis	i. 391; ii. 586, 772, 774

CASES CITED.

Cecil v. Butcher	i. 433
v. Juxon	ii. 716
v. Plaistow	i. 334
Central R. Co. v. Collins	ii. 868
Central Ry. v. Kisch	i. 208
Chace v. Westmore	ii. 791, 793
Chadwick v. Turner	i. 402
Chadwill v. Dollman	i. 433
Chadworth v. Edwards	i. 476
Chaffin v. Chaffin	i. 590
v. Kimball	i. 431
Chalie v. Pickering	ii. 200
Chalk v. Wyatt	ii. 228, 231
Chalmers v. Storrill	ii. 438
Chamberlain v. Agar	i. 264; ii. 106
v. Chamberlain	i. 97, 194; ii. 106, 517, 519
v. Dummer	ii. 218
v. Knapp	ii. 830
v. St. Paul R. Co.	i. 527
Chamberlayne v. Brockett	ii. 495
Chambers v. Brailsford	ii. 401
v. Crabbe	i. 273, 344
v. Goldwin	i. 541, 545
v. King Bridge Manuf.	ii. 206
v. Livermore	ii. 90
v. Minchin	i. 191; ii. 626, 629
v. Perry	ii. 692
v. Watson	i. 191
v. Wright	ii. 768
Chamblin v. Slichter	ii. 12
Champernoon v. Gubbs	i. 695, 696, 697
Champion v. Brown	ii. 48, 107, 108, 110, 111, 170, 171, 560, 575
v. Rigby	i. 318
v. Wenham	i. 260; ii. 789, 792
Champney v. Blanchard	i. 609
Chancey's Case	ii. 462, 463
Chancey v. May	i. 678
Chandler v. Dyer	i. 423
v. Howell	ii. 526
v. Rider	ii. 387
v. Simmons	ii. 683
Chandos v. Brownlow	i. 400
v. Talbot	ii. 107, 349
Chapel v. Clapp	i. 376
Chapin v. First Univ. Soc.	ii. 386
v. Marvin	i. 279
v. Waters	ii. 591
Chaplin v. Chaplin	i. 501, 581; ii. 440, 447
v. Holmes	i. 659
Chapman, In re	ii. 210
Chapman v. Beach	i. 682
v. Chapman	i. 30, 31; ii. 124
v. Coats	i. 109
v. Derby	ii. 769
v. Evans	i. 690
v. Field	i. 157
v. Gibbs	i. 412
v. Hurd	i. 167, 180
v. Kellogg	ii. 700
v. Koops	i. 687, 688
v. Pingree	i. 391
v. Ry. Co.	ii. 866
v. Tanner	ii. 562, 575
Chappedelaine v. Dechenaux	i. 541
Chappell v. Akin	ii. 163
v. Boosey	ii. 254
v. Davidson	ii. 258
v. Sheard	ii. 258
Charge v. Goodyer	ii. 401
Charles v. Coker	ii. 711
Charles River Bridge v. Warren Bridge	ii. 871
Charlestown v. County Commissioners	i. 390
v. Middlesex	i. 121
Charlton v. Durham	ii. 623
v. Low	ii. 298
v. Poulter	i. 676
v. Wright	i. 566
Chase v. Chase	ii. 759
v. Ridding	i. 610, 614
v. Walters	i. 377
v. Westmore	i. 530; ii. 555
v. Woodbury	ii. 580
Chastain v. Smith	ii. 76
Chater v. Becket	i. 480
Chatham v. Hoare	i. 262; ii. 851
v. Niles	i. 542
Chattock v. Muller	ii. 82
Chauncey v. Greydon	i. 289
Chavany v. Van Sommer	i. 675
Chawner, In re	ii. 331
Cheale v. Kenward	ii. 37
Chedworth v. Edwards	i. 626; ii. 214, 259, 549
Cheeseborough v. Millard	i. 477, 495, 497, 506, 507, 516, 517, 518, 521, 526, 527, 571, 573, 578, 637, 642, 645, 647
Cheesman, Ex parte	ii. 587
Cheetham v. Crook	ii. 770, 774
v. Ward	i. 123
Cheever v. Perley	ii. 334, 844
v. Rutland R. Co.	ii. 316
v. Wilson	ii. 875
Chelmsford Co. v. Demarest	i. 338
Chennel v. Churchman	ii. 10
Cherrington v. Abney	ii. 229

CASES CITED.

Chertsey Market, In re	ii. 524
Chesapeake R. Co. v. Miller	ii. 14
Cheslyn v. Dalby	i. 314; ii. 789
Chesman v. Nainby	i. 294
Chesslyn v. Smith	ii. 724
Chester v. Chester	ii. 526
v. Dickerson	i. 214
v. Willis	ii. 340
Chesterfield v. Bolton	i. 104, 344
v. Janssen	i. 143, 199, 201, 203, 212, 254, 266, 298, 303, 305, 309, 329, 339, 340, 341, 343, 348, 349, 350, 353, 385
Chesterman v. Gardner	i. 406
Chewning v. Singleton	i. 87
Chicago R. Co. v. Field	ii. 770
Chichester v. Coventry	ii. 441, 448
v. Donegal	ii. 818
v. Vass	i. 76
Chicot v. Lequesne	ii. 788, 790, 823
Chilcot v. Bromley	ii. 401
Child v. Comber	ii. 70
v. Douglas	ii. 860
v. Godolphin	ii. 69, 70, 73
v. Mann	ii. 152
v. Thorley	ii. 605, 606
Childers v. Wooler	i. 209
Childs v. Connor	i. 365
v. Jordan	ii. 272
v. Stoddard	i. 153, 155
Chillener v. Chillener	ii. 28
Ching v. Ching	ii. 793
Chipman v. Morrill	i. 505
Chirton's Case	ii. 535
Chiswell v. Morris	i. 636
Chitty v. Parker	ii. 113, 534, 552
v. Williams	ii. 592
Cholmondeley v. Ashburton	ii. 398
v. Clinton	i. 62, 66; ii. 258, 278, 310, 333, 373, 844, 845
v. Oxford	ii. 837
Chouteau v. Allen	i. 332
Christian v. Cabell	ii. 102
Christie v. Craig	ii. 260
Christmas v. Oliver	ii. 349
Christopher v. Sparke	ii. 334
Christ's College, Case of	ii. 507
Christ's Hospital v. Hawes	ii. 508
Chubb v. Peckham	ii. 54
v. Stretch	ii. 727
Chudleigh's Case	ii. 269, 293
Chumley, Ex parte	ii. 695
Church v. Mar. Ins. Co.	i. 322
v. Rutland	i. 416
Churchill v. Churchill	ii. 454
Churchill v. Hobson	ii. 623, 625, 626
v. Wells	i. 373
Churchman v. Ireland	ii. 435
Cilley v. Fenton	i. 459
Cincinnati R. Co. v. Washburn	ii. 46
Cipperly v. Cipperly	ii. 542
Citizens' Loan Assoc. v. Lyon	ii. 603
City Bank, Ex parte	ii. 366
v. Bangs	ii. 153, 155
City Ins. Co. v. Olmstead	ii. 49
Clack v. Carlton	ii. 612
Clagett v. Salmon	i. 335, 336
Clancarty v. Latouche	i. 545
Clanricarde v. Henning	i. 318
Clapp v. Emery	ii. 607, 608
v. Ingraham	i. 188
v. Leatherbee	i. 377, 408, 437
Clappier v. Banks	i. 197
Clare v. Bedford	i. 392, 395
Clarendon v. Barham	ii. 572, 583, 584
v. Hornby	i. 662, 667
Claridge v. Hoare	ii. 819
Clark, In re	ii. 495
v. Clark	ii. 40, 166, 167, 168, 534, 624, 628, 675, 761, 764
v. Cost	ii. 768, 772
v. Covenant Ins. Co.	ii. 11, 12, 13
v. Ely	i. 527
v. Ewing	ii. 179, 197, 202
v. Flint	ii. 33, 38, 39
v. Freeman	ii. 254
v. Garfield	ii. 618
v. Grant	i. 173, 174
v. Hackwell	ii. 67
v. Hozle	i. 556, 557
v. Jeffersonville R. Co.	ii. 234
v. Jones	i. 24
v. Malpas	i. 343
v. Martin	ii. 55
v. Pistor	ii. 724
v. Price	ii. 261, 263
v. Richards	ii. 545
v. Ricker	i. 405
v. Royle	ii. 574, 579
v. Seirer	ii. 52
v. Sewel	ii. 438, 440
v. Tennison	i. 278
v. Van Reimsdyk	ii. 856
v. Ward	i. 243
v. Wright	ii. 78, 289
Clarke, In re	ii. 680
v. Abingdon	ii. 650
v. Bancroft	i. 638
v. Byne	ii. 142
v. Cordis	ii. 397
v. Dickson	i. 208
v. Dutcher	i. 111
v. Grant	ii. 73, 92, 93

Clarke v. Guise	ii. 417, 418, 428
v. Hart	ii. 862
v. Henty	ii. 194, 213
v. Hilton	ii. 534, 546
v. Ormonde	i. 561, 562, 563; ii. 199
v. Palmer	ii. 324
v. Parkins	i. 264, 283, 288, 289, 291, 292
v. Perrain	i. 300
v. Tipping	ii. 616
Clarkson v. Hanway	i. 247, 248
v. Scarborough	i. 492
Clason v. Morris	i. 516, 647
Clavering's Case	ii. 805, 806
Clavering v. Clavering	i. 96, 433
v. Westley	i. 691
Clay, Ex parte	i. 684
v. Brittingham	ii. 689
v. Gurley	ii. 611
v. Pennington	ii. 685, 687
v. Sharpe	ii. 331
v. Willis	i. 566
Clayton's Case	i. 460, 462, 464, 465
Clayton v. Freet	i. 120
Cleaver v. Cleaver	ii. 398
Clegg v. Edmonson	i. 333
Cleghorn v. Insurance Bank	i. 684, 687
Cleland v. Fish	i. 311
v. Hedly	ii. 791
Clemens v. Clemens	i. 378
v. Drew	i. 158
Clement v. Cheesman	i. 610, 614
v. Wheeler	ii. 220
Clements v. Hall	i. 333; ii. 861
v. Moore	i. 376
v. Welles	ii. 233
Clemon v. Geach	ii. 863
Clemson v. Davidson	ii. 366
Clere's Case	ii. 389, 390
Clergy Society, In re	i. 191
Clerk v. Clerk	i. 241
v. Miller	ii. 735
v. Wright	ii. 85
Clerke v. Johnston	i. 555
Cleveland Ins. Co. v. Reed	i. 323
Cleveland Iron Co. v. Stephenson	i. 208
Cleverley v. Cleverley	ii. 199
Click v. Click	ii. 534
Clifford v. Brooke	i. 31, 396; ii. 122
v. Doe	ii. 397
v. Francis	ii. 504
v. Lewis	ii. 591
Clifton v. Burt	i. 572, 573, 575, 576, 577, 579, 643
v. Livor	ii. 872
Climer v. Hovey	i. 175
Clinan v. Cooke	i. 168, 174; ii. 74, 75, 76, 77, 82, 85, 87, 93, 127
Clinch v. Financial Corp.	ii. 816, 868
Clinton v. Hooper	ii. 703
v. Myers	i. 5
Clippinger v. Hepbaugh	i. 296
Clive v. Clive	i. 479, 489
Clopton v. Butman	ii. 401
v. Gholson	ii. 281
Closs v. Bopp	ii. 538
Cloud v. Clinkenbeard	ii. 463
Clough v. Bond	ii. 615
v. Clough	i. 609
Clouston v. Shearer	i. 24, 30, 87; ii. 11
Clowes v. Dickinson	ii. 580
v. Higginson	i. 167, 169, 170, 173, 174; ii. 58, 59
v. Staffordshire Co.	ii. 230
Cloyne v. Young	ii. 546
Clulow, In re	i. 481
Clun's Case	i. 482, 484
Coale v. Merryman	i. 154
Coates v. Clarence Ry. Co.	ii. 231
Coats v. Holbrook	ii. 255, 256, 258
Cobb v. Duke	ii. 560
v. New Eng. Ins. Co.	ii. 794
v. Rice	ii. 138, 145
Cobbett v. Woodward	ii. 242
Cochrane v. Chambers	i. 375
v. Willis	i. 118
Cochran's Estate, In re	i. 519
Cock v. Donovan	ii. 837
v. Ravie	ii. 804
v. Richards	i. 275, 276, 280, 281
Cockburn v. Edwards	ii. 316
v. Thomson	i. 677
Cockcroft v. Black	i. 589
Cockerill v. Cholmeley	i. 147
Cocks v. Chandler	ii. 257
v. Foley	i. 95, 693
v. Simmons	i. 660
Cocksedge v. Cocksedge	ii. 754
Cockshott v. Bennett	i. 385
Codd v. Codd	ii. 805
Codrington v. Lindsay	ii. 437
v. Parker	ii. 164
Coe, In re	ii. 688
v. Lake Co.	ii. 225
Coffeen v. Brunton	ii. 256
Coffin v. Loper	i. 535
Cofield v. Pollard	ii. 388
Coglar v. Coglar	ii. 803
Cogswell v. Cogswell	ii. 280
Cohen v. New York Ins. Co.	ii. 654
v. Sharp	ii. 13
v. Wilkinson	ii. 868

Coiron v. Millaudon	i. 310
Coker v. Whitlock	i. 438
Colburn v. Simms	i. 626; ii. 238
Colchester v. Lowton	ii. 10, 11
v. Stamford	i. 571
Colclough v. Sterum	ii. 473
Cole v. Cole	ii. 73
v. Gibbons	i. 309, 339, 342, 348, 353
v. Gibson	i. 268, 269, 309, 353
v. Johnson	i. 411
v. Patterson	i. 492
v. Pilkington	ii. 76
v. Robins	i. 244
v. Scott	ii. 572
v. Wade	ii. 385
v. Warden	i. 567
v. White	ii. 79
v. Young	ii. 210
Coleman, In re	i. 377
v. Britain	ii. 826
v. Eastern Ry. Co.	ii. 868
v. Mellersh	i. 542
v. Norman	i. 234
v. Parker	i. 609, 610
v. Sarrel	i. 433, 434; ii. 9, 22, 116, 117, 273, 289, 290
v. Wathen	ii. 244
v. Winch	i. 422
Cole Mining Co. v. Virginia Water Co.	ii. 181
Coles v. Jones	ii. 366
v. Sims	i. 404; ii. 28, 651, 860
v. Trecothick	i. 256, 323, 328; ii. 75
Colesworth v. Brangwin	ii. 547
Colgate v. Colgate	ii. 429
v. Compagnie Française	i. 30
Collen v. Wright	i. 205, 210
Collet v. Jaques	i. 95, 693, 694
Collier v. Brown	i. 254
v. Jenkins	ii. 103
v. Mason	ii. 54
v. McBean	ii. 103
Collier's Will	ii. 388
Collins, In re	ii. 696
v. Archer	i. 64, 417, 634, 635
v. Blantern	i. 302
v. Denison	i. 218
v. Evans	i. 209
v. Hare	i. 339
v. Lewis	i. 576, 580
v. Plumb	ii. 54
v. Sullivan	ii. 536, 537
Collinson's Case	ii. 483, 487, 507, 509
Collinson v. Lister	i. 407
v. Pattrick	ii. 118, 273, 354
Collyer v. Fallon	i. 355, 363, 379; ii. 577
Colman v. Croker	i. 383
v. St. Albans	ii. 219
Colmer v. Colmer	ii. 758, 759
Colne Co., In re	ii. 617
Colombine v. Penhall	i. 380
Colpoys v. Colpoys	ii. 82
Colquitt v. Thomas	i. 407
Colson v. Leitch	ii. 206
v. Thompson	ii. 83, 87, 95
Colsten v. Chaudet	ii. 387
Colt v. Netterville	ii. 26
v. Wollaston	i. 199
Colton v. King	i. 433
v. Thomas	ii. 258
v. Wilson	ii. 780
Columbia College v. Thacher	ii. 39, 55, 65
Columbine v. Colchester	ii. 44
Columbus Gas Co. v. Freeland	ii. 229
Columbus R. Co. v. Watson	ii. 46
Colvile v. Middleton	ii. 594
Colwell v. Lawrence	ii. 651
v. May's Landing	ii. 234
Colyear v. Mulgrave	ii. 119, 273, 354, 579
Colyer v. Clay	i. 156, 157, 160
v. Langford	ii. 873
Coming, Ex parte	ii. 323
Commendam Case	ii. 390
Commercial Bank v. Cunningham	i. 414
v. Wilkins	i. 684
Commercial Bank v. Western Reserve Bank	i. 514; ii. 580
Commercial Ins. Co. v. McLoon	i. 28; ii. 6
Commissioners v. Glasse	ii. 816
Commonwealth v. Briggs	ii 677
v. Duffield	i. 188
v. Eagle Ins. Co.	ii. 612, 620
v. Reading Bank	i. 180; ii. 315
v. Rush	ii. 230
v. Smith	ii. 14, 15
v. Stauffer	i. 276, 278, 279, 280
v. Wright	ii. 223
Compagnie du Pacifique v. Peruvian Guano Co.	ii. 822
Compton v. Bunker Hill Bank	i. 301
v. Collinson	ii. 731, 732
v. Oxenden	ii. 113, 340
Comstock v. Clemens	ii. 206
v. Comstock	i. 313
v. Johnson	i. 66

Conaway v. Gore	i. 156
Condit v. Blackwell	i. 323
Condon v. Shehan	ii. 770
Conger v. McLaury	i. 483
Congress Spring Co. v. High Rock Spring Co.	ii. 256, 257
Conklin v. Conklin	i. 664
Connecticut v. Bradish	i. 436
v. Jackson	ii. 620
Connell v. Reed	ii. 258
Connelly v. Connelly	ii. 764
v. Fisher	i. 237, 249
Conner v. Fitzgerald	ii. 79, 80
v. Welch	i. 154
Connery v. Swift	ii. 872
Connihan v. Thompson	i. 406
Connolly v. Branstler	i. 392; ii. 866
Conolly v. Parsons	i. 295
Conover v. Van Mater	i. 416
Conrad v. Atlantic Ins. Co.	ii. 607
v. Harrison	i. 640, 643
v. Lane	i. 392
v. Massasoit Ins. Co.	ii. 789
Consequa v. Fanning	i. 543
v. Willings	i. 159
Consolidated Ins. Co. v. Riley	ii. 339
Constantine v. Blache	i. 386
Contract Corp., Ex parte	ii. 825
Converse v. Ferre	ii. 581
Conway v. Alexander	ii. 321
Conyers v. Abergavenny	ii. 174
Conyngham's Appeal	i. 470
Cook, Ex parte	i. 684
v. Addison	ii. 616
v. Barr	ii. 272
v. Bean	ii. 102
v. Bell	ii. 378
v. Castner	ii. 214
v. Clayworth	i. 244, 245; ii. 4
v. Coolingridge	i. 331
v. Craft	ii. 130
v. Dawson	ii. 592
v. Duckenfield	ii. 523
v. Finch	ii. 651
v. Fountain	ii. 528, 529
v. Hutchinson	ii. 530, 538, 541
v. Jennings	i. 480
v. Martyn	ii. 182
v. Rosslyn	ii. 149
v. Tombs	i. 480
v. Walker	ii. 547
Cooke, Ex parte	ii. 549, 607, 608, 615
In re	ii. 80
v. ——	i. 512
v. Clayworth	ii. 856
v. Forbes	ii. 231
v. Moore	i. 663
v. Nathan	i. 146, 207
Cookes v. Hellier	i. 95; ii. 436
Cookney v. Anderson	i. 692
Cookson v. Ellison	ii. 823
Coomb, Ex parte	ii. 323
Coomes v. Elling	ii. 709
Cooney v. Woodburn	ii. 713
Coope v. Twynam	i. 509, 511
Cooper v. Bigley	i. 411
v. Cooper	i. 263
v. De Tastet	ii. 146, 147, 150
v. Denne	ii. 64
v. Evans	i. 508, 509
v. Gordon	ii. 263
v. Martin	i. 187
v. Pena	ii. 96
v. Phibbs	i. 112, 113, 118
v. Regina	i. 297
v. Reilly	ii. 357
v. Remsen	i. 292
v. Spottiswoode	ii. 569
v. Tappan	i. 306
v. Tyler	ii. 198
Cooth v. Jackson	i. 297; ii. 71, 73, 78, 84, 85, 855
Cope v. Cope	i. 579, 581, 582, 584
v. District Fair	i. 19, 59
Copeman v. Gallant	ii. 608
Copis v. Middleton	i. 254, 256, 359, 360, 361, 365, 372, 505, 506, 515, 519, 520, 522, 524
Copland v. Tentman	i. 460
Copley v. Copley	ii. 449
Coppage v. Barnett	i. 431
Coppin v. Coppin	i. 97; ii. 571
Coppinger v. Fernyhough	i. 400
Coppock v. Bower	i. 296
Coquillard v. Suydam	i. 469
Corbet v. Brown	i. 208
v. Tottenham	ii. 685
Corbett v. Barker	ii. 333, 334
v. Poelhitz	ii. 731
Corbin v. Tracy	ii. 41
Corbitt v. Corbitt	i. 654
Corby v. Bean	i. 65, 80
Corbyn v. French	ii. 514
Cordel v. Noden	ii. 546
Corder v. Morgan	ii. 331
Cordova v. Hood	ii. 562
Cordwill v. Mackrill	i. 408
Corking v. Pratt	i. 129, 133, 155, 311
Cork Ry. Co., In re	i. 304
Corley v. Stafford	i. 314
Corneforth v. Geer	i. 135; ii. 790
Cornell v. Edwards	i. 510
v. Hall	ii. 320
v. Lovett	i. 276, 278, 279, 280
v. Radway	i. 359
Cornfoote v. Fowke	i. 211
Corning v. Lowerre	ii. 226, 231, 232

Cornish v. Clark	i. 369, 374
Cornish v. Tanner	ii. 137
Cornwall, In re	i. 367; ii. 842
v. Cornwall	i. 580, 683, 684
Corrothers v. Board of Education	ii. 14
Corsbie v. Free	ii. 750
Cortelyou v. Lansing	ii. 308, 322, 335, 336
Corwine v. Corwine	ii. 591, 592
Cory v. Cory	i. 124, 133, 142, 245, 250
Cosens v. Bognor Ry. Co.	ii. 233
Coslake v. Till	ii. 41, 101
Costley v. Allen	ii. 198
Cothay v. Sydenham	i. 397; ii. 324
Cott v. Tourle	ii. 42
Cotter v. Layer	ii. 718
Cottin v. Blane	i. 648
Cottington v. Fletcher	ii. 69, 70, 73, 536
Cotton v. Cotton	ii. 398, 400, 700
v. Wood	ii. 541
Couch v. Terry	i. 509
Coulson v. Walton	ii. 95, 843
v. White	ii. 229
Coulter's Case	ii. 130
Council Bluffs v. Stewart	ii. 234
Court v. Jeffery	ii. 728
Courtenay v. Godshall	i. 456
Courthope v. Mapplesden	ii. 234, 235
Coutant v. Schuyler	i. 616
Coutts v. Ockworth	ii. 23, 431
v. Walker	ii. 557
Covell v. Cole	ii. 104
Covenhoven v. Shuler	i. 605; ii. 167, 168
Coventry v. Attorney-Gen.	ii. 631
v. Burslen	i. 540
v. Coventry	i. 584; ii. 598
v. Hall	i. 533, 534
Coverdale v. Eastwood	ii. 290
Coverdill v. Coverdill	ii. 764
Covington v. Powell	i. 117, 118
Coward v. Hughes	i. 118
Cowden's Estate	ii. 579
Cowdry v. Day	i. 314
Cowell v. Edwards	i. 505
v. Simpson	ii. 565, 570, 573
v. Sykes	i. 178, 685
Cowen v. Milner	i. 309
Cowes v. Higginson	i. 144
Cowles v. Gale	ii. 99
v. Pollard	ii. 611
v. Whitman	ii. 24, 39
Cowper v. Baker	ii. 236
v. Clerk	ii. 175
v. Cowper	i. 12, 17, 60, 62, 63, 262
Cowtan v. Williams	ii. 142
Cox's Case	i. 381, 561
Cox v. Baleman	ii. 630
v. Bishop	i. 694
v. Curwen	ii. 398
v. Dolman	ii. 851
v. Donelly	i. 302
v. Douglass	ii. 234, 236
v. Land Co.	ii. 242
v. McBurney	i. 683
v. Mobile R. Co.	ii. 203
v. Parker	ii. 530
v. Smith	i. 659, 668
v. Tyson	i. 337
v. Wheeler	ii. 332
v. Wilder	i. 374
v. Willoughby	i. 669
Coxe v. Basset	ii. 492
Coy v. Coy	i. 406
Crabb v. Crabb	ii. 542
Crabtree v. Bramble	i. 68
Crackelt v. Bethune	ii. 610
Craft v. Lathrop	ii. 210
v. Moore	i. 518, 522
Cragg v. Holme	i. 245
Craig v. Franklin	ii. 495
v. Hobbs	i. 216
v. Hulschizer	i. 691
v. Leslie	i. 69; ii. 112, 113, 114, 115, 551, 590
v. Parkis	ii. 367
v. People	ii. 224
v. Ward	i. 214
Crallan v. Oulton	ii. 852, 853
Crampton v. Zabriskie	ii. 180
Crane v. Burntrager	ii. 143
v. Drake	ii. 470
v. Hancks	i. 96
v. McCoy	ii. 159
Cranmer, Ex parte	ii. 696
Cranson v. Smith	i. 374
Cranstown v. Johnston	ii. 60, 62, 208, 209, 633, 634
Crapster v. Griffith	i. 654
Crassen v. Swoveland	ii. 320
Craven, Ex parte	i. 377
v. Winter	ii. 273
Crawford v. Austin	i. 377
v. Creswell	ii. 674, 688
v. Fisher	ii. 140, 148
v. Summers	i. 95
v. Wick	i. 293; ii. 79
Crawshay v. Collins	ii. 794
v. Maule	i. 661, 673, 679, 680
v. Thompson	ii. 255, 256, 258
v. Thornton	ii. 134, 135, 137, 142, 143, 147, 148, 149, 150, 151
Cray v. Mansfield	i. 323

CASES CITED.

Cray v. Willis — i. 604
Craythorne v. Swinburne — i. 505, 509, 510, 511, 512, 515, 516, 518, 520
Creagh v. Blood — i. 238
— v. Wilson — i. 277
Creditors of Cox, Case of, — i. 558, 559, 565, 567
Creed v. Scraggs — i. 67
Creely v. Bay State Brick Co. — ii. 182
Creighton v. Paine — i. 412
Creuse v. Hunter — ii. 676
Crevier v. New York — ii. 13, 14
Crews v. Burcham — ii. 14
Crim v. Handley — ii. 198, 202, 203
Cripps v. Jee — ii. 533
Crisp, Ex parte — i. 506, 518
Crockford v. Alexander — ii. 235, 236
Croft v. Goldsmid — ii. 654
— v. Lyndsey — i. 98; ii. 192
— v. Powell — ii. 331
Crome v. Ballard — i. 250, 251, 309, 322, 323, 353, 354
Cromer v. Pinckney — ii. 397, 398
Crompton v. Pratt — i. 460
Cromwell v. Brooklyn Ins. Co. — ii. 602
— v. Sac — i. 416
Crook v. Brooking — ii. 272
— v. Glen — ii. 333, 847
— v. Seaford — ii. 861
Crooke v. Andrews — ii. 12
— v. De Vandes — ii. 403, 404
Crookes v. Petter — ii. 244
Croome v. Lediard — ii. 857
Crop v. Norton — ii. 535, 537
Crosbie v. McDonal — ii. 109
— v. Murray — ii. 416
Crosby v. Church — ii. 730
— v. Loop — i. 492
— v. Middleton — i. 167, 179
— v. Taylor — ii. 342
Crosier v. Acer — i. 150
Crosley v. Marriot — ii. 802
Cross v. Addenbroke — ii. 112
— v. Button — i. 497
Crosse v. Crosse — i. 97
— v. Smith — ii. 192, 627
Crosskill v. Bower — ii. 612
Crossley v. Derby Gas Light Co. — ii. 239
— v. Elworthy — i. 369
Crossling v. Crossling — i. 182
Crossly v. Clare — ii. 401
Crossman v. Crossman — ii. 272, 282
Croton Turnpike Co. v. Ryder — ii. 232
Crouk v. Trumble — ii. 75
Crousillat v. McCall — i. 444, 448
Crowder v. Stewart — i. 590
— v. Tinkler — ii. 224, 226
Crowfoot v. Gurney — ii. 348, 366

Croxton v. May — ii. 752
Croyston v. Baynes — ii. 69
Crubb v. Bray — i. 331
Cruger v. Douglas — ii. 764
— v. McLaury — i. 492, 494, 496
Cruikshank v. Duffin — ii. 331
Cruikshanks v. Robarts — ii. 165, 210
Crum v. Thornley — i. 607
Crumb, Ex parte — ii. 674
Crump v. Lambert — ii. 229
Cruse v. Barley — ii. 114, 115, 534, 551, 552
— v. Paine — ii. 37
Crutterell v. Lye — i. 294
Cruwys v. Colman — ii. 268, 401, 411
Cud v. Rutter — ii. 26, 32, 43, 128, 129
Cull v. Showell — ii. 433
Cullingworth v. Lloyd — i. 386
Culpepper v. Aston — i. 575
Cumberland v. Codrington — i. 587; ii. 272, 346, 596
Cumberland Coal Co. v. Sherman — i. 333
Cumberland R. Co.'s Appeal — ii. 265, 868
Cumberland Valley Ry. v. McLanahan — ii. 865
Cummings v. Cummings — ii. 429
— v. Fletcher — ii. 328
— v. National Bank — ii. 15
Cummins v. Fletcher — i. 517
Cunard v. Atlantic Ins. Co. — ii. 549
Cundy v. Lindsay — i. 150, 152
Cunningham v. Blake — ii. 64, 81
— v. Dwyer — i. 376
— v. Plunkett — ii. 23
— v. Taylor — ii. 206
Cunninghame v. Glasgow Bank — ii. 619
Cuppy v. Hixon — ii. 75, 76
Curnick v. Tucker — ii. 406
Curran v. Holyoke Water Co. — ii. 125
Curre v. Bowyer — ii. 553
Currie v. Goold — i. 122
Currier v. Esty — ii. 872
— v. Howard — ii. 110
— v. Railroad — ii. 820
Curson v. African Co. — ii. 603, 770
Curteis, In re — ii. 541
Curtess v. Smallridge — ii. 203
Curtis v. Auber — ii. 378
— v. Buckingham — ii. 259
— v. Curtis — i. 533, 534, 627, 628, 629, 631, 634, 696; ii. 559, 676
— v. Hutton — ii. 512, 518
— v. Perry — i. 189, 300
— v. Price — i. 378
— v. Rippon — ii. 408, 411, 412, 673

CASES CITED.

Curtis v. Smith	ii. 278
Curtiss v. Sheldon	ii. 321
Cushing v. Drew	ii. 651
v. Townshend	i. 350, 352
Cushman v. Thayer Jewelry Co.	ii. 37
Cuthbert v. Kuhn	i. 496
Cutler, In re	ii. 756
v. Coxeter	ii. 471
v. Tuttle	ii. 535, 538
Cutter v. Doughty	ii. 397
v. Emery	i. 511
v. Powell	i. 479, 480
v. Tuttle	i. 301, 302, 378
Cutting v. Carter	ii. 789, 790, 873
Cuyler v. Brandt	i. 403
v. Ensworth	i. 518

D.

Dabbs v. Nugent	i. 455
Da Costa v. De Pas	ii. 493, 502, 522
v. Mellish	ii. 673, 675
Daggett v. Rankin	i. 120
Dahl v. Page	i. 406
Dailey v. Kastell	i. 201, 247, 406
Daily v. Litchfield	ii. 28
Dails v. Lloyd	i. 85, 154
Dakens v. Berisford	ii. 713
Dalbiac v. Dalbiac	i. 237, 254, 261
Dalby v. Pullen	ii. 103
Dale, Ex parte	ii. 616
v. Cooke	ii. 767, 773, 774
v. McEvers	ii. 327
v. Smithson	ii. 257
v. Sollet	ii. 767
Dallas v. Timberlake	i. 456
Dalton v. Coatsworth	i. 93, 198, 260, 261
v. Currier	i. 377
v. Dalton	i. 249
v. Dean	ii. 546
v. Lemburth	ii. 872
v. Poole	i. 61
Dalton R. Co. v. McDaniel	i. 557
Daly v. Kelly	ii. 214, 215, 259
v. Palmer	ii. 244
v Sheriff	ii 210
Dalzell v. Welch	ii. 401
Dambmann v. Schulting	i. 109, 149
Dameron v. Jameson	i. 661
Damus's Case	ii. 507, 508
Dana v. Valentine	ii. 229
Danbury v. Robinson	ii. 828
Danbury Ry. v. Wilson	ii. 868
Dane v. Mallory	ii. 335
Danforth v. Streeter	ii. 372
Daniel v. Dudley	ii. 399
Daniel v. Green	i. 659
v. Kent	i. 406
v. Skipwith	ii. 330
v. Sorrels	i. 415
Daniell v. Mitchell	i. 155
v. Sinclair	i. 112, 119
Daniels v. Davidson	i. 406; ii. 110, 560
Danklessen v. Braynard	ii. 358
Danser v. Warwick	ii. 271, 272
Danvers v. Manning	i. 190, 191
Darby v. Darby	i. 661, 684
v. Whitaker	i. 676
D'Arcy v. Blake	i. 629, 634; ii. 274
Darcey v. Chute	ii. 701
Darden v. Cowper	i. 473
Dare Valley Ry. Co., In re	ii. 792, 793
Darke v. Williamson	ii. 324
Darkin v. Darkin	ii. 702
Darley v. Darley	ii. 703, 710, 711
Darlington v. Bowes	ii. 177
Darlington v. Putney	i. 102, 184, 189; ii. 433
Darnell v. Rowland	i. 249
Darnley v. London Ry. Co.	ii. 46
Darst v. Brockway	i. 303
Dart v. Orme	ii. 13
Darthez v. Clemens	i. 457
v. Winter	ii. 152
Dartmouth College v. Woodward	ii. 871
Darvill v. Terry	i. 376
Dashwood v. Bithazey	ii. 330
v. Bulkley	i. 288
v. Peyton	ii. 406, 425, 427
Daubeney v. Cockburn	i. 387
Daubigny v. Davallen	ii. 821
Davenport v. Kelly	i. 556
v. Mason	ii. 85
v. Rylands	ii. 129
Davers v. Dewes	ii. 547
Davey v. Durrant	ii. 332
David v. Park	i. 215
Davidson v. Barclay	ii. 130
v. Carroll	i. 525
v. Carter	i. 305
v. Greer	i. 154
v. Lanier	i 365, 377, 379, 380
Davie v. Beardsham	ii. 110
v. Verelst	ii. 836
Davies, In re	ii. 385
v. Austen	i. 64; ii. 339
v. Davies	i. 96; ii. 863
v. Dodd	i. 94, 95
v. Humphreys	i. 505, 509
v. London Ins. Co.	i. 234, 334
v. Otty	i. 305
v. Sears	i. 406; ii. 861
v. Stainbank	i. 512

CASES CITED.

Davies v. Thorneycroft	ii. 713
v. Topp	i. 574, 581, 588
v. Wottier	i. 100
Davis's Case	ii. 691
Davis v. Austin	i. 424, 426
v. Bagley	i. 116
v. Bemis	i. 214
v. Boston	ii. 12
v. Christian	i. 411
v. Cook	ii. 327
v. Davis	i. 528
v. Dowding	ii. 331
v. Gardner	ii. 592
v. Gray	ii. 197
v. Henry	i. 309; ii. 789
v. Herndon	ii. 359
v. Hone	ii. 57, 98
v. Jones	ii. 51, 52
v. Leo	ii. 219
v. Marlborough	i. 297, 339, 341, 342, 343, 348, 353; ii. 10, 158, 159, 163, 164, 348, 355, 356
v. Mason	i. 294
v. May	ii. 620
v. Meeker	i. 223, 225
v. Monkhouse	i. 98
v. Morriss	i. 592
v. Old Colony R. Co.	ii. 868
v. Parker	ii. 53, 61, 90
v. Pearson	ii. 561
v. Shepherd	ii. 90
v. Smith	ii. 725, 735
v. Strathmore	i. 400, 413
v. Symonds	i. 167, 168, 169, 170, 173
v. Thomas	i. 179
v. Turvey	i. 662
v. West	ii. 645, 646
v. Zimmerman	i. 392
Davis Machine Co. v. Barnard	i. 238
Davison v. Atkinson	ii. 710
v. Davison	ii. 76
Davor v. Spurrier	i. 394
Davoue v. Fanning	i. 329, 330; ii. 549
Davy v. Davy	i. 693, 695, 696, 697; ii. 57
v. Hooper	ii. 385
v. Pollard	ii. 739
Dawes v. Head	i. 597
v. Tredwell	ii. 285
Dawkins v. Gill	i. 297
v. Saxe-Weimar	ii. 211
Daws v. Benn	i. 540
Dawson v. Bank of Whitehaven	i. 636
v. Beeson	i. 294
v. Chater	ii. 781
v. Clarke	i. 601; ii. 546
Dawson v. Collis	ii. 19
v. Dawson	i. 541; ii. 458, 760, 801, 802, 803
v. Hardcastle	ii. 145, 146
v. Lawes	i. 334, 335
v. Massey	i. 324, 325, 327
v. Oliver-Massey	i. 279
v. Small	ii. 495
v. Whitehaven	ii. 326
Day v. Brownrigg	ii. 239, 256, 257
v. Cummings	i. 80
v. Day	i. 313; ii. 433
v. Lubke	ii. 99
v. Merry	ii. 220
v. Perkins	i. 683
Dayton v. Fargo	ii. 359
Deacon v. Smith	ii. 578
Deaderick v. Watkins	i. 256
Dean v. Anderson	ii. 49
v. Charlton	i. 67
v. Dalton	ii. 546
v. Davis	ii. 15
v. Emerson	i. 293, 294
v. Izard	ii. 32, 128, 129
v. McDowell	i. 332, 674
v. O'Meara	i. 664
v. Smith	ii. 801
Dearborn v. Taylor	ii. 315
Deare v. Soutten	ii. 756
Dearle v. Hall	i. 425; ii. 339, 340, 379, 529
Deas v. Harvie	i. 79
Deaver v. Eller	ii. 374
De Beauvoir v. De Beauvoir	ii. 397
Debenham v. Ox	i. 250, 268, 269
De Berenger v. Hammel	i. 682
De Bernales v. Fuller	ii. 363
Debeze v. Mann	ii. 453, 457, 460
Debigge v. Howe	ii. 818
De Camp v. Crane	ii. 99
De Caters v. Le Ray de Chaumont	ii. 315
Dech's Appeal	ii. 96
Decker v. McGowan	ii. 14
Decks v. Strutt	i. 552, 598, 599, 600
Decorah Mill Co. v. Greer	i. 390
De Costa v. Jones	i. 298
Decouche v. Sevetier	ii. 844
Dedham Bank v. Chickering	i. 338
Deem v. Phillips	i. 313
Deerhurst v. St. Albans	ii. 287
Deering v. Winchelsea	i. 477, 486, 502, 505, 509, 510, 511
v. York Ry. Co.	ii. 868
Deeze, Ex parte	ii. 556
Deg v. Deg	i. 565, 566, 567, 569; ii. 535, 548
De Garcin v. Lawson	ii. 514, 518

CASES CITED.

Degge, Ex parte	ii. 690, 693, 695
Dehon v. Foster	ii. 60, 210
Deiz v. Lamb	ii. 257
De la Garde v. Lempriere	ii. 752
Delaine Co. v. James	i. 215
Delany v. Macdermot	ii. 494
Delapole v. Delapole	ii. 222
Delavan v. Delavan	ii. 99
Delaware Ins. Co. v. Hogan	i. 171
Delaware R. Co. v. Erie R. Co	ii. 265, 867
v. Raritan R. Co	ii. 265
Delmare v. Rebello	i. 191
Delmonico v. Guillaume	i. 684
Deloraine v. Browne	ii. 849
Delver v. Barnes	ii. 791, 793
v. Hunter	i. 632
Demainville v. Mann	i. 494, 495
Demandry v. Metcalf	ii. 336, 338
De Manneville v. De Manneville	ii. 665, 666, 667, 670, 675, 676, 678
De Manville v. Compton	i. 216, 274
Demarest v. Wyncoop	i. 416; ii. 315, 724
De Mattos v. Gibson	ii. 348
De Montmorency v. Devereux	i. 314
Dempsey v. Bush	i. 518
Denham v. Williams	i. 639
Denison v. Gibson	i. 334
Dennison v. Gothring	ii. 288
Denniston v. Little	ii. 94
Denny v. Hancock	ii. 90, 103
v. Steakly	ii. 570
Densmore Oil Co. v. Densmore	i. 323
Dent v. Auction Mart Co.	ii. 182
v. Bennett	i. 321
v. Dent	ii. 816
Denton v. Denton	ii. 759, 803
v. Stewart	ii. 66, 80, 91, 124, 126, 128
Denver v. Roane	i. 685
Denyer v. Druce	ii. 502
De Pierres v. Thorn	ii. 49
Derby v. Athol	ii. 633
De Reimer v. De Cantillon	ii. 874
De Rivafinoli v. Corsetti	ii. 34, 804
Dermott v. Wallack	ii. 615
Desbody v. Boyville	i. 288
Desborough v. Harris	ii. 145
Desper v. Continental Co.	i. 692; ii. 40
De Themmines v. De Bonneval	ii. 502, 503, 515, 518, 522
Detroit v. Dean	ii. 603
Detroit R. Co. v. Gregg	ii. 771
Devaynes v. Noble	i. 177, 460, 685
De Veney v. Gallagher	i. 621; ii. 234
Deveney v. Mahoney	i. 683
Devenish v. Baines	i. 61, 194, 264; ii. 106
Devese v. Pontet	ii. 444, 459, 463
Devis v. Turnbull	ii. 837
De Visme, In re	ii. 539
De Voll v. Scales	ii. 198
Devonsher v. Newenham	ii. 177, 780
Devonshire's Case	i. 446
Dew v. Clarke	ii. 832, 838
Dewar v. Maitland	ii. 434, 436, 437
Dewdney, Ex parte	ii. 844, 852
Dewey v. Allen	ii. 614
v. White	ii. 152
De Witt v. Ackerman	i. 659
v. Schoonmaker	i. 599, 606
De Witte v. Palin	ii. 685
De Wolf v. Pratt	i. 301
Dexheimer v. Gautier	i. 609
Dexter v. Arnold	ii. 844
v. Gardner	ii. 494
v. Phillips	i. 479, 481
Dey v. Dunham	i. 402, 408, 409; ii. 344
v. Williams	ii. 463
Dhegetoft v. London Assur. Co.	ii. 379, 381
Dias v. Bouchaud	i. 522
Dibble v. Scott	ii. 374
Dick v. Milligan	ii. 793
v. Swinton	ii. 803
Dickerson v. Stoll	i. 621
Dickey v. Beatty	i. 156
v. Lyon	i. 406
v. Thompson	ii. 580
Dickinson v. Burrell	ii. 372
v. Corniff	ii. 280
v. Dickinson	ii. 475
v. Lewis	i. 545
v. Lockyer	i. 427
v. Seaver	ii. 359
Dicks v. Brooks	ii. 239
v. Yates	ii. 242, 248
Dickson's Trust	i. 277, 280, 289
Dickson v. Chorn	i. 638
v. Montgomery	ii. 491
v. Swansea Ry. Co.	ii. 367
Dietrich v. Koch	i. 378
Dietrichsen v. Cabburn	ii. 42
Digby, Ex parte	i. 499
v. Cornwallis	i. 554
v. Howard	ii. 759
Diggle v. Higgs	i. 308
Diggs v. Wolcott	ii. 210
Digman v. McCollum	i. 410
Dillaway v. Butler	i. 413
Dilley v. Doig	ii. 173
Dillon v. Copper	ii. 116, 120
v. Grace	ii. 719

CASES CITED.

Dillon v. Parker ii. 415, 418, 426, 431, 433, 434, 435, 437
Dilworth v. Rice ii. 387
Diman v. Providence R. Co. i. 111, 150, 157
Dimmock v. Hallett i. 204, 295
Dimpfell v. Ohio R. Co. ii. 603
Dingwood v. Stowmarket Co. ii. 230
Dinham v. Bradford i. 673, 676; ii. 86, 794
Dinwiddie v. Bailey i. 453, 456, 457, 467
Disney v. Robertson ii. 175
Dixon, Ex parte ii. 774
— v. Dixon ii. 398, 574, 630, 702
— v. Ewart i. 189
— v. Hammond ii. 147
— v. Holden ii. 240
— v. Muckleston ii. 324
— v. Olmius ii. 711
— v. Samson ii. 428
— v. Saville ii. 314
Doane v. Badger ii. 581
— v. Russell ii. 335, 336
Dobbs v. St. Joseph Ins. Co. ii. 197
Dobbyn's Case ii. 805
Dobson v. Litton ii. 82
— v. Pearce ii. 210, 211
— v. Swan ii. 91
Docker v. Somes i. 471; ii. 609, 620
Doddington v. Hallet i. 473; ii. 588
Dodds v. Snyder i. 572, 638, 639
— v. Wilson i. 248
Dodge v. Cole ii. 694
— v. Essex Ins. Co. ii. 842
— v. Morse ii. 611
— v. Pond ii. 553
— v. Strong ii. 203, 204
Dodgson's Case i. 211
Dodkin v. Brunt ii. 279
Dodsley v. Kinnersley ii. 55
— v. Varley ii. 555, 561, 577
Doe v. Alsop i. 401
— v. Ball i. 379
— v. Bancks ii. 658
— v. Gray i. 599
— v. Hassell i. 325
— v. Joinville ii. 411, 412
— v. Lewis i. 433
— v. Manning i. 358, 429, 430
— v. Routledge i. 358, 360, 361, 362, 364, 368, 430
— v. Sandham i. 105
— v. Smith ii. 412
— v. Staples ii. 717, 718
Doggett v. Lane i. 321
Dohle, Ex parte i. 369
Dole v. Lincoln i. 607, 610
Dole v. Wooldredge i. 29, 669
Doloret v. Rothschild ii. 36, 37, 39, 44, 99, 101
Dolphin v. Aylward i. 429, 639, 640
Dolton v. Hewen ii. 394, 473
Donald v. Suckling ii. 335, 336
Donaldson v. Donaldson i. 489; ii. 119
Done's Case i. 540; ii. 804
Donegal's Case i. 250
Donne v. Hart ii. 736, 743, 744, 747
— v. Lewis i. 581, 588
Donnell v. Bennett ii. 35, 42
Donoghue v. Chicago i. 629
Donovan v. Firemen's Ins. Co. ii. 861
Doody v. Higgins ii. 397
Doolin v. Ward i. 295
Doolittle v. Hilton ii. 592
— v. Lewis ii. 331
Door v. Geary i. 191
Doran v. Simpson i. 428, 592
Dorchester v. Effingham ii. 429
Dorison v. Westbrook ii. 43
Dormer's Case ii. 695
Dormer v. Fortescue i. 91, 93, 260, 533, 534, 535, 628, 629, 631, 633; ii. 182
Dornford v. Dornford i. 561; ii. 620
Dorr v. Fisher ii. 19
— v. Shaw i. 571, 572, 644, 651
Dorset v. Girdler ii. 831, 832
Doty v. Martin i. 293
— v. Whittlesey i. 96
Doughty v. Bull ii. 112
Douglas v. Clay i. 560
— v. Culverwell i. 343
— v. Douglas ii. 438
— v. Grant i. 153
Douglass v. Russell ii. 354, 378
— v. Sutterlee ii. 624
— v. Wiggins ii. 219
Douglass Co. v. Union Pacific R. Co. i. 69
Doungsworth v. Blair i. 181; ii. 354
Dousman v. Wisconsin Mining Co. i. 218
Dove v. Dove ii. 261, 262
Dover v. Gregory ii. 591, 593, 594
Dow v. Chicago ii. 14
— v. Sayward i. 687
Dowbiggin v. Bourne i. 506, 515, 518, 519, 521
Dowdale's Case i. 593
Dowell v. Dew ii. 717
— v. Mitchell i. 78
Dowling v. Bergin ii. 80
— v. Betzemann ii. 33
— v. Hudson ii. 473

Downam v. Matthews	ii. 765, 769
Downe v. Morris	ii. 326
Downer v. Smith	ii. 865
Downes v. Glazebrook	ii. 332
Downey v. Thorp	ii. 773
Downin v. Lessors	ii. 672
Downing v. Traders' Bank	i. 640
Downs v. Timperon	ii. 720
Downshire v. Sandys	ii. 218, 220
Doyle v. Blake	ii. 626
v. Hort	i. 210
Doyley v. Attorney-Gen.	ii. 398
Doyly v. Perfull	ii. 743
Dozier v. Mitchell	i. 156; ii. 317, 318, 319, 327
Drake v. Glover	ii. 866
v. Green	ii. 631
v. Jones	ii. 14
Drakeford v. Walker	i. 264
Draper's Company v. Davis	i. 320
v. Yardloy	i. 406
Draper v. Borlau	i. 395
v. Springport	i. 157
Dresel v. Jordan	ii. 99, 102
Drew v. Norbury	i. 411
v. Power	i. 545
v. Wakefield	ii. 398
Drewe v. Hanson	ii. 102, 103, 105
Drewry v. Thacker	i. 562, 563
Drinkwater v. Drinkwater	i. 379, 384
Drohan v. Drohan	i. 427
Drown v. Smith	i. 535
Druce v. Denison	ii. 745
Drummond v. Pigou	ii. 201
Drury v. Drury	i. 473
v. Ewing	ii. 242, 244
v. Hayden	i. 158
v. Hooke	i. 267, 268
v. Natick	ii. 495
v. Smith	i. 611, 617
Dryden v. Hanway	ii. 534
Drysdale v. Piggott	i. 647
Du Bois v. Baum	ii. 95
Dubois v. Hole	ii. 699
Dubost, Ex parte	ii. 117, 449, 453, 456, 460, 461
Duddy v. Gresham	i. 278, 279, 280
Dudley v. Batchelder	ii. 536
v. Dudley	i. 634; ii. 299
v. Mallery	ii. 24
v. Witter	i. 412
Duff v. Dalzell	i. 186
v. Fisher	ii. 32
Duffield v. Elwes	i. 434, 607, 611, 612, 613, 615, 616; ii. 21, 22, 23, 116, 118
Dufour v. Ferrara	ii. 108
Dugdale v. Dugdale	i. 576, 580
Duggan, In re	ii. 348
Duggan v. Kelly	i. 292
Duhine v. Young	i. 431
Duke v. Balme	ii. 570
Dulany v. Rogers	i. 111, 150
Dumas, Ex parte	ii. 607
Dumey v. Schoeffler	i. 279
Dummer v. Chippenham	ii. 823, 824
Dumpor's Case	i. 494, 496
Dunaway v. Robertson	i. 378
Dunbar v. Tredennick	i. 322, 354
Duncamban v. Stint	i. 554, 604
Duncan's Appeal	i. 273
Duncan v. Duncan	ii. 757, 758, 760, 805
v. Hayes	ii. 231
v. Lyon	i. 445, 449, 451, 529; ii. 204, 767, 773, 775, 789
v. North Wales Bank	i. 516
v. Philips	i. 278
v. Warrall	ii. 11, 13
Dunch v. Kent	ii. 346
Duncomb v. Duncomb	ii. 293
Duncombe v. Mayer	ii. 18
Duncuft v. Albrecht	ii. 37, 44
Dundas v. Dutens	i. 375, 382; ii. 88, 290
Dungey v. Angove	ii. 141, 142, 143
Dunham v. Downing	ii. 872
v. Gillis	i. 529
v. Presley	i. 301
Dunklin v. Wilkins	ii. 359
Dunlop, In re	i. 497
Dunn v. Coates	ii. 820
v. Dunn	ii. 716
v. Sargent	ii. 736
Dunnage v. White	i. 130, 137, 139, 140, 141, 142, 143, 245
Dunne v. Dunne	ii. 530
Dunnell Mfg. Co. v. Pawtucket	i. 121
Dunning v. Aurora	ii. 224
Dunscomb v. Dunscomb	ii. 620, 621
Durando v. Durando	ii. 553
Durant v. Bacot	i. 155
v. Durant	i. 166, 172
v. Einstein	i. 470
v. Titley	ii. 763
Durell v. Pritchard	ii. 230
Dureth v. Briggs	ii. 570
Durfee v. Old Colony, &c R. Co.	ii. 867, 869
Durham & Sunderland Ry. Co. v. Wawn	ii. 264
Dursley v. Fitzhardinge	ii. 816, 827, 833
Durst v. Burton	i. 214
Dutton v. Furness	ii. 152
v. Morrison	i. 684, 687, 688
v. Poole	i. 194; ii. 106
Duvall v. Craig	ii. 278

Duvall v. Terrey	ii. 649
Duvalls v. Ross	i. 78
Dwight v. Tyler	i. 156
Dwinel v. Brown	ii. 651
Dyckman v. Valiente	i. 473
Dyer v. Dyer	ii. 531, 537, 538, 539
v. Hargrave	ii. 102, 103, 125
v. Kearsley	i. 562
Dyke's Estate, In re	i. 184
Dyke, Ex parte	ii. 659

E.

Eade v. Eade	ii. 408, 412
Eades v. Harris	ii. 215
Eager v. Barnes	ii. 619
Eaglesfield v. Londonderry	i. 207
Eames v. Sweetser	ii. 756
Earl v. Stocker	ii. 789
East v. Cook	ii. 431, 432
v. Thornbury	i. 122
Eastabrook v. Scott	i. 272, 386
Easterbrooks v. Tillinghast	ii. 534
Easterly v. Keney	ii. 277
Eastern R. Co., In re	ii. 630
East India Co. v. Boddam	i. 70, 88, 89, 90, 95, 96
v. Campion	ii. 155, 649, 850
v. Donald	i. 163, 180; ii. 855
v. Henchman	i. 468
v. Neave	i. 180, 298, 302
v. Tritton	i. 111
v. Vincent	i. 394
Eastladd v. Reynolds	i. 264, 289
East Lewisburg Mfg. Co. v. Marsh	ii. 348
Eastman v. Amoskeag Co.	ii. 228
v. Foster	i. 527
v. Plumer	ii. 96
v. St. Anthony Falls Co.	i. 150
Eastwoode v. Vincke	ii. 438
Easum v. Cato	ii. 768
Eaton v. Eaton	i. 156, 158; ii. 271
v. Jaques	ii. 368
v. Lyon	ii. 656
v. Watts	ii. 406
Ebbett's Case	ii. 861
Ebelmesser v. Ebelmesser	i. 331
Eberts v. Eberts	i. 325
Ebrand v. Dancer	ii. 537, 541
Ecclesiastical Com. v. Northern Ry. Co.	ii. 848, 850
Echliff v. Baldwin	ii. 215, 259
Eckelkamp v. Schrader	ii. 234

Eckman v. Eckman	ii. 12
Eddie v. Davidson	i. 688
Eddleston v. Vick	ii. 257
Eddy v. Traver	i. 524
Ede v. Knowles	i. 367
Edelsten v. Edelsten	ii. 255, 256
Eden v. Smyth	ii. 20, 22
Edensor v. Roberts	ii. 145
Edes v. Brereton	ii. 691
Edgell v. Haywood	i. 375
Edick v. Crim	i. 209
Edinburgh v. Aubery	ii. 518, 519, 636
Edmond's Appeal	i. 153
Edmonds v. Crenshaw	ii. 623, 628
v. Plews	i. 294
Edmunds v. Fessey	ii. 397
Edsell v. Buchanan	i. 62
Edson v. Munsell	i. 242
Edward's Appeal	ii. 553
Edward v. Jones	i. 434
Edwards, In re	ii. 286
v. Abrey	ii. 758
v. Allouez Mining Co.	ii. 229
v. Browne	i. 343
v. Burt	i. 344, 345
v. Child	i. 171
v. Freeman	i. 97, 99, 528, 584; ii. 303
v. Grand Junc. Ry. Co.	i. 296
v. Graves	i. 553
v. Jones	i. 607; ii. 22, 23, 116, 117, 118, 120
v. Meyrick	i. 313, 314, 316, 318, 319, 321, 329
v. Mitchell	i. 377
v. Moore	ii. 536
v. Morgan	ii. 437
v. Parkhurst	ii. 372
v. Warwick	i. 488, 489; ii. 115
Edwin v. East India Co.	i. 171; ii. 641
Eedes v. Eedes	ii. 738, 744
Effinger v. Ralston	ii. 570
Egberts v. Wood	ii. 344
Egmont v. Smith	ii. 65
Eland v. Eland	ii. 469, 471, 473, 474
Elborough v. Ayres	i. 24, 30; ii. 372, 373
Elder v. Elder	i. 175
Elderton, In re	ii. 677
Eldred v. Hazlett	ii. 863
Eldridge v. Eldridge	i. 636
v. Hill	ii. 172, 173, 174, 176, 177, 211
v. Smith	ii. 11
Elibank v. Montelieu	ii. 749
Elkins v. Page	ii. 790
Ellard v Llandaff	i. 230; ii. 90, 103
Ellerhorst, In re	i. 639

CASES CITED.

Elliot v. Brown	i. 683
v. Collier	i. 549
v. Davenport	ii. 21
v. Edwards	ii. 572
v. Fitchburg R. Co.	ii. 231
v. Merryman	i. 427; ii. 468, 469, 470, 471, 473
Elliott v. Balcom	ii. 874
v. Cordell	ii 740, 741, 742, 744, 745, 746, 747, 758
v. Royal Ass. Co.	ii. 794
v. Sackett	i. 158
v. Turner	ii. 645
Ellis v. Atkinson	ii. 723
v. Davis	i. 198, 441; ii. 779
v. Ellis	ii. 737, 749
v. Grey	ii. 358
v. Lanier	i. 30
v. Nimmo	i. 184, 188, 380, 435; ii. 119, 120, 273, 290, 291, 354
v. Ohio Life Ins. Co.	i. 205, 390
v. Secor	i. 607, 609
v. Selby	ii. 496
v. State Bank	i. 359
v. Temple	ii. 576
v. Woods	ii. 710
Ellison v. Chapman	i. 673
v. Cookson	ii. 449, 457
v. Ellison	i. 433, 434; ii. 23, 109, 116, 117, 118, 289, 290, 631
v. Elwyn	ii. 746
v. Moffat	i. 546
Ellsworth v. Ellsworth	i. 117
v. Hale	ii. 211, 234
v. Lockwood	i. 518
Elmendorf v. Taylor	ii. 278, 844
Elmsley v. Macauley	ii. 158
v. Young	ii. 397, 400, 401, 402
Elter, Ex parte	i. 684
Elton v. Elton	i. 291
v. Shepard	ii. 721
Elwell v. Chamberlin	i. 214
Elwin v. Elwin	ii. 113
Elworthy v. Bird	ii. 763
Elwyn v. Williams	ii. 746
Ely v. McKay	ii. 41
v. Stewart	i. 215
v. Wilcox	i. 411, 416; ii. 12
Elyton Land Co. v. Ayres	ii. 14
Emerson v. Davies	ii. 248
v. Staton	i. 89
v. Udall	ii. 198, 790, 873, 876
Emery v. Cochran	ii. 12
v. Hill	ii. 519, 636
v. Lawrence	ii. 349
v. Wase	ii. 51, 789, 791, 795
Emmons v. Bradley	i. 572, 639
Empringham v. Short	ii. 161
Empson's Case	ii. 863
Enders v. Brune	i. 522
v. Williams	i. 431
Engel v. Scheuerman	ii. 210, 211
England, In re	ii. 687
v. Curling	i. 674, 676; ii. 34, 40
v. Downs	i. 270, 272, 273, 274
v. Lavers	ii. 454, 464
English v. Miller	ii. 210
Eno v. Calder	i. 557
Enos v. Hamilton	ii. 228
Ensign v. Kellogg	ii. 28, 66
Eppes v. Randolph	i. 522
Eppinger v. McGreal	ii. 95
Equitable Soc. v. Fuller	ii. 617
Era Ins. Co., In re	ii. 868
Erie R. Co. v. Delaware R. Co.	ii. 868
Errington v. Aynesly	ii. 29, 45, 129, 645
v. Attorney-Gen.	ii. 141
Erving's Case	i. 593
Erwin v. Down	i. 205
v. Hanmer	i. 190
Esdaile v. Stephenson	ii. 102
Eslava v. Crampton	i. 65; ii. 327
Espey v. Lake	i. 326
Espin v. Pemberton	i. 413; ii. 324
Esron v. Nicholas	i. 392
Essell v. Hayward	i. 682
Essex v. Atkins	ii. 718, 724
v. Berry	ii. 873
Estes v. Mansfield	ii. 792
Estwick v. Caillaud	ii. 343
Esty v. Clark	ii. 398
Etches v. Lance	ii. 801, 804
Eton College v. Beauchamp	i. 95, 694
Etting v. Bank of U. S.	i. 164, 234
Etty v. Bridges	i. 425; ii. 340, 379
European Bank, In re	i. 413, 414
Evans's Appeal	i. 116; ii. 437
Evans v. Bacon	ii. 851
v. Bicknell	i. 90, 199, 203, 204, 205, 221, 227, 389, 393, 395, 396, 397; ii. 324
v. Bremridge	i. 179, 512
v. Charles	ii. 399
v. Cheshire	i. 353
v. Edmonds	i. 210
v. Ellis	i. 318
v. Evans	ii. 761, 857
v. Harris	ii. 70
v. Llewellyn	i. 130, 134, 138, 143, 250, 260
v. Smithson	i. 586, 587
v. Wood	ii. 37

Evansville v. Pfisterer	ii. 861
Evants v. Strode	i. 120
Evartson v. Tappan	i. 331
Evelyn v. Evelyn	i. 581, 583, 584, 586, 587; ii. 391, 395, 599
v. Lewis	ii. 161
Everard v. Warren	ii. 855
Everitt v. Everitt	i. 324; ii. 23
Everston v. Miles	i. 209
Evertson v. Booth	i. 516, 642
Evestorn v. Tappan	ii. 519, 620
Evitt v. Price	ii. 258
Evroy v. Nichols	i. 392
Ewell v. Greenwood	ii. 225
Ewelme Hospital v. Andover	ii. 173, 174
Ewen v. Bannerman	ii. 493
Ewer v. Corbet	i. 427; ii. 470
v. Moyle	i. 483
Ewing v. Ewing	ii. 631
Ewins v. Gordon	ii. 110
Exchange Bank v. Rice	ii. 362, 602
v. Russell	i. 158
Eyre v. Bartrop	ii. 195
v. Dolphin	i. 400, 401, 403, 406, 407
v. Eyre	i. 302; ii. 95
v. Good	ii. 795
v. Ivison	ii. 70
v. Popham	ii. 69
v. Shaftesbury	ii. 482, 483, 521, 663, 666, 674, 675, 683, 691, 693
Eyres v. Broderick	ii. 785
Eyton v. Eyton	i. 260

F.

Fabre v. Colden	ii. 740
Fairbanks v. Belknap	ii. 145, 147, 149, 150, 152, 611
Fairbrother v. Nerot	ii. 139, 140, 145
v. Prattent	ii. 139, 140, 145
Fairchild v. Adams	ii. 791
v. Lynch	ii. 341
v. McArthur	i. 67
Fairfax v. Derby	i. 696
v. Fairfax	ii. 624
Fairfield v. Fairfield	i. 556
Fairthorne v. Weston	i. 679
Falcke v. Gray	ii. 33, 38
Fales v. Russell	i. 87
Falkland v. Bertie	i. 59; ii. 484
Falkner v. O'Brien	i. 250
Fall v. Hayebrigg	ii. 73
Fallon v. Railroad Co.	ii. 46

Falls v. Carpenter	ii. 58
Falls Village Waterpower Co. v. Tibbetts	ii. 225
Falmouth v. Innys	ii. 177, 235
Fanar v. Winterton	ii. 552
Fane v. Fane	i. 157, 160
Fanning v. Dunham	i. 306; ii. 7
Farebrother v. Gibson	ii. 865
v. Wodehouse	i. 509, 515
Farewell v. Coker	i. 129, 138, 144, 162
Farhall v. Farhall	i. 591
Farina v. Silverlock	ii. 258
Farish v. Wilson	i. 599
Farmer v. Arundel	ii. 605
v. Calvert Lith. Co.	ii. 246
v. Kimball	ii. 401
v. Russel	ii. 361
Farmers' Bank v. Detroit	i. 151, 152
v. King	ii. 616
v. Rathbone	i. 512
v. Teeters	ii. 828
Farmers' Loan Trust Co. v. Maltby	i. 410
Farmville Ins. Co. v. Butter	i. 121
Farnan v. Brooks	i. 324, 328, 330, 333
Farnham v. Campbell	ii. 14
v. Clements	ii. 89
v. Phillips	ii. 458, 459
Farnsworth v. Childs	i. 401
Farnum v. Bascom	i. 580
Farquharson v. Cave	i. 609
v. Floyer	i. 580
v. Pitcher	ii. 202
Farr v. Middleton	ii. 577
v. Newnham	i. 589
Farrant v. Lovell	ii. 219, 220
Farrell v. Lloyd	ii. 539
Farres v. Newnham	i. 565
Farrington v. Knightley	i. 549, 553, 600, 601; ii. 547
Farrow v. Rees	i. 402
Farwell v. Harding	ii. 12
v. Jacobs	i. 599
Faulder v. Silk	i. 242
Faulds v. Yates	i. 683
Faulkner v. Daniel	i. 499, 500
Fawcett v. Gee	i. 385
v. Lowther	ii. 530
v. Whitehouse	ii. 544, 609
Fawell v. Heelis	ii. 569, 572, 575
Featherstonhaugh v. Fenwick	i. 680
v. Turner	i. 674
Feistel v. King's College	ii. 356
Feit v. Vanatta	ii. 397
Felch v. Hooker	i. 68, 592
Fellows v. Fellows	ii. 609
v. Gwydyr	i. 227
v. Lewis	i. 359, 374

CASES CITED.   xliii

Fellows v. Mitchell	ii. 623, 625, 627
Fells v. Read	ii. 24, 25, 33, 213
Felton v. Justice	ii. 234
Fenhoulhet v. Passavant	i. 575
Fenn v. Edmands	ii. 145
Fenner v. Taylor	ii. 753
Fenton v. Browne	i. 223
v. Hughes	ii. 823, 824
Fenwick v. Laycock	ii. 848
Fergus v. Gore	ii. 852
Ferguson v. Waters	i. 76, 78
v. Wilson	ii. 91
Ferne v. Bullock	ii. 67
Ferrand v. Prentice	i. 604, 605
Ferrars v. Cherry	i. 406, 416
Ferrer v. Barrett	i. 648
Ferrers v. Shirley	i. 562
v. Tanner	i. 695
Ferres v. Ferres	i. 243
Ferries v. Adams	i. 297
Ferris v. Irving	ii. 81
v. Newby	i. 693, 695
Ferson v. Drew	ii. 789
Fetrow v. Merriwether	ii. 372
Fettiplace v. Gorges	ii. 107, 718, 720
Feversham v. Watson	ii. 97
Fiddey, In re	ii. 864
Field v. Beaumont	ii. 204, 235, 236
v. Craig	i. 473
v. Evans	i. 313
v. Hamilton	i. 525
v. Maghee	ii. 354
v. Moore	ii. 437
v. Oliver	ii. 770
v. Schieffelin	ii. 470
v. Sowle	ii. 723, 724, 728, 735
Fielden v. Fielden	i. 563
v. Slater	i. 406; ii. 233
Fielding v. Bound	ii. 511
Fiero v. Fiero	i. 611
Filley v. Fassett	ii. 257
Filmer v. Gott	i. 168, 248
Finch v. Brown	ii. 317
v. Finch	i. 186; ii. 535, 539, 812, 815, 819, 822
v. Hattersley	ii. 593, 594
v. Newnham	i. 261
v. Tucker	ii. 291
v. Winchelsea	i. 567; ii. 561, 576, 598
Finden v. Stephens	ii. 406
Findon v. Parker	ii. 372
Finger v. Finger	i. 549
Fink v. Denny	i. 373
Finley v. Lynn	i. 171
Firmin v. Pulham	i. 344
First Baptist Church v. Robberson	ii. 139, 153
First Baptist Church v. Utica R. Co.	ii. 225
First Church v. Stewart	ii. 263
First National Bank v. Balcom	i. 607
v. Gage	i. 556
First National Ins. Co. v. Salisbury	ii. 619
First Orthod. Church v. Walrath	ii. 651
Firth v. Denny	ii. 423
Fish v. Cleland	i. 311
v. Howland	ii. 574
v. Lightner	ii. 59
Fishback v. Weaver	i. 504, 514
Fisher v. Fields	ii. 269, 274, 275, 283
v. Skillman	ii. 401
v. Thirkell	ii. 225
Fishmongers' Co. v. East India Co.	ii. 229
Fisk v. Attorney-Gen.	ii. 495, 505, 534
v. Norton	i. 559
v. Wilbur	ii. 229, 231
Fiske v. McIntosh	ii. 729
Fitch v. Fitch	i. 350
Fitter v. Macclesfield	ii. 845
Fitts v. Davis	ii. 13
Fitzer v. Fitzer	i. 364, 371
Fitzgerald, In re	ii. 671, 695, 696
v. Falconberg	i. 414
v. Fitzgerald	ii. 701
v. Holmes	ii. 180
v. Peck	i. 135
v. Rainsford	i. 251
v. Stewart	ii. 362, 365
Fitzhugh v. Lee	ii. 837
Fitzsimmons v. Guestier	i. 63, 65
v. Joslin	i. 211
v. Ogden	i 416; ii. 826
Flack v. Holm	ii. 800, 801, 803, 804
Flagg v. Manhattan Ry. Co.	i. 333
v. Mann	i. 64, 407; ii. 70, 825, 856
Flanagan v. Flanagan	ii. 114
v. Great Western Ry. Co.	ii. 91
Flanders v. Chamberlain	ii. 335
Flarty v. Odlum	ii. 355, 357
Fleet v. Perrins	ii. 736
Fleming v. Beaver	i. 518
v. Buchanan	i. 188
v. Chunn	i. 694
v. McHale	ii. 536
v. McKesson	i. 555
Fletcher v. Ashburner	i. 69; ii. 112, 551
v. Bealey	ii. 229, 230
v. Fletcher	ii. 759, 764
v. Green	ii. 630

Fletcher v. Hubbard	ii. 790
v. Peck	i. 387, 436
v. Warren	ii. 198
Flewellen v. Crane	i. 359
Flight v. Bolland	ii. 43, 65, 109
v. Cook	i. 604; ii. 48, 168, 259
v. Leman	ii. 372
Flint, Ex parte	ii. 769
v. Brandon	ii. 29, 45
Flitcroft's Case	ii. 603
Flocks v. Peake	i. 455
Flood's Case	ii. 509
Flood v. Finley	i. 173
Florence Sewing Machine Co. v. Grover Sewing Machine Co.	ii. 637
Flower v. Lloyd	ii. 873
v. Marten	i. 434; ii. 19, 20, 21, 22
Floyd v. Jayne	ii. 198
v. Priester	i. 542
Floyer v. Bankes	ii. 276, 583
v. Sydenham	ii. 817
Fludyer v. Cocker	i. 533
Fluharty v. Beatty	ii. 89
Foden v. Finney	ii. 755, 756
Fogerty v. Jordan	ii. 373
Foley v. Burnell	i. 605; ii. 167
v. Hill	i. 80, 333; ii. 283
v. Kirk	ii. 15, 19
Foll's Appeal	ii. 37, 91
Follansbee v. Parker	i. 390
Follett v. Reese	ii. 569
Folliott v. Ogden	i. 648
Folly v. Hill	ii. 843
Folsom v. Marsh	ii. 242, 249, 252
Foly's Case	i. 567, 568
Fonda v. Jones	ii. 569
v. Sage	ii. 12
Fontain v. Ravenel	ii. 491
Foot v. Farrington	ii. 851
Foote v. Foote	ii. 271
v. Perry	ii. 872
Forbes v. Ball	ii. 405, 411
v. Dennister	i. 400
v. Jackson	i. 514, 515
v. Moffatt	ii. 342
v. Peacock	ii. 384
v. Ross	i. 331; ii. 549
Ford v. Foster	ii. 258
v. Fowler	ii. 406, 407, 408
v. Hennessey	i. 333
v. Loomis	i. 391
v. Peering	ii. 18, 19, 23, 830
Fordy v. Williams	ii. 109
Fordyce v. Willis	ii. 272
Forman v. Homfray	i. 677
v. Wright	i. 118, 129
Formby v. Pryor	i. 296
Forrest v. Elwes	ii. 36, 43, 44, 125, 128, 610
v. Prescott	ii. 393
Forrester v. Cotton	ii. 427, 433
v. Leigh	i. 575, 576
Forshaw v. Welsby	ii. 22
Forster v. Forster	ii. 291
v. Hale	ii. 82, 86
Fortescue v. Barnett	i. 188, 380, 434; ii. 23, 118, 120
v. Hennah	i. 272
Forth v. Chapman	ii. 404
Fosdick v. Fosdick	ii. 276
Foster v. Ames	i. 640
v. Blackstone	i. 400, 402, 424, 425, 426; ii. 339, 340, 367, 379, 574, 579
v. Blagnen	ii. 512
v. Charles	i. 215, 219
v. Cockerell	i. 425; ii. 339, 340
v. Cook	i. 576; ii. 429
v. Deacon	ii. 348
v. Denny	ii. 674, 675
v. Donald	i. 680
v. Foster	ii. 554, 601, 620
v. Fox	ii. 367
v. Grigsby	i. 377
v. Hilliard	i. 500, 502
v. Hodgson	i. 546; ii. 816
v. Munt	ii. 546
v. Roberts	i. 343
v. Spencer	i. 457
v. Vassall	ii. 62, 209, 634
v. Wightman	i. 67
v. Wood	ii. 204
Fothergill v. Fothergill	i. 180, 182; ii. 119
v. Rowland	ii. 42
Fowkes v. Chadd	ii. 782
v. Pascoe	ii. 539, 541
Fowle v. Lawrason	i. 454
v. Torrey	ii. 702
Fowler, In re	ii. 619, 697
v. Adams	i. 154
v. Bott	i. 105
v. Fowler	ii. 462, 725
v. Garlike	ii. 282, 517, 531
v. Lee	ii. 206
v. Redican	ii. 82
Fowley v. Palmer	i. 459
Fox, In re	i. 638
v. Hanbury	i. 687
v. Mackreth	i. 164, 229, 230, 231, 248, 310, 323, 328
v. Scard	ii. 28
v. Wright	i. 350, 354, 355
Foxcraft v. Parris	i. 539

CASES CITED.

Foxcroft v. Lister	ii. 77
Foxworth v. Bullock	ii. 564
Frame v. Dawson	ii. 75, 78, 79, 85
Frampton v. Frampton	ii. 761
France v. France	i. 662, 668
Francis v. Wigzell	ii. 725, 726
Franciscus v. Reigart	i. 493, 494
Franco v. Alvares	i. 600, 603
v. Bolton	i. 300; ii. 8, 819
v. Franco	ii. 743
Frank v. Frank	i. 110, 123, 124, 142; ii. 437
v. Standish	ii. 417
Franklin v. Hosier	ii. 556
v. Osgood	ii. 384, 387
v. Redenhous	ii. 851
v. Tuton	ii. 48
Franklyn v. Thomas	i. 689
Franks v. Bollans	i. 328
v. Cooper	i. 589
Frazer v. Jordan	i. 336
v. Lee	i. 331
v. Thompson	i. 380
Frazier v. Gelston	ii. 866
Freake v. Cranefeldt	ii. 851, 852
Frederick v. Aynscompe	ii. 785
v. Coxwell	ii. 50, 52
v. Ewrig	ii. 12
v. Groshon	i. 26; ii. 234
Freeland v. Freeland	i. 379
v. Heron	i. 544
Freelove v. Cole	ii. 91
Freeman v. Bishop	i. 339
v. Boynton	i. 111, 118
v. Cooke	ii. 863
v. Curtis	i. 129
v. Fairlie	i. 605; ii. 17, 18, 165, 166, 616, 619
v. Freeman	i. 342, 674; ii. 80, 335, 336
v. Pope	i. 365, 369
v. Stewart	i. 684, 685
Freemantle v. Bankes	ii. 459
Freemoult v. Dedire	i. 567; ii. 598
Freke v. Barrington	ii. 425
French v. Burns	ii. 321
v. Chichester	ii. 471
v. Davies	ii. 429
v. De Bow	i. 158
v. French	i. 380
v. Mehan	i. 379
v. Shotwell	ii. 874
French Bank Case	ii. 163, 189
Frere v. Moore	i. 423
Freshfield, In re	ii. 364, 367
Frewin v. Lewis	ii. 260
Friend v. London Ry. Co.	ii. 821
Frier v. Peacock	ii. 503
Frietas v. Don Santos	i. 75, 456, 457, 467
Frink v. Lawrence	ii. 231
Frisby v. Parkhurst	ii. 109
Frith v. Cameron	ii. 675
Frogley v. Phillips	ii. 398
Frost v. Beekman	i. 410, 423
v. Belmont	i. 296; ii. 603
Frowd v. Lawrence	ii. 200
Frue v. Loring	i. 456, 458
Fry v. Porter	i. 12, 15, 290
v. Tapson	ii. 615
Fryer v. Bernard	ii. 209
v. Butler	i. 606
Fuchs v. Treat	i. 153, 156, 157
Fuggle v. Bland	ii. 162
Fulham v. Jones	ii. 112
Fulkerson v. Davenport	ii. 770, 773
Fulkner v. Hebard	ii. 868
Fullager v. Clark	i. 203
Fuller v. Abbott	i. 480
v. Gibson	ii. 145
v. Hovey	ii. 95
v. Percival	i. 28; ii. 6, 10, 13
v. Wilson	i. 212
v. Yates	ii. 428, 429, 430
Fullwood v. Fullwood	ii. 842
Fulton v. Fulton	ii. 428
Fulton Bank v. New York Canal Co.	i. 79
Funk v. Eggleston	ii. 388
Furman v. Clark	ii. 33, 38
Furnival v. Carew	ii. 40, 47
Furnold v. Bank of Missouri	i. 514
Fursor v. Penton	ii. 700, 702
Fyler v. Fyler	ii. 612, 617
Fytche v. Fytche	ii. 436

G.

Gabbett v. Lawder	i. 330
Gage v. Abbott	ii. 11
v. Acton	ii. 701
v. Billings	ii. 12
v. Chapman	ii. 12
v. Rohrback	ii. 12
Gaines v. Chew	i. 197, 441
v. Gaines	ii. 757, 759
v. Thompson	ii. 260
Gainsborough v. Gifford	ii. 192, 203, 872
Gairity v. Russell	ii. 871
Galbraith v. Galbraith	ii. 80
Gale v. Archer	ii. 99
v. Gale	i. 201, 435; ii. 289, 290, 436

CASES CITED.

Gale v. Kalamazoo	i. 293
v. Leckie	i. 672
v. Lindo	i. 269, 271
v. Luttrell	ii. 770
v. Morris	ii. 322
v. Nourse	i. 479, 496
v. Williamson	i. 374
Galland v. Galland	ii. 756
Gallatiani v. Cunningham	i. 309
Gallejo v. Attorney-Gen.	ii. 488
Galloway v. Jenkins	ii. 260
Galton v. Hancock	i. 573, 579, 581
Galway v. Fullerton	ii. 366
Gamble v. Folsom	ii. 844
Gammon v. Stone	i. 506, 519, 647
Ganard v. Lauderdale	ii. 117
Gannett v. Albree	ii. 646
Ganse v. Perkins	ii. 234
Garbut v. Hilton	i. 291
Garden Gully Co. v. McLister	ii. 661
Gardner v. ——	ii. 802
v. Adams	ii. 359
v. Cole	i. 431
v. Collins	ii. 397
v. Diedricks	i. 529
v. Gardner	ii. 342, 590, 725, 726, 730
v. Hershey	ii. 197
v. Marshall	ii. 755
v. Newburgh	ii. 231
v. Parker	i. 611, 612
v. Pullen	ii. 43
v. Short	i. 380
v. Townsend	ii. 577
v. Walker	ii. 737, 749, 750
Gardiner v. Shannon	i. 561
v. Slater	i. 277
Garforth v. Fearon	i. 298
Garland v. Salem Bank	i. 155
Garlick v. James	ii. 336
Garnier, In re	ii. 697
Garrard v. Frankel	i. 150
v. Grinling	i. 173
v. Lauderdale	ii. 344, 345, 364, 379, 529
Garret v. White	i. 658
Garretson v. Weaver	i. 680
Garrett v. Lynch	i. 87
v. Pretty	i. 2 0
Garson v. Green	ii. 560, 566, 567, 571
Garth v. Cotton	i. 199, 534, 537; ii. 219, 292, 293, 294
v. Townsend	i. 184
v. Ward	i. 411
Garthshore v. Chalie	ii. 445, 446, 459, 548
Gartside v. Gartside	ii. 789
Gartside v. Isherwood	i. 236, 237, 247, 248, 249, 256, 310
Garvin v. Garvin	i. 662
v. Williams	i. 327
Gascoine v. Douglas	ii. 633
Gascoyne v. Thuring	ii. 535
Gaskeld v. Durdin	i. 611, 612; ii. 215
Gaskell v. Chambers	ii. 870
v. Gaskell	i. 661, 664, 665; ii. 117, 273, 364
Gaskill v. Line	ii. 580
Gaskins v. Rogers	i. 579; ii. 513
Gason v. Wordsworth	ii. 838
Gass v. Mason	i. 249
v. Simpson	i. 609
v. Stinson	i. 460, 461, 462, 463
Gatewood v. Toomer	i. 666
Gatling v. Newell	i. 227; ii. 865
Gaunt v. Fynney	ii. 229
Gause, In matter of,	ii. 697
Gawler v. Standerwick	i. 604
Gay v. Butler	ii. 367
v. Parpart	i. 660
Gayer v. Wilkinson	ii. 744
Gaylord v. Norton	ii. 789
Gayne v. Boisregard	ii. 15
Gayoso Sav. Inst. v. Fellows	ii. 367
Gear v. Schrel	i. 373
Geary v. Norton	ii. 237
Geast v. Barker	i. 74
Gedge v. Traill	ii. 165
Gedye v. Matson	i. 515
Gee, Ex parte	i. 524
v. Gee	i. 496
v. Pritchard	ii. 250, 252
Gell v. Vermedun	ii. 57
Gelston v. Hoyt	i. 78, 79, 80; ii. 820, 822
v. Sigmund	ii. 81
General Credit Co. v. Glegg	ii. 652
General Smith, The	ii. 587
Gengell v. Horne	ii. 198
Gent v. Harrison	i. 535, 537, 538
Gentry v. Rogers	ii. 96
George v. Alexander	i. 86
v. Kent	ii. 580
v. Milbank	i. 188, 366
v. Tutt	ii. 202
v. Wood	i. 411; ii. 580
Georgia Loan Assoc. v. McGowan	ii. 14
German v. Machin	ii. 66
German Ins. Co. v. Davis	i. 153
German Seminary v. Keifer	i. 546
Gerrard v. Lauderdale	ii. 272
Gerry v. Stimson	ii. 532
Gervis v. Gervis	i. 580
Gething v. Keighley	i. 542

Getman v. Beardsley	i. 171
Gherson v. Eyre	i. 537
Giacometti v. Prodgers	ii. 751
Gibb v. Rose	i. 120
Gibbens v. Eyden	i. 576
Gibbons v. Baddall	ii. 569, 571
v. Bressler	ii. 872
v. Caunt	i. 116, 140, 141
v. Dawley	i. 554
v. Fairlamb	ii. 398
Gibbs's Case	ii. 769
Gibbs v. Harding	ii. 53
Gibert v. Gonord	ii. 616
Gibson, Ex parte	ii. 805
v. Crehore	i. 500, 636; ii. 341
v. East India Co.	i. 297
v. Foote	ii. 534
v. Goldthwaite	ii. 148
v. Ingo	i. 402; ii. 17
v. Jeyes	i. 315, 316, 317, 318, 320, 321, 328; ii. 696
v. Patterson	ii. 99
v. Russell	i. 321
v. Scudamore	ii. 689
v. Seagrim	i. 637, 640, 644
v. Wells	ii. 221
v. Winter	ii. 378
Giddings v. Eastman	ii. 609
v. Giddings	i. 330
v. Palmer	ii. 589
v. Hart	ii. 164
v. Williams	i. 659
Gifford, Ex parte	i. 123, 335, 505, 512, 513, 516; ii. 195
v. New Jersey Ry. Co.	ii. 868
Gilbee v. Gilbee	ii. 694
Gilbert v. Arnold	ii. 263
v. Bennett	ii. 412
v. Cooksey	ii. 82
v. East Newark Co.	ii. 76
v. Gilbert	ii. 539
v. Haire	ii. 329
v. Manchester	ii. 863
v. Neely	i. 514
v. Showerman	ii. 231
v. Sykes	i. 298
Gilchrist v. Cator	ii. 749, 758
Giles v. Giles	i. 191, 192
Gilham v. Locke	i. 381, 561
Gill v. Attorney-Gen.	ii. 628, 629
v. Lyon	ii. 579
v. Shelley	ii. 401
Gillespie v. Moon	i. 167, 169, 170, 173, 175
v. Thomas	i. 495
Gillet v. Wray	i. 277
Gillett v. Peppercorne	i. 323, 329
Gilliam v. Brown	ii. 462

Gilliam v. Chancellor	ii. 440
v. Esselman	i. 337
Gillis v. Hall	i. 294
Gillott v. Esterbrook	ii. 255, 258
v. Kettle	ii. 258
Gilman v. Bell	i. 100
v. Brown	i. 530; ii. 560, 570
v. Dwight	i. 294
Gilman R. Co. v. Kelley	i. 333
Gilmore v. Driscoll	ii. 235
v. North Am. Land Co.	i. 368
Gilpin v. Southampton	i. 558, 561
Gilroy v. Alis	ii. 90
Gilson v. Hutchinson	i. 359
Ginesi v. Cooper	i. 294
Girard v. Philadelphia	ii. 503
Girard Ins. Co. v. Farmers' Bank	i. 662
Girdlestone v. North British Assur. Co.	ii. 816
Girling v. Lee	i. 566, 567
Gittings v. McDermott	ii. 397, 401
Givens v. Calder	ii. 85
Gjerness v. Mathews	i. 417
Gladstone v. Birley	ii. 556, 559, 582
v. Hadwen	ii. 347
Glasgow, In re	ii. 619
Glass v. Dunn	i. 582
v. Hulbert	i. 155, 171, 175; ii. 73, 74, 76, 89, 90
v. Pullen	i. 637
Glasscott v. Copper Miners' Co.	ii. 824
Glegg v. Legh	ii. 815
v. Rees	ii. 345, 364
Glen v. Gregg	ii. 498
Glen Mfg. Co. v. Hall	ii. 258
Glenorchy v. Bosville	ii. 286
Glenwaters v. Miller	i. 323
Glidewell v. Spaugh	ii. 534
Glissen v. Ogden	i. 311
Gloag, In re	i. 216, 217
Gloucester v. Wood	ii. 402, 408
Glover v. Hayden	i. 313
Glyn v. Baster	ii. 718
v. Duesbury	ii. 137
Glynn v. Bank of England	i. 93, 94; ii. 854
v. Houston	ii. 819
Goate v. Fryer	i. 562
Gobble v. Linder	ii. 651
Godard v. Gray	ii. 875
Goddard v. Carlisle	i. 309, 314
v. Hodges	i. 461
v. Keate	i. 698
v. Monitor Ins. Co.	i. 152
v. Snow	i. 272, 273, 274
Godden v. Kimmell	ii. 844, 850
Godfray v. Godfray	i. 342

xlviii   CASES CITED.

Godfrey v. Littel	i. 624
v. Saunders	i. 444
Goetchius v. Sanborn	ii. 79
Goilmere v. Battison	ii. 108
Going v. Emery	ii. 491
Goldman v. Page	i. 89
Goldney v. Crabb	ii. 404, 405
Goldsmid v. Goldsmid	i. 264; ii. 444, 445
v. Tunbridge Com'rs	ii. 230
Goldsmith v. Bruning	i. 268, 303
v. Guild	ii. 99
Goldsworthy, In re	ii. 678
Goltra v. Sanasack	i. 112
Gooch's Case	i. 358; ii. 825
Gooch v. Assoc. for Relief	ii. 494
Goodall v. Crofton	ii. 231
v. Harris	ii. 675, 683
Goodburn v. Stevens	i. 683
Goodchild v. Ferrett	i. 566
Goode v. McPherson	ii. 511
Goodell v. Blumer	ii. 14, 15
Goodfellow v. Burchett	ii. 462, 463
Goodier v. Ashton	ii. 330
Goodin v. Cincinnati R. Co.	ii. 868
Goodman v. Grierson	ii. 322
Goodman v. Kine	ii. 320
v. Randall	ii. 81
v. Sayers	i. 111, 140; ii. 793
v. Whitcomb	i. 676, 682
Goodrich v. Proctor	ii. 468, 469, 471
Goodrick v. Shotbolt	ii. 154
Goodright v. Parker	ii. 292
Goodson v. Whitfield	i. 273, 275
Goodtitle v. Bailey	ii. 419
v. Otway	i. 50
Goodwin v. Goodwin	i. 187, 331, 433
Gordon, In matter of	ii. 696
v. Close	ii. 833
v. Gordon	i. 124, 133, 140, 142, 163, 164, 166, 235, 335, 473
v. Hope	ii. 397
v. Lewis	ii. 767, 771
v. Manning	i. 95; ii. 561, 570
v. Simpkinson	i. 540
Gordon v. Uxbridge	i. 174
Gore v. Brazier	i. 436
v. Knight	ii. 716
v. Stackpole	ii. 331
Gorham Co. v. White	ii. 255
Goring v. Nash	ii. 5, 289, 290, 291
Gormbel v. Arnett	i. 377
Goring v. Bickerstaff	ii. 348
Gosling v. Warburton	ii. 421
Goss v. Tracy	i. 194, 264
Gossmour v. Pigge	i. 140
Gott v. Atkinson	i. 565, 567
Gotwalt v. Neal	ii. 6, 8
Gough v. Manning	i. 278; ii. 428
Gould v. Boston Dock Co.	ii. 231
v. Gould	i. 441; ii. 845
v. Mather	ii. 387
v. Okeden	i. 251
v. Steinburg	ii. 11
Gourlay v. Somerset	ii. 794
Gourley v. Linsinbigler	i. 609, 610
v. Woodbury	i. 659
Gout v. Aleploglu	ii. 255
Gouverneur v. Lynch	i. 644; ii. 580
Gower v. Andrew	i. 322, 330, 333
v. Mainwaring	ii. 503
Gowland v. De Faria	i. 343, 354
Grace v. Newman	ii. 242
Grafftey v. Humpage	ii. 399
Graham, Ex parte	i. 512
In re	ii. 682
v. Craig	ii. 848
v. Graham	i. 629, 662; ii. 289, 538
v. Hockwith	i. 91, 95
v. Horton	ii. 260
v. Johnson	ii. 367
v. Londonderry	ii. 704, 707, 708
v. Long	ii. 272
v. Newman	ii. 314
v. Oliver	ii. 104
v. Roseburgh	ii. 459, 463
v. Sam	ii. 41
Gram v. Wasey	ii. 648
Granard v. Dunkin	ii. 253
Grand Chute v. Winegar	i. 31
Granger v. Bassett	i. 479, 488
Grant v. Austen	ii. 362, 363
v. Bissett	i. 423
v. Duane	ii. 328
v. Grant	ii. 398, 649, 804
v. Jackson	i. 79
v. Lathrop	ii. 197
v. Lyman	ii. 401
v. Meunt	ii. 103, 125
v. Mills	ii. 569, 570, 573, 574, 575
v. Quick	ii. 211
Granville v. Beaufort	ii. 518
Granville Ry. v. Coleman	ii. 868
Grapengether v. Fejervary	i. 156
Grave v. Salisbury	ii. 456, 457, 460
Graves v. Boston Marine Ins. Co.	i. 167
v. Dolphin	ii. 277
v. Graves	ii. 591, 592
v. Griffith	ii. 804
v. Key	i. 389, 391
v. Mattison	ii. 303

CASES CITED.

Graves v. White	i. 215
Gray v. Agnew	i. 390
v. Chiswell	i. 177, 684, 685
v. Cockeril	ii. 18
v. Gray	ii. 539
v. Mannock	ii. 291
v. Mathias	i. 300; ii. 8, 9, 10, 15
v. Minnethorp	i. 582
v. Pitman	ii. 155
v. Robinson	i. 151
v. Russell	ii. 245
v. Seckham	i. 524
v. St. John	i. 377
v. Wilson	ii. 794
Graydon v. Hicks	i. 290, 292; ii. 546, 641
Great Eastern Ry. Co. v. Turner	i. 304
Greatley v. Noble	ii. 728, 733
Great Northern Ry. Co. v. Eastern Counties Ry. Co.	ii. 868
Great Northern Ry. v. Manchester Ry.	ii. 870
Greatorex v. Cary	ii. 429
Greatrex v. Greatrex	i. 675
Great Western Ry. Co. v. Birmingham Ry. Co.	ii. 259
Great Western Ry. Co. v. Rushout	ii. 868
Great Western Ry. Co. v. Sutton	ii. 265
Greaves, Ex parte	ii. 614
v. Powell	i. 569
Greedup v. Franklin	ii. 15
Green's Appeal	ii. 398
Green, Ex parte	ii. 685, 687
v. Ball	ii. 89
v. Baverstock	i. 295
v. Belcher	ii. 391
v. Biddle	i. 411; ii. 130, 132, 133, 583, 584, 586
v. Briggs	ii. 588
v. Butler	ii. 321
v. Demoss	ii. 574
v. Drummond	ii. 534
v. Farmer	i. 530; ii. 767
v. Folghamb	ii. 258
v. Green	ii. 418, 423, 424, 425
v. Ingham	ii. 367
v. Johnson	ii. 554
v. Lake	ii. 231
v. Lowes	ii. 214, 259
v. Pigott	i. 604; ii. 42
v. Price	i. 294
v. Putnam	i. 664
v. Rutherforth	ii. 498
v. Sargent	i. 331
v. Slayter	i. 406, 424
v. Smith	ii. 110
v. Spaulding	i. 30
Green v. Spicer	ii. 278
v. Stephens	ii. 286
v. Sutton	ii. 716
v. Weaver	ii. 819, 820
v. Winter	i. 323, 330; ii. 280, 549, 586
v. Wynn	i. 336
Greenaway v. Adams	ii. 28, 50, 65, 66, 91, 124, 125, 126, 129
Greene v. Bishop	ii. 242, 244
v. Darling	ii. 766, 767, 769, 770
v. West Cheshire Ry. Co.	ii. 32, 40, 46
Greenhill v. Church	ii. 791
v. Greenhill	ii. 112
Greenleaf v. Queen	ii. 819
Greenside v. Benson	i. 552
Greenway, Ex parte	i. 50, 70, 89, 90, 106
Greenwood v. Firth	i. 558; ii. 331
v. Greenwood	i. 344
v. Taylor	i. 571, 637, 640
Greetham v. Cotton	ii. 471
Gregg v. Hamilton	ii. 74
Gregor v. Kemp	i. 272
Gregory v. Haworth	i. 431
v. Howard	ii. 822
v. Ingwersen	ii. 40
v. Lockyer	ii. 728
v. Marks	i. 81
v. Mighell	ii. 80
v. Wilson	i. 84; ii. 616, 654, 655
v. Winston	i. 275
Grell v. Levy	ii. 373, 374
Grenfell v. Windsor	ii. 355, 358, 844, 846, 851
Gresham v. Crossland	ii. 163
Gresley v. Adderley	ii. 164
v. Mousley	i. 319
Gretton v. Haward	ii. 419, 423, 425
Grey v. Northumberland	ii. 235
Grider v. Payne	i. 522
Gridley v. Watson	i. 373; ii. 12
Grier v. Grier	ii. 286
Grierson v. Eyre	i. 624
Griffies v. Griffies	i. 662
Griffin v. Cunningham	ii. 54
v. De Veulle	i. 247
v. First National Bank	i. 362
v. Griffin	ii. 322, 550
v. Orman	ii. 170
Griffith v. Bird	ii. 686
v. Griffith	i. 402
v. Harrison	ii. 390
v. Hood	ii. 700
v. Robins	i. 248, 333
v. Rogers	ii. 548

CASES CITED.

Griffith v. Spratley	i. 251, 254, 255, 340
v. Townley	i. 118
Griffiths v. Evans	ii. 386
v. Porter	i. 331
Grigby v. Cox	ii. 718, 728
Grigg v. Cocks	ii. 607
v. Landis	ii. 100, 659
Griggs v. Gibson	ii. 423, 437
Grigsby v. Breckenridge	ii. 249
v. Clear Lake Water Co.	ii. 228
Grimes v. French	ii. 182
v. Harmon	ii. 483, 488, 491, 493, 503
Grim's Appeal	i. 580
Grimston v. Bruce	ii. 646, 659
Grimstone, Ex parte	ii. 669, 670, 689, 690, 693, 695, 696
Grisley v. Lother	i. 266
Grissel's Case	ii. 769
Grissell v. Swinhoe	ii. 430
Grocers' Bank v. Clark	ii. 359
Groff v. Rohrer	ii. 541
Grogan v. Cooke	i. 375
Groot v. Story	ii. 350
Grosvenor, Ex parte	ii. 806
v. Allen	i 64
v. Austin	i. 684
v. Sherratt	i. 344
Grove v. Bastard	ii. 780
v. Young	ii. 780
Groves v. Clarke	ii. 752
v. Groves	i. 659
v. Perkins	i. 141; ii. 752
Gryll, In re	ii. 398
Grymes v. Blofield	ii. 420
v. Hone	i. 609, 610, 611
v. Sanders	i. 109, 151, 154
Guardhouse v. Blackburn	i. 191
Guchenback v. Rose	i. 383
Guckian v. Riley	i. 117
Gudon v. Gudon	i. 130
Guerand v. Dandelet	i. 293
Guest v. Homfray	ii. 102
Guidott v. Guidott	ii. 112
Guild v. Butler	i. 514
Guion v. Knapp	ii. 580
Gullan v. Grove	i. 187
Gully v. Holloway	i. 588
Gumbleton, Ex parte	ii. 805
Gump's Appeal	i. 158, 180
Gunter v. Halsey	ii. 69, 77, 85
Gurlick v. Clark	ii. 591
Guthrie's Appeal	ii. 397
Guy v. Pearkes	i. 375; ii. 756
v. Sharpe	ii. 457
Guynn v. McCauley	ii. 120
Gwillim v. Stone	ii. 126, 127, 129
Gwinett v. Bannister	ii. 787, 788
Gwynne v. Edwards	i. 516, 571, 637
v. Heaton	i. 256, 339, 342, 343, 344, 348, 353, 354, 355

H.

Habergham v. Vincent	ii. 286
Habershon v. Blurton	i. 687, 688
v. Troby	ii. 822
v. Vardon	ii. 493
Hablitzel v. Latham	ii. 872
Hack v. Leonard	ii. 653
v. Norris	i. 533
Hackett v. Webb	ii. 141
Haffey v. Haffey	ii. 801, 803
Hagar v. American Ins. Co.	ii. 654
v. Buck	ii. 654
Hager v. Burlington	i. 390
v. Shindler	ii. 11, 12
v. Thomson	i. 542
Hagey v. Hill	i. 336
Haggerty v. Palmer	ii. 565
Haigh, Ex parte	ii. 323
v. Jagger	ii. 222
v. Kaye	i. 303; ii. 271, 532, 536, 538
Haine's Appeal	i. 30
Haines v. Carpenter	ii. 158
v. Thompson	ii. 321
Hakewill, In re	ii. 677
Hale v. Barlow	ii. 233
v. Cushman	i. 31
v. Darter	i. 621
v. Harrison	i. 510
v. Saloon Omnibus Co.	i. 376
v. Sharpe	i. 302
v. Skinner	i. 391
v. Thomas	ii. 221, 649
v. Webb	i. 100, 480, 481
v. Wilkinson	ii. 59
v. Wilson	i. 691
Hales v. Cox	i. 638, 639
v. Margerum	ii. 721
v. Van Berchem	ii. 74
Halfman v. Ellison	i. 359
Halford v. Hetch	i. 698
Halkett, Ex parte	ii. 587
Hall, Ex parte	i. 242
v. Buffalo	ii. 366
v. Claggett	i. 170
v. Click	ii. 574
v. Cushman	i. 515
v. Hall	i. 158, 429, 676, 679, 680; ii. 23, 675
v. Hallett	i. 332

CASES CITED.

Hall v. Hardy	ii. 49, 795	Hamilton v. Young	i. 328, 329
v. Hill	ii. 463	Hamilton Woollen Co. v. Goodrich	
v. Hoddesdon	ii. 834		i. 542
v. Huntoon	i. 300	Hamlon v. Sullivant	i. 154
v. Hutchens	i. 514	Hammer v. McEldowney	ii. 82
v. Jack	i. 411	Hammersley v. De Biel	ii. 290
v. Joiner	i. 30; ii. 33	Hammersmith Skating Rink Co.	
v. Light	ii. 290	v. Dublin Skating Rink Co.	ii. 239
v. Luckup	ii. 401	Hammond v. Fuller	ii. 231
v. Piddock	i 663, 664	v. Messenger	ii. 379
v. Potter	i. 266, 268	Hamor v. Moore	i. 611
v. Robinson	i. 514	Hampden v. Hampden	i. 199, 261, 262
v. Smith	i. 406; ii. 99	Hampshire v. Peirce	i. 190, 191
v. Timmons	i. 392	Hampton v. Phipps	i. 527
v. Warren	ii. 65	Hanbury v. Hussey	i. 654
v. Whiston	ii. 13	v. Kirkland	ii. 615
v. Whittier	ii. 74	v. Litchfield	i. 407; ii. 102
v. Williams	i. 356	v. Walker	ii. 675
v. Wood	i. 460, 464	Hance v. Truwhitt	ii. 435, 436
Hallet v. Thompson	ii. 277	Hancock v. Carlton	i. 86
Hallett, In re	ii. 606, 608, 609, 616	Hancom v. Allen	ii. 615, 617
v. Bonsfield	i. 504	Hanington v. Du Chatel	ii. 7, 9
v. Wylie	i. 105	Hankey v. Smith	ii. 768
Halliday v. Holgate	ii. 335, 336	v. Vernon	ii. 203, 204, 206
Hallifax v. Lyle	i. 205	Hankin v. Middleditch	ii. 837
Halliwell v. Tanner	i. 585	Hanley v. Pearson	i. 154
Hallock v. Smith	ii. 569	Hannah v. Hodson	i. 344
Halsey v. Brotherhood	ii. 238, 239	Hannam v. Sims	ii. 414
v. Grant	ii. 28, 29, 36, 63, 102, 103, 105, 125	Hannay v. Eve	i. 59
		Hannewinkle v. Georgetown	ii. 14
v. Whitney	ii. 343, 344, 345	Hanning v. Ferrers	i. 389, 395
Halsley v. Fultz	i. 301	Hannon v. Christopher	ii. 353
Haly v. Goodson	ii. 260	Hansard v. Robinson	i. 90, 93, 94, 95
Hamaker v. Schroers	ii. 648		
Hambleton v. Durrington	ii. 406	Hanson, Ex parte	ii. 773, 774
Hambley v. Trott	i. 476, 535	v. Gardiner	ii. 173, 174, 234, 235
Hamblin v. Dinneford	ii. 34		
Hambling v. Lister	ii. 458	v. Hancock	i. 301, 302
Hambrook v. Smith	i. 80	v. Keating	ii. 740, 742, 743, 744, 749
Hambrooke v. Simmons	i. 616, 617		
Hamersley v. Lambert	i. 685	v. Meyer	ii. 555
Hames v. Hames	ii. 399	Haraden v. Larrabee	i. 496
Hamilton v. Cummings	ii. 10, 13	Harbert's Case	i. 485, 486, 497
v. Denny	ii. 582	Harcourt v. White	i. 535
v. Fond du Lac	ii. 12	Hardcastle v. Smithson	i. 539
v. Gilbert	ii. 575	Harden v. Parsons	ii. 618
v. Hector	ii. 53	Hardin v. Jones	ii. 11
v. Houghton	ii. 345	Harding v. Glynn	i. 103, 106; ii. 385, 405
v. Knott	ii. 821		
v. Marks	ii. 137	v. Handy	ii. 6, 8
v. Rankin	ii. 790	v. Harding	i. 555
v. Royal	i. 404	v. Larned	ii. 618
v. Russell	i. 358	Hardman v. Johnson	i. 330
v. Schwer	i. 638	Hardwick v. Forbes	i. 199
v. Van Hook	ii. 770	v. Mynd	i. 99, 528
v. Watson	i. 334	Hardwicke v. Vernon	i. 476
v. Whitridge	ii. 229	Hardy v. Brier	i. 28, 216
v. Wright	i. 329, 330	v Donellan	i. 687, 689

Hardy v. Martin	ii. 645
v. Mills	i. 659
v. Yarmouth	ii. 144
Hare v. Beecher	ii. 699
v. Burges	ii. 646
v. Groves	i. 105
v. Shearwood	ii. 74
Hargrave v. Conroy	i. 469
Hargraves v. Rothwell	i. 414
Hargreaves v. Michell	ii. 852
Harker, Ex parte	ii. 801
Harkness v. Public Works	ii. 157
v. Remington	ii. 90
Harlan v. Maglaughlin	i. 365
Harland v. Trigg	ii. 406, 408, 411
Harman v. Brewster	ii. 370
v. Cannon	i. 123
v. Clark	i. 684
v. Harman	i. 378
Harmon v. Brown	i. 279
Harms v. Parsons	i. 294
Harmer v. Plane	ii. 236, 238
Harner v. Price	i. 117, 118
Harnett v. Baker	ii. 90
v. Yeilding	ii. 27, 29, 32, 65, 82, 83, 86, 87, 90, 91
Harney v. Charles	i. 121, 122
Harold v. Weaver	i. 156
Harper's Appeal	ii. 320
Harper v. Harper	ii. 271
v. Mansfield	i. 331
v. Munday	ii. 594
v. Ravenhill	ii. 751
Harpham v. Shacklock	i. 417
Harrell v. Ellsworth	ii. 232
Harriman v. Egbert	i. 337
Harrington v. Churchward	i. 451
v. Du Chastel	i. 298
v. Grant	i. 305, 313
v. Harrington	ii. 291
v. Harte	i. 188
v. Long	ii. 348, 372, 373, 374, 376, 377
Harris v. Clark	i. 607, 611; ii. 366
v. Cotterell	ii. 780, 832, 838, 839
v. Galbraith	ii. 202
v. Harris	ii. 617
v. Ingledew	i. 497
v. Mitchell	ii. 790
v. Morris	ii. 756
v. Mott	ii. 729
v. Newton	ii. 397
v. Pepperill	ii. 90
v. Pugh	ii. 555
v. Pullman	ii. 210
v. Tremenheere	i. 316, 318, 320, 321
v. Troup	ii. 658, 659

Harrison, Ex parte	ii. 588
v. Armitage	i. 677, 679
v. Austin	i. 181
v. Buckle	ii. 737, 749
v. Dewey	i. 473, 541, 542, 545
v. Field	i. 178
v. Forth	i. 415
v. Gardner	i. 294
v. Good	ii. 229, 231
v. Gurney	ii. 208
v. Hallum	i. 549
v. Harrison	i. 595; ii. 429, 610
v. Hart	ii. 335
v. Henderson	i. 589
v. Jaquess	i. 376
v. McCarty	ii. 180
v. Mirge	i. 178
v. Nettleship	ii. 202
v. North	i. 104
v. Phillips	i. 515
v. Phillips Academy	i. 376
v. Southcote	ii. 18, 810, 817
v. Tennant	i. 681
v. Ward	ii. 397
Harrow School v. Alderton	ii. 221
Harston v. Tenison	ii. 630
Hart v. Albany	ii. 228, 233
v. Farmers' Bank	i. 414; ii. 280, 828
v. Goldsmith	i. 306
v. Hart	ii. 74, 86, 761
v. Ten Eyck	i. 626; ii. 335, 617, 627, 856
Harter v. Christolph	i. 111, 153, 154
v. Coleman	i. 422; ii. 328
Hartford Ore Co. v. Miller	i. 158
Hartford, &c. Ry. v. Crosswell	ii. 867
Hartland v. Murrell	ii. 594
Hartley v. Cummings	i. 294
v. Hurle	ii. 712
v. O'Flaherty	i. 639; ii. 580
v. Rice	i. 275, 298
v. Russell	ii. 373, 374, 376, 377
v. Tapley	ii. 349
Hartly v. Hitchcock	ii. 555
Hartman v. Woehr	i. 682
Hartop v. Whitmore	ii. 456
Hartopp v. Hartopp	i. 313; ii. 453
Hartshorn v. South Reading	ii. 225
Hartshorne v. Hartshorne	i. 627
Hartwell v. Chitters	i. 565
v. Hartwell	i. 298
v. Smith	i. 509, 511
Harvey, Ex parte	i. 379
v. Aston	i. 285, 288, 289, 290, 291, 292
v. Blakeman	ii. 627

CASES CITED.

Harvey v. Cooke	i. 139, 140, 142
v. Crickett	i. 672
v. Harvey	ii. 687, 703, 709
v. Ledbetter	ii. 536
v. Montague	i. 413
v. Morris	ii. 822
v. Richards	i. 597
v. Seashol	ii. 203
v. Tebbutt	i. 79
v. Varney	i. 302, 305, 378, 692; ii. 535, 538
v. Wood	ii. 773
Harville v. Lowe	ii. 570
Harwood v. Fisher	ii. 745
v. Oglander	i. 74, 581, 587, 588
v. Schmedes	i. 541
v. Tooker	i. 269, 350; ii. 354
Hasbrouck v. Vandervoort	ii. 336
Haselfoot, In re	i. 463
Haselinton v. Gill	ii. 715
Haskell v. Allen	i. 621
v. Haskell	ii. 816
v. New Bedford	ii. 233
Haskins v. Burr	i. 469
v. Kelly	ii. 335
Haslett v. Pattle	i. 100
Haslewood v. Pope	i. 68, 569, 576, 577, 582
Hassall v. Smithers	ii. 365, 607
Hassam v. Day	i. 659
Hassard v. Rowe	ii. 280
Hassell v. Hassell	ii. 592
Hassie v. G. I. Congregation	ii. 349
Hastings v. Whitby	i. 294
Hatch v. Atkinson	i. 610
v. Cobb	ii. 128
v. Dana	i. 557
v. Hatch	i. 303, 316, 317, 320, 321, 326, 328
v. Vermont Central Ry. Co.	ii. 234
Hatfield v. Gulden	i. 296
v. McWhorter	ii. 148
Hathaway v. Seaman	ii. 711
Hatton v. Hatton	i. 601
Haughton v. Haughton	i. 292
Haughwout v. Murphy	ii. 95
Hause v. Hause	i. 603
Hauser v. Shore	ii. 474
Haven v. Adams	i. 411
v. Foster	i. 111, 113, 159
v. Wakefield	i. 690
Havens v. Sackett	ii. 424, 427
Hawes v. Oakland	ii. 603
v. Wyatt	i. 250, 251, 311
Hawk v. Thorn	ii. 359
Hawker, Ex parte	i. 297
Hawkes v. Saunders	i. 599
Hawkins's Appeal	i. 326
Hawkins v. Day	i. 97, 98, 553, 602
v. Freeman	ii. 769
v. Hawkins	i. 216, 404
v. Holmes	ii. 74, 78
v. Kelly	i. 491, 492
v. Maltby	ii. 37
v. Skeggs	i. 278
Hawkshaw v. Parkins	i. 689; ii. 10, 259
Hawksworth v. Hawksworth	ii. 680
Hawley v. Clowes	i. 536; ii. 221
v. Cramer	i. 328, 329, 456
v. Mancius	i. 331
Hawralty v. Warren	ii. 32, 43, 52
Hay, In re	i. 237
v. Estell	i. 659
v. Palmer	i. 488, 489, 490
Hayes v. Bement	i. 690
v. Harmony Grove Cem.	ii. 64
v. Hayes	ii. 161, 169
v. Little	i. 337
v. Ward	i. 334, 337, 506, 507, 508, 516, 517, 526, 527, 642, 643, 645, 647, 648, 649; ii. 48, 170
Haygarth v. Wearing	i. 206
Haygood v. Marlowe	ii. 566
Haynes v. Littlefear	i. 601
v. Mico	ii. 445
v. Nice	i. 460
Hays v. Quay	ii. 536
Hayter v. Trego	ii. 517
Haytor v. Rod	ii. 299
Hayward v. Andrews	ii. 380
v. Angell	ii. 616, 647, 653
v. Dimsdale	ii. 10, 11
v. National Bank	i. 332
Haywood v. Hutchins	i. 456
v. Judson	i. 662, 666, 667, 668
Hazel v. Hagan	ii. 387
Hazeltine v. Granger	ii. 321
Head v. Boston Mar. Ins. Co.	i. 171
v. Egerton	ii. 23
v. Godlee	i. 313
v. Head	ii. 757, 758, 759
v. Randall	ii. 398, 401
Headen v. Rosher	i. 343; ii. 724
Heams v. Bance	i. 422
Heane v. Rogers	i. 389, 391
Heapy v. Hill	ii. 99
Heard v. Stanford	i. 59
Hearle v. Greenbank	ii. 436
Hearst v. Pujol	i. 85
Heasman v. Pearse	i. 489
Heath v. Bucknell	ii. 230

CASES CITED.

Heath v. Dendy	i. 580
v. Erie R. Co.	ii. 820
v. Hall	ii. 366
v. Hay	i. 336
v. Nugent	i. 488
v. Perry	i. 604
v. Waters	i. 686
Heatly v. Thomas	ii. 722, 730, 732, 735
Heaton v. Dearden	i. 664
v. Fryberger	i. 120
Heavenridge v. Mondy	i. 114
Heburn v. Warner	ii. 729
Hecht v. Spears	ii. 570
Heck v. Kleppenger	ii. 398
Heckard v. Sayre	ii. 99
Hedges v. Everard	ii. 125, 129
v. Harpur	ii. 404
v. Hedges	i. 607
Heidingsfelder v. Slade	i. 377
Heine v. Vogel	ii. 341
Heister v. Fortner	i. 410
Heli, In re	ii. 671
Heller, In re	i. 664
Helme v. Phila. Ins. Co.	ii. 654, 659
Heming v. Clutterbuck	ii. 464
Hemings v. Pugh	i. 333
Hemming v. Gurrey	ii. 464
v. Maddick	ii. 170
Hemmings v. Munckley	i. 277, 291
Henderson v. Ayres	i. 590
v. Dickey	i. 156
v. Huey	i. 335
v. Lacon	i. 209
v. McDuffee	i. 510
v. Vaulx	ii. 24
Hendrick v. Whittemore	i. 511
v. Wood	i. 692
Hendricks v. Hopkins	i. 244
v. Kelly	i. 406
v. Toole	i. 31
Hendrickson v. Hinckley	ii. 876
Heneage v. Hunloke	i. 172
Henkle v. Royal Assur. Co.	i. 166, 167, 170, 171, 172; ii. 93
Henley v. Cooke	i. 141
Henn v. Walsh	i. 680
Hennell v. Kelland	ii. 203
Henry v. Railroad Co.	i. 557
v. Tupper	ii. 653, 655
v. Winnebago	ii. 851
Hensman v. Fryer	i. 576, 580
Henty v. Wrey	i. 263
Henvell v. Whitaker	ii. 593, 594
Hepburn v. Auld	ii. 102, 103, 125
v. Dunlop	i. 76, 127, 173, 222; ii. 92, 99, 102
Herbert's Case	ii. 580, 691
Herbert v. Herbert	ii. 711, 716
v. Lownes	i. 194
v. Mechanics' Assoc.	i. 640
v. Salisbury Ry. Co.	ii. 645
v. Wren	i. 629, 636
Hercy v. Birch	i. 673
Heriot's Hospital v. Gibson	ii. 55, 233
Hermann v. Hodges	ii. 49
Hern v. Nichols	i. 214
Herne v. Bembow	ii. 221
v. Meyrick	i. 575, 577
Heron v. Heron	i. 311; ii. 535
v. Newton	ii. 547
Herrick v. Ames	i. 674
v. Belknap	ii. 794
v. Blair	ii. 791
Herriman v. Skillman	i. 639
Herrington v. Williams	ii. 11
Hertford v. Boore	ii. 99
Hervey v. Savery	i. 153
v. Young	i. 223
Hess's Estate	i. 525
Hess v. Voss	i. 29, 667
Hessing v. McCloskey	i. 377
Heuser v. Harris	ii. 494, 502, 503, 521
Heward v. Slagle	i. 555
Hewes v. Dehon	i. 584; ii. 595
Hewison v. Guthrie	ii. 570
Hewitt's Case	i. 654
Hewitt v. Crane	i. 311
v. Kaye	i. 611
v. Loosemore	i. 402
v. Phelps	ii. 281
v. Sturdevant	ii. 588
v. Wright	ii. 113, 115
Heydon v. Heydon	i. 687
Heyland v. Badger	ii. 335
Heyman v. Dubois	i. 516
Heyn's Case	ii. 805
Heysham v. Heysham	ii. 687
Heywood, Ex parte	i. 530; ii. 365, 554
v. Waring	ii. 555
Hibbard v. Eastman	ii. 193
v. Lambe	ii. 631
Hibbert v. Cooke	ii. 583
v. Hibbert	i. 673; ii. 398
v. Rollestone	i. 189
Hichens v. Congreve	i. 678, 679
Hickenbotham v. Blackledge	i. 662
Hickman v. Painter	i. 88
Hicks v. Chapman	ii. 683
v. Hastings	i. 624
v. Hunt	ii. 866
Hickson v. Darlow	ii. 332
Hicock v. McKay	ii. 362
Hide v. Pettit	ii. 62, 262
Higbee v. Camden R. Co.	ii. 225

Higgen v. Lyddal	i. 421
Higgens's Case	i. 178
Higginbotham v. Cornwell	ii. 428
v. Hawkins	i. 535, 537
Higgins v. Mills	ii. 855
v. Samels	ii. 90, 102
Higginson v. Clowes	i. 174
Higgs v. Dorkis	i. 662
High v. Worley	ii. 554
Highberger v. Stiffler	i. 313
Hightower v. Rigsby	ii. 560, 574
Hileman v. Wright	i. 154
Hill, Ex parte	i. 377
v. Ahern	i. 376, 408
v. Barclay	ii. 45, 644, 645, 646, 648, 653, 655, 656, 658, 661
v. Beebe	ii. 342
v. Boyle	ii. 359
v. Buckley	i. 157; ii. 104
v. Chapman	i. 611
v. Curtis	i. 549
v. Davies	ii. 239, 240
v. Fullbrook	i. 663
v. Gray	i. 223
v. Kelly	i. 519
v. Lane	i. 30, 199
v. London	ii. 530, 534, 590
v. More	ii. 794
v. Palmer	i. 673
v. Paul	ii. 356, 358
v. Pine River Bank	ii. 541
v. Robbins	i. 460
v. Rockingham Bank	ii. 24, 37, 39
v. Rowland	ii. 654
v. Simpson	i. 427, 428, 588, 589, 590, 591; ii. 470, 606
v. Spencer	i. 303
v. South Staffordshire Ry. Co.	ii. 861
v. Thompson	ii. 238
v. Turner	i. 601, 602
v. Walker	i. 590
Hilles v. Parrish	ii. 869
Hillman, Ex parte	i. 369
Hills v. Croll	ii. 42
v. Loomis	ii. 321
v. Miller	ii. 231
Hilton v. Barrow	ii. 9
v. Biron	ii. 805
v. Eckersley	i. 293
v. Scarborough	ii. 175
v. Woods	ii. 129, 372
Himes v. Keller	i. 506, 514, 518
Hinchcliffe v. Hinchcliffe	ii. 446, 449
Hinchinbrooke v. Seymour	i. 263
Hinchley v. Greany	i. 30, 69, 87; ii. 179
Hincksman v. Smith	i. 343, 346
Hinde v. Longworth	i. 364, 367, 368
Hindley v. Emery	ii. 129
v. Westmeath	ii. 756, 763
Hinds v. Ballou	ii. 341
Hindson v. Weatherill	i. 320
Hine v. Dodd	i. 407, 409, 410
v. Handy	ii. 259
Hines v. Perkins	ii. 570
v. Rawson	ii. 210
v. Citizens Ins. Co.	i. 153
v Hinton	i. 250
v Parker	i. 551, 552
v Sparkes	ii. 651, 652
Hipp v. Babin	i. 30
Hipwell v. Knight	ii. 100
Hiram, The	i. 175
Hirst v. Denham	ii. 255
Hiscock v. Phelps	i. 683
Hise v. Foster	ii. 651
Hitch v. Davis	i. 609
v. Wells	ii. 782
Hitchcock v. Coker	i. 294
v. Giddings	i. 155, 160
Hitchen v. Hitchen	ii. 430
Hitchins v. Hitchins	i. 634
v. Pettingill	i. 154, 155, 171, 175; ii. 90
Hixam v. Witham	i. 567, 568, 569
Hoare v. Bremridge	i. 27, 28, 31, 199; ii. 6
v. Contencin	i. 177, 456
v. Osborne	ii. 494, 505
Hobart v. Suffolk	ii. 534
Hobbs v. Davis	i. 377
v. Norton	i. 61, 393
Hobday v. Peters	i. 314, 320; ii. 614
Hobson v. Bass	i. 524
v. Blackburn	ii. 512
v. Sherwood	i. 663
v. Trevor	ii. 353, 354
Hocker v. Gentry	ii. 554
Hoddy v. Hoard	i. 91, 95
Hodgens v. Hodgens	ii. 751, 752, 753, 754
Hodges v. Griggs	ii. 11
v. Hodges	ii. 756
v. Smith	ii. 142
v. Tennessee Ins. Co.	ii. 321
v. Waddington	i. 99
Hodgson v. Anderson	ii. 348
v. Butts	i. 360, 361
v. Dean	i. 397
v. Murray	ii. 214
v. Shaw	i. 505, 506, 515, 518, 519, 520, 522, 523
Hodsdon v. Dancer	ii. 388
v. Butts	ii. 587
Hoffman v. Beard	i. 659

CASES CITED.

Hogan v. Curtin	i. 276, 277, 278, 280
v. Delaware Ins. Co.	i. 175
Hogg v. Cook	ii. 398
v. Kirby	ii. 236, 237, 254
Hoggart v. Cutts	ii. 146
v. Scott	ii. 102
Hoghton v. Hoghton	i. 310, 312
Hoig v. Adrian College	ii. 120
Holbird v. Anderson	i. 378; ii. 343
Holbrook v. Connor	i. 206
v. Harrington	ii. 383
v. Sharpey	i. 307; ii. 6, 8
Holdane v. Coldspring	ii. 863
Holden v. Gilbert	ii. 332
v. Phelps	ii. 5
v. Pike	ii. 579
Holder v. Chambury	i. 95, 693, 696
Holdich v. Holdich	ii. 430
Holditch v. Mist	i. 649
Holdridge v. Gillespie	ii. 317, 321, 550
Holdsworth v. Davenport	ii. 526
Holland v. Anderson	i. 215
v. Holland	i. 662; ii. 630
v. Hughes	ii. 617
v. Moon	i. 156
v. Prior	i. 428, 592
Hollier v. Eyre	ii. 195
Hollinrake v. Lister	ii. 646, 653
Hollis v. Claridge	ii. 555
v. Edwards	ii. 32, 74
v. Whiting	ii. 88
v. Wyse	ii. 652
Hollister v. Shaw	ii. 388
Holliway v. Holliway	i. 27, 256
Holloway v. Clarkson	ii. 399
v. Headington	i. 380, 435; ii. 23, 87, 120, 273, 290, 291, 354
v. Holloway	ii. 257
Holman v. Johnson	i. 59
Holmes's Estate	i. 318
Holmes, In re	i. 314
v. Clark	i. 365
v. Coghill	i. 181, 182
v. Custance	i. 191
v. Day	i. 519
v. Dring	ii. 618, 619
v. Higgins	i. 669, 672
v. Holmes	i. 75; ii. 80, 443, 447
v. McGinty	ii. 314
v. Mead	ii. 495
v. Penney	i. 376
v. Shepard	i. 694
v. Taber	i. 490
Holroyd v. Marshall	ii. 349
Holstcomb v. Rivers	i. 547; ii. 855
Holt v. Bancroft	i. 557
Holt v. Frederick	ii. 539
v. Holt	i. 98; ii. 44
v. Rice	ii. 424
v. Rogers	ii. 95
Holton v. Meighen	ii. 320
Holtzapffell v. Baker	i. 105
Holworthy v. Mortlock	ii. 206
Home v. Pringle	ii. 613
Home Ins. Co. v. Meyer	i. 158
Homer v. Homer	ii. 272
Homfray v. Fothergill	ii. 41
Hone v. Brother	i. 160
Honner v. Morton	ii. 743, 744, 745, 746, 747, 748
Honore v. Hutchings	ii. 542
Hood v. Adams	ii. 332
v. Aston	ii. 214, 259
v. Northeastern Ry. Co.	ii. 40
Hook v. Payne	ii. 620
Hooker v. Pynchon	ii. 28
Hooley v. Hatton	ii. 464
Hooper, Ex parte	ii. 75, 78, 323
v. Brodrick	ii. 263
v. Eyles	ii. 535
Hoosac Tunnel Co. v. O'Brien	ii. 789, 791
Hoover v. Calhoun	ii. 53
Hope v. Carnegie	i. 592; ii. 199, 210
v. Hayley	ii. 349
v. Hope	i. 296
Hopgood v. Parkin	ii. 614
Hopkins, Ex parte	ii. 675
v. Adams	i. 87
v. Fechter	ii. 194
v. Gilman	ii. 40, 81, 86
v. Hopkins	ii. 270, 286
Hopkinson v. Burghley	ii. 816
Hopper v. Conyers	i. 549
v. Hopper	ii. 43
Hopson v. Shipp	i. 116
Hopton v. Dryden	i. 590
Hopwood v. Hopwood	ii. 447
Hord v. Miller	ii. 41
Horde v. Suffolk	ii. 493
Horn v. Gilpin	i. 473
v. Horn	i. 375; ii. 473
v. Ketaltas	ii. 321
v. Ludington	ii. 75
Hornby v. Gordon	ii. 153
Horncastle v. Charlesworth	i. 654
Horne v. Pringle	ii. 628
Horniblow v. Shirley	ii. 102
Hornsby v. Finch	ii. 546
v. Lee	ii. 747
Horrell v. Waldron	i. 553, 602, 603
Horridge v. Ferguson	ii. 401
Horrocks v. Rigby	ii. 104, 125

CASES CITED.

Horsburg v. Baker	ii. 652, 819
Horton v. Chester Church	ii. 145
v. McCoy	ii. 688, 689
v. Smith	i. 415
Horwood v. West	ii. 405, 412
Hosack v. Rogers	i. 123; ii. 366
Hosea v. Jacobs	ii. 504
Hosford v. Merwin	i. 661, 668
Hoskins v. Hoskins	ii. 548
Hotel Co. v. Hampson	ii. 631
Hotham v. Stone	i. 518, 521, 524
Hotten v. Arthur	ii. 242
Houck v. Wachter	ii. 228
Hough v. Richardson	ii. 851
Houghton, Ex parte	ii. 542
v. Hapgood	i. 502
v. Houghton	i. 684
v. Kendall	ii. 153, 397
v. Troughton	i. 422
Houldsworth v. Glasgow Bank	i. 211, 212, 213, 214
House v. Grant	i. 610
v. Thompson	i. 651
Houser v. Lamont	ii. 68
Houston, Ex parte	i. 524
Hout v. Hout	i. 156
Hoveden v. Annesley	i. 516; ii. 278, 812, 814, 849
Hovey v. Blakeman	ii. 626
How v. Broomsgrove	ii. 174
v. Rogers	ii. 80
v. Russell	ii. 321
v. Synge	i. 480
v. Vigures	ii. 330
Howard v. Brown	i. 598
v. Carpenter	ii. 81
v. Castle	i. 295
v. Digby	ii. 705, 724, 725, 759
v. Edgell	i. 256
v. Henriques	ii. 255, 256
v. Howard	i. 554
v. Moffat	ii. 740
v. Peace Soc.	ii. 491, 493
v. Snelling	i. 431
v. Woodward	ii. 651
Howarth, In re	ii. 680, 685
v. Deem	i. 406
v. Dewell	ii. 406
Howden v. Rogers	ii. 803, 804
v. Simpson	i. 296
Howe v. Conley	ii. 96
v. Dartmouth	i. 606; ii. 615
v. Howe	i. 606
v. Nickerson	ii. 41
v. Rogers	ii. 817
v. Sheppard	ii. 767, 771
v. Wheldon	i. 256, 259, 310
Howel v. George	ii. 50, 51, 52, 59
Howel v. Hanforth	i. 490
Howell v. Baker	i. 321
v. Buffalo	ii. 13
v. Price	i. 581, 582, 583, 584, 587; ii. 316, 395
v. Ransom	i. 318
Howells v. Jenkins	ii. 423
Howland v. Blake	i. 153; ii. 537
v. Norris	ii. 125
v. Woodruff	i. 391
Howse v. Chapman	ii. 494
Hoxie v. Carr	i. 684; ii. 544, 589
v. Price	ii. 702
Hoxsie v. Hoxsie	ii. 231
Hoy v. Bramhall	ii. 580
v. Smythies	ii. 90
Hoysradt v. Holland	i. 527
Hubbard v. Curtis	i. 689
v. Eastman	ii. 874
v. Hubbard	i. 590, 662
v Martin	i. 293
v. Miller	i. 294
v. Shaw	ii. 317
Hubbell v. Courrin	i. 26
v. Currier	i. 387
v. Meigs	i. 206
v. Van Schoening	ii. 95, 99
Huckabee v. Smith	i. 557
Huckenstine's Appeal	ii. 229, 231
Huddlestone v. Huddlestone	i. 627
Hudson v. Buck	ii. 81
v. Cheyney	i. 394
v. Densmore	i. 390
v. Hudson	ii. 548
v. King	ii. 55
v. Kline	ii. 202
v. Marietta	ii. 180
v. Stalwood	i. 519
Hudson Iron Co. v. Stockbridge Iron Co.	i. 113, 116, 153
Hudson River R. Co. v. Loeb	ii. 225
Hudspeth v. Thomason	i. 87
Huff v. Ripley	i. 30
v. Shepard	ii. 81, 86
Huffman v. Hummer	ii. 99, 111
Huger v. Huger	i. 331
Huggins, Ex parte	i. 297
v. Alexander	ii. 432
Hughes v. Boyd	i. 278
v. Davies	i. 539
v. Edwards	ii. 321, 844
v. Hatchett	ii. 164
v. Kearney	ii. 560, 563, 566, 567, 569, 571, 572, 574
v. Morden College	ii. 187
v. Nelson	i. 158
v. Science	ii. 664, 666, 683, 684, 691

Hughes v. Stubbs	ii. 117
v. Wynne	ii. 852
Hughes-Hallett v. Indian Mines Co.	i. 648
Huguenin v. Baseley	i. 248, 251, 256, 263, 310, 322, 323, 339; ii. 162, 181, 261
Huish, In re	i. 263; ii. 103
Hulett v. Whipple	ii. 576
Hull v. Sherwood	i. 519
v. Sturdivant	ii. 28
Hulme v. Coles	ii. 195
v. Hulme	ii. 623
v. Tenant	ii. 718, 720, 725, 726, 727, 728, 730, 732, 734, 735
Humbard v. Humbard	ii. 59
Humble v. Bill	i. 427; ii. 470
Hume v. Dixon	i. 65
v. Bentley	i. 217
v. Pocock	ii. 103
v. Richardson	ii. 615
Humphreys v. Allen	ii. 327
v. Burleson	i. 331, 555
v. Harrison	ii. 220
v. Leggett	ii. 876
Humphries v. Brogden	ii. 235
Hunnewell v. Charlestown	ii. 14
Hunsdon, Case of	i. 262
Hunsden v. Cheyney	i. 272
Hunt v. Beach	ii. 464
v. Coachman	ii. 206
v. Elmes	i. 413
v. Frazier	i. 156
v. Hunt	i. 187, 249
v. Matthews	i. 261
v. Peake	ii. 235
v. Rousmaniere	i. 110, 111, 113, 114, 115, 117, 119, 120, 121, 122, 123, 124, 125, 126, 127, 130, 131, 135, 146, 147, 155, 167, 168, 175, 177
v. Scott	i. 606
Hunter v. Atkins	i. 314, 317, 319
v. Belcher	i. 468, 469
v. Bullock	ii. 495
v. Daniel	ii. 372, 373, 374
v. Hunter	ii. 623
v. Nolf	i. 298
Huntington v. Allen	ii. 12
v. Gilmore	i. 609
v. Nicoll	ii. 174, 176, 211
Hurd v. Eaton	i. 644
Hurdman v. Northeastern Ry. Co.	ii. 230
Hurlbert v. Pacific Ins. Co.	ii. 767
Hurlbut v. Mayo	ii. 873
v. Phelps	i. 141
Hurley v. Brown	ii. 37, 82
Hurlock v. Smith	ii. 574
Hurry v. Hurry	i. 662
Hurst v. Beach	i. 600, 601, 603, 613; ii. 464
v. Hurst	i. 581
v. Sheldon	ii. 153
v. Winchelsea	ii. 391
Hurt v. Wilson	ii. 367
Husband v. Aldrich	i. 29, 529, 659, 667
Huss v. Morris	i. 116, 154, 156, 158, 188
Hussey v. Christie	ii. 587
v. Coffin	ii. 631
Huston v. Cantril	i. 372
v. Roosa	i. 28
v. Schindler	i. 28
Hutchins v. Heywood	ii. 277, 535, 536
Hutchinson v. Crane	ii. 575
v. Massareene	ii. 159
v. Simon	ii. 363
Hutson v. Furness	i. 151
Hutton v. Moore	ii. 574
v. Simpson	i. 533, 631
Hyde v. Cooper	ii. 81
v. Hyde	i. 577
v. Parrat	i. 605; ii. 166, 167
v. Tracey	i. 511
v. White	i. 350
v. Whitfield	ii. 801, 804
Hylton v. Hylton	i. 268, 321, 325, 326, 327
v. Morgan	ii. 817
Hyman v. Devereux	ii. 314
Hyslop v. Clarke	ii. 343, 344
Hythe v. East	ii. 129

I.

Ibbitson, In re	ii. 553
Ibbotson v. Rhodes	i. 397
Ilchester v. Carnarvon	i. 583, 586
Indiana R. Co. v. Tyng	i. 205, 210
Inches v. Hill	ii. 281
Inchiquin v. French	i. 582; ii. 272
Incledon v. Northcote	i. 578; ii. 707
Incorporated Society v. Richards	ii. 490
Indianapolis Co. v. Indianapolis	ii. 234
Ingalls v. Morgan	i. 637, 638
Ingersoll v. Sergeant	i. 493, 494, 495
Ingham v. Bickerdike	ii. 674
Ingle v. Hartman	i. 322
v. McCurry	ii. 206
Inglehart v. Crane	ii. 580
v. Lee	ii. 203
Inglis v. Sailors' Snug Harbor	ii. 503, 504

CASES CITED.

Ingraham v. Dunnell	ii. 229
v. Wheeler	ii. 344
Ingram v. Pelham	i. 416
Innes v. East India Co.	i. 297
v. Jackson	ii. 51, 703
v. Mitchell	ii. 396, 397
Insurance Co. v. Bailey	i. 27, 28; ii. 6
v. Eggleston	ii. 654
v. McCain	ii. 654
Inwood v. Twynne	ii. 688, 689
Ireland v. Wilson	i. 621
Ireson v. Denn	ii. 328
Irick v. Black	i. 648
v. Fulton	i. 156
Irion v. Mills	i. 365
Irish v. Nutting	i. 609
Irnham v. Child	i. 111, 124, 130, 167, 168, 169, 260; ii. 89
Irons v. Smallpiece	i. 607
Irvin v. Bond	i. 555
Irvine v. Armistead	i. 629
v. Sullivan	ii. 406
Irving v. Young	i. 514, 515
Irwin v. Baily	ii. 66, 77, 90
v. Dixon	ii. 234
v. Farrer	ii. 721
v. Johnson	ii. 21
v. Parham	i. 256
Isaac v. Defriez	ii. 398
Isaacson v. Harwood	ii. 630
Isham v. Gilbert	i. 76, 81
Israel v. Douglas	ii. 348, 361
Ithell v. Beane	i. 427; ii. 289, 290
Ive v. Ash	i. 298
Ives v. Ashley	i. 331
v. Medcalfe	ii. 789, 792, 823
Ivie v. Ivie	ii. 18, 19
Ivinson v. Hutton	i. 153, 154
Ivory v. Burns	ii. 272
Ivy v. Gilbert	ii. 391
v. Kekewick	ii. 815

J.

Jackman v. Mitchell	i. 385, 386; ii. 7, 11
Jackson, In re	ii. 672, 688
v. Burgott	i. 195, 401
v. Burke	i. 469
v. Burtis	ii. 387
v. Butler	ii. 18, 24
v. Caldwell	i. 383
v. Cator	i. 394
v. Cleveland	ii. 532
v. Cocke	ii. 44
v. Cutright	ii. 75
v. De Witt	ii. 341
Jackson v. Duchaise	i. 388
v. Edwards	i. 660
v. Ferris	ii. 384, 387
v. Given	i. 416
v. Hammond	ii. 526
v. Hankey	ii. 687
v. Henry	i. 416
v. Jackson	i. 676; ii. 543, 544, 598, 617
v. King	i. 203
v. Leap	i. 555, 560, 562
v. Lever	i. 105
v. Lomas	i. 385
v. McChesney	ii. 828
v. Moore	ii. 535
v. Nealy	i. 406
v. Petrie	ii. 62, 634, 801
v. Phillips	ii. 495, 503, 510, 521
v. Robinson	ii. 773
v. Rowe	i. 397
v. Sharp	i. 401
v. Small	i. 69
v. Town	i. 364, 372, 431
v. West	i. 401
Jacobs v. Allard	ii. 230
v. Amyatt	ii. 713
v. Jacobs	ii. 397
v. Morange	i. 113, 122
v. Peterborough R. Co.	ii. 77
Jacobson v. Williams	ii. 744
Jalabert v. Chandos	i. 175
James, Ex parte	i. 329, 330
v. Allen	ii. 492
v. Couchman	ii. 739, 752
v. Dean	ii. 550
v. Downes	ii. 201
v. Drake	i. 407
v. Faulk	i. 600
v. Hubbard	ii. 580
v. James	ii. 257, 331, 629
v. Kynnier	ii. 769, 770
v. Litchfield	i. 406; ii. 104
v. Marcy	ii. 339, 341
v. Morey	i. 426
v Morgan	i. 202, 339; ii. 638
Jamison v. Barelli	ii. 576
v. Petit	i. 621
Jandon v. National Bank	ii. 280
Janney v. Buell	i. 59
Janson v. Rany	ii. 855
v. Solarte	ii. 826
January v. Rutherford	ii. 630
Jaques v. Methodist Ep. Church	ii. 718
v. Millar	ii. 41, 81
Jarman v. Wooloton	ii. 715
Jarratt v. Aldam	ii. 23
Jarret v. Andrews	ii. 688

CASES CITED.

Jarrett v. Kennedy	i. 210
Jarrold v. Heywood	ii. 261
Jarvis v. Brooks	i. 684, 687, 689
v. Chandler	ii. 198, 203
v. Duke	i. 203, 221, 227
v. Rogers	ii. 338
Jee v. Thurlow	ii. 763
Jefferson v. Durham	ii. 183, 215
Jeffery v. Stephens	ii. 94
Jefferys, In re	ii. 385
v. Jefferys	i. 184, 380, 435; ii. 23, 116, 120, 290, 291, 354
Jeffrey v. Bigelow	i. 214
v. Bowles	ii. 247
Jeffries v. Jeffries	ii. 64, 348
v. Wiester	i. 322
Jeffryes v. Agra Bank	ii. 772
Jeffs v. Wood	ii. 461, 765, 769, 770
Jegon v. Vivian	ii. 129
Jencks v. Alexander	ii. 332
Jenkins v. De Groot	i. 685
v. Eldredge	ii. 536
v. Hill	ii. 469
v. Kemis	i. 106
v. Lester	ii. 632, 635
v. Pye	i. 311, 312
v. Parkinson	ii. 801
v. Stetson	i. 347; ii. 353
Jenkyn v. Vaughan	i. 369
Jenner v. Jenner	i. 313, 344
v. Morgan	i. 490, 491
v. Morris	ii. 18
Jennings v. Boughton	ii. 865
v. Jordan	ii. 328
v. McConnell	i. 318
v. Moore	i. 413
v. Whittemore	ii. 872
Jennor v. Harper	ii. 508
Jerome v. Scudder	ii. 91, 104
Jerrard v. Saunders	i. 63, 64, 416, 635; ii. 827
Jerrold v. Houlston	ii. 244, 248
Jervis v. White	ii. 9, 10, 16
Jervoise v. Northumberland	ii. 281, 285, 286, 287, 288
Jesse v. Roy	i. 479
Jeston v. Key	ii. 288
Jesus College v. Bloom	i. 71, 73, 74, 75, 476, 535, 536, 537, 538
Jeter v. Barnard	i. 555
Jew v. Thirkenell	i. 487
v. Wood	ii. 142
Jewell v. Lee	ii. 55
Jewett, Ex parte	ii. 688
Jewon v. Grant	i. 99, 528
Jewson v. Moulson	i. 380, 602; ii. 347, 576, 736, 737, 739, 740, 743, 744
Jodrell v. Jodrell	i. 489; ii. 705, 707, 762
Joest v. Williams	i. 237
Johnes's Case	i. 465
Johnes v. Lockhart	ii. 711, 713
Johns v. Norris	ii. 95
v. Sewell	ii. 574, 575
Johnson, In re	i. 361, 376; ii. 163
v. Atkinson	ii. 142
v. Bowden	ii. 74
v. Brooks	ii. 33, 37, 41
v. Brown	i. 424
v. Cornett	ii. 315
v. Cummins	ii. 735
v. Curtis	i. 541, 542, 544, 545
v. Cushing	i. 188
v. De La Creuze	i. 604
v. Dougherty	ii. 532
v. Fesemeyer	i. 318
v. Gallagher	ii. 734, 735
v. Goss	i. 579
v. Hopkins	ii. 96
v. Huston	ii. 321
v. Johnson	i. 97, 506; ii. 541, 745, 750, 751
v. Kennett	ii. 474, 475
v. Kimbro	i. 665
v. Lyttle's Iron Agency	ii. 661
v. Medlicott	i. 243, 244
v. Mills	i. 604; ii. 168
v. Murphy	ii. 7
v. Ogilby	i. 297
v. Osenton	i. 377
v. Pye	i. 252, 392
v. Quarles	ii. 536
v. Skillman	ii. 74
v. Spies	i. 611
v. Stear	ii. 335
v. Strong	i. 410
v. Sugg	ii. 569
v. Thorndike	ii. 180
v. Twist	ii. 547
v. Vaughn	i. 510
v. Waters	i. 378
v. West	i. 373
Johnston v. Aston	ii. 165
v. Haynes	ii. 688
v. Johnston	ii. 80
v. Renton	ii. 16
v. Swan	ii. 493
Johnstone, In re	ii. 673
v. Beattie	ii. 682, 683
Joliet R. Co. v. Healey	i. 5
Joliffe v. Baker	i. 209
Jolland v. Stainbridge	i. 407, 409
Jollie v. Jaques	ii. 243
Jones, In re	ii. 673
v. Alephsin	ii. 803
v. Badley	ii. 526

CASES CITED.

	PAGE
Jones v. Bamford	i. 414
v. Barkley	i. 385
v. Bennett	ii. 795
v. Blanton	i. 510
v. Bolles	i. 199
v. Boston Mill Corp.	ii. 792, 793, 795
v. Boulter	i. 364, 372, 373
v. Bowles	ii. 826
v. Caswell	i. 295
v. Clifford	i. 112, 118, 156
v. Croucher	i. 358, 429
v. Curry	ii. 391
v. Davids	i. 515, 519, 522
v. De Graffenreid	ii. 11
v. Doss	ii. 570
v. Dow	i. 638, 640
v. Dexter	i. 332, 674
v. Deyer	i. 609
v. Edwards	ii. 554
v. Hall	i. 429
v. Harris	ii. 725, 728, 734
v. Higgins	ii. 864
v. Jones	i. 77, 199, 276, 277, 278, 279, 441, 614; ii. 779, 781
v. Kearney	i. 392
v. King	i. 362
v. Lewis	ii. 614, 615
v. Lloyd	ii. 693
v. Lock	ii. 273
v. Marsh	i. 380, 383
v. Martin	i. 260, 261, 272, 388
v. Matthie	ii. 332
v. Monroe	i. 122
v. Morgan	i. 499; ii. 439, 447, 453
v. Newhall	i. 26, 27, 28, 29, 30, 31, 444; ii. 32, 43
v. Noble	ii. 100
v. Noy	i. 681
v. Ogle	i. 488
v. Oliver	ii. 397
v. Perry	ii. 11, 13
v. Powell	i. 561
v. Quinipiack Bank	i. 527
v. Randall	ii. 397
v. Ricketts	i. 343
v. Roe	ii. 349, 353, 354
v. St. John's College	ii. 641, 794
v. Sampson	ii. 803
v. Selby	i. 607, 611, 614
v. Sheriff	i. 175
v. Smith	i. 218, 397, 402, 403, 407, 422; ii. 324, 328, 335, 336, 337, 338
v. Southall	ii. 388

	PAGE
Jones v. Suffolk	ii. 641
v. Thomas	i. 316, 318, 321; ii. 144
v. Tripp	i. 314
v. Waite	ii. 763
v. Westcome	ii. 548
v. Whittaker	i. 437
v. Williams	i. 404, 405; ii. 494
v. Yates	i. 691
Jope v. Morshead	i. 654, 659
Jordan v. Black	i. 273
v. Money	ii. 191
v. Stevens	i. 129
Jordon v. Corley	ii. 203
Jortin, Ex parte	ii. 511
Joslin v. Brewitt	ii. 547
Joslyn v. Smith	i. 337
Joy v. Campbell	ii. 626, 627, 628
v. Joy	ii. 19
Joynes v. Statham	i. 169, 173, 175; ii. 58, 89, 92, 93, 94
Julian v. Reynolds	i. 328
Juliana, The	i. 340

K.

Kain v. Old	i. 173
Kampshire v. Young	ii. 788
Kane v. Bloodgood	ii. 278, 844
v. Roberts	i. 361, 365, 590, 591
Kann's Estate	ii. 688, 689
Kansas Constr. Co. v. Topeka R. Co.	ii. 46, 61
Katz v. Moore	ii. 191
Kauffman's Appeal	ii. 43
Kay v. Scates	ii. 397
Keane v. Kyne	ii. 11
v. Robarts	ii. 470
Kearney v. Macomb	ii. 436
v. Sascer	154, 180
Kearsley v. Cole	i. 336
Keat v. Allen	i. 269, 270
Keating v. Sparrow	ii. 656, 661
Keaton v. Miller	i. 638
Keats v. Cadogan	i. 216
Keble v. Thomson	ii. 629
Keech v. Hall	ii. 319
Keeler v. Taylor	i. 294; ii. 90, 91
Keeling v. Brown	ii. 592
Keen v. Coleman	i. 392
v. Jordan	i. 87
Keene v. Clark	ii. 254
v. Kimball	ii. 254
v. Wheatley	ii. 254
Keepfer v. Force	i. 156
Keighler v. Savage Manuf. Co.	ii. 191
Keily v. Keily	i. 263
v. Monck	i. 285, 286, 291, 617

CASES CITED.

Keisselbrack v. Livingston i. 175, 176	Kennell v. Abbott i. 192, 193, 196
Keith v. Globe Ins. Co. i. 158, 171	Kenny v. Clarkson i. 159
v. Goodwin i. 179	v. Udall ii. 692, 737, 739, 745
Kekewich's Case i. 176	Kensington, Ex parte ii. 323
Kekewich v. Manning i. 433; ii. 119, 339	v. Dollond ii. 712, 713
	v. Mansell ii. 818
v. Marker ii. 220	Kenson's Case ii. 508
Keller v. Equitable Ins. Co. i. 215, 404	Kent, Ex parte ii. 685
v. Lewis ii. 652	v. Elstob ii. 787, 792
v. Williams i. 509, 511	v. Freehold ii. 862
Kelley v. Jenness ii. 534, 536	v. Kent i. 541
Kellock's Case i. 639	v. Lasley i. 154
Kellogg v. Ames ii. 342	v. Pickering i. 562; ii. 199
Kelly v. Herrick i. 527	v. Riley i. 359, 369, 377
v. Hurt ii. 842	Kenyon v. Clarke ii. 179, 197
v. Hutton ii. 258	v. Welty i. 122
v. McGrath i. 273	v. Worthington i. 559, 560, 562
v. Power ii. 302	
v. Solari i. 85, 118, 148, 154, 159, 162	Kepple v. Bailey ii. 54, 348
	Ker's Case ii. 619
v. Turner i. 116, 122; ii. 709	Ker v. Ker i. 638
Kelso v. Kelly ii. 40, 81	v. Wauchope ii. 425
v. Tabor ii. 735	Kerrich v. Bransby i. 194, 196, 197, 198, 441
Kemble v. Farren ii. 651, 652	
v. Kean ii. 42, 261, 263	Kerrigan v. Rantigan i. 373
Kemp v. Finden i. 505, 508	Kerrison v. Sparrow ii. 226
v. Mackrell ii. 206	Kershaw v. Thompson i. 412; ii. 262
v. Prayer i. 11, 61, 63, 70, 89, 90; ii. 3, 13	Kesner v. Trigg ii. 704, 708
	Ketchum v. Stout i. 156
v. Westbrook ii. 335, 336	Kettleby v. Attwood ii. 112, 289
Kempe v. Antill i. 571	Kettlewell v. Barstow ii. 816, 818
Kemper v. Kemper i. 609	v. Watson i. 403, 405, 413
Kempshall v. Stone ii. 127, 128	Key v. Bradshaw i. 275, 276, 279
Kempson v. Ashbee i. 312	v. Flint ii. 768
Kendall, Ex parte i. 177, 178, 571, 572, 573, 637, 647, 651, 652, 685; ii. 604	v. Jones i. 550
	Keys v. Williams ii. 323
	Keyser v. Rice ii. 60
v. Almy ii. 86, 87, 90, 95	Kidder v. Page i. 572, 639
v. Davis ii. 256	Kidney v. Coussmaker i. 362, 365, 366, 368, 569; ii. 432, 438, 592
v. Dow ii. 179, 197	
v. Granger ii. 495	Kiefer v. Rogers i. 215
v. Mann ii. 532, 534, 537	Kilborn v. Robbins ii. 342
v. United States ii. 363	Kildare v. Eustace ii. 62, 209, 633
v. Winsor ii. 210	Kilgannon v. Jenkinson i. 621
Kenestons v. Sceva i. 611	Kilgore v. Jordan i. 392
Kenge v. Delavall ii. 733	Kilgour v. Crawford i. 640, 662
Kennard v. George i. 120	Kill v. Hollister ii. 794
Kennedy v. Brown i. 542	Killian v. Badgett i. 237
v. Carpenter i. 178	v. Ebbinghaus ii. 138, 140
v. Cassillis ii. 208	Kilmer v. Smith i. 85, 110, 111, 150, 154
v. Cresswell i. 556, 557	
v. Daly i. 416	Kilmorey v. Thackeray ii. 41
v. Elliott i. 494	Kilvert, In re ii. 504
v. Green i. 218, 402, 404, 405, 413	Kimball v. Ætna Ins Co. i. 208
	Kimball v. Merchants' Trust Co. ii. 14
v. McKay i. 214	v. Story ii. 398
v. Parke ii. 367	Kimber v. Barber i. 322, 324
v. Stainsby ii. 547	Kimberley v. Dick i. 456; ii. 794

CASES CITED.

	PAGE
Kimberley v. Jennings	ii. 91, 261
Kimpland v. Courtney	ii. 348
Kinaston v. Clark	ii. 559
Kinder v. Jones	ii. 236
Kine v. Balfe	ii. 80
King, Ex parte	ii. 328
v. Baldwin	i. 24, 76, 89, 334, 335, 337, 454, 456, 506, 516, 517, 648, 649; ii. 170, 195
v. Bardeau	ii. 102
v. Bennet	i. 527
v. Burr	ii. 819
v. Carpenter	ii. 11
v. Clark	i. 79
v. Cotton	i. 274
v. De Mannville	ii. 678
v. Denison	ii. 530, 589, 590, 591
v. Doolittle	i. 113, 159
v. Dupine	i. 375
v. Free Fishers of Whitstable	i. 531
v. Greenhill	ii. 677
v. Gridley	i. 580
v. Hamilton	ii. 65, 91, 92, 95, 101
v. Hamlet	i. 347, 348, 354; ii. 214
v. King	ii. 214, 805
v. Moon	i. 203
v. Morris	ii. 233
v. Paterson R. Co.	i. 405
v. Rossett	i. 457
v. Ruckman	ii. 99
v. Savage	ii. 397
v. Smith	i. 538; ii. 220, 317, 331
v. Talbot	ii. 620
v. Thompson	ii. 120
v. Treasury	ii. 357
v. Watson	ii. 343
v. Whitely	ii. 288, 341
v. Wilson	ii. 101, 104
King of Sicilies v. Wilcox	ii. 820
Kingham v. Lee	i. 536
Kingman v. Perkins	ii. 366
Kingsbury v. Flowers	ii. 228, 229
Kingsland v. Clark	i. 495
v. Rapelye	ii. 397
Kingsman v. Kingsman	ii. 73
Kinley v. Irvine	i. 328
Kinnaird v. Webster	i. 514
Kinnoul v. Money	ii. 326
Kinyon v. Young	ii. 828
Kirby v. Carr	i. 681
v. Marlborough	i. 464, 466
Kirk v. Clark	ii. 700
v. Eddowes	ii. 450
v. Webb	ii. 535, 536
Kirkbank v. Hudson	ii. 493
Kirkby Ravensworth Hospital, Ex parte	ii. 498

	PAGE
Kirkham v. Smith	i. 499
Kirkman v. Kirkman	ii. 445
v. Miles	ii. 112, 115
Kirksey v. Kirksey	ii. 68
Kirkwood v. Thompson	ii. 332
Kitchen v. St. Louis Ry. Co.	i. 333
Kitchin v. Hawkins	i. 116, 121, 122
v. Herring	ii. 32
Kitson v. Kitson	ii. 429
Kittredge v. Betton	i. 325, 327
Klein v. Caldwell	i. 392
v. Ins. Co.	ii. 653, 654, 655
Kleine v. Catara	ii. 792, 793
Kleiser v. Scott	i. 525
Kleppner v. Laverty	ii. 397
Kline v. Baker	i. 203
Knapp v. Marshall	ii. 620
Knatchbull v. Hallett	i. 28, 55; ii. 616
Knecht's Appeal	i. 580
Knifong v. Hendricks	ii. 204
Knight v. Boughton	ii. 407, 410
v. Bowyer	ii. 847
v. Cameron	i. 291
v. Davis	i. 577
v. Ellis	ii. 404
v. Knight	ii. 405, 407, 408, 409, 413, 713
v. Plimouth	ii. 614, 615, 616, 617
Knightly v. Knightly	ii. 591, 592
Kniskern v. Lutheran Church	ii. 525
Knoll v. Harvey	ii. 77
Knott, Ex parte	i. 421, 423, 438; ii. 337, 554
v. Cottee	ii. 406
v. Morgan	ii. 255
Knotts v. Tarver	i. 458
Knowles v. Carpenter	ii. 342
v. Haughton	i. 302, 677, 678
v. Inches	ii. 177
Knowlton v. Amy	i. 216
Knox v. Dunn	ii. 12
v. Gye	i. 686
v. New York	ii. 225
v. Symmonds	ii. 789, 791, 792, 793
Knye v. Moore	ii. 17, 18, 24
Kost v. Bender	i. 206
Krehl v. Burrell	ii. 182
Kreiser's Appeal	ii. 437
Kruger v. Wilcocks	i. 530
Kruse v. Steffens	i. 331
Krutz v. Fisher	i. 323
Kuhn v. McNeil	ii. 14
v. Stansfield	i. 373, 377, 379, 380
Kuhner v. Butler	i. 306
Kurtz v. Hibner	i. 664; ii. 80
v. Sponable	ii. 314

L.

Labadie *v.* Hewitt i. 30, 69, 87
Labouchere *v.* Dawson i. 294
Lacam *v.* Mertins i. 571, 572, 573, 584
Lacey, Ex parte i. 329, 330, 475
Lackawanna Canal Co., In re i. 488
Lacon *v.* Mertins ii. 69, 70, 73, 74, 77, 80, 85
Lacy *v.* Anderson ii. 421
Ladd *v.* Pleasants i. 156
Laid *v.* Scott i. 372
Laidlaw *v.* Organ i. 109, 149, 164, 205, 208, 221, 231, 233
Laight *v.* Morgan i. 80, 81
Laing *v.* McKee ii. 89
Laird *v.* Birkenhead Ry. Co. ii. 862
Lake *v.* Brutton i. 515
v. Craddock i. 683; ii. 544, 581
v. De Lambert ii. 631
v. Gibson ii. 542, 544, 589
v. Meacham i. 154
Lake Bigler Road Co. *v.* Bedford ii. 11
Lakin, Ex parte ii. 685
Lamb *v.* Hinman ii. 76
Lambe *v.* Eames ii. 398, 406, 411
Lambert *v.* Lambert ii. 757, 758
v. Thwaites ii. 385
Lamlee *v.* Hanman i. 270, 271
Lamotte, In re ii. 694
Lampert *v.* Lampert ii. 700, 701
Lampet's Case ii. 167, 292, 347
Lamphir *v.* Creed ii. 716
Lamplugh *v.* Lamplugh ii. 532
v. Smith i. 355
Lamprey *v.* Lamprey ii. 22, 273
Lamprière *v.* Lange i. 252
Lampson *v.* Arnold i. 377
Lancashire *v.* Lancashire ii 798
Lancaster Ry. Co. *v.* N. W. Ry. Co. ii. 869
Lance *v.* Norman i. 273
Landell *v.* Baker i. 668
Lane *v.* Dighton ii. 535, 536, 538, 548, 549, 608
v. Husband ii. 273, 344
v. Marshall i. 26
v. Morrill ii. 260
v. Newdigate ii. 231
v. Stacey i. 527
v. Williams i. 685
Lanesborough *v.* Jones ii. 769, 770
Laney *v.* Jasper ii. 234
Lang *v.* Bank of United States i. 138
v. Brevard i. 337
Lange *v.* Work i. 294
Langford, In re ii. 617
Langford *v.* Gascoyne ii. 615, 626
Langham *v.* Nenny ii. 389, 722, 739
v. Sandford i. 601
Langley *v.* Brown i. 146, 167
v. Oxford ii. 379, 470
v. Thomas ii. 396
Langstaffe *v.* Fenwick i. 144
v. Taylor i. 320
Langston, Ex parte ii. 323
v. Langston ii. 401
v. Ollivant ii. 629
Langstone *v.* Boylston ii. 138, 139, 140, 141, 145
Langthorne *v.* Swinburne i. 337
Langton *v.* Horton ii. 340, 349, 350, 353, 354, 378, 826, 828
v. Waite ii. 37
Lanier *v.* Hill i. 157
Lanning *v.* Carpenter i. 119
Lanoy *v.* Athol i. 570, 571, 573, 637, 641; ii. 580, 687
Lansden *v.* McCarthy ii. 349
Lansdowne *v.* Lansdowne i. 113, 126, 131, 135, 136, 146, 534, 535, 536, 537
Lansing *v.* Eddy ii. 204, 206, i. 872
v. Van Alstyne i. 495
Lant's Appeal i. 119
Lantry *v.* Lantry ii. 271
Lapham *v.* Clapp ii. 591
Lapp *v.* Lapp i. 117
Largan *v.* Bowen i. 562
Large's Appeal ii. 554
Larkin *v.* Mann i. 662
Larkins *v.* Biddle i. 113, 121
Larmon *v.* Jordan ii. 13
Lasbrook *v.* Tyler ii. 759
Lasher, In re ii. 696
Lassells *v.* Cornwallis i. 182, 188
Lassence *v.* Tierney ii. 437
Latham *v.* Morrow i. 226, 295
v. Staples ii. 575
Lathrop's Appeal i. 518, 522
Lathrop *v.* Smalley ii. 630, 631
Latimer *v.* Aylesbury Ry. Co. ii. 264
Latouche *v.* Dunsany i. 409, 410, 423
Latourette *v.* Williams ii. 736
La Trobe *v.* Hayward i. 542
Latymer, In re ii. 511
Laughter's Case ii. 641
Laughton *v.* Harden i. 361, 365
Laurencel *v.* De Boom ii. 272
Lavassar *v.* Washburne i. 203
Lavender *v.* Blackstone i. 383
v. Stanton ii. 475
Laver *v.* Dennett i. 114
Lavette *v.* Sage i. 243
Law *v.* East India Co. i. 337
v. Garret ii. 794

CASES CITED.

Law v. Law	i. 266, 268, 298
Lawder, In re	i. 637, 638, 639, 640
Lawes, In re	ii. 441, 443, 447
Lawless v. Shaw	ii. 408
Lawley v. Hooper	i. 200
Lawrence v. Beverly	ii. 112
v. Cornell	i. 516
v. Lawrence	i. 87; ii. 95, 422, 429
v. Smith	ii. 236, 237, 241, 242
Lawrence Mfg. Co. v. Lowell Mills	ii. 255, 258
Lawson v. Hudson	i. 584
v. Laude	ii. 87
v. Lawson	i. 607; ii. 548
Lawton, In re	i. 489
Layard v. Maud	ii. 324
Layer v. Nelson	i. 504
Lea v. Barber	i. 480
v. Hinton	i. 647
v. Whitaker	ii. 652
Leach v. Beattie	i. 473
v. Duvall	i. 273
v. Fobes	ii. 37, 41
Leadbetter, —— v.	ii. 247
Leaf v. Coles	i. 681
Leaird v. Smith	ii. 100
Leak v. Morrice	ii. 75
Leake v. Leake	ii. 448, 804
Leardet v. Johnson	ii. 240
Learned v. Foster	ii. 851
Leary v. Cheshire	i. 514
Leather Cloth Co. v. American Leather Cloth Co.	ii. 258
Leather Cloth Co. v. Lorsont	i. 293, 294
Leavitt v. La Force	i. 310, 333
v. Pratt	ii. 341
Lechmere v. Carlisle	ii. 112, 273, 289, 441, 445
v. Charlton	i. 583, 584; ii. 302, 595
v. Fletcher	i. 178
v. Lavie	ii. 408
Leddell v. McDougal	i. 219
v. Starr	i. 313; ii. 21
Ledyard v. Butler	i. 387, 433
v. Hartford Ins. Co.	i. 111
Lee v. Alston	i. 74, 451, 537, 538
v. Angas	ii. 16
v. Brook	i. 337
v. Browder	ii. 536
v. Cox	ii. 445
v. Green	i. 377
v. Haley	ii. 255, 256
v. Howell	i. 325
v. Howlett	ii. 339
Lee v. Kirby	ii. 54
v. Kirkpatrick	ii. 865
v. Lee	i. 30, 69, 87; ii. 672, 673, 675, 684
v. Muggeridge	ii. 718, 722
v. Munroe	i. 395
v. Overstreet	ii. 651
v. Park	i. 561
v. Pearce	i. 235
v. Prieaux	ii. 710, 711
v. Rook	i. 618; ii. 48, 171
v. Ruggles	ii. 12
v. Sankey	ii. 623
Leech's Appeal	ii. 320
Leech v. Leech	ii. 620
v. Trollop	ii. 830
Leeds v. Amherst	i. 538
v. Marine Ins. Co.	ii. 556, 559, 773, 774
v. New Radnor	i. 74, 95, 456, 625, 693, 696
v. Powell	i. 95, 103, 625, 695
v. Strafford	i. 624
Lecke v. Bennett	i. 605
Lees v. Mosley	ii. 401
v. Nuttall	i. 322, 323; ii. 550
Legal v. Miller	i. 173
Legard v. Hodges	ii. 577
v. Johnson	ii. 756, 757, 759, 763
Legg v. Goldwire	i. 173
Legge v. Asgill	ii. 514
Leggett v. Dubois	ii. 538
v. Postley	i. 79
Leggott v. Barrett	i. 294
Le Guen v. Gouverneur	ii. 204
Lehigh Valley R. Co. v. McFarlan	ii. 173
Leicester v. Foxcroft	i. 194
v. Rose	i. 334, 386
Leigh v. Barry	ii. 623
v. Macauley	ii. 165, 606, 608
v. Norbury	ii. 401
Leighton v. Leighton	ii. 176, 177, 450, 780
Leitch v. Wells	i. 411
Leland v. Smith	ii. 632
Leman v. Newnham	i. 584
v. Whitley	ii. 71, 529, 533
Lemay v. Johnson	i. 638
Le Merchant v. Le Merchant	ii. 406
Lemon v. Hansbarger	ii. 675
v. Phoenix Ins. Co.	i. 180
Lemont v. Singer Stone Co.	ii. 15
Lempster v. Pomfret	i. 78; ii. 18, 19
Lench v. Lench	ii. 536, 538, 548, 578, 608
Le Neve v. Le Neve	i. 201, 400, 401

CASES CITED.

Lennon v. Napper	i. 96, 97; ii. 57, 64, 98, 313
Leonard v. Leonard	i. 130, 131, 133, 134, 139, 140, 142, 155, 163, 164, 235
v. Simpson	i. 563
v. Sussex	ii. 286
Leonis v. Lazzarovich	i. 156
Le Pypre v. Farr	i. 81
Lerow v. Wilmarth	i. 373
Leroy v. Veeder	i. 76, 91
Lesley v. Shock	ii. 197
Leslie v. Bailie	i. 159
v. Guthrie	ii. 347, 378
Lester v. Kinne	ii. 77
L'Estrange v. L'Estrange	ii. 355
Le Texier v. Anspach	ii. 821
Lethulier v. Castlemain	i. 620, 621
Lett v. Morris	ii. 362, 363, 364
Letton v. Goodden	ii. 175, 232
Leverton v. Waters	i. 661
Levy v. Barker	i. 242
v. Brush	ii. 89
v. Levy	ii. 781
Lewellin v. Cobbold	i. 273
Lewin v. Oakley	i. 68, 566
Lewis, Ex parte	ii. 805
v. Allenby	ii. 526
v. Chapman	ii. 263
v. Denkgrave	ii. 197
v. Fullerton	ii. 242, 246
v. Hillman	i. 318, 322
v. Lechmere	ii. 43
v. Lewis	i. 577; ii. 596
v. Llewellyn	ii. 391
v. Madocks	ii. 548, 578, 608
v. Mew	i. 411
v. Palmer	i. 518
v. Pead	i. 248
v. Stein	ii. 230
Lewisburg Mfg. Co. v. Marsh	ii. 350
Lexington R. Co. v. Elwell	i. 338
Ley v. Ley	i. 495
Lick v. Ray	ii. 12
Liddard v. Lopes	i. 480
Liddell v. Norton	i. 331
Lidderdale v. Montrose	ii. 355
Liebman v. Harcourt	ii. 549, 608
Life Ins. Co. v. Cutler	ii. 580
Light v. Scott	ii. 529
Lightner v. Menzel	ii. 651
Like v. Beresford	ii. 745, 753
Liles, Succession of	ii. 612
Liley v. Hay	ii. 401
Lilford v. Powys-Keck	i. 575, 576
Lilia v. Airey	ii. 700, 733, 734, 735
Lilly v. Hayes	ii. 362
Lime Rock Bank v. Phetteplace	i. 683
Lincoln v. Newcastle	ii. 275, 286, 287, 288
v. Pelham	ii. 401
v. Rutland R. Co.	ii. 139
v. Wright	i. 303, 405
Lindenau v. Desborough	i. 235
Lindley, Ex parte	ii. 493
Lindsay v. Bates	ii. 314, 367, 574
v. Lynch	ii. 79, 82, 83, 85, 86, 87, 94
v. Pleasants	ii. 112
v. Price	ii. 365
Lindsley v. James	ii. 820, 822
Lingan v. Simpson	i. 674; ii. 24, 25, 35
Lingard v. Bromley	i. 529
Lingen v. Sowray	ii. 112
Lingood v. Croucher	ii. 823
Lingwood v. Eade	ii. 790
Lining v. Peyton	ii. 476
Linkous v. Cooper	ii. 102
Linn v. Barkey	i. 154
Linton v. Hart	i. 492, 493
v. Hurley	ii. 359
v. Hyde	ii. 529
Linzee v. Mifer	ii. 55, 348
Lippencott v. Barker	ii. 343
Lippincott v. Lippincott	ii. 383
Lipscom v. Lipscom	i. 495
Lishy v. Perry	i. 374
Lisle v. Liddle	ii. 10, 16
Lister v. Hodgson	ii. 23
v. Pickford	ii. 608
Litchfield v. Webster	ii. 15
Litterdale v. Robinson	i. 522
Little v. Cooper	i. 81
Littlefield v. Littlefield	ii. 80
v. Tinseley	ii. 102
Littleton v. Littleton	i. 273
Livermore v. Aldrich	ii. 532
v. Peru	i. 118
Liverpool Assoc. v. Fairhurst	i. 392
Liverpool Co. v. Hunter	ii. 210
Livingston v. Clarkson	i. 666
v. Livingston	i. 693, 694, 696; ii. 222, 233, 235, 236, 699, 703
v. Newkirk	i. 68, 581, 582, 588
v. Ogden	ii. 233
v. Tompkins	ii. 652, 656
v. Woodworth	ii. 237
Llewellyn v. Rous	i. 489
Lloyd v. Atwood	i. 331
v. Banks	i. 407
v. Branton	i. 277, 279, 288, 289, 290
v. Brooks	ii. 273, 286

CASES CITED.

Lloyd v. Collet	ii. 99
v. Galbraith	i. 574, 639
v. Gurdon	ii. 214
v. Johnes	i. 500
v. Loaring	ii. 25
v. Lloyd	ii. 494
v. Read	ii. 537, 538, 541
v. Spillet	ii. 270, 532, 535, 536, 538
v. Williams	ii. 751, 753
Lobdell v. Baker	i. 209
v. Lobdell	ii. 80
Loch v. Bagley	ii. 286
Lock v. Fulford	ii. 580
v. Lyman	i. 674
Locke v. Lomas	ii. 476
v. Stearns	i. 214
Lockett v. Hurt	ii. 12
Lockey v. Lockey	i. 533; ii. 80
Locking v. Parker	ii. 313, 332
Lockley v. Eldridge	i. 481
Lockton v. Lockton	ii. 384
Lockwood v. Ewer	ii. 335, 336
v. Thorne	i. 545
Lodge v. Furman	ii. 320
v. Lysely	ii. 828
Loffus v. Maw	ii. 76
Loftin v. Espy	ii. 24
Logan v. Fairlie	ii. 687
v. Simmons	i. 273, 275
v. Thrift	ii. 711
v. Wienholt	ii. 28, 66, 109
Loker v. Rolle	i. 623
Lomas v. Wright	i. 575, 576
Lombard v. Boyden	ii. 397
London v. Levy	ii. 812
v. Mitford	ii. 659
v. Nash	ii. 44, 58, 128
v. Perkins	ii. 175
v. Pugh	ii. 40
v. Richmond	i. 694
London Assurance Co. v. Mansel	i. 28
London Bank v. Lamprière	ii. 735
London Banking Co. v. Lewis	i. 412
London Ry. Co. v. Lancashire Ry. Co.	ii. 234
London Ry. Co. v. Winter	ii. 69, 92, 93
Loney v. Penniman	ii. 60
Long v. Allen	i. 480
v. Bowring	ii. 28
v. Dennis	i. 289
v. Heinrich	ii. 378
v. Rickets	i. 290
v. Smith	ii. 203
v. Stewart	ii. 610
v. Towl	ii. 651
v. Watkinson	ii. 399
Longford v. Eyre	i. 186
Longhurst v. Star Ins. Co.	i. 121
Longley v. Hudson	ii. 15
Longman v. Winchester	ii. 244
Longuet v. Scawen	ii. 322
Lonsdale v. Littledale	ii. 787, 788, 823
Loomes v. Stotherd	i. 589
Loomis's Appeal	i. 580
Loomis v. Loomis	ii. 367
Lopdell v. Creagh	i. 547
Loraine v. Thomlinson	i. 480
Lord v. Jeffkins	i. 354, 355
v. Lord	ii. 428
v. Wormleighton	i. 562
Lorenty v. Lorenty	ii. 76, 80
Lorimer v. Lorimer	i. 532, 663
Loring, Ex parte	ii. 569, 570
v. Beacon	ii. 581
v. Marsh	ii. 387
v. Thorndike	ii. 397
Loscomb v. Wintringham	ii. 495
Loscee v. Murray	ii. 54
Loss v. Obry	i. 180; ii. 872
Loud v. Charlestown	ii. 14, 144
Lousada v. Templer	i. 75
Lovat v. Ranelagh	ii. 659
Love v. Baker	ii. 208, 209
v. Carpenter	i. 674
v. Cobb	ii. 55, 91
v. Sierra Nev. Mining Co.	i. 120, 157; ii. 322
v. Sortwell	ii. 90
Loveridge v. Cooper	ii. 339, 379, 529
Lovering v. Worthington	ii. 276
Low v. Barchard	i. 254
v. Burron	ii. 291
v. Harmony	ii. 397
v. Ward	ii. 242, 248
Lowe v. Allen	i. 153
v. Bryant	ii. 77
v. Joliffe	ii. 783
v. Peers	i. 275, 276, 279; ii. 651
v. Richardson	ii. 146
Lowell v. Daniels	i. 392
Lowndes v. Bettle	ii. 234
v. Cornford	ii. 140
v. Lane	i. 220; ii. 103
Lownsberry v. Purdy	ii. 13
Lowry v. Bourdieu	i. 302
v. Buffington	ii. 59, 73
v. Howard	i. 377
v. Spear	i. 344; ii. 47
Lowson v. Copeland	ii. 619
Lowther v. Carlton	i. 414, 416
v. Lowther	i. 323; ii. 25
Lowthian v. Hasel	i. 418, 422; ii. 337

	PAGE		PAGE
Loyd v. Loyd	i. 662	Lyon v. Richmond	i. 120, 122, 123, 127, 136, 146, 148
Lubbock v. Potts	i. 302		
Lucas v. Beach	i. 669	v. Tweddell	i. 682
v. Calcraft	i. 632	Lyons v. Blenkin	ii. 675, 676
v. Commerford	ii. 29, 45	v. Miller	i. 80
v. King	i. 661	Lysaght v. Royse	ii. 672, 694, 695, 696
v. Lucas	ii. 704, 710		
v. Worswick	i. 162	v. Walker	i. 460, 466
Luckenbach v. Anderson	ii. 197, 206	Lytle v. Beveridge	i. 331
Luckett v. Williamson	ii. 71	Lytton v. Devey	ii. 249, 250, 251
Lucy, Ex parte	i. 116, 140	v. Great Northern Ry. Co.	ii. 870
Ludlow v. Dutch Ry. Co.	ii. 660		
v. Grayall	ii. 561		
v. Greenhouse	ii. 124, 484, 490, 499	**M.**	
v. Simond	i. 73, 76, 89, 335, 449, 451, 454, 456, 470, 541	Maber v. Hobbs	ii. 273, 364, 713
Lufton v. White	i. 476	Macaulay v. Philips	ii. 743, 745, 748, 750, 751, 752, 761
Luigart v. Ripley	i. 278		
Luker v. Dennis	ii. 54, 348	Macauley v. Shackell	ii. 818, 835, 836, 838
Lukin v. Aird	i. 362		
Lumb v. Milnes	ii. 711, 712, 713	Macbryde v. Weekes	ii. 99
Lumley v. Wagner	ii. 34, 35, 42, 261, 263	MacCabe v. Hussey	ii. 7
		Macdonald v. Bell	i. 526
Lumsden v. Buchanan	ii. 619	v. Macdonald	i. 579, 595
Lunn v. Thornton	ii. 349	MacFarlan v. Rolt	ii. 821
Lupton v. Lupton	i. 99, 582; ii. 591	Mack v. Petter	ii. 244
v. White	i. 626	Mackay v. Brackett	ii. 200
Lush, In re	i. 392; ii. 753, 866	v. Commercial Bank	i. 212, 213, 214
v. Wilkinson	i. 362, 365, 368, 371		
		v. Douglas	i. 369
Lutheran Church v. Maschop	ii. 263	Mackensie v. Robinson	ii. 331
Lutkins v. Leigh	i. 574, 575, 576, 585, 643	Mackenzie v. Coulson	i. 171
		v. Johnston	i. 333, 455, 456, 457, 458, 470
Luttrell v. Waltham	i. 260, 264		
Lyddon v. Moss	i. 319	Mackintosh v. Townsend	ii. 518, 519
Lyde v. Mynn	ii. 41, 47, 598	McAfee v. Ferguson	i. 273
Lyman v. Bonney	i. 332	McAleer v. Horsey	i. 209
v. Califer	i. 158	McAllister v. McAllister	i. 629
v. Cessford	i. 365	McAnally v. O'Neal	i. 359
v. Estes	ii. 770	McBee, Ex parte	ii. 554
v. Lyman	i. 637; ii. 580	v. Myers	i. 347
v. United Ins. Co.	i. 167, 170, 171	McBride v. Little	ii. 203
		McCaa v. Wolf	i. 69; ii. 736
Lyme v. Allen	ii. 872	McCabe v. Swap	i. 636; ii. 341, 342
Lynch, In re	i. 638	McCall's Appeal	i. 662
v. Paraguay	i. 595	McCall v. Harrison	ii. 602
v. Rotan	ii. 672	McCandless's Estate	ii. 847
v. Sumrall	i. 77	McCann v. White	ii. 576
Lyne, —— v.	ii. 711	McCarnack v. Sage	ii. 81
Lynes v. Coley	i. 594	McCarogher v. Whieldon	ii. 446
v. Hayden	ii. 81	McCarroll v. Alexander	ii. 536
Lynn v. Gephart	ii. 553	McCartee v. Orph. Asylum Soc.	ii. 279
Lyon v. Acker	ii. 401	M'Carthy v. Goold	i. 297, 375; ii. 318, 355
v. Home	i. 333		
v. Lyon	i. 140; ii. 535	McCarthy v. Decaix	i. 118, 129, 147
v. McIlvaine	ii. 342	McCartney v. Calhoun	i. 328
v. Mitchell	ii. 404	v. Garnhart	ii. 255

CASES CITED.

	PAGE		PAGE
McClane v. Shepherd	ii. 847	McKay v. Green	i. 557, 560
McCleary v. Beirne	i. 518	McKecknie v. Sterling	i. 105
McClellan v. Darrah	ii. 96	McKee v. Judd	ii. 359
v. Sanford	i. 154	McKelway v. Armour	i. 157
v. Scott	i. 215	McKenzie v. Johnston	i. 71; ii. 3
McClintic v. Ochiltree	ii. 716	M'Kenzie v. Powis	ii. 849
McClintock v. Laing	ii. 49, 81	McKeogh v. McKeogh	i. 388
McClure v. Harris	ii. 569	McKibben v. Brown	ii. 40, 81, 86
v. Lewis	i. 325	McKim v. Voorhes	ii. 210
McClurg's Appeal	i. 293	McKimell v. Robinson	i. 308
McCollum v. Prewitt	ii. 818	McKinney v. Hensley	i. 313
McComas v. Easley	ii. 59, 94	McKnight v. Robbins	ii. 34
McConnell v. Beattie	i. 527	v. Taylor	ii. 843, 845, 846
McCord v. Ochiltree	ii. 483, 488, 491	v. Walsh	ii. 612, 620, 686, 687
McCormack v. McCormack	ii. 849		
McCormick's Appeal	i. 639, 644, 684	McLane v. Johnson	i. 362, 365
McCormick v. Garnett	i. 113, 159	McLaughlin v. Bank of Potomac	i. 367
v. Knox	ii. 327	v. Barnum	ii. 129, 583
v. Wheeler	i. 414	v. McLaughlin	i. 66
McCrea v. Holdsworth	ii. 244	McLaurie v. Thomas	ii. 570
McCulloch v. Gregory	ii. 780	McLean v. Fleming	ii. 255
McCullum v. Gourley	i. 302	v. Longlands	ii. 704
v. Turpie	ii. 580	v. Presley	ii. 331, 332
McCune v. Belt	i. 514	v. Walker	ii. 335
McDermutt v. Strong	ii. 557	McLearn v. McLellan	ii. 560, 561, 595, 596
McDole v. Purdy	ii. 570		
McDonald v. Neilson	i. 65, 254	McLellan v. Osborne	i. 473
McDonough v. Shewbridge	ii. 330	McLemore v. Powell	i. 336, 337
McDougal v. Armstrong	ii. 168	McLenahan v. McLenahan	ii. 595
McDougald v. Capron	ii. 328	McLeod v. Drummond	i. 427, 428, 429, 588, 589, 590, 591; ii. 4, 470
McDowell v. Blackstone Canal Co.	i. 460		
v. Lucas	ii. 80	McMahan v. Smith	i. 314
M'Durmut v. Strong	i. 375	McMahon v. Fawcett	i. 522
McElwer v. Sutton	i. 79	v. McGraw	i. 323
M'Fadden v. Jenkins	ii. 119, 273	McMurray v. Spicer	ii. 82
McFarland's Appeal	i. 580	v. St. Louis Oil Co.	i. 116
McGarvey v. Hall	ii. 33	McNeil v. Ames	ii. 14, 15
McGavock v. Drery	i. 404	v. Cahill	i. 270, 386, 388
McGill, In re	i. 525	v. Magee	ii. 95, 825
McGillicuddy v. Cook	i. 609	McNeill v. McNeill	i. 555
McGinniss v. Edgell	ii. 539	McNeilledge v. Barclay	ii. 398
McGough v. Insurance Bank	i. 26	v. Galbraith	ii. 398
McGowan v. McGowan	ii. 536	McPherson v. Housel	i. 411
McGowin v. Remington	i. 80; ii. 33	v. Snowdon	ii. 397
McGrath v. Reynolds	i. 607, 609, 610	McPike v. Pen	ii. 12, 15
McGregor v. Topham	ii. 782	McQueen v. Farquhar	i. 263, 416
McGregory v. McGregory	i. 87	McRoberts v. Washburne	ii. 175, 232
McGuire v. Stephens	ii. 74, 81	McVickar v. Wolcott	ii. 204
McHenry v. Davies	ii. 735	McWilliams v. Webb	ii. 366
v. Hazard	ii. 144	Macclesfield v. Davis	ii. 25
v. Lewis	ii. 211	Macedon Pl. Road Co. v. Lapham	ii. 867
McIlvaine v. Smith	ii. 277		
McIntier v. Shaw	ii. 320	Machinists' Bank v Field	ii. 37
McIntire v. Zanesville	ii. 503	Machine Co. v. Perry	ii. 11
McIntosh v. Saunders	i. 151	Machir v. Morse	i. 308
McIntyre v. Storey	ii. 234	Mackett v. Mackett	ii. 406
McKay's Case	i. 332	Macklin v. Richardson	ii. 249
		Macklot v. Davenport	ii. 14

CASES CITED.

Macknet v. Macknet i. 112, 113, 117; ii. 437, 438
Macomber v. Peck i. 362
Mackreth v. Symmons i. 65, 400, 421; ii. 110, 535, 560, 561, 562, 563, 564, 566, 567, 568, 570, 571, 572, 573, 575, 576
Macy v. Nantucket ii. 14, 144, 611
Maddeford v. Austwick i. 237, 333
Maddison v. Alderson i. 208
— v. Andrew ii. 385, 538
Maddox v. Maddox i. 279
Madeiros v. Hill ii. 641
Madeley v. Booth i. 217
Madgwick v. Wimble i. 680
Maffit v. Rynd ii. 272
Magdalena Nav. Co., In re i. 304; ii. 862
Magee v. Lavell ii. 651, 652
— v. Leggett i. 525
— v. Magee ii. 575
Magee Furnace Co. v. Le Barron ii. 256, 257, 258
Magoffin v. Holt ii. 99
Magraff v. Muir ii. 90, 103
Magrath v. Morehead ii. 286
Magruder v. Campbell ii. 367
— v. Peter i. 524
Maguire, In re ii. 504
Mahana v. Blunt ii. 79
Mahon v. Savage ii. 401
Mahone v. Williams ii. 316, 318
Mahoney v. Hunter i. 203
Mahurin v. Harding i. 205, 209, 210
Main v. Melbourn ii. 74
Mainwaring, In re ii. 286
— v. Newman i. 690
Maitland v. Backhouse i. 325
— v. Irving i. 311
Major v. Lansley ii. 710, 719, 720, 746, 747, 748
Makeham v. Hooper ii. 512
Makepeace v. Rogers i. 309, 468, 469
Malcolm v. Andrews ii. 801
— v. Charlesworth ii. 378
— v. O'Callaghan i. 289, 291
Malden v. Merrill i. 107, 148, 179
Male v. Smith i. 399
Malin v. Garnsey i. 379
— v. Malin i. 247
Malins v. Brown ii. 12
— v. Freeman ii. 91, 92
Mallan v. May i. 294
Mallory v. Mallory ii. 534
Malmesbury Ry. Co. v. Budd ii. 196, 790
Malone v. Marriott ii. 320
Malony v. Rourke i. 151, 153
Maloy v. Sloans ii. 542
Maltby's Case i. 234
Malvin v. Keighley ii. 405, 406
Man v. Ward i. 199
Manahan v. Gibbons ii. 627
Manaton v. Molesworth ii. 182
— v. Squire i. 659
Manby v. Bewicke ii. 851
— v. Robinson ii. 141
Mandeville v. Mandeville ii. 158, 163, 165
— v. Welch ii. 323, 349, 363, 378
Manhattan Co. v. Barker ii. 225
— v. Wood ii. 258
Manlove v. Bale ii. 574
Manly v. Slason ii. 566, 569, 570
Mann v. Ballet ii. 510
— v. Betterly i. 249
— v. Flower ii 190
— v. Utica ii. 15
Manning's Case ii. 167, 292
Manning v. Lechmere ii. 854
— v. Manning ii. 612, 620
— v. Spooner i. 581
— v. Wadsworth i. 674; ii. 35
Mansel v. Mansel ii. 294
Mansell v. Payne i. 545
Mansfield's Case i. 242
Manson v. Thacker i. 217
Manville v. Gay i. 495
Many v. Beekman Iron Co. ii. 812
Maple v. Junior Army Stores ii. 242
Mapps v. Sharpe ii. 314
Maquoketa v. Willey i. 337
Marak v. Abel i. 302
Marble v. Whitney i. 116
Marble Co. v. Ripley i. 676; ii. 32, 34, 43
Marbury v. Brooks ii. 343, 344, 346
March v. England ii. 15
— v. Davison i. 79; ii. 812, 820
Marchington v. Vernon ii. 362
Marcus v. Boston ii. 68
Mardree v. Mardree ii. 736
Margetts v. Barringer ii. 712
Margrave v. Le Hooke ii. 328
Marine Ins. Co. v. Hodgson i. 86, 106; ii. 198, 202, 203, 205, 206
Markby, In re i. 481
Markham v. Howell ii. 218
Marks v. Pell ii. 321
Marksbury v. Taylor i. 203
Marlatt v. Warwick i. 301
Marlborough v. Godolphin i. 106; ii. 717
Marlin v. Jewell ii. 179, 197
Marlow v. Adams ii. 130
Marples v. Bainbridge i. 288, 290

CASES CITED. lxxi

Marquand v. New York Mfg. Co.	i. 688
Marr v. Bennett	i. 404
v. Lewis	i. 572
Marriot v. Thompson	i. 589
Marriott v. Marriott	i. 194, 196, 551, 598
Marryatts v. White	i. 461, 464
Marsh v. Billings	ii. 255, 256, 257
v. Brooklyn	ii. 15
v. Burroughs	i. 557
v. Lee	i. 418, 419
Marshal v. Crutwell	ii. 539, 541
Marshall v. Baltimore & O. R. Co.	i. 296
v. Berridge	ii. 41, 81
v. Berry	i. 609
v. Caldwell	ii. 281
v. Collet	i. 147
v. Colman	i. 674, 682
v. Crow	i. 654
v. Crowther	i. 501
v. Moon	i. 614
v. Moseley	i. 490
v. Ross	ii. 258
v. Rutton	ii. 725, 732, 763
v. Stephens	i. 328
v. Watson	i. 676
Marshfield v. Weston	i. 445; ii. 855
Marston v. Moore	ii. 11
v. Rowe	ii. 12
Martel v. Somers	i. 407
Martidale v. Martin	ii. 481
Martin v. Clarke	ii. 373
v. Dwelly	i. 120, 156
v. Graves	i. 26; ii. 12
v. Headon	ii. 129
v. Heathcote	ii. 846
v. Jordan	i. 206
v. Marghan	ii. 510
v. Martin	i. 68, 313, 558, 560, 562; ii. 199, 200, 751
v. Mitchell	ii. 51, 52
v. Mohr	ii. 767, 768
v. Morgan	i. 233, 234
v. Nicolls	ii. 212
v. Nutkin	ii. 261
v. Rebow	ii. 547
v. Righter	ii. 863
v. Stiles	ii. 231
v. Veeder	ii. 96, 373
v. Wade	i. 299
v. Wright	ii. 238
v. Zellerbach	i. 390
Martinetti v. Maguire	ii. 241
Martinius v. Helmuth	ii. 140, 145
Martinson v. Clowes	i. 332
Martyn v. Hind	ii. 362
v. Perryman	i. 661, 665
Martyn v. Westbrook	i. 203
Marvin v. Ellwood	ii. 139
Marwood v. Turner	ii. 295
Mason, In re	i. 465; ii. 821
v. Armitage	i. 173; ii. 43, 59
v. Bogg	i. 639
v. Day	ii. 688, 689
v. Gardiner	i. 65, 306
v. Goodburne	ii. 830, 832, 833
v. Hamilton	ii. 151
v. Kaine	i. 674
v. Mason	ii. 847
v. Masters	ii. 737
v. Payne	ii. 99
v. Pearson	i. 159
v. Ring	i. 314
Massey v. Banner	i. 456, 457, 458; ii. 615, 616
v. Davies	i. 322, 468
v. Parker	ii. 711, 713
v. Sherman	ii. 405
Massie v. Watts	ii. 60, 62, 209, 635
Massy v. Rowen	ii. 713
Master v. Fuller	ii. 732, 735
v. Kirton	i. 682
Masters v. Masters	i. 577; ii. 441
Mastin v. Barnard	ii. 387
v. Marlow	ii. 47
Match v. Hunt	i. 209
Mather v. Fraser	ii. 179
Mathews v. Cartwright	ii. 337
v. Jones	ii. 259
Matlock v. Todd	i. 215
Matthai v. Heather	i. 365
Matthewman's Case	ii. 734
Matthew's Appeal	i. 331
Matthews v. Aiken	i. 518
v. Cartwright	i. 418, 421
v. Feaver	i. 375
v. Heyward	ii. 688
v. Jarrett	ii. 81, 82
v. Matthews	ii. 789
v. Newby	i. 554
v. Warner	ii. 798
v. Wolwyn	i. 542
Matthewson v. Stockdale	ii. 244
Matthie v. Edwards	ii. 332
Mattingly v. Nye	i. 362
Mattison v. Tunfield	ii. 401
Mattocks v. Tremain	ii. 804
Mauck v. Mauck	i. 683
Maul v. Rider	i. 407, 411
Maunder v. Lloyd	i. 692
Maundrell v. Maundrell	i. 399, 417, 418, 634; ii. 720, 826
Maundy v. Maundy	i. 194
Mawhorter v. Armstrong	ii. 9
Mawman v. Tegg	ii. 240, 248

CASES CITED.

Mawson v. Stork	i. 386
Maxon v. Ayres	ii. 13
Maxwell, In re	i. 479
v. Hyslop	ii. 436
v. Montacute	ii. 321
May v. Bennett	i. 100
v. Coffin	i. 118
v. Hook	ii. 200
v. Leclaire	ii. 129, 608
v. May	ii. 23
v. Rice	i. 496
v. Western Union Tel. Co.	i. 205, 210
Mayer v. Murray	i. 533; ii. 316
v. Mutual Ins. Co.	ii. 654
Mayfield v. Kilgour	i. 377
Mayhew v. Boyd	i. 336
v. Crickett	i. 334, 337, 511, 515, 516
Mayn v. Mayn	ii. 286
Mayne v. Bredwin	ii. 677
Mayo v. Carrington	i. 256
Mayott v. Mayott	ii. 401
Mays v. Dwight	i. 153
Meach v. Meach	i. 607
Meacham v. Sterne	ii. 614
Meacher v. Young	ii. 686, 687
Mead, In re	i. 610
v. Bunn	i. 215
v. Combs	i. 376
v. Merritt	ii. 62, 208, 210, 211, 632
v. New York R. Co.	i. 592
v. Orrery	i. 406, 411, 412, 427, 428, 590; ii. 319
Meader v. Norton	ii. 851
Meadows v. Kingston	i. 196
Meals v. Meals	i. 602
Meason v. Kaine	ii. 35
Mechanics' Assoc. v. Conover	i. 640
Mechanics' Bank v. Seton	ii. 44, 606
Mechanics' Bank of Alexandria v. Lynn	ii. 91, 98, 101
Medlicot v. Bowes	ii. 773
Medlicott v. O'Donel	i. 417, 423, 438, 636
Medsker v. Bonebrake	ii. 702
Meek v. Chamberlain	i. 636
v. Kettlewell	i. 436; ii. 47, 116
v. Perry	i. 325, 327
Meeley v. Webber	i. 491
Meguire v. Corwine	i. 296
Meily v. Wood	i. 684
Meliorucchi v. Royal Exchange Ass. Co.	ii. 769
Mellen v. Whipple	ii. 362
Meller v. Woods	ii. 331
Mellish v. Mellish	i. 191
Meloy v. Dougherty	ii. 13
Meluish v. Milton	i. 441, 548; ii. 779
Mendes v. Barnard	ii. 812
Mendizabel v. Machado	ii. 837
Menominee Co. v. Langworthy	i. 158
Mercantile Ins. Co. v. Jaynes	i. 158
Merceron v. Dowson	i. 494, 495
Merchants' Bank v. Davis	i. 80
Merchants' Bank of Providence v. Packard	ii. 155
Merchants' Line v. Waganer	ii. 603
Merchant Tailors' Co. v. Attorney-Gen.	ii. 511
Mercier v. West Kansas City Land Co.	ii. 739, 752
Meredith v. Heneage	ii. 406, 407, 408
v. Wynn	ii. 97
Merewether v. Shaw	i. 272, 396
Merriam v. Boston R. Co.	i. 392
v. Cunningham	i. 252, 392
v. Hassam	ii. 278, 847
Merrifield v. Worcester	ii. 230
Merrill v. Allen	i. 29
v. Bullock	ii. 711
v. Englesby	ii. 365
v. Humphrey	i. 66
v. Merrill	ii. 290
Merriman v. Cannovan	ii. 202
Merritt, Ex parte	ii. 200
v. Bartholick	ii. 315
v. Brown	ii. 95, 99
v. Shrewsbury Ry. Co.	ii. 869
Merry v. Ryves	i. 264
Mertins v. Joliffe	i. 404, 416
Mesgrett v. Mesgrett	i. 264
Messenburgh v. Ash	ii. 275
Messiter v. Wright	i. 636
Mestaer v. Gillespie	i. 189, 264; ii. 104, 106
Metcalf v. Gilmore	ii. 197
v. Hervey	ii. 136, 141, 142, 152, 815
v. Hovey	i. 80
v. Pulvertoft	i. 412; ii. 215
Metcalfe v. Beckwith	i. 620, 622
v. York	ii. 578
Methodist Church v. Remington	ii. 503
Methodist Ep. Church v. Jaques	ii. 718, 722, 724, 725
Methwold v. Walbank	i. 297
Metropolitan R. Co. v. Chicago	ii. 223
Metropolitan Soc. v. Brown	i. 111, 150
Metzler v. Wood	ii. 255, 258
Meux v. Bell	i. 402; ii. 155, 339, 367
v. Howell	ii. 343
v. Maltby	i. 406
Meyer v. Gregson	i. 480
Meyn v. Belcher	i. 263

CASES CITED.   lxxiii

Michoud v. Girod	ii. 848
Michel v. Tinsley	i. 154, 157
Michigan Plaster Co. v. White	ii. 139, 140, 141
Mickles v. Thayer	ii. 789
Micklethwait v. Micklethwait	i. 538
Middlecome v. Marlow	i. 380
Middleditch v. Sharland	i. 467
Middlesex Manufacturing Co. v. Lawrence	i. 338
Middleton's Case	ii. 487
Middleton v. Jackson	ii. 175
v. Middleton	i. 201
v. Selby	ii. 77
v. Spicer	ii. 512, 530, 547
Middletown Bank v. Russ	i. 70, 76, 81, 454
Milan Steam Mills v. Hickey	ii. 234
Milbourn v. Ewart	ii. 701
Mildmay v. Hungerford	i. 123, 125, 134
v. Mildmay	ii. 222, 759
Mildred v. Austin	ii. 326
Mildway v. Quicke	ii. 554
v. Smith	i. 389
Miles v. Caldwell	ii. 872
v. Mellwraith	i. 213, 296
v. Williams	ii. 347
Milhau v. Sharp	ii. 225, 228
Milkman v. Ordway	ii. 91, 126
Millard v. Eyre	ii. 631
v. Thanet	ii. 101
Millegan v. Cooke	ii. 104
Miller's Appeal	ii. 397
Miller v. Atkinson	ii. 493
v. Barber	i. 208
v. Blandist	ii. 68
v. Cook	i. 350
v. Davis	ii. 538
v. Ewer	ii. 869
v. Gable	ii. 515, 525
v. Harris	ii. 673
v. Jeffries	i. 607
v. Life Ins. Co.	ii. 654
v. Marriott	i. 668
v. McIntire	i. 546; ii. 843, 845
v. Miller	i. 607, 610, 611, 614, 616; ii. 99
v. Morse	i. 86
v. Ord	i. 516, 527
v. Palmer	ii. 197, 198
v. Proctor	i. 683
v. Rowan	ii. 493
v. Sawbridge	i. 216
v. Sawyer	i. 514
v. Simonds	i. 311
v. Tobie	ii. 130
Miller v. Warmington	i. 621, 623, 624, 654, 656, 661, 668
v. Wells	i. 95
Milles v. Wikes	ii. 711
Millican v. Millican	i. 313
Milligan's Appeal	i. 519
Millingar v. Sorg	ii. 861
Millington v. Fox	ii. 254, 255
Millnight v. Smith	i. 684
Mills, ——— v.	ii. 788
Mills v. Banks	ii. 326, 391, 394
v. Dennis	ii. 330
v. Eden	i. 516, 571
v. Evansville Seminary	i. 154, 156
v. Farmer	ii. 480, 487, 501, 502, 504, 506, 507, 513, 514, 515, 521
v. Fowkes	i. 460
v. Hyde	i. 510
v. Jennings	i. 422; ii. 327, 328
v. Lockwood	i. 156
v. Mills	i. 296, 606
v. Townshend	ii. 142
v. Trumper	i. 490
Millsops v. Pfeiffer	i. 70
Milltown v. Stewart	ii. 7
Milmine v. Burnham	i. 153
Milne v. Morwood	i. 208
v. Walton	ii. 342
Milner v. Mills	ii. 112
v. Milner	i. 190, 191
Milnes v. Busk	ii. 702, 724, 725, 726
v. Slater	i. 581, 582, 587, 588
Milward v. Hallett	ii. 587
v. Thanet	ii. 95
Milwaukee R. Co. v. Milwaukee R. Co.	ii. 359
Mims v. Lockett	ii. 76, 77
Miner v. Beekman	ii. 583
v. Hess	i. 153
v. Pierce	i. 653, 684, 689
v. Jackson	i. 365
Minet v. Hyde	ii. 752
v. Morgan	ii. 821, 822
v. Vulliamy	ii. 519, 636
Mining Co. v. Coal Co.	i. 150, 151, 157
Minke v. Hopeman	ii. 224, 228
Minnesota Oil Co. v. Palmer	ii. 157
Minnier v. Minnier	ii. 701
Minot v. Boston Asylum	ii. 504
v. Mitchell	ii. 271
v. Taylor	ii. 611
Minshaw v. Jordan	ii. 10
Minter v. Wraith	ii. 398
Minturn v. Seymour	i. 433; ii. 23, 119, 120, 290
Mirehouse v. Scaife	i. 580; ii. 846

CASES CITED.

Mississippi v. Johnson	ii. 260
Missouri R. Co. v. Commissioners	ii. 260
Mitchel v. Bunch	ii. 208, 210, 632, 803, 804
Mitchell's Case	ii. 861
Mitchell v. Butt	ii. 570
v. Chancellor	i. 89
v. Denson	i. 184
v. Dorrs	ii. 235
v. Harris	ii. 794
v. Hayne	ii. 138, 139, 154, 155
v. Kingman	i. 240
v. Milwaukee	ii. 14
v. Mitchell	i. 588
v. Moberly	ii. 526
v. Reynolds	i. 293, 294
v. Smith	ii. 821
v. Steward	ii. 860
v. Winslow	ii. 349, 378
Mitford v. Mitford	ii. 347, 575, 576, 741, 744, 745, 747
v. Reynolds	ii. 494, 519
Mix v. Beach	ii. 99
Mixer's Case	i. 211
Mobile v. Kimball	ii. 91, 126
Mobile Bldg. Assoc. v. Robertson	ii. 321
Mocatta v. Murgatroyd	i. 395
Mocher v. Reed	ii. 198
Mogg v. Hodges	i. 575, 579; ii. 512
Moggridge v. Thackwell	ii. 408, 480, 487, 492, 501, 502, 509, 513, 515, 521, 522, 523, 525
Mohawk Bridge Co. v. Utica & Schenectady R. Co.	ii. 223, 224, 228
Mohawk & Hudson R. Co. v. Artcher	ii. 229, 232
Mohawk &c. R. Co v. Clute	ii. 137, 143, 154, 155
Mold v. Wheatcroft	ii. 865
Mole v. Mansfield	i. 662
v. Smith	i. 417, 634
Molesworth, Ex parte	ii. 685
Monaghan, In re	ii. 696
Monck v. Monck	ii. 460
Monell v. Monell	ii. 626, 627, 628, 675
Moneypenny v. Bristow	ii. 774
Monis v. Nixon	ii. 321
Monk v. Cooper	i. 104, 105
Monroe v. Graves	ii. 272, 282
v. Skelton	i. 85, 154, 156
Montague v. Dudman	ii. 201, 202, 811, 812, 819, 822
v. Sandwich	i. 366
Montecute v. Maxwell	i. 339, 382; ii. 88
Montefiore v. Browne	i. 408
Montefiore v. Guedalla	ii. 458
Montefiori v. Montefiori	i. 272
Montesquieu v. Sandys	i. 316, 317, 318, 319, 321
Montgomery v. Sayre	ii. 12, 14
Montgomery County v. Elston	i. 67
Montgomery R. Co. v. Branch	i. 557
Moodalay v. Morton	i. 78; ii. 812, 821, 824, 837
Moody v. Holcomb	ii. 12
v. Payne	i. 687, 689
v. Reid	i. 184, 187
v. Walters	ii. 281, 294, 295
v. Wright	ii. 349
Moor v. Black	i. 629, 632
v. Rainsbeck	ii. 553
v. Rycault	i. 379
Moore v. Blake	ii. 59, 95, 101
v. Bowman	ii. 866
v. Burke	i. 205, 208
v. Cable	ii. 586
v. Craven	ii. 822
v. Crowder	ii. 59, 66, 77, 90
v. Darton	i. 609
v. Edwards	ii. 70, 71, 84
v. Ellis	ii. 700
v. Fessenbeck	ii. 180
v. Freeman	ii. 702
v. Greg	ii. 45
v. Macnamara	i. 411; ii. 215
v. Moore	i. 98, 99; ii. 503, 701
v. Pickett	ii. 272
v. Usher	ii. 137, 139, 373
v. White	i. 546
v. Wood	i. 362
v. Worthy	ii. 566
Moorehead v. Moorehead	i. 660
Moorehouse v. Colvin	ii. 109
Moorman v. Collier	i. 117
Moors v. Stone	ii. 397
Moravian Soc., In re	ii. 631
Mordant v. Thorold	i. 628, 632, 633
Mordaunt v. Benwell	ii. 554
Mordue v. Palmer	ii. 795
More v. Bonnet	i. 293
v. More	ii. 691
Morecock v. Dickens	i. 409
Morely v. Bonge	ii. 855
Morenhout v. Higuera	i. 659
Mores v. Huish	ii. 718
Morgan, Ex parte	ii. 578
v. Berger	ii. 73
v. Dillon	ii. 664, 665, 666, 667, 674
v. Gronow	ii. 276
v. Higgins	i. 319
v. Mallison	ii. 23

Morgan v. Marsack	ii. 140
v. Mather	ii. 790, 791, 793
v. Minett	i. 314, 317, 318
v. Morgan	i. 606; ii. 101, 103
v. Perhamus	i. 293
v. Seymour	i. 505, 506
v. Sherrard	i. 567
v. Skidmore	i. 684
Morice v. Durham	ii. 408, 410, 492, 515
Morison v. Salmon	ii. 256
Morley v. Morley	ii. 328, 614
v. Rennoldson	i. 279, 286
v. Thompson	ii. 146
v. Wright	ii. 747
Mornington v. Keane	ii. 577
Mornsby v. Blamire	ii. 401
Morphett v. Jones	ii. 74, 78, 79, 80
Morrall v. Marlow	ii. 347
Morret v. Parke	i. 323, 418, 421, 422; ii. 549
Morrice v. Bank of England	i. 555, 557, 558, 560, 562, 567, 569; ii. 199
Morris v. Bacon	i. 180; ii. 315
v. Berkeley	ii. 232
v. Burroughs	i. 311
v. Clarkson	i. 263
v. Colman	i. 293; ii. 263
v. Hoyt	ii. 99
v. Kearsley	i. 684
v. Kelly	ii. 254
v. McCullough	i. 298, 303, 305
v. McNeil	ii. 803
v. Morris	i. 309, 538, 684; ii. 261
v. Munroe	i. 140
v. Nixon	i. 332
v. Potter	ii. 397
v. Remington	ii. 60, 61
v. Shannon	i. 391
v. Stephenson	ii. 49, 50, 52
Morris Canal Co. v. Emmatt	i. 162, 220, 221
Morris Coal Co. v. Barclay Coal Co.	i. 293
Morris R. Co. v. Prudden	ii. 229
Morrison v. Arbuthnot	i. 269, 271
v. Arnold	ii. 779, 780, 839
v. Clark	i. 373
v. Hershire	i. 66
v. Moat	ii. 258
v. Peay	ii. 80
v. Rossignol	ii. 40, 81
v. Turnour	ii. 70
Morse v. Bassett	i. 579; ii. 315
v. Dearborn	i. 210
v. Hill	i. 328; ii. 844
Morse v. Huntington	i. 336
v. Martin	i. 156
v. Morse	i. 188
v. Rathbun	ii. 651
v. Roach	ii. 785
v. Royal	i. 320, 330, 353, 354
v. Stearns	ii. 153
Morse Twist Co. v. Morse	i. 293
Mortimer v. Bell	i. 295; ii. 91
v. Capper	i. 105, 140, 163, 166
v. Orchard	ii. 85, 856
Mortlock v. Buller	i. 200; ii. 4, 51, 73, 125
Morton v. Naylor	ii. 363, 364, 366
Moseley v. Simpson	ii. 791
Mosely v. Virgin	ii. 29, 45
Moses v. Levi	ii. 623, 626
v. Lewis	i. 457, 467
v. Macferland	ii. 605
v. Mobile	i. 19; ii. 175
v. Moses	i. 331
v. Murgatroyd	i. 68, 565; ii. 272, 346
Moshier v. Norton	ii. 317
Moss v. Adams	i. 637
v. Bainbrigge	i. 318
v. Barton	ii. 40
v. Gallimore	ii. 319
Mossop v. Eadon	i. 94
Mostyn v. Brooke	ii. 675
Motley v. Dowman	ii. 254
Mott v. Buxton	ii. 286
Motteux v. London Assur. Co.	i. 167, 171, 172; ii. 93
Moulson v. Moulson	ii. 459
Mount v. Potts	ii. 580
Mountfort, Ex parte	ii. 323, 336, 673, 677, 685
Mt. Holly Co. v. Ferree	ii. 141
Mower, In re	i. 640
Moxey v. Bigwood	ii. 90
Moxon v. Bright	i. 333, 469
Moyl v. Horne	ii. 68
Moyse v. Gayles	ii. 542
Muckleston v. Brown	i. 300; ii. 547
Muggeridge, In re	ii. 277
Muir v. Leitch	i. 684
v. Schenck	i. 426; ii. 347, 348
v. Schenectady	ii. 339
Mulford v. Peterson	ii. 342
Mulhall v. Quinn	ii. 349
Mulheran v. Gillespie	ii. 463
Mulhern v. McDavitt	ii. 686
Mullens v. Miller	i. 211
Muller v. Dows	ii. 60
v. Rhuman	i. 153
Mulligan v. Baring	ii. 13, 14

CASES CITED.

Mullings v. Trinder ii. 103
Mulloy v. Backer i. 480
Mulock v. Mulock i. 156
Mumford v. Murray ii. 627, 629, 744
— v. Nicoll ii. 588
Mumma v. Potomac Co. ii. 603
Mundy v. Howe ii. 386, 686, 687
— v. Mundy i. 627, 629, 657; ii. 330
Munns v. Isle of Wight Ry. Co. ii. 233
Munsell v. Loree ii. 81
Munson v. Munson ii. 872
Murphy v. Clark ii. 24
Murray v. Ballou i. 399, 411, 412; ii. 215, 606, 609
— v. Barlee ii. 726, 731
— v. Clarendon ii. 260
— v. Clayton ii. 822
— v. Coster ii. 844
— v. Dake i. 167
— v. Elibank ii. 736, 739, 740, 750, 751, 752
— v. Finster i. 399, 412
— v. Graham ii. 202
— v. Lylburn i. 426; ii. 215, 347, 366, 607, 608, 609
— v. Murray i. 688; ii. 604
— v. Palmer i. 354
— v. Toland i. 544; ii. 773
Murrell v. Cox ii. 623, 625
Murrill v. Neill i. 684
Murtagh v. Costello i. 683
Musgrave's Case ii. 37
Musselman v. Cravens i. 237
— v. Marquis ii. 234
Mussleman's Appeal ii. 102
Mustain v. Jones ii. 13
Mycock v. Beatson i. 682
Myer v. Myer ii. 801
Myers v. Forbes ii. 40, 81, 82
— v. O'Hanlon i. 198
Myerscough, Ex parte ii. 673, 685
Myres v. De Mier ii. 60

N.

Nab v. Nab ii. 272
Naill v. Maurer i. 627
Nairn v. Prowse ii. 562, 566, 567, 571, 572
Naldred v. Gilham i. 433
Nantes v. Corrock i. 248, 375; ii. 725, 726
Nant-y-glo-Iron Works Co. v. Grave i. 332
Nash v. Derby ii. 661
Nash v. New England Ins. Co. ii. 182, 231, 234
— v. Morley ii. 491, 494
Natal Investment Co., In re ii. 366
National Bank, Ex parte i. 463; ii. 324
— v. Bangs i. 205, 390
— v. Barry ii. 605, 607
— v. Ins. Co. ii. 616
— v. Rogers i. 158
— v. Sprague i. 295, 683
National Exchange v. Drew i. 212
National Ins. Co. v. Crane i. 171
National Land Co. v. Perry ii. 648, 656
Natusch v. Irving ii. 867
Navulshaw v. Brownrigg i. 469
Nayler v. Wetherell ii. 435
Naylor v. Winch i. 124, 130, 133, 140, 254
Neal's Case ii. 704, 716
Neal v. Gregory i. 157
Neale v. Cripps ii. 222
— v. Neale i. 124, 138, 140; ii. 80
Neall v. Hill ii. 163
Near v. Lowe i. 473
Neate v. Marlborough ii. 557, 560
Neave v. Alderton i. 573
Neblett v. Macfarland i. 227
Nedby v. Nedby ii. 714
Needles v. Martin ii. 493, 847
Neigel v. Walsh ii. 234
Neilson v. Blight ii. 272, 346
Neimcewicz v. Gahn ii. 703
Nellis v. Lathrop i. 492, 493
Nelson v. Booth ii. 620
— v. Bridges ii. 123
— v. Davis i. 111, 113
— v. Duncombe ii. 695
— v. Goree ii. 153
— v. Hagerstown Bank ii. 95, 553
— v. Oldfield i. 194
— v. Skinner ii. 89
— v. Stocker i. 392
Nelthorp v. Hill i. 98, 99
Nesbit v. Lockman i. 318, 320
— v. Murray ii. 547
Nesbitt v. Berridge i. 343
— v. Tredenick ii. 550
Nesham v. Selby ii. 41, 81
Ness v. Fisher i. 673
Nestor, The Brig ii. 305
Nethersole v. School for Blind ii. 526
Neuman v. Godfrey ii. 823
Neven v. Speckerman i. 529
Neves v. Scott ii. 288
Nevill v. Snelling i. 342
Neville v. Fortescue i. 606
— v. Robinson i. 61

CASES CITED.

Neville v. Wilkinson	i. 204, 212, 237, 270, 271, 302, 303, 393
New v. Bonaker	ii. 503, 505, 517, 519
v. Wamback	i. 167
New Albany R. Co. v. Fields	i. 403
New Bedford Sav. Inst. v. Fairhaven Bank	i. 527
New Brunswick Ry. Co. v. Conybeare	i. 208
New Brunswick Ry. Co. v. Muggeridge	i. 208; ii. 864
Newburgh v. Bickerstaffe	i. 533
Newburgh Turnpike Co. v. Miller	ii. 232
Newbury, In re	ii. 680
Newcastle v. Pelham	ii. 18, 817
Newcomb v. Bonham	ii. 321
v. Brooks	i. 329
Newell v. Wheeler	ii. 12
New England Bank v. Lewis	ii. 344
Newham v. May	ii. 122, 123, 125, 127
Newland v. Champion	i. 428, 592
Newlands v. Paynter	ii. 710, 714, 828
Newman, In re	ii. 651, 652
v. Alvord	ii. 256, 257
v. Barton	i. 99, 528; ii. 602
v. Franco	ii. 819
v. Milner	ii. 9, 17
v. Newman	ii. 434, 437
v. Payne	i. 320, 542
v. Rogers	ii. 99
v. Rusham	i. 437
New Orleans v. United States	ii. 223
New River Co. v. Graves	ii. 175
Newry Ry. Co. v. Ulster Ry.	ii. 870
Newsom v. McLendon	i. 651
New South Church, In re	ii. 524
Newstead v. Johnstone	ii. 546, 548
v. Searle	ii. 289
Newton's Trusts	ii. 397
Newton v. Bennett	i. 68, 566
v. Chorlton	i. 514, 515
v. Hunt	i. 345, 346
v. Newton	ii. 280, 324
v. Porter	ii. 605, 607
v. Preston	ii. 535
v. Reid	ii. 713
v. Rowse	i. 480
v. Stanley	i. 580
New York v. Baumberger	ii. 225
v. Mapes	ii. 229
New York Guar. Co. v. Memphis Water Co.	ii. 380
New York Printing & Dyeing Estab. v. Fitch	ii. 234
New Zealand Banking Co., Ex parte	ii. 366
Niagara Falls Bridge Co. v. Great Western Ry. Co.	ii. 228
Nicholas v. Adams	i. 607
v. Nicholas	i. 602, 603
Nicholls v. Danvers	ii. 758
v. Leeson	i. 123
v. Peak	ii. 476
Nichols v. Chalie	ii. 787, 788, 789
v. Crisp	ii. 546
v. Davis	ii. 356
v. Eaton	ii. 277, 281
v. Glover	ii. 562
v. Gould	i. 343
v. Judkin	ii. 463
v. Levy	i. 355
v. Nichols	i. 250
v. Norris	i. 336
v. Roe	ii. 786, 792
v. Rowe	ii. 789
v. Stratton	i. 294
v. Williams	ii. 81
Nicholson v. Hooper	i. 391
v. Revell	i. 123, 336, 512, 513
v. Sherman	i. 549
v. Squire	ii. 691
Nickels v. Hancock	ii. 790
Nickerson v. Loud	ii. 14, 15
Nickolson v. Knowles	ii. 147
Nicoll v. Mumford	i. 687, 688; ii. 272, 344, 346, 589
Nicols v. Pitman	ii. 252, 253
Nield v. Smith	ii. 107
Niell v. Morley	i. 242
Nightingale v. Goulburn	ii. 492, 494
v. Lawson	i. 500
Nisbit v. Smith	i. 334, 337, 648; ii. 170, 194
Niven v. Belknap	ii. 85
Nives v. Nives	ii. 95
Nixon's Appeal	ii. 534
Noble v. Googins	i. 156, 157, 162
v. Noble	i. 379
v. Walker	i. 306
Noel v. Robinson	i. 98, 99, 528, 553, 602; ii. 602
v. Ward	ii. 19
Nokes v. Gibbon	ii. 654
Norcott v. Gordon	i. 580
Norcross v. Widgery	i. 401
Norfolk v. Myers	ii. 174
Norman v. Morrill	i. 577
Normanby v. Devonshire	ii. 55
Norrington, In re	ii. 281
Norris's Appeal	i. 621
Norris v. Chambers	i. 692
v. Larrabee	i. 116
v. Le Neve	i. 322, 330

CASES CITED.

Norris v. Norris	i. 575
v. Thompson	ii. 491, 492
v. Wilkinson	ii. 323, 324
North v. Ansall	i. 259
v. Pardon	ii. 546
v. Strafford	i. 625, 693, 696, 698
Northcote v. Duke	ii. 653, 656
Northen v. Carnegie	ii. 534
Northey v. Northey	ii. 707
North Hudson R. Co. v. Booraem	ii. 583
Northrop v. Boom	ii. 73
v. Graves	i. 117, 118
Norton v. Boston	ii. 14, 144
v. Coons	i. 509
v. Frecker	i. 532, 631; ii. 291, 852
v. Mascall	ii. 795
v. Norton	i. 365
v. Phelps	ii. 281
v. Reid	ii. 170
v. Turvill	ii. 728, 734
v. Webb	ii. 316
v. Woods	ii. 204
Norway v. Rowe	i. 682; ii. 164, 234, 236
Norwich R. Co. v. Storey	i. 811
Nott v. Hill	i. 339
Nourse v. Finch	ii. 548
v. Gregory	i. 78
Nowell v. Roake	ii. 389
Nowlan v. Nellighan	ii. 411
Noyes v. Crawley	i. 686
v. Loring	i. 205
v. Marsh	ii. 81, 86
Noys v. Mordaunt	ii. 417, 418, 422
Nudd v. Powers	i. 28, 30; ii. 844
Nugent v. Bates	ii. 14
v. Clifford	i. 427
v. Gifford	i. 589, 590; ii. 470
Nunn v. Fabian	ii. 79, 80, 861
v. Hancock	ii. 675
Nurse v. Craig	ii. 734, 735
Nussbaum v. Heilbron	i. 78
Nutbrown v. Thornton	ii. 25, 26, 43, 213, 229
Nutt v. Nutt	i. 190
Nye v. Mosely	i. 303

O.

Oakes v. Turquand	i. 212; ii. 862
Oakley v. Hurlbut	ii. 11, 844
v. Pound	ii. 734
O'Bannon v. Miller	i. 684
Oberle v. Leech	ii. 554
O'Brien v. Egan	i. 330
O'Brien v. Lewis	i. 314
O'Byrne v. Feeley	ii. 397
Oceanic Nav. Co. v. Sutherberry	ii. 467, 471
Ocean Ins. Co. v. Field	ii. 198
O'Conner v. Rempt	i. 243, 244
v. Spaight	i. 448, 451, 456, 531; ii. 772
O'Connor v. Cook	ii. 798
O'Dell v. Crone	ii. 402
Odineal v. Barry	i. 297
Oelrichs v. Spain	i. 27, 29
O'Fallon v. Kennerly	ii. 99
Offley v. Offley	ii. 704
Offutt v. King	i. 367
Ogden's Appeal	ii. 714
Ogden v. Gibbons	ii. 232, 233
v. Larrabee	ii. 620
v. Prentice	i. 365
Ogilvie v. Currie	i. 30
v. Foljambe	i. 174; ii. 92
v. Jeaffreson	i. 402, 413, 414
v. Knox Ins. Co.	i. 557
Ogle v. Cooke	ii. 782, 783
O'Gorman v. Comyn	ii. 557
O'Hara v. O'Neal	ii. 536
v. Stack	ii. 263
v. Strange	i. 621
O'Hare v. Downing	ii. 179
O'Herlihy v. Hedges	ii. 75
Ohio Ins. Co. v. Ledyard	i. 527
Oil Run Co. v. Gale	ii. 138
Oke v. Heath	ii. 717
Okeden v. Okeden	ii. 391
Okeefe v. Casey	ii. 674
Okill v. Whittaker	i. 156, 157
Olcott v. Bynum	ii. 536
Old Colony R. Co. v. Evans	ii. 43
Oldham v. Carleton	ii. 546
v. Hand	i. 320, 321
v. James	ii. 91
v. Litchford	i. 61, 264; ii. 89, 106
v. Oldham	ii. 851
Olin v. Bate	i. 301
Oliphant v. Hendrie	ii. 517, 518, 519
Oliver v. Court	i. 333; ii. 619, 629
v. Hamilton	i. 680
v. Jernigan	i. 659
v. Memphis R. Co.	ii. 15
v. Mutual Ins. Co.	i. 171
v. Piatt	ii. 549, 606, 607
Olive v. Smith	ii. 768
Olliver v. King	i. 379
Olney v. Eaton	ii. 60
Omerod v. Hardman	ii. 92, 99
Ommanney v. Butcher	ii. 282, 407, 408, 495, 515, 517, 522, 530

CASES CITED.   lxxix

	PAGE
O'Neil v. Chandler	i. 378
Onge v. Truelock	i. 505
Onions v. Tyrer	i. 103
Onslow v. ——	ii. 219
v. Mitchell	ii. 448
Onyon v. Washbourne	ii. 201
Oppenheim v. Wolf	ii. 139
Orby v. Trigg	ii. 322
Ord v. Noel	ii. 608
Oregon Nav. Co. v. Winsor	i. 293
O'Reilly v. Nicholson	ii. 427
v. Thompson	ii. 79, 85, 86
Orford v. Churchill	ii. 401
Orger v. Spark	i. 660
Oriental Co. v. Overend	i. 335, 512
Ormond v. Hutchinson	i. 143, 236, 330, 468
v. Kynersley	i. 536
Ormrod v. Huth	i. 209
Orr v. Johnston	ii. 209, 255, 256, 258
v. Kaines	i. 97, 98, 99
Orrell v. Orrell	ii. 436
Orrok v. Binney	ii. 165
Osborn v. Bank of United States	ii. 213, 214, 233
v. Morgan	ii. 746
v. Osborn	i. 668; ii. 222
Osborne v. Brooklyn R. Co.	ii. 226
v. Phelps	i. 175
v. Williams	i. 297, 301, 302, 305
Osbrey v. Bury	ii. 295
Oscanyan v. Arms Co.	i. 296
Osgood v. Franklin	i. 255, 256; ii. 124
v. Lovering	ii. 397
v. Strode	ii. 289, 290
Osmond v. Fitzroy	i. 246, 247, 266, 310, 343
Oswell v. Probert	ii. 744
Otis v. Beckwith	i. 433, 435; ii. 21, 119
v. McClellan	ii. 276
v. Prince	i. 279
Ottley v. Browne	i. 300
Otway v. Hudson	ii. 112
Otway-Cave v. Otway	i. 664
Outram v. Round	ii. 50
Overend v. Oriental Corp.	i. 336
Overing v. Foote	ii. 13
Overton v. Banister	i. 392
Owen v. Davies	ii. 74
v. Griffith	i. 532
v. Paul	ii. 12
v. Phillips	ii. 231
Owens v. Bean	ii. 504
v. Dickenson	i. 559, 560; ii. 388, 722, 725, 726, 729, 730, 735
v. Missionary Soc.	ii. 503
v. Ranstead	ii. 206
Ownes v. Ownes	i. 302, 305, 378; ii. 535, 538
Oxenden v. Compton	ii. 113, 114, 669, 670, 689, 690, 693, 694, 695, 696, 758, 759
v. Oxenden	ii. 758, 759
Oxenham v. Esdaile	ii. 556, 561
Oxford v. Provand	ii. 46
Oxford & Cambridge Universities v. Richardson	ii. 231, 237, 238, 240

P.

	PAGE
Pacific R. Co. v. Missouri Pacific Ry.	i. 218
Packer v. Wyndham	ii. 743, 750
Packet Co. v. Sickles	ii. 237
Paddock v. Palmer	ii. 191, 872
v. Shields	i. 657
Padwick v. Stanley	i. 333
Page v. Broom	ii. 95, 98, 345, 529
v. Montgomery	ii. 11
v. Page	ii. 547
v. Patton	i. 590
Paget v. Gee	i. 490, 491, 492
v. Grinfall	ii. 448
v. Marshall	i. 110, 150
Paice v. Canterbury	ii. 522
Paige v. Banks	ii. 261
Pain v. Coombs	ii. 79
v. Smith	ii. 323, 331
Paine v. First Div. St. Paul R. Co.	ii. 12
v. Hutchinson	ii. 37
v. Upton	i. 156, 157
v. Wagner	ii. 401
Pale v. Mitchell	ii. 736
Palin v. Hills	ii. 399, 401
Palmer's Case	i. 465
Palmer, In re	ii. 265
v. Bate	i. 298; ii. 356
v. Bethard	i. 180
v. Casperson	i. 627
v. De Witt	ii. 254
v. Harris	ii. 258
v. Johnson	i. 217
v. Mason	i. 604
v. Neave	i. 271
v. Stebbins	i. 294
v. Stevens	ii. 275
v. Waller	i. 563
v. Wheeler	i. 263
v. Whettenhal	i. 693, 696, 697; ii. 57
Pamphrey v. Brown	ii. 536

Pamplin v. Green	i. 554
Pannell v. McMechen	i. 335
Panton v. Panton	i. 476, 626
Papillon v. Voice	ii. 18, 286
Paradine v. Jane	i. 104, 478; ii. 641
Paramore v. Yardley	i. 599
Parbury's Case	i. 212
Parchman v. McKinney	i. 460
Pardee v. Treat	ii. 341
Pardo v. Bingham	i. 567
Parham v. Green	i. 528
v. McCrary	ii. 850
v. Randolph	i. 215
Paris v. Gilham	ii. 140, 142, 144
v. Hulett	i. 527
v. Stone	i. 607, 609
Park v. Johnson	ii. 54, 90
Parker v. Barker	ii. 141, 152
v. Benjamin	i. 171
v. Blythmore	i. 416, 635
v. Brooke	i. 406, 408; ii. 702, 710
v. Browning	ii. 161, 200
v. Butcher	ii. 645, 652
v. Clarke	ii. 404
v. Clarkson	ii. 476
v. Coburn	ii. 462
v. Converse	ii. 275
v. Dee	i. 72, 74, 454
v. Dun. Nav. Co.	ii. 868
v. Flagg	i. 359, 379
v. Gerrard	i. 659, 661
v. Grant	i. 230
v. Harvey	ii. 707
v. Housefield	ii. 331
v. Marchant	ii. 591, 594
v. Marston	i. 607
v. Nickerson	i. 322, 324
v. Nightingale	ii. 55, 348
v. Phetteplace	i. 203
v. Pistor	i. 689
v. Sowerby	ii. 428
v. Taswell	ii. 90
v. Winnipiseogee Co.	i. 27
Parkes v. White	ii. 718, 720, 724, 725
Parkhurst v. Alexander	i. 409, 410, 423
v. Howell	ii. 460
v. Lowten	ii. 821
v. Van Cortlandt	i. 173; ii. 77, 78, 82, 83, 86, 87, 124, 128
Parkin v. Thorold	ii. 99
Parkinson v. Hanbury	ii. 217
Parkist v. Alexander	i. 323
Parks v. Evansville Ry.	ii. 862
v. Jackson	ii. 154
Parmelee v. Cameron	i. 344
Parr v. Eliason	i. 436
Parshall v. Eggart	ii. 335
Parslow v. Weaden	i. 383
Parsons v. Baker	ii. 405
v. Bignold	i. 167
v. Bradford	i. 54
v. Briddock	i. 517, 518
v. Hughes	i. 227
v. Parsons	i. 191; ii. 397
v. Ruddock	i. 647
v. Thompson	i. 298
v. Winslow	i. 280, 288, 289
Parteriche v. Powlet	i. 170; ii. 87, 542
Partridge v. Gopp	i. 359, 360, 368, 375
v. Hood	ii. 240
v. Menck	ii. 255
v. Smith	i. 411
v. Walker	ii. 481
Parvis v. Corbet	i. 422
Pascall v. Pickering	i. 262
Paschall v. Ketterich	i. 553, 566, 604
Pascoe v. Swan	i. 663
Pasley v. Freeman	i. 204, 215, 219, 389
Passyunk Building Assoc.'s Appeal	i. 458
Patch v. Shore	ii. 388
v. Ward	i. 261; ii. 197, 816, 873
Patman v. Harland	i. 405
Patmore v. Morris	i. 124
Paton v. Rogers	ii. 104, 105
Patrick v. Harrison	ii. 214
Patten v. Casey	i. 361
Patterson v. Bloomer	ii. 90
v. Donner	i. 297
v. Lawrence	i. 392; ii. 866
v. McCamant	ii. 177
v. Patterson	ii. 757
v. Yeaton	ii. 130
Pattison v. Hull	i. 462, 463; ii. 367
v. Skillman	ii. 24
Patton v. Campbell	i. 87
Patty v. Pease	i. 531, 644; ii. 580
Paul v. Compton	ii. 406
v. Paul	ii. 272, 283, 529
v. York	ii. 688
Paulling v. Creagh	i. 542, 543
Pawlet v. Delaval	ii. 703, 710
v. Ingres	ii. 174
Pawlett v. Attorney-Gen.	ii. 312, 314
Paxton v. Douglas	i. 558, 560, 562; ii. 199
Payne, Ex parte	ii. 408, 412
v. Avery	ii. 580
v. Compton	i. 64, 634, 636; ii. 825, 826

CASES CITED.   lxxxi

Payne v. Little	ii. 702
v. Meller	ii. 101
Payson v. Lamson	i. 31
Payton v. Bladwell	i. 269, 270
Peabody v. Flint	i. 218
v. Norfolk	i. 295
v. Tarbell	ii. 129
Peachy v. Somerset	ii. 646, 647, 661
Peacock, In re	ii. 450
v. Evans	i. 66, 256, 341, 342, 343, 345, 348, 354
v. Monk	ii. 709, 717, 719, 720, 728, 734
v. Peacock	i. 673, 679
v. Stockford	ii. 530
Peak v. Hayden	ii. 218
Peake, Ex parte	ii. 569, 575
v. Highfield	ii. 13, 16
Pearce v. Creswick	i. 71, 75, 81, 453; ii. 3
v. Crutchfield	ii. 691
v. Gamble	i. 314
v. Green	i. 468, 470
v. Olney	ii. 196, 210, 211
v. Pearce	ii. 623
Pearl v. Deacon	i. 514
v. Harris	ii. 81, 794
Pearly v. Smith	i. 488, 489
Pearne v. Lisle	ii. 25
Pearpont v. Graham	ii. 343
Pearse v. Chamberlain	i. 681
v. Green	ii. 619
Pearson's Case	i. 332
Pearson v. Benson	i. 314
v. Cardon	ii. 137, 145, 147, 150, 151
v. Concord R. Co.	i. 333
v. Lord	i. 155
v. Morgan	i. 215, 216, 230, 393, 395
v. Pearson	ii. 429
v. Ward	ii. 837
Pease v. Kelly	ii. 570
v. Pilot Knob Iron Co.	ii. 390
Peat v. Crane	ii. 615, 617
Peck v. Arehart	i. 153
v. Ashley	ii. 812
v. Conway	ii. 348
v. Crane	ii. 201
v. Matthews	ii. 232
Peckham v. Barker	ii. 76, 77, 79
Pecot v. Armelin	i. 683
Pedder, In re	ii. 115
Peek v. Gurney	i. 208; ii. 862
Peeples v. Horton	i. 577
Peer v. Kean	ii. 39
Peers v. Baldwin	ii. 649
v. Needham	i. 667
Peet v. Beers	ii. 341
Peiffer v. Lytle	ii. 541
Pelham v. Aldrich	i. 429, 431
Pell v. Northampton Ry. Co.	ii. 233, 265
Pelletrave v. Jackson	ii. 342
Pells v. Brown	ii. 404
Pelton v. National Bank	ii. 15
Pember v. Matthews	i. 175; ii. 89, 171, 855, 856
Pemberton v. Barnes	i. 662
v. Johnson	ii. 729
v. Oakes	i. 460, 465
v. Pemberton	i. 198; ii. 779, 781, 782
Pembroke v. Beighden	ii. 112
v. Thorpe	ii. 45, 67, 78
Pence v. Pence	ii. 554
Pendarvis v. Hicks	i. 289
Pendleton v. Dalton	ii. 90
v. Wambersie	i. 458
Penfold v. Mould	ii. 752
Pengal v. Ross	ii. 75, 76, 77, 85
Penn v. Baltimore	i. 138, 625; ii. 47, 61, 62, 107, 209, 261, 632
v. Hayward	ii. 60
v. Reynolds	ii. 872
Pennell v. Millar	i. 352
Penney v. Watts	i. 402
Pennington v. Gittings	i. 611, 614, 616
Pennsylvania Co. v. Stokes	ii. 424, 427
Penny v. Martin	i. 86, 106, 162
Penrhyn v. Hughes	i. 500, 502
Pentland v. Stokes	i. 409
People v. Albany R. Co.	ii. 869
v. Brown	i. 390
v. Canal Board	ii. 260
v. Janssen	i. 335
v. Mercein	ii. 677, 761, 762
v Utica Ins. Co.	i. 19
People's Bank's Appeal	i. 206
Peoria v. Johnson	i. 80
Perceval v. Phipps	ii. 250, 251, 253
Percival v. Dunn	ii. 366
Perens v. Johnson	i. 333
Perfect v. Lane	i. 343
Perkins's Case	ii. 697
Perkins v. Clay	i. 294
v. Coddington	ii. 55
v. Finnegan	ii. 674
v. Hart	i. 541, 543, 544
v. Hays	i. 356; ii. 277
v. Kershaw	i. 518
v. Lyman	i. 294, 295
Perkyns v. Bayntun	i. 586
Perrett's Case	ii. 862
Perrin v. Lyon	i. 292

CASES CITED.

	PAGE
Perrot v. Perrot	ii. 219
Perry v. Barker	ii. 330
v. Grant	ii. 560
v. Phelps	i. 557, 558, 560, 561, 562; ii. 199, 548
v. Porter	i. 414
v. Roberts	ii. 367
v. Truefit	ii. 254, 255, 258
Perry-Herrick v. Attwood	i. 396
Persons v. Persons	ii. 541
Persse v. Persse	i. 142, 143
Petch v. Tutin	ii. 349
Peter v. Beverly	ii. 383
v. Rich	i. 505, 510
v. Russell	i. 397, 398
Peterborough v. Lancaster	i. 118
Peters v. Anderson	i. 464
v. Bacon	i. 662
v. Florence	i. 112, 117
v. Grote	ii. 758
v. Mortimer	i. 307
v. Rule	i. 76
v. Soame	ii. 767, 770
Petit's Case	ii. 697
Petit v. Smith	i. 67, 554, 601; ii. 547
Peto v. Brighton Ry. Co.	ii. 46
Petre v. Bruen	i. 569
v. Eastern Counties Ry.	i. 296
v. Espinasse	i. 378, 429; ii. 273
v. Petre	ii. 23, 687
Petter v. Nicolls	i. 429
Pettes v Bank of Whitehall	ii. 873
Pettinger v. Ambler	ii. 388
Pettit v. Shepherd	ii. 5, 11
Pettiton v. Hipple	i. 301
Petty v. Cooke	i. 335
v. Petty	i. 273
v. Styward	ii. 543
Peugh v. Davis	ii. 321
Peyroux v. Howard	ii. 587
Peyster v. Clendining	ii. 384
Peyton's Case	ii. 420
Peyton v. Bury	i. 264, 290, 292
v. Green	ii. 855
v. Rawlins	i. 244
v. Stith	ii. 843
Pharis v. Leachman	i. 359
Phayre v. Peree	ii. 608
Phelan v. Gardner	i. 237
Phelps v. Curts	i. 362
v. Decker	i. 302
v. Green	i. 658, 659, 662
v. White	i. 209, 210, 215, 217
Phené v. Gillan	i. 648
Phenix Bank v. Sullivan	ii. 345
Philadelphia v. Fox	ii. 503
Philanthropic Soc. v. Kemp	ii. 512, 513
Phillippi v. Phillippi	ii. 848

	PAGE
Phillips, Ex parte	ii. 663, 667, 669, 689, 694
Phillips v. Allen	i. 535
v. Berger	ii. 41
v. Blatchford	i. 680, 687
v. Bordman	ii. 234
v. Bucks	i. 220
v. Carew	ii. 835
v. Chamberlain	i. 191; ii. 721
v. Dexter	i. 488
v. Foxall	i. 334
v. Homfray	ii. 90, 103
v. Hunter	ii. 874
v. Parker	i. 571, 581
v. Phillips	i. 309, 469; ii. 548, 615, 826
v. Pitts	ii. 13
v. Soule	ii. 45, 46
v. Stauch	ii. 52, 53, 104
v. Thompson	ii. 78, 82, 86, 124, 128, 129
v. Trezevant	i. 680
v. Wooster	i. 379
v. Worth	ii. 200
Phillipson v. Kerry	ii. 23
Philpott v. Jones	i. 460
Phippen v. Stickney	i. 295
Phipps v. Annesley	i. 604, 605
Phœnix Ins. Co. v. Abbott	ii. 729
Piatt v. McCullough	i. 186
v. Vattier	i. 546; ii. 278, 279, 843, 845
Picard v. Hine	ii. 735
v. McCormick	ii. 206
Pickard, Ex parte	ii. 695
v. Roberts	ii. 724, 748
v. Sears	i. 389, 391; ii. 863
Pickens v. Finney	i. 337
Pickering v. Cape Town Ry. Co.	ii. 790
v. Dawson	i. 173, 226
v. Ilfracombe Ry. Co.	ii. 349
v. Pickering	i. 127, 130, 140, 141, 145
v. Stamford	i. 62; ii. 432
Picket v. Loggon	i. 251, 260
Pickman v. Trinity Church	i. 24
Pickstork v. Lyster	i. 378; ii. 343, 344
Picot v. Colombet	i. 473
Pidcock v. Bishop	i. 164, 205, 234, 334, 388
Pidding v. How	ii. 258
Piddock v. Brown	i. 542
Pier v. Fond du Lac	ii. 14
Pierce, In re	i. 378
v. Brooks	ii. 273
v. Catron	ii. 73, 76
v. Fuller	i. 293, 294
v. Fynney	ii. 773

CASES CITED.

Pierce v. Lamson	ii. 17
v. Milwaukee Constr. Co.	i. 557
v. Thornly	ii. 737, 739, 744, 745
v. Waring	i. 326
v. Webb	ii. 9, 10, 11
v. Woodward	i. 294
Piercy v. Fynney	i. 691
v. Roberts	ii. 277
Piersall v. Elliot	ii. 9, 10, 15
Pierson v. Garnett	i. 106; ii. 407, 411
v. Hutchinson	i. 90
v. Shore	ii. 689
Piffard v. Beeby	ii. 816
Piggott v. Green	ii. 401
v. Williams	ii. 770, 772
Pigott v. Bagley	ii. 438
v. Thompson	ii. 362
Pike v. Fay	i. 206
v. Hoare	i. 625; ii. 62
v. Miles	i. 365
v. Nicholas	ii. 244, 261
v. Pettus	ii. 77
v. Williams	ii. 80
Pillage v. Armitage	i. 231, 394
Pillgrim v. Pillgrim	ii. 848
Pilling v. Armitage	ii. 855
Pinch v. Anthony	ii. 577
Pincke v. Curtit	ii. 99
v. Thorneycroft	ii. 849
Pinckston v. Brown	i. 305
Pingree v. Coffin	ii. 60, 91
Pingry v. Washburn	i. 296
Pink, In re	ii. 694
Pinney v. Fellows	ii. 536
Pinto Silver Mining Co., In re	ii. 851
Pitcairne v. Ogbourne	i. 167, 168, 169, 170, 171, 173, 270, 272
Pitcher v. Hennessey	i. 113, 114, 119
v. Rawlins	i. 404
v. Rigby	i. 320
Pitney v. Brown	ii. 401
Pitt v. Cholmondeley	i. 543, 544, 545
v. Hunt	ii. 743
v. Jackson	ii. 414
v. Jones	i. 662
Pitt's Will, In re	i. 193
Pittman's Appeal	i. 638
Pitts v. Cable	ii. 320
Place v. Sweetyer	i. 687
Platt v. Stewart	i. 665
v. Stonington Bank	ii. 90
Playford v. United Kingdom Tel. Co.	i. 205
Pleasanton's Appeal	i. 337
Pledge v. Buss	i. 515
Plimpton v. Fuller	i. 582
Plumb v. Fluitt	i. 395, 396, 397, 400, 402, 408; ii. 324
Plume v. Belle	i. 196
Plumer v. Marchant	i. 589
Plunket v. Brereton	i. 695
v. Lewis	ii. 441
Plunkett v. Penson	i. 567, 570
Plymouth v. Throgmorton	i. 479
Plympton v. Plympton	ii. 423, 428
Pockman v. Meatt	i. 662
Pocock v. Reddington	ii. 610
Podmore v. Gunning	ii. 89, 407, 408, 412
Poirier v. Fetter	ii. 234
Pole v. Pole	ii. 540
Polk v. Cosgrove	i. 411
v. Pendleton	ii. 11
v. Reynolds	ii. 12
Pollard, In re	ii. 534
v. Bailey	i. 557
Pollen v. James	ii. 729
Pollexfen v. Moore	i. 573, 575; ii. 110, 563, 571, 598
Pollitt v. Long	ii. 231
Pollock, In re	ii. 441, 447, 448
Polson v. Young	i. 314
Pomeroy v. Bailey	i. 373
v. Partington	ii. 390
Pomfret v. Perring	i. 187
v. Winsor	i. 423, 438, 546
Pond v. Framingham R. Co.	ii. 180, 231
Ponder v. Scott	i. 425
Pool v. Doster	i. 527, 528
v. Lloyd	i. 78, 79
Poole v. Bott	i. 289
v. Ray	i. 98
Pooley v. Budd	ii. 33, 38, 39
v. Harradine	ii. 195
v. Quilter	i. 330
v. Ray	i. 155
Poore v. Clark	ii. 174
Pope v. Crashaw	ii. 745
v. Curl	ii. 249, 250
v. Garland	ii. 92
v. Gwynn	i. 567
v. Onslow	ii. 328
v. Pope	ii. 408
v. Whitcomb	ii. 401
Popham v. Bamfield	i. 59, 290; ii. 646, 652, 653
v. Lancaster	ii. 175
Portarlington v. Soulby	i. 307; ii. 61, 208, 209
Port Clinton R. Co. v. Cleveland R. Co.	ii. 31, 32, 34, 46, 65
Porter v. Bank of Rutland	i. 414; ii. 710
v. Barclay	i. 411
v. Bradley	ii. 404

CASES CITED.

Porter v. Jones	ii. 6, 8
v. Lopes	i. 662
v. Peckham	i. 318
v. Read	ii. 328
v. Rice	ii. 15
v. Spencer	i. 456, 470; ii. 802, 803
Portis v. Fall	i. 19
Portland R. Co. v. Grand Trunk R. Co.	ii. 94
Portlock v. Gardner	ii. 844, 847
Portman v. Mill	ii. 103
Portmore v. Morris	i. 168
v. Taylor	i. 348
Port Royal Co. v. Hammond	ii. 60
Portsmouth v. Effingham	ii. 830
v. Fellows	ii. 631
Post v. Kimberly	i. 89, 451, 456, 470
v. Marsh	ii. 90, 91
Postley v. Kain	i. 660
Postmaster Gen. v. Furber	i. 460, 461, 465
Poston v. Balch	i. 305
v. Jones	i. 495
Pothonier v. Dawson	ii. 337
Potter v. Chapman	ii. 295
v. Jacobs	ii. 73
v. Sanders	ii. 107
v. Stevens	ii. 314
Potts v. Curtis	i. 343
v. Surr	i. 314
v. Whitehead	ii. 81, 100
Powell v. Cleaver	ii. 460
v. Evans	ii. 615, 617, 619
v. Hankey	ii. 725
v. Hellicar	i. 610
v. Knowler	ii. 373
v. Monson Mfg. Co.	i. 629, 636; ii. 535, 606
v. Mouchett	i. 192
v. Powell	i. 107
v. Powis	ii. 175
v. Price	i. 179
v. Redfield	ii. 661
v. Riley	ii. 395
v. Robins	ii. 592
v. Stewart	ii. 203
v. White	i. 506, 518, 521, 524
Power v. Alston	i. 362
v. Bailey	ii. 107, 577, 735
v. Knowler	i. 298
Power's Appeal	ii. 47, 353
Powers v. Bowman	ii. 14
v. Mayo	ii. 54
v. Powers	ii. 602
Powerscourt v. Powerscourt	ii. 493
Powitt v. Guyon	ii. 471
Powlet v. Herbert	ii. 610
Powsey v. Armstrong	i. 670
Powys v. Blagrave	ii 219
v. Mansfield	ii. 439, 450, 452, 453, 459, 461
Pratt v. Barker	i. 321
v. Brent	ii. 219
v. Carroll	ii. 95
v. Clemens	i. 63
v. Law	ii. 101, 124, 125, 128
v. Pond	i. 26, 27, 30; ii. 12
v. Sladden	ii. 516
v. Taunton Copper Co.	ii. 37
v. Thornton	i. 328
v. Tuttle	i. 309, 333, 469
v. Tyler	i. 285
Pray v. Clark	ii. 41, 81
Preachers Soc. v. Rich	ii. 491, 499, 503
Prebble v. Boghurst	ii. 701
Predgers v. Langham	i. 387
Prees v. Coke	i. 332
Prendergast v. Turton	ii. 660, 861
Presbyterian Cong. v. Wallace	ii. 579
Prescott, Ex parte	ii. 768, 770
v. More	i. 601
Preston v. Croput	i. 436
v. Luck	i. 116
Prevost v. Clarke	ii. 405
v. Gratz	i. 329; ii. 278, 844, 847
Price v. Bridgman	ii. 838
v. Dewhurst	i. 197
v. Dyer	i. 174; ii. 92
v. Edmunds	ii. 195
v. Evans	i. 562; ii. 199
v. Fastnedge	i. 422, 423
v. Griffith	ii. 125
v. Jenkins	i. 369, 435; ii. 289, 290
v. Ley	i. 110, 150
v. Lovett	i. 297
v. Neal	i. 205, 390
v. North	ii. 591
v. Price	ii. 117
v. Strange	ii. 399, 401
v. White	i. 411
v. Williams	ii. 793
Price's Candle Co. v. Bauwen's Candle Co.	i. 78
Prichard v. Ames	ii. 711
v. Gee	ii. 837
Prickett v. Prickett	i. 607
Priddy v. Rose	ii. 355, 361, 363, 366, 529
Pride v. Boyce	i. 522
v. Bubb	ii. 719
Pridgeon v. Pridgeon	ii. 701

CASES CITED.

Priest v. Parrot	i. 381
Primmer v. Patten	ii. 818
Primrose v. Bromley	i. 510
Prince v. Rowson	i. 590
Princeton v. Adams	ii. 525
Pring v. Pring	ii. 546
Pringle v. Dunkley	i. 279
Printup v. Fort	i. 690
Prior v. Williams	i. 157, 178
Prison Charities, In re	ii. 511
Pritchard v. Madren	ii. 12
v. Ovey	ii. 41
v. Todd	ii. 99
Pritt v. Clay	i. 542
Probate Court v. May	i. 157
Probert v. Clifford	ii. 707
Probosco v. Johnson	ii. 322
Proctor v. Heyer	ii. 281, 511
Prodgers v. Langham	i. 436
Professional Insur. Co., In re	i. 639
Proof v. Hines	i. 251, 319, 339
Prosser v. Edmonds	ii. 347, 349, 359, 362, 372, 374, 376
Protheroe v. Forman	ii. 203, 204
Proudly v. Fielder	ii. 722
Providence Bank v. Billings	ii. 871
v. Wilkinson	ii. 145
Prudential Assur. Co. v. Knott	ii. 239, 240
v. Thomas	ii. 140
Pryor v. Adams	i. 78
v. Hill	ii. 744, 745
Pudsey Coal Gas Co. v. Bradford	ii. 868
Pugh v. Arton	ii. 179
Pulbrook, In re	ii. 676
Pullen v. Ready	i. 116, 123, 125, 134, 166, 289
Pullerton v. Agnew	ii. 638
Pulliam v. Newberry	i. 376
v. Pensoneau	ii. 790
Pulsford v. Richards	ii. 861
Pulteney v. Darlington	ii. 423, 424, 425, 550
v. Warren	i. 473, 532, 533, 534, 535, 536, 537, 540, 630; ii. 649, 850
Pultney v. Shelton	ii. 218
Pulvertoft v. Pulvertoft	i. 429, 430, 433, 434; ii. 22, 116, 117, 289, 290
Pumfrey, In re	ii. 616
Purcell v. McNamara	i. 323
v. Miner	ii. 76, 77
v. Purcell	ii. 757
Purdew v. Jackson	ii. 353, 736, 744, 745, 746, 747, 748
Purefoy v. Purefoy	ii. 328
Purinton v. Northern Ill. R. Co.	ii. 82
Purse v. Snaplin	i. 191
Purviance v. Holt	i. 91, 95
Pusey v. Desbouvrie	i. 127, 221
v. Pusey	ii. 25
Pushman v. Filliter	ii. 410, 412
Putnam v. Collamore	ii. 341
v. Ritchie	i. 664; ii. 130, 131, 132, 584, 586
v. Story	i. 431
Pybus v. Mitford	ii. 532
v. Smith	ii. 717, 722, 724
Pye, Ex parte	i. 433; ii. 109, 116, 117, 118, 449, 450, 453, 456
v. Gorges	ii. 280, 294
Pym v. Blackburn	i. 105; ii. 85, 89
v. Lockyer	ii. 439, 441, 442, 449, 450, 454, 457, 460
Pyncent v. Pyncent	ii. 19
Pyrke v. Waddingham	ii. 64

Q.

Quarrell v. Beckford	ii. 164
Quarrier v. Colston	ii. 7
Quartz Hill Mining Co. v. Beall	ii. 239
Queensbury v. Shebbeare	ii. 249
Quilter v. Mapleson	ii. 659
Quinn v. Roath	ii. 59, 99
Quinton v. Frith	i. 326
Quivey v. Baker	i. 157, 180

R.

Raby v. Ridehalgh	ii. 609
Race v. Weston	ii. 81, 90
Rachfield v. Careless	i. 549; ii. 546
Racouillat v. Rene	i. 411
v. Sansevain	i. 411
Radcliff v. Brooklyn	ii. 225
Radde v. Norman	ii. 256, 257
Radnor v. Vanderberdy	i. 399, 417, 634
Raffety v. King	ii. 333, 334
Raggett, In re	i. 417, 420; ii. 327
Ragsdale v. Holmes	i. 549
Raguert v. Cowles	i. 308
Railroad Co. v. Neal	ii. 206
v. Telegraph Co.	ii. 77, 90
Railton v. Mathews	i. 334, 338
Rainey v. Nance	i. 684
Rakestraw v. Brewer	ii. 317
Ramsay v. Bell	i. 659
v. Warner	i. 460
Ramsbotham v. Senior	ii. 684
Ramsbottom v. Gosden	i. 169, 173; ii. 93, 94

CASES CITED.

Ramsbottom v. Parker	i. 251, 339
Ramsden v. Hylton	i. 129, 131, 134, 138, 139, 144, 162, 380, 383
v. O'Keefe	ii. 873
Ramsey v. Smith	i. 111, 150
Ramshire v. Bolton	i. 29, 30, 199
Ramsour v. Ramsour	ii. 428
Rancliffe v. Parkins	ii. 418, 425, 430
Randall v. Bookey	ii. 547
v. Latham	ii. 54
v. Marble	i. 279
v. Morgan	i. 383
v. Phillips	i. 378; ii. 543
v. Randall	i. 172, 684
v. Russell	i. 330, 606; ii. 721
v. Willis	i. 172, 388
Randel v. Ely	i. 546
Randell v. Trimen	i. 205
Randle v. Carter	i. 604
Ranelagh v. Melton	ii. 99
Ranelaugh v. Hayes	i. 648; ii. 48, 123, 170, 171
Ranger v. Great Western Ry. Co.	i. 212; ii. 651
Ranken v. Huskisson	ii. 232
v. Patten	i. 311, 325
Rankin v. Lay	ii. 646
v. Rankin	ii. 383
v. Weguelin	i. 610
Ransom v. Keyes	i. 511
Ransome v. Burgess	ii. 386, 686
Rapelee v. Stewart	i. 379
Raphael v. Boehm	i. 472; ii. 620
v. Thames Valley Ry. Co.	ii. 40
Rappleye v. International Bank	i. 377
Raritan Water Works v. Veghte	ii. 861
Rashdall v. Ford	i. 207
Rashleigh v. Master	i. 489; ii. 112, 113
Rastel v. Hutchinson	ii. 537
Ratcliff v. Davies	ii. 335
Ratcliffe v. Barnard	ii. 324
v. Graves	ii. 621
Rathbone v. Warren	i. 24, 76, 451, 454, 456
Rathbun v. Colton	ii. 582
Raunie v. Irving	i. 294
Ravald v. Russell	ii. 334
Raw v. Potts	i. 61, 394
Rawbone's Bequest	i. 407
Rawden v. Shadwell	i. 302, 307, 308; ii. 819
Rawlings v. Landes	ii. 554
Rawlins v. Powell	ii. 461, 463
v. Wickham	i. 150, 209, 210, 682
Rawson v. Samuel	ii. 768, 771, 772
Rawstone v. Parr	i. 179
Ray, Ex parte	ii. 711, 712
v. Bogart	i. 546
v. Ray	i. 589; ii. 848
v. Womble	i. 256
Raymond v. Sellick	i. 607
Rayner v. Koehler	i. 549
v. Pearsall	i. 427, 546
v. Stone	ii. 45
Raynham v. Cantou	i. 159
Rea v. Longstreet	ii. 13, 15
Reach v. Kennigate	i. 264
Read v. Brokman	i. 90
v. Read	ii. 759, 802
v. Stedman	ii. 546, 547
Reade v. Bentley	ii. 261
v. Conquest	ii. 244
v. Livingston	i. 361, 362, 364, 365, 366, 367, 371, 382
v. Lowndes	i. 528
v. Reade	ii. 441, 447
Redding v. Wilkes	i. 382; ii. 78, 88
Rede v. Farr	ii. 657, 658
Redfearn v. Ferrier	i. 424, 426
Redfern v. Smith	ii. 221
Redfield v. Buck	i. 365
Redgrave v. Hurd	i. 109, 110, 149, 206, 209, 210, 211, 215
Redheimer v. Pyson	ii. 476
Redington v. Redington	i. 499, 501
Redman v. Graham	i. 391
v. Redman	i. 269, 271, 394
Redmond v. Packersham	ii. 13
Reech v. Kenningall	i. 194; ii. 106
Reed v. Bank of Newburg	ii. 5, 10
v. Breeden	ii. 100
v. Norris	i. 323, 506, 515, 519; ii. 550
v. Noxon	i. 203
v. Peterson	i. 330
v. Tyler	i. 67; ii. 12
v. Ward	i. 492
v. White	i. 122
Rees v. Berrington	i. 335; ii. 170, 194
Reese v. Reese	ii. 81
Reese Silver Mining Co. v. Smith	i. 110, 150, 209, 210
Reeve v. Attorney-Gen.	ii. 522
v. Hicks	ii. 334
v. Parkins	ii. 214
Reeves v. Denicke	ii. 258
v. Reeves	ii. 18
Refeld v. Woodfolk	ii. 171
Reffell v. Reffell	i. 191
Reformed Soc. v. Draper	ii. 263
Regent's Canal Co. v. Ware	ii. 54
Regina v. Shaw	ii. 696
v. Smith	ii. 677
Rehden v. Wesley	ii. 615

CASES CITED. lxxxvii

Reichart v. Castelor	i. 379
Reickhoff v. Brecht	i. 314
Reid v. Gifford	ii. 231, 233
v. Shergold	i. 185; ii. 721
v. Stearn	ii. 149
Reilly v. Mayer	i. 640
Reimers v. Druce	ii. 866
Reinskoffe v. Rogge	i. 237
Remington v. Campbell	ii. 536, 537
v. Higgins	i. 120, 157
Remsen v. Remsen	ii. 855
Renals v. Colishaw	ii. 348
Rendell v. Carpenter	ii. 852
Rengo v. Binns	i. 324
Rennie v. Young	ii. 861
Reppy v. Reppy	ii. 770
Reubens v. Joel	ii. 557
Revell v. Hussey	ii. 5
Revett v. Harvey	i. 325, 326
Rex v. Arundel	i. 90, 93, 262
v. Boston	ii. 537
v. Hare	i. 40, 57
v. Hopkins	ii. 677
v. Morely	ii. 677
v. Standish	i. 42, 43
Reynard v. Spence	ii. 436
Reynell v. Sprye	i. 209, 302
Reynish v. Martin	i. 283, 289, 290, 291, 603, 604
Reynolds v. McCurry	i. 324
v. Nelson	ii. 99, 213
v. Pitt	ii. 644, 649, 653, 655, 656, 659
v. Smith	ii. 653
v. Teynham	ii. 675
v. Vilas	i. 431
v. Waller	i. 244
Rhenish v. Martin	i. 490
Rhett v. Mason	ii. 406
Rhodes v. Bate	i. 318, 320, 333, 344
v. Childs	i. 609; ii. 863
v. Cook	i. 313
v. Outcalt	i. 152, 179
Rhys v. Dare Ry. Co.	i. 533
Rice v. Barnard	i. 683
v. Dewey	i. 527
v. Harbeson	i. 575, 595, 637, 638
v. Rice	i. 65
v. St. Paul R. Co.	ii. 163
Rich v. Aldred	ii. 135
v. Austin	i. 468
v. Cockell	ii. 425, 703, 710, 711, 720
v. Doane	ii. 12, 320
v. Jackson	i. 167, 173, 174; ii. 87, 92
v. Sydenham	i. 245
v. Whitfield	ii. 553
Richards, Ex parte	ii. 673
v. Baker	i. 288
v. Baurman	i. 679, 681
v. Chambers	ii. 722, 723, 724, 748
v. Davies	i. 679
v. Noble	i. 537
v. Revett	i. 294
v. Salter	ii 137, 140
v. Symes	i. 613; ii. 21, 22, 118, 204
v. Todd	i. 682
v. White	i. 379
Richardson, In re	ii. 331
v. Bank of England	i. 675
v. Boynton	ii. 618
v. Campbell	ii. 587
v. Chapman	ii. 384
v. Elphinstone	ii. 445
v. Goodwin	ii. 94
v. Greese	ii. 463
v. Hall	i. 579, 580; ii. 611
v. Horton	i. 177, 178
v. Nourse	ii. 793
v. Silvester	i. 204
v. Smallwood	i. 362, 364, 365, 366, 367
v. Smith	i. 407; ii. 41, 86, 794
v. Wallis	ii. 317
v. Williamson	i. 205
v. Younge	ii. 333
Richie v. Cowper	i. 333
Richmond v. Aiken	ii. 334
v. Dubuque R. Co.	ii. 42
v. Gray	ii. 102
v. London	i. 694
v. Robinson	ii. 52, 99
v. White	i. 590
Ricker v. Ham	i. 376, 408, 431
v. Pratt	ii. 203
Rickets v. McCully	i. 367
v. Turquand	ii. 785
Ricketts, Ex parte	ii. 357
v. Hitchins	ii. 206
Rickle v. Dow	ii. 192
Rickman v. Morgan	ii. 442, 445
Rico v. Gualtier	ii. 803
Riddick v. Moore	ii. 770
Riddle v. Mandeville	i. 98, 99; ii. 380, 601, 602
Rider v. Kidder	i. 302, 304, 375; ii. 537, 541
v. Powell	i. 110, 111, 150, 167
v. Wager	ii. 458
Ridges v. Morrison	i. 579; ii. 512
Ridgway v. Darwin	ii 696
v. Underwood	i. 433

CASES CITED.

	PAGE
Ridler, In re	i. 369
v. Ridler	i. 241
Ridout v. Pain	i. 135; ii. 790, 792
v. Plymouth	ii. 707, 708
Riesy's Appeal	ii. 52
Rife v. Geyer	ii. 277
Rigby v. Connol	ii. 263
Rigden v. Vallier	ii. 542, 543, 544
Riggan v. Green	i. 238, 242
Rindge v. Coleraine	ii. 359
Ringhouse v. Keever	i. 629
Riopelle v. Doellner	i. 30
Ripley v. Waterworth	i. 683; ii. 399, 534, 544
v. Wightman	i. 497
Ripon v. Hobart	ii. 223, 225, 227, 229, 264
Rippon v. Dawding	ii. 107, 700, 701, 718
Rishton v. Whatmore	ii. 81
Risk's Appeal	ii. 401
Ritchie v. Atkinson	i. 480
Ritson v. Brumlow	i. 495
Ritter v. Cost	ii. 341
River's Case	i. 191
Rivers v. Durr	i. 662; ii. 683
Riverview Cem. Co. v. Turner	i. 659
Rives v. Dudley	ii. 864
v. Rives	i. 500
Rivett's Case	ii. 487, 504, 507, 508
Roach v. Garvan	ii. 674, 676, 687, 691
v. Haynes	ii. 720
Roake v. Denn	ii. 389
Roberdeau v. Rous	ii. 62, 262, 635
Roberts v. Anderson	i. 436
v. Bell	ii. 147
v. Bury	ii. 641
v. Croft	ii. 324
v. Dixwell	ii. 275
v. Eberhardt	i. 680
v. Kuffin	i. 543
v. Oppenheim	ii. 816
v. Roberts	i. 268, 269, 303, 309; ii. 259, 749
v. Spicer	ii. 712
v. Ware	ii. 534, 536
v. Wynne	i. 194
Robertson v. Norris	ii. 332
Robins v. Quinliven	ii. 397
Robinson v. Alexander	ii. 846
v. Bland	i. 307, 480
v. Briggs	i. 314
v. Byron	ii. 231
v. Campbell	i. 27, 54
v. Comyn	ii. 295
v. Cumming	ii. 855
v. Davison	i. 418

	PAGE
Robinson v. Fife	ii. 333
v. Gee	i. 300
v. Geldard	i. 579
v. Gilbraith	i. 78
v. Harbour	ii. 574
v. Holt	i. 376
v. Hook	i. 546
v. Joplin	ii. 12
v. Kettletas	ii. 40
v. Litton	ii. 219, 320
v. McDonnel	ii. 378
v. Preston	ii. 542
v. Ridley	ii. 583
v. Robinson	ii. 820
v. Stewart	i. 362
v. Taylor	ii. 534
v. Tonge	ii. 557, 559
v. Wall	i. 295
v. Willoughby	ii. 320
v. Wilson	i. 517, 518, 521, 527, 647
Robson v. Collins	ii. 92
Rocarrick v. Barton	ii. 312
Roche v. O'Brien	i. 354
Rochester v. Alfred Bank	i. 121
Rochford v. Hackman	ii. 277
Rochfort v. Ely	ii. 669
Rockwell v. Hobby	ii. 322
Rockwood v. Rockwood	i. 194
Rodgers v. McCluer	i. 518
v. Nowill	ii. 256, 257
Rodick v. Gandell	ii. 370
Rodney v. Chambers	ii. 763
Roe v. Lincoln	ii. 13, 14, 15
v. Mitton	ii. 290
v. Roe	ii. 423
Roebuck v. Chadebet	i. 662
Rogers v. Blackwell	i. 238, 242
v. Dallimore	ii. 793
v. Gwinn	ii. 210, 211, 213
v. Ingham	i. 115, 118
v. Jones	i. 402
v. Leele	i. 416
v. Mackenzie	i. 505, 510, 529
v. Meyers	i. 639
v. Place	i. 216, 403
v. Rathbun	i. 306
v. Rogers	ii. 214, 259
v. Seale	i. 635
v. Skillicome	ii. 474
v. Torbert	ii. 327
v. Traders' Ins. Co.	ii. 355
v. Tudor	ii. 646
v. Vosburgh	ii. 198
v. Walker	ii. 696
v. Ward	ii. 734, 735
Rogers Locomotive Works v. Erie Ry. Co.	ii. 265, 868

Rohan v. Hanson	i. 460
Rohrer v. Turrill	ii. 153
Rolfe v. Gregory	i. 439
v. Harris	ii. 656, 659
Rolland v. Hart	i. 400, 402, 414
Rollfe v. Budder	ii. 710
Rollins v. Hinks	ii. 238, 239, 240
Rondeau v. Wyatt	ii. 67, 69, 71
Rook v. Worth	ii. 45, 689
Roome v. Roome	ii. 453, 460
Roosevelt v. Fulton	i. 254
v. Thurman	ii. 793
Root v. Railway Co.	ii. 237
Roper v. Day	ii. 562
v. Radcliffe	ii. 115
v. Williams	ii. 232
Ropes v. Upton	i. 293; ii. 28, 651, 652
Rorke, In re	i. 639
Rose v. Clarke	ii. 380
v. Cunynghame	ii. 112
v. Hart	ii. 768
v. Rose	ii. 646
v. Watson	i. 682
Rosenthal v. Freeburger	ii. 79
Rosewell v. Bennett	ii. 460
Roshi's Appeal	ii. 525
Roskelly v. Godolphin	i. 589
Ross v. Armstrong	ii. 729
v. Cobb	i. 661
v. Drake	ii. 554
v. Heintzen	ii. 574
v. Union Pacific R. Co.	ii. 37, 46
Rotch v. Emerson	ii. 494
Rotheram v. Franshaw	ii. 207
Rothwell v. Cook	i. 480
v. Rothwell	ii. 165
Roundell v. Breary	ii. 577
Rous v. Noble	i. 604, 605
Rouse v. Barker	i. 624
Rousillon v. Rousillon	i. 294
Routh v. Webster	ii. 254
Row v. Dawson	ii. 361, 363, 366
Rowe v. ——	ii. 837
v. Beckett	ii. 372
v. Jackson	ii. 752
v. Teed	ii. 71
v. Williams	ii. 794
v. Wood	ii. 164
Rowland v. First School District	ii. 14
v. Gorsuch	ii. 400
Rowley v. Rowley	ii. 761
Roworth v. Wilkes	ii. 244
Rowth v. Howell	ii. 615
Roy v. Beaufort	i. 250
Royal Bank v. Grand Junc. R. Co.	ii. 851
Royle v. Wynne	ii. 198
Rucker v. Moore	ii. 206
Ruckman v. Bergholz	i. 322
v. Ransom	ii. 792
Ruddell v. Ambler	i. 306
Rudge v. Hopkins	ii. 174
Ruding, In re	ii. 388
Ruffin, Ex parte	i. 684, 685; ii. 604
Ruffner v. McConnell	i. 153
Ruggles v. Barton	ii. 315
Ruhling v. Hackett	i. 152
Rumball v. Metropolitan Bank	i. 391
Rumbold v. Rumbold	i. 516, 571
Rumbolds v. Parr	i. 373
Rundell v. Rivers	i. 561
Runyan v. Coster	ii. 869
Rusden v. Pope	ii. 153
Rush v. Higgs	i. 555, 556, 558
Rushforth, Ex parte	i. 334, 515, 518, 524, 527, 647
Rusk v. Fenton	i. 392
Russell, Ex parte	i. 365, 369
In re	i. 425
v. Ashby	ii. 802, 803
v. Bodvil	ii. 757
v. Branham	i. 404
v. Clark	i. 76, 78, 199, 453; ii. 602, 606
v. Darwin	ii. 41
v. Deshon	ii. 11, 12
v. Dudley	i. 379
v. Grinnell	i. 356
v. Hammond	i. 361, 362, 371, 380
v. Loscombe	i. 677, 679, 682
v. Madden	i. 454
v. Ransom	i. 406
v. Russell	ii. 263, 322, 331
v. Smythies	ii. 113
v. Southard	ii. 321
v. Woodward	ii. 344
Russell Road Moneys, In re	ii. 301
Ruth's Appeal	ii. 576
Rutherford v. Ruff	i. 244
Rutland v. Rutland	i. 549
Ryall v. Rowles	i. 425, 614; ii. 305, 306, 335, 366, 378, 608, 770
v. Ryall	ii. 535, 536, 538, 549
Ryan v. Boyd	ii. 206
v. Brown	ii. 234
v. Doyle	ii. 280
v. Duncan	ii. 12
v. Macmath	i. 696; ii. 9, 10, 16
v. Martin	ii. 651
Ryder v. Benthan	ii. 233
v. Bickerton	ii. 618
Ryer v. Gass	ii. 341
Ryle v. Brown	i. 343
v. Haggie	i. 71, 73, 74, 75, 454; ii. 3

S.

Saagar v. Wright	i. 330
Saberton v. Skeels	ii. 399
Sable v. Maloney	ii. 844
Sackvill v. Ayleworth	ii. 816, 834
Sackville-West v. Holmesdale	ii. 288, 291
Saddler v. Lee	i. 681
Sadler, Ex parte	i. 386
v. Hobbs	ii. 626, 628, 629
Saffold v. Wade	i. 527
Saffron Building Soc. v. Rayner	i. 414
Sagitary v. Hide	i. 360, 368, 516, 573
Sainsbury v. Jones	ii. 126
Sainter v. Ferguson	i. 294
Sale v. Crutchfield	ii. 129, 583
v. McLean	ii. 11
v. Moore	ii. 407, 411, 412
Salem Rubber Co. v. Adams	i. 215
Salisbury v. Andrews	ii. 182
Salmon v. Bennett	i. 370
v. Cutts	i. 314
Salter, Ex parte	ii. 643, 685
v. Bradshaw	i. 344
Saltern v. Melhuish	i. 262
Saltmarsh v. Barrett	ii. 546
Saltonstall v. Sanders	ii 495
Salvin v. Brancepeth Co.	ii. 229
Sample v. Barnes	ii. 203, 876
Sampson v. Shaw	i. 293
v. Smith	ii. 226, 228
Samuel v. Wiley	ii. 861
Samuell v. Howarth	ii. 195
Sanborn v. Kittredge	i. 75
Sandby, Ex parte	i. 100, 480
Sander v. Heathfield	i. 589
Sanders v. McAffee	ii. 569
v. Pope	ii. 645, 646, 653, 722
v. Sanders	ii. 851
Sanderson, In re	ii. 534
v. Bayley	ii. 398
v. C. & W. Ry. Co.	ii. 870
Sandford v. Handy	i. 214
v. Remington	ii. 821
Sandfoss v. Jones	ii. 89, 91
Sandon v. Hooper	ii. 318, 319
Sands v. Hildreth	i. 436
v. N. Y. Ins. Co.	ii. 654
Sanfley v. Jackson	i. 313
Sankey Coal Co., In re	ii. 349
Saratoga v. Dryor	ii. 173
Sargeant v. Bigelow	i. 86
Sargent v. Parsons	i. 446
v. Sargent	i. 479
Sarver's Appeal	ii. 263
Satterfield v. John	ii. 630, 631
Saunders v. Dehaw	i. 400; ii. 280
Saunders v. Frost	ii. 316
v. Leslie	ii. 566, 567, 569
v. Smith	ii. 247, 263
Saunderson v. Harrison	i. 495
v. Stockdale	i. 359
Savage v. Brocksopp	ii. 4, 99, 856
v. Burnham	ii. 428
v. Carroll	ii. 79, 82, 548
v. Foster	i. 389, 392, 394; ii. 76
v. Murphy	i. 365
Savannah Bank v. Haskins	i. 87, 94
Savannah R. Co. v. Shiels	ii. 225
Savery v. Dyer	ii. 396
v. King	i. 314
Saville v. Saville	i. 499, 501
v. Tankred	ii. 24
Savin v. Bowdin	i. 481
Savory v. Dyer	ii. 182
Sawer v. Shute	ii. 742
Sawyer v. Sawyer	ii. 609
Saxby v. Easterbrook	ii. 239
Saxon Life Assurance Co., In re	i. 118
Say v. Barwick	i. 244, 354
Sayer v. Bennet	i. 681
v. Pierce	i. 74, 533, 536
Sayre v. Fredericks	i. 361
v. Hughes	ii. 539
v. Sayre	ii. 275
Scales v. Maude	ii. 273
Scarborough v. Arrant	ii. 99
v. Borman	ii. 713, 714
Scawin v. Scawin	ii. 539, 541
Schaferman v O'Brien	i. 376; ii. 372
Schafroth v. Ambs	ii. 714
Schibsby v. Westenholz	ii. 875
Schieffelin v. Stewart	i. 331; ii. 620, 621, 622
Schmeling v. Kriesel	ii. 82
Schnitzel's Appeal	i. 517
Scholefield v. Templer	i. 180, 211, 337
Scholey v. Worcester	i. 378
School District v. First National Bank	ii. 616
v. Weston	ii. 140
Schoole v. Sall	ii. 198
Schoonover v. Dougherty	i. 111, 150
Schorr's Appeal	ii. 525
Schotsman v. Lancashire Ry. Co.	ii. 129
Schreiber v. Dinkel	ii. 704
Schroeppell v. Shaw	i. 337
Schryver v. Teller	i. 644; ii. 580
Schultz's Appeal	i. 333
Schultz v. Carter	i. 522
Schumpert, Ex parte	ii. 677
Schwoerer v. Boylston Market Assoc.	ii. 182
Scobey v. Decatur	ii. 15

Scofield v. Lansing	ii. 13, 14	Selby v. Selby	i. 516, 571, 574, 575, 637; ii. 563, 573
Scott v. Avery	ii. 794	Selden v. Keen	i. 279
v. Beecher	i. 583, 586; ii. 596	Seley v. Rhodes	i. 323
v. Colburn	ii. 870	Selkrig v. Davies	i. 683; ii. 544
v. Curle	ii. 515	Sellack v. Harris	ii. 89
v. Davis	i. 328	Sellors v. Matlock Board	ii. 225, 229
v. Fenhoullet	ii. 301, 535	Selwood v. Mildmay	i. 191
v. Guernsey	i. 663	Semmes v. Boykin	i. 640
v. Hanson	i. 223	v. Worthington	ii. 73, 109
v. Jones	ii. 852	Senhouse v. Earl	ii. 827, 830
v. Liverpool	i. 458; ii. 794, 864	Senior v. Pawson	ii. 129
v. Nesbit	i. 306, 427; ii. 582	Sergeson v. Sealy	i. 242, 501; ii. 689
v. Porcher	ii. 362, 364, 365	Serle v. St. Eloy	i. 582
v. Rand	ii. 605	Sessions v. Moseley	i. 609
v. Rayment	i. 674; ii. 35	Seton v. Slade	i. 96, 97; ii. 99, 111, 115, 310, 312, 313, 321, 637
v. Scott	i. 271, 272, 393, 394, 576, 577; ii. 114	Severn v. Fletcher	i. 75
v. Stanford	ii. 242	Sevier v. Greenway	ii. 620
v. Surman	i. 470; ii. 347, 576, 607	Sewall v. Sparrow	ii. 770
v. Tyler	i. 277, 282, 283, 285, 287, 288, 289, 290, 291, 427, 590	Seward v. Jackson	i. 361, 364, 431; ii. 708
v. Ware	i. 556; ii. 158, 316, 319	Sewell v. Freeston	ii. 203
Scribner v. Hitchcock	i. 495	Sexton v. Wheaton	i. 365, 367
Scriven v. Tapley	ii. 751	Seybourne v. Clifton	ii. 827
Scrope's Case	ii. 389	Seymore v. Tresilian	ii. 707
Scruggs v. Blair	i. 683	Seymour v. Davis	i. 485
v. Memphis R. Co.	i. 533; ii. 316	v. Delancy	ii. 7, 58, 90
		v. Hazard	ii. 801
Scudder v. Vanarsdale	ii. 554	v. Long Dock Co.	i. 456
Sculthorpe v. Tipper	ii. 614	v. Miller	ii. 198
Scurfield v. Howes	ii. 626, 627	v. Seymour	i. 78, 79, 555
Seabury v. Brewer	ii. 401	v. Van Slyck	i. 461
Seackel v. Litchfield	i. 331	Shackell v. Macaulay	ii. 819
Seager v. Cooley	i. 406	Shackle v. Baker	i. 294
Seagood v. Meale	ii. 75, 85	Shadford v. Temple	ii. 114
Seagram v. Knight	i. 535	Shaftoe v. Shaftoe	ii. 760, 802, 803
Seagrave v. Kirwan	i. 195	Shafts v. Adams	i. 344
Sea Ins. Co. v. Stebbins	ii. 160	Shaftsbury v. Arrowsmith	ii. 811, 816, 817
Seaman v. Aschermann	ii. 76	Shaiffer v. Chambers	ii. 316
Sear v. Ashwell	i. 433	Shakel v. Marlborough	ii. 49
Searing v. Searing	ii. 736	Shallcross v. Findon	ii. 591
Searle v. Choat	ii. 161, 197	Shallenberger's Appeal	i. 80
Sears v. Russell	ii. 276	Shand v. Aberdeen Canal Co.	ii. 187
v. Shafer	i. 311	Shank, Ex parte	ii. 556
v. Smith	ii. 569	Shanks v. Klein	i. 683
v. Vincent	ii. 795	Shanley v. Baker	ii. 523
Seaving v. Brinkerhoff	ii. 344	Shannon v. Bradstreet	i. 186, 394
Sebright v. Moore	i. 391	v. Hoboken	ii. 366
Second National Bank v. Williams	i. 611	v. Howard Assoc.	ii. 645
Secor v. Woodward	ii. 206	Shargold v. Shargold	i. 614
Segar v. Pratt	i. 30	Sharman v. Bell	ii. 793
Segee v. Thomas	i. 156	Sharp v. Carter	ii. 160
Seighortner v. Weissenborn	i. 682	v. Ropes	ii. 348
Seixo v. Provizende	ii. 255, 256	v. St. Saveur	ii. 553
Selby v. Pomfret	i. 517	v. Thompson	ii. 327
		v. Trimmer	ii. 99

CASES CITED.

Sharpe v. Foy	ii. 753
v. San Paulo Ry. Co.	ii. 794
v. Scarborough	i. 567
Shattock v. Shattock	i. 188
Shattuck v. Gay	i. 153
Shaver v. Radley	ii. 278
v. White	i. 688
Shaw v. Borrer	ii. 393, 468, 469, 470, 471, 472
v. Coster	ii. 141, 150, 152
v. Dwight	ii. 191
v. Fisher	ii. 37
v. Foster	i. 425
v. Jersey	ii. 239
v. Lawless	ii. 406
v. Neale	i. 319
v. Picton	i. 464
v. Spencer	i. 406, 427; ii. 280
Shays v. Norton	ii. 12
Shearer v. Shearer	i. 684
Shearman v. Shearman	ii. 803
Sheboygan v. Sheboygan R. Co.	ii. 226
Shedd v. Bank of Brattleboro	i. 639
Sheddon v. Goodrich	ii. 436
Sheehy v. Mandeville	i. 178
Sheets v. Selden	ii. 191
Sheffield v. Buckinghamshire	i. 194, 195; ii. 779
Sheffield Water Works v. Yeomans	ii. 173
Shegogg v. Perkins	i. 593
Shelburne v. Inchiquin	i. 166, 167, 170, 175, 176
Sheldon v. Conn. Ins. Co.	ii. 654
v. Coxe	i. 400, 413
v. Fortescue	ii. 663, 669, 695, 696
v. Rice	i. 331
Shelley v. Nash	i. 345, 355
v. Shelley	ii. 291
v. Spillman	ii. 14
v. Westbroke	ii. 676
Shelly's Case	i. 505; ii. 275
Shelton v. Alcox	ii. 795
v. Farmer	i. 335, 510
Shepard v. Brown	i. 27, 30, 444, 455
v. Jones	i. 533; ii. 316, 317, 318
v. Merrill	ii. 791
v. Thomas	ii. 574
Shepherd's Case	ii. 37
Shepherd v. Churchill	i. 660
v. Guernsey	i. 68, 580
v. McEvers	ii. 272, 346
v. Titley	i. 421; ii. 337
v. Towgood	i. 472
v. Wright	i. 504
Sheppard v. Kent	i. 558, 559, 569
v. Oxenford	i. 680
Sheriff v. Coates	ii. 236, 237
Sheriff of Middlesex, Ex parte	ii. 152
Sherman v. Fitch	ii. 12, 13, 15
v. Sherman	i. 544, 546, 603
v. Wright	ii. 59
Sherrard v. Sherrard	i. 489
Sherratt v. Mountford	ii. 398
Sherwood v. Salmon	i. 223
v. Sanderson	ii. 663, 669, 696
v. Sherwood	i. 191
v. Sutton	i. 546; ii. 845
Shewen v. Vanderhorst	ii. 852
Shey v. Bennett	i. 558
Shiel v. McNett	ii. 651
Shields v. Alsup	i. 590
v. Smith	ii. 387
Shillaber v. Robinson	ii. 321, 331, 332
Shine v. Gough	ii. 586
Shinn v. Budd	i. 647
v. Fredericks	ii. 570
Shipbrook v. Hinchinbrook	ii. 615, 626, 628, 676, 691
Shiphard v. Lutwidge	i. 566
Ship Packet, The	ii. 587
Shirk's Appeal	i. 542
Shirley v. Ferrers	ii. 837
v. Martin	i. 267, 353
v. Shankey	i. 298
v. Shirley	ii. 710
v. Stratton	ii. 103
Shitz v. Dieffenbach	ii. 322
Shonk v. Brown	ii. 712
Shorer v. Shorer	ii. 112
Shormate v. Lockridge	ii. 12
Short v. Lee	ii. 798
v. Stevenson	i. 323
v. Waller	ii. 614
Shorter v. Frazer	i. 404
v. Smith	ii. 843
Shortridge v. Lamplugh	ii. 532
Shottenkirk v. Wheeler	ii. 873
Shotwell v. Mott	ii. 481
v. Murray	i. 111, 120, 123, 127, 140, 146
v. Smith	i. 30, 69; ii. 820
Shreve v. Brereton	ii. 651
Shrewsbury v. Hornby	ii. 515
v. North Staff. Ry. Co.	i. 296
v. Shrewsbury	i. 499, 500, 501; ii. 392
Shrewsbury Ry. Co. v. Shrewsbury & B. Ry. Co.	ii. 259
Shropshire v. Brown	ii. 81
Shubrick v. Selmond	ii. 641

CASES CITED.

Shudal v. Jekyll	ii. 453, 457, 460
Shufeldt v. Boehm	i. 556
Shull v. Johnson	ii. 398
v. Kennon	i. 660
Shute v. Hamilton	ii. 648
Shutter's Case	i. 58
Shuttleworth v. Bruce	ii. 366
v. Laycock	i. 422; ii. 328
Sibbering v. Balcarras	i. 354
Sibley v. Baker	i. 637, 640
v. Perry	ii. 401
Sichel v. Mosenthal	i. 674; ii. 35
Sidmouth v. Sidmouth	ii. 539
Sidney v. Shelly	ii. 302
v. Sidney	ii. 753, 754
Siegel v. Outagamic	ii. 12
Siemon v. Schurck	ii. 13, 280
Sieveking v. Behrens	ii. 138, 144
Silcox v. Bell	ii. 401
Silk v. Prime	i. 68, 566
Silloway v. Brown	i. 374
Silver v. Norwich	ii. 160
v. Udell	i. 662
Silvey v. Dowell	i. 528
Simmonds v. Palles	ii. 344, 345
Simmons v. Cornelius	ii. 68, 85
v. Gooding	ii. 397
v. Kinnaird	i. 79
v. Simmons	i. 469
v. Thomas	ii. 702
v. Williams	ii. 767
Simond v. Hilbert	ii. 576
Simons v. Horwood	ii. 712
Simonton v. Bacon	i. 237
Simpler v. Lord	i. 313
Simpson v. Fogo	ii. 875
v. Hart	ii. 204, 206, 770, 872
v. Howden	i. 27, 296; ii. 9, 10, 15, 202
v. McAllister	ii. 562, 566
v. Montgomery	i. 158, 179
v. Vaughan	i. 167, 171, 177
Sims v. Aughtery	i. 80
v. Sims	ii. 459
v. Urrey	i. 175
v. Walker	i. 607
Simson v. Cooke	i. 460
v. Ingham	i. 460, 461
Sinclair v. Fraser	ii. 874
v. Winona	ii. 13
Singer Mfg. Co. v. Domestic Sewing Machine Co.	ii. 239
v. Loog	ii. 256, 257
v. Wilson	ii. 256
Singleton v. Love	ii. 553
Sinnett v. Herbert	ii. 526
Sipthorp v. Moxon	ii. 21
Sisk v. Garry	ii. 790
Sitwell v. Bernard	ii. 113
Six v. Shaner	ii. 534
Sjoerds v. Luscombe	ii. 641
Skapholme v. Hart	ii. 373
Skeel v. Spraker	i. 531, 644; ii. 580
Skeeles v. Shearley	i. 402; ii. 826
Skelton v. Cole	i. 381
Skett v. Whitmore	ii. 74, 89
Skillern v. May	ii. 6
Skinner, Ex parte	ii. 677, 680
v. Dayton	ii. 645, 647, 651, 656
v. Judson	i. 81
v. Warner	ii. 675
v. White	ii. 651
Skip v. Harwood	i. 687, 689; ii. 159
v. Huey	i. 335
Skipper v. Stokes	ii. 349
Skirras v. Craig	i. 64
Skottowe v. Williams	ii. 864
Slack v. Buchannan	ii. 822
Slade v. Barlow	i. 659
Slanning v. Style	i. 602, 604, 605; ii. 167, 704, 710, 716
Slater v. Dangerfield	ii. 397
v. Lawson	ii. 852
Slaughter v. Genson	i. 209
Sleech's Case	i. 465, 686
Sleech v. Thorington	ii. 740, 750, 758
Sleight v. Dawson	ii. 875
Slemmer's Appeal	i. 681
Slim v. Croucher	i. 390, 393
Slingsby v. Boulton	ii. 139, 152
Sloan v. Frothingham	ii. 853
v. Moore	i. 680
Sloane v. Cadogan	ii. 23, 118, 120
v. Heatfield	i. 74
Sloman v. Walter	ii. 644
Sluman v. Wilson	ii. 847
Small v. Atwood	i. 204
v. Currie	i. 338
v. Marwood	ii. 343, 344, 346
Smallcomb's Case	ii. 862
Smart v. Prujean	ii. 500, 518
Smedberg v. Mark	ii. 802, 804
Smiley v. Smiley	ii. 700
Smith's Case	ii. 772
Smith, In re	i. 688, 690
v. Acton	ii. 851
v. Allen	ii. 872
v. Alsop	i. 122
v. Applegate	i. 296
v. Ashton	i. 101, 185
v. Attersoll	ii. 272
v. Auditor-Gen.	i. 66

CASES CITED.

Smith v. Aykerill i. 268
   v. Bank of Scotland i. 164, 205, 221, 234, 334, 388
   v. Bate ii. 674
   v. Beaufort ii. 818
   v. Bell ii. 412, 721
   v. Bicknell i. 95
   v. Bromley i. 59, 301, 303, 305, 307, 385
   v. Bruning i. 268, 303
   v. Brush ii. 856
   v. Burnham ii. 86
   v. Byers ii. 617
   v. Camelford ii. 725
   v. Campbell ii. 401, 402
   v. Carll ii. 17
   v. Chadwick i. 204, 209, 219
   v. Chicago R. Co. ii. 378
   v. Clarke i. 226, 295
   v. Clay i. 62, 546; ii. 277, 844, 845
   v. Collyer ii. 222, 235
   v. Conner ii. 327
   v. Cooke i. 74, 537; ii. 18
   v. Critchfield ii. 152
   v. Davidson ii. 842, 843
   v. Day i. 424
   v. Drake ii. 583
   v. Eustis i. 636
   v. Evans i. 159
   v. Everett i. 682; ii. 364, 366
   v. Felton ii. 770
   v. Fromont ii. 53
   v. Gibson i. 425
   v. Guild ii. 424
   v. Hammond ii. 140, 147, 148
   v. Harrison i. 203; ii. 779
   v. Hays ii. 194
   v. Haytwell ii. 214
   v. Hibbard ii. 110
   v. Hickman ii. 13
   v. Hitchcock i. 116
   v. Hollenback ii. 271
   v. Hubbard ii. 561
   v. Hughes i. 109
   v. Hurst ii. 557
   v. Hutchinson i. 390
   v. Jeges i. 679
   v. Jewett ii. 652
   v. Johnson ii. 91
   v. Jordan i. 115
   v. Kane ii. 740, 744
   v. Kay i. 310, 318, 333
   v. Kelly ii. 91
   v. Land Corporation i. 210
   v. Laveaux i. 455, 458, 469
   v. Lawrence ii. 96
   v. Lloyd i. 461; ii. 794

Smith v. Low i. 406
   v. Lowry ii. 203, 204
   v. Lucas ii. 285
   v. Lytle ii. 110
   v. Maitland i. 192
   v. Marsack i. 205
   v. McCluskey i. 105
   v. McConnell ii. 12
   v. McVeigh ii. 77
   v. Murphy i. 65
   v. New York Ins. Co. ii. 61
   v. Packhurst i. 181
   v. Perry ii. 606, 607, 608
   v. Pincombe i. 141
   v. Plummer ii. 587
   v. Railroad Co. i. 556
   v. Reese Mining Co. i. 404
   v. Richards i. 201
   v. Robinson i. 306
   v. Rockwell i. 87
   v. Smith i. 407, 661; ii. 13, 182, 462, 618, 691, 692
   v. Spencer i. 198; ii. 530
   v. Steele i. 528
   v. Stowell ii. 509
   v. Streatfield i. 192
   v. Strong ii. 459
   v. Target ii. 143
   v. Turner ii. 79
   v. Turrentine i. 187
   v. Vreeland i. 380
   v. Walker ii. 203
   v. Walser ii. 280
   v. Watson i. 590
   v. Wheeler ii. 344, 346
   v. White i. 301
   v. Wigley i. 465
   v. Woodruff ii. 258
Smithers v. Hooper ii. 554
Smyth, Ex parte i. 477, 478, 479, 481, 482, 485, 489, 491, 492
   v. Griffin ii. 16
Sneed v. Culpepper i. 572
Snelgrove v. Bailey i. 611
Snell v. Dwight i. 301
   v. Elam ii. 532
   v. Ins. Co. i. 121, 154, 155
Snelling v. Flatman ii. 805
Snelson v. Corbett ii. 707
Snider v. Newsom i. 278
Snow v. Weber ii. 214
   v. Whitehead ii. 230
Snowdon, Ex parte i. 509
Snowman v. Harford ii. 99
Snyder's Appeal i. 580
Snyder v. Marks ii. 14
   v. Robinson ii. 341

CASES CITED. XCV

Société Générale v. Tramways Co.	ii. 339, 379
Soc. for Propagating the Gospel v. Att.-Gen.	ii. 517
Sockett v. Wray	ii. 718, 722, 725
Sofer v. Kemp	ii. 580
Sohier v. Burr	ii. 153
v. Eldredge	i. 481; ii. 583
v. Loring	i. 336
Sollory v. Leaver	ii. 163, 164
Solomon v. Laing	ii. 868
Soltau v. De Held	ii. 225, 228, 261
Somerby v. Buntin	i. 673, 674; ii. 35, 41
Somerset's Case	ii. 421
Somerset v. Cookson	ii. 25
Somersetshire Coal Co. v. Harcourt	ii. 865
Somerville v. Mackay	i. 674
Somes v. Skinner	i. 240
Sorrell v. Carpenter	i. 411
South, Ex parte	ii. 362, 363, 366, 579
v. Bloxam	i. 640
Southall v. ——	ii. 819
v. McKean	ii. 130
Southampton v. Greaves	i. 599
Southampton Dock Co. v. Southampton Board	i. 458
Southby v. Stonehouse	ii. 717
Southcot v. Watson	ii. 547, 548
Southcote's Case	ii. 697
Southern Ins. Co. v. Booker	ii. 654
Southey v. Sherwood	ii. 241, 249
South Sea Co. v. Bumstead	ii. 789, 791
v. D'Oliffe	i. 167, 169, 171, 172
v. Wymondsell	ii. 849
South Wales Ry. Co. v. Wythes	ii. 46
Southwell v. Thompson	i. 624
Southwick v. Morrell	ii. 623
Sowarsby v. Lacy	ii. 475
Sowden v. Sowden	ii. 548
Sowerby v. Fryer	ii. 220
Sowler v. Day	i. 158
Spader v. Davis	i. 375
Spain v. Hamilton	i. 306
Spalding v. Alexander	ii. 99
v. Preston	i. 308
v. Thompson	i. 463
Spangler's Appeal	ii. 231
Sparhawk v. Buell	ii. 686
v. Cloon	i. 356; ii. 277
v. Union Ry. Co.	ii. 225
Sparkes v. Cator	ii. 448, 449
Sparkman v. Place	i. 367
Sparks v. Liverpool Water Works	ii. 660
Sparrow v. Paris	ii. 651
Spaulding v. Backus	ii. 767, 770
Spaulding v. Shalmer	ii. 471
Spear v. Grant	ii. 603
v. Hayward	i. 300
v. Orendorf	ii. 79, 80
Speer v. Bidwell	ii. 791, 792
v. Crawter	i. 618, 619, 621, 623, 624
Speight, In re	ii. 617
v. Gaunt	ii. 614, 615
Speiglemyer v. Crawford	i. 518
Speke v. Walrond	i. 655
Spence, In re	ii. 675
v. Dunlap	i. 373
Spencer v. Carr	i. 393
v. Chesterfield	ii. 674
v. Clarke	ii. 324
v. London & Birmingham Ry. Co.	ii. 226, 228
v. Parry	i. 505
v. Pearson	i. 417
v. Peck	ii. 832
v. Topham	i. 318
Sperling v. Rochfort	ii. 724, 734
Sperry v. Gibson	ii. 193
Spettigue v. Carpenter	ii. 788
Spicer, In re	i. 378
Spike v. Harding	i. 624
Spiller v. Spiller	i. 412
Spinks v. Robins	ii. 453
Spirett v. Willows	i. 369; ii. 752
Spooner v. Payne	ii. 356
Spoor v. Tyzzer	ii. 789
Sporrer v. Eifler	i. 65, 306
Spottiswoode v. Clarke	ii. 238, 240
Sprague v. West	ii. 138, 139, 154
Spring v. Gray	i. 546
v. South Car. Ins. Co.	ii. 144, 343, 379
Springett v. Jenings	ii. 526
Springfield v. Conn. River Ry. Co.	ii. 869
v. Edwards	ii. 180
v. Harris	ii. 231
Springhead Spinning Co. v. Riley	ii. 240
Springport v. Teutonia Bank	ii. 15
Springs v. Sanders	ii. 43
Sproles v. Powell	i. 87
Sproule v. Pryor	i. 573, 575, 587
Sprout v. Crowley	i. 691
Spurr v. Benedict	i. 157
v. Snyder	ii. 773
Spurrett v. Spiller	i. 385
Spurrier v. Fitzgerald	ii. 69, 70
Square v. Dean	ii. 725
Squire v. Campbell	ii. 87, 92, 232, 233
v. Harder	ii. 534
St. Albyn v. Harding	i. 343

CASES CITED.

St. Amand v. Jersey	i. 371
St. Andrew's Church v. Tomkins	i. 423
St. Dunstan v. Beauchamp	ii. 483, 498
St. George v. Wake	i. 274
St. Helen's Smelting Co. v. Tipping	ii. 229, 233, 262
St. Jago de Cuba, The	ii. 587
St. James Church v. Arrington	ii. 229
St. John v. Benedict	ii. 58
v. Conger	i. 411
v. Hodges	i. 595
v. Holford	ii. 337
v. St. John	i. 300, 302; ii. 7, 8, 10, 13, 761, 762, 764
St. Louis v. Clemens	ii. 349
St. Luke's v. Leonard's Parish	i. 622
St. Paul v. Dudley	i. 499; ii. 342
v. Morris	i. 540
St. Paul Division v. Brown	ii. 49, 65
Stackhouse v. Barnstown	i. 62, 546; ii. 814
Stackpole v. Beaumont	i. 276, 277, 280, 282, 285, 288, 290, 291; ii. 692, 753
Stacy v. Pearson	i. 80
Stafford v. Buckley	ii. 347
v. Fetters	i. 113
v. Nutt	i. 664
v. Stafford	ii. 860
v. Van Rensselaer	ii. 574
Stains v. Banks	ii. 319
Stainton v. Chadwick	i. 79
Stakie, Ex parte	ii. 685
Stall v. Hart	i. 156
Stallings v. Freeman	i. 328, 331
Stallworth v. Preslar	i. 528
Stamford v. Hobart	ii. 286
Stammers v. Elliott	ii. 773
Stamper v. Barker	ii. 747
Standen v. Standen	ii. 391
Stanfield v. Simmons	i. 378
Stanford v. Harlstone	ii. 234
v. Marshall	ii. 735
v. Roberts	ii. 18
Stanhope v. Roberts	i. 81
v. Verney	ii. 339, 825
Stanley v. Coulthurst	ii. 286
v. Cramer	i. 454
v. McGauran	i. 215
Stannard v. St. Giles	ii. 190, 234
Stansfield v. Habergham	ii. 219, 220, 294, 534
v. Hobson	ii. 851
Stanton v. Allen	i. 293
v. Embry	ii. 196
v. Hall	ii. 710, 711, 713, 741, 745, 746, 747
Stantons v. Thompson	ii. 342
Stapilton v. Stapilton	i. 124, 137, 138, 140, 142, 181; ii. 273
Staples v. Parker	ii. 651
v. Staples	i. 331
Stark v. Starr	i. 157
Starnes v. Newsom	ii. 34
Starr v. Bennett	i. 404
v. Heckart	ii. 198
v. Starr	i. 611
State v. Alder	i. 26, 30
v. Warren	ii. 493, 504
State Bank v. Fearing	i. 205
State Railroad Tax Cases	ii. 12, 14, 191
Stawell v. Atkyns	i. 540
Stead v. Clay	ii. 214, 259
v. Nelson	ii. 729
Stearns v. Barrett	i. 294
v. Beckham	ii. 59, 90
v. Cooper	i. 477
v. Page	ii. 844
Stebbing v. Walkey	i. 190, 191
Stebbins v. Eddy	i. 162, 220, 221
Stedman v. Hart	i. 242
Steed v. Preece	ii. 114, 554
Steel v. Brown	i. 379
v. Dixon	i. 514
Steele v. Babcock	i. 331; ii. 550
v. Branch	ii. 99
v. Ellmaker	i. 295
v. Stuart	i. 692
Steere v. Hoagland	i. 549
v. Steere	ii. 535
Steevens Hospital v. Dyas	ii. 861
Steff v. Andrews	ii. 793
Stein v. Herman	i. 376
Steinmetz v. Halthin	ii. 739, 752
Stent v. Bailis	i. 199
Stephen v. Beall	i. 329
Stephens, Ex parte	ii. 766, 772, 773
v. Baird	i. 389
v. Callanan	ii. 142
v. Howard	ii. 686
v. James	ii. 687
v. Olive	i. 365, 366, 371, 373
v. Trueman	ii. 289
Stephenson, In re	i. 638
v. Abingdon	ii. 398
v. Wilson	ii. 206
Sterndale v. Hankinson	i. 465, 559
Sterne v. Beck	ii. 646
Sterry v. Arden	i. 406, 430, 436
Stevens v. Bagwell	i. 301; ii. 348, 357, 358, 373
v. Benning	ii. 261
v. Church	i. 639

CASES CITED.

Stevens v. Cooper i. 497, 516, 526, 527, 642, 647; ii. 579
— v. Dedham Inst. for Sav. ii. 333
— v. Dennett i. 390, 391
— v. Hampton i. 410
— v. Keating ii. 238
— v. Lynch i. 110, 111, 118
— v. Mid-Hants Ry. Co. ii. 342
— v. Morse i. 431
— v. Perrier i. 295
— v. Praed ii. 206
— v. Robinson i. 373
— v. Rut. & Bur. Ry. Co. ii. 867
— v. Savage ii. 692
— v. Stevens i. 607
— v. Warren ii. 153
Stevenson v. Anderson ii. 141, 145
— v. Lombard i. 494
— v. Snow i. 480
Steward v. Blakeway i. 670, 683
— v. Bridger i. 95
— v. East India Co. ii. 822
— v. Winters ii. 39
Stewart v. Careless ii. 70, 73
— v. Denton ii. 85
— v. E. Transp. Co. ii. 265, 867
— v. Graham ii. 801, 803
— v. Hall ii. 587
— v. Jones ii. 404, 414
— v. Kirkwall ii. 725, 726, 728, 730, 732, 733, 735
— v. Metcalf ii. 94
— v. Munford i. 391
— v. Nicholls ii. 334
— v. Sanderson ii. 617
— v. Stewart i. 116, 118, 134, 135, 136, 138, 140, 141, 145, 148, 555
— v. Stokes i. 86
Stickney v. Crane i. 377
Stiff v. Eastburne ii. 194
Stiffe v. Everitt ii. 713, 747
Stileman v. Ashdown i. 362; ii. 331, 557
Stillman v. Stillman ii. 580
Stillwell v. Wilkins i. 256; ii. 162
— v. Williams ii. 162
Stines v. Hays i. 154, 157
Stirling v. Forrester i. 486, 498, 502, 505, 506, 509, 513, 516, 647
Stockbridge Iron Co. v. Hudson Iron Co. i. 113, 115, 116, 155
Stockdale v. Allery i. 674
— v. Nicholson ii. 399
Stocken v. Stocken ii. 686, 687
Stocker v. Brockelbank ii. 34, 42
— v. Stocker i. 388

Stocker v. Wedderborn i. 674; ii. 35
Stockley v. Stockley i. 115, 123, 124, 133, 137, 140, 141, 142, 245
Stockton v. Union Oil Co. ii. 104
Stoddard v. Dennison ii. 335
Stoddart v. Nelson ii. 398
Stoell v. Botelar ii. 805, 806
Stokeman v. Dawson i. 392
Stokes v. Holden ii. 349, 353, 354
— v. Huron ii. 396
— v. Knarr ii. 206
— v. Mendon i. 516
— v. Moore ii. 78
Stokoe v. Robson i. 95
Stone v. Compton i. 334
— v. Covell i. 210
— v. Fargo ii. 771
— v. Godfrey i. 116
— v. Hackett i. 431, 433; ii. 119
— v. Hale i. 120, 158, 179
— v. Lane i. 422
— v. Liddesdale i. 297; ii. 348, 353, 355, 356
— v. Seaver ii. 873
— v. Stone ii. 847
— v. Yea ii. 373
Stones v. Cooke ii. 759, 802, 803
Stoney v. Shultz ii. 580
Stonor, In re ii. 285
— v. Corwen ii. 275, 286
Stook's Appeal ii. 398
Stopford v. Canterbury ii. 686
Storer v. Great Western Ry. Co. ii. 29, 40
Storey v. Johnson i. 662, 663, 666, 667
Storm v. Mann ii. 234
Storring v. Borren ii. 437
Storrs v. Barker i. 111, 120, 121, 122, 123, 127, 146, 148, 390, 394, 395
— v. Scougale i. 243, 333
Storry v. Walsh ii. 471
Story v. Holcombe ii. 242
— v. Tompkins ii. 335
— v. Windsor i. 74, 536
Stout v. Cook ii. 13
Stover v. Eycleshimer ii. 353
— v. Mitchell i. 140
Stow v. Russell ii. 99
Stowe v. Bowen ii. 623, 625
Stowell v. Cole i. 541
— v. Haslett ii. 11
Straat v. Uhrig ii. 534
Strachan v. Brander i. 301; ii. 373
Strafford v. Welch i. 28
Strand v. Music Hall Co. ii. 861
Strange v. Harris i. 554, 604; ii. 165
— v. Smith i. 264

CASES CITED.

Strasburgh v. New York	ii. 15
Strathmore v. Bowes	i. 274
Stratton v. Stratton	ii. 74
Straus v. Goldsmid	ii. 494
Stray, Ex parte	ii. 863
Streatfield v. Streatfield	ii. 417
Streeper v. Williams	ii. 651
Street v. Blay	ii. 19
v. Rigby	i. 676; ii. 789, 794, 821
v. Street	ii. 803
Streeter v. Rush	ii. 651
Strelly v. Winson	i. 473
Stribblehill v. Brett	i. 268, 270
Stribley v. Hawkie	ii. 62, 181, 261
Strickland v. Aldrich	i. 300
v. Strickland	i. 628, 630, 634, 658, 660
Striker v. Mott	i. 664
Strode v. Parker	ii. 652
Strong v. Blanchard	ii. 317, 865
v. Jackson	i. 405; ii. 315
v. Strong	ii. 789
v. Williams	ii. 463
Stronge v. Hawkins	i. 639
Stroud v. Gwyer	ii. 606, 608, 609, 616, 620
v. Stroud	i. 683
Stroughill v. Anstey	ii. 474, 594
Strozier v. Howes	ii. 210
Struve v. Childs	ii. 332
Stuart v. Coalter	i. 621
v. Cockerell	i. 425
v. Kissam	ii. 711
v. Welch	ii. 143, 144
Stubbs v. Sargon	ii. 282, 385, 407, 408, 517, 530
Studer v. Seyer	ii. 120
Studholme v. Hodgson	i. 604
Sturgis v. Champneys	i. 66; ii. 740, 742, 743, 744, 749
v. Corp.	ii. 718, 724, 748
v. Morse	ii. 848
Sturt v. Mellish	i. 546; ii. 267
Sturtevant v. Jaques	ii. 102
Sturz v. De La Rue	ii. 236
Stuyvesant v. Hall	ii. 580
Suckling v. Morley	ii. 819
Suessenguth v. Birgenheimer	i. 207
Suffolk v. Green	ii. 819, 832, 833
Suggitt, In re	ii. 752
Suidam v. Beals	ii. 876
Suisse v. Lowther	ii. 451, 454, 457, 460, 464
Sullivan v. Blackwell	i. 324, 326
v. Finnegan	ii. 11
v. Portland R. Co.	ii. 844
v. Tuck	ii. 33, 34
Summers v. Hoover	i. 367
Sumner v. Powell	i. 177, 178
v. Thorpe	i. 541
Superintendent of Pub. Schools v. Heath	ii. 366
Supervisors v. Herrington	ii. 847
Surber v. McClintic	ii. 336
Surman v. Barlow	i. 406
Suter v. Matthews	i. 26, 27, 28
Sutherland v. Briggs	ii. 77
v. Brush	ii. 627
v. Sutherland	i. 609
Sutphen v. Cushman	i. 545
Sutton, In re	ii. 493
v. Chetwynd	ii. 273
v. Fowler	ii. 60, 62
v. Montford	ii. 232
v. Wilders	ii. 614
Swain v. Cato	ii. 564
v. Fidelity Ins. Co.	ii. 102
v. Wall	i. 486, 510, 511, 514
Swaine v. Denby	i. 668
Swaisland v. Dearsley	ii. 90
Swan v. Frick	ii. 273
v. Swan	i. 663, 668; ii. 584
Swannock v. Lefford	i. 399, 417, 634; ii. 326
Swansea Ry. Co. v. Budd	ii. 816
Swasey v. Bible Soc.	ii. 504
Swedesborough Church v. Shivers	i. 694
Sweeny v. Williams	i. 30, 87, 89, 603
Sweet v. Shaw	ii. 247
v. Southcote	i. 416
Sweetapple v. Bindon	ii. 112
Swift, Ex parte	ii. 687
v. Beneficial Soc.	ii. 495
v. Jewsbury	i. 212
v. Winterbotham	i. 212
Swire v. Francis	i. 212, 213
Sword v. Allen	ii. 234
Sydney v. Shelley	ii. 286
Sykes v. Sykes	ii. 255, 256, 257, 258, 276
Symes v. Hughes	i. 303
Symonds, Ex parte	i. 177
Symondson v. Tweed	ii. 69, 82
Symons v. James	ii. 592
v. Rutter	ii. 112
Sympson v. Turner	ii. 270
Synge v. Hales	ii. 285, 287
v. Synge	ii. 424

T.

Tabor v. Brooks	ii. 281
v. Cilley	i. 151

CASES CITED. xcix

Taggart v. Taggart	i. 172; ii. 286
v. Wood	ii. 206
Tainter v. Clark	ii. 494
v. Cole	ii. 91, 126
Tait, Ex parte	ii. 210
Talbot v. Frere	i. 463
v. Radnor	ii. 432
v. Scott	ii. 222
v. Shrewsbury	ii. 461, 675
v. Staniforth	i. 344
Talcott, Ex parte	i. 639
Taliaffero v. Branch Bank	ii. 203
Tallahassee Mfg. Co., In re	ii. 320
Tallis v. Tallis	i. 294
Tallmadge v. East River Bank	ii. 230
Tamm v. Lavalle	ii. 91
Tamworth v. Ferrers	ii. 220
Tanfield v. Davenport	ii. 749
Tanguery v. Bowles	i. 369
Tanner v. European Bank	ii. 153
v. Wise	i. 81; ii. 18
Tanqueray-Williaume, In re	ii. 594
Tantum v. Miller	ii. 6, 8
Tapling v. Jones	ii. 230
Tapp v. Lee	i. 208
Tappan v. De Blois	ii. 503
v. Evans	i. 557
Tarleton v. Tarleton	ii. 874
Tarsey, In re	ii. 713
Tarver v. Tarver	i. 197
Tassell v. Smith	ii. 328
Tatam v. Williams	ii. 843, 846
Tate v. Austin	ii. 703
v. Evans	ii. 767
v. Hilbert	i. 607, 608, 609, 616; ii. 116
v. Leithead	i. 609
Tatham v. Wright	ii. 781, 782
Tatum v. McLellan	ii. 612
Tay v. Slaughter	ii. 598
Tayleur, In re	ii. 834
Taylor, In re	ii. 677
v. Abingdon	i. 532
v. Allen	ii. 158
v. Ashton	i. 207, 215
v. Atwood	i. 201
v. Baker	i. 402
v. Beech	ii. 74, 88
v. Blanchard	i. 293, 294
v. Bryn Mawr College	ii. 517, 518, 519
v. Buck	i. 382
v. Davis	i. 675
v. Dean	i. 379
v. Ferguson	i. 81
v. Fields	i. 687, 688, 689; ii. 604
v. Fore	ii. 203
v. Foster	ii. 583
Taylor v. Grange	i. 668
v. Great Indian Ry. Co.	i. 396
v. Hawkins	i. 427
v. Haylin	i. 541, 542, 545
v. Johnson	ii. 554
v. Johnston	i. 311
v. Jones	i. 360, 361, 364, 366, 371, 375
v. Knight	ii. 657
v. Kymer	i. 460, 461
v. Longworth	ii. 65, 95, 98, 100, 101
v. Neville	ii. 38
v. Okey	ii. 770
v. Palmer	ii. 349
v. Patrick	i. 244
v. Pillow	ii. 261
v. Pine Bluff	i. 19
v. Plumer	ii. 150, 549, 607
v. Popham	ii. 646, 653
v. Porter	i. 497
v. Pugh	i. 274, 275
v. Roberts	ii. 622
v. Rochfort	i. 340, 354
v. Salmon	i. 323, 679
v. Savage	i. 506, 511
v. Sheppard	ii. 203, 204
v. Short	ii. 580
v. Stibbert	i. 400, 406; ii. 110
v. Stone	ii. 711
v. Taylor	i. 310
v. Watson	ii. 397
v. Williams	ii. 59, 90
Teal v. Woodworth	i. 663
Teale v. Teale	ii. 839
Teall v. Watts	i. 662
Teasdale v. Sanderson	i. 663
v. Teasdale	i. 391
Teas's Appeal	i. 580
Tebbs v. Carpenter	ii. 615, 619
Techell v. Watson	ii. 372
Telegraph Co. v. Davenport	i. 392
Tempest, Ex parte	i. 377
In re	ii. 631
v. Camoys	ii. 281
Tendril v. Smith	i. 311
Ten Eyck v. Holmes	i. 527
Tenham v. Herbert	ii. 174, 175, 177
Tennant v. Braie	i. 292
Tennent v. Patton	ii. 557
Teresy v. Gorey	i. 92, 94
Terretts v. Sharon	ii. 180
Terrewest v. Featherby	i. 562, 563
Terrill v. Richards	i. 672
Terry v. Harrison	ii. 259
v. Little	i. 557
v. Tubman	i. 557
Tew v. Winterton	ii. 601

CASES CITED.

	PAGE
Thacher v. Churchill	i. 216
v. Phinney	i. 365, 373
Thackwell v. Gardiner	i. 187
Thalhimer v. Brinkerhoff	ii. 347, 370, 373, 374
Thalman v. Canon	ii. 536
Thames Iron Works v. Patent Derrick Co.	ii. 370
Thatcher v. Humble	i. 25
Thellusson v. Woodford	ii. 415, 417, 425, 433, 434, 435, 436
Therasson v. Hickock	i. 365
Therman v. Abell	i. 481
Thetford School, Case of	ii. 481
Thigpen v. Pitt	ii. 6
Thomas, Ex parte	ii. 685
v. Bartow	i. 155
v. Bennett	ii. 725
v. Britnell	ii. 591
v. Brownville R. Co.	i. 332
v. Canterbury	i. 552
v. Chicago	ii. 534, 541
v. Cooper	i. 306
v. Coultas	i. 66
v. Cronie	i. 308
v. Davies	i. 679
v. Dering	ii. 105
v. Farmers' Bank	i. 663
v. Frazer	i. 171, 177, 178
v. Freeman	ii. 348
v. Gyles	i. 661
v. James	ii. 234
v. Jones	ii. 233
v. McCormick	i. 175
v. Oakley	ii. 235, 236
v. Porter	ii. 661
v. Thomas	i. 500, 582, 588
v. Tyler	ii. 818
v. Williams	ii. 239, 240
Thompson v. Attfield	i. 181
v. Brown	i. 460, 557, 558, 559; ii. 199, 200, 617
v. Bruen	ii. 96
v. Charnock	i. 676
v. Dunn	ii. 818
v. Ebbets	ii. 143, 154
v. Finch	ii. 623
v. Fisher	ii. 286, 403
v. Graham	ii. 6, 7
v. Griffin	ii. 686
v. Harcourt	ii. 25
v. Harrison	i. 272
v. Heywood	ii. 341
v. Hodgson	i. 607
v. Hudson	i. 463; ii. 318, 646
v. Leach	i. 241
v. Leake	i. 189
Thompson v. Lynch	ii. 11, 13
v. Noel	ii. 795
v. Perkins	ii. 607
v. Pyland	ii. 574
v. Saco Water Power Co.	i. 479, 496
v. Simpson	i. 392
v. Smith	i. 189; ii. 259
v. Stanhope	ii. 250, 253
v. Thompson	i. 116, 300, 302
v. Todd	ii. 70, 71
v. Young	ii. 398
Thompsonville Co. v. Osgood	i. 111, 150
Thoms v. Thoms	ii. 702
Thomson v. Grant	i. 590
v. Ludington	ii. 397
v. Shakespeare	ii. 495
Thorley's Co. v. Massam	ii. 239
Thorn v. Thorn	i. 313
Thornber v. Sheard	i. 310
Thornborough v. Baker	ii. 316
Thornborrow v. Whiteacre	ii. 638, 641
Thorndike v. Collington	i. 693, 694, 697
v. Hunt	i. 549
v. Loring	ii. 276
Thorne v. Thorne	i. 180, 181; ii. 80
Thornhill v. Evans	i. 339
Thornton v. Dixon	i. 683
v. Marginal Ry. Co.	i. 460
v. Ramsden	ii. 861
v. Tandy	i. 377
v. Thornton	i. 468, 660
Thoroughgood's Case	i. 58
Thorp v. Keokuk Coal Co.	ii. 341
v. McCallum	i. 187
v. Pettit	ii. 96
Thorpe v. Dunlap	ii. 570
v. Gartside	ii. 331
v. Holdsworth	ii. 324
v. Jackson	i. 177, 178, 685, 686
v. Macauley	ii. 819, 837
Threlfall v. Lunt	ii. 16
Throckmorton v. Crowley	ii. 771
Thrupp v. Collett	ii. 514
Thruston v. Minke	i. 662
Thurlow v. Mackeson	ii. 331
Thurmond v. Clark	i. 122
v. Reese	i. 359
Thurston v. Clifton	ii. 437
v. Hancock	ii. 235
Thynn v. Duvall	i. 502
v. Thynn	i. 61, 194, 264
Thynne v. Glengall	ii. 437, 447, 458
Tibbets v. George	ii. 366
Tibbits v. Tibbits	ii. 405, 406, 408, 424, 425, 436

CASES CITED.

Tichborne v. Tichborne	i. 555
Tichener, In re	i. 407
Tickel v. Short	i. 544
Tidd v. Lister	i. 638
Tiernan v. Gibney	ii. 81
v. Jackson	ii. 348, 362, 363, 364, 378
v. Roland	ii. 437
v. Thurman	i. 404
v. Woodruff	i. 336
Tiffany v. Crawford	i. 653
Tiffin v. Tiffin	ii. 299
Tilley v. Bridges	i. 532, 533, 631
v. Thomas	ii. 99
Tillinghast v. De Wolf	ii. 397
v. Wheaton	i. 611
Tillmes v. Marsh	i. 621
Tilton v. Cofield	i. 411
Timson v. Ramsbottom	i. 400, 402, 424, 426; ii. 339, 377
Tinney v. Stebbins	i. 654
v. Tinney	ii. 87
Tinsley v. Anderson	i. 518, 522
Tipping v. Tipping	i. 575; ii. 707
Tipton Green Colliery Co. v. Tipton Moat Colliery Co.	ii. 319
Tirrell v. Branch Bank of Mobile	i. 414
Tisdale v. Bailey	i. 273, 275
Tissen v. Tissen	ii. 166
Titcomb v. Morrill	ii. 271, 532, 535
Tittenson v. Peat	ii. 792, 823
Titus v. Titus	i. 580
Tobey v. Bristol	ii. 81, 86, 794
v. Moore	ii. 348
Todd v. Barlow	ii. 791
v. Gee	ii. 104, 124, 125, 126, 127, 128, 129
v. Grove	i. 311
v. Taft	ii. 37, 95
Toker v. Toker	ii. 23
Toller v. Carteret	ii. 60, 209, 633
Tollett v. Tollett	i. 106, 181, 182, 185; ii. 384
Tolson v. Collins	ii. 449, 463
Tombes v. Elers	ii. 674, 675
Tombs v. Roch	i. 580
Tomkins v. Colthurst	i. 580
v. Willshear	i. 444
Tomlinson v. Harrison	ii. 801
v. Savage	i. 226
Tommy v. Ellis	ii. 194
Tompkins v. Bernet	i. 302
v. Sprout	i. 310, 376
v. Tompkins	ii. 679, 686
Tomplin v. James	ii. 90, 96
Tomson v. Judge	i. 314, 317, 333
v. Tomson	i. 592
Tongue v. Nutwell	i. 67
Tonnerlau v. Poyntz	i. 191
Tonnins v. Prout	ii. 214
Tonson v. Walker	ii. 240
Tooke v. Hartely	ii. 330
v. Hastings	ii. 578
Tool Co. v. Norris	i. 296
Toole v. Medlicott	ii. 82
Topham v. Portland	i. 263
Toplis v. Baker	ii. 21, 334
Topp v. Williams	i. 621
Torr v. Torr	ii. 82
Torrance v. Bolton	i. 203
Torrent v. Booming Co.	ii. 15
Torrey v. Bank of New Orleans	i. 323
Tottenham v. Emmett	i. 344, 352
Totty v. Nesbitt	i. 90
Toulman v. Price	i. 90
v. Steere	i. 401, 424; ii. 342
Tourle v. Rand	i. 396, 397; ii. 324
Tourson's Case	i. 243
Tourville v. Naish	ii. 379
Tovey v. Young	ii. 203
Tower v. Appleton Bank	i. 87
Towers v. Davys	ii. 23
Towle v. Swasey	i. 580, 582
Town v. Needham	i. 663
v. Wood	i. 545
Townsend v. Ash	i. 532, 533, 535
v. Carpenter	ii. 380
v. Crowdy	i. 85, 118, 154
v. Ives	ii. 783
v. Lowfield	i. 202
v. Marquard	i. 365
v. Toker	ii. 23
v. Townsend	ii. 779
v. Westacott	i. 369
v. Windham	i. 188, 358, 361, 362, 364, 371, 578; ii. 366, 703, 707, 725
Townshend v. Devaynes	i. 683; ii. 544
v. Stangroom	i. 111, 116, 124, 130, 143, 167, 169, 170, 174, 226, 260; ii. 87, 92, 93, 94
Towsley v. Denison	i. 545
Tracy v. Albany Exch. Co.	ii. 81
Trafford v. Ashton	ii. 391, 392
v. Boehm	ii. 617
Trafton v. Hawes	i. 431
Traip v. Gould	i. 80
Transatlantic Co. v. Pietroni	i. 592
Trash v. White	ii. 334
Travers v. Bulkeley	ii. 699
v. Travers	ii. 546
Treackle v. Coke	i. 694
Treadwell v. Brown	ii. 818

CASES CITED.

Treadwell v. Cordis	ii. 611
v. Salisbury Mfg. Co.	ii. 231, 611
Treasurer v. Commercial Mining Co.	ii. 37
Tregonwell v. Sydenham	ii. 534
Trelawney v. Booth	ii. 112
Tremble v. Hill	i. 308
Tremblestown v. Lloyd	i. 198
Trench v. Fenn	ii. 768
Trenchard v. Wanley	i. 199, 202
Trevor v. McKay	ii. 203
v. Perkins	ii. 596
v. Trevor	ii. 288, 289
Trexler v. Miller	i. 198
Trierson v. General Assembly	ii. 495
Trimmer v. Bayne	i. 517, 571, 574, 575, 587, 637; ii. 110, 449, 453, 457, 563
Trist v. Child	i. 296
Trith v. Sprague	i. 159
Tritton v. Foote	ii. 40
Troops v. Snyder	i. 154
Troost v. Davis	ii. 129
Trott v. Buchanan	ii. 590
v. Vernon	ii. 592
Trotter v. Hughes	ii. 341
Troughton v. Binkes	i. 428, 592; ii. 328, 329
v. Troughton	i. 188
Troy v. Clarke	ii. 100
Trower v. Newcome	i. 204, 223
Trull v. Bigelow	i. 436
v. Eastman	i. 350; ii. 47, 348, 349, 353
Truly v. Wanzer	ii. 198, 876
Truman v. London Ry. Co.	ii. 225
Trumper v. Trumper	i. 330
Trustees of Schools v. Otis	i. 151
Tuck v. Calvert	i. 525
Tucke v. Buchholz	i. 325, 326
Tucker v. Campbell	i. 511
v. Conwell	ii. 13
v. Howard	ii. 182
v. Kenniston	ii. 15, 179
v. Laing	i. 335
v. Madden	i. 154
v. Oxley	i. 684; ii. 773, 774
v. Phipps	i. 198, 261, 442
v. Seamen's Aid Soc.	ii. 504
v. Wilson	ii. 335
Tuckfield v. Buller	i. 661
Tuckley v. Thompson	i. 639
Tudor v. Samyne	ii. 743
Tuffnell v. Constable	i. 434, 436; ii. 21, 22, 116, 118
v. Page	ii. 508
Tufton v. Harding	ii. 201
Tufts v. Larned	i. 153
v. Tapley	ii. 321
Tulk v. Moxhay	ii. 55
Tullett v. Armstrong	ii. 714, 730
Tullit v. Tullit	ii. 689
Tulloch v. Hartley	i. 625
Tunnicliff's Case	ii. 805
Tunstall v. Boothby	ii. 353, 355, 356, 357, 358
v. Christian	ii. 235
v. Trappes	ii. 558
Tupper v. Phipps	i. 198
Turley v. Nowell	ii. 54
Turner's Case	ii. 743
Turner, In re	i. 217
v. Burkinshaw	i. 468
v. Collins	i. 311
v. Davies	i. 511
v. Harvey	i. 204, 226, 229, 230; ii. 4
v. Ivie	ii. 397
v. Kelly	i. 156
v. Kerr	ii. 320
v. McCarty	ii. 362
v. Morgan	i. 664
v. Nye	ii. 272, 290
v. Ogden	ii. 494
v. Turner	i. 146, 567
v. Wright	i. 538
Turnipseed v. Hudson	i. 390
Turton v. Benson	i. 271
Tuscumbia R. Co. v. Rhodes	ii. 767, 768
Tuttle v. Standish	i. 87
Tweddell v. Tweddell	i. 586, 587; ii. 596
Tweedale v. Coventry	i. 582
v. Tweedale	ii. 396
Twining v. Morrice	i. 130, 226, 295
Twin Lick Co. v. Marbury	i. 332
Twisden v. Twisden	ii. 445, 418
Twiss v. Massey	i. 684
Twistleton v. Griffith	i. 339, 342, 348
Twitchell v. Bridge	i. 210
Twogood, Ex parte	ii. 773
v. Swanston	i. 543
Twort v. Twort	ii. 221
Twyne's Case	i. 358, 360, 361, 373, 375, 381
Twypont v. Warcup	i. 220
Tyler v. Barrows	ii. 349
v. Hamersley	ii. 190
v. Lake	ii. 711, 712
v. Yates	i. 350
Tyndale v. Warre	ii. 557, 559
Tynes v. Grimstead	i. 322
Tynham v. Mullens	i. 361

CASES CITED.

Tynt v. Tynt	ii. 707
Tyrie v. Fletcher	i. 480
Tyrrell v. Bank of London	i. 318, 322, 324, 331, 674; ii. 612
v. Hope	ii. 710, 711
Tyson v. Brown	ii. 13
v. Cox	ii. 195
v. Fairclough	ii. 163
v. Tyson	i. 129
Tysor v. Lutterloh	ii. 198
Tyus v. Rust	ii. 147, 148, 149

U.

Udell v. Atherton	i. 212
Uhler v. Semple	i. 323, 683
Uhlfelder v. Carter	i. 306
Uhlrich v. Muhlke	i. 322
Ulrich v. Litchfield	i. 190
Underhill v. Harwood	i. 171, 177, 178, 251, 256; ii. 5
v. Van Cortlandt	ii. 789, 791, 793, 797
Underwood v. Courtown	i. 139, 400, 409, 410
v. Hatton	i. 97, 560
v. Hitchcox	ii. 58
v. Stevens	ii. 615, 626, 628
Unfried v. Heberer	i. 392
Ungless v. Tuff	ii. 617
Ungley v. Ungley	ii. 79
Union Bank v. Bell	i. 306
v. Ingram	ii. 319
v. Kerr	ii. 137
Union Ins. Co. v. Pottker	ii. 654, 659
Union Pacific Ry. Co. v. Cheyenne	ii. 14, 191
Union Pacific R. Co. v. Credit Mobilier	i. 332, 333
United States v. Bank of Virginia	ii. 819
v. Cushman	i. 178
v. Eckford	i. 461, 465, 466
v. Green	ii. 678
v. Howland	i. 27, 54; ii. 346
v. Hunter	i. 522; ii. 346
v. January	i. 461, 465, 466
v. Keokuk	ii. 210
v. Kirkpatrick	i. 337, 460, 461, 465, 466
v. McRae	ii. 652, 819, 820
v. Morrison	ii. 555
v. Price	i. 178
United States v. Ruggles	ii. 225
v. Throckmorton	ii. 197
v. Wardwell	i. 460, 461, 465, 466
Upham v. Wyman	ii. 773
Upjohn v. Richland	ii. 227, 230, 233
Upperton v. Nickolson	ii. 100
Upwell v. Halsey	ii. 167
Urann v. Coates	ii. 272
Urquhart v. King	ii. 547
Ushborne v. Ushborne	ii. 320
Utterson v. Mair	ii. 158
Uvedale v. Ettrick	ii. 631

V.

Vachel v. Vachel	ii. 167
Vachell v. Jefferies	ii. 547
Vail v. Foster	ii. 569
Vallance v. Blagdon	i. 299
Valliant v. Dodemede	i. 694
Valpy, Ex parte	ii. 324
Van Alen v. American Bank	ii. 616
Van Bergen v. Van Bergen	ii. 231
Van Campen v. Knight	ii. 99
Vance v. Andrews	i. 79
v. Blain	i. 673
v. Burbank	ii. 197
v. Smith	i. 365
v. Wood	ii. 159
Vandergucht v. De Blaquiere	ii. 734, 760, 802
Vanderheyden v. Mallory	ii. 727, 728
Vanderplank v. King	ii. 414
Vanderveer, In re	i. 203
Vandervoort v. Smith	i. 173
Vanderwerker v. Vt. Cent. R. Co.	ii. 790, 793
Vanderzee v. Willis	ii. 336, 338
Van Doren v. New York	ii. 11, 16
v. Robinson	ii. 86
Van Douge v. Van Douge	i. 158
Van Duyne v. Vreeland	ii. 109, 110, 167, 168
Van Duzer v. Van Duzer	ii. 692, 749, 750
Vandyck v. Herritt	i. 301, 302
Van Dyke's Appeal	ii. 436
Vane v. Vane	ii. 693, 851
Van Epps v. Van Deusen	ii. 692, 737, 744
v. Van Epps	i. 323, 328
Van Horn v. Fonda	ii. 549
Van Horne v. Crain	i. 494
Van Houten v. Post	ii. 449
Van Meter v. Dieffenbach	ii. 322
v. Ely	i. 572, 639

CASES CITED.

Van Meter v. Jones	i. 311
v. Sickler	i. 555
Van Rensselaer v. Bradley	i. 492, 493, 494, 495
v. Chadwick	i. 482, 493, 494, 495
v. Gallup	i. 495
v. Gifford	i. 493, 495
Van Riper v. Van Riper	ii. 462
Van Vronker v. Eastman	ii. 318
Van Wert v. Benedict	ii. 388
Van Wyck v. Knevels	ii. 12
Varick v. Briggs	ii. 828
v. New York	ii. 187
Varnum v. Meserve	ii. 554
Varrell v. Wendell	ii. 398
Vattier v. Hinde	ii. 826
Vaughan, Ex parte	ii. 656
v. Bibb	ii. 620
v. Buck	ii. 737
v. Burslem	ii. 288
v. Fitzgerald	ii. 834
v. Lovejoy	i. 278
v. Marable	ii. 332
v. Vandersteegen	i. 188
v. Welsh	ii. 198
Vauxhall Bridge Co. v. Spencer	i. 266, 272, 296
Vavasseur v. Krupp	ii. 260
Veal v. Veal	i. 610, 614
Veazie v. Williams	i. 226, 295
Venning v. Leckie	i. 672
Verdier v. Verdier	i. 588
Verney v. Verney	i. 500
Vernon's Case	i. 309; ii. 421
Vernon v. Bethell	ii. 321, 322
v. Keys	i. 225, 227
v. Vawdry	i. 542, 515; ii. 630
v. Vernon	i. 492; ii. 289
Verplanck v. Strong	i. 364
Verplank v. Sterry	i. 368, 372
Verselius v. Verselius	i. 359, 379
Vesey v. Jamson	ii. 495
Vickers v. Vickers	ii. 41, 81, 86, 794
Vidal v. Girard	ii. 491
Viers v. Montgomery	i. 433
Vigers v. Pike	i. 227; ii. 90, 95, 844
Villa v. Rodriguez	i. 332; ii. 321
Villareal v. Galway	ii. 428
Villers v. Villers	ii. 298
Villiers v. Beaumont	i. 433
Vincent v. Beverlye	i. 695
Viney v. Chaplin	ii. 96
Vint v. Padget	ii. 328
Vipan v. Mortlock	ii. 201
Voeghtly v. Pittsburgh R. Co.	i. 482, 493, 494, 496
Voll v. Smith	ii. 68, 85
Voorhees v. Dow	ii. 373
Voorhis v. Murphy	i. 154
Vose v. Grant	ii. 603
v. Reed	ii. 165
Vrooman v. Turner	ii. 341
Vulliamy v. Noble	i. 685; ii. 773, 774
Vyse v. Foster	ii. 620
Vyvyan v. Vyvyan	ii. 847

W.

W—— v. B——	i. 305
Waddell v. Lanier	i. 359
v. Wolfe	i. 217
Waddingham v. Loker	i. 203
Waddington v. Oliver	i. 480
Wade v. Colvert	i. 244
v. Coope	i. 515
v. Howard	ii. 342
v. Paget	i. 186
Wadham v. Calcraft	ii. 646, 653, 656
Wadsworth v. Davis	i. 557, 560
v. Williams	i. 376; ii. 315
Wafer v. Mocato	ii. 653, 659
Wager v. Wager	ii. 546
Wagstaff v. Smith	ii. 711, 718, 720, 735
v. Wagstaff	i. 186
Wainwright v. Bendlowes	i. 582
Wait, In re	i. 687, 688
v. Smith	i. 156
Waite v. Horwood	ii. 549
Wake v. Conyers	i. 618, 620, 621, 623, 625
v. Wake	ii. 438
Wakeman v. Dalley	i. 204, 206
v. Groner	ii. 344
Walburn v. Ingilby	i. 678
Walcot v. Hall	i. 99, 528
v. Walker	ii. 241
Walcott v. Keith	ii. 335
Walden v. Murdock	i. 377
Waldo v. Caley	ii. 493, 522
v. Martin	i. 298
Waldon v. Dicks	ii. 248
Waldron, Ex parte	ii. 677
Wales v. Mellen	ii. 316
Walker, In matter of	ii. 739
In re	ii. 752, 754, 757
v. Allen	ii. 581
v. Bradley	i. 99
v. Brooks	i. 78, 79; ii. 379, 380, 637, 767
v. Burroughs	i. 358, 360, 362, 365, 366, 371
v. Childs	ii. 512, 523
v. Covar	i. 639
v. Denne	ii. 113, 114, 530

Walker v. Hill	i. 99
v. House	i. 680
v. Jackson	i. 582, 583; ii. 417
v. Johnson	ii. 272
v. Jones	ii. 194
v. Locke	ii. 536
v. Meagher	i. 568, 569
v. Mottram	i. 294
v. Perkins	i. 300
v. Preswick	ii. 110
v. Robbins	ii. 206, 876
v. Smallwood	i. 408; ii. 469
v. Smith	i. 314, 318, 320
v. Symonds	i. 202, 235; ii. 618, 619
v. Taylor	i. 427
v. Walker	i. 176; ii. 74, 88, 321, 612, 620
v. Wetherell	ii. 687, 688
v. Witte	ii. 874
Wall v. Arvington	i. 179
v. Stubbs	i. 222
v. Wall	ii. 437
Wallace v. Greenwood	ii. 554
v. Holmes	ii. 683
v. Pomfret	ii. 449
v. Wallace	i. 313
Waller v. Armistead	i. 325
v. Portland	i. 301
Wallis v. Carpenter	ii. 651
v. Crimes	ii. 646, 647
v. Pipon	i. 552
v. Portland	ii. 373, 818, 819
v. Smith	ii. 651, 652
v. Woodland	ii. 404
Wallop v. Portsmouth	ii. 391
Wallwyn v. Coutts	ii. 117, 272, 273, 290, 315, 364, 379, 529
v. Lee	i. 416; ii. 24
Walmesley v. Booth	i. 313, 319, 321, 342, 343
Walmsley v. Child	i. 89, 90, 91, 93, 94, 95
Walsh v. Gladstone	ii. 510
v. Wason	ii. 752
Walter v. Hodge	ii. 704
v. Saunders	ii. 743
v. Selfe	ii. 229
v. Walter	ii. 701
Walters v. Morgan	ii. 71
v. Northern Coal Co.	i. 694
v. Walters	i. 590
Waltham's Case	i. 201
Walton v. Hargroves	ii. 576
v. Hobbs	ii. 855
Walworth v. Holt	i. 677
Wanless v. United States	ii. 358
Ward v. Arredondo	ii. 62
Ward v. Audland	ii. 23, 118
v. Buckingham	ii. 26, 39
v. Byrne	i. 294
v. Dudley	i. 584, 634
v. Jenkins	ii. 343
v. Morrison	ii. 367
v. Peck	i. 78
v. Shallet	i. 380
v. Society of Attorneys	ii. 867
v. Turner	i. 607, 608, 610, 611, 614, 616
v. Webber	i. 178
Wardell v. Union Pacific R. Co.	i. 332
Warden v. Jones	i. 382; ii. 290
v. Richards	ii. 387
Warder v. Tucker	i. 111, 118
Wardlaw v. Wardlaw	i. 180
Wardour v. Binsford	i. 261
Wardwell v. Wardwell	ii. 673
Ware v. Egmont	i. 218, 404, 405
v. Gardner	i. 365, 367
v. Horwood	ii. 5, 173, 206, 211
v. Owens	i. 683
v. Polhill	ii. 689
v. Regent's Canal Co.	ii. 866
v. Thompson	i. 306
v. Watson	ii. 530
Warfield v. Booth	i. 293
v. Fisk	ii. 694
Waring v. Ayres	ii. 82
v. Hotham	i. 622, 625
v. Lewis	ii. 206
v. Ward	ii. 599
v. Waring	i. 238, 250
Warlick v. White	ii. 704
Warmstrey v. Tanfield	ii. 348
Warner v. Bates	ii. 406
v. Baynes	i. 662, 664
v. Bennett	ii. 652
v. Conant	ii. 873
v. Gouverneur	ii. 164
v. Jacob	ii. 332
v. Willington	ii. 81
Warnton v. May	ii. 208
Warre, Ship, in re	ii. 354, 378
Warren v. Rudall	ii. 416
v. Swett	i. 218, 402, 405
v. Warren	i. 574, 637; ii. 449
Warrick v. Queen's College	ii. 816
Warrington v. Wheatstone	ii. 141
Warwick v. Warwick	i. 179, 414
Washburn v. Bank of Bellows Falls	i. 653, 683, 684
v. Miller	ii. 234
v. Pond	ii. 336
Washington v. Barnes	ii. 206
Wass v. Mugridge	ii. 96

CASES CITED.

Wasson v. Davis	ii. 570
Wastneys v. Chappell	ii. 291
Waterbury Bank v. Lawler	ii. 14
Waterer v. Waterer	i. 683
Waterhouse v. Stansfield	ii. 60
Waterlow v. Bacon	ii. 193
Waterman v. Seeley	ii. 534
Waters v. Howard	ii. 33
v. Mattinglay	i. 199
v. Riley	i. 178
v. Taylor	i. 676, 677, 681, 682, 688; ii. 211
v. Tazewell	i. 278
v. Travis	ii. 103, 104
v. Waters	ii. 782
Watertown v. Cowen	ii. 223, 231
Watford Ry. Co. v. London Ry. Co.	i. 456
Wathan v. Smith	ii. 445
Watkins v. Cheek	i. 591; ii. 473, 474, 475
v. Flanagan	i. 524
v. Maule	i. 103; ii. 47
v. Peck	i. 405
v. Specht	ii. 278
v. Worthington	i. 518
Watkinson v. Bernardiston	ii. 587
Watkyns v. Watkyns	ii. 701, 750, 758, 759, 761
Watmough, In re	ii. 526
Watney v. Wells	i. 332, 673
Watson, In re	ii. 694
v. Allcock	i. 338
v. Erb	ii. 537
v. Hunter	i. 537; ii. 222
v. Lincoln	ii. 458, 459
v. Mahan	ii. 80
v. Mid-Wales Ry. Co.	ii. 772
v. Northumberland	i. 657, 659
v. Planters' Bank	i. 216
v. Reid	ii. 95
v. Saul	ii. 847
v. Sutherland	i. 25
v. Watson	i. 117, 118; ii. 424, 437, 450
v. Wellington	ii. 364, 365, 378
Watt v. Grove	i. 323; ii. 124
v. Scofield	i. 406
v. White	ii. 574, 576
Watts v. Burnett	i. 216
v. Brooks	i. 302
v. Cummins	i. 157
v. Girdlestone	ii. 609, 618
v. Kinney	i. 522
v. Shuttleworth	i. 335
v. Waddle	ii. 95, 103
Way v. Patty	ii. 569
Weakley v. Gurley	i. 556
Weal v. Lower	i. 107; ii. 349
Weale v. Water Works Co.	ii. 58
Weall v. Rice	ii. 439, 440, 442, 447, 448, 453, 456
Weaver, In re	ii. 694
v. Poyer	ii. 206
v. Shryork	i. 177, 178
Web v. Web	i. 693
Webb, In matter of	ii. 695, 696
v. Alexandria	i. 112, 113, 122
v. Cleverden	i. 194, 198, 199
v. Hewitt	i. 336
v. Hughes	ii. 100
v. Lymington	ii. 19
v. Manchester Ry. Co.	ii. 867
v. Parker	i. 154
v. Sadler	ii. 399, 553
v. Shaftesbury	i. 489, 490; ii. 435, 689
Webber v. Hunt	ii. 620
v. Smith	ii. 653
v. Webber	i. 604
Webster's Appeal	i. 514
Webster v. Bailey	i. 215
v. Cecil	ii. 90
v. Cook	i. 344
v. Gray	ii. 75
v. Pawson	ii. 838
v. Stark	i. 109
v. Van Steenburgh	i. 416
v. Woodford	i. 240
Wedderburn, In re	ii. 617
v. Wedderburn	i. 325, 473, 686; ii. 848
Wedel v. Herman	i. 156
Wedgewood v. Adams	ii. 59
Weed v. Weed	i. 116
Weeds v. Bristow	ii. 398
Weeks v. Gore	i. 590
v. Staker	ii. 174
v. Weeks	i. 262
Weir v. Bell	i. 212, 213, 214
v. Mundell	ii. 41
Weise's Appeal	ii. 90, 103
Wekett v. Raby	ii. 21, 22
Welby v. Rutland	ii. 175
v. Welby	i. 243; ii. 423, 425, 433, 434
Welch v. Burris	ii. 686
v. Mandeville	ii. 378
v. Parran	i. 524
v. Priest	i. 416
Weld v. Lancaster	i. 295
v. Rees	i. 256
Well v. Thornagh	i. 194
Welland Canal Co. v. Hathaway	i. 389

CASES CITED.

Wellbeloved v. Jones	ii. 484
Weller v. Smeaton	ii. 175, 177
v. Weyand	ii. 52
Welles v. Middleton	i. 314, 317, 320, 321
Wellesley v. Beaufort	ii. 667, 672, 673, 674, 676
v. Mornington	i. 263
v. Wellesley	ii. 47, 221, 577, 578, 662, 667, 668, 674, 678, 679, 681, 682, 683, 685
Wellington v. Mackintosh	i. 676
Wellman v. Bowring	ii. 399
Wells v. Banister	i. 394
v. Beall	i. 627
v. Carpenter	i. 691
v. Cooper	i. 457, 470
v. Doane	ii. 493
v. Foster	i. 297; ii. 353, 356, 357
v. Hubbell	i. 529
v. McCall	ii. 714
v. Millett	ii. 90, 103
v. Morrow	i. 407
v. Newton	ii. 401
v. Tucker	i. 607, 609, 611, 616
v. Wells	ii. 398
v. Yates	i. 157
Welsh, In re	i. 333
v. Bayand	ii. 81
v. Freeman	i. 662
v. Usher	ii. 322
v. Welsh	i. 359, 379, 384
Wendell v. Van Rensselaer	i. 321, 390, 395
Wentworth v. Lloyd	i. 323
Werner v. Leisen	i. 680, 682
Wertz's Appeal	ii. 592
Wesson v. Washburn Iron Co.	ii. 228
West v. Belches	i. 522
v. Erissey	i. 172, 173, 179; ii. 289
v. Forsythe	ii. 674
v. Knight	ii. 483, 504, 521
v. Randall	ii. 854
v. Raymond	ii. 373
v. Reid	i. 397; ii. 324
v. Shuttleworth	ii. 493, 494
v. Skip	i. 687; ii. 589, 604
v. Sloan	i. 331
Westerdell v. Dale	ii. 368
Westerlo v. DeWitt	i. 610
Western v. McDermott	ii. 232, 860
v. Russell	i. 254
Western Assur. Soc., Ex parte	ii. 564, 570
Western Bank v. Addie	i. 213
Western R. Co. v. Bayne	ii. 32, 179, 180
Western Transp. Co. v. Lansing	ii. 81
Westfaling v. Westfaling	i. 574; ii. 559
West Jersey R. Co. v. Thomas	ii. 792
Westley v. Clarke	ii. 625, 627
Westmeath v. Salisbury	ii. 761, 762, 763, 764
v. Westmeath	ii. 761, 762, 763
Westmoreland v. Powell	i. 373
Weston v. Barker	ii. 272, 346
v. Collins	ii. 99
v. Metropolitan Asylum Dist.	ii. 656
v. Wilson	i. 151
Wetherbee v. Baker	i. 557
v. Dunn	i. 103, 621
Wetherby v Dixon	ii. 460
Wethered v. Wethered	i. 269, 350; ii. 353, 354
Wetmore v. Parker	ii. 495
v. White	ii. 77
Weymouth v. Boyer	i. 79
Whale v. Booth	i. 565, 589, 591
Whaley v. Bagenal	ii. 71, 73, 85
v. Dawson	i. 510, 625, 660
v. Norton	i. 300
Whalley v. Whalley	i. 339; ii. 850
Wharton v Durham	ii. 447, 453, 456, 457
v. May	i. 350, 353, 542; ii. 209
Wheatley v. Chrisman	ii. 230
v. Slade	ii. 125
Wheatly v. Westminster Coal Co.	ii. 34
Wheaton v. Calhoun	i. 522
v. Peters	ii. 247
Wheeler, Ex parte	ii. 673
v. Bingham	i. 289, 290
v. Caryl	i. 380
v. Conn. Ins. Co.	ii. 653, 655
v. Horne	i. 446, 448
v. Kirtland	i. 180; ii. 598
v. Le Merchant	i. 78; ii. 821
v. Reynolds	ii. 68, 76, 77
v. Sheers	ii. 546, 547
v. Smith	i. 116; ii. 282, 491
v. Sumner	ii. 313
v. Tootel	i. 489
v. Wheeler	ii. 315
Whelan v. McCreary	i. 64, 414
v. Reilly	ii. 398
v. Sullivan	ii. 81
Wheldale v. Partridge	ii. 113
Whelen's Appeal	i. 118, 130
Whichcote v. Lawrence	i. 327
Whicherly v. Whicherly	ii. 855
Whicker v. Hume	ii. 494
Whistler v. Newman	ii. 734
v. Webster	ii. 431, 433, 434, 438

CASES CITED.

Whitaker v. Bond	ii. 91
v. Newman	ii. 781
v. Rush	ii. 767, 769, 773, 776, 778
v. Wright	i. 560
Whitbread, Ex parte	ii. 323
v. Brockhurst	ii. 71, 74, 78, 85
Whitcher v. Hall	ii. 195
Whitchurch v. Bevis	ii. 69, 71, 73, 78, 83, 84, 88, 89
v. Golding	i. 90, 91
v. Whitchurch	ii. 298, 299, 302
Whitcomb v. Minchin	i. 330
White, —— v.	ii. 128
v. Arlett	ii. 648
v. Baring	ii. 587
v. Buss	i. 308
v. Butcher	ii. 58
v. Cox	i. 244
v. Crow	i. 261; ii. 197, 206
v. Cudden	ii. 66
v. Damon	i. 255; ii. 59
v. Dobson	ii. 101
v. Evans	ii. 546, 547
v. Hall	ii. 62, 209, 634
v. Hampton	i. 455
v. Hicks	ii. 388
v. Hillacre	i. 422, 558; ii. 328
v. Howard	ii. 113
v. Hussey	i. 384
v. Langdon	ii. 863
v. Lincoln	i. 476
v. Madison	i. 205
v. McNett	ii. 734
v. Nutt	i. 105
v. Parnther	i. 428, 592; ii. 328, 333, 334, 338, 843, 844, 846
v. Peterborough	ii. 158, 163, 164
v. Polleys	i. 572, 638, 640
v. Port Huron R. Co.	ii. 652
v. Sawyer	i. 214
v. Sheldon	ii. 535
v. Small	i. 247
v. Smith	i. 311
v. Stover	ii. 574
v. Thornborough	ii. 288
v. Ward	i. 323
v. Warner	ii. 656, 659
v. White	i. 500; ii. 398, 480, 494, 501, 502, 504, 523, 792
v. Williams	i. 451, 601; ii. 90
v. Wilson	i. 179; ii. 781
Whitehead, In re	i. 27, 30
v. Bennett	ii. 654
v. Brown	i. 179
Whitehead v. Kitson	ii. 239, 240
v. Wooten	ii. 316
Whitehouse v. Partridge	ii. 801, 803, 804
Whitehurst v. Green	ii. 197
Whitfield, Ex parte	ii. 663, 685
v. Bewit	i. 535, 537
v. Faussat	i. 64, 88, 90, 92; ii. 354
v. Hales	ii. 676
Whiting v. Burke	i. 509, 510, 512
v. Hill	i. 309
v. Whiting	i. 659, 667
Whitlock v. Duffield	ii. 40, 81
Whitmel v. Farrel	ii. 57
Whitmore, Ex parte	ii. 759, 803
v. Mackeson	i. 31
v. Oxborn	i. 558
v. Thornton	ii. 204
Whitney v. Smith	ii. 617
v. Stone	ii. 28
v. Union R. Co.	ii. 55
v. Wheeler	i. 609
Whitridge v. Parkhurst	ii. 77
Whittemore v. Farrington	i. 109, 149
v. Gibbs	ii. 314
v. Whittemore	ii. 104
Whitten v. Russell	i. 59, 106, 264
Whittingham v. Burgoyne	ii. 214
Whittington v. Wright	i. 392
Whittle v. Henning	ii. 437
v. Skinner	ii. 335
Whitworth v. Guagain	ii. 828
v. Harris	i. 674; ii. 35
Whorewood v. Whorewood	ii. 757, 759
Whyte v. Ahrens	ii. 822
v. O'Brien	ii. 771
Wibdey v. Cooper Co.	i. 122
Wicherly v. Wicherly	i. 445
Wickenden v. Rayson	i. 640
Wickes v. Clarke	i. 361, 364, 380; ii. 708, 709, 750
Wickham v. Wickham	ii. 222
Wickiser v. Cook	i. 324
Wickliffe v. Breckenridge	i. 412
Wicks, Ex parte	i. 297
Widmore v. Woodroffe	ii. 398, 483
Widows' Case	i. 678
Wier v. Tucker	i. 545; ii. 822
Wigg v. Nicholl	i. 579; ii. 513
Wiggen v. Swett	i. 496
Wiggin v. Bush	i. 386
v. Dorr	i. 514, 637, 642
v. Heywood	i. 413; ii. 557
v. Wiggin	ii. 74
Wiggins v. Burkam	i. 544, 545
v. Ingleton	i. 480
Wiggle v. Owen	ii. 688

Wigglesworth v. Steers	i. 244
Wigley v. Beauchamp	ii. 429
Wigsell v. Wigsell	i. 499
Wikoff v. Davis	ii. 580
Wilbur v. Howe	i. 295
Wilcox v. Drake	ii. 673
— v. Fairhaven Bank	i. 515
— v. Wheeler	ii. 228, 234
— v. Wilcox	i. 580, 684; ii. 445, 446
Wilcoxon v. Galloway	ii. 104
Wild v. Banning	ii. 534
— v. Hobson	i. 441
— v. Milne	i. 661
Wildbridge v. Paterson	i. 384
Wilde v. Gibson	i. 413
Wilder v. Lee	i. 86
— v. Pigott	ii. 693
Wildgrove v. Wayland	i. 407
Wiley v. Mahood	i. 637
Wilhelm v. Caylor	ii. 842
Wilkerson v. Cheatham	i. 377
Wilkes v. Clarke	i. 431
— v. Collin	ii. 342
— v. Ferris	ii. 343
— v. Holmes	i. 186
— v. Smith	ii. 570
— v. Steward	ii. 618
— v. Wilkes	ii. 9, 761
Wilkin v. Wilkin	i. 444, 659, 662
Wilkins v. Aiken	ii. 237, 240, 242, 244, 245, 246
— v. Finch	i. 556
— v. Hogg	ii. 615
— v. Rotherham	i. 488
— v. Stearns	ii. 607
Wilkinson, In re	ii. 388
— v. Barber	ii. 526
— v. Brayfield	i. 243
— v. Clements	ii. 45
— v. Dent	ii. 430, 431
— v. Henderson	i. 177, 685, 686
— v. Joughin	i. 193
— v. L'Eaugler	i. 308
— v. Lindgren	ii. 494
— v. Nelson	i. 184
— v. Simson	ii. 318, 341
— v. Stafford	i. 472
Willamin v. Dunn	i. 310
Willan v. Lancaster	ii. 592
— v. Willan	i. 129, 130, 135, 144, 248; ii. 5
Willard v. Eastham	ii. 729, 735
— v. Reas	ii. 570
— v. Taylor	ii. 96
— v. Ware	ii. 388
Willcox v. Foster	i. 152, 153
Willcox v. Lucas	i. 156, 157, 158
Willett v. Blandford	i. 332
Willey v. Thompson	i. 590
Williams's Appeal	i. 263
Williams, Ex parte	ii. 604
— In re	ii. 494
— v. Ayrault	ii. 211
— v. Briscoe	ii. 81
— v. Callow	ii. 758
— v. Carle	i. 273
— v. Chitty	ii. 591
— v. Cooke	i. 541
— v. Craddock	ii. 829
— v. Davies	ii. 771, 772
— v. Evans	ii. 76
— v. Everett	ii. 348, 362, 363, 364
— v. Fitzhugh	i. 306
— v. Flight	ii. 10
— v. Griffith	i. 460
— v. Halbert	ii. 141
— v. Harden	i. 79
— v. Hart	ii. 96
— v. Jackson	ii. 279
— v. Jersey	ii. 230, 262
— v. Jones	ii. 546
— v. Jordan	ii. 81
— v. Kershaw	ii. 496, 512
— v. Lambe	i. 64, 416, 634, 635
— v. Lee	ii. 203, 204
— v. Lonsdale	ii. 530
— v. Lucas	ii. 598
— v. Neville	ii. 67
— v. New York Central R. Co.	ii. 232
— v. Nixon	ii. 624, 628
— v. Nolan	ii. 197
— v. Owens	i. 424, 515
— v. Prince of Wales Assur. Co.	ii. 253
— v. Protheroe	ii. 370, 374, 377
— v. Purdy	i. 590
— v. Rawlinson	i. 466
— v. Sand	i. 141
— v. Smith	ii. 230
— v. Steward	ii. 57, 58, 107
— v. Stratton	ii. 322
— v. Thorp	ii. 379
— v. Urmston	ii. 730
— v. Vreeland	ii. 105
— v. Walker	ii. 141
— v. Wiggand	i. 661
— v. Williams	i. 314, 405; ii. 258, 406, 491, 503
— v. Wright	ii. 141
Williamson v. Barbour	i. 413, 512
— v. Codrington	ii. 289
— v. Curtis	ii. 471

CASES CITED.

Williamson v. Gihon	i. 268, 270
v. Moriarty	i. 314
v. Naylor	ii. 852
Willie v. Lugg	ii. 328
Willis v. Brown	ii. 493
v. Jernegan	i. 247, 248, 339, 544
v. Matthews	ii. 80
v. Parkinson	i. 624
v. Vallette	i. 218, 404, 406
Willisford v. Watson	ii. 794
Willison v. Watkins	i. 546; ii. 845
Willmot v. Barber	i. 85, 118, 154; ii. 91
Willoughby v. Bridcoke	i. 344
v. Middleton	ii. 437
v. Willoughby	ii. 298, 301, 302, 825
Wills v. Maccarmic	ii. 789
v. Sayers	ii. 711, 712
v. Slade	i. 661, 664, 668
v. Stradling	ii. 74, 79, 80, 85
Willson v. Barton	ii. 341
Wilmot v. Maccabe	ii. 819
Wilson's Case	i. 387; ii. 324
Wilson, Ex parte	i. 337; ii. 319
v. Atkinson	ii. 397
v. Cluer	ii. 316
v. Coxwell	i. 590
v. Darlington	i. 584
v. Duncan	i. 662
v. Farrand	ii. 210
v. Fielding	i. 565, 567, 574
v. Foreman	ii. 548
v. Furness Ry. Co.	ii. 40
v. Greenwood	i. 680
v. Harman	i. 489
v. Hart	i. 405; ii. 233, 348
v. Hunter	i. 407
v. Ivat	i. 601
v. Jones	ii 615
v. Mason	ii. 606
v. McKeehan	i. 580
v. Miller	i. 331
v. Moore	ii. 605, 606
v. Northampton Ry. Co.	ii. 821
v. O'Leary	ii. 464
v. Pack	ii. 704
v. Paul	i. 567
v. Pigott	ii. 445
v. Riddle	i. 455
v. Stewart	i. 518
v. Thornbury	ii. 437
v. Townshend	ii. 417, 435
v. Troup	ii. 326, 550
v. Turner	ii. 386
v. West Hartlepool Ry. Co.	ii. 46, 861
v. Wills Valley R. Co.	ii. 867
Wilson v. Wilson	ii. 53, 424, 739, 759, 762
v. Wormal	i. 437
Wilt v. Franklin	ii. 344
Wilton v. Harwood	ii. 74
Wiltshire v. Rabbits	ii. 339
Winans v. Wilkie	ii. 341
Winch v. Brutton	ii. 410
v. James	ii. 692
v. Page	ii. 737
v. Rich. Ry. Co.	ii. 868
v. Winchester	i. 173, 174, 220; ii. 92
Winchelsea v. Norcliffe	ii. 689
v. Norfolk	i. 554
Winchester v. Ball	ii. 335
v. Beaver	ii. 215
v. Charter	i. 373
v. Fournier	ii. 10
v. Grosvenor	i. 155
v. Guddy	i. 374
v. Knight	i. 74, 476, 534, 536
v. Paine	i. 411, 412; ii. 215
Wind v. Jekyll	i. 549, 553, 600; ii. 348
Winegar v. Newland	i. 30
Wing v. Ayer	i. 636
v. Harvey	ii. 654, 659
v. Merchant	i. 609, 610, 614
Wingate v. Haywood	ii. 198, 872
Winged v. Lefebury	ii. 110
Winn v. Williams	i. 399
Winne v. Reynolds	ii. 98, 103
Winona R. Co. v. St. Paul R. Co.	i. 70
Winship v. Pitts	ii. 222
Winslow v. Cummings	ii. 504
Winstone's Case	i. 670
Winston v. Browning	i. 156
v. McAlpine	i. 528
Winter v. Anson	ii. 566, 569
v. D'Evreux	ii. 49
Winterfield v. Strauss	ii. 206
Winton v. Fort	ii. 130
Winty v. Weakes	ii. 55
Wisden v. Wisden	ii. 592
Wise v. Fuller	i. 207
Wiseley v. Findlay	i. 661
Wiseman v. Beake	i. 343
v. Roper	ii. 57
v. Westland	i. 409
Wiser v. Blachley	i. 167, 179
Withers v. Pinchard	ii. 49, 50
Withington v. Warren	ii. 789
Withy v. Cottle	ii. 41, 43, 125
v. Mangles	ii. 397, 398, 402
Witley v. Price	i. 355
Witt v. Grand Gros	i. 394
Witte v. Clarke	i. 637, 639

CASES CITED.

Witter v. Witter	ii. 689
Witts v. Boddington	ii. 385
v. Dawkins	ii. 722
Woffington v. Shaw	i. 519
v. Sparks	i. 506
Wofford v. Board of Police	ii. 12
Wolcott v. Jones	ii. 202, 767
Wolf v. Smith	i. 637, 639
Wolf Creek Co. v. Shultz	ii. 648
Wolff v. Shelton	ii. 790
Wollaston v. Hakewell	i. 494, 495
v. King	ii. 431
v. Tribe	ii. 23
Wollstonecraft, Ex parte	ii. 677, 678
Wolverhampton Bank v. Marston	i. 377
Wolverhampton Ry. Co. v. London & N. Ry. Co.	ii. 42
Wommack v. Whitmore	i. 661
Wonson v. Fenno	ii. 91, 126
Wood v. Abrey	i. 251, 344, 345
v. Birch	ii. 582
v. Burnham	ii. 275
v. Cochrane	i. 410
v. Cone	ii. 112
v. Cox	ii. 282, 407, 408, 412, 530
v. Dixie	i. 376
v. Downes	i. 314, 317, 320, 321, 326, 353, 354; ii. 330, 372, 373
v. Dummer	ii. 603, 604
v. Griffith	ii. 103, 104, 373, 374, 376, 792, 793, 795
v. Hubbell	i. 105
v. Humphrey	ii. 794
v. Keyes	ii. 112
v. Mann	i. 61; ii. 825, 827
v. McCann	i. 296
v. Myrick	ii. 615
v. Norman	ii. 582
v. Patterson	i. 154
v. Rabe	i. 311
v. Rowcliffe	ii. 24, 32, 38, 39
v. Scarth	ii. 90
v. Steele	770
v. Sullens	ii. 570
v. Truax	ii. 689
v. White	ii. 383, 469
v. Woad	ii. 263
v. Wood	ii. 401, 717
Woodbury v. Luddy	ii. 53, 104
Woodbury Bank v. Charter Oak Ins. Co.	i. 121, 155
Woodcock's Case	i. 387
Woodcock v. Bennet	ii. 109, 124, 127, 128
Woode v. Fenwick	i. 252
Woodford v. Stephens	ii. 536
Woodgate v. Field	i. 559
Woodhouse v. Hoskins	ii. 295
v. Meredith	i. 305, 322
v. Shipley	i. 275, 280, 281
v. Woodhouse	ii. 847
Woodman v. Blake	ii. 646
v. Freeman	i. 27
v. Kilbourn Manuf. Co.	ii. 225
Woodmeston v. Walker	ii. 710, 713
Woodreff v. Barton	i. 261
Woodroffe v. Farnham	i. 307
Woodruff v. Erie Ry. Co.	ii. 41
Woods v. Huntingford	i. 586
v. Monroe	ii. 11
v. Reeves	ii. 554
v. Woods	ii. 398
Woodward, Ex parte	ii. 677
v. Aspinwall	ii. 34
v. Schatzell	ii. 804
Woodworth v. Campbell	i. 664, 668
v. Gorton	ii. 14
v. Paige	i. 402
v. Van Buskerk	ii. 198
Woody v. Old Dominion Ins. Co.	ii. 41
Woolam v. Hearn	i. 167, 168, 170, 174; ii. 87
Woolaston v. Wright	ii. 143
Wooldridge v. Norris	i. 514, 527
Wooley v. Drew	i. 249, 256
Woollam v. Hearn	ii. 92, 94
Woollands v. Crowcher	ii. 748
Woolscombe, Ex parte	ii. 673
Woolstencroft v. Woolstencroft	ii. 596
Woolstoncroft v. Long	i. 568
Wooten v. Bellinger	ii. 560
Worcester v. Eaton	i. 302, 303
Workman v. Mifflin	i. 496
Wormald v. Maitland	i. 405, 418
Wormley v. Wormley	ii. 471, 476, 609
Worral v. Worral	i. 433
Worrall's Appeal	ii. 618
Worrall v. Jacob	i. 123; ii. 761, 762, 763
v. Morlar	ii. 576
v. Munn	ii. 111
Worseley v. De Mattos	i. 376, 398, 400, 427
v. Johnson	ii. 401
v. Scarborough	i. 411, 414
Worthen v. Badgett	ii. 15
Worthington v. Evans	i. 292
Worthy v. Tate	i. 26, 93
Wortley v. Birkhead	i. 419, 422; ii. 827
Wortman v. Price	ii. 714
Wotherspoon v. Currie	ii. 255, 256, 257

CASES CITED.

Wotten v. Copeland	i. 664
Wragge's Case	ii. 347
Wray v. Steele	ii. 535, 542
v. Williams	i. 634
Wren v. Bradley	i. 292
v. Weild	ii. 239
Wrexham v. Hudleston	i. 681
Wride v. Clarke	i. 567, 568, 570
Wright v. Atkyns	ii. 401, 407, 408, 411
v. Bell	ii. 36, 39, 41
v. Bircher	ii. 350, 353
v. Booth	i. 243
v. Cadogan	ii. 702, 718, 719
v. Cartwright	ii. 167, 292
v. Englefield	ii. 717, 719
v. Goff	i. 111, 150
v. Hake	i. 334
v. Hunter	i. 509, 510, 529
v. Laing	i. 461
v. Leonard	i. 392
v. Maidstone	i. 87
v. Morley	i. 337, 506, 515, 516, 517, 518, 521, 524, 527, 647; ii. 741, 758
v. Naylor	ii. 675, 683
v. Newton	i. 390
v. Nutt	i. 618
v. Pilling	i. 421
v. Pitt	i. 694
v. Proud	i. 314, 315, 320, 325, 326
v. Redgrave	ii. 189
v. Rider	i. 293
v. Ross	ii. 335
v. Russell	i. 178
v. Simpson	i. 336, 337, 524, 571, 647, 648, 649; ii. 170
v. Southwestern R. Co.	ii. 15
v. Tinsley	ii. 109
v. Troutman	ii. 575
v. Vanderplank	i. 311, 313
v. Ward	ii. 140, 148
v. Wilson	i. 256
v. Wright	i. 590, 616; ii. 81, 349, 353, 354
Wrightson v. Hudson	i. 408, 409
Wrigley v. Swainson	i. 273, 274
Wuesthoff v. Seymour	ii. 102
Wurt v. Page	ii. 554
Wyatt v. Barwell	i. 402, 409, 413
Wych v. Meal	ii. 824
Wyche v. Greene	i. 113
Wycherley v. Wycherley	ii. 109, 289
Wykham v. Wykham	i. 490
Wykoff v. Wykoff	ii. 280
Wyllie v. Wilkes	ii. 646
Wyman v. Babcock	ii. 321
v. Brown	i. 431
Wynch, Ex parte	ii. 404
Wynn v. Morgan	ii. 99, 102
v. Newborough	ii. 160
v. Williams	i. 417, 634
Wynne v. Callendar	i. 307; ii. 7, 10
v. Hank	ii. 406
v. Hawkins	ii. 408, 412
v. Warren	ii. 617
Wynstanley v. Lee	ii. 229, 232
Wynter v. Bold	ii. 303
Wyse v. Russell	ii. 41, 81
Wythe v. Henniker	i. 575, 576, 585
Wythes v. Labouchere	i. 414, 512

X.

Ximènes v. Franco	ii. 214

Y.

Yale v. Dederer	ii. 735
Yallop, Ex parte	ii. 542
Yarborough v. Thompson	ii. 137
Yard v. Ford	ii. 228
Yare v. Harrison	i. 604; ii. 165
Yates v. Bell	ii. 362, 363, 364
v. Boen	i. 242
v. Cole	i. 190
v. Compton	ii. 112
v. Finn	i. 332
v. Hambley	i. 532, 537
v. Madden	ii. 396
Yauger v. Skinner	ii. 13
Yeates v. Groves	ii. 366
Yeomans v. Chatterton	i. 386
v. Williams	ii. 21
York v. Landis	i. 515, 518
v. Pilkington	i. 540, 622, 625; ii. 175, 202
York Bank v. Carter	i. 377
York & Jersey Co. v. Associates of Jersey Co.	i. 640
Yost v. Devault	ii. 52
v. Mallicote	i. 156
Youell v. Allen	ii. 91
Young's Estate	ii. 736
Young, Ex parte	i. 473
v. Atkins	ii. 570
v. Cason	i. 152, 179, 396
v. Dumas	i. 377
v. Holmes	i. 599
v. Hughes	i. 322
v. Keighley	ii. 604
v. McGown	i. 111, 150

Young v. Morgan	i. 158, 514	**Z.**	
v. Peachy	i. 250, 311; ii. 89, 535, 536	Zamboco v. Casavetti	ii. 387
v. Rathbone	ii. 55, 102	Zane's Will	ii. 481
v. Smith	ii 286	Zebach v. Smith	ii. 387
v. Walter	ii. 792, 793	Zeigler v. Hughes	i. 314
v. Wood	ii. 570	Zeisweiss v. James	ii. 493, 504
v. Young	i. 433; ii. 22, 109, 290, 716	Zettelle v. Myers	i. 468
		Zoellner v. Zoellner	ii. 844
Youngblood v. Youngblood	i. 30	Zollman v. Moore	i. 112, 121
Younge, Ex parte	ii. 588	Zouch v. Parsons	i. 252, 253
v. Furse	i. 277, 288	Zule v. Zule	i. 496
Yovatt v. Winyard	ii. 258		

COMMENTARIES

ON

EQUITY JURISPRUDENCE.

COMMENTARIES

ON

EQUITY JURISPRUDENCE.

CHAPTER I.

THE TRUE NATURE AND CHARACTER OF EQUITY JURISPRUDENCE.

1. IN treating of the subject of Equity it is material to distinguish the various senses in which that word is used. For it cannot be disguised that an imperfect notion of what, in England, constitutes Equity Jurisprudence is not only common among those who are not bred to the profession, but that it has often led to mistakes and confusion in professional treatises on the subject. In the most general sense we are accustomed to call that Equity which in human transactions is founded in natural justice, in honesty and right, and which properly arises ex æquo et bono. In this sense it answers precisely to the definition of justice, or natural law, as given by Justinian in the Pandects. 'Justitia est constans et perpetua voluntas jus suum cuique tribuendi.' 'Jus pluribus modis dicitur. Uno modo, cum id quod semper æquum et bonum, jus dicitur, ut est jus naturale.' 'Juris præcepta sunt hæc; honeste vivere, alterum non lædere, suum cuique tribuere.'[1] And the word 'jus' is used in the same sense in the Roman law, when it is declared that 'jus est ars boni et æqui,'[2] where it means what we are accustomed to call jurisprudence.[3]

---

[1] Dig. Lib. 1, tit. 1, l. 10, 11.   [2] Dig. Lib. 1, tit. 1, l. 1.

[3] Grotius, after referring to the Greek word used to signify Equity, says, 'Latinis autem æqui prudentia vertitur, quæ se ita ad æquitatem habet, ut jurisprudentia ad justitiam.' Grotius de Æquitate, ch. 1, § 4. This distinction is more refined than solid, as the citation in the text shows. See also

2. Now it would be a great mistake to suppose that Equity, as administered in England or America, embraced a jurisdiction so wide and extensive as that which arises from the principles of natural justice above stated. Probably the jurisprudence of no civilized nation ever attempted so wide a range of duties for any of its judicial tribunals. Even the Roman law, which has been justly thought to deal to a vast extent in matters ex æquo et bono, never affected so bold a design.[1] On the contrary it left many matters of natural justice wholly unprovided for, from the difficulty of framing any general rules to meet them, and from the doubtful nature of the policy of attempting to give a legal sanction to duties of imperfect obligation, such as charity, gratitude, and kindness, or even to positive engagements of parties, where they are not founded in what constitutes a meritorious consideration.[2] Thus it is well known that in the Roman law, as well as in the common law, there are many pacts, or promises of parties (nude pacts), which produce no legal obligation capable of enforcement in foro externo, but which are left to be disposed of in foro conscientiæ only.[3] 'Cum nulla subest causa propter conventionem, hic constat non posse constitui obligationem. Igitur nuda pactio obligationem non parit.'[4] And again: 'Qui autem promisit sine causa, condicere quantitatem non potest, quam non dedit, sed ipsam obligationem.'[5] And hence the settled distinction, in that law, between natural obligations, upon which no action lay, but which were merely binding in conscience, and civil obligations, which gave origin to actions.[6] The latter were sometimes called

Taylor's Elements of the Civil Law, pp. 90 to 98. Cicero, Topic. § 2; II. ad Heren. 13; III. ad Heren. 2. Bracton has referred to the various senses in which 'jus' is used. 'Item,' says he, 'jus quandoque ponitur pro jure naturali, quod semper bonum et æquum est; quandoque pro jure civili tantum; quandoque pro jure prætorio tantum; quandoque pro eo tantum, quod competit ex sententia.' Bracton, lib. 1, ch. 4, p. 3. See Dr. Taylor's definition of 'lex' and 'jus.' Elem. Civ. Law, pp. 147, 148; Id. 178; Id. 40 to 43; Id. 55, 56; Id. 91.

[1] See Heinecc. Hist. Edit. L. 1, ch. 6; De Edictis Prætorum, §§ 7, 8, 9, 10, 11, 12; Id. §§ 18, 21 to 30; De Lolme on Eng. Const. B. 1, ch. 11.

[2] Ayliffe, Pand. B. 4, tit. 1, p. 420, &c.; 1 Kaims, Equity, Introd. p. 3; Francis, Maxims, Introd. pp. 5, 6, 7.

[3] Ayliffe, Pand. B. 4, tit. 2, pp. 424, 425; 1 Domat, Civ. Law, B. 1, tit. 1, § 5, arts. 1, 6, 9, 13.

[4] Dig. Lib. 2, tit. 14, l. 7, § 4.   [5] Dig. Lib. 12, tit. 7, l. 1.

[6] Ayliffe, Pand. B. 4, tit. 1, pp. 420, 421.

just, because of their perfect obligation in a civil sense; the former merely equitable, because of their imperfect obligation. 'Et justum appellatur,' says Wolfius, 'quicquid fit secundum jus perfectum alterius; æquum vero, quod secundum imperfectum.'[1] Cicero has alluded to the double sense of the word 'Equity' in this very connection. 'Æquitatis,' says he, 'autem vis est duplex; cujus altera directi et veri et justi, ut dicitur, æqui et boni ratione defenditur; altera ad vicissitudinem referendæ gratiæ pertinet; quod in beneficio gratia, in injuria ultio nominatur.'[2] It is scarcely necessary to add that it is not in this latter sense, any more than in the broad and general sense above stated, which Ayliffe has with great propriety denominated 'Natural Equity,' because it depends on and is supported by natural reason, that equity is spoken of as a branch of English Jurisprudence. The latter falls appropriately under the head of 'Civil Equity,' as defined by the same author, being deduced from and governed by such civil maxims as are adopted by any particular state or community.[3]

3. But there is a more limited sense in which the term is often used, and which has the sanction of jurists in ancient as well as in modern times, and belongs to the language of common life as well as to that of juridical discussions. The sense here alluded to is that in which it is used in contradistinction to strict law, or strictum et summum jus. Thus Aristotle has defined the very nature of equity to be the correction of the law wherein it is defective by reason of its universality.[4] The same sense is repeatedly recognized in the Pandects. 'In omnibus quidem, maxime tamen in jure, æquitas spectanda sit. Quotiens æquitas, desiderii naturalis ratio, aut dubitatio juris moratur, justis decretis res temperanda. Placuit in omnibus rebus præ-

---

[1] Wolff. Instit. Jur. Nat. et Gent. P. 1, ch. 3, § 83.
[2] Cic. Orat. Part. § 37.
[3] Ayliffe, Pand. B. 1, tit. 7, p. 37.
[4] Arist. Ethic. Nicom. L. 5, ch. 14, cited 1 Wooddes. Lect. (Lect. vii.) p. 193; Taylor, Elem. of Civ. Law, pp. 91, 92, 93; Francis, Maxims, 3; 1 Fonbl. Eq. B. 1, § 2, p. 5, note (e). Cicero, speaking of Galba, says that he was accustomed, 'Multa pro æquitate contra jus dicere.' Cic. de Oratore, Lib. 1, § 57. See also other passages, cited in Taylor's Elem. of the Civ. Law, 90, 91. Bracton defines equity as contradistinguished from law ('jus'), thus: 'Æquitas autem est rerum convenientia, quæ in paribus causis paria desiderat jura, et omnia bene coæquiparat; et dicitur æquitas, quasi æqualitas.' Bracton, Lib. 1, ch. 4, § 5, p. 3.

cipuam esse justitiæ æquitatisque, quam stricti juris rationem.'[1] Grotius and Puffendorf have both adopted the definition of Aristotle; and it has found its way, with approbation, into the treatises of most of the modern authors who have discussed the subject.[2]

4. In the Roman Jurisprudence we may see many traces of this doctrine, applied to the purpose of supplying the defects of the customary law, as well as to correct and measure the interpretation of the written and positive code. Domat accordingly lays it down, as a general principle of the civil law, that if any case should happen which is not regulated by some express or written law, it should have for a law the natural principles of equity, which is the universal law, extending to everything.[3] And for this he founds himself upon certain texts in the Pandects, which present the formulary in a very imposing generality. 'Hæc Æquitas suggerit, etsi jure deficiamur,' is the reason given for allowing one person to restore a bank or dam in the lands of another, which may be useful to him, and not injurious to the other.[4] (*a*)

---

[1] Dig. Lib. 50, tit. 17, 1. 85, 90; Cod. Lib. 3, tit. 1, 1. 8.

[2] Grotius de Æquitate, ch. 1, § 3; Puffend. Law of Nature and Nat. B. 5, ch. 12, § 21, and Barbeyrac's note (1); 1 Black. Comm. 61; 1 Wooddes. Lect. vii. p. 193; Bac. de Aug. Scient. Lib. 8, ch. 3, Aphor. 32, 35, 45. Grotius says, ' Proprie vero et singulariter æquitas est virtus voluntatis, correctrix ejus, quo lex propter universalitatem deficit.' Grotius de Æquitate, ch. 1, § 2. ' Æquum est id ipsum, quo lex corrigitur.' Id. Dr. Taylor has with great force paraphrased the language of Aristotle. ' That part of unwritten law,' says he, ' which is called Equity, or τὸ Ἐπιεικές, is a species of justice distinct from what is written. It must happen either against the design and inclination of the lawgiver, or with his consent. In the former case, for instance, when several particular facts must escape his knowledge; in the other, when he may be apprized of them indeed but by reason of their variety is not willing to recite them. For if a case admits of an infinite variety of circumstances, and a law must be made, that law must be conceived in general terms.' Taylor, Elem. Civ. Law, 92. And of this infirmity in all laws the Pandects give open testimony. ' Non possunt omnes articuli singillatim aut legibus, aut senatusconsultis comprehendi; sed cum in aliqua causa sententia eorum manifesta est, is, qui jurisdictioni præest, ad similia procedere, atque ita jus dicere debet.' Dig. Lib. 1, tit. 3, 1. 12; Id. 1. 10.

[3] 1 Domat, Prel. Book, tit. 1, § 1, art. 23. See also Ayliffe, Pand. B. 1, tit. 7, p. 38.

[4] Dig. Lib. 39, tit. 3, 1. 2, § 5. Domat cites other texts not perhaps quite

---

(*a*) It is held however that equity will not aid the doing of what would work no good to the plaintiff but only hardship to the defendant. Joliet

NATURE OF EQUITY.

5. The jurisdiction of the prætor doubtless had its origin in this application of equity, as contradistinguished from mere law. 'Jus autem civile,' say the Pandects, 'est, quod ex legibus, plebiscitis, senatusconsultis, decretis principum, auctoritate prudentum venit. Jus prætorium est, quod prætores introduxerunt, adjuvandi, vel supplendi, vel corrigendi juris civilis gratia, propter utilitatem publicam; quod et honorarium dicitur, ad honorem prætorum sic nominatum.'[1] But broad and general as this language is, we should be greatly deceived if it were to be supposed that even the prætor's power extended to the direct overthrow or disregard of the positive law. He was bound to stand by that law in all cases to which it was justly applicable, according to the maxim of the Pandects, 'Quod quidem perquam durum est; sed ita lex scripta est.'[2]

---

so stringent; such as Dig. Lib. 27, tit. 1, l. 13, § 7; Id. Lib. 47, tit. 20, l. 7. Dr. Taylor has given many texts to the same purpose. Elem. Civ. Law, pp. 90, 91. There was a known distinction in the Roman law on this subject. Where a right was founded in the express words of the law, the actions grounded on it were denominated Actiones Directæ; where they arose upon a benignant extension of the words of the law to other cases, not within the terms, but within what we should call the equity of the law, they were denominated Actiones Utiles. Taylor, Elem. Civ. Law, 93.

[1] Dig. Lib. 1, tit. 1, l. 7; Id. tit. 3, l. 10. 'Sed et eas actiones, quæ legibus proditæ sunt,' say the Pandects, 'si lex justa ac necessaria sit, supplet prætor in eo, quod legi deest.' Dig. Lib. 19, tit. 5, l. 11. Heineccius, speaking of the prætor's authority, says, 'His Edictis multa innovata, adjuvandi, supplendi, corrigendi juris civilis gratia, obtentuque utilitatis publicæ.' 1 Heinecc. Elem. Pand. P. 1, Lib. 1, § 42.

[2] Dig. Lib. 40, tit. 9, l. 12, § 1. See also 3 Black. Comm. 430, 431; 1 Wooddes. Lect. vii. pp. 192 to 200. Dr. Taylor (Elem. of the Civil Law, p. 214) has therefore observed, that for this reason this branch of the Roman law was not reckoned as part of the jus civile scriptum by Papinian, but stands in opposition to it. And thus, as we distinguish between common law and equity, there were with that people actiones civiles et prætoriæ, et obligationes civiles, et prætoriæ. The prætor was therefore called 'Custos, non conditor juris; judicia exercere potuit; jus facere non potuit; dicendi, non condendi juris potestatem habuit; juvare, supplere, interpretari, mitigare jus civile potuit; mutare vel tollere non potest.' The prætorian edicts are not properly law, though they may operate like law. And Cicero, speaking of contracts bonæ fidei, says, in allusion to the same jurisdiction, 'In his magni esse judicis statuere (præsertim cum in plerisque essent judicia contraria), quid

---

R. Co. v. Healy, 94 Ill. 416. But while equity will not aid in enforcing a mere legal right in such a case, it is held that equity will not enjoin the owner of the right from proceeding to exercise it. Clinton v. Myers, 46 N. Y. 511.

6. But a more general way in which this sense of Equity, as contradistinguished from mere law, or strictum jus, is applied, is to the interpretation and limitation of the words of positive or written laws; by construing them, not according to the letter, but according to the reason and spirit of them.[1] Mr. Justice Blackstone has alluded to this sense in his Commentaries, where he says: 'From this method of interpreting laws, by the reason of them, arises what we call Equity;'[2] and more fully in another place, where he says, 'Equity, in its true and genuine meaning, is the soul and spirit of all law; positive law is construed, and rational law is made by it. In this, Equity is synonymous with justice; in that, to the true and sound interpretation of the rule.'[3]

7. In this sense Equity must have a place in every rational system of jurisprudence, if not in name, at least in substance.[4] It is impossible that any code, however minute and particular, should embrace or provide for the infinite variety of human affairs, or should furnish rules applicable to all of them. 'Neque leges, neque senatusconsulta ita scribi possunt,' says the Digest, 'ut omnes casus, qui quandoque inciderint, comprehendantur; sed sufficit ea, quæ plerumque accidunt, contineri.'[5] Every system

---

quemque cuique præstare oporteret;' that is, he should decide according to equity and conscience. Cic. de Officiis, Lib. 3, cap. 17. Dr. Taylor has, in another part of his work, gone at large into equity and its various meanings in the civil law. Taylor, Elem. of Civil Law, pp. 90 to 98.

[1] Plowden, Comm. pp. 465, 466.
[2] 1 Black. Comm. pp. 61, 62.
[3] 3 Black. Comm. p. 429. See also Taylor, Elem. Civil Law, pp. 96, 97; Plowd. Comm. p. 465, Reporter's note. Dr. Taylor has observed that the great difficulty is to distinguish between that equity which is required in all law whatsoever, and which makes a very important and a very necessary branch of the jus scriptum, and that equity which is opposed to written and positive law, and stands in contradistinction to it. Taylor, Elem. Civil Law, p. 90.
[4] See 1 Fonbl. Equity, B. 1, § 3, p. 24, note (*h*); Plowden, Comm. p. 465, 466. Lord Bacon said, in his Argument on the jurisdiction of the Marches, 'There is no law under heaven which is not supplied with Equity; for "Summum jus summa injuria;" or as some have it, " Summa lex summa crux." And therefore all nations have equity.' 4 Bac. Works, p. 274. Plowden, in his note to his Reports, dwells much (pp. 465, 466) on the nature of equity in the interpretation of statutes, saying, 'Ratio legis est anima legis.' And it is a common maxim in the law of England that 'Apices juris non sunt jura.' Branch's Maxims, p. 12; Co. Litt. 304 (*b*).
[5] Dig. Lib. 1, tit. 3, l. 10.

of laws must necessarily be defective; and cases must occur to which the antecedent rules cannot be applied without injustice, or to which they cannot be applied at all. It is the office therefore of a judge to consider whether the antecedent rule does apply, or ought, according to the intention of the lawgiver, to apply to a given case; and if there are two rules nearly approaching to it, but of opposite tendency, which of them ought to govern it; and if there exists no rule applicable to all the circumstances, whether the party should be remediless, or whether the rule furnishing the closest analogy ought to be followed. The general words of a law may embrace all cases; and yet it may be clear that all could not have been intentionally embraced, for if they were, the obvious objects of the legislation might or would be defeated. So words of a doubtful import may be used in a law, or words susceptible of a more enlarged or of a more restricted meaning, or of two meanings equally appropriate.[1] The question in all such cases must be, in what sense the words are designed to be used; and it is the part of a judge to look to the objects of the Legislature, and to give such a construction to the words as will best further those objects. This is an exercise of the power of equitable interpretation. It is the administration of equity as contradistinguished from a strict adherence to the mere letter of the law. Hence arises a variety of rules of interpretation of laws according to their nature and operation, whether they are remedial, or are penal laws, whether they are restrictive of general right, or in advancement of public justice or policy; whether they are of universal application, or of a private and circumscribed intent.

---

[1] It is very easy to see from what sources Mr. Charles Butler drew his own statement (manifestly, as a description of English Equity Jurisprudence, incorrect, as Professor Park has shown), 'That equity, as distinguished from law, arises from the inability of human foresight to establish any rule which, however salutary in general, is not in some particular cases evidently unjust and oppressive, and operates beyond or in opposition to its intent, &c. The grand reason for the interference of a Court of Equity is, that the imperfection of the legal remedy, in consequence of the universality of legislative provisions, may be redressed.' 1 Butler's Reminisc. 37, 38, 39; Park's Introd. Lect. 5, 6. Now Aristotle or Cicero, or a Roman prætor, or a Continental jurist, or a publicist of modern Europe, might have used these expressions as a description of general Equity; but it would have given no just idea of equity as administered under the municipal jurisprudence of England.

But this is not the place to consider the nature or application of those rules.[1]

8. It is of this equity, as correcting, mitigating, or interpreting the law, that not only civilians but common law writers are most accustomed to speak;[2] and thus many persons are misled into the false notion that this is the real and peculiar duty of Courts of Equity in England and America. St. German, after alluding to the general subject of Equity, says: 'In some cases it is necessary to leave the words of the law, and to follow that reason and justice requireth, and to that intent equity is ordained, that is to say, to temper and mitigate the rigor of the law, &c. And so it appeareth that equity taketh not away the very right, but only that that seemeth not to be right by the general words of the law.'[3] And then he goes on to suggest the other kind of equity, as administered in chancery, to ascertain 'Whether the plaintiff hath title in conscience to

---

[1] See Grotius De Jure Belli ac Pacis, Lib. 3, ch. 20, § 47, pp. 1, 2; Grotius De Æquitate, ch. 1. This paragraph is copied very closely from the article 'Equity,' in Dr. Lieber's Encyclopædia Americana, a license which has not appropriated another person's labors. There will be found many excellent rules of interpretation of laws in Rutherforth's Institutes of Natural Law, B. 2, ch. 7; in Bacon's Abridgment, title 'Statute;' in Domat on the Civil Law (Prelim. Book, tit. 1, § 2); and in 1 Black. Comm. Introduction, pp. 58 to 62.

There are yet other senses in which Equity is used, which might be brought before the reader. The various senses are elaborately collected by Oldendorpius, in his work De Jure et Æquitate Disputatio; and he finally offers what he deems a very exact definition of Equity in its general sense. 'Æquitas est judicium animi, ex vera ratione petitum, de circumstantiis rerum, ad honestatem vitæ pertinentium, cum incidunt, recte discernens quid fieri aut non fieri oporteat.' This seems but another name for a system of ethics. Grotius has in one short paragraph (De Æquitate, ch. 1, § 2) brought together the different senses in a clear and exact manner. 'Et ut de Æquitate primum loquamur, scire oportet, æquitatem aut æquum de omni interdum jure dici, ut cum jurisprudentia ars boni et æqui dicitur; interdum de jure naturali absolute, ut cum Cicero ait, jus legibus, moribus, et Æquitate constare; alias vero de hisce rebus, quas lex non exacte definit, sed arbitrio viri boni permittit. Sæpe etiam de jure aliquo civili proprius ad jus naturale accedente, idque respectu alterius juris, quod paulo longius recedere videtur, ut jus prætorium et quædam jurisprudentiæ interpretationes. Proprie vero et singulariter Æquitas est virtus voluntatis, correctrix ejus, in quo lex propter universalitatem deficit.'

[2] See Merlin Répertoire, Equité; Grounds and Rudim. of the Law (attributed sometimes to Francis), pp. 3, 5, edit. 1751; 1 Fonbl. Equity, B. 1, ch. 1, § 2, note (e); 1 Wooddes. Lect. vii. pp. 192 to 200; Pothier, Pand. Lib. 1, tit. 3, art. 4, § 11 to 27.

[3] Dialogue, 1, ch. 16.

recover or not.'[1] And in another place he states: 'Equity is a rightwiseness, that considereth all the particular circumstances of the deed, which is also tempered with the sweetness of mercy.'[2] Another learned author lays down doctrines equally broad. 'As summum jus,' says he, 'summa est injuria, as it cannot consider circumstances; and as this [equity] takes in all the circumstances of the case, and judges of the whole matter, according to good conscience, this shows both the use and excellency of equity above any prescribed law.' Again: 'Equity is that which is commonly called equal, just, and good; and is a mitigation or moderation of the common law, in some circumstances, either of the matter, person, or time; and often it dispenseth with the law itself.'[3] 'The matters, of which equity holdeth cognizance in its absolute power, are such as are not remediable at law; and of them the sorts may be said to be as infinite, almost, as the different affairs conversant in human life.'[4] And he adds that 'equity is so extensive and various, that every particular case in equity may be truly said to stand upon its own particular circumstances; and therefore under favor I apprehend precedents not of that great use in equity, as some would contend, but that equity thereby may possibly be made too much a science for good conscience.'[5]

9. This description of equity differs in nothing essential from that given by Grotius and Puffendorf,[6] as a definition of general equity as contradistinguished from the equity which is recognized by the mere municipal code of a particular nation. And indeed it goes the full extent of embracing all things which the law has not exactly defined, but leaves to the arbitrary discretion of a judge; or, in the language of Grotius, ' de hisce rebus, quas lex non exacte definit, sed arbitrio viri boni permittit.'[7] So that in this view of the matter an English Court of Equity would

[1] Dialogue, 1, ch. 17.　　　　　　　　　　[2] Id. ch. 16.
[3] Grounds and Rudim. pp. 5, 6, edit. 1751.　　[4] Id. p. 6.
[5] Grounds and Rudim. pp. 5, 6, edit. 1751. Yet Francis (or whoever else was the author) is compelled to admit that there are many cases in which there is no relief to be had either at law or in equity itself; but the same is left to the conscience of the party, as a greater inconvenience would thence follow to the people in general. Francis, Max. p. 5.
[6] Grotius De Æquitate, ch. 1, §§ 3, 12; Puffend. Elem. Juris. Univ. L. 1, §§ 22, 23, cited 1 Fonbl. Eq. B. 1, ch. 1, § 2, note (e), p. 5.
[7] Grotius De Æquitate, ch. 1, § 2; 1 Fonbl. Equity, B. 1, ch. 1, § 2, note (e).

seem to be possessed of exactly the same prerogatives and powers as belonged to the prætor's forum in the Roman law.[1]

10. Nor is this description of the Equity Jurisprudence of England confined to a few text writers. It pervades a large class, and possesses the sanction of many high authorities. Lord Bacon more than once hints at it. In his Aphorisms he lays it down, 'Habeant similiter Curiæ Prætoriæ potestatem tam subveniendi contra rigorem legis, quam supplendi defectum legis.'[2] And on the solemn occasion of accepting the office of Chancellor, he said: 'Chancery is ordained to supply the law, and not to subvert the law.'[3] Finch, in his Treatise on the Law, says, that the nature of equity is to amplify, enlarge, and add to the letter of the law.[4] In the Treatise of Equity attributed to Mr. Ballow, and deservedly held in high estimation, language exceedingly broad is held on this subject. After remarking that there will be a necessity of having recourse to the natural principles, that what is wanting to the finite may be supplied out of that which is infinite, and that this is properly what is called equity, in opposition to strict law, he proceeds to state: 'And thus, in chancery, every particular case stands upon its own circumstances; and although the common law will not decree against the general rule of law, yet chancery doth, so as the example introduce not a general mischief. Every matter therefore that happens inconsistent with the design of the legislator, or is contrary to natural justice, may find relief here. For no man can be obliged to anything contrary to the law of nature; and indeed no man in his senses can be presumed willing to oblige another to it.'[5]

11. The Author has indeed qualified these propositions with the suggestion: 'But if the law has determined a matter with

[1] Dig. Lib. 1, tit. 1, l. 7. See also Heinecc. De Edict. Prætorum, Lib. 1, ch. 6, §§ 8 to 13; Id. §§ 18 to 30; Dr. Taylor's Elem. Civil Law, pp. 213 to 216; Id. 92, 93; De Lolme on Eng. Const. B. 1, ch. 11. Lord Kaims does not hesitate to say that the powers assumed by our Courts of Equity are in effect the same that were assumed by the Roman prætor from necessity, without any express authority. 1 Kaims, Eq. Introd. 19.

[2] Bac. De Aug. Scient. Lib. 8, ch. 3, Aphor. 35, 45.

[3] Bac. Speech, 4; Bac. Works, 488.

[4] Finch's Law, p. 20.

[5] 1 Fonbl. Eq. B. 1, ch. 1, § 3. The author of Eunomus describes the original jurisdiction of the Court of Chancery as a Court of Equity, to be 'the power of moderating the summum jus.' Eunomus, Dial. 3, § 60.

all its circumstances, equity cannot intermeddle.' But even with this qualification the propositions are not maintainable in the Equity Jurisprudence of England, in the general sense in which they are stated. For example, the first proposition, that equity will relieve against a general rule of law, is (as has been justly observed) neither sanctioned by principle nor by authority.[1] For though it may be true that equity has in many cases decided differently from Courts of Law, yet it will be found that these cases involved circumstances to which a Court of Law could not advert, but which, in point of substantial justice, were deserving of particular consideration, and which a Court of Equity, proceeding on principles of substantial justice, felt itself bound to respect.[2]

12. Mr. Justice Blackstone has taken considerable pains to refute this doctrine. 'It is said,' he remarks, 'that it is the business of a Court of Equity in England to abate the rigor of the common law.[3] But no such power is contended for. Hard was the case of bond creditors, whose debtor devised away his real estate; rigorous and unjust the rule which put the devisee in a better condition than the heir; yet a Court of Equity had no power to interfere. Hard is the common law still subsisting, that land devised or descending to the heir should not be liable to simple contract debts of the ancestor or devisor, although the money was laid out in purchasing the very land; and that the father shall never immediately succeed as heir to the real estate of the son. But a Court of Equity can give no relief; though in both these instances the artificial reason of the law, arising from feudal principles, has long since ceased.'[4] And illustrations of the same character may be found in every State of the Union. In some States bond debts have a privilege of priority of payment over simple contract debts, in cases of insolvent intestate estates. In others judgments are a privileged lien on lands. In many, if not in all, a debtor may prefer one creditor to another, in discharging his debts, when his assets are wholly insufficient to pay all the debts. And (not to multiply in-

---

[1] Com. Dig. Chancery, 3, F. 8.
[2] 1 Fonbl. Eq. B. 1, ch. 1, § 3, note (*g*); 1 Dane's Abridg. ch. 9, art. 1, §§ 2, 3; Kemp *v.* Prayer, 7 Ves. 249, 250.
[3] Grounds and Rudim. p. 74 (Max. 105), edit. 1751.
[4] 3 Black. Comm. 430. See Com. Dig. Chancery, 3 F. 8.

stances) what can be more harsh or indefensible than the rule of the common law by which a husband may receive an ample fortune in personal estate through his wife, and by his own act or will strip her of every farthing and leave her a beggar?

13. A very learned judge in equity, in one of his ablest judgments, has put this matter in a very strong light.[1] 'The law is clear,' said he, 'and Courts of Equity ought to follow it in their judgments concerning titles to equitable estates; otherwise great uncertainty and confusion would ensue. And though proceedings in equity are said to be "secundum discretionem boni viri;" yet when it is asked, "Vir bonus est quis?" the answer is "Qui consulta patrum, qui leges juraque servat." And as it is said in Rook's case (5 Rep. 99. b.), that discretion is a science, not to act arbitrarily, according to men's wills and private affections; so that discretion which is executed here is to be governed by the rules of law and equity, which are not to oppose, but each in its turn to be subservient to the other. This discretion in some cases follows the law implicitly; in others assists it, and advances the remedy; in others again it relieves against the abuse, or allays the rigor of it. But in no case does it contradict or overturn the grounds or principles thereof, as has been sometimes ignorantly imputed to the court. That is a discretionary power which neither this nor any other court, not even the highest, acting in a judicial capacity, is by the constitution entrusted with.'[2]

14. The next proposition, that every matter that happens inconsistent with the design of the legislator, or is contrary to natural justice, may find relief in equity, is equally untenable. There are many cases against natural justice, which are left wholly to the conscience of the party, and are without any redress, equitable or legal. And so far from a Court of Equity supplying universally the defects of positive legislation, or peculiarly carrying into effect the intent as contradistinguished from the text of the Legislature, it is governed by the same rules of

---

[1] Sir Joseph Jekyll, in Cowper *v.* Cowper, 2 P. Will. 753.

[2] Sir Thomas Clarke, in pronouncing his judgment in the case of Burgess *v.* Wheate (1 W. Black. R. 123), has adopted this very language, and given it his full approbation. See also 1 Fonbl. Eq. B. 1, ch. 1, § 3, note (*g*). See also Fry *v.* Porter, 1 Mod. R. 300; Grounds and Rudim. p. 65 (Max. 92), edit. 1751.

interpretation as a Court of Law, and is often compelled to stop where the letter of the law stops. It is the duty of every court of justice, whether of law or of equity, to consult the intention of the Legislature. And in the discharge of this duty a Court of Equity is not invested with a larger or a more liberal discretion than a Court of Law.[1]

15. Mr. Justice Blackstone has here again met the objection in a forcible manner. 'It is said,' says he, 'that a Court of Equity determines according to the spirit of the rule and not according to the strictness of the letter. But so also does a Court of Law. Both, for instance, are equally bound, and equally profess, to interpret statutes according to the true intent of the Legislature. In general, all cases cannot be foreseen; or, if foreseen, cannot be expressed. Some will arise which will fall within the meaning, though not within the words, of the legislator; and others, which may fall within the letter, may be contrary to his meaning, though not expressly excepted. These cases, thus out of the letter, are often said to be within the equity of an Act of Parliament; and so cases within the letter are frequently out of the equity. Here, by Equity we mean nothing but the sound interpretation of the law, &c. But there is not a single rule of interpreting laws, whether equitably or strictly, that is not equally used by the judges in the Courts both of Law and Equity. The construction must in both be the same; or, if they differ, it is only as one Court of Law may happen to differ from another. Each endeavors to fix and adopt the true sense of the law in question. Neither can enlarge, diminish, or alter that sense in a single tittle.'[2]

16. Yet it is by no means uncommon to represent that the peculiar duty of a Court of Equity is to supply the defects of the common law, and next, to correct its rigor or injustice.[3] Lord Kaims avows this doctrine in various places and in language singularly bold. 'It appears now clearly,' says he, 'that a Court of Equity commences at the limits of the common law, and enforces benevolence where the law of nature makes it our duty. And thus a Court of Equity, accompanying the law of nature, in its general refinements enforces every natural duty

---

[1] 1 Fonbl. Eq. B. 1, ch. 1, § 3, note (*h*).
[2] 3 Black. Comm. 431; 1 Dane, Abr. ch. 9, art. 3, § 3.
[3] 1 Kaims on Equity, B. 1, p. 40.

that is not provided for at common law.'[1] And in another place he adds, a Court of Equity boldly undertakes 'to correct or mitigate the rigor, and what in a proper sense may be termed the injustice of the common law.'[2] And Mr. Wooddeson, without attempting to distinguish accurately between general or natural, and municipal or civil, equity, asserts that 'Equity is a judicial interpretation of laws which, presupposing the legislator to have intended what is just and right, pursues and effectuates that intention.'[3]

17. The language of judges has often been relied on for the same purpose; and from the unqualified manner in which it is laid down, too often justifies the conclusion. Thus Sir John Trevor (the Master of the Rolls), in his able judgment in Dudley v. Dudley,[4] says: 'Now equity is no part of the law, but a moral virtue, which qualifies, moderates, and reforms the rigor, hardness, and edge of the law, and is a universal truth. It does also assist the law, where it is defective and weak in the constitution (which is the life of the law), and defends the law from crafty evasions, delusions, and mere subtilties, invented and contrived to evade and elude the common law, whereby such as have undoubted right are made remediless. And thus is the office of equity to protect and support the common law from shifts and contrivances against the justice of the law. Equity therefore does not destroy the law nor create it, but assists it.' Now however true this doctrine may be sub modo, to suppose it true in its full extent would be a grievous error.

18. There is another suggestion which has been often repeated; and that is, that Courts of Equity are not, and ought not to be, bound by precedents, and that precedents therefore are of little or no use there; but that every case is to be decided upon circumstances, according to the arbitration or discretion of

---

[1] 1 Kaims on Equity, Introd. p. 12.
[2] Id. Introd. p. 15. Lord Kaims's remarks are entitled to the more consideration, because they seem to have received in some measure at least the approbation of Lord Hardwicke (Parke's Hist. of Chan. Appx. 501, 502; Id. 333, 334); and also from Mr. Justice Blackstone's having thought them worthy of a formal refutation in his Commentaries. (3 Black. Comm. 436.)
[3] 1 Wooddeson, Lect. vii. p. 192.
[4] Preced. in Ch. 241, 244; 1 Wooddes. Lect. vii. p. 192.

the judge, acting according to his own notions ex æquo et bono.[1] Mr. Justice Blackstone, addressing himself to this erroneous statement, has truly said: 'The system of our Courts of Equity is a labored connected system, governed by established rules, and bound down by precedents from which they do not depart, although the reason of some of them may perhaps be liable to objection, &c. Nay, sometimes a precedent is so strictly followed, that a particular judgment, founded upon special circumstances, gives rise to a general rule.'[2] And he afterwards adds: 'The system of jurisprudence in our Courts of Law and Equity are now equally artificial systems, founded on the same principles of justice and positive law, but varied by different usages in the forms and mode of their proceedings.'[3] The value of precedents and the importance of adhering to them were deeply felt in ancient times, and nowhere more than in the prætor's forum. 'Consuetudinis autem jus esse putatur id,' says Cicero, 'quod, voluntate omnium, sine lege, vetustas comprobarit. In ea autem jura sunt, quædam ipsa jam certa propter

---

[1] See Francis, Max. pp. 5, 6; Selden, cited in 3 Black. Comm. 432, 433, 435; 1 Kaims, Eq. pp. 19, 20.

[2] 3 Black. Comm. 432, 433.

[3] 3 Black. 434; Id. 440, 441; 1 Kent, Comm. Lect. 21, pp. 489, 490 (2d edition). The value and importance of precedents in chancery were much insisted upon by Lord Keeper Bridgman, in Fry v. Porter (1 Mod. R. 300, 307). See also 1 Wooddes. Lect. vii. pp. 200, 201, 202. Lord Hardwicke in his letter to Lord Kaims on the subject of Equity, in answer to the question whether a Court of Equity ought to be governed by any general rules, said, 'Some general rules there ought to be; for otherwise the great inconvenience of jus vagum et incertum will follow. And yet the prætor must not be so absolutely and invariably bound by them as the judges are by the rules of the common law. For if they were so bound, the consequence would follow, which you very judiciously state, that he must sometimes pronounce decrees which would be materially unjust, since no rule can be equally just in the application to a whole class of cases that are far from being the same in every circumstance.' (Parke's Hist. of Chancery, pp. 501, 506.) This is very loosely said, and the reason given equally applies to every general rule; for there can be none which will be found equally just in its application to all cases. If every change of circumstance is to change the rule in equity, there can be no general rule. Every case must stand upon its own ground. Yet Courts of Equity now adhere as closely to general rules as Courts of Law. Each expounds its rules to meet new cases; but each is equally reluctant to depart from them upon slight inconveniences and mischiefs. See Mitford, Plead. in Eq. p. 4, note (b); 1 Fonbl Eq. B. 1, ch. 1, § 3, note (k). The late Professor Park of King's College, London, has made some very acute remarks on this whole subject in his Introductory Lecture on Equity (1832).

vetustatem; quo in genere et alia sunt multa, et eorum multo maxima pars, quæ prætores edicere consuerunt.'[1] And the Pandects directly recognize the same doctrine. 'Est enim juris civilis species, *consuetudo;* enimvero, diuturna consuetudo pro jure et lege, in his, quæ non ex scripto descendunt observari, solet, &c. Maxime autem probatur consuetudo ex rebus judicatis.'[2]

19. If indeed a Court of Equity in England did possess the unbounded jurisdiction which has been thus generally ascribed to it, of correcting, controlling, moderating, and even superseding the law, and of enforcing all the rights, as well as the charities, arising from natural law and justice, and of freeing itself from all regard to former rules and precedents, it would be the most gigantic in its sway, and the most formidable instrument of arbitrary power, that could well be devised. It would literally place the whole rights and property of the community under the arbitrary will of the judge, acting, if you please, arbitrio boni judicis, and, it may be, ex æquo et bono, according to his own notions and conscience; but still acting with a despotic and sovereign authority. A Court of Chancery might then well deserve the spirited rebuke of Selden: 'For law we have a measure, and know what to trust to. Equity is according to the conscience of him that is chancellor; and as that is larger or narrower, so is equity. 'T is all one as if they should make the standard for the measure the chancellor's foot. What an uncertain measure would this be! One chancellor has a long foot, another a short foot, a third an indifferent foot. It is the same thing with the chancellor's conscience.'[3] And notions of this sort were, in former ages, when the Chancery Jurisdiction was opposed with vehement disapprobation by common lawyers, very industriously propagated by the most learned of English antiquarians, such as Spelman, Coke, Lambard, and Selden.[4] We might indeed under such circumstances adopt the language of Mr. Justice Blackstone, and say: 'In short if a Court of

---

[1] Cicero de Invent. Lib. 2, cap. 22. My attention was first called to these passages by a note of Lord Redesdale. Mitford, Plead. Eq. p. 4, note (*b*). See Heineccius De Edictis Prætorum, Lib. 1, cap. 6, §§ 13, 30.

[2] Pothier, Pand. Lib. 1, tit. 3, art. 6, n. 28, 29; Dig. Lib. 1, tit. 3, l. 33, l. 34.

[3] Selden's Table Talk, title 'Equity;' 3 Black. Comm. 432, note (*y*).

[4] See citations, 3 Black. Comm. 433; Id. 54, 55; Id. 440, 441.

Equity in England did really act, as many ingenious writers have supposed it (from theory) to do, it would rise above all law, either common or statute, and be a most arbitrary legislator in every particular case.[1] So far however is this from being true, that one of the most common maxims upon which a Court of Equity daily acts is, that equity follows the law, and seeks out and guides itself by the analogies of the law.[2]

20. What has been already said upon this subject cannot be more fitly concluded than in the words of one of the ablest judges that ever sat in equity. 'There are,' said Lord Redesdale, 'certain principles on which Courts of Equity act, which are very well settled. The cases which occur are various, but they are decided on fixed principles. Courts of Equity have in this respect no more discretionary power than Courts of Law. They decide new cases, as they arise, by the principles on which former cases have been decided; and may thus illustrate or enlarge the operation of those principles. But the principles are as fixed and certain as the principles on which the Courts of Common Law proceed.[3] In confirmation of these remarks it may be added that the Courts of Common Law are, in like manner, perpetually adding to the doctrines of the old jurisprudence, and enlarging, illustrating, and applying the maxims which were at first derived from very narrow and often obscure sources. For instance, the whole law of Insurance is scarcely a century old; and more than half of its most important principles and distinctions have been created within the last fifty years.

21. In the early history of English Equity Jurisprudence there might have been, and probably was, much to justify the suggestion that Courts of Equity were bounded by no certain limits or rules; but they acted upon principles of conscience and natural justice, without much restraint of any sort.[4] And as the chancellors were for many ages almost universally either eccle-

---

[1] 3 Black. Comm. 433; Id. 440, 441, 442. De Lolme, in his work on the Constitution of England, has presented a view of English Equity Jurisprudence far more exact and comprehensive than many of the English text-writers on the same subject. The whole chapter (B. 1, ch. 11) is well worthy of perusal.

[2] Cowper v. Cowper, 2 P. Will. 753.

[3] Bond v. Hopkins, 1 Sh. & Lefr. R. 428, 429. See also Mitford on Plead. Eq. p. 4, note (b).

[4] 1 Kent, Comm. Lect. 21, pp. 490, 491, 492 (2d edit.).

siastics or statesmen, neither of whom are supposed to be very scrupulous in the exercise of power, and as they exercised a delegated authority from the Crown as the fountain of administrative justice, whose rights, prerogatives, and duties on this subject were not well defined, and whose decrees were not capable of being resisted, it would not be unnatural that they should arrogate to themselves the general attributes of royalty, and interpose in many cases which seemed to them to require a remedy more wide or more summary than was adopted by the common Courts of Law.

22. This is the view which Mr. Justice Blackstone seems to have taken of the matter; who has observed that in the infancy of our Courts of Equity, before their jurisdiction was settled, the chancellors themselves, 'partly from their ignorance of the law (being frequently bishops or statesmen), partly from ambition and lust of power (encouraged by the arbitrary principles of the age they lived in), but principally from the narrow and unjust decisions of the Courts of Law, had arrogated to themselves such unlimited authority as hath totally been disclaimed by their successors for now (1765) above a century past. The decrees of the Court of Equity were then rather in the nature of awards, formed on the sudden, pro re nata, with more probity of intention than knowledge of the subject, founded on no settled principles, as being never designed, and therefore never used, as precedents.'[1]

23. It was fortunate indeed that even in those early times the knowledge which the ecclesiastical chancellors had acquired of general equity and justice from the civil law enabled them to administer them with a more sound discretion than could otherwise have been done. And from the moment when principles of decision came to be acted upon and established in chancery, the Roman law furnished abundant materials to erect a superstructure at once solid, convenient, and lofty, adapted to human wants, and enriched by all the aids of human wisdom, experience, and learning. To say that later chancellors have borrowed much from these materials, is to bestow the highest praise upon their judgment, their industry, and their reverential regard to their duty. It would have been little to the commendation of

[1] 3 Black. Comm. 433; Id. 440, 441.

such learned minds that they had studiously disregarded the maxims of ancient wisdom, or had neglected to use them, from ignorance, from pride, or from indifference.[1]

24. Having dwelt thus far upon the inaccurate or inadequate notions which are frequently circulated as to Equity Jurisprudence in England and America, it may be thought proper to give some more exact and clear statement of it. This may be better done by explanatory observations than by direct definitions, which are often said in the law to be perilous and unsatisfactory.

25. In England and in the American States, which have derived their jurisprudence from that parental source, Equity has a restrained and qualified meaning. The remedies for the redress of wrongs and for the enforcement of rights are distinguished into two classes: first, those which are administered in Courts of Common Law; and secondly, those which are administered in Courts of Equity. Rights which are recognized and protected, and wrongs which are redressed, by the former courts, are called legal rights and legal injuries. Rights which are recognized and protected, and wrongs which are redressed, by the latter courts only, are called equitable rights and equitable injuries.(a) The former are said to be rights and wrongs

---

[1] The whole of the late Professor Park's Lecture upon Equity Jurisprudence, delivered in King's College in November, 1831, on this subject, is well deserving of a perusal by every student. There is much freedom and force in his observations; and if his life had been longer spared, he would probably have been a leader in a more masculine and extensive course of law studies by the English bar. There are also two excellent articles on the same subject in the American Jurist, one of which, published in 1829, contains a most elaborate review and vindication of the jurisdiction of Courts of Equity; and the other, in 1833, a forcible exposition of the prevalent errors on the subject (2 Amer. Jurist, 314; 10 Amer. Jurist, 227). I know not where to refer the reader to pages more full of useful comment and research.

(a) Equity has no criminal jurisdiction. Cope v. District Fair, 99 Ill. 489; Portis v. Fall, 34 Ark. 375; Taylor v. Pine Bluff, Ib. 603; Moses v. Mobile, 52 Ala. 198. Its jurisdiction is limited to the protection of civil rights. Attorney-Gen. v. Tudor Ice Co., 104 Mass. 239, 240. In the case last cited the proceedings of a private trading corporation were objected to solely on the ground that they were not authorized by the charter of the company, and were for that reason against public policy. The court declined to grant an injunction on behalf of the State. Attorney-Gen. v. Utica Ins. Co., 2 Johns. Ch. 371; People v. Utica Ins. Co., 15 Johns. 358; Attorney-Gen. v. Reynolds, 1 Eq. Cas. Abr. 131 (3d ed.). Several English cases

at common law, and the remedies therefore are remedies at common law; the latter are said to be rights and wrongs in equity, and the remedies therefore are remedies in equity. Equity Jurisprudence may therefore properly be said to be that portion of remedial justice which is exclusively administered by a Court of Equity as contradistinguished from that portion of remedial justice which is exclusively administered by a Court of Common Law.

26. The distinction between the former and the latter courts may be further illustrated by considering the different natures of the rights they are designed to recognize and protect, the different natures of the remedies which they apply, and the different natures of the forms and modes of proceeding which they adopt, to accomplish their respective ends. In the Courts of Common Law, both of England and America, there are certain prescribed forms of action to which the party must resort to furnish him a remedy; and if there be no prescribed form to reach such a case, he is remediless; for they entertain jurisdiction only of certain actions, and give relief according to the particular exigency of such actions, and not otherwise. In those actions a general and unqualified judgment only can be given, for the plaintiff or for the defendant, without any adaptation of it to particular circumstances.

27. But there are many cases in which a simple judgment for either party, without qualifications or conditions or peculiar arrangements, will not do entire justice ex æquo et bono to either party. Some modifications of the rights of both parties may be required; some restraints on one side, or on the other, or perhaps on both sides; some adjustments involving reciprocal obligations or duties; some compensatory or preliminary or concurrent proceedings to fix, control, or equalize rights; some

were distinguished as cases of suits against public bodies or officers exceeding their powers, or against corporations vested with the power of eminent domain or doing acts which were deemed inconsistent with rights of the public. Attorney-Gen. *v.* Norwick, 16 Sim. 225; Attorney-Gen. *v.* Guardians of Poor, 17 Sim. 6; Attorney-Gen. *v.* Andrews, 2 Macn. & G. 225; Attorney-Gen. *v.* Great Northern Ry. Co., 1 Drew. & S. 154. It was declared that there were but two cases in Massachusetts in which informations in equity were proper: (1) public nuisances requiring immediate interposition; (2) trusts for charitable purposes when the beneficiaries are so numerous and indefinite as to make this the only efficient mode of proceeding.

qualifications or conditions, present or future, temporary or permanent, to be annexed to the exercise of rights or the redress of injuries. In all these cases Courts of Common Law cannot give the desired relief. They have no forms of remedy adapted to the objects. They can entertain suits only in a prescribed form, and they can give a general judgment only in the prescribed form.[1] From their very character and organization they are incapable of the remedy which the mutual rights and relative situations of the parties, under the circumstances, positively require.

28. But Courts of Equity are not so restrained. Although they have prescribed forms of proceeding, the latter are flexible, and may be suited to the different postures of cases. They may adjust their decrees so as to meet most if not all of these exigencies; and they may vary, qualify, restrain, and model the remedy so as to suit it to mutual and adverse claims, controlling equities, and the real and substantial rights of all the parties. Nay, more; they can bring before them all parties interested in the subject matter, and adjust the rights of all, however numerous; whereas Courts of Common Law are compelled to limit their inquiry to the very parties in the litigation before them, although other persons may have the deepest interest in the event of the suit. So that one of the most striking and distinctive features of Courts of Equity is that they can adapt their decrees to all the varieties of circumstances which may arise, and adjust them to all the peculiar rights of all the parties in interest; whereas Courts of Common Law (as we have already seen) are bound down to a fixed and invariable form of judgment in general terms, altogether absolute, for the plaintiff or for the defendant.[2]

29. Another peculiarity of Courts of Equity is that they can administer remedies for rights, which rights Courts of Common

---

[1] Mitford on Plead. pp. 3, 4; 1 Wooddes. Lect. vii. pp. 203 to 206.

[2] 1 Wooddes. Lect. vii. pp. 203 to 206; 3 Black. Comm. 438. Much of this paragraph has been abstracted from Dr. Lieber's Encyclopædia Americana, article 'Equity.' The late Professor Park, of King's College, London, in his Introductory Lecture on Equity (1831, p. 15), has said, 'The editors of the Encyclopædia Americana have stated the real case with regard to what we call Courts of Equity much more accurately than I can find it stated in any English law books;' and he thus admits the propriety of the exposition contained in the text.

Law do not recognize at all; or if they do recognize them they leave them wholly to the conscience and good-will of the parties. Thus what are technically called Trusts, that is, estates vested in persons upon particular trusts and confidences, are wholly without any cognizance at the common law; and the abuses of such trusts and confidences are beyond the reach of any legal process. But they are cognizable in Courts of Equity, and hence they are called equitable estates; and an ample remedy is there given in favor of the cestuis que trust (the parties beneficially interested) for all wrongs and injuries, whether arising from negligence or positive misconduct.[1] There are also many cases (as we shall presently see) of losses and injuries by mistake, accident, and fraud; many cases of penalties and forfeitures; many cases of impending irreparable injuries or meditated mischiefs; and many cases of oppressive proceedings, undue advantages and impositions, betrayals of confidence, and unconscionable bargains; in all of which Courts of Equity will interfere and grant redress, but which the common law takes no notice of or silently disregards.[2]

30. Again; the remedies in Courts of Equity are often very different in their nature, mode, and degree from those of Courts of Common Law, even when each has a jurisdiction over the same subject matter. Thus a Court of Equity, if a contract is broken, will often compel the party specifically to perform the contract; whereas Courts of Law can only give damages for the breach of it. So Courts of Equity will interfere by way of injunction to prevent wrongs; whereas Courts of Common Law can grant redress only when the wrong is done.[3]

31. The modes of seeking and granting relief in equity are also different from those of Courts of Common Law. The latter proceed to the trial of contested facts by means of a jury; and the evidence is generally to be drawn, not from the parties, but from third persons, who are disinterested witnesses. But Courts of Equity try causes without a jury; and they address themselves to the conscience of the defendant, and require him to

---

[1] 3 Black. Comm. 439; 1 Wooddes. Lect. vii. pp. 209 to 213; 2 Fonbl. Equity, B. 2, ch. 1, § 1; Id. ch. 7; Id. ch. 8.

[2] 1 Wooddes. Lect. vii. pp. 203, 204; 3 Black. Comm. 434, 435, 438, 439; 1 Fonbl. Eq. B. 1, ch. 1, § 3, note (*f*).

[3] 1 Wooddes. Lect. vii. pp. 206, 207.

CHAP. I.] NATURE OF EQUITY. 23

answer upon his oath the matters of fact stated in the bill, if they are within his knowledge; and he is compellable to give a full account of all such facts, with all their circumstances, without evasion or equivocation; and the testimony of other witnesses also may be taken to confirm or to refute the facts so alleged.[1] Indeed every bill in equity may be said to be in some sense a bill of discovery, since it asks for the personal oath of the defendant, to purge himself in regard to the transactions stated in the bill. It may readily be perceived how very important this process of discovery may be, when we consider how great the mass of human transactions is, in which there are no other witnesses, or persons having knowledge thereof, except the parties themselves.

32. Mr. Justice Blackstone has in a few words given an outline of some of the more important powers and peculiar duties of Courts of Equity. He says that they are established 'to detect latent frauds and concealments which the process of Courts of Law is not adapted to reach; to enforce the execution of such matters of trust and confidence as are binding in conscience, though not cognizable in a Court of Law; to deliver from such dangers as are owing to misfortune or oversight; and to give a more specific relief, and more adapted to the circumstances of the case, than can always be obtained by the generality of the rules of the positive or common law.'[2] But the general account of Lord Redesdale (which he admits however to be imperfect and in some respects inaccurate) is far more satisfactory as a definite enumeration. 'The jurisdiction of a Court of Equity,' says he,[3] ' when it assumes a power of decision, is to be exercised, (1) where the principles of law, by which the ordinary courts are guided, give a right, but the powers of those courts are not sufficient to afford a complete remedy, or their modes of proceeding are inadequate to the purpose; (2) where the courts of ordinary jurisdiction are made instruments of injustice; (3) where the principles of law, by which the ordinary courts are guided, give no right, but upon the principles of universal justice the interference of the judicial power is necessary to prevent a wrong and the positive law is silent. And it may

---

[1] 3 Black. Comm. 437, 438; 1 Wooddes. Lect. vii. p. 207.
[2] 1 Black. Comm. 92.
[3] Mitford, Eq. Pl. by Jeremy, pp. 111, 112.

also be collected that Courts of Equity, without deciding upon the rights of the parties, administer to the ends of justice by assuming a jurisdiction, (4) to remove impediments to the fair decision of a question in other courts; (5) to provide for the safety of property in dispute pending a litigation, and to preserve property in danger of being dissipated or destroyed by those to whose care it is by law entrusted, or by persons having immediate but partial interests; (6) to restrain the assertion of doubtful rights in a manner productive of irreparable damage; (7) to prevent injury to a third person by the doubtful title of others; and (8) to put a bound to vexatious and oppressive litigation, and to prevent multiplicity of suits. And further, that Courts of Equity, without pronouncing any judgment which may affect the rights of parties, extend their jurisdiction (9) to compel a discovery, or obtain evidence which may assist the decision of other courts; and (10) to preserve testimony when in danger of being lost before the matter to which it relates can be made the subject of judicial investigation.'[1]

33. Perhaps the most general if not the most precise description of a Court of Equity, in the English and American sense, is that it has jurisdiction in cases of rights, recognized and protected by the municipal jurisprudence,(a) where a plain, adequate, and complete remedy cannot be had in the Courts of Common Law.[2] The remedy must be plain; for if it be doubtful and obscure at law, Equity will assert a jurisdiction.[3] (b)

---

[1] Dr. Dane, in his Abridgment and Digest, ch. 1, art. 7, §§ 33 to 51 (1 Dane, Abrid. 101 to 107), has given a summary of the differences between Equity Jurisdiction and Legal Jurisdiction in regard to contracts, which may be read with utility. See also Mitford, Eq. Pl. by Jeremy, 4, 5.

[2] Cooper, Eq. Pl. 128, 129; Mitford, Eq. Pl. by Jeremy, 112, 123; 1 Wooddes. Lect. vii. pp. 214, 215.

[3] Rathbone *v.* Warren, 10 John. R. 587; King *v.* Baldwin, 17 John. R. 284.

(a) See Elborough *v.* Ayres, L. R. 10 Eq. 367, and note at the end of this section.

(b) If the remedy at law involve delay, and is inconvenient and circuitous, equity will assume jurisdiction. Clouston *v.* Shearer, 99 Mass. 209. But of course the mere fact that there is doubt in the mind of a party whether he can maintain an action at law will not give jurisdiction to equity. Allen *v.* Storer, 132 Mass. 372; Clark *v.* Jones, 5 Allen, 379. Nor will the fact that the evidence in a cause will be voluminous and tedious give equity jurisdiction. Bowen *v.* Chase, 94 U. S. 812. Damages alone cannot become a ground of equitable relief. Pickman *v.* Trinity Church, 123 Mass. 1. Further see note (b), p. 25.

It must be adequate; for if at law it falls short of what the party is entitled to, that founds a jurisdiction in equity.(a) And it must be complete; that is, it must attain the full end and justice of the case. It must reach the whole mischief and secure the whole right of the party in a perfect manner at the present time and in future; otherwise equity will interfere and give such relief and aid as the exigency of the particular case may require.[1] The jurisdiction of a Court of Equity is therefore sometimes concurrent with the jurisdiction of a Court of Law; it is sometimes exclusive of it, and it is sometimes auxiliary to it.[2] (b)

[1] See Dr. Lieber's Ency. Americana, art. 'Equity;' Mitford, Eq. Pl. by Jeremy, 111, 112, 117, 123; 1 Wooddes. Lect. vii. pp. 214, 215; Hinde's Pract. 153; Cooper, Eq. Pl. Sir James Mackintosh, in his Life of Sir Thomas More, says: 'Equity, in the acceptation in which the word is used in English Jurisprudence, is no longer to be confounded with that moral equity which generally corrects the unjust operation of law, and with which it seems to have been synonymous in the days of Selden and Bacon. It is a part of laws formed from usages and determinations which sometimes differ from what is called Common Law in its subjects; but chiefly varies from it in its modes of proof, of trial, and of relief. It is a jurisdiction so irregularly formed, and often so little dependent upon general principles, that it can hardly be defined or made intelligible otherwise than by a minute enumeration of the matters cognizable by it.' There is much of general truth in this statement; but it is perhaps a little too broad and undistinguishing for an accurate equity lawyer. Equity, as a science and part of jurisprudence built upon precedents as well as upon principles, must occasionally fail in the mere theoretical and philosophical accuracy and completeness of all its rules and governing principles. But it is quite as regular and exact in its principles and rules as the common law, and probably as any other system of jurisprudence established generally by positive enactments or usages or practical expositions in any country, ancient or modern. There must be many principles and exceptions in every system, in a theoretical sense arbitrary if not irrational, but which are yet sustained by the accidental institutions or modifications of society in the particular country where they exist. There are wide differences between the philosophy of law as actually administered in any country and that abstract doctrine which may in matters of government constitute in many minds the law of philosophy.

[2] Fonbl. Eq. B. 1, ch. 1, § 3, note (f).

(a) Watson v. Sutherland, 5 Wall. 74; Thatcher v. Humble, 67 Ind. 444.

(b) *Existence of a Remedy at Law.* — How far the existence of a remedy at law in general operates to prevent jurisdiction in equity is considered in many of its features in the text; and it is there shown that there are not a few cases in which equity has a concurrent jurisdiction with Courts of Law in cases in which all needful relief may be given in those courts. Some special questions of concurrent jurisdiction remain to be considered.

In the beginnings of the distinct jurisdiction of the chancellor, — for

34. Many persons, and especially foreigners, have often expressed surprise that distinct courts should in England and the chancellor at first sat with the other judges in the ordinary tribunals (Bigelow's History of Procedure, 19), — that functionary held court mainly for two purposes, so far as litigation was concerned: first, for the protection of the poor and the weak against the rich and the strong, — who, when they found the king's judges unwilling to aid them sufficiently, were seldom above overawing the courts themselves; secondly, for alleviating the misfortune that had come about in the thirteenth century by the narrowing of the jurisdiction of the ordinary courts to certain specific modes of relief, as seen especially in the forms of action of the common law. Ib. 198; Bigelow, Elements of Equity, 5-7. The relief given by the Stat. of West. 2, ch. 24, authorizing actions on the case, was but partial.

The first of these grounds of jurisdiction substantially disappeared long ago, though not without leaving traces of its existence in the law of to-day. See Worthy v. Tate, 44 Ga. 152 (statutory law as to poverty); Frederick v. Groshon, 30 Md. 436, 446 (powerful corporations). It is enough now, in ordinary cases, so far as any question of poverty of the plaintiff or power of the defendant is concerned, that the cause of action may be satisfactorily tried at law, assuming of course that it is not a case of concurrent jurisdiction in equity. The second ground is the one on which jurisdiction in equity is at this day mainly entertained. It is the case in which the plaintiff has no plain, adequate, and complete remedy at law.

Our American Courts of Equity have had much difficulty under this head, distinct from the difficulties which the English Chancery has encountered; or at least they have failed to agree upon any consistent rule of jurisdiction with regard to cases remediable at law. Many of our courts derive their powers from statute; and it is probably accurate to say that if, and in so far as, the statute has actually derogated from the powers of the common-law tribunals, the law must be strictly construed, and not taken to confer the broad jurisdiction of equity in England, unless the statute itself indicate the contrary intention. For the converse case see Lane v. Marshall, 1 Heisk. 30; and see State v. Alder, Ib. 543, 547; McGough v. Insurance Bank, 2 Ga. 151, 154.

But the chief difficulty arises with statutes which do not apparently derogate from the powers of the law courts. The statute of Massachusetts may be taken as a typical case for consideration. That statute in conferring equity jurisdiction upon the Supreme Court of the State declares that 'the court may hear and determine in equity all causes hereafter mentioned, when the parties have not a plain, adequate, and complete remedy at the common law,' and then enumerates the ordinary heads of equity. Pub. Stats. ch. 151, § 2. There the statute stopped, until in 1877 another section was added, to be noticed presently.

This statute — as it stood before 1877 — has always been strictly construed, and not as declaratory of any existing rule, or as equivalent to the adoption of the jurisdiction of the English Court of Chancery; indeed the courts have looked with scant favor upon jurisdiction in equity. Bassett v. Brown, 100 Mass. 355; Pratt v. Pond, 5 Allen, 59; Martin v. Graves, Ib. 601; Jones v. Newhall, 115 Mass. 244, 251; Suter v. Matthews, Ib. 253; Hubbell v. Courrin, 10 Allen, 333. For example, though fraud in procuring a deed to land (or of any written contract, valid on its face, Simp-

NATURE OF EQUITY.

America be established for the administration of equity, instead of the whole administration of municipal justice being confided

son v. Howden, 3 Mylne & C. 97; Hoare v. Bremidge, L. R. 8 Ch. 22; British Assur. Co. v. Great Western Ry. Co., 38 L. J. Ch. 132; s. c. on appeal, Ib. 314) affords in England a clear ground for jurisdiction in equity; Simpson v. Howden, supra; and see Holliway v. Holliway, 77 Mo. 392; post, § 700; — in Massachusetts, before 1877 (and perhaps still), if the aggrieved party was in a position to maintain a writ of entry, he could not have relief in equity from such a deed. It would not be treated as a cloud to be removed by equity, though after the recovery in the writ of entry the deed would still be in existence and might be on record. Bassett v. Brown, 100 Mass. 355, Pratt v. Pond, 5 Allen, 59. (But cases like this may be deemed to have fallen to some extent under the influence of special statute in relation to quieting titles.) Indeed a strict construction of the statute, consistently maintained, would virtually exclude all concurrent jurisdiction except in cases where a defective remedy at law has been perfected. Jones v. Newhall, 115 Mass. 244, 250, 252.

In contrast with the construction of the Massachusetts statute, the Federal Judiciary Act of 1789, ch. 20, § 16, which declares that 'suits in equity shall not be sustained in either of the courts of the United States in any case where plain, adequate, and complete remedy may be had at law,' had already been repeatedly pronounced to be merely declaratory of the pre-existing rule; it was not intended to narrow jurisdiction in equity, but on the contrary to affirm the general doctrine of Courts of Equity, as handed on from England. Mr. Justice Story directly says that the equity jurisdiction of the United States Courts does not depend upon what is exercised by Courts of Equity or Courts of Law in the several States, but upon what is a proper subject of equitable relief in Courts of Equity in England. Bean v. Smith, 2 Mason, 252, 270, citing Robinson v. Campbell, 3 Wheat. 212, 221; United States v. Howland, 4 Wheat. 108, 115. See also, to the effect that the act is merely declaratory of the pre-existing rule, Oelrichs v. Spain, 15 Wall. 211, 228; Parker v. Winnipiseogee Co., 2 Black, 545, 551; Boyce v. Grundy, 3 Peters, 210, 215; Woodman v. Freeman, 25 Maine, 531, 541; Baker v. Biddle, Baldw. 394, 403. But the Supreme Court, while admitting the jurisdiction, appear to have departed from the rule in one case. Insurance Co. v. Bailey, 13 Wall. 616, where cancellation of a policy of insurance for fraud was refused. See infra as to this point. And as to asserting the jurisdiction but declining to exercise it, see Hoare v. Bremridge, L. R. 14 Eq. 522; s. c. 8 Ch. 22, 27; Shepard v. Brown, 4 Giff. 208, 218; In re Whitehead, 28 Ch. D. 614; also infra, near the end of this note.

The disfavor shown in Massachusetts towards enlarged jurisdiction in equity culminated with the cases of Jones v. Newhall, 115 Mass. 244, and Suter v. Matthews, Ib. 253; in the first of these cases especially, the court, by Mr. Justice Wells, defending and applying, in an elaborate judgment, the narrower view of jurisdiction which had been persistently maintained in that State. The case was a bill to enforce, in favor of the vendor, a contract for the sale of land and other property which would have been sustained, it seems, in England on the principle of mutuality of relief to vendor and purchaser. Post, § 723. In the course of the opinion (p. 252), refusing jurisdiction, the court sought to fortify their position by decisions of the Supreme Court of the United

to one and the same class of courts without any discrimination between law and equity.[1] But this surprise is founded almost

[1] 3 Black. Comm. 441, 442.

States above cited; but an examination of the cases cited will show that the only one which affords the court any support is Insurance Co. v. Bailey, 13 Wall. 616; and that case itself would not have been held good law in Massachusetts (not to mention England) at the time of Jones v. Newhall. Commercial Ins. Co. v. McLoon, 14 Allen, 351, cited with approval in Fuller v. Percival, 126 Mass. 381.

The result of the two cases referred to was the passage in 1877 of a statute declaring that the Supreme Court 'shall also have jurisdiction in equity of all cases and matters of equity cognizable under the general principles of equity jurisdiction, and in respect of all such cases and matters shall be a court of general equity jurisdiction.' Pub. Stats. ch. 151, § 4.

It would seem that under this provision there could be no doubt that the Legislature intended to confer upon the court jurisdiction as developed in equity in England at that time (1877). See Knatchbull v. Hallett, 13 Ch. D. 696, 710, Jessel, M. R., quoted in note to § 56, infra. At all events it appears to have been the view of the court in Nudd v. Powers, 136 Mass. 273, 278, that the existence in Massachusetts of a remedy at law, though perhaps plain, adequate, and complete, was not ground for refusing jurisdiction of a case arising within the jurisdiction of the English Chancery. The bill 'may be sustained,' said Holmes, J., 'to declare and enforce a charge, the legal remedies for which, if any, are either derived from equity . . . *or* are inadequate.'

It has also been held in Massachusetts since 1877 that equity will entertain jurisdiction to decree the delivery up for cancellation of an apparently valid overdue negotiable note, not already sued upon, to which there would be an available defence of fraud at law. Fuller v. Percival, 126 Mass. 381. And see the suggestion of the court in sustaining a demurrer to the bill in Anthony v. Valentine, 130 Mass. 119, — a bill to enjoin a suit at law upon a promissory note. 'There is no allegation that it was obtained by *fraud*, accident, or mistake.' And that equity will, elsewhere at least, grant relief against a forged note valid on its face, see Strafford v. Welch, 59 N. H. 46; Huston v. Roosa, 43 Ind. 517; Huston v. Schindler, 46 Ind. 38; Hardy v. Brier, 91 Ind. 91; post, §§ 700, 701. The case of Fuller v. Percival, supra, was clearly correct on general equity jurisdiction, if not on a narrow rule, for no remedy at law can be as adequate as cancellation; and Suter v. Matthews, 115 Mass. 253, though decided before 1877, may well be doubted, in any view. Before the decision of this case of Suter v. Matthews the same court had sustained a bill alleging that the defendant had obtained a policy of insurance by fraud, whereby an apparent cause of action had arisen against the plaintiff, and praying the court to order the policy to be given up for cancellation. Commercial Ins. Co. v. McLoon, 14 Allen, 351, cited with approval in Fuller v. Percival, supra. To the same effect, London Assur. v. Mansel, 11 Ch. D. 363, Jessel, M. R.; Hoare v. Bremridge, L. R. 14 Eq. 522; s. c. 8 Ch. 22; British Assur. Co. v. Great Western Ry. Co., 38 L. J. Ch. 132; s. c. on appeal, Ib. 314. But see Insurance Co. v. Bailey, 13 Wall. 616, supra.

And since 1877 the broad rule has been conceded that cancellation may

wholly upon an erroneous view of the nature of Equity Jurisprudence. It arises from confounding the general sense of

be had of any invalid contract in the possession of a defendant, if the invalidity thereof is not apparent on the face of the paper, and if there is danger that the evidence to support a defence to it at law may be lost by the delay of the other party to sue upon it. Anthony *v.* Valentine, 130 Mass. 119. Indeed this ought to be true in any view of the statute, without the act of 1877. To an action at law upon a written instrument of any kind, apparently valid, there may indeed be a perfect and complete defence; but (1) the opportunity to make that defence may be lost by studied delay of the other party to sue, and (2) in any event mere defence, however perfect, is not relief. The relief desired is different in kind and efficiency from the defence available. Compare the language of the court in Oelrichs *v.* Spain, 15 Wall. 211, 228, quoting Boyce *v.* Grundy, 3 Peters, 210, 215, that the remedy at law must be ' as practical and *efficient*' as the remedy in equity, to cut off equitable jurisdiction. See also Merrill *v.* Allen, 38 Mich. 487. It is conceived that where A has wrongfully obtained or wrongfully withholds from B a written instrument which, not disclosing its own invalidity, may therefore be used unjustly and harmfully against B or his privies, A should be required to surrender the same, at least if he does not bring suit upon it. See further as to cancellation, infra, § 86; infra, § 700, and the editor's note thereto.

But on the other hand the Supreme Court of Massachusetts have recently decided in Husband *v.* Aldrich, 135 Mass. 317, contrary to the rule in Hess *v.* Voss, 52 Ill. 472, that equity has no jurisdiction in that State to order partition of land between tenants in common; though equity has apparently had exclusive jurisdiction of such cases in England ever since 1835, when the writ of partition was abolished; 3 and 4 Will. 4. ch. 27, § 36; Bailey *v.* Sisson, 1 R. I. 233, 236; and before that time equity had concurrent jurisdiction. Hess *v.* Voss, supra; Burhans *v.* Burhans, 2 Barb. Ch. 398, 404; Bailey *v.* Sisson, supra; post, §§ 646 et seq. Husband *v.* Aldrich however proceeded mainly on statutes relating to partition, and the jurisdictional act of 1877 was not mentioned. See again Dole *v.* Wooldredge, 135 Mass. 140, where the court speak hesitatingly about jurisdiction.

The result is that Equity Jurisdiction in Massachusetts is in a state of uncertainty even with the statute of 1877. Indeed while jurisdiction has certainly been enlarged, it may be difficult to determine what the statute means, though properly considered to have extended the jurisdiction to the bounds of the English Chancery. In so doing has it brought with it the nice distinctions, sometimes standing upon no clear principle, that have been adopted and are still maintained in England? See e. g. Ramshire *v.* Bolton, L. R. 8 Eq. 294, 299. However it is clear that the Legislature of Massachusetts intended, by the act of 1877, to do away with the test of a ' plain, adequate, and complete remedy ' to be had at law under the jurisprudence of that State, and to substitute the broader jurisdiction of the English Chancery. To admit, as was admitted in Jones *v.* Newhall, that the English courts would take jurisdiction of the case, would now be decisive, if the intention of the Legislature is fully carried out.

Cases of mutuality of relief, cancellation, and partition are not the only ones that have created confusion in regard to jurisdiction. In some States it has been held that if disclosure of

equity, which is equivalent to universal or natural justice, ex æquo et bono, with its technical sense, which is descriptive of

the facts sought by a bill of discovery can be had in a suit at law in aid or defence of which the disclosure is desired, a bill of the kind, not seeking other proper relief, cannot be maintained. Hall *v.* Joiner, 1 S. Car. 186; Riopelle *v.* Doellner, 26 Mich. 102 ('per curiam'); post, p. 78, note (*b*). But this has been denied. Colgate *v.* Compagnie Française, 23 Fed. Rep. 82, 85. See post, p. 70, note (*b*). And except upon the narrow construction of the terms 'plain, adequate, and complete remedy at law,' it cannot be upheld. Shepard *v.* Brown, 4 Giff. 208, 218.

There are doubtless still other cases. With regard to the mooted question of fraud as a ground of jurisdiction in equity, it may be conceded perhaps that in a simple case in which nothing is sought in the bill but damages, equity should not in this country entertain jurisdiction. Ambler *v.* Choteau, 107 U. S. 586. And in England see Ogilvie *v.* Currie, 37 L. J. Ch. 541. But see Hill *v.* Lane, L. R. 11 Eq. 215, 220; Ramshire *v.* Bolton, L. R. 8 Eq. 294. And possibly so, as a matter of discretion *merely*, of fraud generally, where all relief asked for can clearly be given as well at law; though not where there is any doubt on that point. Green *v.* Spaulding, 76 Va. 411; Youngblood *v.* Youngblood, 54 Ala. 486; Hipp *v.* Babin, 19 How. 278; Huff *v.* Ripley, 58 Ga. 11; Ellis *v.* Lanier, 44 Ga. 9. Nor will intent to commit a fraud give jurisdiction to equity if the act to which the intent attaches is not a matter for equitable cognizance. Winegar *v.* Newland, 44 Mich. 367. And there are also special cases, as in removing clouds or quieting title to lands, and in obtaining relief from illegal taxes or assessments, in regard to which the jurisdiction of equity is deemed to have been restrained by statute. See the editor's note to § 700, post.

But the test of the existence of a remedy at law, however adequate, cannot be final even upon a narrow construction of statutes creating Courts of Equity; for it may be that a remedy once incomplete at law, and therefore giving occasion for the interference of equity which has been improved, has been enlarged and made complete in the ordinary tribunals. This will not take away jurisdiction from equity. Shotwell *v.* Smith, 5 C. E. Green, 79; Sweeny *v.* Williams, 36 N. J. Eq. 627; Segar *v.* Pratt, 20 Gratt. 672; Hinchley *v.* Greany, 118 Mass. 596; Clouston *v.* Shearer, 99 Mass. 209; Pratt *v.* Pond, 5 Allen, 59; Labadie *v.* Hewitt, 85 Ill. 341; Lee *v.* Lee, 55 Ala. 590, 598; Nudd *v.* Powers, 136 Mass. 273, 278; Jones *v.* Newhall, 115 Mass. 244, 250. Contra, Hall *v.* Joiner, 1 S. Car. 186, 190; Riopelle *v.* Doellner, 26 Mich. 102, 105. The last two are the cases on discovery already referred to.

Again Courts of Equity will assume jurisdiction over their own officers (e. g. solicitors) though the Common Law Courts might afford redress. Chapman *v.* Chapman, L. R. 9 Eq. 276, 294. See In re Whitehead, 28 Ch. D. 614. And, at least in England, the sovereign power may also claim relief where it will. Attorney-Gen. *v.* Tudor Ice Co., 104 Mass. 239, 243; Attorney-Gen. *v.* Galway, 1 Molloy, 95, 103. And see State *v.* Alder, 1 Heisk. 543. On the other hand it is said that the Legislature cannot give a court which acts without a jury power to determine a legal right except upon some equitable ground. Haine's Appeal, 73 Penn. St. 169. And of course equity cannot enforce supposed rights not recognized by municipal law. Elborough *v.* Ayres, L. R. 10 Eq. 367;

the exercise of jurisdiction over peculiar rights and remedies. Such persons seem to labor under the false notion that Courts of Law can never administer justice with reference to principles of universal or natural justice, but are confined to rigid, severe, and uncompromising rules, which admit of no equitable considerations. Now such a notion is founded in the grossest mistake of our systems of jurisprudence. Courts of Common Law, in a great variety of cases, adopt the most enlarged and liberal principles of decision, and indeed often proceed, as far as the nature of the rights and remedies which they are called to administer will permit, upon the same doctrines as Courts of Equity. This is especially true in regard to cases involving the application of the law of nations and of commercial and maritime

Carlton v. Salem, 103 Mass. 141; Hale v. Cushman, 6 Met. 425; Hendricks v. Toole, 29 Mich. 340.

It is said however that even in courts of general chancery powers, that is, in the English Chancery, the common practice in matters of concurrent jurisdiction is to remit parties to their remedy at law if that is plain and adequate, unless there is some peculiar advantage afforded by equity or some other controlling fact. Wells, J., in Jones v. Newhall, 115 Mass. 244, 252, referring to Clifford v. Brooke, 13 Ves. 131; Whitmore v. Mackeson, 16 Beav. 126; Hammond v. Messenger, 9 Sim. 327; Hoare v. Bremridge, L. R. 14 Eq. 522; s. c. 8 Ch. 22. It may be conceded that equity will not enjoin proceedings pending at law which for any reason can be more suitably prosecuted there; unless on terms imposed upon and consented to by the plaintiff in equity — such as giving judgment at law — which will result in drawing the cause wholly into equity. And this, with the interesting intimation of Lord Selborne just stated (L. R. 8 Ch. at p. 27), is the extent of Hoare v. Bremridge, supra, the most important case upon the subject. To the same effect, that pending proceedings at law will not be enjoined in such cases, see Grand Chute v. Winegar, 15 Wall. 373; Payson v. Lamson, 134 Mass. 593; Anthony v. Valentine, 130 Mass. 119. That is easy to understand.

On the whole it is to be regretted that the State courts have not always taken the view maintained in the Federal courts, that the words 'plain, adequate, and complete remedy at law' are merely descriptive, in a broad way, of jurisdiction in equity, and not narrowly definitive. The way is still open in some, probably in many, of the States. A statute which merely copies common language cannot be considered ordinarily to have been adopted with the careful verbal consideration and exact definition of a statute newly worked out and studiously framed. It is hardly probable that legislators in adopting the common language of the books had in mind any specific and exact limits, except where, as recently in Massachusetts, attention had been plainly and forcibly directed thereto. It cannot be seriously doubted that the broader jurisdiction is generally desired and desirable. Comp. Chapman v. Chapman, L. R. 9 Eq. 276, 294. ' Under its improved course of practice it would seem to be the duty of this court to extend its jurisdiction as far as possible,' &c. Stuart, V. C.

law and usages, and even of foreign municipal law. And Mr. Justice Blackstone has correctly said, that 'where the subject matter is such as requires to be determined secundum æquum et bonum, as generally upon actions on the case, the judgments of the Courts of Law are guided by the most liberal equity.'[1]

35. Whether it would or would not be best to administer the whole of remedial justice in one court, or in one class of courts, without any separation or distinctions of suits, or of the form or modes of proceeding and granting relief, is a matter upon which different minds in the same country, and certainly in different countries, would probably arrive at opposite conclusions. And whether, if distinctions in rights and remedies and forms of proceeding are admitted in the municipal jurisprudence, it would be best to confide the whole jurisdiction to the same court or courts, is also a matter upon which an equal diversity of judgment might be found to exist. Lord Bacon, upon more than one occasion, expressed his decided opinion that a separation of the administration of equity from that of the common law was wise and convenient. 'All nations,' says he, 'have equity. But some have law and equity mixed in the same court, which is worse; and some have it distinguished in several courts, which is better.'[2] And again, among his aphorisms, he says: 'Apud nonnullos receptum est, ut jurisdictio, quæ decernit secundum æquum et bonum, atque illa altera, quæ procedit secundum jus strictum, iisdem curiis deputentur; apud alios autem et diversis. Omnino placet curiarum separatio. Neque enim servabitur distinctio casuum, si fiat commixtio jurisdictionum; sed arbitrium legem tandem trahet.'[3] Lord Hardwicke held the same opinion;[4] and it is certainly a common opinion in countries governed by the common law. In civil law countries the general if not the universal practice is the other way;[5] whether more for the advancement of public justice, is a matter of doubt with many learned minds.

36. But whether the one opinion or the other be most correct in theory, it is most probable that the practical system adopted

---

[1] 3 Black. Comm. 436. See Eunomus, Dial. 3, § 60.
[2] Bac. Jurisd. of the Marches; 4 Bac. Works, 274.
[3] Bac. De Aug. Scient. Lib. 8, cap. 3, Aph. 45; 7 Bac. Works, 448.
[4] Parkes, Hist. Chan. App. pp. 504, 505.
[5] 1 Kaims on Eq. Introd. pp. 27 to 30.

by every nation has been mainly influenced by the peculiarities of its own institutions, habits, and circumstances; and especially by the nature of its own jurisprudence and the forms of its own remedial justice. The union of equity and law in the same court, which might be well adapted to one country, or even to one age, might be wholly unfit for another country, or for another age. The question in all such cases must be a mixed question of public policy and private convenience, and never can be susceptible of any universal solution applicable to all times and all nations and all changes in jurisprudence.

37. Accordingly we find that in the nations of antiquity different systems existed. And in Rome, with whose juridical institutions we are best acquainted, not only were different jurisdictions entrusted to different magistrates, but the very distinction between law and equity was clearly recognized.[1] Thus civil jurisdiction and criminal jurisdiction were confided to different magistrates.[2] The Roman prætors generally exercised the former only. In the exercise of this authority a broad distinction was taken between Actions at Law and Actions in Equity, the former having the name of Actiones Civiles, and the latter of Actiones Prætoriæ. And in the same way a like distinction was taken between Obligationes Civiles and Obligationes Prætoriæ, between Actiones Directæ and Actiones Utiles.[3] And in modern nations it is not uncommon for different portions of judicial jurisdiction to be vested in different magistrates or tribunals. Thus questions of state or public law, such as prize causes and causes touching sovereignty, are generally confided to special tribunals; and maritime and commercial questions often belong to Courts of Admiralty, or other courts constituted for commercial purposes. There is then nothing incongruous, much less absurd, in separating different portions

---

[1] 3 Black. Comm. 50; Parkes, Hist. Chan. 28; Butler's Horæ Subsecivæ [43], p. 66; 1 Collect. Jurid. 25; Pothier, Pand. Lib. 1, tit. 2, §§ 2 to 24; Id. tit. 10, §§ 1, 2, 3; Id. tit. 11, §§ 1 to 9; Id. tit. 14, §§ 1, 2; Id. tit. 20.

[2] Taylor's Elem. Civil Law, 211, 213, 215, 216; Pothier, Pand. Lib. 2, tit. 1, art. 2, §§ 5 to 8; Id. § 10.

[3] Taylor's Elem. Civil Law, 213, 214; Id. 93, 94, 95; Pothier, Pand. Lib. 50, tit. 16; De Verb. Signif. Actio; Inst. Lib. 4, tit. 6, §§ 3, 8; Inst. Lib. 3, tit. 14, § 1; Heinecc. De Edict. Prætor. Lib. 1, cap. 6; 3 Black. Comm. 50; Parkes, Hist. Ch. 28. See 1 Collect. Jurid. 33; De Lolme on Eng. Const. B. 1, ch. 11.

of municipal jurisprudence from each other in the administration of justice ; or in denying to one court the power to dispose of all the merits of a cause, when its forms of proceeding are ill adapted to afford complete relief, and giving jurisdiction of the same cause to another court better adapted to do entire justice by its larger and more expansive authority.

CHAPTER II.

THE ORIGIN AND HISTORY OF EQUITY JURISPRUDENCE.

38. HAVING thus ascertained what is the true nature and character of Equity Jurisprudence as it is administered in countries governed by the common law, it seems proper, before proceeding to the consideration of the particulars of that jurisdiction, to take a brief review of its origin and progress in England, from which country America has derived its own principles and practice on the same subject. It is not intended here to speak of the Common Law Jurisdiction of the Court of Chancery, or of any of its specially delegated jurisdiction in exercising the prerogatives of the Crown, as in cases of infancy and lunacy; or of its statutable jurisdiction in cases of bankruptcy.[1] The inquiry will mainly relate to its equitable, or, as it is sometimes called, its extraordinary jurisdiction.[2]

39. The origin of the Court of Chancery is involved in the same obscurity which attends the investigation of many other questions of high antiquity relative to the common law.[3] The administration of justice in England was originally confided to the Aula Regis, or great Court or Council of the King, as the Supreme Court of Judicature, which in those early times undoubtedly administered equal justice according to the rules of both law and equity, or of either, as the case might chance to require.[4] When that court was broken into pieces, and its principal jurisdiction distributed among various courts, the Common Pleas, the King's Bench, and the Exchequer, each received a

[1] See Com. Dig. Chancery, C. 1; 1 Madd. Ch. Pr. 262; 2 Madd. Ch. Pr. 447; Id. 565; 3 Black. Comm. 426, 427, 428.
[2] 3 Black. Comm. 50; Com. Dig. Chancery, C. 2; 4 Inst. 79; 2 Inst. 552.
[3] Mitford, Pl. Equity, 1; Com. Dig. Chancery, A. 1; 4 Inst. 79; 1 Wooddes. Lect. vi.
[4] 3 Black. Comm. 50; 1 Reeves, Hist. 62, 63.

certain portion, and the Court of Chancery also obtained a portion.[1] But at that period the idea of a Court of Equity as contradistinguished from a Court of Law does not seem to have subsisted in the original plan of partition, or to have been in the contemplation of the sages of the day.[2] Certain it is that among the earliest writers of the common law, such as Bracton, Glanvill, Britton, and Fleta, there is not a syllable to be found relating to the equitable jurisdiction of the Court of Chancery.[3] Fleta indeed mentions the existence of a certain office called the Chancery, and that to the office 'it belongs to hear and examine the petitions and complaints of plaintiffs, and to give them, according to the nature of the injuries shown by them, due remedy by *the writs of the King.*'[4]

40. That the Court of Chancery, in the exercise of its ordinary jurisdiction, is a court of very high antiquity, cannot be doubted. It was said by Lord Hobart that it is an original and fundamental court, as ancient as the kingdom itself.[5] The name of the court, Chancery (Cancellaria), is derived from that of the presiding officer, Chancellor (Cancellarius), an officer of great distinction, whose office may be clearly traced back before the Conquest, to the times of the Saxon kings, many of whom had their chancellors.[6] Lord Coke supposes that the title ' Cancellarius' arose from his cancelling (a cancellando) the king's letters patent when granted contrary to law, which is the highest point of jurisdiction.[7] But the office and name of Chancellor (Mr. Justice Blackstone has observed) was certainly known to the courts of the Roman emperors, where it originally seems to have signified a chief scribe, or secretary, who was afterwards invested

---

[1] 3 Black. Comm. 50; Com. Dig. Chancery, A. 1, 2, 3; 1 Collect. Jurid. 27 to 30; Parkes, Hist. Chan. 16, 17, 28, 56; 1 Eq. Abridg. 129; Courts, B. note (a); 1 Wooddes. Lect. vi. pp. 174, 175; Gilb. For. Roman. 14; 1 Reeves, Hist. 59, 60, 63; Bac. Abridg. Court of Chancery, C.

[2] 3 Black. Comm. 50. The Legal Judic. in Chanc. stated (1727), ch. 2, p. 24.

[3] Id. 50; Parkes, Hist. Chan. 25; 4 Inst. 82; 1 Reeves, Hist. 61; 2 Reeves, Hist. 250, 251.

[4] Parkes, Hist. Chan. 25; Fleta, Lib. 2, cap. 13; 4 Inst. 78.

[5] Hobart, R. 63; Com. Dig. Chancery, A. 1, 2; 2 Inst. 551, 552; 4 Inst. 78, 79.

[6] Com. Dig. Chancery, A. 1; 4 Inst. 78; 1 Wooddes. Lect. vi. pp. 161 to 165; Prynne's Animadv. 48; 1 Coll. Jurid. 26; 1 Rep. in Chan. App. 5, 7.

[7] 4 Inst. 88; Eunomus, Dial. 3, § 60.

CHAP. II.] ORIGIN AND HISTORY. 37

with several judicial powers, and a general superintendency over the rest of the officers of the prince.[1] From the Roman emperors it passed to the Roman Church, ever emulous of imperial state; and hence every bishop has to this day his chancellor, the principal judge of his consistory. And when the modern kingdoms of Europe were established upon the ruins of the empire, almost every state preserved its chancellor, with different jurisdictions and dignities, according to their different constitutions. But in all of them he seems to have had the supervision of all charters, letters, and such other public instruments of the Crown as were authenticated in the most solemn manner; and therefore when seals came in use he always had the custody of the king's great seal.[2]

41. It is not so easy to ascertain the origin of the equitable or extraordinary jurisdiction of the Court of Chancery. By some

---

[1] See Parkes, Hist. Chan. 14; 1 Wooddes. Lect. vi. p. 160; Hist. of Chancery (1726), 3, 4.

[2] 3 Black. Comm. 46, 47; 1 Wooddes. Lect. vi. pp. 159, 160; 1 Collect. Jurid. 25; Parkes, Hist. Chan. 14; 1 Reeves, Hist. 61; 2 Reeves, Hist. 250, 251. Camden, in his Britannia, p. 180, states the matter in this manner: 'The Chancery drew that name from a chancellor, which name, under the ancient Roman emperors, was not of so great esteem and dignity, as we learn out of Vopiscus. But now-a-days a name it is of the highest honor, and chancellors are advanced to the highest pitch of civil dignity; whose name Cassiodorus fetcheth from cross-grates, or lattices, because they examined matters within places (secretum) severed apart, enclosed with partitions of such cross-bars, which the Latins called Cancelli. Regard (saith he to a chancellor) what name you bear. It cannot be hidden, which you do within lattices. For you keep your grates lightsome, your bars open, and your doors transparent as windows. Whereby it is very evident that he sat within grates, where he was to be seen on every side; and thereof it may be thought he took his name. But minding it was his part, being, as it were, the prince's mouth, eye, and ear, to strike and slash out with cross lines, lattice like, those letters, commissions, warrants, and decrees, passed against law and right, or prejudicial to the Commonwealth, which, not improperly, they called "to cancel," some think the name of chancellor came from this cancelling. And in a glossary of a later time this we read: A chancellor is he whose office it is to look into and peruse the writings of the emperor; to cancel what is written amiss, and to sign that which is well.' However antiquaries differ much upon the origin of the word 'chancellor.' Some derive it 'a cancellis,' or latticed doors, and hold that it was a denomination of those ushers who had the care of the 'cancelli,' or latticed doors, leading to the presence-chamber of the emperors and other great men. See 1 Wooddes. Lect. vi. pp. 159, 160; Bythewood's Eunomus, Dial. 3, § 60, note (a), p. 564; Brissonius, Voce, Cancellarius. Vicat, Vocab. Voce, Cancellarius; 1 Savigny's Hist. of Roman Law, translated by Cathcart, pp. 51 to 83.

persons it has been held to be as ancient as the kingdom itself.[1] Others are of a different opinion. Lambard, who (according to Lord Coke) was a keeper of the Records of the Tower, and a Master in Chancery, says that he could not find that the chancellor held any Court of Equity, nor that any causes were drawn before the chancellor for help in equity before the time of Henry IV.; in whose days, by reason of intestine troubles, feoffments to uses did first begin, as some think.[2] Lord Coke says it has been thought that this Court of Equity began in the reign of Henry V., and increased in the reign of Henry VI.; but that its principal growth was during the chancellorship of Cardinal Wolsey, in the reign of Henry VIII.[3] And he adds, in another place, that we find no cases in our books reported before the reign of Henry VI.[4] Lord Coke's known hostility to the jurisdiction of the Court of Chancery would very much abate our confidence in his researches, if they were not opposed by other pressing authorities.[5]

[1] Com. Dig. Chancery, A. 2; Jurisd. of Chancery Vind. 1 Rep. in Chan. App. 9, 10; 1 Collect. Jurid. 28, 29, 30, 62 : Discourses on Judicial Authority of the Master of Rolls, 2; Id. Edit. of 1728, Preface, cxi. to cxix. (ascribed to Lord Hardwicke); Barton, Equity, Introd. 2 to 13. This was Lord Hobart's opinion (as we have seen), who added: 'That part of equity being opposite to regular law, and in a manner an arbitrary discretion, is still administered by the king himself, and his chancellor in his name, ab initio, as a special trust committed to the king, and not by him to be committed to another.' Hob. Rep. 63. Camden (Britannia, p. 181) says: 'It is plain and manifest that chancellors were in England before the Normans' Conquest.' In the Vindication of the Judgment, given by King James, in the case of the Court of Chancery (1 Collectanea Juridica, pp. 23, 61, 62), it is said: 'It cannot be denied but that the chancery, as it judgeth in equity, is a part of the law of the land and of the ancient common law;' 'for equity is, and always hath been, a part of the law of the land.'

[2] 2 Inst. 552. But see 1 Wooddes. Lect. vi. p. 176, note (*b*); Parkes, Hist. Chan. 27; Id. 34; Jurisdiction of Chan. Vind. 1 Rep. in Chan. App. 7, 8; 1 Collect. Jurid. 27; Legal Judic. in Chan. stated (1727), pp. 28, 29.

[3] 2 Inst. 553.   [4] 4 Inst. 82.

[5] 3 Black. Comm. 54; 1 Collect. Jurid. 23, &c.; Com. Dig. Chancery, A. 2; 1 Wooddes. Lect. vi. pp. 176, 177. Camden (Britannia, p. 181) says: 'To this chancellor's office, in process of time, much authority and dignity hath been adjoined by authority of Parliament; especially ever since that lawyers stood so precisely upon the strict points of law, and caught men with the traps and snares of their law terms; that of necessity there was a Court of Equity to be erected, and the same committed to the chancellor, who might give judgment according to equity and reason, and moderate the extremity of law, which was wont to be thought extreme wrong.'

Mr. Cooper, in his Lettres sur la Cour de la Chancellerie (Lettr. 25, p. 182),

42. Lord Hale's account of the matter is as follows: 'There were many petitions referred to the Council (meaning either the Privatum Concilium or Legale Concilium Regis) from the Parliament; sometimes the answers to particular petitions, and sometimes whole bundles of petitions in Parliament which by reason of a dissolution could not be there determined, were referred, in the close of the Parliament, sometimes to the Council in general, and sometimes to the chancellor. And this I take to be the true original of the Chancery Jurisdiction in matters of equity, and gave rise to the multitude of equitable causes to be there arbitrarily determined.' And he afterwards adds: 'Touching the equitable jurisdiction (in chancery), though in ancient time no such thing was known, yet it hath now so long obtained, and is so fitted to the disposal of lands and goods, that it must not be shaken, though in many things fit to be bounded or reformed. Two things might possibly give original [jurisdiction], or at least much contribute to its enlargement. (1) The usual committing of particular petitions in Parliament, not there determined, unto the determination of the chancellor, which was as frequent as to the Council; and such a foundation being laid for a jurisdiction, it was not difficult for it to acquire more. (2) By the invention of *uses* (that is, *trusts*), which were frequent and necessary, especially in the times of dissension touching the Crown. In these proceedings the chancellor took himself to be the only dispenser of the king's conscience; and possibly the Council was not called, either as assistants or co-judges.'[1] We shall presently see how far these suggestions have been established.

43. Lord Hardwicke seems to have accounted for the jurisdiction in another manner. The chancery is the grand Officina Justitiæ, out of which all original writs issue under the great

says that there is not a doubt that the jurisdiction now exercised by the chancellor to mitigate the severity of the common law has always been a part of the law of England. And he cites, in proof of it, the remark, stated in Burnet's Life of Lord Hale, p. 106, that he (Lord Hale) did look upon equity as a part of the common law, and one of the grounds of it. There is no doubt that this remark is well founded; but it may well be doubted whether Lord Hale meant anything more than a general assertion, that in the administration of the common law there often mingled equitable considerations and constructions, and not merely a strict and rigid summum jus.

[1] Parkes, Hist. Chan. App. pp. 502, 503. See also Hist. Chan. (1726), 11, 12, 13, 14; Parkes, Hist. Chan. 56.

seal, returnable into the Courts of Common Law, to found proceedings in actions competent to the Common Law Jurisdiction. The chancellor therefore (according to Lord Hardwicke) was the most proper judge whether upon any petition so referred such a writ could not be framed and issued by him as might furnish an adequate relief to the party; and if he found the common-law remedies deficient, he might proceed according to the extraordinary power committed to him by the reference: Ne Curia Regis deficeret in justitia exercenda.[1] Thus the exercise of the equitable jurisdiction took its rise from his being the proper officer to whom all applications were made for writs to ground actions at the common law; and from many cases being brought before him in which that law would not afford a remedy, and thereby being induced through necessity or compassion to extend a discretionary remedy.[2] If (Lord Hardwicke added) this account of the original of the jurisdiction in equity in England be historically true, it will at least hint one answer to the question how the forum of common law and the forum of equity came to be separated with us. It was stopped at its source, and in the first instance; for if the case appeared to the chancellor to be merely of equity, he issued no original writ, without which the Court of Common Law could not proceed in the cause, but he retained the cognizance to himself.[3] The jurisdiction then may be deemed in some sort a resulting jurisdiction in cases not submitted to the decision of other courts by the Crown, or Parliament, as the great fountain of justice.[4]

44. Lord King (or whoever else was the author of the treatise entitled, 'The Legal Judicature in Chancery stated')[5]

[1] An account, nearly similar, of the Court of Chancery, is given in Bacon's Abridg. Court of Chancery, A. C.
[2] Parkes, Hist. Chan. App. pp. 503, 504.
[3] Id. Rex v. Hare, 1 Str. Rep. 150, 151. Per Yorke arguendo.
[4] Id. 502; Hist. of Chan (1726), pp. 9, 10, 12, 13; Parkes, Hist. of Chan. 56. Sir James Mackintosh, in his elegant Life of Sir Thomas More, has sketched out a history of chancery jurisdiction not materially different from that given by Lord Hardwicke, aided, as he was, by the later discoveries of the Commissioners of the Public Records, as stated in their printed reports. I would gladly transcribe the whole passage, if it might not be thought to occupy too large a space for a work like the present.
[5] Mr. Cooper, in his Lettres sur la Cour de la Chancellerie, 85, note (1), expresses a doubt whether Lord King was the author of this pamphlet, stating that it was written by the same person who wrote the History of the Chancery,

deduced the jurisdiction of the Court of Chancery from the prerogative of the king to administer justice in his realm, being sworn by his coronation oath to deliver his subjects æquam et rectam justitiam. This it was impossible for him to do in person; and therefore of necessity he delegated it, by several portions, to ministers and officers deputed under him. But inasmuch as positive laws must in their nature consist of general institutions, there was of necessity a variety of particular cases still happening where no proper or adequate remedy could be given by the ordinary courts of justice. Therefore to supply this want, and correct the rigor of the positive law, recourse was had to the king as the fountain of justice, to obtain relief in such cases. The method of application was by bills or petitions to the king, sometimes in Parliament and sometimes out of Parliament, commonly directed to him and his Council; and the granting of them was esteemed not a matter of right, but of grace and favor. When Parliament met, there were usually petitions of all sorts preferred to the king; and the distinguishing of these petitions and giving proper answers to them occasioned a weight and load of business, especially when Parliament sat but a few days.[1] Accordingly in the 8th of the reign of Edward I. an ordinance passed by which petitions of this sort were to be referred, according to their nature, to the chancellor and the justices; and in matters of grace, to the chancellor. And if the chancellor and others could not do without the king, then they were to bring the matter with their own hands before the king, to know his pleasure. So that no petitions should come before the king and his Council, but by the hands of the chancellor and other chief ministers.[2] And hence the writer deduces the

---

relating to the judicial power of that court and the rights of the Masters (1726). Bishop Hurd, in his Life of Warburton, says that they were both written by Mr. Burrough, with the aid of Bishop Warburton. The discourse of the Judicial Authority of the Master of the Rolls is said to have been written by Lord Hardwicke alone, or in conjunction with Sir Joseph Jekyll. Cooper, Lettres, &c., p. 334, App. C.; Id. p. 85, note.

[1] Parkes, Hist. Chan. 56.
[2] Legal Judic. in Chan. (1727), pp. 27, 28, 29. The Ordinance (8 Edw. I.), is cited at large in the work, The Legal Judicature, &c., p. 27, and is as follows. It recites that the people who came to Parliament were often 'delayed and disturbed, to the great grievance of them and of the court, by the multitude of petitions laid before the king, the greatest part whereof might be despatched by the chancellor and by the justices; therefore it is

conclusion that at this time all matters of grace were determinable only by the king. And he added that he did not find any traces of a Court of Equity in chancery in the time of Edward II., and that it seemed to him that the equity side of the court began in the reign of Edward III.,[1] when by proclamation he referred matters of grace to the cognizance of the chancellor.[2]

provided that all the petitions which concern the seal shall come first to the chancellor; and those which touch the exchequer, to the exchequer; and those which concern the justices and the law of the land, to the justices; and those which concern the Jews, to the justices of the Jews; and if the affairs are so great, or if they are of grace, that the chancellor and others cannot do it without the king, then they shall bring them with their own hands before the king, to know his pleasure; so that no petitions shall come before the king and his Council, but by the hands of his said chancellor and other chief ministers; so that the king and his Council may, without the load of other business, attend to the great business of his realm and of other foreign countries.' The same ordinance will be found in Ryley, Placit. Parliam. p. 442, and Parkes, Hist. Chan. 29, 30.

[1] Legal Judic. in Chan. (1727), p. 28.

[2] Id. 30, 31 (22 Edw. III.). See Parkes, Hist. Chan. 35; 1 Equity Abr. Courts, B. note (*a*). The proclamation is given in the Legal Judicature, &c., pp. 30, 31, and in Parkes, History of Chancery, p. 35. It is as follows: ' The King to the sheriffs of London greeting: Forasmuch as we are greatly and daily busied in various affairs concerning us and the state of our realm of England: We will, That whatsoever business, relating as well to the common law of our kingdom as our special grace, cognizable before us, from henceforth be prosecuted as followeth, viz. The common law business, before the Archbishop of Canterbury elect, our chancellor, by him to be despatched; and the other matters, grantable by our special grace, be prosecuted before our said chancellor, or our well-beloved clerk, the Keeper of the Privy Seal, so that they, or one of them, transmit to us such petitions of business which without consulting us they cannot determine, together with their advice thereupon, without any further prosecution to be had before us for the same; that upon inspection thereof we may further signify to the aforesaid chancellor or keeper our will and pleasure therein; and, that none other do for the future pursue such kind of business before us, we command you immediately, upon sight hereof, to make proclamation of the premises,' &c. Mr. Lambard, in his work on the Jurisdiction of Courts, says of the Court of Chancery, that ' the king did at first determine causes in equity in person; and about the 20th of Edward III., the king, going beyond sea, delegated this power to the chancellor;' and then, he says, ' Several statutes were made to enlarge the jurisdiction of this court, 17 Rich. II. ch. 6,' &c. Bigland arguendo in Rex *v.* Standish (1 Mod. R. 59). And Bigland then adds, ' But the chancellor took not upon him, ex officio, to determine matters in equity, till Edward the Fourth's time ; for till then it was done by the king in person, who delegated to whom he pleased.' This last remark seems, from the recent publication of the Record Commissioners, to be founded in error. 1 Cooper, Public Rec. p. 354, ch. 18.

And the jurisdiction was clearly established and acted on in the reign of Richard II.[1]

45. Mr. Justice Blackstone seems to rely on the same general origin of the jurisdiction of chancery, as arising from the reference of petitions from the Privy Council to the chancellor; and also from the introduction of uses of land, about the end of the reign of Edward III.[2] Mr. Wooddeson deduces the jurisdiction from the same source, and lays great stress on the proclamation of 22 Edw. III.; and also on the statute of 36 Edw. III. (stat. 1, ch. 9), which he, as well as Spelman, considers as referring many things to the sole and exclusive cognizance of the chancellor.[3] And he adds, that it seems incontrovertible that the chancery exercised an equitable jurisdiction, though its practice perhaps was not very flourishing or frequent through the reign of Edward III.[4]

46. But all our juridical antiquaries admit that the jurisdiction of chancery was established, and in full operation, during the reign of Richard II.; and their opinions are supported by the incontrovertible facts contained in the remonstrances and other acts of Parliament. At this period the extensive use or abuse of the powers of chancery had become an object of jealousy with Parliament, and various efforts were made to restrain and limit its authority. But the Crown steadily supported it.[5] And the invention of the writ of subpœna by John Waltham, Bishop

---

[1] Id. 29, 32, 33; Parkes, Hist. Chan. 39 to 44, 51; Rex v. Standish, 1 Mod. R. 59, Bigland's Argument.

[2] 3 Black. Comm. 50 to 52; Parkes, Hist. Chan. 56.

[3] 1 Wooddes. Lect. vi. p. 176, and note (f); 2 Inst. 553; Parkes, Hist. Chan. 35; 1 Eq. Abr. Courts, B. note (a).

[4] 1 Wooddes. Lect. vi. pp. 178, 179 to 183; see also 7 Dane's Abridg. ch. 225, art. 4, § 1. Mr. Reeves, in his History of the English Law, traces the origin of the Court of Chancery to the reign of Richard II.; and refers the probable origin of its jurisdiction to the reference of petitions to the chancellor by Parliament or by the king's Council; and conjectures that he soon afterwards, as the king's adviser, began to grant redress, without any such reference, by the mere authority of the king. 3 Reeves, Hist. of English Law, pp. 188 to 191. Mr. Jeremy, in the Introduction to his Treatise on Equity Jurisdiction (pp. i. to xxi.), has given a sketch of the origin and progress of that jurisdiction in England. It is certainly a valuable though concise review of it. But it does not seem to contain any remarks important to be taken notice of, beyond what are furnished by the other authors already cited. See also Barton on Eq. Pract. Introd. pp. 2 to 13.

[5] Parkes, Hist. Chan. 39 to 44.

of Salisbury, who was Keeper of the Rolls, about the 5th of Richard II., gave great efficiency, if not expansion, to the jurisdiction.[1] In the 13th of Richard II. the Commons prayed that no party might be required to answer before the chancellor or the Council of the king for any matter where a remedy is given by the common law, unless it be by writ of scire facias in the county where it is found by the common law. To which the king answered that he would preserve his royalty, as his progenitors had done before him.[2] And the only redress granted was by Stat. 17 Richard II., ch. 6, by which it was enacted that the chancellor should have power to award damages to the defendant, in case the suggestions of the bill were untrue, according to his discretion.[3] The struggles upon this subject were maintained in the subsequent reigns of Henry IV. and V. But the Crown resolutely resisted all appeals against the jurisdiction; and finally, in the time of Edward IV., the process by bill and subpœna was become the daily practice of the court.[4]

47. Considerable new light has been thrown upon the subject of the origin and antiquity of the equitable jurisdiction of the Court of Chancery by the recent publication of the labors of the Commissioners on the Public Records. Until that period the notion was very common (which was promulgated by Lord Ellesmere) that there were no petitions of the chancery remaining in the office of record before the 15th year of the reign of Henry VI. But it now appears that many hundreds have been lately found among the records of the Tower for nearly fifty years antecedent to the period mentioned by Lord Ellesmere, and commencing about the time of the passage of the statute of 17 Rich. II.

---

[1] 3 Reeves, Hist. 192 to 194; Id. 274, 379, 380, 381; 3 Black. Comm. 52; Bac. Abr. Court of Chancery, C. In the third year of the reign of Henry V., the Commons, in a petition to the king, declared themselves aggrieved by writs of subpœna sued out of chancery for matters determinable at the common law, 'which were never granted or used before the time of the late King Richard, when John Waltham, heretofore Bishop of Salisbury, of his craft, made, formed, and commenced such innovations.' Parkes, Hist. Chan. 47, 48; 1 Wooddes. Lect. vi. pp. 183, 184. See also Gilb. Forum Roman. 17.

[2] Parkes, Hist. Chan. 41; 4 Inst. 82.

[3] Parkes, Hist. Chan. 41, 42; 3 Black. Comm. 52; 4 Inst. 82, 83; 1 Wooddes. Lect. vi. p. 183; 3 Reeves, Hist. 194.

[4] 3 Black. Comm. 53; Parkes, Hist. Chan. 45 to 57; 1 Wooddes. Lect. vi. pp. 183 to 186; 3 Reeves, Hist. 193, 194, 274, 379, 380.

ch. 6.[1] But there is much reason to believe that upon suitable researches many petitions or bills addressed to the chancellor will be found of a similar character during the reigns of Edward I., Edward II., and Edward III.[2]

48. From the proceedings which have been published by the Record Commissioners it appears that the chief business of the Court of Chancery in those early times did not arise from the introduction of uses of land, according to the opinion of most writers on the subject. Very few instances of applications to the chancellor on such grounds occur among the proceedings of the chancery during the first four or five reigns after the equitable jurisdiction of the court seems to have been fully established. Most of these ancient petitions appear to have been presented in consequence of assaults and trespasses and a variety of outrages which were cognizable at common law, but for which the party complaining was unable to obtain redress in consequence of the maintenance and protection afforded to his adversary by some powerful baron, or by the sheriff, or by some officer of the county in which they occurred.[3]

---

[1] 1 Cooper, Pub. Rec. 355. I extract this statement from the Preface to the Calendars of the Proceedings in Chancery, &c., published by the Record Commissioners in 1827, and now before me. That Preface is signed by John Bayley, Sub-Commissioner. But it would seem that it was in fact drawn up by Mr. Lysons more than ten years before. Mr. Cooper, in his very valuable account of the Public Records, has published this preface verbatim, and has also extracted a letter of Mr. Lysons, written on the same subject in 1816. The preface and letter seem almost identical in language. 1 Cooper, Pub. Rec. ch. 18, p. 354; Id. 384, note (b); Id. 455 to 458. In the English Quarterly Jurist for January, 1828, there will be found, in a review of these Calendars, a very succinct but interesting account of the contents of the early Chancery Cases printed by the Record Commissioners.

[2] Mr. Cooper says that he 'has made some inquiries which induce him to think that there still exist among the records at the Tower many petitions or bills addressed to the chancellor during the reigns of Edw. I., Edw. II. and Edw. III., similar to those addressed to that judge during the reign of Richard II., selections from which have been printed. Upon a very slight research several documents of this description are stated to have been discovered, but only one of them has been seen by the compiler. It is dated the 38th year of Edward III.' 1 Cooper, Publ. Rec. Addenda, pp. 454, 455. Mr. Barton says that so early as the reign of Edward I. the chancellor began to exercise an original and independent jurisdiction, as a Court of Equity in contradistinction to a Court of Law. Barton on Eq. Pr. Introd. p. 7.

[3] This passage is a literal transcript from the Preface to the Calendars in Chancery; and it is fully borne out by the examples of those bills and petitions given at large in the same work. Mr. Cooper, in his own work on the

49. If this be a true account of the earliest known exercises of equitable jurisdiction, it establishes the point that it was principally applied to remedy defects in the common-law proceedings; and therefore that equity jurisdiction was entertained upon the same ground which now constitutes the principal reason of its interference, viz., that a wrong is done, for which there is no plain, adequate, and complete remedy in the Courts of Common Law.[1] And in this way great strength is added to the opinions of Lord Hale and Lord Hardwicke, that its jurisdiction is in reality the residuum of that of the Commune Concilium or Aula Regis, not conferred on other courts, and necessarily exercisable by the Crown as a part of its duty and prerogative to administer justice and equity.[2] The introduction of Uses or Trusts (*a*) at a later period may have given new activity and extended operation to the jurisdiction of the court, but it did not found it. The redress given by the chancellor in such cases was merely a new application of the old principles of the court, since there was no remedy at law to enforce the observance of such uses or trusts.[3]

Public Records has given an abstract or marginal note of all the examples thus given, from the reign of Richard II. to the reign of Richard III., amounting in number to more than one hundred. 1 Cooper, Pub. Rec. 359, 373; Id. 377 to 385. As we recede from the reign of Richard II. and advance to modern times, the cases become of a more mixed character, and approach to those now entertained in chancery.

[1] See Treatise on Subpœna, ch. 2; Harg. Law Tracts, pp. 333, 334.

[2] See Eunomus, Dial. 3, § 60; 1 Eq. Abrid. Courts, B. note (*a*). Ante, § 42. See the British and Foreign Quarterly Review, No. 27, Dec. 1842, pp. 167, 168, 172, 173.

[3] See 3 Black. Comm. 52; 3 Reeves, Hist. 379, 381; 1 Wooddes. Lect. vi. pp. 174, 176, 178, 182; Eunomus, Dial. 3, § 60; Parkes, Hist. Chan. 28 to 31. The view which is here taken of the subject is confirmed by the remarks of the commissioners under the chancery commission, in the 50th George III., whose report was afterwards published by Parliament in 1826. The passage to which allusion is made is as follows: 'The proceedings in the Courts of Common Law are simple, and generally founded on certain writs of great antiquity, conceived in prescribed forms. This adherence to prescribed forms has been considered as important to the due administration of justice in common cases. But in progress of time cases arose in which full justice could not be done in the Courts of Common Law according to the practice then prevailing. And for the purpose of obtaining an adequate remedy in such cases resort was had to the extraordinary jurisdiction of the Courts of Equity, which

---

(*a*) Upon this subject see an article by Mr. Justice Holmes in the April No., 1885, of the Law Quarterly Review.

50. From this slight review of the origin and progress of equitable jurisdiction in England, it cannot escape observation how naturally it grew up in the same manner, and under the same circumstances, as the equitable jurisdiction of the prætor at Rome. Each of them arose from the necessity of the thing in the actual administration of justice, and from the deficiencies of the positive law (the lex scripta), or from the inadequacy of the remedies, in the prescribed forms, to meet the full exigency of the particular case. It was not an usurpation for the purpose of acquiring and exercising power, but a beneficial interposition, to correct gross injustice and to redress aggravated and intolerable grievances.[1]

51. But be the origin of the equity jurisdiction of the Court of Chancery what it may, from the time of the reign of Henry VI. it constantly grew in importance;[2] and in the reign

alone had the power of examining the party on oath, and thereby acting through the medium of his conscience, and of procuring the evidence of persons not amenable to the jurisdiction of the Courts of Common Law, and whose evidence therefore it was in many cases impossible to obtain without the assistance of a Court of Equity. The application to this extraordinary jurisdiction, instead of being in the form of a writ prescribed by settled law, seems always to have been in the form of a petition of the party or parties aggrieved, stating the grievance, the defect of remedy by proceedings in the Courts of Common Law, and the remedy which it was conceived ought to be administered. This mode of proceeding unavoidably left every complaining party to state his case according to the particular circumstances, always asserting that the party was without adequate remedy at the common law.' The reviewer of the Early Proceedings in Chancery, in the English Jurist for January, 1828, concludes his observations in the following manner: 'It is, we think, established to demonstration, that the general jurisdiction of the court was derived from that extensive judicial power which in early times the king's ordinary council had exercised; but that it arose gradually and insensibly as circumstances occurred and occasions seemed to demand it; and that having so arisen, it afterwards settled down by equally slow degrees, and in consequence of occasional resistance, excited to its encroaching and despotic spirit, appears to us to be equally as demonstrable.' 1 English Quarterly Jurist, p. 350.

[1] 1 Kaims on Equity, Introd. p. 19; Butler's Horæ Jurid. § v. 3, pp. 43 to 46; Id. App. note 3, p. 130. Those who have a curiosity to trace the origin and history of the prætor's authority in Rome, and the gradual development or assumption of jurisdiction by him, will find ample means for this purpose in Taylor's Elements of the Civil Law, pp. 210 to 216, and in Heineccius De Edictis Prætorum, Lib. 1, cap. 6, per tot. The same complaints were made at Rome as in England, of the excess and abuse of authority by the prætors, and the complaints commonly ended in the same way. The jurisdiction was occasionally restricted, but it was generally confirmed. See Butler's Horæ Jurid. § v. 3, pp. 43 to 46.

[2] Parkes, Hist. Chan. 55, 56; 3 Reeves, Hist. 379 to 382.

of Henry VIII. it expanded into a broad and almost boundless jurisdiction under the fostering care and ambitious wisdom and love of power of Cardinal Wolsey.[1] Yet (Mr. Reeves observes), after all, notwithstanding the complaints of the Cardinal's administration of justice, he has the reputation of having acted with great ability in the office of chancellor, which lay heavier upon him than it had upon any of his predecessors, owing to the too great care with which he entertained suits, and the extraordinary influx of business, which might be attributed to other causes.[2] Sir Thomas More, the successor to the Cardinal, took a more sober and limited view of Equity Jurisprudence, and gave public favor as well as dignity to the decrees of the court. But still there were clamors from those who were hostile to equity during his time, and especially to the power of issuing injunctions to judgments and other proceedings, in order to prevent irreparable injustice.[3] This controversy was renewed with much greater heat and violence in the reign of James I., upon the point whether a Court of Equity could give relief for or against a judgment at common law; and it was mainly conducted by Lord Coke against, and by Lord Ellesmere in favor of, the chancery jurisdiction. At last the matter came directly before the king, and upon the advice and opinion of very learned lawyers to whom he referred it, his Majesty gave judgment in favor of the equitable jurisdiction in such cases.[4] Lord Bacon succeeded

[1] 4 Reeves, Hist. 368, 369; Parkes, Hist. Chan. 61, 62; 4 Inst. 91, 92. It seems that the first delegation of the powers of the Lord Chancellor to commissioners was in the time of Cardinal Wolsey. It will be found in Rymer's Fœdera, tom. 14, p. 299; Parkes, Hist. of Chan. 60, 61. It was in the same reign that the Master of the Rolls (it is said), under a like appointment, first set apart and used to hear causes at the Rolls in the afternoon. The Master who thus first heard causes was Cuthbert Tunstall. 4 Reeves, Hist. of the Law, 368, 369; 5 Reeves, Hist. 160. But see Discourse on the Judicial Authority of the Master of the Rolls (1728), § 3, p. 83, &c.; Id. § 4, p. 110, &c., ascribed to Sir Joseph Jekyll.

[2] 4 Reeves, Hist. 370.

[3] Sir James Mackintosh's Life of Sir Thomas More; 4 Reeves, Hist. 370 to 376; Parkes, Hist. Chan. 63 to 65.

[4] 1 Collect. Jurid. 23, &c.; 1 Wooddes. Lect. vi. p. 186; 3 Black. Comm. 54; Parkes, Hist. Chan. 80. The controversy gave rise to many pamphlets, not only at the time but in later periods. The learned reader who is inclined to enter upon the discussion of these points, now of no importance except as a part of the juridical history of England, may consult advantageously the following works: Observations concerning the Office of Lord Chancellor, published in 1651, and ascribed (though it is said incorrectly) to Lord Elles-

Lord Ellesmere; but few of his decrees which have reached us are of any importance to posterity.[1] But his celebrated ordinances for the regulation of chancery gave a systematical character to the business of the court; and some of the most important of them (especially as to bills of review) still constitute the fundamental principles of its present practice.[2]

52. From this period down to the time when Sir Heneage Finch (afterwards Earl of Nottingham) was elevated to the Bench (in 1673), little improvement was made either in the principles or in the practice of chancery;[3] and none of the persons who held the seal were distinguished for uncommon attainments or learning in their profession.[4] With Lord Nottingham a new era commenced. He was a person of eminent abilities and the most incorruptible integrity. He possessed a fine genius, great liberality of views, and a thorough comprehension of the true principles of equity; so that he was enabled to disentangle the doctrines from any narrow and technical notions, and to expand the remedial justice of the court far beyond the aims of his predecessors. In the course of nine years, during which he presided in the court, he built up a system of jurisprudence and jurisdiction upon wide and rational foundations, which served as a model for succeeding judges, and gave a new character to the court;[5] and hence he has been emphatically called 'the father of

---

mere (Discourse concerning the Judicial Authority of the Master of Rolls, 1728, p. 51); A Vindication of the Judgment of King James, &c., printed in an Appendix to the first volume of Reports in Chancery, and in 1 Collect. Jurid. 23, &c.; the several Treatises on the Writ of Subpœna in Chancery, and the Abuses and Remedies in Chancery, in Hargrave's Law Tracts, pp. 321, 425; and 4 Reeves, Hist. of the Law, pp. 370 to 377; 2 Swanst. 24, note. There is a curious anecdote related of Sir Thomas More, who invited the judges to dine with him, and after dinner showed them the number and nature of the causes in which he had granted injunctions to judgments of the Court of Common Law; and the judges, upon full debate of the matters, confessed that they could have done no otherwise themselves. The anecdote is given at large in Mr. Cooper's Lettres sur la Cour de la Chancellerie, Lett. 25, p. 185, note 1, from Roper's Life of Sir Thomas More.

[1] 3 Black. Comm. 55.
[2] See Bacon's Ord. in Chancery, by Beames.
[3] 3 Black. Comm. 55.
[4] See Parkes, Hist. Chan. 92 to 210.
[5] Mr. Justice Blackstone has pronounced a beautiful eulogy on him, in 3 Black. Comm. 56, from which the text is with slight alterations borrowed. See also 4 Black. Comm. 442.

Equity.'[1] His immediate successors availed themselves very greatly of his profound learning and judgment. But a successor was still wanted, who with equal genius, abilities, and liberality should hold the seals for a period long enough to enable him to widen the foundation and complete the structure begun and planned by that illustrious man. Such a successor at length appeared in the person of Lord Hardwicke. This great judge presided in the Court of Chancery during the period of twenty years; and his numerous decisions evince the most thorough learning, the most exquisite skill, and the most elegant juridical analysis. There reigns throughout all of them a spirit of conscientious and discriminating equity, a sound and enlightened judgment as rare as it is persuasive, and a power of illustration from analogous topics of the law as copious as it is exact and edifying. Few judges have left behind them a reputation more bright and enduring; few have had so favorable an opportunity of conferring lasting benefits upon the jurisprudence of their country; and still fewer have improved it by so large, so various, and so important contributions. Lord Hardwicke, like Lord Mansfield, combined with his judicial character the still more embarrassing character of a statesman, and in some sort of a minister of state. Both of them of course encountered great political opposition (whether rightly or wrongly it is beside the purpose of this work to inquire); and it is fortunate for them that their judicial labors are embodied in solid volumes, so that when the prejudices and the passions of the times are past away, they may remain open to the severest scrutiny, and claim from posterity a just and unimpeachable award.[2]

---

[1] 1 Madd. Ch. Pr. Preface, 13. See Parkes, Hist. Chan. 211, 212, 213, 214; 1 Kent, Comm. Lect. 21, p. 492 (2d edition).

[2] See 1 Kent, Comm. Lect. 21, p. 494 (2d edit.), and Lord Kenyon's opinion in Goodtitle v. Otway, 7 T. R. 411. Mr. Charles Butler, in his Reminiscences, has given a sketch of Lord Hardwicke and Lord Mansfield, which no lawyer can read without high gratification. Few men were better qualified to judge of their attainments. 1 Butler's Reminis. § 11, n. 1, 2, pp. 104 to 116. Lord Eldon, in Ex parte Greenway, 8 Ves. R. 312, said, 'He (Lord Hardwicke) was one of the greatest judges that ever sat in Westminster Hall.' Those who wish to form just notions of the great chancellors of succeeding times down to our own may well consult the same interesting pages, in which Lord Camden, Lord Thurlow, Lord Roslyn, Sir William Grant, and though last, not least, the venerable Lord Eldon, are spoken of in terms of high but discriminating praise. See 4 Kent's Comm. Lect. 21, pp. 494, 495 (2d edit.).

53. This short and imperfect sketch of the origin and history of Equity Jurisdiction in England will be here concluded. It has not been inserted in this place from the mere desire to gratify those whose curiosity may lead them to indulge in antiquarian inquiries, laudable and interesting as it may be. But it seemed, if not indispensable, at least important, as an introduction to a more minute and exact survey of that jurisdiction as administered in the present times. In the first place, without some knowledge of the origin and history of Equity Jurisdiction, it will be difficult to ascertain the exact nature and limits of that jurisdiction, and how it can or ought to be applied to new cases as they arise. If it be a mere arbitrary or usurped jurisdiction, standing upon authority and practice, it should be confined within the very limits of its present range; and the terra incognita and the terra prohibita ought to be the same as to its boundaries. If, on the other hand, its jurisdiction be legitimate, and founded in the very nature of remedial justice, and in the delegation of authority in all cases where a plain, adequate, and complete remedy does not exist in any other court, to protect acknowledged rights and to prevent acknowledged wrongs (that is, acknowledged in the Municipal Jurisprudence), then it is obvious that it has an expansive power to meet new exigencies; and the sole question, applicable to the point of jurisdiction, must from time to time be, whether such rights and wrongs do exist, and whether the remedies therefor in other courts, and especially in the Courts of Common Law, are full, and adequate to redress them. If the present examination (however imperfect) has tended to any result, it is to establish that the latter is the true and constitutional predicament and character of the Court of Chancery.

54. In the next place a knowledge of the origin and history of Equity Jurisdiction will help us to understand, and in some measure to explain, as well as to limit, the anomalies which do confessedly exist in the system. We may trace them back to their sources, and ascertain how far they were the result of accidental or political or other circumstances; of ignorance or perversity or mistake in the judges; of imperfect development of principles; of narrow views of public policy; of the seductive influence of prerogative; or finally of a spirit of accommodation to the institutions, habits, laws, or tenures of the age, which

have long since been abolished, but have left the scattered fragments of their former existence behind them. We shall thus be enabled to see more clearly how far the operation of these anomalies should be strengthened or widened; when they may be safely disregarded in their application to new cases and new circumstances; and when, though a deformity in the general system, they cannot be removed without endangering the existence of other portions of the fabric, or interfering with the proportions of other principles which have been moulded and adjusted with reference to them.

55. In the next place such a knowledge will enable us to prepare the way for the gradual improvement as well of the science itself as of the system of its operations. Changes in law, to be safe, must be slowly and cautiously introduced and thoroughly examined. He who is ill-read in the history of any law must be ill-prepared to know its reasons as well as its effects. The causes or occasions of laws are sometimes as important to be traced out as their consequences. The new remedy to be applied may otherwise be as mischievous as the wrong to be redressed. History has been said to be philosophy teaching by examples; and to no subject is this remark more applicable than to law, which is emphatically the science of human experience. A sketch, however general, of the origin and sources of any portion of jurisprudence may at least serve the purpose of pointing out the paths to be explored, and by guiding the inquirer to the very places he seeks, may save him from the labor of wandering in the devious tracks, and of bewildering himself in mazes of errors as fruitless as they may be intricate.

56. In America Equity Jurisprudence had its origin at a far later period than the jurisdiction properly appertaining to the Courts of Common Law. In many of the colonies, during their connection with Great Britain, it had either no existence at all, or a very imperfect and irregular administration.[1] Even since

---

[1] Equity Jurisprudence scarcely had an existence, in any large and appropriate sense of the terms, in any part of New England during its colonial state. (1 Dane, Abridg. ch. 1, art. 7, § 51; 7 Dane, Abridg. ch. 225, art. 1, 2.) In Massachusetts and Rhode Island it still has but a very limited extent. In Maine and New Hampshire more general equity powers have been, within a few years, given to their highest Courts of Law. In Vermont and Connecticut it had an earlier establishment; in the former State since the Revo-

the Revolution, which severed the ties which bound us to the parent country, it has been of slow growth and cultivation; and there are still some States in whose municipal jurisprudence it has no place at all, or no place as a separate and distinct science. Even in those States in which it has been cultivated with the most success and for the greatest length of time, it can scarcely be said to have been generally studied or administered as a system of enlightened and exact principles until about the close of the eighteenth century.[1] Indeed until a much later period, when Reports were regularly published, it scarcely obtained the general regard of the profession beyond the purlieus of its immediate officers and ministers. Even in the State of New York, whose rank in jurisprudence has never been second to that of any State in the Union (if it has not been the first among its peers) equity was scarcely felt in the general administration of justice until about the period of the Reports of Caines and of Johnson. And perhaps it is not too much to say that it did not attain its full maturity and masculine vigor until Mr. Chancellor Kent brought to it the fulness of his own extraordinary learning, unconquerable diligence, and brilliant talents. If this tardy progress has somewhat checked the study of the beautiful and varied principles of equity in America, it has on the other hand enabled us to escape from the embarrassing effects of decisions

---

lution, and in the latter a short time before the Revolution. 2 Swift, Dig. p. 15, edit. 1823. In Virginia there does not seem to have been any court having chancery powers earlier than the Act of 1700, ch. 4. 3 Tucker's Black. App. 7. In New York the first Court of Chancery was established in 1701; but it was so unpopular, from its powers being vested in the Governor and Council, that it had very little business until it was reorganized in 1778. (1 John. Ch. Rep. Preface; Campb. and Camb. American Chancery Digest, Preface, 6; Blake's Chan. Introduct. viii.) In New Jersey it was established in 1705. (1 Fonbl. Eq. by Laussat, edit. 1831, p. 14, note.) Mr. Laussat, in his Essay on Equity in Pennsylvania (1826), has given an account of its origin and progress and present state in that Commonwealth (pp. 16 to 31). From this account we learn that the permanent establishment of a Court of Equity was successfully resisted by the people during the whole of its colonial existence; and that the year 1790 is the true point at which we must fix the establishment of Equity in the Jurisprudence of Pennsylvania. It has since been greatly expanded by some legislative enactments. See also 7 Dane, Abridg. ch. 225, art. 1, 2. (a)

[1] 1 Dane, Abridg. ch. 1, art. 7, § 51; 7 Dane, Abridg. ch. 225, art. 1, 2.

(a) See 1 Quarterly Law Rev. 455. A Court of Chancery existed in Pennsylvania between the years 1720 and 1736. Ib. 456.

which might have been made at an earlier period, when the studies of the profession were far more limited and the benches of America were occasionally, like that of the English Chancery in former ages, occupied by men who, whatever might have been their general judgment or integrity, were inadequate to the duties of their stations, from their want of learning or from their general pursuits. (*a*) Indeed there were often other circumstances which greatly restricted or impeded a proper choice; such as the want of the due enjoyment of executive or popular favor by men of the highest talents, or the discouragement of a narrow and incompetent salary.

57. The Equity Jurisprudence at present exercised in America is founded upon, co-extensive with, and in most respects conformable to, that of England. It approaches even nearer to the latter than the jurisdiction exercised by the Courts of Common Law in America approaches to the common law as administered in England. The common law was not, in many particulars, applicable to the situation of our country when it was first introduced. Whereas Equity Jurisprudence in its main streams flows from the same sources here that it does in England, and admits of an almost universal application in its principles. The Constitution of the United States has in one clause conferred on the National Judiciary cognizance of cases in equity as well as in law; and the uniform interpretation of that clause has been that by cases in equity are meant cases which, in the jurisprudence of England (the parent country), are so called as contradistinguished from cases at the common law.[1] So that in the Courts

[1] Robinson *v.* Campbell, 3 Wheaton, R. 212, 221, 223; Parsons *v.* Bradford, 3 Peters, Sup. Ct. R. 433, 447; 3 Story, Comm. on Const. 506, 507; Id. 644, 645; U. S. *v.* Howland, 4 Wheaton, R. 115; 7 Dane, Abridg. ch. 225, art. 1.

(*a*) 'It must not be forgotten that the rules of Courts of Equity are not, like the rules of the common law, supposed to have been established from time immemorial. It is perfectly well known that they have been established from time to time, — altered, improved, and refined from time to time. In many cases we know the names of the chancellors who invented them. No doubt they were invented for the purpose of securing the better administration of justice, but still they were invented. Take such things as these : the separate use of a married woman, the restraint on alienation, the modern rule against perpetuities, and the rules of equitable waste. We can name the chancellors who first invented them, and state the date when they were first introduced into Equity Jurisprudence; and therefore in cases

of the United States Equity Jurisprudence generally embraces the same matters of jurisdiction and modes of remedy as exist in England. (*a*)

58. In nearly all the States in which Equity Jurisprudence is recognized it is now administered in the modes and according to the forms which appertain to it in England; that is, as a branch of jurisprudence separate and distinct from the remedial justice of Courts of Common Law.[1] In Pennsylvania it was formerly administered through the forms, remedies, and proceedings of the common law; and was thus mixed up with legal rights and titles in a manner not easily comprehensible elsewhere.[2] This anomaly has been in a considerable degree removed by some recent legislative enactments. In some of the States in the Union distinct Courts of Equity are established; in others the powers are exercised concurrently with the Common Law Jurisdiction by the same tribunal, being at once a Court of Law and a Court of Equity, somewhat analogous to the case of the Court of Exchequer in England. In others again no general equity powers exist; but a few specified heads of Equity Jurisprudence are confided to the ordinary Courts of Law, and constitute a limited statutable jurisdiction.[3] (*b*)

[1] Fonblanq. on Eq. by Laussat (edit. 1831), pp. 13 to 20; 7 Dane's Abridg. ch. 225, art. 1, 2.

[2] Id. 18 to 20.

[3] Mr. Chancellor Kent, in a note to his Commentaries, has given a brief statement of the actual organization of Equity Jurisdiction in all the States; to which I gladly refer the learned reader. 4 Kent, Comm. Lect. 58, p. 163, note (*d*). A fuller account may be found in the Preface to Campbell and Cambreleng's American Chancery Digest (edit. 1828), in Mr. Laussat's edi-

---

of this kind the older precedents in equity are of very little value. The doctrines are progressive, refined, and improved; and if we want to know what the rules of equity are, we must look of course rather to the more modern than the more ancient cases.' Jessel, M. R. in Knatchbull *v.* Hallett, 13 Ch. D. 696, 710.

(*a*) By act of Parliament, Aug. 5, 1873, 36 and 37 Vict. ch. 66, the Courts of Chancery, Queen's Bench, Common Pleas, Exchequer, Admiralty, Probate, Divorce and Matrimonial Causes, and the London Court of Bankruptcy were consolidated into one court of two chief divisions, called Her Majesty's High Court of Justice and Her Majesty's High Court of Appeal. The act provides that if a plaintiff or a defendant claims any equitable estate or relief or defence, in any case before any judge, he shall have the same relief as ought to have been given in the Court of Chancery before the act.

(*b*) As to the legislation of the States on the subject, see Bispham, Equity, pp. 16-23.

tion of Fonblanque on Equity, vol. 1, pp. 11 to 20 (edit. 1831); and in Mr. Laussat's Essay on Equity in Pennsylvania. App. (1826). As the systems of the different States are in many cases subject to legislative authority, which is frequently engaged in introducing modifications, a more minute detail would scarcely be of any permanent importance to the profession. The article on Chancery Jurisdiction, in the first volume of the American Jurist, p. 314, contains many very valuable suggestions on this subject; and exhibits in a striking manner the importance of Equity Jurisprudence. See also 7 Dane's Abridg. ch. 225, art. 1, 2.

CHAPTER III.

GENERAL VIEW OF EQUITY JURISDICTION.

59. HAVING traced out the nature and history of Equity Jurisprudence, we are naturally led to the consideration of the various subjects which it embraces and the measure and extent of its jurisdiction. Courts of Equity in the exercise of their jurisdiction may in a general sense be said to differ from Courts of Common Law in the modes of trial, in the modes of proof, and in the modes of relief. One or more of these elements will be found essentially to enter as an ingredient into every subject over which they exert their authority. Lord Coke has in his summary manner stated that three things are to be judged of in the Court of Conscience or Equity, — covin, accident, and breach of confidence;[1] or, as we should now say, matters of fraud, accident, and trust. Mr. Justice Blackstone has also said that Courts of Equity are established 'to detect latent frauds and concealments which the process of the Courts of Law is not adapted to reach; to enforce the execution of such matters of trust and confidence as are binding in conscience, though not cognizable in a Court of Law; to deliver from such dangers as are owing to misfortune or oversight; and to give a more specific relief, and more adapted to the circumstances of the case than can always be obtained by the generality of the rules of the positive or common law.'[2]

60. These, as general descriptions, are well enough; but they are far too loose and inexact to subserve the purposes of those

---

[1] 4 Inst. 84; Com. Dig. Chancery, Z.; 3 Black. Comm. 431; 1 Eq. Abr. Courts, B. § 4, p. 130; 1 Dane's Abridg. ch. 9, art. 1, § 3; Earl of Bath v. Sherwin, Prec. Ch. 261; s. c. 1 Bro. Parl. Cas. 266; Rex v. Hare & Mann, 1 Str. 149, 150, Yorke, arguendo; 1 Wooddes. Lect. vii. pp. 208, 209; Bac. Abridg. Court of Chancery, C.

[2] 1 Black. Comm. 92; and see 3 Black. Comm. 429 to 432.

who seek an accurate knowledge of the actual or supposed boundaries of Equity Jurisdiction. Thus, for example, although fraud, accident, and trust are proper objects of Courts of Equity, it is by no means true that they are exclusively cognizable therein. On the contrary, fraud is in many cases cognizable in a Court of Law. Thus, for example, reading a deed falsely to an illiterate person, whether it be so read by the grantee or by a stranger, avoids it as to the other party at law.[1] And sometimes fraud, such as fraud in obtaining a will, or devise of lands, is exclusively cognizable there.[2] Many cases of accident are remediable at law, such as losses of deeds, mistakes in accounts and receipts, impossibilities in the strict performance of conditions, and other like cases. And even trusts, though in general of a peculiar and exclusive jurisdiction in equity, are sometimes cognizable at law; as, for instance, cases of bailments, and that larger class of cases where the action for money had and received for another's use is maintained ex æquo et bono.[3]

61. On the other hand there are cases of fraud, of accident, and of trust, which neither Courts of Law nor of Equity presume to relieve or mitigate.[4] Thus a man may most unconscientiously wage his law in an action of debt; and yet the aggrieved party will not be relieved in any Court of Law or Equity.[5] And where the law has determined a matter, with all its circumstances, equity cannot (as we have seen) intermeddle against the positive rules of law.[6] And therefore equity will not interfere in such cases, notwithstanding accident or unavoidable necessity.[7] This was long ago remarked by Lord Talbot, who, after saying, 'There are instances indeed in which a Court of Equity gives remedy where the law gives none,' added: 'But where a particular remedy is given by law, and that remedy is bounded and circumscribed by particular rules, it would be very improper for this court to take it up where the

---

[1] Thoroughgood's case, 2 Co. 9 a.; Hobart, R. 296; Id. 126, 330, 426; Shutter's case, 12 Co. R. 90; Jenkins' Cent. 166.
[2] 1 Hovenden on Frauds, Introd. p. 16; Id. ch. 10, p. 252; 1 Dane, Abridg. ch. 9, art. 1, § 3; 3 Wooddes. Lect. lvi. p. 477.
[3] 3 Black. Comm. 431, 432; 1 Wooddes. Lect. vii. pp. 208, 209.
[4] 1 Fonbl. Eq. B. 1, ch. 1, § 3, p. 16.
[5] Francis, Max. Introd. 6, 7.
[6] 1 Fonbl. Eq. B. 1, ch. 1, § 3; 1 Hovend. on Frauds, Introd. pp. 12, 13.
[7] Ibid.; 1 Dane's Abridg. ch. 9, art. 1, § 2.

law leaves it, and extend it further than the law allows.'[1] (a) And upon this ground relief was refused to a creditor of the wife against her husband after her death, though he had received a large fortune with her on his marriage.[2] So a man may by accident omit to make a will, appointment, or gift, in favor of some friend or relative, or he may leave his will unfinished; and yet there can be no relief.[3] And many cases of the non-performance of conditions precedent are equally without redress.[4] So cases of trust may exist, in which the parties must abide by their own false confidence in others, without any aid from courts of justice. Thus in cases of illegal contracts, or those in which one party has placed property in the hands of another for illegal purposes, as for smuggling, if the latter refuses to account for the proceeds and fraudulently or unjustly withholds them, the former must abide by his loss; for, 'In pari delicto melior est conditio possidentis et defendentis,' is a maxim of public policy equally respected in Courts of Law and Courts of Equity.[5] And on the other hand where the fraud is perpetrated by one party only, still, if it involves a public crime, and redress cannot be obtained except by a discovery of the facts from him personally, the law will not compel him to accuse himself of a crime; and therefore the case is one of irremediable injury.[6] (b)

62. These are but a few among many instances which might be selected to establish the justice of the remark that even in

[1] Heard v. Stanford, Cas. Temp. Talb. 174.
[2] Ibid.
[3] See Whitten v. Russell, 1 Atk. 448, 449; 1 Madd. Ch. Pr. 39; Id. 45, 46; 1 Wooddes. Lect. vii. p. 214; Com. Dig. Chancery, 3 F. 8; 1 Fonbl. B. 1, ch. 3, § 7, and note (x); Francis, Max. M. 9, § 4.
[4] 1 Madd. Ch. Pr. 35; Popham v. Bamfield, 1 Vern. R. 83; Lord Falkland v. Bertie, 2 Vern. 333; 7 Dane's Abridg. ch. 225, art. 4, § 6.
[5] Holman v. Johnson, Cowper, R. 341; Armstrong v. Toler, 11 Wheaton, R. 258; Hannay v. Eve, 3 Cranch, R. 242; Grounds and Rudim. of the Law, M. 347, p. 260, edit. 1751; 7 Dane's Abridg. ch. 226, art. 18; Smith v. Bromley, Doug. R. 696, note. The civil law has a like maxim: 'Paria delicta mutua compensatione tolluntur.' Breviar. Advocat. title, Delictum. 'Paria sunt non esse aliquid, vel non esse legitime.' Id. Paria; Batty v. Chester, 5 Beavan, R. 103.
[6] Grounds and Rudim. of the Law, Introd. 6, 7; Id. M. 306, p. 225, edit. 1751; 2 Fonbl. Eq. B. 6, ch. 3, § 5.

(a) Janney v. Buell, 55 Ala. 408, 411.
(b) Equity has no criminal jurisdiction. Supra, note to § 25; Cope v. District Fair, 99 Ill. 489.

cases professedly within the scope of Equity Jurisdiction, such as fraud, accident, and trust, there are many exceptions; and that all that can be ascribed to such general allegations is general truth.[1] The true nature and extent of Equity Jurisdiction as at present administered must be ascertained by a specific enumeration of its actual limits in each particular class of cases falling within its remedial justice.[2] This will accordingly be done in the subsequent pages.

63. Before proceeding however to this distribution of the subject, it may be well to take notice of some few maxims and rules of a general nature which are of constant and tacit and sometimes of express reference in most of the discussions arising in equity, in order that we may understand the true nature and extent of the meaning attached to them.

64. In the first place it is a common maxim that equity follows the law, ' Æquitas sequitur legem.'[3] This maxim is susceptible of various interpretations. It may mean that equity adopts and follows the rules of law in all cases to which those rules may in terms be applicable; or it may mean that equity, in dealing with cases of an equitable nature, adopts and follows the analogies furnished by the rules of law.[4] Now the maxim is true in both of these senses, as applied to different cases and different circumstances. It is universally true in neither sense; or rather it is not of universal application.[5] Where a rule either of the common or the statute law is direct, and governs the case with all its circumstances or the particular point, a Court of Equity is as much bound by it as a Court of Law, and can as little

---

[1] See Com. Dig. Chancery, 3 F. 1 to 9; 7 Dane's Abridg. ch. 225, § 6; 1 Wooddes. Lect. vii. pp. 200 to 215.

[2] Dr. Dane, in his Abridgment and Digest, has devoted two large chapters to the consideration of the System and Practice of Equity, especially in the Courts of the United States. The diligent student will not fail to avail himself of this ample source of information. 7 Dane's Abridg. ch. 225, 226, from pp. 516 to 639.

[3] 1 Dane's Abridg. ch. 9, art. 1, § 2; Grounds and Rudim. of the Law, M. 9 (edit. 1751). See Earl of Bath *v.* Sherwin, 10 Mod. R. 1, 3; Cowper *v.* Cowper, 2 P. Will. 753.

[4] 3 Wooddes. Lect. lvi. pp. 479 to 482.

[5] Sir Thomas Clarke (Master of the Rolls), in one of his elaborate opinions, has remarked, in regard to uses and trusts, that at law the legal operation controls the intent; but in equity the intent controls the legal operation of the deed. Burgess *v.* Wheate, 1 W. Black. R. 137.

justify a departure from it.[1] If the law commands or prohibits a thing to be done, equity cannot enjoin the contrary or dispense with the obligation. Thus since the law has declared in England that the eldest son shall take by descent the whole undevised estate of his parent, a Court of Equity cannot disregard this canon of descent, but must give full effect and vigor to it in all controversies in which the title is asserted.[2] And yet there are cases in which equity will control the legal title of an heir, general or special, when it would be deemed absolute at law; and in which therefore, so far from following the law, it openly abandons it. Thus if a tenant in tail, not knowing the fact, should upon his marriage make a settlement on his wife, and the heir in tail should engross the settlement and conceal the fact, although at law his title would be absolute, a Court of Equity would award a perpetual injunction against asserting it to the prejudice of the settlement.[3] So if an heir-at-law should by parol promise his father to pay his sisters' portions if he would not direct timber to be felled to raise them; although discharged at law, he would in equity be deemed liable to pay them in the same way as if they had been charged on the land.[4] And many cases of a like nature may be put.[5]

64 a.[6] So in many cases equity acts by analogy to the rules of law in relation to equitable titles and estates. Thus although the Statutes of Limitations are in their terms applicable to Courts of Law only, yet equity by analogy acts upon them, and refuses relief under like circumstances. Equity always discountenances laches, and holds that laches is presumable in cases where it is positively declared at law. Thus in cases of equitable titles in land, equity requires relief to be sought within the same period

---

[1] Kemp v. Pryor, 7 Ves. 249 to 251; 2 Bac. Abridg. Court of Chancery, C.

[2] Grounds and Rudim. of the Law, M. 9, p. 16 (edit. 1751); Doct. and Stud. Dial. 1, ch. 20.

[3] Raw v. Potts, Prec. Ch. 35; s. c. 2 Vern. R. 239.

[4] Dalton v. Poole, 1 Vent. R. 318.

[5] 1 Fonbl. Eq. B. 1, ch. 3, § 4; Hobbs v. Norton, 1 Vern. R. 135; Neville v. Robinson, 1 Bro. Ch. C. 543; Devenish v. Baines, Pre. Ch. 3; Oldham v. Litchfield, 2 Freem. R. 284; Thynn v. Thynn, 1 Vern. R. 296; 11 Ves. 638, 639; Gilb. Lex Prætor. 336; Sugden, Vendors (7th edit.), pp. 717, 718; 3 Woodles. Lect. lix. pp. 479 to 482; Id. 486, 490, 491.

[6] This section and the succeeding sections to § 65 were in the former editions misnumbered and repeated; and they are therefore now marked § 64 a, § 64 b, &c. to § 64 k, after which the numbers regularly proceed, as before.

in which an ejectment would lie at law ; and in cases of personal claims it also requires relief to be sought within the period prescribed for personal suits of a like nature.[1] And yet there are cases in which the statutes would be a bar at law, but in which equity would, notwithstanding, grant relief; and on the other hand there are cases where the statutes would not be a bar at law, but where equity, notwithstanding, would refuse relief.[2] But all these cases stand on special circumstances which Courts of Equity can take notice of when Courts of Law may be bound by the positive bar of the statutes. And there are many other cases where the rules of law and equity on similar subjects are not exactly co-extensive as to the recognition of rights or the maintenance of remedy.[3] Thus a person may be tenant by the curtesy of his wife's trust estate, but she is not entitled to dower in his trust estate.[4] (a) So where a power is defectively executed, equity will often aid it; whereas at law the act is wholly nugatory.[5]

64 b. Other illustrations of the same maxim may be drawn from the known analogies of legal and trust estates. In general, in Courts of Equity the same construction and effect are given to perfect or executed trust estates as are given by Courts of Law to legal estates. The incidents, properties, and consequences of the estates are the same. The same restrictions are applied as to creating estates and bounding perpetuities and giving absolute dominion over property. The same modes of construing the

[1] Blanshard on Limit. ch. 4, p. 61; Edsell v. Buchanan, 1 Ves. R. 83; Com. Dig. Chanc. 1; Mitford, Pl. Eq. 269 to 274; 1 Madd. Ch. Pr. 79, 80; 2 Madd. Ch. Pr. 244; Smith v. Clay, 3 Bro. Ch. R. 640, note; Cholmondeley v. Clinton, 2 Jack. & Walk. 156; post, § 529.

[2] See Pickering v. Lord Stamford, 2 Ves. jr. 289; Id. 582; 2 Madd. Ch. Pr. 244 to 247; Mitford, Pl. Eq. 269 to 274; Blanshard on Limit. ch. 4, pp. 61, 81, 82, 83; 1 Fonbl. Eq. B. 1, ch. 4, § 27, note (q); Stackhouse v. Barnstown, 10 Ves. 466; Bond v. Hopkins, 1 Sch. & Lef. 413; 1 Fonbl. Eq. B. 1, ch. 1, § 3, note (g); Cowper v. Cowper, 2 P. Will. 753.

[3] See Earl of Bath v. Sherwin, 10 Mod. R. 1, 3; s. c. 1 Bro. Parl. C. 270; Doct. and Stud. Dial. 1, ch. 20.

[4] Cruise, Dig. tit. 12, ch. 2, § 15; 1 Fonbl. Eq. B. 1, ch. 6, § 9, note (t).

[5] 1 Fonbl. Eq. B. 1, ch. 1, § 7, and note ibid.; Id. B. 1, ch. 4, § 25, note (h).

(a) This subject has been much affected by legislation since the author wrote.

language and limitations of the trusts are adopted.[1] But there are exceptions as well known as the rule itself. Thus executory trusts are treated as susceptible of various modifications and constructions not applicable to executed trusts.[2] And even at law the words in a will are or may be differently construed when applied to personal estate from what they are when applied to real estate. In short it may be correctly said that the maxim that equity follows the law is a maxim liable to many exceptions; and that it cannot be generally affirmed that where there is no remedy at law in the given case there is none in equity; or on the other hand that equity in the administration of its own principles is utterly regardless of the rules of law.[3]

64 c. Another maxim is, that where there is equal equity the law must prevail.[4] And this is generally true; for in such a case the defendant has an equal claim to the protection of a Court of Equity for his title as the plaintiff has to the assistance of the court to assert his title; and then, the court will not interpose on either side; for the rule there is, 'In æquali jure melior est conditio possidentis.'[5] (a) And the equity is equal between persons who have been equally innocent and equally diligent. It is upon this account that a Court of Equity constantly refuses to interfere either for relief or discovery against a bona fide purchaser of the legal estate for a valuable consideration without notice of the adverse title, if he chooses to avail himself of the defence at the proper time and in the proper mode.[6] And it extends its protection equally if the purchase is originally of an

[1] 3 Wooddes. Lect. lix. pp. 479 to 482; 1 Fonbl. Eq. B. 1, ch. 3, § 1, p. 147, note (b); Cowper v. Cowper, 2 P. Will. 753.
[2] 3 Wooddes. Lect. lix. pp. 480 to 482; 1 Fonbl. Eq. B. 1, ch. 3, § 1, p. 147, note (b).
[3] Kemp v. Pryor, 7 Ves. 249, 250.
[4] 1 Fonbl. Eq. B. 1, ch. 4, § 25, and note; Id. ch. 5, § 3; 2 Fonbl. Eq. B. 6, ch. 3, § 3, and note (c); Id. B. 3, ch. 3, § 1; Mitford, Pl. Eq. 274; Jeremy, Eq. Jurisd. 285; Fitzsimmons v. Guestier, 7 Cranch, 2, 18; Caldwell v. Ball, 1 T. R. 214.
[5] Mitf. Pl. Eq. [215] 274; 1 Fonbl. Eq. B. 1, ch. 4, § 25; Id. ch. 5, § 3; 1 Madd. Ch. Pr. 170, 171; Jeremy on Equity Jurisd. 283; Jerrard v. Saunders, 2 Ves. jr. 454; 2 Fonbl. Eq. B. 3, ch. 3, § 1.
[6] See Sugden on Vendors (7th edit.), ch. 16, p. 713, &c. § 10; Id. ch. 18, pp. 757, 762, 763; Grounds and Rudim. of the Law, M. 236 (edit. 1751); Story on Eq. Pl. § 603, 604, 805, 806.

(a) Pratt v. Clemens, 4 W. Va. 443.

equitable title without notice, (*a*) and afterwards with notice the party obtains or buys in a prior legal title in order to support his equitable title.[1] This doctrine applies strictly in all cases where the title of the plaintiff seeking relief is equitable. But it yet remains a matter of some doubt whether it is applicable to the case of a plaintiff seeking relief upon a legal title.[2] The purchaser however in all cases must hold a legal title, or be entitled to call for it, in order to give him the full protection for this defence ; for if his title be merely equitable, then he must yield to a legal and equitable title in the adverse party.[3] So the purchaser must have paid his purchase-money before notice, for otherwise he will not be protected, (*b*) and if he have paid a part only, he will be protected pro tanto only.[4]

[1] See Sugden on Vendors (7th edit.), ch. 16, pp. 713, 728; 1 Fonbl. Eq. B. 1, ch. 4, § 25, note (*e*); Post, §§ 108, 139, 154, 265, 381, 409, 434, 436; Grosvenor *v.* Allen, 9 Paige, R. 74, 76, 77.

[2] Sugden on Vendors, ch. 18 (7th edit.), pp. 762, 763; Id. ch. 18, 2 vol. 309, 310 (9th edit.); Jeremy, Eq. Juris. 295. It is an apparent anomaly in the general doctrine, that it should be inapplicable to a bill for relief founded on a legal title. Against such a bill Lord Thurlow decided that a plea of a bona fide purchase, without notice, was no protection; Williams *v.* Lambe, 3 Bro. Ch. C. 264. Lord Loughborough seems to have entertained a different opinion; and the point has been contested by some elementary writers, and supported by others. Mr. Belt, in his note to the case, 3 Bro. Ch. C. 264, insists on Lord Thurlow's doctrine being right; so do Mr. Roper and Mr. Beames. But Mr. Sugden treats it as incorrect. See Jerrard *v.* Saunders, 2 Ves. jr. 454, 458; Sugden on Vendors (7th edit.), 762, 763; Id. ch. 18 (9th ed.), 2 vol. 309, 310; Roper, Husband and Wife, 446, 447; Post, § 410, note (1); Id. §§ 436, 630, 631. In Collins *v.* Archer, 1 Russ. & Mylne, 284, 292, Sir John Leach followed the case of Williams *v.* Lambe, and held that the fact that the party was a bona fide purchaser for a valuable consideration without notice was not available as a defence against a plaintiff who relies upon a legal title. On the other hand Lord Abinger, in Payne *v.* Compton (2 Y. & Coll. 457, 461), held that such a purchase was a good defence against any claim in equity by the owner of the legal estate. See also Wood *v.* Mann, 1 Sumner, R. 504.

[3] Sugden on Vendors (7th ed.), and Id. ch. 18 (9th ed.), 2 vol. p. 309, 310; Id. ch. 18, p. 757 to 763; Grounds and Rudim. of the Law, M. 236 (ed. 1751); Com. Dig. Chancery, 4 W. 12; Davies *v.* Austen, 1 Ves. jr. 247; Skirras *v.* Craig, 7 Cranch, R. 34; Whitfield *v.* Faussat, 1 Ves. 387; Jeremy on Equity Jurisd. 286.

[4] Wood *v.* Mann, 1 Sumner, R. 506, 578; Flagg *v.* Mann, 2 Sumner, R. 487; Post, § 1502.

(*a*) A bona fide purchaser from a trustee, without notice of the trust, will be protected against the cestui que trust. Caskell *v.* Lathrop, 63 Ga. 96.

(*b*) Whelan *v.* McCreasy, 64 Ala. 319.

64 *d*. But even when the title of each party is purely equitable, it does not always follow that the maxim admits of no preference of the one over the other. For where the equities are in other respects equal, still another maxim may prevail, which is, 'Qui prior est in tempore, potior est in jure;' for precedency in time will under many circumstances give an advantage or priority in right.[1](*a*) Hence when the legal estate is outstanding, equitable incumbrances must be paid according to priority of time.[2] And whenever the equities are unequal, there the preference is constantly given to the superior equity.[3]

64 *e*. Another maxim of no small extent is that he who seeks equity must do equity.[4](*b*) This maxim principally applies to the party who is seeking relief in the character of a plaintiff in the court. Thus for instance if a borrower of money upon usurious interest seeks to have the aid of a Court of Equity in cancelling or procuring the instrument to be delivered up, the court will not interfere in his favor unless upon the terms that he will pay the lender what is really and bona fide due to him.(*c*) But if the lender comes into equity to assert and enforce his own claim under the instrument, there the borrower may show the invalidity of the instrument, and have a decree in his favor and a dismissal of the bill without paying the lender anything; for the court will never assist a wrong-doer in effectuating his wrongful and illegal purpose.[5] And the like principles will govern in

---

[1] 1 Fonbl. Equity, B. 1, ch. 4, § 25; Fitzsimmons *v.* Guestier, 7 Cranch, 2; Berry *v.* Mutual Ins. Co., 2 John. Ch. R. 608; Beckett *v.* Cordley, 1 Brown, Ch. R. 358; Mackrett *v.* Symmons, 15 Ves. R. 354. See Post, § 421 *a*; Miner *v.* Schenck, 3 Hill, N. Y. R. 228.

[2] Ibid note (*e*). See Blake *v.* Hungerford, Prec. Ch. 158.

[3] Jeremy, Eq. Jurisd. 285, 286.

[4] Grounds and Rudim. of the Law, M. 175; Id. 179 (edit. 1751); Com. Dig. Chan 3 F. 3; McDonald *v.* Neilson, 2 Cowp. R. 139.

[5] 1 Fonbl. Eq. B. 1, ch. 1, § 3, note (*h*); Id. B. 1, ch. 2, § 13; Mason *v.* Gardiner, 4 Bro. Ch. C. 435.

(*a*) But not where the junior equity has the superior merit. Hume *v.* Dixon, 37 Ohio St. 66; Rice *v.* Rice, 2 Drew. 73; Cave *v.* Cave, 15 Ch. D. 639, 648.

(*b*) Smith *v.* Murphy, 58 Ala. 630; and note infra.

(*c*) Sporrer *v.* Eifler, 1 Heisk. 633; Eslava *v.* Crampton, 61 Ala. 507; Campbell *v.* Murray, 62 Ga. 86. On the other hand if the grantee in a usurious deed comes to equity to reform it, he must abate the usury. Corby *v.* Bean, 44 Mo. 379. See post, § 301.

other similar cases where the transaction is not as between the parties grossly fraudulent,(a) or otherwise liable to just exception.[1] Many other illustrations of the maxim of a different nature may readily be put. As where a second incumbrancer seeks relief against a prior incumbrancer who has a claim to tack a subsequent security, he shall not have it before paying both securities. So where a husband seeks to recover his wife's property, and he has made no settlement upon her, he shall not have it without making a suitable settlement. So where an heir seeks possession of deeds in the possession of a jointress, he shall not have relief unless upon the terms of confirming her jointure. So where a party seeks the benefit of a purchase made for him in the name of a trustee who has paid the purchase-money, but to whom he is indebted for other advances, he shall not be relieved but upon payment of all the money due to the trustee.[2] (b)

[1] Peacock v. Evans, 16 Ves. 511; Grounds and Rudim. of the Law, M. 175, 179 (edit. 1751).

[2] Com. Dig. Chancery, 3 F. 3; Sturgis v. Champneys, 5 Mylne & Craig, 97, 101, 102. In this case Lord Cottenham said: 'Undoubtedly for many purposes this court, acting upon the principle of following the law, deals with property coming under its cognizance from the legal estate being outstanding, according to the rights which would exist at law; but that is far from being universally true. Cholmondeley v. Clinton (2 Mer. 171; 2 J. & W. 1), and the authorities upon which that decision was founded, are instances to the contrary. There are many cases in which this court will not interfere with a right which the possession of a legal title gives, although the effect be directly opposed to its own principles as administered between parties having equitable interests only, such as in case of subsequent incumbrancers without notice gaining a preference over a prior incumbrancer by procuring the legal estate.

(a) Equity does not require one from whom a contract has been obtained by fraud to show that he has offered performance of the same as a condition to relief from it. Thomas v. Coultas, 76 Ill. 493.

(b) The books are full of illustrations of this maxim. A few may be added to those of the text. If a party seek relief against interference with his water privilege, he may be required to discontinue a wrongful use of defendant's land connected with it. Comstock v. Johnson, 46 N. Y. 615. So an heir asking to set aside his deed to a widow, and for an account, must allow one third of the income, though her dower has not been set out. Ames v. Ames, 1 Cinn. Sup. Ct. 559. And a person asking for partition in equity must pay his proportion of a mortgage paid by the other party. Campbell v. Campbell, 21 Mich. 438. So a widow asking for her dower must account for what she has occupied beyond her third. McLaughlin v. McLaughlin, 5 C. E. Green, 190. One asking for relief from an over-assessment must pay what is justly due. Morrison v. Hershire 32 Ia. 271; Smith v. Auditor-General, 20 Mich. 398; Merrill v. Humphrey, 24 Mich.

64 *f.* Another maxim of general use is, that equality is equity; or, as it is sometimes expressed, equity delighteth in equality.[1] And this equality, according to Bracton, constitutes equity itself: ' Æquitas est rerum covenientia, quæ paribus in causis paria jura desiderat, et omnia vere co-æquiparat, et dicitur æquitas, quasi æqualitas.'[2] This maxim is variously applied; as, for example, to cases of contribution between co-contractors, sureties, and others; to cases of abatement of legacies, where there is a deficiency of assets; to cases of apportionment of moneys due on incumbrances among different purchasers and claimants of different parcels of the land; and especially to cases of the marshall-

It may be to be regretted, that the rights of property should thus depend upon accident, and be decided upon, not according to any merits, but upon grounds purely technical. This however has arisen from the jurisdiction of law and equity being separate, and from the rules of equity (better adapted than the simplicity of the common law to the complicated transactions of the present state of society), though applied to subjects without its own exclusive jurisdiction, not having, in many cases, been extended to control matters properly subject to the jurisdiction of the courts of common law. Hence arises the extensive and beneficial rule of this court, that he who asks for equity must do equity; that is, this court refuses its aid to give to the plaintiff what the law would give him if the courts of common law had jurisdiction to enforce it, without imposing upon him conditions which the court considers he ought to comply with, although the subject of the condition should be one which this court would not otherwise enforce. If therefore this court refuses to assist a husband who has abandoned his wife, or the assignee of an insolvent husband who claims against both, in recovering property of the wife, without securing out of it for her a proper maintenance and support, it not only does not violate any principle, but acts in strict conformity with a rule by which it regulates its proceedings in other cases.'

[1] Grounds and Rudim. of the Law, M. 91 (edit. 1751); Petit *v.* Smith, 1 P. Will. 9.

[2] Bracton, Lib. 1, cap. 3, § 20; Plowden, Comm. 467; Co. Litt. 24.

170; Montgomery County *v.* Elston, 32 Ind. 27. But it must clearly appear how much is due. Dean *v.* Charlton, 23 Wis. 590. And a co-surety, seeking relief from a judgment against him from the whole debt, must pay his just proportion of the contribution. Creed *v.* Scraggs, 1 Heisk. 590. So one asking to be relieved from an invalid tax-deed as a cloud upon the title must pay all the taxes which the holder of the deed has paid. Reed *v.* Tyler, 56 Ill. 288. And the principle applies as well to a defendant as to a plaintiff. Tongue *v.* Nutwell, 31 Md. 302. The grantee of a mortgagor of land cannot, because of fraud practised by the mortgagee on the mortgagor in obtaining the mortgage, maintain a bill against an assignee of the mortgagee to restrain a sale of the mortgaged premises, without paying the entire debt secured by the mortgage, though the mortgage was assigned to the defendant as security for a smaller sum. Foster *v.* Wightman, 123 Mass. 101; Fairchild *v.* McArthur, 15 Gray, 526.

ing and distribution of equitable assets.[1] For although out of legal assets payment must be made of debts in the course of administration according to their dignity and priority of right, yet as to equitable assets all debts are generally deemed by Courts of Equity to stand in pari jure, and are to be paid proportionally, without reference to their dignity, or priority of right at law.[2] And here we have another illustration of the doctrine that equity does not always follow the law.[3]

64 *g*. Another and the last maxim which it seems necessary to notice is, that equity looks upon that as done which ought to have been done. The true meaning of this maxim is, that equity will treat the subject-matter as to collateral consequences and incidents in the same manner as if the final acts contemplated by the parties had been executed exactly as they ought to have been, not as the parties might have executed them.[4] But equity will not thus consider things in favor of all persons, but only in favor of such as have a right to pray that the acts might be done.[5] And the rule itself is not in other respects of universal application; although Lord Hardwicke said that it holds in every case except in dower.[6] (*a*) The most common cases of the application of the rule are under agreements. All agreements are considered as performed which are made for a valuable consideration in favor of persons entitled to insist upon their performance. They are to be considered as done at the time when, according to the tenor thereof, they ought to have been performed. (*b*) They are also

---

[1] Grounds and Rudim. of the Law, M. 91 (edit. 1751); 1 Wooddes. Lect. lvi. pp. 486, 487, 488, 490; Shepherd *v.* Guernsey, 9 Paige, R. 357.

[2] 3 Wooddes. Lect. lviii. pp. 466 to 468; Shepherd *v.* Guernsey, 9 Paige, R. 357.

[3] 1 Fonbl. Eq. B. 4, Pt. 2, ch. 2, § 1, and note; 1 Madd. Ch. Pr. 466; Martin *v.* Martin, 1 Ves. 211; 2 Black. Comm, 511, 512; Lewin *v.* Oakley, 2 Atk. 50; Newton *v.* Bennet, 1 Brown, Ch. Cas. 185; Silk *v.* Prime, 1 Bro. Ch. Cas. 138, note; Haslewood *v.* Pope, 3 P. Will. 322; Moses *v.* Murgatroyd, 1 John. Ch. R. 119; Livingston *v.* Newkirk, 3 John. Ch. R. 319.

[4] 1 Fonbl. Eq. B. 1, ch. 6, § 9; Francis, Maxims, M. 196 (edit. 1751); 1 W. Black. 129.

[5] Burgess *v.* Wheate, 1 W. Black. 123, 129; Crabtree *v.* Bramble, 3 Atk. 687; 1 Fonbl. Equity, B. 1, ch. 6, § 9, note (*s*).

[6] Crabtree *v.* Bramble, 3 Atk. 687.

(*a*) The maxim will not be applied against the interests of third persons. Casey *v.* Cavaroc, 96 U. S. 467.

(*b*) Felch *v.* Hooper, 119 Mass. 52, 57.

deemed to have the same consequences attached to them; so that one party, or his privies, shall not derive benefit by his laches or neglect; and the other party, for whose profit the contract was designed, or his privies, shall not suffer thereby.[1] Thus money covenanted or devised to be laid out in land is treated as real estate in equity and descends to the heir. And on the other hand where land is contracted or devised to be sold, the land is considered and treated as money.[2] (*a*) There are exceptions to the doctrine where other equitable considerations intervene, or where the intent of the parties leads the other way; (*b*) but these demonstrate, rather than shake, the potency of the general rule.[3]

64 *h*. There are also one or two rules as to the extent of maintaining jurisdiction, which deserve notice in this place, as they apply to various descriptions of cases, and pervade whole branches of Equity Jurisprudence, and cannot therefore with propriety be exclusively arranged under any one head.

64 *i*. One rule is, that if originally the jurisdiction has properly attached in equity in any case, on account of the supposed defect of remedy at law, that jurisdiction is not changed or obliterated by the Courts of Law now entertaining jurisdiction in such cases, when they formerly rejected it. This has been repeatedly asserted by Courts of Equity, and constitutes in some sort the pole-star of portions of its jurisdiction. (*c*) The reason is that it cannot be left to Courts of Law to enlarge or to restrain the powers of Courts of Equity at their pleasure. The jurisdiction of equity, like that of law, must be of a permanent and fixed character. There can be no ebb or flow of jurisdiction dependent upon external changes. Being once vested

[1] Grounds and Rudim. of the Law, M. 106 (edit. 1751).
[2] 1 Fonbl. Eq. B. 1, ch. 6, § 9, note (*t*); Gilbert, Lex Prætor, 243, 244; Fletcher *v*. Ashburner, 1 Bro. Ch. C. 497; Craig *v*. Leslie, 3 Wheat. R. 563, 577; 3 Wooddes. Lect. lviii. pp. 466, 468.
[3] Ibid. The whole of this doctrine was very much considered by the Supreme Court in the case of Craig *v*. Leslie, 3 Wheat. R. 563, where a very elaborate opinion was delivered by Mr. Justice Washington.

(*a*) Jackson *v*. Small, 34 Ind. 241; Brewer *v*. Herbert, 30 Md. 301; McCaa *v*. Wolf, 42 Ala. 389.

(*b*) As where the sale is conditional. Douglass Co. *v*. Union Pacific R. Co., 5 Kans. 615.

(*c*) Shotwell *v*. Smith, 5 C. E. Green, 79; Hinchley *v*. Greany, 118 Mass. 595; Labadie *v*. Hewitt, 85 Ill. 341; Lee *v*. Lee, 55 Ala. 590, 598; ante, p. 30, note.

legitimately in the court, it must remain there until the Legislature shall abolish or limit it; for without some positive act, the just inference is that the legislative pleasure is that the jurisdiction shall remain upon its old foundations. This doctrine has been a good deal canvassed in modern times; and it has been especially the subject of commentary by some of the greatest equity judges who have ever adorned the bench.[1] (a) Lord Eldon upon one occasion said: 'Upon what principle can it be said [that] the ancient jurisdiction of this court is destroyed, because Courts of Law now very properly perhaps exercise that jurisdiction which they did not exercise forty years ago? Demands have been frequently recovered in equity which now could be without difficulty recovered at law, &c. I cannot hold that the jurisdiction is gone, merely because the Courts of Law have exercised an equitable jurisdiction.'[2] (b)

64 k. Another rule respects the exercise of jurisdiction when the title is at law and the party comes into equity for a discovery, and for relief as consequent on that discovery. In many cases it has been held that where a party has a just title to come into equity for a discovery and obtains it, the court will go on and give him the proper relief, and not turn him round to the expenses and inconveniences of a double suit at law. The jurisdiction having once rightfully attached, it shall be made effectual for the purposes of complete relief. (c) And it has accordingly been laid down by elementary writers of high reputation, that 'The court, having acquired cognizance of the suit for the purpose of discovery, will entertain it for the purpose of relief in most cases of fraud, account, accident, and mistake.'[3] The ground is stated to be the propriety of preventing a multiplicity

---

[1] See Atkinson v. Leonard, 3 Bro. Ch. R. 218; Ex parte Greenway, 6 Ves. 812; East India Company v. Boddam, 9 Ves. 468, 469; Bromeley v. Holland, 7 Ves. 19 to 21; Cooper, Eq. Pl. ch. 3, pp. 126, 129.

[2] Kemp v. Pryor, 7 Ves. 249, 250.

[3] 1 Fonbl. Eq. B. 1, ch. 1, § 3, note (*f*); Coop. Eq. Pl. Introd. p. xxxi; Middletown Bank v. Russ, 3 Connect. R. 135.

(a) See also Biddle v. Moore, 3 Barr, 161.

(b) A change in the law of evidence, giving the right to one party to call the adverse party as a witness, does not take away the jurisdiction of equity over discovery. Cannon v. McNab, 48 Ala. 99; Millsops v. Pfeiffer, 44 Miss. 805; ante, p. 30.

(c) Winona R. Co. v. St. Paul R. Co., 26 Minn. 179.

'of suits;[1] a ground of itself quite reasonable and sufficient to justify the relief, and one upon which Courts of Equity act, as we shall presently see, as a distinct ground of original jurisdiction.[2]

---

[1] The passage from Fonblanque on Equity deserves to be quoted at large. 'The concurrence of jurisdiction may, in the greater number of cases in which it is exercised, be justified by the propriety of preventing a multiplicity of suits; for as the mode of proceeding in Courts of Law requires the plaintiff to establish his case, without enabling him to draw the necessary evidence from the examination of the defendant, justice could never be attained at law in those cases where the principal facts to be proved by one party are confined to the knowledge of the other party. In such cases therefore it becomes necessary for the party wanting such evidence to resort to the extraordinary powers of a Court of Equity, which will compel the necessary discovery; and the court having acquired cognizance of the suit, for the purpose of discovery, will entertain it for the purpose of relief, in most cases of fraud, account, accident, and mistake.'

[2] See Jesus College v. Bloom, 3 Atk. 262, 263. In Pearce v. Creswick, 2 Hare, R. 293, Mr. Vice-Chancellor Wigram said: 'The first proposition relied upon by the plaintiff in support of the equity of his bill was this, that the case was one in which the right to discovery would carry with it the right to relief. And undoubtedly dicta are to be met with tending directly to the conclusion that the right to discovery may entitle a plaintiff to relief also. In Adley v. The Whitstable Company (17 Ves. 329), Lord Eldon says: "There is no mode of ascertaining what is due, except an account in a Court of Equity, but it is said the party may have discovery, and then go to law. The answer to that is, that the right to the discovery carries along with it the right to relief in equity." In Ryle v. Haggie (1 Jac. & Walk. 236), Sir Thomas Plumer said: "When it is admitted that a party comes here properly for the discovery, the court is never disposed to occasion a multiplicity of suits by making him go to a Court of Law for the relief." And in McKenzie v. Johnston (4 Madd. 373), Sir J. Leach says: "The plaintiff can only learn from this discovery of the defendants how they have acted in the execution of their agency, and it would be most unreasonable that he should pay them for that discovery if it turned out that they had abused his confidence; yet such must be the case if a bill for relief will not lie."

'Now in a case in which I think that justice requires the court if possible to find an equity in this bill, to enable it once for all to decide the question between the parties, I should reluctantly deprive the plaintiff of any remedy to which the dicta I have referred to may entitle him. But I confess the arguments founded upon these dicta appear to me to be exposed to the objection of proving far too much. They can only be reconciled with the ordinary practice of the court by understanding them as having been uttered with reference in each case to the subject-matter to which they were applied, and not as laying down any abstract proposition so wide as the plaintiff's argument requires. I think this part of the plaintiff's case cannot be stated more highly in his favor than this, that the necessity a party may be under (from the very nature of a given transaction) to come into equity for discovery, is a circumstance to be regarded in deciding upon the distinct and independent question

65. It is observable that the guarded language used is, 'in most cases,' although it is certainly difficult to perceive any solid ground why the jurisdiction should not extend to all cases embraced by the general principle. But the qualification is made with reference to the bearing of some of the authorities. The learned author of the Treatise on Equity [1] has laid down the principle in the broadest terms. 'And when,' says he, 'this court can determine the matter, it shall not be a handmaid to the other courts, nor beget a suit to be ended elsewhere.' [2] There are many authorities which go to support this proposition. But there are many also which are irreconcilable with it, or at least which contain exceptions to it.

66. Mr. Fonblanque has remarked: 'There are some cases in which, though the plaintiff might be relieved at law, a Court of Equity, having obtained jurisdiction for the purpose of discovery, will entertain the suit for the purpose of relief. But there certainly are other cases where, though the plaintiff be entitled to discovery, he is not entitled to relief. To strike out the distinguishing principle upon which Courts of Equity in such cases have proceeded, would be extremely useful. But after having given considerable attention to the subject, I find myself incapable of reconciling the various decisions upon it.' [3] What the learned author desired to ascertain has been found equally embarrassing to subsequent inquirers; and there is a distressing uncertainty in this branch of Equity Jurisdiction in England. [4]

67. In cases of account there seems a distinct ground upon which the jurisdiction for discovery should incidentally carry the jurisdiction for relief. In the first place the remedy at law in most cases of this sort is imperfect or inadequate. In the next place, where this objection does not occur, the discovery sought must often be obtained through the instrumentality of a master or of some interlocutory order of the court; in which case it would seem strange that the court should grant some,

of equitable jurisdiction; further than this I have not been able to follow this branch of the plaintiff's argument.'

[1] Mr. Ballow.
[2] 2 Fonbl. Eq. B. 6, ch. 3, § 6. This is the very language of the Lord Keeper (afterwards Lord Chancellor Nottingham) in Parker *v.* Dee, 2 Ch. Cas. 200, 201.
[3] 2 Fonbl. B. 6, ch. 3, § 6, note (*r*).
[4] Coop. Eq. Pl. ch. 3, § 3, pp. 188, 189.

and not proceed to full, relief.[1] In the next place in cases not falling under either of these predicaments the compelling of the production of vouchers and documents would seem to belong peculiarly to a Court of Equity and to be a species of relief. And in the last place, where neither of the foregoing principles applies, there is great force in the ground of suppressing multiplicity of suits, constituting, as it does, a peculiar ground for the interference of equity.[2]

68. Cases of accident and mistake furnish like reasons for extending the jurisdiction to relief where it attaches for discovery. The remedy at law is not in such cases (as we shall presently see) either complete or appropriate. And cases of fraud are least of all those in which the complete exercise of the jurisdiction of a Court of Equity in granting relief ought to be questioned or controlled; since in addition to all other reasons fraud constitutes the most ancient foundation of its power; and equity sifts the conscience of the party, not only by requiring his own answer under oath, but by subjecting it to the severe scrutiny of comparison with other competent testimony, thus narrowing the chances of successful evasion, and compelling the party to do equity, as it shall appear upon a full survey of the whole transaction. Indeed in many cases of fraud, what should be the nature and extent of the redress, whether it should be wholly legal or wholly equitable, or a mixture of both, can scarcely be decided but upon a full hearing upon all the proceedings in the cause.

69. But there are cases, if not leading authorities, which it is not easy to reconcile with the principles already stated in matters of fraud, accident, mistake, and account.[3] Some of them may

[1] 3 Black. Comm. 437; Mitf. Eq. Pl. by Jeremy, p. 119, 120, 123; Corporation of Carlisle v. Wilson, 13 Ves. 278, 279.

[2] See Jesus College v. Bloom, 3 Atk. 262; s. c. Ambler, R. 54. The full concurrency of jurisdiction of Courts of Equity for relief in all matters of account, whether there be a remedy at law or not, seems to have been largely insisted on by Lord Erskine, in The Corporation of Carlisle v. Wilson (13 Ves. 278, 279). And it was positively asserted by the Court of Errors in New York, in Ludlow v. Simond (2 Caines, Cas. in Err. 38, 39, 53, 54). In Ryle v. Haggie (1 Jac. & Walk. 234), the Master of the Rolls said: 'When it is admitted that a party comes here properly for a discovery, the court is never disposed to occasion a multiplicity of suits by making him go to a Court of Law for the relief.'

[3] 2 Fonbl. Eq. B. 6, ch. 3, § 6, note (r).

have been adjudged upon their own peculiar circumstances, or they may stand upon some ground which leaves these principles untouched. Others are not susceptible of such a classification, and must either be rejected altogether, or be admitted to a considerable extent to overturn these principles.[1]

[1] In Parker *v.* Dee (2 Chan. Cas. 200), the bill was against an executor for a discovery of assets, and payment; and relief was decreed by Lord Nottingham. In Bishop of Winchester *v.* Knight (1 P. Will. 406), the bill was for a discovery and an account of ore, dug by a tenant during his life, and by his heir, against the executor and heir; and the court maintained the suit, directing a trial at law, and after the trial granted relief. In Story *v.* Lord Windsor (2 Atk. 630), the bill was for an account of the profits of a colliery, upon a legal title asserted by the plaintiff; Lord Hardwicke sustained the bill for the account, because, he said, this is not a title of land, but of a colliery, which is a kind of trade; and therefore an account of the profits may be taken here. (See also Jesus College *v.* Bloom, 3 Atk. 262.) The same learned chancellor, in Sayer *v.* Pierce (1 Ves. 232), seems to have proceeded on the same ground, holding that the party, being out of possession of lands, generally, was not entitled to maintain a bill for an account of profits alone; but he retained the bill in that case, directing a trial at law upon the ground that it asked to ascertain boundaries. In Lee *v.* Alston (1 Bro. Ch. R. 194), a bill for an account of timber cut by a tenant for life, impeachable for waste, was entertained by Lord Thurlow, and relief granted. In Jesus College *v.* Bloom (3 Atk. 262; s. c. Ambler, R. 54), which was a bill for an account and satisfaction for waste, in cutting down timber before the assignment, against an assignee of the lessee of the plaintiffs, Lord Hardwicke said: 'Upon the opening of the case, the bill seems improper, and an action of trover is the proper remedy. Where the bill is for an injunction, and waste has been already committed, the court, to prevent a double suit, will decree an account and satisfaction for what is past.' And because the bill sought an account only against the assignee for waste before the assignment, and without praying an injunction, his lordship dismissed the bill. The same point was held in Smith *v.* Cooke (3 Atk. R. 378, 381). In Geast *v.* Barker (2 Bro. Ch. 61), the bill was for a discovery of the quantity of coal and coke sold from a mine let by plaintiff to defendant upon a reservation of one shilling for every stack of coal sold, &c., and prayed an issue, to try what quantity a stack should contain, and suggested a custom of the country. The Master of the Rolls (Lord Kenyon) said if it were now necessary either to decree account or dismiss the bill, he would do the latter, as he was clear the remedy was at law. (s. c. cited in Harwood *v.* Oglander, 6 Ves. 225.) Why the remedy and account should not be given in equity is not stated; and it is difficult to see, since it is clear that the bill was good for the discovery, and it was obtained. In Sloane *v.* Heatfield (Bunb. R. 18), the bill was for a discovery of treasure-trove and relief; and the court held it good for discovery, but that the plaintiff could not have relief, because he might bring trover at law. In Ryle *v.* Haggie (1 Jac. & Walk. 234) an opposite course was adopted, upon the professed ground of avoiding a multiplicity of suits, the party having a good ground to seek a discovery, and there being a remedy at law. In The Duke of Leeds *v.* New Radnor (2 Bro. Ch. R. 338, 519), Lord Thurlow reversed the decree of the Master of the

GENERAL MAXIMS.

70. But when we depart from matters of fraud, accident, mistake, and account, as the foundations of a suit in equity, it is far more difficult to ascertain the boundary where the right of a Court of Equity to entertain a bill for relief as consequent upon the jurisdiction for discovery begins, and where it ends.[1] The difficulty is increased by the recent rule adopted in the Courts of Equity in England (of which we shall have occasion to speak more fully hereafter), that if the party seeks relief as well as discovery, and he is entitled to discovery only, a general demurrer will lie to the whole bill.[2] The effect of this rule is, that a plaintiff may be compelled, in a doubtful case, to frame his bill for a discovery in the first instance; and having obtained it, he may be compelled to ask leave to amend (which will not ordinarily be granted, unless it is clear that the proper relief is in equity), and then he may try the question whether he is entitled to relief or not.[3]

71. In America a strong disposition has been shown to follow out a convenient and uniform principle of jurisdiction, and to adhere to that which seems formerly (as we have seen) to have received the approbation of Lord Nottingham.[4] The principle is, that where the jurisdiction once attaches for discovery, and the discovery is actually obtained, the court will further entertain the bill for relief, if the plaintiff prays it. This has been broadly asserted in many cases, (a) and certainly possesses the recommendation of simplicity and uniformity of application; and escapes from what seems to be the capricious and unintelligible line of

---

Rolls, denying relief, because there was a remedy at law, upon the ground that the bill being retained for a year, the right to grant relief in equity was thus far admitted, and it ought to give entire relief. See Mr. Fonblanque's comments on this case, in 1 Fonbl. Eq. B. 1, ch. 3, § 3, note (g), p. 156. See Mr. Blunt's note to the case of Jesus College v. Bloom, Ambler, 54; 1 Fonbl. Eq. B. 1, ch. 3, § 3, note (g); ante, § 64 k, and note.

[1] See Ryle v. Haggie, 1 Jac. & Walk. 234; Pearce v. Creswick, 2 Hare, R. 243; Post, § 690.
[2] Ante, § 64 k, §§ 71 to 74; Story, Eq. Plead. §§ 312, 545.
[3] Post, §§ 690, 691; Mitford, Eq. Pl. by Jeremy, pp. 183, 184, note (n); Cooper, Eq. Pl. ch. 1, § 3, p. 58; Id. ch. 3, § 3, p. 188; Story on Equity Pleadings, § 312, and note (1); Lousada v. Templer, 2 Russ. R. 564; Frietas v. Don Santos, 1 Y. & Jerv. 577; Severn v. Fletcher, 5 Sim. R. 457.
[4] Ante, § 65, note 2; Post, § 691.

(a) See Sanborn v. Kittredge, 20 Vt. 632; Holmes v. Holmes, 36 Vt. 525.

demarcation pointed out in the English authorities. Thus it has been laid down in the courts of New York, upon more than one occasion, as a settled rule, that when the Court of Chancery has gained jurisdiction of a cause for one purpose, it may retain it generally for relief.[1] A similar doctrine has been asserted in other States,[2] and it has been affirmed in the Supreme Court of the United States. On one occasion it was laid down by the last-named court, 'That if certain facts essential to the merits of a claim purely legal be exclusively within the knowledge of the party against whom that claim is asserted, he may be required in a Court of Chancery to disclose those facts; and the court, being thus rightly in possession of the cause, will proceed to determine the whole matter in controversy.'[3]

72. This doctrine however, though generally true, is not to be deemed of universal application.[4] To justify a Court of Equity in granting relief as consequent upon discovery in cases of this sort, it seems necessary that the relief should be of such a nature as a Court of Equity may properly grant in the ordinary exercise of its authority. If therefore the proper relief be by an award of damages, which can alone be ascertained by a jury, there may be a strong reason for declining the exercise of the jurisdiction, since it is the appropriate function of a Court of Law to superintend such trials. And in many other cases where a question arises purely of matters of fact fit to be tried by a jury, and the relief is dependent upon that question, there is equal reason that the jurisdiction for relief should be altogether declined; or, at all events, that if the bill is retained, a trial at law should be directed by the court, and relief granted or withheld according to the final issue of the trial. (*a*) Thus if a bill seeks the discovery of a contract for the sale of goods and chattels, or of a wrongful

---

[1] Armstrong *v.* Gilchrist, 2 John. Cas. 424; Rathbone *v.* Warren, 10 John. R. 587, 596; King *v.* Baldwin, 17 John. R. 384. See also Leroy *v.* Veeder, 1 John. Cas. 417; s. c. 2 Cain. Cas. in Err. 175; Hepburn *v.* Dunlop, 1 Wheat. R. 197; Ludlow *v.* Simond, 2 Cain. Err. 1, 38, 51, 52.

[2] Chichester's Executor *v.* Vass's Administrator, 1 Munf. R. 98; Isham *v.* Gilbert, 3 Connect. R. 166; Ferguson *v.* Waters, 3 Bibb, 303; Middletown Bank *v.* Russ, 3 Connect. R. 139.

[3] Russell *v.* Clarke's Executors, 7 Cranch, 69.

[4] Middletown Bank *v.* Russ, 3 Connect. R. 135, 140; Id. 166.

(*a*) As to the English practice, see 28 L. J. Ch. 246. And see Black *v.* Peters *v.* Rule, 5 Jur. N. S. 61; s. c. Lamb, 1 Beasl. 108.

conversion of goods and chattels, and the breach of the contract, or the conversion of the goods and chattels, is properly remediable in damages, to be ascertained by a jury, the relief seems properly to belong to a Court of Law. In like manner questions of fraud in obtaining and executing a will of real estate, and many cases of controverted titles to real estate, dependent partly on matters of fact and partly on matters of law, are properly triable in an ejectment, and may well be left to the common tribunals.[1] And it has accordingly been laid down in some of the American courts, that under such circumstances, where the verdict of a jury is necessary to ascertain the extent of the relief, the plaintiff should be left to his action at law after the discovery is obtained.[2]

73. The distinction here pointed out furnishes a clear line for the exercise of Equity Jurisdiction in cases where relief is sought upon bills of discovery; and if it should receive a general sanction in the American courts, it will greatly diminish the embarrassments which have hitherto attended many investigations of the subject. In the present state of the authorities however little more can be absolutely affirmed than these propositions: first, that in bills of discovery seeking relief, if any part of the relief sought be of an equitable nature, the court will retain the bill for complete relief; secondly, that in matters of account, fraud, mistake, and accident, the jurisdiction for relief will generally, but not universally, be retained and favored; and thirdly, that in cases where the remedy at law is more appropriate than the remedy in equity, or the verdict of a jury is indispensable to the relief sought, the jurisdiction will either be declined, or, if retained, will be so subject to a trial at law.

74. From what has been already stated, it is manifest that the jurisdiction in cases of this sort attaches in equity solely on the ground of discovery. If therefore the discovery is not obtained, or it is used as a mere pretence to give jurisdiction, it would be a gross abuse to entertain the suit in equity when the whole foundation on which it rests is either disproved, or it is shown to be a colorable disguise for the purpose of changing the forum of litigation. Hence to maintain the jurisdiction for relief as consequent on discovery, it is necessary in the first place to

[1] Jones v. Jones, 3 Meriv. R. 161.
[2] Lynch v. Sumrall, 1 Marsh. Kentuck. R. 469.

allege in the bill that the facts are material to the plaintiff's case, and that the discovery of them by the defendant is indispensable as proof; (a) for if the facts lie within the knowledge of witnesses who may be called in a Court of Law, that furnishes a sufficient reason for a Court of Equity to refuse its aid. The bill must therefore allege (and if required the fact must be established) that the plaintiff is unable to prove such facts by other testimony.[1](b) In the next place, if the answer wholly denies the matters of fact, of which discovery is sought by the bill, the latter must be dismissed; for the jurisdiction substantially fails by such a denial.[2](c)

[1] Gelston v. Hoyt, 1 John. Ch. R. 543; Seymour v. Seymour, 4 John. Ch. R. 409; Pryor v. Adams, 1 Call, R. 382; Duvalls v. Ross, 2 Munf. R. 290, 296; Bass v. Bass, 4 H. & Munf. 478.

[2] Russell v. Clarke's Executors, 7 Cranch, 69; Ferguson v. Waters, 3 Bibb, R. 303; Nourse v. Gregory, 3 Litt. R. 378; Robinson v. Gilbraith, 4 Bibb, R. 184.

(a) As to the discovery of communications alleged in defence to be privileged, see Wheeler v. Le Merchant, 17 Ch. D. 675.

(b) See Nussbaum v. Heilbron, 63 Ga. 312. In Massachusetts a bill for discovery cannot be maintained, it has been held, where the discovery prayed is only incidental to the relief sought, or is obtainable at law by interrogatories. Ahrend v. Odiorne, 118 Mass. 261; Pool v. Lloyd, 5 Met. 525; Ward v. Peck, 114 Mass. 121. Sed qu. since 1877. See ante, p. 30, note.

(c) So in general where the equitable relief sought fails for defect of proof, or other cause, the court is without jurisdiction to proceed further, and should dismiss the bill without prejudice. Dowell v. Mitchell, 105 U. S. 430; Price's Candle Co. v. Bauwen's Candle Co. 4 Kay & J. 727; Bailey v. Taylor, 1 Russ. & M. 73. See Walker v. Brooks, 125 Mass. 241; Pool v. Lloyd, 5 Met. 525; Ahrend v. Odiorne, 118 Mass. 261.

Jurisdiction for Discovery. — The following consideration of the grounds of Equity Jurisdiction for discovery, written by the late Chief Justice Redfield, appears in previous editions of this work (subject to some changes and abridgment now made) as §§ 74 a–74 e.

The uncertainty in the jurisdiction of equity to obtain discovery appears to have arisen chiefly from not discriminating sufficiently between that discovery which is sought in support of the bill as evidence merely, or in aid or anticipation of a suit at law (Lord Hardwicke in Lempster v. Pomfret, Ambl. 154; Moodalay v. Morton, 1 Bro. C. C. 469), and that appeal to the conscience of the defendant which is based upon some alleged misconduct either in withholding documents or in suppressing facts to which the plaintiff is entitled, — which but for the defendant's conduct he would have had, and thus have been able to obtain redress at law.

In the former case the plaintiff charges no wrong upon the defendant, so far as the discovery is concerned. He asks it as a favor to enable him to obtain redress in equity if the subject-matter of the suit is appropriate for such remedy; and if not, then to enable him to obtain redress at law. And where the discovery is sought merely in aid of a suit at law, then, whether it is obtained or not, the plaintiff upon the coming in of the answer is bound to discontinue and pay the costs. Cartwright *v.* Hateley, 1 Ves. jr. 292, 293. See also Simmons *v.* Kinnaird, 4 Ves. 746; 1 Madd. Ch. Pr. 217. Though as to the matter of costs, if the defendant on reasonable request refuse to make the admission, and thus drive the plaintiff to equity, where he succeeds, the defendant will not be entitled to them. Weymouth *v.* Boyer, 1 Ves. jr. 416, 423; Deas *v.* Harvie, 2 Barb. Ch. 448. Such costs are sometimes taxed in the action at law. 1 Madd. Ch. Pr. 217; Grant *v.* Jackson, Peake, 203. See further as to costs, Burnett *v.* Sanders, 4 Johns. Ch. 504; McElwer *v.* Sutton, 1 Hill, Ch. 32; King *v.* Clark, 3 Paige, 76; Harvey *v.* Tebbutt, 1 Jac. & W. 197; Fulton Bank *v.* New York Canal Co., 4 Paige, 127.

But in a bill for discovery merely in aid of redress, and where no wrong is charged upon the defendant in withholding documents or facts, it is not competent for the plaintiff, according to the English and the better practice, to pray relief unless his case is one which in itself is a proper subject of equitable cognizance. Walker *v.* Brooks, 125 Mass. 241; Pool *v.* Lloyd, 5 Met. 525; Ahrend *v.* Odiorne, 118 Mass. 261. If his case is not of this character, he must ask for the discovery in aid of a contemplated or a pending suit at law. And if he asks relief in a case which is not proper for the interference of equity, the bill is demurrable. He must show not only a case in which he is entitled to discovery, he must also state the true ground of such discovery, that the court may see whether the proceeding is proper. A bill, for instance, will be sustained in aid of a defence at law to a bond or other instrument based upon the ground of illegality in the consideration, while if relief had been prayed the bill must have been dismissed; the court could give no relief in such a case. Benyon *v.* Nettleford, 3 Macn. & G. 94. See however the author's observations, supra, § 70. All that is required to be alleged in a bill for discovery in aid of a suit at law is to show that the plaintiff has such a case that the discovery is needful for him. Vance *v.* Andrews, 2 Barb. Ch. 370; Deas *v.* Harvie, Ib. 448; Williams *v.* Harden, 1 Barb. Ch. 298; Welford, Eq. Pl. 99; Stainton *v.* Chadwick, 3 Macn. & G. 575.

Nor is it necessary in such a case, according to the better view, to allege that the plaintiff is unable to establish his case or defence by other witnesses, or to make any affidavit to that effect, except for the purpose of obtaining an injunction to stay proceedings at law. Vance *v.* Andrews, 2 Barb. Ch. 370; Appleyard *v.* Seton, 16 Ves. 223; March *v.* Davison, 9 Paige, 580; post, §§ 148–150. But see Gelston *v.* Hoyt, 1 Johns. Ch. 543; Seymour *v.* Seymour, 4 Johns. Ch. 409; Leggett *v.* Postley, 2 Paige, 599, which, it is apprehended, are not sound law. As the law stood, when parties could not be witnesses, either party might claim discovery from the other to save expense, delay, or uncertainty. But the necessity for such bills having ceased, this kind of discovery has become practically obsolete. And while it was in full force it required no other check to prevent abuse than the payment of all the expenses without regard to the result.

If however discovery in the broad sense has become a recognized ground of equity jurisdiction in this country, it will not be relinquished because courts of law have advanced to the same position. But it is an American doctrine of equity entirely, springing mainly, as has already been suggested, from confusing that discovery which is merely matter of general evidence, whether sought for purposes of relief in equity or at law, with that which is necessary because of the wrongful conduct of the defendant, which alone, as where it involves a breach of confidence, may be sufficient ground for equity jurisdiction; springing partly also, it seems, from pushing beyond its just meaning the maxim that where equity obtains jurisdiction of a cause for any purpose it will retain it for final relief. Day *v.* Cummings, 19 Vt. 496; Bank of United States *v.* Biddle, 2 Pars. Ch. 54; McGowin *v.* Remington, 12 Penn. St. 63; Shallenberger's Appeal, 9 Harris, 340; Brooks *v.* Stotley, 3 McLean, 523; Traip *v.* Gould, 15 Maine, 82; Boyd *v.* Hunter, 44 Ala. 705; Peoria *v.* Johnson, 56 Ill. 45; Corby *v.* Bean, 44 Miss. 379. But this maxim, it is apprehended, has no proper application where the court has no legitimate jurisdiction of the *cause* or some portion of it.

But when a party comes into equity for general discovery merely, the court acquires no general jurisdiction over the cause or any part of it. Discovery is something which a party may claim in every cause at law, whether he be plaintiff or defendant, and in every transaction which may fairly be expected to become the foundation of an action thereafter; and that too whether destitute of other evidence or not. He may claim the discovery to save expense or uncertainty in the proof of his case. Story, Eq. Pl. § 319; Stacy *v.* Pearson, 3 Rich. Eq. 148, 152; Mitford, Eq. Pl. 307, Jeremy. It follows that if such discovery were really a ground of Equity Jurisdiction for ulterior purposes, it would be sufficient to bring any case, proper only for a court of law, into equity, to call for the discovery of facts from the defendant. See Foley *v.* Hill, 2 Clark & F. 28, 37, Lord Cottenham. And see Hambrook *v.* Smith, 9 Eng. L. & E. 226.

This reductio ad absurdum has led the American courts from time to time to annex limitations to the application of the rule of giving relief as a consequence of entertaining a bill for discovery. It is laid down as necessary for a party who seeks to transfer to equity a cause appropriate for a court of law, on the ground of discovery alone, to allege in his bill, and to verify the allegation by affidavit, that he has no other means of proving his case. Gelston *v.* Hoyt, 1 Johns. Ch. 543; Merchants' Bank *v.* Davis, 3 Kelly, 112; Bank of United States *v.* Biddle, 2 Pars. Ch. 31 ; Emerson *v.* Staton, 3 B. Mon. 116, 118; Bullock *v.* Boyd, 2 A. K. Marsh. 322; Stacy *v.* Pearson, 3 Rich. Eq. 148, 152; Laight *v.* Morgan, 1 Johns. Cas. 429; s. c. 2 Caines' Cas. 344; Lyons *v.* Miller, 6 Gratt. 427, 428; Sims *v.* Aughtery, 4 Strobh. Eq. 103, 121. But to make any such fact as the party's want of other evidence the basis of Equity Jurisdiction, the allegation should be traversable, and the jurisdiction should fail upon its disproof. And another necessary qualification of the rule will then arise, to wit, that the existing evidence to defeat the jurisdiction must be in the knowledge, or at least within the reach, of the plaintiff; unless it be so, it is the same to him as if it did not exist. This inquiry whether the plaintiff is destitute of other evidence would raise a collateral issue not capable of decision. The limitation in question, which was at first made to apply to all bills for discovery (Gelston *v.* Hoyt, 1 Johns. Ch. 543), has been abandoned as to bills which do not seek to transfer a merely legal cause to equity.

The only distinct ground of Equity Jurisdiction over cases of a purely legal nature, based upon mere discovery, is where, as has been stated above, the defendant has been charged with a wrong and a virtual fraud in withholding legal evidence. Sometimes such a case is founded upon the defendant's duty to disclose deeds, writings, and documents in his keeping. Madd. Ch. Pr. 199; Metcalf *v.* Hovey, 1 Ves. sr. 248. As where an heir claims under the deed withheld, or is obstructed by an attempt to set up an outstanding and false title. Bond v. Hopkins, 1 Sch. & L. 428, 429; Tanner v. Wise, 3 P. Wms. 295, 296. So a bill of this sort will lie against one who conceals a bankrupt's estate. Boden v. Dillow, 1 Atk. 289. Also where a confusion of boundaries has occurred through the fault of the defendant. Aston v. Exeter, 6 Ves. 288, 293; post, § 620. And where the defendant declines to give knowledge of the goods put on board a ship insured and lost. Le Pypre v. Farr, 2 Vern. 716. But see Taylor v. Ferguson, 4 Har. & J. 46. In these cases of trust and confidence and fraudulent breach of duty equity will retain the bill and give relief. See also Stanhope v. Roberts, 2 Atk. 214. But these cases are broadly distinguished from general bills of discovery. For American cases which take the distinction under consideration, see Gregory v. Marks, 1 Rand. 355; Burroughs v. McNeill, 2 Dev. & B. Eq. 297.

In cases where Courts of Law and of Equity exercise concurrent jurisdiction, as in matters of fraud, accident, mistake, and account, there will often be occasion for the exercise of discretion. Whether this should be exercised in favor of retaining a bill for final relief must often depend upon special circumstances, such as the complication of facts, the number and variety of interests involved, and the like. But there are many cases still in which no prayer for discovery should induce equity to proceed to relief; such as the case of a mere claim to damages for a fraudulent misrepresentation. In Pearce v. Creswick, 2 Hare, 286, Wigram, V. C. says: 'I think this part of the plaintiff's case cannot be stated more highly in his favor than this, — that the necessity a party may be under, from the very nature of the transaction, to come into a Court of Equity for discovery is a circumstance to be regarded in deciding upon the distinct and independent question of equitable jurisdiction. Further than this I have not been able to go.' See Middletown Bank v. Russ, 3 Conn. 135; Isham v. Gilbert, Ib. 166; Norwich R. Co. v. Storey, 17 Conn. 364; Taylor v. Ferguson, 4 Har. & J. 46; Brown v. Edsall, 1 Stockt. Ch. 256; Little v. Cooper, 2 Stockt. 273; Skinner v. Judson, 8 Conn. 528; Avery v. Holland, 2 Tenn. 71; Laight v. Morgan, 1 Johns. Cas. 429; s. c. 2 Caines, Cas. 344.

CHAPTER IV.

CONCURRENT JURISDICTION OF EQUITY. — ACCIDENT.

75. HAVING disposed of these matters, which may in some sort be deemed preliminary, the next inquiry which will occupy our attention is to ascertain the true boundaries of the jurisdiction at present exercised by Courts of Equity. The subject here naturally divides itself into three great heads, — the concurrent, the exclusive, and the auxiliary or supplemental jurisdiction.[1] As the concurrent jurisdiction is that which is of the greatest extent and most familiar occurrence in practice, I propose to begin with it.

76. The concurrent jurisdiction of Courts of Equity may be truly said to embrace, if not all, at least a very large portion of the original jurisdiction inherent in the court from its very nature, or first conferred upon it upon the dissolution or partition of the powers of the Great Council, or Aula Regis, of the king. We have already seen that it did not take its rise from the introduction of technical uses or trusts, as has sometimes been erroneously supposed.[2] Its original foundation then may be more fitly referred to what Lord Coke deemed the true one, fraud, accident, and confidence.[3] In many cases of this sort Courts of Common Law are, and for a long time have been, accustomed to exercise jurisdiction and to afford an adequate remedy. And in many other cases in which anciently no such remedy was allowed, their jurisdiction is now expanded so as effectually to

---

[1] In this division I follow Mr. Fonblanque and Mr. Jeremy; and though a more philosophical division might be made, I am by no means certain that it would be more convenient. Mr. Maddock has made a different division; but upon reflection I have not been inclined to give it a preference. 1 Fonbl. Eq. B. 1, ch. 1, § 3, note (*f*); Jeremy on Eq. Jurisd. Introd. p. xxvii.

[2] Ante, §§ 42, 43; 1 Cooper's Public Records, 357.

[3] 4 Inst. 84; Earl of Bath *v.* Sherwin, 10 Mod. 1; 3 Black. Comm. 431.

reach them.[1] Still however there are many cases of fraud, accident, and confidence which either Courts of Law do not attempt to redress at all or if they do the redress which they afford is inadequate and defective.[2] The concurrent jurisdiction then of equity has its true origin in one of two sources: either the Courts of Law, although they have general jurisdiction in the matter, cannot give adequate, specific, and perfect relief; or under the actual circumstances of the case they cannot give any relief at all. The former occurs in all cases when a simple judgment for the plaintiff or for the defendant does not meet the full merits and exigencies of the case; but a variety of adjustments, limitations, and cross claims are to be introduced and finally acted on; and a decree meeting all the circumstances of the particular case between the very parties is indispensable to complete distributive justice. The latter occurs when the object sought is incapable of being accomplished by the Courts of Law; as for instance a perpetual injunction, or a preventive process to restrain trespasses, nuisances, or waste.[3] It may therefore be said that the concurrent jurisdiction of equity extends to all cases of legal rights where, under the circumstances, there is not a plain, adequate, and complete remedy at law.[4]

77. The subject, for convenience, may be divided into two branches: (1) that in which the subject-matter constitutes the principal (for it rarely constitutes the sole) ground of the jurisdiction; and (2) that in which the peculiar remedies afforded by Courts of Equity constitute the principal (although not always the sole) ground of the jurisdiction. Of these we shall endeavor to treat successively in their order, beginning with that of the subject-matter where the relief is deemed more adequate, complete, and perfect in equity than at common law; but where the remedy is not, or at least may not be, of a peculiar and exclusive character.[5] It is proper however to add that

[1] 3 Black. Comm. 431, 432.
[2] See 7 Dane's Abridg. ch. 225, art. 5, § 10; art. 6, § 1; Com. Dig. Chancery, 3 F. 8.
[3] See Jeremy on Eq. Jurisd. 292; Id. 307; 3 Wooddes. Lect. lvi. p. 397, &c.; Beames, Eq. Pl. ch. 3, pp. 77, 78.
[4] Com. Dig. Chancery, 3 F. 9.
[5] See Mitford, Pl. Eq. by Jeremy, 111; 1 Fonbl. Eq. B. 1, ch. 1, § 3, note (*f*), p. 12.

as the grounds of jurisdiction often run into each other, any attempt at a scientific method of distribution of the various heads would be impracticable and illusory.

78. And in the first place let us consider the cases where the jurisdiction arises from accident. (*a*) By the term *accident* is

(*a*) *Accident and Negligence.* — Accident means happening; and its consequences therefore, falling upon one who seeks relief from them, fall there without that one's intention. On this ground — the absence of intention on the part of the plaintiff — relief is granted. Some forfeiture or some final loss is about to transpire, without the intention of the sufferer, in consequence of what has merely happened.

Jurisdiction of the courts may indeed be cut off by force of the terms of a contract; as where a promise to pay rent is absolute, or a promise to do something on a certain day or within a certain time is made in such terms as to show that the understanding was, that performance on that particular day or within that time was the very thing, or one of the very things, agreed upon. That is, in common language, such performance is of the essence of the contract. See e. g. Brown *v.* Vandergrift, 80 Penn. St. 142; Gregory *v.* Wilson, 9 Hare, 683. True, the result — the non-performance — may have happened without the party's intention; but accident is excluded from consideration, because the parties have agreed that nothing of the sort shall be taken into the account. The case may still be one for equitable interference against the agreed result; but where that is the fact, it will be found that interference is based, not on the ground of accident, but of some other consideration, such as the fact that a forfeiture provided is named by way of penalty, and not of liquidated damages. See infra, §§ 1314-1318.

Negligence consists in failing to exercise due care, prudence, or diligence in the particular situation, — the care, prudence, or diligence, that is to say, which a good citizen would there exercise. Will negligence have the effect to bar one of relief from the consequences of accident? Clearly it will, if it shows that the particular fact came about by the intention of the party seeking relief; clearly not, in principle, if it does not substantially show that.

Now it is often said, and for certain purposes it is well enough to say, that a man is held to intend the natural consequences of his conduct. But that rule has only a particular application. It does not express the whole conception of negligence even when applied to that subject. It merely means that for the purpose of punishment or damages, or of saving another from harm and injustice, the act or omission may be deemed to have had its natural result, and the result treated as if it had been foreseen, as it ought to have been. The party must for such purpose be deemed to have intended what he should have expected. But a man does not, broadly speaking, lose his rights by mere negligence. Negligence cannot e. g. work a gift. The rule that a man intends the natural consequences of his conduct cannot be pressed into service to deprive a man arbitrarily of his property; the rule is applied only where the position of an innocent person has been influenced and changed by such conduct.

But relief from the consequences of accident is never granted where the equities of the defendant are equal — as in the case just put — to those of the plaintiff. If however the defendant stands in no position deserving the sup-

here intended not merely inevitable casualty, or the act of Providence, or what is technically called vis major, or irresistible

port of the court, the case of the plaintiff, negligent though he may have been, is virtually that of one who denies having made a gift, and seeks the aid of the court to recover or to retain his own. The court therefore cannot refuse its aid from a desire to protect the defendant, and refusal must be in the nature of punishment to the plaintiff. Can this be proper?

A chancellor is, it is true, apt to be impatient with a party who seeks relief based even in part on his own negligence; but it is submitted that this ought never to go to the extent of refusing justice where there are no adverse interests deserving attention. It is well-settled law in England that negligence in the payment of money will not bar the payer from recovering it back if the payment was made under mistake; and this has been declared to be good law by chancellors as well as by common-law judges. Willmott v. Barber, 15 Ch. D. 96; Kelly v. Solari, 9 Mees. & W. 54; Bell v. Gardiner, 4 Man. & G. 11; Dails v. Lloyd, 12 Q. B. 531; Townsend v. Crowdy, 8 C. B. N. S. 477. The authorities are not so clear in this country, but it is apprehended that the rule stated is the true one. See Kilmer v. Smith, 77 N. Y. 226; Monroe v. Skelton, 36 Ind. 302; post, note to § 140. Now the situation of the defendant in such a case is generally more deserving of consideration than that of a defendant in a case of accident; besides, there has been actual intention in the case of mistake, though the intention would have been different, probably, — who can say certainly? — had the situation been understood. And the plaintiff is in the same predicament in both cases; he has been guilty of negligence.

The question of the effect of negligence may be forcibly brought out by considering the case of the loss of a negotiable instrument, in which case equity, generally speaking, grants relief upon a suitable tender of indemnity to the defendant. Can it be that the plaintiff will be barred of relief on the ground that the loss of the instrument was due to his own negligence? What if the result *was* the natural effect of the plaintiff's want of care? The defendant is no worse off for that than if the instrument had been lost without negligence; and the plaintiff did not intend to give up his right.

Take the case of pay-day passed, involving a certain proper forfeiture. If payment on the very day is of the essence of the contract, it must be made then; if not, payment on a subsequent day, within a reasonable time, will be good, in equity at least, by necessary consequence. See Hearst v. Pujol, 44 Cal. 230; Beecher v. Beecher, 43 Conn. 556. The parties have not fixed a day absolute. Tender within a reasonable time after the day named will save the forfeiture for the strongest reason, if the failure to pay on the day was due to accident; and the case cannot be different though the accident was due to negligence, or, to put the case directly, though the *failure* was due to negligence, if the neglect to pay was not wilful. So long as the other party's position has not been changed to his detriment, and there is no binding agreement for a forfeiture absolute, a forfeiture ought not to be decreed for negligence per se in the face of the tender. There has been no gift or abandonment of rights.

In the case of wilful neglect with foresight of the specific result, and with no obstacle entirely preventing performance of an obligation, no doubt equity will refuse its aid to prevent consequences made a dis-

force ; but such unforeseen events, misfortunes, losses, acts, or omissions as are not the result of any negligence or misconduct

tinct and proper part of the contract, though there may still be something short of actual intention to confer a gift. Hancock v. Carlton, 6 Gray, 39, 52, 57. There is something like an abandonment of a right in such a case. It will be noticed that the author usually speaks of 'gross misconduct,' 'gross negligence,' or 'rashness,' as barring relief. Supra, § 78; post, § 105. He speaks very cautiously of mere negligence. 'That perhaps may induce a Court of Equity to withhold its assistance;' § 90, at end. It might have that effect where attended with forecast of the result, if no sufficient obstacle prevented action ; otherwise it is apprehended it would not necessarily. (Of course knowledge alone of e. g. the time of performance would not bar relief from the effect of accident. Bargent v. Thompson, 4 Giff. 473, where prompt performance was prevented by the weather, time not being of the essence of the contract.)

Indeed it may be that wilful negligence with forecast of the specific result will bar relief, though a preventing obstacle existed, if that preventing obstacle would not have been in the way but for the plaintiff's negligence. In the case of Bargent v. Thompson, just cited, it is probable that the party would not have been relieved had the performance of his contract (to make repairs) been delayed by his negligence till the bad weather at last set in and prevented the completion of what might well have been done notwithstanding the weather. But that would be because of *wilful* negligence, — negligence with forecast, not because of negligence as such, or negligence that another of better judgment might have seen would end in the particular loss. That is, there is something, if not equivalent to a gift, at all events capable of being treated as an abandonment.

There is a similar distinction with reference to negligence after the day of performance (not of the essence of the contract) has passed with knowledge on the part of the obligor. Neglect of tender in such a case will be evidence, more or less cogent according to circumstances, of acquiescence; and acquiescence with knowledge may no doubt make decisive that which otherwise would be indecisive.

There is also a case with regard to which a settled and sound public policy applies, touching accident resulting from negligence, and that is the conduct of causes. Courts are of small use if they cannot put a stop to litigation. 'Interest reipublicæ ut litium finis sit;' and if litigants were allowed to upset decisions on grounds of their own negligence, causes might never be at an end. This is the case to which the rule applies, that the courts aid 'vigilantibus non dormientibus;' and this is the case of the decisions referred to by the author. Penny v. Martin, 4 Johns. Ch. 566; Marine Ins. Co. v. Hodgson, 7 Cranch, 532, 536. See also Sargeant v. Bigelow, 24 Minn. 370; Wilder v. Lee, 64 N. Car. 50; Miller v. Morse, 23 Mich. 365; George v. Alexander, 6 Cold. 641.

Aside from this class of cases it is apprehended that the courts have nothing to do with the mere negligence of a plaintiff asking for relief from the consequences of accident. The question of rights is the only one legitimately before the court.

The following may be enumerated among recent specific cases of relief: —

Death of a sheriff before making conveyance, but after having duly made sale, received the purchase-money, and made return of his acts. Stewart v. Stokes, 33 Ala. 494. De-

in the party.[1] Lord Cowper, speaking on the subject of accident as cognizable in equity, said: 'By accident is meant, when a case

[1] Grounds and Rudim. of the Law, M. 120, p. 81 (edit. 1781). See Jeremy on Equity Jurisd. B. 3, Pt. 2, Introd. p. 358. Mr. Jeremy defines accident, in the sense used in a Court of Equity, to be 'an occurrence in relation to a contract, which was not anticipated by the parties when the same was entered into, and which gives an undue advantage to one of them over the other in a Court of Law.' Jeremy on Eq. Jurisd. B. 3, Pt. 2, p. 358. Accidents, in the sense of a Court of Equity, may arise in relation to other things besides contracts, and therefore the confining of the definition to contracts is not entirely accurate. The definition is defective in another respect; for it does not exclude cases of unanticipated occurrences, resulting from the negligence or misconduct of the party seeking relief.

struction of the records of the court ordering a sale in a particular case. Garrett v. Lynch, 45 Ala. 205. Destruction of the whole record of a cause. Sproles v. Powell, 10 Heisk. 693. But it is held that equity cannot restore the lost records of another court. Keen v. Jordan, 13 Fla. 327. Loss of a mortgage deed on land to secure personal support. Lawrence v. Lawrence, 42 N. H. 109. Loss of a deed containing an error reformable in equity, with decree of a new and correct deed. Hudspeth v. Thomason, 46 Ala. 470. Loss of sealed instrument. Patton v. Campbell, 70 Ill. 72. Lost negotiable paper. Hopkins v. Adams, 20 Vt. 407; Adams v. Edmunds, 55 Vt. 352; Chewning v. Singleton, 2 Hill, Ch. (S. Car.) 371. Further as to the loss of negotiable paper, see Fales v. Russell, 16 Pick. 315; Almy v. Reed, 10 Cush. 421; Boston Lead Co. v. McGuirk, 15 Gray, 87; Tower v. Appleton Bank, 3 Allen, 387; Tuttle v. Standish, 4 Allen, 481; Smith v. Rockwell, 2 Hill, 482; Bridgeford v. Masonville Manuf. Co., 34 Conn. 546; Savannah Bank v. Haskins, 101 Mass. 370; McGregory v. McGregory, 107 Mass. 543; Wright v. Maidstone, 1 Kay & J. 701. The last-named case shows that when the paper, though negotiable, has been *destroyed*, the jurisdiction is at law and not in equity. And where, as in some States is deemed to be the case, adequate indemnity can be required at law, the Courts of Law will entertain suits on lost as well as on destroyed negotiable instruments. Bridgeford v. Masonville Manuf. Co., supra; Tuttle v. Standish, supra; McGregory v. McGregory, supra. But it is held in Tuttle v. Standish that where the suit is against an *indorser*, a mere bond of indemnity may not afford adequate protection to the defendant, since he may need the instrument for the purpose of suit against a prior party. And in Savannah Bank v. Haskins, supra, it was held that such a bond would not sufficiently serve an acceptor of a bill, since he may need the paper as a voucher in settling his accounts with the drawer. But as to the maker of a note it was considered to be settled law in Massachusetts that tender of a suitable bond would justify the Law Courts in entertaining the indorsee's action. In any event however jurisdiction will exist in equity unless it is clear that it has been taken away by statute. Labadie v. Hewitt, 85 Ill. 341; Lee v. Lee, 55 Ala. 590, 598; Hinchley v. Greany, 118 Mass. 595; Clouston v. Shearer, 99 Mass. 209; Sweeny v. Williams, 36 N. J. Eq. There, it seems, all the parties to the paper can be brought before the court, and their respective rights adjusted. Compare § 28, supra.

is distinguished from others of the like nature by unusual circumstances;'[1] a definition quite too loose and inaccurate, without some further qualifications; for it is entirely consistent with the language, that the unusual circumstances may have resulted from the party's own gross negligence, folly, or rashness.

79. The jurisdiction of the court arising from accident, in the general sense already suggested, is a very old head in equity and probably coeval with its existence.[2] But it is not every case of accident which will justify the interposition of a Court of Equity.[3] The jurisdiction being concurrent will be maintained only: first, when a Court of Law cannot grant suitable relief; and secondly, when the party has a conscientious title to relief. (a) Both grounds must concur in the given case; for otherwise a Court of Equity not only may, but is bound to, withhold its aid. Mr. Justice Blackstone has very correctly observed that 'Many accidents are supplied in a Court of Law; as loss of deeds, mistakes in receipts and accounts, wrong payments, deaths, which made it impossible to perform a condition literally, and a multitude of other contingencies. And many cannot be redressed even in a Court of Equity; as if by accident a recovery is ill suffered, a devise ill executed, a contingent remainder destroyed, or a power of leasing omitted in a family settlement.'[4]

[1] Earl of Bath *v.* Sherwin, 10 Mod. R. 1, 3; Com. Dig. Chancery, 4 D. 10.
[2] See East India Company *v.* Boddam, 9 Ves. 466; Armitage *v.* Wadsworth, 1 Madd. R. 189 to 193.
[3] Whitfield *v.* Faussat, 1 Ves. 392, 393.
[4] 3 Black. Comm. 431; Com. Dig. Chancery, 3 F. 8. Even this language is true in a general sense only; for (as we shall presently see) omissions in a family settlement, and many other defects in private and legal proceedings, may be redressed or rather supplied in equity. 1 Fonbl. Eq. B. 1, ch. 1, § 7; Mitford, Pl. Eq. 127, 128 (4th edit.), by Jeremy. In Whitfield *v.* Faussat (1 Ves. 392), Lord Hardwicke is reported to have said: 'The loss of a deed is not always a ground to come into Courts of Equity for relief; for if there was no more in the case, although he (the plaintiff) is entitled to have a discovery of that, whether lost or not, Courts of Law [sometimes] admit evidence of the loss of a deed, proving the existence of it, and the contents, just

(a) See e. g. Hickman *v.* Painter, 11 W. Va. 386, where the plaintiff had lost a receipt given him by the defendant acknowledging possession of choses in action given him by the plaintiff for collection. The bill prayed discovery of the facts in regard to the same, and that the lost receipt might be set up. The prayer was granted, and a decree rendered for damages for moneys collected by the defendant and not paid over.

80. The first consideration then is, whether there is an adequate remedy at law, not merely whether there is some remedy at law.[1] And here a most material distinction is to be attended to. In modern times Courts of Law frequently interfere, and grant a remedy under circumstances in which it would certainly have been denied in earlier periods. And sometimes the Legislature by express enactments has conferred on Courts of Law the same remedial faculty which belongs to Courts of Equity. Now (as we have seen) in neither case, if the Courts of Equity originally obtained and exercised jurisdiction, is that jurisdiction overturned or impaired by this change of the authority at law in regard to legislative enactments; for unless there are prohibitory or restrictive words used, the uniform interpretation is that they confer concurrent and not exclusive remedial authority. (*a*) And it would be still more difficult to maintain that a Court of Law by its own act could oust or repeal a jurisdiction already rightfully attached in equity.[2]

81. One of the most common interpositions of equity under this head is in the case of lost bonds, or other instruments under seal.[3] (*b*) Until a very recent period the doctrine prevailed that there could be no remedy on a lost bond in a Court of Common Law, because there could be no profert of the instru-

as a Court of Equity does.' The other parts of his Lordship's opinion show that the word 'sometimes' should be inserted as a qualification of the language.

[1] Cooper, Eq. Pl. 129.

[2] Mitf. Pl. Eq. 113, 114; 1 Fonbl. Eq. B. 1, ch. 1, § 3, note (*f*), pp. 15, 16, 17; Atkinson *v.* Leonard, 3 Bro. Ch. R. 218; Ex parte Greenway, 6 Ves. 812; Bromley *v.* Holland, 7 Ves. 19, 20; East India Company *v.* Boddam, 9 Ves. 466; Walmsley *v.* Child, 1 Ves. 341; Kemp *v.* Pryor, 7 Ves. 248 to 250; Cooper, Eq. Pl. ch. 3, p. 129; Ludlow *v.* Simond, 2 Caines, Cas. in Err. 1; King *v.* Baldwin, 17 John. R. 384; Post *v.* Kimberly, 9 John. R. 470.

[3] Mr. Reeves (Hist. of English Law, vol. 3, p. 189) has remarked, that by the old common law, 'When a person was to found a claim by virtue of a deed, which was detained in the hands of another, so that he was prevented from making a profert of it, he was utterly deprived of the means of obtaining justice according to the forms of law. If a deed of grant of rent, common, or annuity were lost, as these claims could only be substantiated by the evidence of a deed, they vanished together with it.'

(*a*) Sweeny *v.* Williams, 36 N. J. Eq.; ante, p. 30.
(*b*) Goldman *v.* Page, 59 Miss. 404. See Mitchell *v.* Chancellor, 14 W. Va. 22, where relief was refused because the bond was not payable to the plaintiff.

ment, without which the declaration would be fatally defective.[1] At present however the Courts of Law do entertain the jurisdiction, and dispense with the profert, if an allegation of loss by time and accident is stated in the declaration.[2] But this circumstance is not permitted in the slightest degree to change the course in equity.[3]

82. Independent of this general ground of the inability to make a proper profert of the deed at law, there is another satisfactory ground for the interference of a Court of Equity. It is, that no other court can furnish the same remedy with all the fit limitations which may be demanded for the purposes of justice, by granting *relief* only upon the terms of the party's giving (when proper) a suitable bond of indemnity. Now a Court of Law is incompetent to require such a bond of indemnity as a part of its judgments, although it has sometimes attempted an analogous relief (it is difficult to understand upon what ground) by requiring the previous offer of such an indemnity.[4] But such an offer may in many cases fall far short of the just relief; for in the intermediate time there may be a great change of the circumstances of the parties to the bond of indemnity.[5] In joint bonds there are still stronger reasons, for the equities may be different between the different defendants.[6] And besides, a Court of Equity, before it will grant *relief* (it is otherwise where *discovery* only is sought) will insist that the defendant shall have the protection of the oath and affidavit of the plaintiff to the fact of the loss; thus requiring, what is most essential to the interests of justice, that the party should pledge his conscience by his oath that the instrument is lost.[7]

---

[1] Whitfield *v.* Faussat, 1 Ves. 392, 393; Co. Litt. 35 (*b*); Rex *v.* Arundel, Hob. R. 109; Atkins *v.* Leonard, 3 Bro. Ch. R. 218; Ex parte Greenway, 5 Ves. 812; Bromley *v.* Holland, 7 Ves. 19, 20; East India Company *v.* Boddam, 9 Ves. 466; Toulman *v.* Price, 5 Ves. 238.

[2] Read *v.* Brokman, 3 T. R. 151; Totty *v.* Nesbitt, 3 T. R. 153, note.

[3] Ibid. Walmsley *v.* Child, 1 Ves. 341; Kemp *v.* Pryor, 7 Ves. 249, 250; Cooper, Eq. Pl. 129, 130; Evans *v.* Bicknell, 6 Ves. R. 182.

[4] Ex parte Greenway, 6 Ves. 812; Pierson *v.* Hutchinson, 2 Camp. 211; s. c. 6 Esp. 126; Hansard *v.* Robinson, 7 B. & Cressw. 90.

[5] East India Company *v.* Boddam, 9 Ves. 466; Ex parte Greenway, 6 Ves. 812.

[6] Ibid.

[7] Bromley *v.* Holland, 7 Ves. 19, 20; Ex parte Greenway, 6 Ves. 812; 1 Fonbl. Eq. B. 1, ch. 1, § 3, note (*f*), pp. 16, 17; Whitchurch *v.* Golding,

83. We have seen that in cases of the loss of sealed instruments equity will entertain a suit for relief as well as for discovery, upon the party's making an affidavit of the loss of the instrument and offering indemnity. The original ground of granting the relief was the supposed inadequacy of a Court of Law to afford it in a suitable manner from the impossibility of making a profert.[1] But where discovery only and not relief is the object of the bill, there equity will grant the discovery without any affidavit of loss or offer of indemnity; and in a variety of cases this is all that the plaintiff may desire.[2] The ground of this distinction is, that when relief is prayed the proper forum of jurisdiction is sought to be changed from law to equity; and in all such cases an affidavit ought to be required, to prevent abuse of the process of the court. But when discovery only is sought, the original jurisdiction remains at law, and equity is merely auxiliary. The jurisdiction for discovery alone would therefore seem upon principle to be universal. But the jurisdiction for relief is special, and limited to peculiar cases; and in all these cases there must be an affidavit of the loss, (a) and when proper, an offer of indemnity also in the bill.[3]

2 P. Will. 541; Anon 3 Atk. 17; Mitf. Eq. Pl. by Jeremy, 29, 54, 123, 124; Walmsley v. Child, 1 Ves. 344, 345; Cooper, Eq. Pl. ch. 3, pp. 126, 129, 130; Id. Introd. pp. xxviii, xxix; Leroy v. Veeder, 1 John. Cas. 417.

[1] Ibid. Anon. 2 Atk. 61; Mitf. Eq. Pl. by Jeremy, 113, 114.

[2] Dormer v. Fortescue, 3 Atk. 132; Whitchurch v. Golding, 2 P. Will. 541; Walmsley v. Child, 1 Ves. 344, 345.

[3] In Walmsley v. Child (1 Ves. R. 344), Lord Hardwicke is reported to have said that there are but three cases in which a bill for discovery and relief on lost instruments can be maintained in equity. The passage however is singularly obscure and of difficult interpretation; and I have not been able entirely to satisfy my mind what Lord Hardwicke's real doctrine was, or what were the three cases to which he alluded. Two of them are easily made out; but the perplexity is in ascertaining the third, as contradistinguished from the other two. The passage is as follows: 'But there are cases upon which you may come into equity on a loss, though remedy may be at law; and one is clear upon a bill for discovery. But if you come into equity, not only for discovery, but to have relief on the foundation of loss, that changes the jurisdiction. And there are but three cases in which you are entitled to that; in every one of which you are obliged to annex an affidavit to the bill to prove the loss. If the deed or instrument upon which the demand arises is lost, and you only come for discovery, you are entitled thereto without affidavit; but if relief is prayed beyond that discovery, to have payment of the debt, affidavit of the

(a) See Hoddy v. Hoard, 2 Ind. 474. But see Graham v. Hockwith, 1 A. K. Marsh. 424; **Purviance v. Holt**, 3 Gilm. (Ill.) 395.

84. It has been remarked by Lord Hardwicke, that the loss of a deed is not always a ground to come into a Court of Equity for relief; for if there is no more in the case, although the party may be entitled to a discovery of the original existence and validity of the deed, Courts of Law may afford just relief, since they will admit evidence of the loss and contents of a deed, just as a Court of Equity will do.[1] To enable the party therefore in case of a lost deed to come into equity for relief, he must establish that there is no remedy at all at law, or no remedy which is adequate, and adapted to the circumstances of the case. In the first place he may come into equity for payment of a lost bond; for in such a case his bill need not be for a discovery only, but may also be for relief, since the jurisdiction attached when there was no loss must be annexed; for that changes the jurisdiction. If the deed lost concerned the title of lands, and possession prayed to be established, such affidavit must be annexed. Another case is of a personal demand, where [there is] loss of a bond, and a bill in equity on that loss, to be paid the demand; there a bill for discovery will not be sufficient, but it must be to be paid the money thereon; but an affidavit must be annexed. The reason of the difference between a bond and a note is, that in an action at law a profert in curia of the bond must itself be made; otherwise oyer cannot be demanded by the defendant; and if oyer is not given, the plaintiff cannot proceed. But that is not necessary in the case of notes; no oyer is demanded upon them, the proving the contents being sufficient; and nothing standing in the plaintiff's way. Another case in which you may come into this court on a loss is, to pray satisfaction and payment of it upon terms of giving security. In an action at law the plaintiff might offer, but the defendant could not be compelled to take; but in equity that would be a consideration whether they were reasonable. That was the case of Teresy *v.* Gorey, as Lord Nottingham has taken the name in an authentic record I have of it; which was Easter, 28 C. 2, where a bill of exchange was drawn on the defendant, and indorsed, in the third place, to the plaintiff, by whom the bill was either lost or mislaid, as appeared by the affidavit annexed. And the bill prayed that the defendant might be decreed to pay the plaintiff the money, as last indorsee, according to the acceptance, the plaintiff first giving security to save the defendant harmless against all former assignments; which was so decreed, but without damages and costs. In a book called Finch's Reports, 301, the decree is somewhat larger, and the acceptance of the defendant was after the third indorsement, and it is in that book, though not so in the manuscript report. And indeed I do take it to be as in the book; and then there is no doubt of the plaintiff's right; but if that be material, it shall be inquired into. In that case, if the plaintiff could at law prove the contents of his bill, and the indorsement, and the loss of it, he might have brought his action at law upon that bill without coming into this court. But he was apprehensive the course of trade might stand in his way at law, and therefore came into this court upon terms, submitting it to the judgment of the court, whether they were not reasonable.'

[1] Whitfield *v.* Faussat, 1 Ves. 392, 393; ante, § 79, note (4).

remedy at law for want of a due profert.[1] In the next place he may come into equity when a deed of land has been destroyed, or is concealed by the defendant; for then, as the party cannot know which alternative is correct, a Court of Equity will make a decree (which a Court of Law cannot) that the plaintiff shall hold and enjoy the land until the defendant shall produce the deed or admit its destruction.[2] (a) So if a deed concerning land is lost, and the party in possession prays discovery, and to be established in his possession under it, equity will relieve; for no remedy in such a case lies at law.[3] And where the plaintiff is out of possession, there are cases in which equity will interfere upon lost or suppressed title deeds, and decree possession to the plaintiff; but in all such cases there must be other equities, calling for the action of the court.[4] Indeed the bill must always lay some ground besides the mere loss of a title deed, or other sealed instrument, to justify a prayer for relief; as that the loss obstructs the right of the plaintiff at law, or leaves him exposed to undue perils in the future assertion of such right.[5]

85. Although upon a lost bond equity will decree payment for the reason already stated, yet it has been said that it will not entertain jurisdiction for relief upon a lost negotiable note, or other unsealed security, so as to decree payment upon the mere fact of loss; for no such supposed inability to recover at law exists in the case of such a note or unsealed contract which is lost, as exists for want of a profert of a bond at law. No profert is necessary, and no oyer allowed at law, of such a note or security;[6] and a recovery can be had at law, upon mere proof of the loss.[7] But then a Court of Law cannot (as we have seen) insist

---

[1] Id. Walmsley v. Child, 1 Ves. 344, 345; Post, § 88.
[2] Rex v. Arundel, Hob. R. 108 b; 1 Ves. 392.
[3] Walmsley v. Child, 1 Ves. 434, 435. See also **Dalton v. Coatsworth**, 1 P. Will. 731; Dormer v. Fortescue, 3 Atk. 132.
[4] Dormer v. Fortescue, 3 Atk. 132.
[5] See 1 Fonbl. Eq. B. 1, ch. 1, § 3, note (*f*); Id. ch. 3, § 3. See Mitf. Eq. Pl. by Jeremy, 113, 114.
[6] Walmsley v. Child, 1 Ves. 345; Glynn v. Bank of England, 2 Ves. 38, 41.
[7] Walmsley v. Child, 1 Ves. 345; Glynn v. Bank of England, 2 Ves. 38, 41. In Hansard v. Robinson (7 B. & Cres. 90) it was expressly decided that no action would lie by the indorsee of a bill of exchange against the acceptor, where the bill was lost and not produced at the trial, although the loss was

(a) See Worthy v. Tate, 44 Ga. 152.

upon an indemnity, or at least cannot insist upon it in such a form as may operate a perfect indemnity.[1] In such a case therefore a Court of Equity will entertain a bill for relief and payment upon an offer in the bill to give a proper indemnity under the direction of the court, and not without. And such an offer entitles the court to require an indemnity not strictly attainable at law, and founds a just jurisdiction.[2] (a)

86. In the cases which we have been considering, the lost note or other security was negotiable. And according to the authorities this circumstance is most material; for otherwise it would seem that no indemnity would be necessary,[3] and consequently no relief could be had in equity. The propriety of this exception has been somewhat doubted; for the party is entitled, upon payment of such a note or security, to have it delivered up to him as voucher of the payment and extinguishment of it; and it may have been assigned in equity to a third person.[4] And although in such a case the assignee would be affected by all the equities between the original parties, yet the promisor may not always, after a great length of time, be able to establish those equities by competent proof; and at all events he may be put to serious expense and trouble to establish his exoneration from the charge. The jurisdiction of Courts of Equity under such circumstances seems perfectly within the principles on which such courts ordinarily proceed to grant relief, not only in cases of absolute loss, but of impending or probable mischief or incon-

---

established to have been after it became due. The ground of the decision was, that by the custom of merchants the acceptor was entitled to the possession of the bill as his voucher for the payment; and the extreme inconvenience of requiring the acceptor to prove the loss, if he should be required so to do, in a suit by another person as holder. The court said the proper remedy was in equity, where an offer of indemnity might be made and enforced.

[1] Ante, § 82; 2 Camp. 211; 7 B. & Cressw. 90.

[2] Walmsley v. Child, 1 Ves. 344, 345; Teresy v. Gorey, Finch, R. 301; s. c. 1 Ves. 345; Glynn v. Bank of England, 1 Ves. 446; 2 Ves. 38; Mossop v. Eadon, 16 Ves. 430, 434; Chitty on Bills (8th edit. 1833), p. 290; Bromley v. Holland, 7 Ves. 19 to 21; Davies v. Dodd, 4 Price, 176; s. c. 1 Wils. Exch. R. 110.

[3] Mossop v. Eadon, 16 Ves. 430, 434; see Chitty on Bills (8th edit. 1833), p. 291, note.

[4] Hansard v. Robinson, 7 Barn. & Cressw. 90; Story on Promissory Notes, §§ 106 to 116, §§ 243 to 245, § 445.

(a) See Savannah Bank v. Haskins, 101 Mass. 370; ante, p. 87, editor's note.

venience. And a bond of indemnity, under such circumstances, is but a just security to the promisor against the vexation and accumulated expenses of a suit.[1] (*a*)

87. It is upon grounds somewhat similar that Courts of Equity often interfere, where the party, from the long possession or exercise of a right over property, may fairly be presumed to have had a legal title to it, and yet has lost the legal evidence of it, or is now unable to produce it. Under such circumstances equity acts upon the presumption arising from such possession as equivalent to complete proof of the legal right. Thus where a rent has been received and paid for a long time, equity will enforce the payment, although no deed can be produced to sustain the claim, or the precise lands out of which it is payable cannot from confusion of boundaries, or other accident, be now ascertained.[2]

88. In the cases of supposed lost instruments, where relief is sought, it has been seen that, as a guard upon the preliminary exercise of jurisdiction, an affidavit of the loss of the instrument, and that it is not in the possession or power of the plaintiff, is indispensable to sustain the bill.[3] (*b*) And in order to maintain the suit, it is further indispensable that the loss, if not admitted by the answer of the defendant, should at the hearing of the cause be established by competent and satisfactory proofs.[4] For the very foundation of the suit in equity rests upon this most material fact. (*c*) If therefore the plaintiff should fail at the

---

[1] See Hansard *v.* Robinson, 7 B. & Cressw. 90; East India Company *v.* Boddam, 9 Ves. 468, 469; Davies *v.* Dodd, 4 Price, R. 176.

[2] 1 Fonbl. Eq. B. 1, ch. 3, § 3, and note (*g*); Steward *v.* Bridger, 2 Vern. 516; Collet *v.* Jaques, 1 Ch. Cas. 120; Cocks *v.* Foley, 1 Vern. 359; Eton College *v.* Beauchamp, 1 Cas. Ch. 121; Holder *v.* Chambury, 3 P. Will. 255; Duke of Leeds *v.* Powell, 1 Ves. 171; Duke of Bridgewater *v.* Edwards, 4 Bro. Parl. C. 139; Duke of Leeds *v.* New Radnor, 2 Bro. Ch. C. 338, 518; Benson *v.* Baldwin, 1 Atk. 598; Cooper, Eq. Pl. 130.

[3] East India Co. *v.* Boddam, 9 Ves. 466; Cooper, Eq. Pl. 125, 126.

[4] Stokoe *v.* Robson, 3 Ves. & B. 50; Smith *v.* Bicknell, Id. note.; Cookes *v.* Hellier, 1 Ves. 234, 235; Walmsley *v.* Child, 1 Ves. 344, 345; Cooper, Eq.

(*a*) Gordon *v.* Manning, 44 Miss. 756, 762.

(*b*) Hoddy *v.* Hoard, 2 Ind. 474. But see Graham *v.* Hockwith, 1 A. K. Marsh. 424; Purviance *v.* Holt, 3 Gilm. (Ill.) 395.

(*c*) Finding the instrument after suit will not defeat jurisdiction. See Crawford *v.* Summers, 3 J. J. Marsh. 300; Miller *v.* Wells, 5 Mo. 6; Hamlin, 3 Jones, Eq. 191.

hearing to establish the loss of the instrument, or the defendant should overcome the plaintiff's proofs by countervailing testimony of its existence, the suit will be dismissed, and the plaintiff remitted to the legal forum.[1] (a) But if the loss is sufficiently established when it is denied by the defendant's answer, the plaintiff will be entitled to relief, although he may have other evidence, competent and sufficient to establish the existence and contents of the instrument, of which he might have availed himself in a Court of Law.[2] For if the jurisdiction once attaches by the loss of the instrument, a Court of Equity will not drive the party to the hazard of a trial at law when the case is fit for its own interposition and final action, upon a claim to sift the conscience of the party by a discovery.

89. We have thus far been considering cases of accident founded upon lost instruments. But there are many other cases of accident where Courts of Equity will grant both discovery and relief. One of the earliest cases in which they were accustomed to interfere was where by accident a bond had not been paid at the appointed day, and it was subsequently sued; or where a part only had been paid at the day.[3] This jurisdiction was afterwards greatly enlarged in its operation, and applied to all cases where relief is sought against the penalty of a bond, upon the ground that it is unjust for the party to avail himself of the penalty when an offer of full indemnity is tendered. The same principle governs in the case of mortgages, where Courts of Equity constantly allow a redemption, although there is a forfeiture at law.[4] (b) And it may now be stated generally that

Pl. 239; Clavering v. Clavering, 2 Ves. 232; East India Co. v. Boddam, 9 Ves. 466.

[1] See Jeremy on Eq. Jurisd. 359, 360, 361; Cooper, Eq. Pl. 238, 239; Mitf. Eq. Pl. by Jeremy, 222; Armitage v. Wadsworth, 1 Madd. R. 192 to 194; 1 Fonbl. Eq. B. 1, ch. 3, § 3, note (h).

[2] 1 Fonbl. Eq. B. 1, ch. 1, § 3, note (f), p. 17. But see Ante, § 83, p. 91, and note 3.

[3] Cary's Rep. 1, 2; 7 Ves. 273. See also Harg. Law Tracts, pp. 431, 432, Norburie on Chancery Abuses.

[4] Seton v. Slade, 7 Ves. 273, 274; Lenon v. Napper, 2 Sch. & Lefr. 684, 685; Com. Dig. Chancery, 4 A. 5; Mitf. Pl. Ch. by Jeremy, 117, 130; Cooper, Eq. Pl. 130, 131; 2 Fonbl. Eq. B. 3, ch. 3, § 4, and notes. Lord Redesdale

(a) As where a bond has been destroyed or suppressed by the obligee. Davies v. Davies, 6 Ired. 418.

(b) Doty v. Whittlesey, 1 Root, 310; Crane v. Hancks, Ib. 468; Bostwick v. Stiles, 35 Conn. 195.

where an inequitable loss or injury will otherwise fall upon a party from circumstances beyond his own control, or from his own acts done in entire good faith, and in the performance of a supposed duty, without negligence, Courts of Equity will interfere to grant him relief.

90. Cases illustrative of this doctrine may easily be put. In the course of the administration of estates, executors and administrators often pay debts and legacies upon the entire confidence that the assets are sufficient for all purposes. It may turn out, from unexpected occurrences, or from debts and claims made known at a subsequent time, that there is a deficiency of assets. Under such circumstances they may be entitled to no relief at law. But in a Court of Equity, if they have acted with good faith and with due caution, they will be clearly entitled to it upon the ground that otherwise they will be innocently subject to an unjust loss from what the law itself deems an accident.[1] Indeed it has been said that in England no case at law has yet decided that an executor or administrator, once become fully responsible by an actual receipt of a part of his testator's property, for the administration thereof, can found his discharge in respect thereof as against a creditor seeking satisfaction out of the testator's assets, either on the score of inevitable accident, or destruction by fire, or loss by robbery or the like, or of reasonable confidence disappointed, or of loss by any of the other various means which afford an excuse to ordinary agents and bailees in cases of loss without any negligence on their part, and that Courts of Law are disinclined to make such a precedent.[2] If

puts the relief in cases of this sort upon the ground of accident. His language is, 'In many cases of accidents, as lapse of time, the Courts of Equity will also relieve against the consequences of the accident in a Court of Law. Upon this ground they proceed in the common case of a mortgage, where the title of the mortgagee has become absolute at law, upon default of payment of the mortgage money at the time stipulated for payment.' Mitf. Eq. Pl. by Jeremy, 130. I apprehend that this is not the true ground; but that it turns upon the construction of the contract being a mere security, and time not being of the essence of the contract, and the unconscionableness of insisting upon taking the land for the money. Seton v. Slade, 7 Ves. 273, 274; Lenon v. Napper, 2 Sch. & Lefr. 684, 685; Post, §§ 1313, 1314, 1316.

[1] Edwards v. Freeman, 2 P. Will. 447; Johnson v. Johnson, 3 Bos. & Pull. 162, 169; Hawkins v. Day, Ambler, R. 160; Chamberlain v. Chamberlain, 2 Freem. 141. But see Coppin v. Coppin, 2 P. Will. 296, 297; Orr v. Kaines, 2 Ves. 194; Underwood v. Hatton, 5 Beavan, R. 36.

[2] Crosse v. Smith, 7 East, R. 246; Johnson v. Johnson, 3 Bos. & Pull.

this be a true description of the actual state of the law on this subject, it would become an intolerable grievance if Courts of Equity should not be able under any circumstances to interfere in favor of executors and administrators in order to prevent such gross injustice. And in cases of this sort relief has accordingly been often granted by Courts of Equity in mitigation and melioration of the hardship of the common law.[1] But to found a good title to such relief it seems indispensable that there should have been no negligence or misconduct on the part of such executors or administrators in the payment of the assets; for if there has been any negligence or misconduct, that perhaps may induce a Court of Equity to withhold its assistance.[2]

91. Other cases may be easily put, in which an executor or administrator would be entitled to relief in equity. Thus if he should receive money supposed to be due from a debtor to the estate, and it should turn out that the debt had been previously paid, and before the discovery he had paid away the money to creditors of the estate, in such a case the supposed debtor may recover back the money in equity from the executor, and the latter may in the same manner recover it back from the creditors to whom he paid it.[3] In like manner if an executor should recover a judgment and receive the amount, and apply it in discharge of debts, and then the judgment should be reversed, he is compellable to refund the money, and may recover it back from the creditors.[4]

162, 169. But see Orr v. Kaines, 2 Ves. 194; Hawkins v. Day, Ambler, R. 160. But even at law the payment of a simple contract debt without notice of a specialty debt would, in case of a deficiency of assets, protect the executor or administrator. Davis v. Monkhouse, Fitzgib. R. 76; Brooks v. Jennings, 1 Mod. R. 174; Britton v. Bathurst, 3 Lev. 115; Hawkins v. Day, Ambler, R. 160, 162.

In Brisbane v. Dacres (5 Taunt. R. 143, 159), Mr. Justice Chambre seems to have thought that an administrator paying money per capita, in misapplication of the effects of the intestate, might recover it back at law. But Lord Chief Justice Mansfield in the same case doubted it, and said, if he could, it would be only under the principle of æquum et bonum.

[1] Croft's Executors v. Lyndsey, 2 Freem. R. 1; s. c. 2 Eq. Abridg. 452; Holt v. Holt, 1 Cas. Ch. 190; 2 P. Will. 447; Orr v. Kaines, 2 Ves. R. 194; Moore v. Moore, 2 Ves. 600; Nelthorp v. Hill, 1 Cas. Ch. 135; Noel v. Robinson, 1 Vern. 90, 91; 2 Eq. Abridg. Ex'ors, K. p. 452. See Riddle v. Mandeville, 5 Cranch, 330.

[2] See Hovenden's note to 2 Freem. R. 1 n. (3); 1 Cas. Ch. 136; 1 Fonbl. Eq. B. 1, ch. 3, § 3.

[3] Poole v. Ray, 1 P. Will. 355; 2 Eq. Abridg. Ex'ors, 452, pl. 5.

[4] Ibid.

92. Upon analogous grounds a Court of Equity will interpose in favor of an unpaid legatee to compel the other legatees who have been paid their full legacies to refund in proportion, if there was an original deficiency of assets to pay all the legacies and the executor is insolvent; but not, as it should seem, if there was no such original deficiency, and there has been a waste by the executor.[1] The reason of the distinction seems to be, that the other legatees in the first case have received more than their just proportion of the assets; but in the last case no more than their just proportion. And therefore there is nothing inequitable on their part in availing themselves of their superior diligence.[2] But legatees are always compellable to refund in favor of creditors, because the latter have a priority of right to satisfaction out of the assets.[3]

93. Other illustrations of the doctrine of relief in equity upon the ground of accident may be stated. Suppose a minor is bound as apprentice to a person subject to the bankrupt laws,

---

[1] Orr v. Kaines, 2 Ves. 194; Moore v. Moore, 2 Ves. 600; Anon. 1 P. Will. 495; Walcot v. Hall, Id. Cox's note; s. c. 1 Bro. Ch. R. 305, and Belt's notes; Noel v. Robinson, 1 Vern. 94, Raithby's note (1); Edwards v. Freeman, 2 P. Will. 447.

[2] Id.; 2 Fonbl. Eq. B. 4, Pt. 1, ch. 2, § 5, note (*p*); Lupton v. Lupton, 2 John. Ch. R. 614, 626. But it seems that the executor himself cannot in a case of deficiency of assets compel the legatees to refund in favor of another legatee who is unpaid, where the executor has made a voluntary payment, but only where the payment has been compulsive. 2 Fonbl. Eq. B. 4, Pt. 1, ch. 2, § 5, note (*p*); Hodges v. Waddington, 2 Vent. 360; Newman v. Barton, 2 Vern. R. 205; Orr v. Kaines, 2 Ves. 194. And in cases of creditors he cannot compel legatees to refund if he knew of the debts at the time of the payment, but only when the debts were then unknown to him. Nelthorp v. Hill. 1 Ch. Cas. 136; Jewon v. Grant, 3 Swanst. 659; Hodges v. Waddington, 2 Vent. 360; 2 Fonbl. Eq. B. 4, Pt. 1, ch. 2, § 5, note (*p*). So that the rights of the executor himself and that of legatees and creditors are not precisely the same in all cases of a deficiency of assets. See 2 Eq. Abridg. Legacies, B. 13, p. 554; 17 Mass. R. 384, 385. In Massachusetts an executor who has voluntarily paid a legatee can, on the subsequent discovery of a deficiency of assets, recover back the money at law. And so if he has paid some creditors in full, and there is afterwards a deficiency of assets, he may recover back from the creditors so paid in proportion to the deficiency. Walker v. Hill, 17 Mass. R. 380; Walker v. Bradley, 3 Pick. R. 261. See Riddle v. Mandeville, 5 Cranch, 329, 330.

[3] Noel v. Robinson, 1 Vern. 90, 94; Id. 460; Newman v. Barton, 2 Vern. 205; Nelthorp v. Hill, 1 Ch. Cas. 136; 2 Fonbl. Eq. B. 4, Pt. 1, ch. 2, § 5, note (*p*); Lupton v. Lupton, 2 John. Ch. R. 614, 626; Anon. 1 Vern. 162; Hardwick v. Mynd, 1 Anst. R. 112.

and a large premium is given for the apprenticeship to the master, and he becomes bankrupt during the apprenticeship; in such a case equity will interfere and apportion the premium upon the ground of the failure of the contract from accident.[1] So if stock of a government is held for the benefit of A during life, and afterwards the growing payments as well as the arrears are to be for the benefit of B, and then a revolution should occur by which the payments should be suspended for several years, and A should die before the arrears are paid, there such revolution would be treated as an accident, and the representatives of A would be entitled to the arrears, and not B, notwithstanding the language of the contract. For the arrears supposed in the contract could mean only such as might ordinarily occur, and not such as should arise from extraordinary events.[2] (a) So if an annuity is directed by a will to be secured by public stock, and an investment is made accordingly sufficient at the time for the purpose, but afterwards the stock is reduced by an act of Parliament, so that the stock becomes insufficient, equity will decree the deficiency to be made up against the residuary legatees, as an accident.[3]

94. In the execution of mere powers it has been said that a Court of Equity will interpose and grant relief on account of accident as well as of mistake. (b) And this seems regularly true where by accident there is a defective execution of the power. But where there is a non-execution of the power by accident there seems more reason to question the doctrine. It is true that it was said by two judges in a celebrated case that if the party appear to have intended to execute his power, and is prevented by death, equity will interpose to effectuate his intent, for it is an impediment by the act of God.[4] But it is

[1] Hale v. Webb, 2 Bro. Ch. R. 78, and Belt's note. See 1 Fonbl. Eq. B. 1, ch. 5, § 8, note (g); Ex parte Sandby, 1 Atk. 149; Post, § 472.
[2] Haslett v. Pattle, 6 Madd. R. 4.
[3] Davies v. Wottier, 1 Sim. & Stu. 463; May v. Bennet, 1 Russell, R. 370.
[4] Earl of Bath & Montague's Case, 3 Ch. Cas. 69, 93; 1 Fonbl. Eq. B. 1, ch. 4, § 25, note (k); Id. B. 1, ch. 1, § 7, note (v); Sugden on Powers, ch. 6, § 2, p. 378 (3d edit.).

(a) So where a vendor reserved a lien 'to be enforced within six years or stand for nought thereafter,' and was prevented by war from enforcing it within that time, equity gave relief. Atkins v. Rison, 25 Ark. 138.

(b) No title or interest vests in the donee of a power until he accepts the power; and equity cannot compel him to accept even for creditors. Gilman v. Bell, 99 Ill. 144.

doubtful whether this doctrine can be maintained unless the party has taken some preparatory steps for the execution, so that it may be deemed a case not of non-execution, but defective execution.[1] And it has been said that equity will also relieve in cases of a defective execution of a power where it is rendered impossible, by circumstances over which the party has no control, for him to execute it; as if he is sent abroad by the Government, and the prescribed witnesses cannot be obtained; or if the remainder man refuses to the party a sight of the deeds creating the power, so that the party cannot ascertain the proper form of executing it.[2]

95. In regard to the defective execution of powers resulting either from accident or mistake or both, and also in regard to agreements to execute powers (which may generally be deemed a species of defective execution),[3] Courts of Equity do not in all cases interfere and grant relief, but grant it only in favor of persons in a moral sense entitled to the same, and viewed with peculiar favor, and where there are no opposing equities on the other side.[4] Without undertaking to enumerate all the qualifications of doctrine belonging to this intricate subject, it may be stated that Courts of Equity, in cases of defective execution of powers, will (unless there be some countervailing equity) interpose, and grant relief in favor of purchasers, creditors, a wife, a child, and a charity; but not in favor of the donee of the power, or a husband, or grandchildren, or remote relations, or strangers generally.[5]

96. But in cases of defective execution of powers we are carefully to distinguish between powers which are created by private parties and those which are specially created by statute; as for instance powers of tenants in tail to make leases. The latter are construed with more strictness; and whatever formalities are

---

[1] See 1 Fonbl. Eq. B. 1, ch. 4, § 25, note (*h*), note (*k*); Smith *v.* Ashton, 1 Ch. Cas. 264; 2 Chance on Powers, ch. 23, § 3, art. 2999 to 3004; Id. § 1, art. 2817 to 2923; Sugden on Powers, ch. 6, § 2, p. 378 (3d edit.).

[2] 1 Fonbl. Eq. B. 1, ch. 5, § 2, note (*h*); Earl of Bath & Montague's Case, 3 Ch. Cas. 68; Gilb. Lex Prætoria, pp. 305, 306.

[3] 2 Chance on Powers, ch. 23, § 1, art. 2824, 2825, 2897 to 2915.

[4] Ibid. ch. 23, § 1, art. 2817 to 2932.

[5] 2 Chance on Powers, ch. 23, § 1, art. 2830 to 2858; Id. 2859 to 2863; Id. 2864 to 2873, 1 Fonbl. Eq. B. 1, ch. 1 § 7, and note (*v*); Id. B. 1, ch. 4, § 25, notes (*h*), (*i*); Id. B. 1, ch 5, § 2, and note (*b*).

required by the statute must be punctually complied with, otherwise the defect cannot be helped, or at least may not perhaps be helped, in equity ; for Courts of Equity cannot dispense with the regulations prescribed by a statute, at least where they constitute the apparent policy and object of the statute.[1]

97. As to the defects which may be remedied, they may generally be said to be any which are not of the very essence or substance of the power. Thus a defect by executing the power by *will* when it is required to be by a deed or other instrument, inter vivos, will be aided. So the want of a seal, (*a*) or of witnessess, or of a signature, and defects in the limitations of the property, estate, or interest, will be aided. And perhaps the same rule will apply to defective executions of powers by femes covert. But equity will not aid defects which are of the very essence or substance of the power; as for instance if the power be executed without the consent of parties who are required to consent to it. So if it be required to be executed by *will*, and it is executed by an irrevocable and absolute *deed ;* for this is apparently contrary to the settler's intention, a will being always revocable during the life of the testator, whereas a deed would not be revocable unless expressly so stated in it.[2]

98. But a class of cases more common in their occurrence as well as more extensive in their operation will be found where trusts, or powers in the nature of trusts, are required to be executed by the trustee in favor of particular persons, and they fail of being so executed, by casualty or accident. In all such cases equity will interpose and grant suitable relief. Thus for instance if a testator should by his will devise certain estates to A, with

---

[1] 1 Fonbl. Eq. B. 1, ch. 1, § 7, and note (*t*); Id. B. 1, ch. 4, § 25, note (*e*); Earl of Darlington *v.* Pultney, Cowp. R. 267. But see 2 Chance on Powers, ch. 23, § 2, art. 2985 to 2997; Post, § 169, 177, and note (3); Bright *v.* Boyd, 1 Story, R. 478.

[2] 2 Chance on Powers, ch. 23, § 1, art. 2874 to 2896; Id. art. 2930; Id. 2980 to 2984. I have contented myself with these general statements on this confessedly involved topic, as a full investigation of all the doctrines concerning it more properly belongs to a treatise on Powers. The learned reader will find the whole subject fully examined, and all the leading authorities brought together, in 2 Chance on Powers, ch. 23, §§ 1, 2, 3, art. 2818 to 3024, and Sugden on Powers, ch. 6, pp. 344 to 393 (3d edition), and Powell on Powers, pp. 54, 155, 243, 280. See Post, §§ 173, 174.

(*a*) See Bernards *v.* Stebbins, 109 U. S. 341, 349; post, note to § 140.

directions that A should at his death distribute the same among his children and relations as he should choose, and A should die without making such distribution, a Court of Equity would interfere and make a suitable distribution; because it is not given to the devisee as a mere power, but as a trust and duty which he ought to fulfil; and his omission so to do by accident or design ought not to disappoint the objects of the bounty. It would be very different if the case were of a mere naked power, and not a power coupled with a trust.[1]

99. Another class of cases is where a testator cancels a former will upon the presumption that a later will made by him is duly executed, when it is not. In such a case it has been decided that the former will shall be set up against the heir in a Court of Equity, and the devisee be relieved there upon the ground of accident.[2] But this class seems more properly to belong to the head of mistake, or of a conditional presumptive revocation, where the condition has failed.[3]

99 *a*. Courts of Equity will also interfere and grant relief (as we shall presently more fully see) where there has been by accident a confusion of the boundaries between two estates.[4] (*a*) So they will also grant relief where by reason of such confusion of boundaries by accident the remedy by distress for a rent charged thereon is gone.[5]

99 *b*. So where by accident or mistake, upon a transfer of a bill of exchange or a promissory note, there has been an omission by the party to indorse it according to the intention of the transfer in such a case, the party, or in case of his death his executor or administrator, may be compelled in equity to make the indorsement, and if the party has since become bankrupt or his estate is insolvent, his assignees will be compelled to make it; for the transaction amounts to an equitable assignment, and a Court of Equity will clothe it with a legal effect and title.[6]

---

[1] Harding *v.* Glynn, 1 Atk. 469, and note by Saunders; Brown *v.* Higgs, 4 Ves. 709; 5 Ves. 495; 8 Ves. 561; 2 Chance on Powers, ch. 23, § 1.

[2] Onions *v.* Tyrer, 1 P. Will. 343, 345; s. c. 2 Vern. 751; Prec. Ch. 459.

[3] 1 P. Will. 345, Cox's note; Burtenshaw *v.* Gilbert, Cowp. R. 49.

[4] Mitf. Eq. Pl. by Jeremy, 117; Post, § 565, §§ 615 to 622.

[5] Duke of Leeds *v.* Powell, 1 Ves. 171; Post, § 622.

[6] Watkins *v.* Maule, 2 Jac. & Walk. 242; Chitty on Bills, ch. 6, p. 263

(*a*) Beatty *v.* Dixon, 56 Cal. 619; Wetherbee *v.* Dunn, 36 Cal. 255.

100. These may suffice as illustrations of the general doctrine of relief in equity in cases of accident. They all proceed upon the same common foundation that there is no adequate or complete remedy at law under all the circumstances; that the party has rights which ought to be protected and enforced; or that he will sustain some injury, loss, or detriment, which it would be inequitable to throw upon him.

101. And this leads us naturally to the consideration of those cases of accident in which no relief will be granted by Courts of Equity. In the first place, in matters of positive contract and obligation created by the party (for it is different in obligations or duties created by law),[1] it is no ground for the interference of equity that the party has been prevented from fulfilling them by accident, or that he has been in no default, or that he has been prevented by accident from deriving the full benefit of the contract on his own side.[2] Thus if a lessee on a demise covenants to keep the demised estate in repair, he will be bound in equity as well as in law to do so, notwithstanding any inevitable accident or necessity by which the premises are destroyed or injured; as if they are burnt by lightning or destroyed by public enemies, or by any other accident, or by overwhelming force. The reason is, that he might have provided for such contingencies by his contract if he had so chosen; and the law will presume an intentional general liability where he has made no exception.[3]

102. And the same rule applies in like cases where there is an express covenant (without any proper exceptions) to pay rent during the term. It must be paid, notwithstanding the premises are accidentally burnt down during the term. And this is equally true as to the rent, although the tenant has covenanted to repair except in cases of casualties by fire, and the premises are burnt down by such casualty; for, 'Expressio unius est

(8th edit. 1833); Bayley on Bills, ch. 5, § 2, pp. 136, 137 (5th edit. 1830); Post, § 729.

[1] Paradine v. Jane, Aleyn, R. 27. See also Story on Bailments, §§ 25, 35, 36.

[2] 1 Fonbl. Eq. B. 1, ch. 5, § 8, note (g). See Com. Dig. Chan. 3 F. 5; Barrisford v. Done, 1 Vern. 98.

[3] Id. Dyer, R. 33 (a); Chesterfield v. Bolton, Com. R. 627; Bullock v. Dommitt, 6 T. R. 650; Brecknock, &c. Canal Company v. Pritchard, 6 T. R. 750; Paradine v. Jane, Aleyn, R. 27; Monk v. Cooper, 2 Str. R. 763; 1 Fonbl. Eq. B. 1, ch. 5, § 8, note (g), p. 374, &c.; Harrison v. Lord North, 1 Ch. Cas. 83.

exclusio alterius.[1] (a) In all cases of this sort of accidental loss by fire the rule prevails, 'Res perit domino;' and therefore the tenant and landlord suffer according to their proportions of interest in the property burnt; the tenant during the term, and the landlord for the residue.

103. And the like doctrine applies to other cases of contract, where the parties stand equally innocent.[2] Thus for instance if there is a contract for a sale at a price to be fixed by an award during the life of the parties, and one of them dies before the award is made, the contract fails; and equity will not enforce it upon the ground of accident, for the time of making the award is expressly fixed in the contract according to the pleasure of the parties, and there is no equity to substitute a different period.[3]

104. So if A should covenant with B to convey an estate for two lives in a church lease to B by a certain day, and one of the lives should afterwards drop before the day appointed for the conveyance, B would be compelled to stand by his contract and to accept the conveyance; for neither party is in any fault, and B by the contract took upon himself the risk, by not providing for the accident.[4] So if an estate should be sold by A to B for a certain sum of money and an annuity, and the agreement should be fair, equity will not grant relief, although the party should die before the payment of any annuity.[5]

105. In the next place Courts of Equity will not grant relief to a party upon the ground of accident, where the accident has arisen from his own gross negligence or fault; for in such a case the party has no claim to come into a court of justice to ask to be saved from his own culpable misconduct. And on this

---

[1] Monk v. Cooper, 2 Str. 763; s. c. 2 Lord Raymond, 1477; Balfour v. Weston, 1 T. R. 310; Fowler v. Bott, 6 Mass. R. 63; Doe v. Sandham, 1 T. R. 705, 710; Hallet v. Wylie, 3 John. R. 44; Hare v. Groves, 3 Anst. 687; Holtzapffell v. Baker, 18 Ves. 115; Pym. v. Blackburn, 3 Ves. 34, 38; 1 Fonbl. Equity, B. 1, ch. 5, § 8, note (g); Cooper, Eq. Pl. 131.

[2] Com Dig. Chancery, 3 F. 5.

[3] Blundell v. Brettargh, 17 Ves. 232, 240

[4] White v. Nutt, 1 P. Will. 61.

[5] Mortimer v. Capper, 1 Bro. Ch. R. 156; Jackson v. Lever, 3 Bro. Ch. R. 605; see also 9 Ves. 246.

(a) See Wood v. Hubbell, 5 Barb. 601; s. c. 10 N. Y. 479. In Brewer v. Herbert, 30 Md. 301, a contract for the sale of a house and land was enforced though the house had burnt down. See also McKecknie v. Sterling, 48 Barb. 330, 335. But see Smith v. McCluskey, 45 Barb. 610, 613.

account, in general, a party coming into a Court of Equity is bound to show that his title to relief is unmixed with any gross misconduct or negligence of himself or his agents.[1]

105 a. In the next place Courts of Equity will not interfere upon the ground of accident where the party has not a clear vested right, but his claim rests in mere expectancy and is a matter, not of trust, but of volition. Thus if a testator intending to make a will in favor of particular persons is prevented from doing so by accident, equity cannot grant relief; for it is not in the power of the court to relieve against accidents which prevent voluntary dispositions of estates;[2] and a legatee or devisee can take only by the bounty of the testator, and has no independent right until there is a title consummated by law. The same principle applies to a mere naked power, such as a power of appointment uncoupled with any trust; if it is unexecuted by accident or otherwise, a Court of Equity will not interfere and execute it as the party could or might have done.[3] But if there be a trust, it will, as we have seen, be otherwise.[4]

106. In the next place no relief will be granted on account of accident, where the other party stands upon an equal equity and is entitled to equal protection. Upon this ground also equity will not interfere to give effect to an imperfect will against an innocent heir at law; for as heir he is entitled to protection, whatever might have been the intent of the testator, unless his title is taken away according to the rules of law.[5]

107. So if a tenant for life or in tail have a power to raise money, and he raises money by mortgage without any reference to the power, and not in conformity to it, the mortgage will not bind the heir in tail.[6] So if a tenant in tail conveys the estate

---

[1] Marine Insurance Company v. Hodgson, 7 Cranch, 336. See Penny v. Martin, 4 John. Ch. R. 569; 1 Fonbl. Eq. B. 1, ch. 3, § 3; Ex parte Greenway, 6 Ves. 812. See also 7 Ves. 19, 20; 9 Ves. 467, 468.

[2] Whitton v. Russell, 1 Atk. 448; 1 Madd. Ch. Pr. 46.

[3] Brown v. Higgs, 8 Ves. 559, 561; Pierson v. Garnet, 2 Brown, Ch. R. 38, 226; Duke of Marlborough v. Godolphin, 2 Ves. 61, and Belt's Supplement, 277, 278; Harding v. Glyn, 1 Atk. 469, and Saunders's note; Tollet v. Tollet, 2 P. Will. 489; 1 Fonbl. B. 1, ch. 4, § 25, note (*h*); Id. note (*k*); 1 Madd. Ch. Pr. 46. [4] Ante, § 98.

[5] See Com. Dig. Chancery, 3 F. 6, 7, 8; 1 Fonbl. Eq. B. 1, ch. 4, § 25, notes (*k*), (*n*); Grounds and Rudim. of the Law, M. 167, p. 128 (edit. 1751).

[6] Jenkins v. Kemis, 1 Cas. Ch. 103; s. c. cited 2 P. Will. 667; 1 Fonbl. Eq. B. 1, ch. 4, § 25, notes (*l*), (*n*).

by bargain and sale, or enters into a contract of sale, and covenants to suffer a fine and recovery, and he dies before the fine or recovery is consummated, the heir in tail or remainder-man is not bound; for he is deemed a purchaser under the donor, and entitled to protection as such; and a Court of Equity will not, further than a Court of Law, carry into effect against him any act of a former tenant in tail.[1]

108. And generally against a bona fide purchaser for a valuable consideration without notice a Court of Equity will not interfere on the ground of accident; for in the view of a Court of Equity such a purchaser has as high a claim to assistance and protection as any other person can have.[2] Principles of an analogous nature seem to have governed in many of the cases in which the want of a surrender of copyholds has been supplied by Courts of Equity.[3]

109. Perhaps upon a general survey of the grounds of equitable jurisdiction in cases of accident it will be found that they resolve themselves into the following: that the party seeking relief has a clear right which cannot otherwise be enforced in a suitable manner; or that he will be subjected to an unjustifiable loss without any blame or misconduct on his own part; or that he has a superior equity to the party from whom he seeks the relief.[4]

[1] 1 Fonbl Eq. B. 1, ch. 1, § 7, and note; Id. ch. 4, § 19, and note; Weal v. Lower, 1 Eq. Abridg. 266; Powell v. Powell, Prec. Ch. 278.
[2] Mitford, Eq. Pl. by Jeremy, 274, X.; Cooper, Eq. Pl. 281 to 285; 2 Fonbl. Eq. B. 2, ch. 6, § 2, and notes; Malden v. Merrill, 2 Atk. 8; Newl. on Contr. ch. 19, p. 342; Ante, § 64 c.; Post, §§ 154, 165, 381, §§ 409 to 411, 416, 434, 436.
[3] 1 Fonbl. Eq. B. 1, ch. 1, § 7, and note (v).
[4] Many of the cases on this subject will be found collected in 1 Madd. Ch. Pr. ch. 2, § 2, p. 41, &c., Jeremy on Equity Jurid. ch. 1, p. 359, &c., and 2 Swift's Digest, ch. 6, p. 92, &c.

CHAPTER V.

MISTAKE.

110. We may next pass to the consideration of the jurisdiction of the Courts of Equity founded upon the ground of mistake. This is sometimes the result of accident in its large sense ; but as contradistinguished from it, it is some unintentional act or omission or error, arising from ignorance, surprise, imposition, or misplaced confidence.[1] Mistakes are ordinarily divided into two sorts, — mistakes in matter of law, and mistakes in matter of fact.

111. And first in regard to mistakes in matter of law.(*a*) It

[1] Mr. Jeremy defines Mistake, in the sense of a Court of Equity, to be 'that result of ignorance of law or of fact which has misled a person to commit that which, if he had not been in error, he would not have done.' Jeremy, Eq. Jurisd. B. 3, Pt. 2, p. 358. This definition seems too narrow, and it does not comprehend cases of omission or neglect. May there not be a mistake from surprise or imposition, as well as from ignorance of law or fact ?

(*a*) *Mistake of Law.* Few subjects of the law present, at first reading of the authorities, so small an attempt at the expression of a pervading principle as the subject of mistake. Much has indeed been done of late towards reducing the mass of cases to order (Pollock, Contract, ch. 8, and Holmes, Common Law, lect. 9), but not a little remains undone. The underlying principles of relief, while seldom if ever sufficiently enunciated by the courts, are reasonably clear, so far at least as the question of relief for mistake of fact is concerned, and, as the writer thinks, of relief for mistake of law as well. These principles, in their relation to contract, may be formulated into the following propositions: —

1. Relief for mistake, either in equity or by an equitable plea at law, is based on mistake in regard to matter of the agreement as distinguished from mistake in respect of the inducements thereto, or in regard to some condition precedent to the same. Something touching the supposed contract must be asserted on the one side and denied on the other to have been agreed. In a word, relief proceeds upon the ground of want of agreement. The minds of the parties have not met. See Pollock, Contract, 409 (3d ed.).

2. The courts therefore will not interfere for mere mistake, however serious, in regard to an external matter not a subject of the agreement or

is a well-known maxim, that ignorance of law will not furnish an excuse for any person, either for a breach or for an omission

a condition precedent to the existence of the same. In case of misapprehension or ignorance of such a matter interference may be expected only when there has been fraud or at least misrepresentation in regard to it by the other side.

3. On the other hand the courts will interfere (*a*) where, in any case, the minds of the parties did not meet, or (*b*) where, in the case of a written contract, they did not meet on the terms expressed in the writing, but did meet on other terms not there appearing.

In regard to all of these propositions it is probably safe to assume, in accordance with the way the first one is framed, that the rule is the same with regard to equitable pleas where fully allowed at law, as in courts of equity; the English statute at all events is held to have done away with the old differences between Courts of Law and Courts of Equity in respect of mistake. Redgrave *v.* Hurd, 20 Ch. D. 1, 12. Hence where equitable pleas are fully allowed, the enforcement of a contract can be resisted by pleading anything which would afford foundation in equity for reforming, enjoining the enforcement of, or rescinding the supposed contract.

In this connection a suggestion upon common language of the cases in regard to materiality may be noticed. The proposition is, that the ground of interference must be mistake in the very agreement, when not in regard to a condition precedent. Now where mistake is found to have been made with reference to an agreed term of a contract, the question of the materiality of the term must be excluded; the parties by making it a subject of agreement have made it material, and the courts can have no right to put a different construction upon it. The familiar case of warranties in insurance policies affords an illustration. It is worse than idle with reference to such a case to say that the subject of the alleged mistake must be material. But where the question is whether a mistake was made, as it usually is, the apparent materiality or immateriality of the subject of the mistake may have a bearing upon the decision of the question. Grymes *v.* Sanders, 93 U. S. 55, well illustrates this. See also Chapman *v.* Coats, 26 Iowa, 288. On the other hand where it is sought to strike out a clause as not agreed upon in the preliminary negotiations, and as inserted by mistake, the materiality of the clause as interpreted by the court *will* be the test of the right to the relief sought.

The second proposition, — that the courts will not interfere for mere mistake as to an external matter not a subject of agreement or a condition precedent thereto, — is a necessary result of the first. Illustrations may be found in recent cases. Dambmann *v.* Schulting, 75 N. Y. 55; Whittemore *v.* Farrington, 76 N. Y. 452; Webster *v.* Stark, 10 Lea (Tenn.), 406. See post, § 210. The proposition covers all that class of cases in which it is held that, in addition to the ignorance of the plaintiff, knowledge on the part of the defendant in respect of the matter in question is not sufficient to justify relief, nor, by the current of authority, even knowledge by the defendant of the plaintiff's ignorance. Laidlaw *v.* Organ, 2 Wheat. 178; Smith *v.* Hughes, L. R. 6 Q. B. 597. See post, §§ 149, 205-207. There must be some misleading act by the defendant to afford ground for relief.

The third proposition comes more frequently into operation: the courts — to repeat it — will interfere (*a*)

of duty; 'Ignorantia legis neminem excusat;' and this maxim is equally as much respected in equity as in law.[1] It probably

[1] Bilbie v. Lumley, 2 East, R. 469; Doct. & Stud. Dial. 1, ch. 26, p. 92; Id. Dial. 2, ch. 46, p. 303; Stevens v. Lynch, 12 East, 38; 1 Fonbl. Eq. B. 1, ch. 2, § 7, note (v); Hunt v. Rousmaniere's Adm'rs, 8 Wheaton, R. 174; s. c. 1 Peters, Sup. C. R. 1; s. c. 2 Mason, R. 342; 3 Mason, R. 294; Frank v. Frank, 1 Ch. Cas. 84. How far money paid under a mistake of law is, as the civil law phrases it, liable to *repetition*, that is, to a recovery back, has been a matter much discussed by civilians, and upon which they are divided in opinion. Pothier and Heineccius maintain the negative; Vinnius and D'Aguesseau the affirmative, the latter especially in a very masterly dissertation. Sir W. D. Evans in the Appendix to his translation of Pothier on Obligations (vol. 2, pp. 408 to 437), has given a Translation of the Dissertations of D'Aguesseau and Vinnius; and Sir W. D. Evans has prefixed to them a view of his own reasoning in support of the same doctrine. (Id. vol. 2, p. 369.) The text of the Roman law seems manifestly on the other side, although the force of the text has been attempted to be explained away, or at least limited. The Digest (Lib. 22, tit. 6, l. 9, §§ 3, 5) says: 'Ignorantia facti, non juris, prodesse; nec stultis solere succurri, sed errantibus;' and still more explicitly the Code says (Lib. 1, tit. 18, l. 10), 'Cum quis jus ignorans indebitatem pecuniam solverit, cessat repetitio; per ignorantiam enim facti tantum repetitionem indebiti soluti competere tibi notum est.' See also 1 Pothier, Oblig. Pt. 4, ch. 3, § 1, n. 834; 1 Evans's Pothier on Oblig. 523, 524; Pothier, Pand. Lib. 22, tit. 6; Cujaccii Opera, Tom. 4, p. 502; Comm. ad Leg. vii. de Jur. et Fact. Ignor. Heinecc. ad Pand. Lib. 22, tit. 6, § 146; 1 Domat, Civil Law, B. 1, tit. 18, § 1, n. 13 to 17. But the question is a very different one, how far

---

where, in any case, the minds of the parties did not meet at all, or (b) where, in the case of a written contract, they did not meet on the terms expressed in the writing, but did meet on other terms. The first of these two cases in its most common form in equity is a case for injunction and rescission, to be followed, if need be, by delivery up for cancellation, though it may of course be a case for defence at law either upon an ordinary or an equitable plea. The only feature of the case that calls for remark here is the fact that in this class of cases mistake of the plaintiff is sufficient of itself to authorize relief; neither injunction, rescission, nor the equivalent equitable defence at law requires any proof of mistake or of fault on the part of the defendant so long as damages are not sought. Redgrave v. Hurd, 20 Ch. D. 1; Arkwright v. Newbold, 17 Ch. D. 301, 320; Reese Silver Mining Co. v. Smith, L. R. 4 H. L. 64; Paget v. Marshall, 28 Ch. D. 255. See Rider v. Powell, 28 N. Y. 310; Kilmer v. Smith, 77 N. Y. 226; Price v. Ley, 4 Giff. 235; s. c. 9 Jur. N. S. 295; Bridges v. McClendon, 56 Ala. 327, 333. A term of the written contract has been inserted or omitted which the plaintiff never agreed to have there, or to have omitted, as the case may be.

The second part (b) of the proposition, upon which an unexpressed term is to be introduced into the writing, or a term therein expunged, covers the case so much considered by the courts under the name of mutual mistake, — not a perfectly accurate term for the case, as the mistake is in the writing and not in the agreement, and the defendant may have intended, or not have been mistaken in regard to, the form of the writing. Rider v.

CHAP. V.] MISTAKE. 111

belongs to some of the earliest rudiments of English Jurisprudence; and is certainly so old as to have been long laid up

a promise to pay is a binding obligation; for a party may not be bound by the latter to pay, although he may not, if he has paid the money, be entitled to recover it back. Heineccius (ubi supra) insists on this distinction, founding himself on the Roman law. Cujaccius also insists on the same distinction. (Cujac. Opera, Tom. 4, 506, 507, edit. 1758.) D'Aguesseau denies the distinction as not founded in reason, and insists on the same right in both cases. Sir W. D. Evans holds to the same opinion, but insists at all events that a mere promise to pay under a mistake of law is not binding. 2 Evans's Pothier on Oblig. 395, &c. There is certainly great force in his reasoning. It has however been rejected by the English courts; and a promise to pay, upon a supposed liability, and in ignorance of the law, has been held to bind the party. Stevens v. Lynch, 12 East, R. 38; Goodman v. Sayers, 2 Jac. & Walk. 263; Brisbane v. Dacres, 5 Taunt. R. 143; East India Company v. Tritton, 3 B. & Cressw. 280. Mr. Chancellor Kent held a doctrine equally extensive in Shotwell v. Murray, 1 John. Ch. R. 512, 516. See also Storrs v. Barker, 6 John. Ch. R. 166; Clarke v. Dutcher, 9 Cowen, R. 674. In Massachusetts it has been held that money, paid under a mistake of law, may be recovered back; and at all events that a promise to pay under a mistake of law cannot be enforced. May v. Coffin, 4 Mass. R. 342; Warder v. Tucker, 7 Mass. R. 452; Freeman v. Boynton, 7 Mass. R. 488. See also Haven v. Foster, 9 Pick. R. 112, in which there is a very learned argument by counsel on each side on the general doctrine, and the opinions of civilians, as well as the common-law decisions, are copiously cited.

Powell, 28 N. Y. 310. See post, note to § 140. However in order to justify the substitution of one term for another in the writing, or the removal of a term, or the insertion of an omitted term, it is plain that, whether the defendant was mistaken or not, the original *intention* of the parties in regard to the result of the proposed change should be one. Rider v. Powell, supra; Kilmer v. Smith, 77 N. Y. 226; Diman v. Providence R. Co., 5 R. I. 130; Thompsonville Co. v. Osgood, 26 Conn. 16; Betts v. Gunn, 31 Ala. 219; Wright v. Goff, 22 Beav. 207; Metropolitan Soc. v. Brown, 26 Beav. 455; Schoonover v. Dougherty, 65 Ind. 463; Nelson v. Davis, 40 Ind. 366; Boyce v. Lorillard Ins. Co., 4 Daly, 246; s. c. 55 N. Y. 366; Dulany v. Rogers, 50 Md. 524; Harter v. Christolph, 32 Wis. 245; Ledyard v. Hartford Ins. Co., 24 Wis. 496; Ramsey v. Smith, 32 N. J. Eq. 28; Young v. McGown, 62 Me. 56. If a new term is to be added, or substituted for one in the writing, the minds of the parties must have met upon it; if it is sought to remove a term without inserting anything in its place, it is of course enough that the plaintiff never agreed to it as part of the contract.

That these propositions are applicable as a general working theory to the case of mistake of law as well as of mistake of fact, must be clear if it be conceded that relief for mistake of law can be granted at all. If relief is to be given, it must be given on the ground of want of union of minds; if the parties have agreed upon the law, then, whether right or wrong their view, there can be no relief. See Irnham v. Child, 1 Bro. C.C. 92; Townshend v. Stangroom, 6 Ves. 328; Hunt v. Rousmaniere, 8 Wheat 174; s. c. 1 Peters, 1.

among its settled elements. We find it stated with great clearness and force in the 'Doctor and Student,' where it is affirmed

An answer to a possible objection based on the second proposition, as to the insufficiency of an external matter, may here be made. Whatever may be said of the machinery of the law, the law itself is not a thing external to the contract; it is not like the secret mine in the vendor's land, or the unknown treaty of peace which will affect the price of a commodity. The law creates, or at least supports, the right; the right does not exist, or does not exist usefully, without the law. It is quite as proper to say, with regard to the existence of the law, that the minds of the parties have not met, as it is to say the same with regard to the existence of the subject of a bargain. That subject is what it is because the law makes it such. To show what constitutes a union of minds with regard to the question of mistake of law will now be the aim of this note.

It is too late certainly at the present day to doubt the existence of jurisdiction in equity to grant relief on the ground of a pure mistake of law; though it must be admitted that such doubt has been entertained since as well as before Mr. Justice Story wrote, and the jurisdiction sometimes directly denied. Peters *v.* Florence, 38 Penn. St. 194; Goltra *v.* Sanasack, 53 Ill. 456; Zollman *v.* Moore, 21 Gratt. 313; Brown *v.* Armistead, 6 Rand. 594. Opposed to this however there is a long line of specific authorities, most of them correct beyond question, in which relief for mistake of law has either been granted, or admitted to be a proper head of Equity Jurisdiction. These will appear throughout the rest of this note.

Want of harmony however exists in regard to the special principle on which relief is to be granted or refused; and it will be noticed upon an examination of the cases that the judges are always glad to discover some special equity, aside from the mistake of law, which with the mistake may make their course more clear. Perhaps judges have sometimes been too ready to steer away from the dangers of the subject. It may be safe with Mr. Justice Story to say, though that is not quite clear, that 'where a party acts or agrees in ignorance of any title in him . . . [he] seems to labor in some sort under a mistake of fact as well as of law.' Infra, § 130. That is very guarded language. Whether it would be safe to put the case in bolder and positive terms, with recent statements (Cooper *v.* Phibbs, L. R. 2 H. L. 149, 170; Beauchamp *v.* Winn, L. R. 6 H. L. 223, 234; Jones *v.* Clifford, 3 Ch. D. 779, 792; Daniell *v.* Sinclair, 6 App. Cas. 181, 190; Macknet *v.* Macknet, 29 N. J. Eq. 54; Webb *v.* Alexandria, 33 Gratt. 168, 176), is still less clear; and there surely is no need in such a case of falling back upon the law of mistake of fact. To do so seems to cast doubt upon the jurisdiction of equity altogether over mistake of law; for the case is or may be one of the clearest cases of mistake of law, as where a conveyance has been made carrying in effect curtesy, when a recent statute, unknown to the grantor, has been passed creating or reviving such an estate. And it is proper at the outset to notice that if the terms 'mistake of law' and 'ignorance of law' were always used with strict propriety, it would be found that the cases in which relief is granted are cases of ignorance and not of mistake; which latter term implies some notice and consideration of the law. But the terms are commonly used as synonymous; or rather the term 'mistake' has nearly usurped the other's place.

that every man is bound at his peril to take knowledge what the law of the realm is, as well the law made by statute as the com-

Nor will it do with Lansdowne *v.* Lansdowne, Mos. 364; s. c. 2 Jac. & W. 205; infra, § 125, and more recent expressions following in the lead of that case (Wyche *v.* Greene, 16 Ga. 58; Jacobs *v.* Morange, 47 N. Y. 57, 61), to relegate the whole maxim concerning ignorance of law to the domain of criminal jurisprudence, and so give to equity a broad and indefinite jurisdiction of relief. The jurisdiction is sufficiently delicate and dangerous when confined within limits. A pretty wide door appears to have been thrown open still, in the dicta of the judges in the cases above referred to (Cooper *v.* Phibbs, Beauchamp *v.* Winn, Macknet *v.* Macknet, and Webb *v.* Alexandria), — wide enough indeed to ease the jurisdiction somewhat, but wide enough also, it would seem, to make doubtful the validity of many contracts and to overturn a good many decisions. According to those dicta the word 'jus' in the maxim 'ignorantia juris haud excusat' refers only to general well-known law, as distinguished from private right generally, and rights arising e. g. from the doubtful construction of a grant. Now, not to mention the difficulty of applying the interpretation (see infra, § 125, where also the beginning of this idea of 'jus' may be seen), it is just this latter class of cases to which the refusal of relief has most frequently been applied in cases of real authority, at least in the United States, as will appear in the consideration of the subject later. True it is held, and doubtless correctly, that the maxim applies only to general public, and not to private, acts of the Legislature or to the laws of another State or country. Such laws may well be treated as facts. King *v.* Doolittle, 1 Head, 77, 84; Haven *v.* Foster, 9 Pick. 112 (foreign laws); McCormick *v.* Garnett, 5 DeG. M. & G. 278 (ib.). But that is a different thing from the interpretation of 'jus' above referred to.

What then is the doctrine to be extracted from the decisions of the courts? So far as the *denial* of relief is concerned, it is apprehended that the true principle is to be found in the much-quoted but sometimes misapplied case of Hunt *v.* Rousmaniere, 8 Wheat. 174; s. c. 1 Peters, 1, particularly in its first phase before the Supreme Court of the United States. In that case a person lending money on the security of ships deliberately, after consulting counsel, took a letter of attorney with power to sell the property, in preference to a mortgage thereon, upon the mistake of law that the security taken would bind the property, in case of the death of the borrower, to the same extent as a mortgage. The debtor dies, and the lender attempts to have the instrument taken reformed so as to make it express the real intention of the parties (if the law should be considered against the interpretation of the counsel); and he fails.

It has sometimes been supposed that this case draws a distinction between mistake made in reducing to writing a contract already agreed upon by the parties, — the mistake being that the language of the writing has a meaning or effect in law different from the intention, — and mistake with regard to the legal meaning or effect of a written instrument agreed upon as representing the contract of the parties. The first case is accordingly supposed to be a case for relief, while the second is not. Larkins *v.* Biddle, 21 Ala. 252; Stockbridge Iron Co. *v.* Hudson Iron Co., 107 Mass. 290, 319. See also Stafford *v.* Fetters, 55 Iowa, 484; Pitcher *v.* Hennessey, 48 N. Y. 415; Nelson *v.* Davis, 40 Ind. 366;

mon law.[1] The probable ground for the maxim is that suggested by Lord Ellenborough, that otherwise there is no saying to what

[1] Doct. & Stud. Dial. 2, ch. 46.

Heavenridge v. Mondy, 49 Ind. 434; Laver v. Dennett, 109 U. S. 90 (a case of laches).

Such a distinction cannot be sound. The writing is agreed upon as stating the contract in the one case as much as in the other. It matters not whether the parties say, 'Here are the facts, and here is what on deliberation we want to do,' and then accept from the draftsman the written instrument and execute it as embodying their intention; or, 'This writing on consideration we accept as truly expressing our intention, and fix our signatures to it accordingly.' The second act may imply more deliberation concerning the writing; but in neither case may the deliberation have touched the legal difficulty which finally arises. That may not have been in the minds of the parties at all. The distinction is trifling; it does not go to the root of the matter.

But Hunt v. Rousmaniere draws no such distinction in either of its stages. The case in its first appearance before the Supreme Court of the United States is clearly stated by Chief Justice Marshall. In giving the opinion of the court he says: 'The agreement stated in the bill is generally that the plaintiff, in addition to the notes of Rousmaniere, should have specific security in the vessels; and it alleges that the parties applied to counsel for advice respecting the most desirable mode of taking this security. On a comparison of the advantages and disadvantages of a mortgage and an irrevocable letter of attorney, counsel advised the latter instrument, and assigned reasons for his advice; the validity of which being admitted by the parties, the power of attorney was prepared and executed, and was received by the plaintiff as full security for the loans.' 8 Wheat. 209.

Here was the whole case; deliberation with knowledge of the safe course (though not as safe) and choice of the unsafe. True on the next page the Chief Justice, in putting the case for decision in general terms, says, 'the parties deliberately, on advice of counsel, agree on a particular instrument,' without adding ' in preference to another before them which would have effectuated the intention,' but the whole case shows that such should be understood as a governing factor in the decision. It is true also that in the second stage of the case, 1 Peters, 1, Mr. Justice Washington, who now delivered the opinion of the court, uses some expressions which, taken apart from the rest, might be thought broad enough to suggest some such distinction as that in question. He says: ' Where an instrument is drawn and executed which professes or is intended to carry into execution an agreement, whether in writing or by parol, previously entered into, but which, by mistake of the draftsman, either as to fact or law, does not fulfil, or which violates, the manifest intention of the parties to the agreement, equity will correct the mistake.' See infra, § 115; Pitcher v. Hennessey, 48 N. Y. 415, 423. But that must be understood with reference to the case before the court, and the learned judge himself so declares. That the doctrine just quoted would not apply where the parties deliberated upon the particular terms or instrument employed, with other effectual terms or instruments before them, making choice of the ineffectual, is the very point decided. The ' intention ' on the evidence was ' manifest ' enough.

extent the excuse of ignorance might not be carried.[1] Indeed one of the remarkable tendencies of the English common law

[1] Bilbie v. Lumley, 2 East, 469, 472.

Indeed the whole case is afterwards well summed up by the same judge. 'We mean to say that when the parties, upon deliberation and advice, reject one species of security and agree to select another, under a misapprehension of the law as to the nature of the security so selected, a Court of Equity will not, on the ground of such misapprehension and the insufficiency of such security . . . direct a new security.' 1 Peters, 17. But the passage first quoted seems to have entirely misled the court in Stockbridge Iron Co. v. Hudson Iron Co., 107 Mass. 290, 319, 320.

The case of Hunt v. Rousmaniere decides then this very intelligible and sound principle, that where a particular course is taken upon deliberation, in preference to another present to the minds of the parties, that action, so far, is final. A letter of attorney was considered as preferable for the matter in hand to a mortgage. There was a choice of ends before the lender, in that both the preferable and the adopted course of action was under consideration; he elected his course; by so doing he bound himself. This affords a suggestion of the specific ground of jurisdiction of mistake.

Indeed the jurisdiction ought, on the point of 'deliberation,' in the ordinary sense, to be somewhat narrower; and cases to be presented will indicate that it has in truth been treated as having a somewhat narrower basis. The working principle is however still that of Hunt v. Rousmaniere. The test to which the question of jurisdiction should be brought is this: Was there in truth a choice of ends open to the complaining party at the time? That is, was a doubt raised in his mind whether the particular word, phrase, term, or instrument was sufficient in law to effectuate the object contemplated at that time by him, and nothing else essentially different? If there was, he was put to a choice; and the choice made, though perhaps not on such deliberation as took place in Hunt v. Rousmaniere, must be binding. If no doubt occurred to the party whether the object contemplated could be accomplished by the step to be taken, with nothing besides radically different, then between the intended effect of that step and the actual course of the law no choice was made, and equity should grant relief. See Stockley v. Stockley, 1 Ves. & B. 31, Lord Eldon; infra, §§ 129, 130. And this though the words used were the words intended. Canedy v. Marcy, 13 Gray, 373; Smith v. Jordan, 13 Minn. 264.

Other cases will now be brought to bear on the test here suggested, first as in Hunt v. Rousmaniere, on the refusal of jurisdiction. The recent English case of Rogers v. Ingham, 3 Ch. D. 351, in the Court of Appeal, though a case into which other considerations, such as laches and change of position, entered, proceeds in part at least upon the ground which governed Hunt v. Rousmaniere. That was a case of the payment of money by an executor to one of two legatees, on advice of legal counsel, taken by both sides to the same effect, with all questions of law under consideration; which payment, two years afterwards, and after distribution of the estate, the other legatee sought to impeach for mistake of law. The decision is finally put thus by Lord Justice James: 'Where people have a knowledge of all the facts, and take advice, and, whether they get proper advice or not, the money is divided and the business is settled, it is not for the good of

upon all subjects of a general nature is, to aim at practical good rather than theoretical perfection; and to seek less to administer

mankind that it should be opened.' Still more clearly Lord Justice Mellish puts the case as one of deliberation and choice. 'Both parties,' he says, 'were well aware that the [legal] question was then [when the transaction took place] to be decided; the plaintiff's attention and the attention of the plaintiff's legal advisers were called to all the facts and circumstances; she took advice upon the point.' See also Stone *v.* Godfrey, 5 DeG. M. & G. 76; Kitchin *v.* Hawkins, L. R. 2 C. P. 22; Preston *v.* Luck, 27 Ch. D. 497. And among cases of the compromise of rights doubtful in law, see Stewart *v.* Stewart, 6 Clark & F. 911, 967; Pullen *v.* Ready, 2 Atk. 587; Gibbons *v.* Caunt, 4 Ves. 840; Ex parte Lucy, 4 DeG. M. & G. 356; Wheeler *v.* Smith, 9 How. 55; infra, § 131.

The same principle may be seen in the case of Weed *v.* Weed, 94 N. Y. 243. There it appeared that a lady, with full knowledge of all the facts, but through a mistaken belief that her interest in certain real estate was not subject to execution, had lost her title through a regular sale, on judgment, execution, and conveyance of the land by the sheriff. She had taken legal advice on the question whether the property, under a peculiar deed which had been made to her, could be taken on execution, and believing the erroneous advice given to be correct, had delayed action until the time of redemption had expired. Relief was properly refused; the party had made up her mind, with the doubt before her. So in a case in Missouri, where the defendants had taken advice concerning the validity of a judgment before purchasing under it. The parties bought, and it was held that they could not allege that the advice given was erroneous. McMurray *v.* St. Louis Oil Co., 33 Mo. 377. So too though parties have misconstrued even a doubtful statute, they must still abide by the construction they have put upon it. Bank of United States *v.* Daniel, 12 Peters, 32; Kelly *v.* Turner, 74 Ala. 513, 519, — in regard to conflicting cases of construction.

Other cases might be referred to more or less to the same effect. See Townshend *v.* Stangroom, 6 Ves. 328; Smith *v.* Hitchcock, 130 Mass. 570; Marble *v.* Whitney, 28 N. Y. 297, 308; Thompson *v.* Thompson, 18 Ohio St. 73 (mistake as to law of descents; see Huss *v.* Morris, 63 Penn. St. 367; but see Hopson *v.* Shipp, 7 Bush, 614); Davis *v.* Bagley, 40 Ga. 181; Norris *v.* Larrabee, 58 Maine, 260. (In Wheeler *v.* Smith, 9 How. 55, the parties were not on equal footing.) And — if we except some decisions based on the distinction above criticised, especially Stockbridge Iron Co. *v.* Hudson Iron Co., 107 Mass. 290, 319, 320 — few cases inconsistent with this view, so far as it is applied to the refusal of relief, can be found.

A peculiar case lately decided in Connecticut may perhaps be thought to be opposed to the view here maintained. Evans's Appeal, 51 Conn. 435. A widow was there allowed to withdraw a renunciation of the provision for her in her husband's will, which renunciation had been made under advice of the Judge of Probate. The advice was wrong in law, and on discovering the error, and before any change of position, the widow asked the same judge for leave to withdraw her renunciation. The request was refused, but the Supreme Court decided that it should have been granted. The opinion is not very instructive. What the nature of the mere act of renunciation alone may be does not appear. It does not become a

justice in all possible cases, than to furnish rules which shall secure it in the common course of human business. If upon the

judgment clearly; it is not an act inter partes; whether before some action has been taken upon it, it is more than what it seems to be, a mere declaration revocable within the period of the statute, is yet to be determined. Further as to the widow's election under mistake, see Macknet *v.* Macknet, 29 N. J. Eq. 54. Also see Ellsworth *v.* Ellsworth, 33 Iowa, 164. And it may be remarked that an election made in ignorance of the existence of a law upon the subject affords a perfectly clear case for relief when asked for soon enough. Watson *v.* Watson, 128 Mass. 152, 155, and cases cited.

A recent decision of the Supreme Court of Michigan may also be noticed. Lapp *v.* Lapp, 43 Mich. 287. A woman, the plaintiff, had married a man who had a wife living to her knowledge, from whom however he had separated under articles of agreement. This fact was known to the plaintiff, but she professed to have supposed at the time that the articles constituted a divorce. No fraud had been practised upon her. On discovering her mistake she sued for divorce with alimony. Both were refused. Mr. Justice Campbell, speaking for the court, said that it could not be presumed (that is, believed) that any person of ordinary intelligence could suppose that marriage could be dissolved by consent of parties. But even supposing such a belief possible, — it might be quite possible in the case of a foreigner, — public policy would probably have led the court to the same conclusion with regard to a question so momentous as marriage and divorce. One should carefully look into the case before marrying a person known by one to have a husband (or wife) living. The plaintiff must at least have been put to a doubt, and that in the view here taken is

enough. So where L after the death of his wife, paid a mortgage made by her on her own property, on the mistaken belief either that the property had become his by descent or that he was bound as his wife's executor to pay it, relief was refused him. The facts show that he was in doubt as to the state of the title and made his election. Peters *v.* Florence, 38 Penn. St. 194. See also Guckian *v.* Riley, 135 Mass. 71; Moorman *v.* Collier, 32 Iowa, 138.

The court in Harner *v.* Price, 17 W. Va. 523, may be thought to have gone contrary to the doctrine of Hunt *v.* Rousmaniere. In that case the plaintiff had acknowledged judgment on a non-negotiable note barred by limitation. He did not know the law, and was induced by the defendant, but not fraudulently as it was found, to make the acknowledgment. Relief was refused. This however was a case where the plaintiff (though the fact is not brought out in the opinion printed) owed the debt in conscience and had come into a court of conscience to obtain relief from a very proper act. Compare Northrop *v.* Graves, 19 Conn. 548; Covington *v.* Powell, 2 Met. (Ky.) 226, 228. The equities on the defendant's side were at least equal to those on the side of the plaintiff. In this view the case is not unlike cases referred to in Hunt *v.* Rousmaniere, of joint obligors, after the death of one of them and discharge of his personal representatives, being still held to the obligee as if the bond had been joint and several, on the ground that they had received the consideration for their promise; and it was to be assumed that they intended to bind themselves severally as well as jointly. This however was treated as doubtful law in our principal case, unless the failure to make the

mere ground of ignorance of the law men were admitted to overhaul or extinguish their most solemn contracts, and especially bond several was due to mistake of fact. See infra, §§ 162–164.

This brings us to the case of money paid under mistake of law, which in England is considered to present the one permanent exception to the right to relief for mistake (Pollock, Contract, 424, 3d ed.); though it must strike the observer as odd that while no amount of negligence can there bar one from the right to recover back money which one has paid under mistake of fact (Willmott v. Barber, 15 Ch. D. 96; Townsend v. Crowdy, 8 C. B. N. S. 477; Kelly v. Solari, 9 Mees. & W. 54), no case of ignorance of the law can give one a right to a return of money paid. Bilbie v. Lumley, 2 East, 469; Rogers v. Ingham, 3 Ch. D. 351; Stewart v. Stewart, 6 Clark & F. 911, 966; Pollock, Contract, supra. But as to the right to resist payment on a contract, see Forman v. Wright, 11 C. B. 481, 492. The doctrine in question has also been declared in the United States (Livermore v. Peru, 55 Maine, 469; Peterborough v. Lancaster, 14 N. H. 383); but it cannot, broadly stated, be said to be settled law here. See Northrop v. Graves, 19 Conn. 548, and Covington v. Powell, 2 Met. (Ky.) 226, 228, showing that where the money was not in conscience or honor due, it may be recovered back.

Why should there be any difference between the case of money paid under mistake of fact and money paid under mistake of law? In the latter case as well as in the former the receiver gets what does not belong to him, what there was no intention to give him, and what there was no consideration for paying. It would be difficult to distinguish such a case from the class of cases already mentioned, in which it is held with perfect unanimity that where a party acts in entire ignorance of any title or right given him by law, or supposes that he has a title or a right when he has not, equity will take jurisdiction and save the right or grant the proper relief. Watson v. Watson, 128 Mass. 152; Bingham v. Bingham, 1 Ves. sr. 126; Cooper v. Phibbs, L. R. 2 H. L. 149; Beauchamp v. Winn, L. R. 6 H. L. 223; Jones v. Clifford, 3 Ch. D. 779; Cochrane v. Willis, 34 Beav. 368; s. c. L. R. 1 Ch. 58; In re Saxon Life Assurance Soc. 2 Johns. & H. 408; Coward v. Hughes, 1 Kay & J. 443; Forman v. Wright, 11 C. B. 481, 492; McCarthy v. Decaix, 2 Russ. & M. 614; Griffith v. Townley, 69 Mo. 13; Blakemore v. Blakemore, 39 Conn. 320; Whelen's Appeal, 70 Penn. St. 410; Baker v. Massey, 50 Iowa, 399; infra, § 130. It has been held too in Massachusetts that an indorser of a promissory note, discharged for want of notice in due time, who on receiving notice promises to pay, under the mistake of law that he is bound, may allege his mistake. Warder v. Tucker, 7 Mass. 449. See May v. Coffin, 4 Mass. 341; Freeman v. Boynton, 7 Mass. 483, 488. This however is opposed to the decision of the King's Bench in Stevens v. Lynch, 12 East, 38, and if there was any moral duty to pay, is also opposed to the West Virginia case of Harner v. Price, above considered.

The doctrine in question is traced back to Bilbie v. Lumley, 2 East, 469; but though Lord Ellenborough is indeed there reported to have laid down the broad rule denying relief, it appears to have been unnecessary to do so, or to do so without qualification. An attempt was made in that case by an insurance company to recover back money paid under a mistake of law concerning the effect of a particular concealment by the assured. All the facts were before

those which have been executed by a complete performance, there would be much embarrassing litigation in all judicial tri-

the underwriters, including the one in question, and they adjusted and paid the loss. The company well knew that concealment in general was ground of discharge of their liability; with such knowledge they considered the particular fact and acted. They elected their course. It may be noticed that Lord Ellenborough does not base the decision of the case upon any ground peculiar to the attempt to recover back money paid; he would, it seems, have applied the same rule to any other case of mistake of law. The distinction itself is much shaken by Daniell *v.* Sinclair, 6 App. Cas. 181.

Thus far of the doctrine in question in respect of the denial of relief. That the converse of it holds equally well, for granting relief, may not perhaps be so decisively shown; still that may be shown with reasonable clearness. From almost every case in which relief has been granted either the element of choice between means or ends — choice between the safe and the unsafe course — was absent, and but one course suggested or thought of by the parties, or some other special equity existed in favor of the plaintiff. In this state of things — a well-defined rule that the exercise of choice is final, and the fact that in the cases in which relief has been granted there has been wanting an opportunity for choice — the inference is reasonable that want of opportunity, that is, absolute ignorance, is a ground of relief. Indeed here appears to be a case for a crucial test of the proposition that want of assent is ground for relief from the consequences of mistake of law. If there is no possibility of choice, there is no true assent, and relief should be granted; that is the proposition to be tried.

Let us turn again to the authorities and apply the test. In Pitcher *v.* Hennessey, 48 N. Y. 415, it appeared that the plaintiff had leased a vessel of the defendant, assuming the 'risk of navigation.' A particular risk inter alia was by mistake of law supposed by the parties to be covered by this term, and the lease was reformed. No occasion for doubt appears to have arisen, and there was therefore no true choice of terms. If the words had been chosen against a doubt of their sufficiency, there would then, and only then, have been an election. The court on p. 424, it may be remarked, barely falls short of this position. The case there affords an illustration of the common missing of the point of Hunt *v.* Rousmaniere, or at least of the failure to bring that point clearly out, — the preference of one writing over another on the matter at issue.

Another case in the same volume of Reports may be mentioned. Lanning *v.* Carpenter, 48 N. Y. 408. It had been agreed that the plaintiff should have a judgment against J. C., which should be a lien upon his property. By mistake of law, but without any doubt as to the proper course, so far as appears, the judgment was docketed in the wrong county, — a county which afterwards turned out to have been illegally organized. Relief was granted. But if the parties had agreed to have the judgment docketed in the particular county in the face of a doubt raised, could any court have interfered and declared the agreement immaterial?

The case of Lant's Appeal, 95 Penn. St. 279, is worthy of special notice. A will was there treated in equity as an antenuptial agreement, in order to effectuate the intention of the parties, which otherwise, by mistake of law, would have miscarried. A lady about to marry had made the will, on a valid

bunals, and no small danger of injustice from the nature and difficulty of the proper proofs.[1] The presumption is, that every

[1] Lyon v. Richmond, 2 John. Ch. R. 51, 60; Shotwell v. Murray, 1 John. Ch. R. 512; Storrs v. Barker, 6 John. Ch. R. 169, 170.

agreement between herself and her intended husband, that she might dispose of her property by will or otherwise as she pleased; which will was revoked by operation of law on her marriage, an event not contemplated in any way. The decision seems perfectly sound; there was no choice between the effectual and the adopted course. The language of the court however is open to objection. It was said that whenever one has a legal right to dispose of property, and means to dispose of it, the form of the instrument adopted for the purpose, if in law ineffectual as it stands, will be disregarded, and equity will enforce the intention. Compare Kennard v. George, 44 N. H. 440; Evants v. Strode, 11 Ohio, 480 ; Clayton v. Freet, 10 Ohio St. 544. Now if this was intended for a broad rule of law, it is not consistent with Hunt v. Rousmaniere. If the particular instrument was chosen, as in that case, in preference to another, on the point at issue, equity will not interfere; but understood with this qualification, the proposition is useful. It may also be noticed that the proposition just criticised would further be too broad for the case of a mistake in the execution by a married woman of a statutory conveyance by her of her own property before the recent enabling acts. Martin v. Dwelly, 6 Wend. 9; Heaton v. Fryberger, 38 Iowa, 185, 201; Gibb v. Rose, 40 Md. 387. Nor would a deed of realty made by a wife directly to her husband on a mistake of law be upheld. Gibb v. Rose. But both of these cases stand on special grounds that do not touch the main doctrine under consideration.

In this connection a case decided by the Supreme Court of California may be noticed. Remington v. Higgins, 54 Cal. 620. Relief was there granted on the following facts: Land bought by A was at his request conveyed to his wife as 'community' property under the laws of California. Such property is not liable for the wife's debts. The wife gave back a mortgage and notes to secure the unpaid purchase-money. The court held that the mortgagee had, without regard to any vendor's lien, an equitable mortgage on the estate for the purchase price. The case clearly falls within the principle under consideration. There was no election. (The court referred to the class of cases of instruments defectively executed, where relief is granted. Love v. Sierra Nev. Mining Co., 32 Cal. 639; Daggett v. Rankin, 31 Cal. 321. But that is a simpler matter.)

A few cases not so clear may be noticed; among them one by the Supreme Court of Alabama. Stone v. Hale, 17 Ala. 557. A father having a daughter unprovided for, whose husband was improvident, determined to vest property in a trustee to her sole and separate use for life, remainder to her children. Instructions were given accordingly to an attorney; but in drawing the deed he omitted the words 'to her sole and separate use,' whereby the estate became vested in the husband for life, and was levied upon by his creditors. The deed was reformed. This looks very much like a mistake of fact; if the omission was witting, it is hard to understand the case, — unless the attorney made a mistake of law and the father, in not noticing the omission, a mistake of fact. There is a similar case in the same court,

person is acquainted with his own rights, provided he has had a reasonable opportunity to know them. And nothing can be more

where the grantor had been his own draftsman and relief was granted. Larkins *v.* Biddle, 21 Ala. 252.

In the recent case of Snell *v.* Insurance Co., 98 U. S. 85, there was a special equity. It appeared that the plaintiff had been induced to act upon the superior knowledge of the defendant's agent. An agreement had been made between A and B that certain insurance should be granted by B on property of a firm of which A was a member. B's agent, but without fraud, *induces* A to have the policy made in his own name, assuring him that in that form it will protect the firm. The court decided that the policy must be reformed to meet the intention of the parties, on the ground that A had trusted B's agent concerning the proper mode of executing the policy. The case was therefore one of trust. To the same effect, Woodbury Bank *v.* Charter Oak Ins. Co., 31 Conn. 517; Longhurst *v.* Star Ins. Co., 19 Iowa, 364. See also Ben. Franklin Ins. Co. *v.* Gillett, 54 Md. 212; Farmville Ins. Co. *v.* Butter, 55 Md. 233. For the converse case of encouraging action, see Storrs *v.* Barker, 6 Johns. Ch. 166; Zollman *v.* Moore, 21 Gratt. 313, 326; Kitchin *v.* Hawkins, L. R. 2 C. P. 22, 31; not cases of agency.

It may also be that where a person by mistake of law acts to his detriment under what may be called compulsion, though compulsion might of itself be lawful, he will be entitled to relief, especially if the other party knew that in the particular case the law did not entitle him to the benefit; and this too though the injured party was seeking at the time to discover what the law required. Thus it is held that a man may have relief from a return of property for taxation when it appears that by mistake of law he included exempt property. Charlestown *v.* Middlesex, 109 Mass. 270. See Dunnell Manuf. Co. *v.* Pawtucket, 7 Gray, 277.

Certain cases of the unauthorized acts of corporations may also clearly fall without the rule in Hunt *v.* Rousmaniere. A corporation has no power beyond that conferred by the Legislature; and if such a body should e. g. issue bonds without authority, the fact that a purchaser was ignorant of the existence of a law making them absolutely void would not help his case in a suit against the corporation, even if it would in a suit against his vendor, supposing he had not bought of the company. In Rochester *v.* Alfred Bank, 13 Wis. 432, it appeared that a public statute had gone into effect, by which the authority of a town to issue bonds had been taken away, of which a purchaser alleged ignorance. But the court said that by taking notice of the time when the statute took effect, and examining the date of the bonds, the want of authority would have appeared.

A difficult question — difficult because of its close relation to deep questions of public policy — is presented by the case of a judicial decision overturning what before had been supposed to be law. If a statute is declared unconstitutional, transactions intermediate must in ordinary cases — see Harney *v.* Charles, 45 Mo. 157 — be readjusted as far as may be (no agreement, it seems, could preclude one from denying the constitutionality of a statute); and the general theory in regard to the overruling of former decisions no doubt is that the law always was what it has been declared to be by the later authority. But the courts are not agreed in the wisdom of pressing the theory to the dangerous extreme of overturning intermediate transactions founded

liable to abuse than to permit a person to reclaim his property upon the mere pretence that at the time of parting with it he was ignorant of the law acting on his title.[1] Mr. Fonblanque has accordingly laid it down as a general proposition that in Courts of Equity ignorance of the law shall not affect agreements nor excuse from the legal consequences of particular acts.[2] And he is fully borne out by authorities.[3]

---

[1] See Storrs *v.* Barker, 6 John. Ch. R. 169.

[2] 1 Fonbl. Eq. B. 1, ch. 2, § 7, note (*v*); 1 Madd. Ch. Pr. 60. But see Moseley's Rep. 364; 1 Ves. 127; Storrs *v.* Barker, 6 John. Ch. R. 169, 170; Hunt *v.* Rousmaniere, 1 Peters, R. 1, 15, 16.

[3] The doctrine was pushed to a great extent (as Mr. Fonblanque has remarked) in Wibdey *v.* Cooper Company, cited in a note to East *v.* Thornbury, 3 P. Will. 127, note B, and Atwood *v.* Lamprey (ibid.), in which a tenant who had paid a rent or annuity charged on land, without deducting the land tax, was not allowed to recover back the amount by a bill in equity. 1 Fonbl. Eq. B. 1, ch. 2, § 7, note (*r*). There is an appearance of hardship in this doctrine; but it has been fully recognized in a late case where an executor paid interest on a legacy without deducting the property tax. Currie *v.* Goold, 2 Madd. R. 163, and Smith *v.* Alsop, 1 Madd. R. 623.

---

on the earlier declaration. Against interference in such cases, Lyon *v.* Richmond, 2 Johns. Ch. 51, 60; Jacobs *v.* Morange, 47 N. Y. 57, 60; Webb *v.* Alexandria, 33 Gratt. 168; Kelly *v.* Turner, 74 Ala. 513, 520; Baker *v.* Pool, 56 Ala. 14; Kenyon *v.* Welty, 20 Cal. 637; Kitchin *v.* Hawkins, L. R. 2 C. P. 22. Contra, Jones *v.* Munroe, 32 Ga. 181; and see Harney *v.* Charles, 45 Mo. 157; infra, § 138; and Reed *v.* White, an unreported case of the Supreme Court of Massachusetts, January term, 1877, in which the point was decided without argument, as the writer is informed. Where the decisions are in an unsettled state, and especially where a question of the true rule of law is known to be pending, parties acting may well be held to have bound themselves by the view of the law they have taken. But see Jones *v.* Munroe, supra. See Lyon *v.* Richmond, supra; Kelly *v.* Turner, supra, at pp. 519, 520; Kenyon *v.* Welty, 20 Cal. 637, 641. Perhaps this should not be invariably so where no doubt of the law had arisen at the time, and the overruling decision followed soon. If then the former situation in the particular case could be restored, there might be ground for interference upon the principle under consideration in this note. But the Legislature is always anxious concerning rights in repealing a statute, and the courts should hardly be less so in overruling former decisions.

It may be observed in concluding this note that a special public policy governs the case of mistake of law or of practice in the conduct of causes. See e. g. Thurmond *v.* Clark, 47 Ga. 500; Jacobs *v.* Morange, 47 N. Y. 57, 59. 'Interest reipublicæ ut litium finis sit.'

The special limitations to the right to relief, growing out e. g. of change of position, the intervention of the rights of others, the amount of evidence necessary to establish the mistake, and like cases, are considered in the editor's note on Mistake of Fact, post, § 140.

Further, Law Quart. Rev., Jan., 1886, art. 'Mistake of Law Again.'

112. One of the most common cases put to illustrate the doctrine is where two are bound by a bond, and the obligee releases one, supposing by a mistake of law that the other will remain bound. In such a case the obligee will not be relieved in equity upon the mere ground of his mistake of the law;[1] (a) for there is nothing inequitable in the co-obligor's availing himself of his legal rights, nor of the other obligor's insisting upon his release, if they have both acted bona fide, and there has been no fraud or imposition on their side to procure the release.[2] So where a party had a power of appointment and executed it absolutely without introducing a power of revocation, upon a mistake of law that being a voluntary deed it was revocable, relief was in like manner denied.[3] If the power of revocation had been intended to be put into the appointment, and omitted by a mistake in the draft, it would have been a very different matter.

113. The same principle applies to agreements entered into in good faith, but under a mistake of the law. They are generally held valid and obligatory upon the parties.[4] Thus where

---

Lord Hardwicke also acted upon the same doctrine in Nicholls v. Leeson, 3 Atk. 573. The cases resolve themselves into an over-payment by mistake of law or of fact, and probably of the former. But it does not appear in any of these cases that the mistake was not mutual. It is a little difficult to reconcile these cases with the doctrine in Bingham v. Bingham, 1 Ves. 126, and Belt's Suppt. 79.

[1] Com. Dig. Chancery, 3 F. 8; Harman v. Cannon, 4 Vin. Abridg. 387, pl. 3; 1 Fonbl. Eq. B. 1, ch. 2, § 7, note (v). See also 1 Peters, Sup. C. R. 17; 1 P. Will. 723, 727; 2 Atk. 591; 2 John. Ch. R. 51; 4 Pick. R. 6, 17; Cann v. Cann, 1 P. Will. 723, 727. But see Ex parte Gifford, 6 Ves. 805, and the comments by Lord Denman on that case in Nicholson v. Revell, 6 Nev. & Mann. 192, 200; s. c. 4 Adolph. & Ellis, 675.

[2] In such a case there is no doubt that the releasee is discharged at law. In Nicholson v. Revell, 6 Nev. & Mann. 192, 200, s. c. 4 Adolph. & Ellis, 675, a discharge of one party on a joint and several note was held to be a discharge of both. S. P. Cheetham v. Ward, 1 Bos. & Pull. 630; Hosack v. Rogers, 8 Paige, R. 229.

[3] Worrall v. Jacob, 3 Meriv. R. 195. See also 1 Peters, Sup. C. R. 16.

[4] Pullen v. Ready, 1 Atk. 591; Stockley v. Stockley, 1 Ves. & B. 23, 30; Frank v. Frank, 1 Ch. Cas. 84; Mildmay v. Hungerford, 2 Vern. R. 243; Shotwell v. Murray, 1 John. Ch. R. 512; Lyon v. Richmond, 2 John. Ch. R. 51; Hunt v. Rousmaniere, 1 Peters, Sup. C. R. 1, 15; Storrs v. Barker, 6 John. Ch. R. 169, 170. Some of the cases commonly cited under this head are cases of family agreements to preserve family honor or family peace; and some of them are compromises of rights thought at the time to be doubtful

(a) See post, § 498 a.

a clause containing a power of redemption, in a deed granting an annuity after it had been agreed to, was deliberately excluded by the parties upon a mistake of law that it would render the contract usurious, the Court of Chancery refused to restore the clause or to grant relief.[1] Lord Eldon, in commenting on this case, said that it went upon an indisputably clear principle; that the parties did not mean to insert in the agreement a provision for redemption, because they were all of one mind that it would be ruinous. And they desired the court to do, not what they intended, for the insertion of that provision was directly contrary to their intention; but they desired to be put in the same situation as if they had been better informed, and consequently had a contrary intention.[2] So where a devise was given upon condition that a woman should marry with the consent of her parents, and she married without such consent, whereby a forfeiture accrued to other parties who afterwards executed an agreement respecting the estate, whereby the forfeiture was in effect waived, the court refused any relief, although it was contended that it was upon a mistake of law. Lord Hardwicke on that occasion said: 'It is said, they (the parties) might know the fact and yet not know the consequence of law. But if parties are entering into an agreement, and the very will out of which the forfeiture arose is lying before them and their counsel while the drafts are preparing, the parties shall be supposed to be acquainted with the consequence of law as to this point; and shall not be relieved on a pretence of being surprised,

---

by all the parties. The cases of Stapilton *v.* Stapilton, 1 Atk. 10; Stockley *v.* Stockley, 1 Ves. & B. 23; Cory *v.* Cory, 1 Ves. 19; Gordon *v.* Gordon, 3 Swanst. R. 463, 467, 471, 474, 477, and perhaps Frank *v.* Frank, 1 Ch. Cas. 84, are of the former sort. And it has been said by Lord Eldon that in family arrangements an equity is administered in equity which is not applied to agreements generally. 1 Ves. & B. 30; Neale *v.* Neale, 1 Keen, 672, 683. Compromises of doubtful rights stand upon a distinct ground; for in such cases the parties are equal, and it is for the public interest to suppress litigation. Cann *v.* Cann. 1 P. Will. 723; 1 Ves. & B. 30; 1 Atk. 10; Naylor *v.* Winch, 1 Sim. & Stu. 564, 565. But of these doctrines a more full discussion belongs to the text. Post, § 120, § 121, § 122, § 126, § 128, § 129, § 130, § 131, § 132.

[1] Irnham *v.* Child, 1 Bro. Ch. R. 92. See 6 Ves. 332, 333; 1 Peters, Sup. C. R. 16, 17.

[2] Marquis of Townshend *v.* Stangroom, 6 Ves. 332. See also Lord Patmore *v.* Morris, 2 Bro. Ch. R. 219; Hunt *v.* Rousmaniere, 2 Mason, R. 366, 367.

CHAP. V.] MISTAKE. 125

with such strong circumstances attending it.'[1] So where the plaintiff was tenant for life, with remainder to his first and other sons in tail, remainder to the defendant in fee, and his wife being then privement ensient of a son, he was advised that if he bought the reversion of the defendant and took a surrender, it would merge his estate for life and destroy the contingent remainder in his sons and give him a fee, and he accordingly bought the reversion and gave security for the purchase-money, and upon a discovery of his mistake of the law he brought a bill to be relieved against the security, it was denied, unless upon payment of the full amount.[2]

114. Another illustration may be derived from a case most vigorously contested and critically discussed, where upon the loan of money for which security was to be given, the parties deliberately took, after consultation with counsel, a letter of attorney, with a power to sell the property (ships) in case of non-payment of the money, instead of a mortgage upon the property itself, upon the mistake of law that the security by the former instrument would, in case of death or other accident, bind the property equally as strongly as a mortgage. The debtor died, and his estate being insolvent, a bill in equity was brought by the creditor against the administrators to reform the instrument or to give him a priority by way of lien on the property in exclusion of the general creditors. The court finally, after the most deliberate examination of the case at three successive stages of the cause, denied relief, upon the ground that the agreement was for a particular security selected by the parties, and not for security generally; and that the court were asked to substitute another security for that selected by the parties, not upon any mistake of fact but upon a mistake of law, when such security was not within the scope of their agreement.[3]

115. It is manifest that the whole controversy in this case turned upon the point whether a Court of Equity could grant relief where a security becomes ineffectual not by fraud or accident, or because it is not what the parties intended it to be, but because, conforming to that intention, the parties in executing it

[1] Pullen v. Ready, 2 Atk. 587, 591.
[2] Mildmay v. Hungerford, 2 Vern. 243.
[3] Hunt v. Rousmaniere, 8 Wheat. R. 174; 1 Peters, Sup. C. R. 1, 13, 14; s. c. 2 Mason, R. 342; 3 Mason, R. 294.

innocently mistook the law. It was the very security the parties had deliberately selected; but by unforeseen events it was not as good a security as they might have selected. It would have been most extraordinary and unprecedented for a Court of Equity under such circumstances to grant relief; for it would be equivalent to decreeing a new agreement not contemplated by the parties, instead of executing that actually made by them. If the party who was to execute the power of attorney had refused that and offered a mortgage, could he have insisted on such a substitute? If a mortgage had been agreed on, could he have compelled the other side to have accepted a letter of attorney? Certainly not. Equity may compel parties to execute their agreements, but it has no authority to make agreements for them or to substitute one for another. If there had been any mistake in the instrument itself, so that it did not contain what the parties had agreed on, that would have formed a very different case; for where an instrument is drawn and executed which professes or is intended to carry into execution an agreement previously entered into, but which by mistake of the draftsman either as to fact or to law does not fulfil that intention, or violates it, equity will correct the mistake so as to produce a conformity to the instrument.[1]

116. In a preceding section[2] it has been stated that agreements made and acts done under a mistake of law are (if not otherwise objectionable) generally held valid and obligatory. The doctrine is laid down in this guarded and qualified manner because it is not to be disguised that there are authorities which are supposed to contradict it, or at least to form exceptions to it. Indeed in one case Lord King is reported to have said that the maxim of law, 'Ignorantia juris non excusat,' was, in regard to the public, that ignorance cannot be pleaded in excuse of crimes; but that it did not hold in civil cases.[3] This broad statement is utterly irreconcilable with the well-established doctrine both of Courts of Law and Courts of Equity. The general rule certainly is (as has been very clearly stated by the Supreme Court of the United States) that a mistake of the law is not a ground for reforming a deed founded on such a mistake. And

---

[1] See the able opinion of Mr. Justice Washington in Hunt v. Rousmaniere's Adm'rs, 1 Peters, Sup. C. R. 13 to 17.   [2] Ante, § 113.
[3] Lansdowne v. Lansdowne, Moseley, R. 364; s. c. 2 Jac. & Walk. 205.

CHAP. V.] MISTAKE. 127

whatever exceptions there may be to this rule, they are not only few in number, but they will be found to have something peculiar in their character, and to involve other elements of decision.[1]

117. In illustration of this remark we may refer to a case commonly cited as an exception to the general rule. In that case the daughter of a freeman of London had a legacy of £10,000 left by her father's will upon condition that she should release her orphanage share; and after her father's death she accepted the legacy and executed the release. Upon a bill afterwards filed by her against her brother, who was the executor, the release was set aside and she was restored to her orphanage share, which amounted to £40,000. Lord Chancellor Talbot in making the decree admitted that there was no fraud in her brother, who had told her that she was entitled to her election to take an account of her father's personal estate, and to claim her orphanage share; but she chose to accept the legacy. His Lordship said: 'It is true, it appears, the son (the defendant) did inform the daughter that she was bound either to waive the legacy given by the father or release her right to the custom, and so far she might know that it was in her power to accept either the legacy or orphanage part. But I hardly think she knew she was entitled to have an account taken of the personal estate of her father; and first to know what her orphanage part did amount to, and that when she should be fully apprised of this, then and not till then she was to make her election; which very much alters the case. For probably she would not have elected to accept her legacy had she known or been informed what her orphanage part amounted unto before she waived it and accepted the legacy.'[2]

---

[1] Hunt v. Rousmaniere, 1 Peters, Sup. C. R. 15; s. c. 8 Wheat. R. 211, 212. See also Hepburn v. Dunlop, 10 Wheat. R. 179, 195; Shotwell v. Murray, 1 John. Ch. R. 512, 515; Lyon v. Richmond, 2 John. Ch. R. 51, 60; Storrs v. Barker, 6 John. Ch. R. 169, 170. Mr. Chancellor Kent has laid down the doctrine in equally strong terms. 'It is rarely,' says he, 'that a mistake in point of law, with a full knowledge of all the facts, can afford ground for relief or be considered as a sufficient indemnity against the injurious consequences of deception practised upon mankind, &c. It would therefore seem to be a wise principle of policy that ignorance of the law with a knowledge of the facts cannot generally be set up as a defence.' Storrs v. Barker, 6 John. Ch. R. 169, 170.

[2] Pusey v. Desbouvrie, 3 P. Will. 315, 321; 2 Ball & Beat. 182. See Pickering v. Pickering, 2 Beavan, R. 31, 56.

118. It is apparent from this language that the decision of his Lordship rested upon mixed considerations, and not exclusively upon mere mistake or ignorance of the law by the daughter. There was no fraud in her brother; but it is clear that she relied upon her brother for knowledge of her rights and duties in point of law, and he, however innocently, omitted to state some most material legal considerations affecting her rights and duty. She acted under this misplaced confidence and was misled by it, which of itself constituted no inconsiderable ground for relief. But a far more weighty reason is that she acted under ignorance of facts; for she neither knew, nor had any means of knowing, what her orphanage share was when she made her election. It was therefore a clear case of surprise in matters of fact as well as of law. No ultimate decision was made in the case, it being compromised by the parties.

119. The case of Evans *v.* Llewellyn[1] is expressly put in the decree upon the ground of surprise, ' the conveyance having been obtained and executed by the plaintiffs improvidently.' It was admitted that there was no sufficient proof of fraud or imposition practised upon the plaintiff (though the facts might well lead to some doubt on that point), and the plaintiff was certainly not ignorant of any of the facts which respected his rights. The Master of the Rolls (Sir Lloyd Kenyon, afterwards Lord Kenyon) said: ' The party was taken by surprise. He had not sufficient time to act with caution; and therefore, though there was no actual fraud, it is something like fraud, for an undue advantage was taken of his situation. I am of opinion that the party was not competent to protect himself; and therefore this court is bound to afford him such protection, and therefore these deeds ought to be set aside as *improvidently* obtained. If the plaintiff had in fact gone back, I should not have rescinded the transaction.'[2]

120. The most general class of cases relied on as exceptions to the rule is that class where the party has acted under a misconception or ignorance of his title to the property respecting which some agreement has been made or conveyance executed. So far as ignorance in point of fact of any title in the party is an ingredient in any of these cases, they fall under a very different con-

[1] 2 Bro. Ch. R. 150; s. c. 1 Cox, R. 333, more full.
[2] 1 Cox, R. 340, 341.

sideration.[1] But so far as the party, knowing all the facts, has acted upon a mistake of the law applicable to his title, they are proper to be discussed in this place. Upon a close survey many although not all of the cases in the latter predicament will be found to have turned not upon the consideration of a mere mistake of law stripped of all other circumstances, but upon an admixture of other ingredients going to establish misrepresentation, imposition, undue confidence, undue influence, mental imbecility, or that sort of surprise which equity uniformly regards as a just foundation for relief.[2] (*a*)

[1] See Ramsden *v.* Hylton, 2 Ves. 304; Cann *v.* Cann, 1 P. Will. 727; Farewell *v.* Coker, cited 2 Meriv. 269; McCarthy *v.* Decaix, 2 Russ. & Mylne, 614. In this last case Lord Chancellor Brougham held that where a husband renounced his title to his wife's property, from whom he had been divorced, under a mistake in point of law that the divorce was valid and he had no longer any title to her property, and under a mistake of fact as to the amount of the property renounced, the information respecting which the other party knew and withheld from him, he was entitled to relief. But the relief seems to have been granted upon mixed considerations. His Lordship in one part of his opinion said: 'What he (the husband) has done was in ignorance of law, possibly of fact; but in a case of this kind that would be one and the same thing.' See also Corking *v.* Pratt, 1 Ves. 400.

[2] See Willan *v.* Willan, 16 Ves. 82. Mr. Jeremy (Eq. Jurisd. Pt. 2, ch. 2, p. 366) seems to suppose that there is something technical in the meaning of the word 'surprise' as used in Courts of Equity; for, speaking upon what he says is technically called a case of surprise, he adds, 'which [surprise] it seems is a term for the immediate result of a certain species of mistake upon which this court will relieve,' a definition or description not very intelligible, and rather tending to obscure than to clear up the subject. In another place (ch. 3, p. 383, note) he says that surprise is often used as synonymous with fraud; but that ' they may perhaps be distinguished by the circumstance that in instances to which the term "fraud" is applied, an unjust design is presupposed; but that in those to which surprise is assigned, no fraudulent intention is to be presumed. In the former case one of the parties seeks to injure the other; in the latter both of them act under an actual misconception of the law.' Whether this explanation makes the matter much clearer may be doubted. The truth is that there does not seem anything technical or peculiar in the word 'surprise' as used in Courts of Equity. The common definition of Johnson sufficiently explains its sense. He defines it to be the act of taking unawares; the state of being taken unawares; sudden confusion or perplexity. When a Court of Equity relieves on the ground of surprise, it does so upon the ground that the party has been taken unawares; that he has acted without due deliberation, and under confused and sudden impressions.

(*a*) See Jordan *v.* Stevens, 51 Maine, 78; Freeman *v.* Curtis, Ib. 140; Forman *v.* Wright, 11 C. B. 481, 492 (innocent misrepresentation of law); Carley *v.* Lewis, 24 Ind. 23; Tyson *v.* Tyson, 31 Md. 134.

121. It has been laid down as unquestionable doctrine, that if a party acting in ignorance of a plain and settled principle of law is induced to give up a portion of his indisputable property to another under the name of a compromise, a Court of Equity will relieve him from the effect of his mistake.[1](a) But where a doubtful question arises, such as a question respecting the true construction of a will, a different rule prevails; and a compromise fairly entered into with due deliberation will be upheld in a Court of Equity as reasonable in itself to terminate the differences by dividing the stake, and as supported by principles of public policy.[2]

122. In regard to the first proposition the terms in which it is expressed have the material qualification that the party has upon plain and settled principles of law a clear title, and yet is in gross ignorance that he possesses any title whatsoever. Thus in England, if the eldest son who is heir at law of all the undisposed-of

---

The case of Evans *v.* Llewellyn, 2 Bro. Ch. R. 150, is a direct authority to this very view of the matter. There may be cases where the word 'surprise' is used in a more lax sense, and where it is deemed presumptive of, or approaching to, fraud. (1 Fonbl. Eq. B. 1, ch. 2, § 8, p. 125; Earl of Bath and Montague's Case, 3 Ch. Cas. 56, 74, 103, 114.) But it will always be found that the true use of it is where something has been done which was unexpected, and operated to mislead or confuse the parties on the sudden, and on that account has been deemed a fraud. See Earl of Bath and Montague's Case, 3 Ch. Ca. 56, 74, 114; Irnham *v.* Child, 1 Bro. Ch. 92; Marquis of Townshend *v.* Stangroom, 6 Ves. 327, 338; Twining *v.* Morrice, 2 Bro. Ch. R. 326; Willan *v.* Willan, 16 Ves. 81, 86, 87. In Evans *v.* Llewellyn, 1 Cox, R. 340, the Master of the Rolls, adverting to the cases of surprise where an undue advantage is taken of the party's situation, said: 'The cases of infants dealing with guardians, of sons with fathers, all proceed upon the same general principles and establish this, that if the party is in a situation in which he is not a free agent, and is not equal to protecting himself, this court will protect him. See 1 Fonbl. Eq. B. 1, ch. 2, § 8. See post, § 234, § 235 and note (1), §§ 236, 237, 238, 239, 240, 242.

[1] Naylor *v.* Winch, 1 Sim. & Stu. 555. See also 1 Ves. 126; Moseley, R. 364; 2 Jac. & Walk. 205; Leonard *v.* Leonard, 2 B. & Beatt. 180; Dunnage *v.* White, 1 Swanst. 137. See Hunt *v.* Rousmaniere, 8 Wheat., R. 211 to 215; s. c. 1 Peters, Sup. C. R. 1, 15, 16; Gudon *v.* Gudon, 3 Swanst. 400. In the very case in which this doctrine is laid down in such general terms, relief was denied because the claim was doubtful, and the compromise was after due deliberation. Naylor *v.* Winch, 1 Sim. & Stu. 555. Is there any distinction between ignorance of a principle of law and mistake of a principle of law as to this point? See 1 Madd. Ch. Pr. 61.

[2] Ibid; Pickering *v.* Pickering, 2 Beavan, R. 31, 56.

(a) Whelen's App. 70 Penn. St. 410.

fee-simple estates of his ancestor, should, in gross ignorance of the law, knowing however that he was the eldest son, agree to divide the estates with a younger brother, such an agreement, executed or unexecuted, would be held in a Court of Equity invalid, and relief would be accordingly granted. In a case thus strongly put there may be ingredients which would give a coloring to the case independent of the mere ignorance of the law. If the younger son were not equally ignorant, there would be much ground to suspect fraud, imposition, misrepresentation, or undue influence on his part.[1] And if he were equally ignorant, the case would exhibit such a gross mistake of rights as would lead to the conclusion of such great mental imbecility, or surprise, or blind and credulous confidence on the part of the eldest son, as might fairly entitle him to the protection of a Court of Equity upon general principles.[2] Indeed where the party acts upon the misapprehension that he has no title at all in the property, it seems to involve in some measure a mistake of fact, that is, of the fact of ownership arising from a mistake of law. A party can hardly be said to intend to part with a right or title of whose existence he is wholly ignorant; and if he does not so intend, a Court of Equity will in ordinary cases relieve him from the legal effect of instruments which surrender such unsuspected right or title.[3]

[1] Jeremy on Eq. Jurisd. Pt. 2, ch. 2, p. 366; Leonard v. Leonard, 2 B. & Beatt. 182.

[2] See Hunt v. Rousmaniere, 8 Wheat. R. 211, 212, 214; s. c. 1 Peters, Sup. C. R. 15, 16; s. c. 2 Mason, R. 342; 3 Mason, R. 294. See Ayliffe's Pand. B. 2, tit. 15, p. 116.

[3] See Ramsden v. Hylton, 2 Ves. 304; 2 Meriv. R. 269. I am aware that generally where the facts are known the mistake of the title of heirship is treated as a mistake of law. Indeed in the civil law it is put as the most prominent illustration of the distinction between ignorance of fact and ignorance of law. 'Si quis nesciat se cognatum esse, interdum in jure, interdum in facto, errat. Nam si et liberum se esse, et ex quibus natus sit, sciat, jura autem cognationis habere se nesciat, in jure errat. At si quis forte expositus, quorum parentum esset, ignoret, fortasse et serviat alicui, putans se servum esse; in facto, magis quam in jure errat.' Dig. Lib. 22, tit. 6, l. 1, § 2; Pothier, Pand. Lib. 22, tit. 6, § 1, n. 1; 1 Domat, Civil Law, B. 1, tit. 18, § 1, n. 4. Is ownership or heirship a conclusion of law, or of fact, or a mixed result of both? Is title to an estate a fact or not? Is ignorance of the title when all the facts on which it legally depends are known, ignorance of a fact, or of law? Mr. Powell puts the case of Lansdowne v. Lansdowne (Moseley, R. 364) as a case of misrepresentation of a fact, that is, that the party was not heir, when in fact he was heir. See 2 Powell on Contracts, 196. An error of law, in relation to

123. One of the earliest cases on this subject is Turner *v.* Turner (in 31 Car. 2),[1] where the plaintiff's father had lent a sum on mortgage to A, who mortgaged lands to the father and his heirs with a proviso that on payment of the money to the father or his *heirs* the premises were to be reconveyed to A. The plaintiff was executor of his father, and claimed the mortgage as vesting in the executor and not in the heirs. The defendant was the son and heir at law of the plaintiff's eldest brother, and set up a release of this mortgage and an allotment of it to him upon an agreement made among the heirs for a division of the personal estate and a subsequent receipt of the mortgage by him. The plaintiff insisted that at the time of the release he looked on the mortgage as belonging to the defendant as heir at law, and knew not his own title thereto; and that the mortgage was worth £8,000, and the shares on the division only £250 apiece. The Lord Chancellor (Lord Nottingham) relieved the plaintiff, stating that the plaintiff had an undoubted right to the mortgaged premises. This case is reported without any statement of the grounds of the decision, so that it is impossible now to ascertain them. There may have been surprise, or imposition, or undue influence; or the defendant might have well known the plaintiff's rights, and suppressed his own knowledge of them. If it proceeded upon the naked ground of a mistake of law, it is not easily reconcilable with other cases. But if it proceeded upon the ground that the plaintiff had no knowledge of his title to the mortgage, and therefore did not intend to release any title to it, the release might well be relieved against as going beyond the intentions of the parties upon a mutual mistake of the law. It might then be deemed in some sort a mistake of fact as well as of law. It was certainly a plain mistake of the settled law; and if both parties acted under a mutual misconception of their actual rights, they could not justly be said to have intended what they did. Mutual misapprehension of

heirship, is not, in the civil law, always fatal to the party. It will not deprive him of a right resulting from his heirship; as if a nephew accounts with an uncle for the whole effects of a deceased brother upon the mistake of law that the uncle was sole heir, he shall be restored to his rights. 1 Domat, Civil Law, B. 1, tit. 18, § 1, n. 15. The rule of the Civil Law is, 'Juris ignorantia non prodest adquirere volentibus; suum vero petentibus non nocet.' Dig. Lib. 22, tit. 6, l. 7.

[1] 2 Rep. in Ch. 81 [154].

124. In Bingham *v.* Bingham [2] there was a devise by A to his eldest son and heir B in fee tail, limiting the reversion to his own right heirs. B left no issue and devised the estate to the plaintiff. The defendant had brought an ejectment for the estate under the will, and the plaintiff purchased the estate of the defendant for £80, under a mistake of law that the devise to him by B could not convey the fee. Having paid the purchase-money, he now brought his bill to have it refunded, alleging in the bill that he was ignorant of the law, and persuaded by the defendant, and his scrivener and conveyancer, that B had no power to make the devise. The Master of the Rolls, sitting for Lord Hardwicke, granted the relief, saying that though no fraud appeared and the defendant apprehended he had a right, yet there was a plain mistake such as the court was warranted to relieve against. It is certainly not very easy to reconcile this case with the general doctrine already stated. It is admitted by the report that the defendant supposed he had a right; and indeed it was probably a case of a family compromise upon a doubted if not a doubtful right, and a mutual claim and a mutual ignorance of the law. If so, it trenches upon that class of cases, and is inconsistent with them. If on the other hand the defendant's title was adverse and not a family controversy, still if the agreement was fairly entered into by the contending parties, it is difficult to perceive why it should have been set aside merely because in the event the title turned out to be in the plaintiff.[3] There were probably some circumstances in the case material to the decision which have not reached us; otherwise it would conflict with other cases already cited.[4]

[1] Willan *v.* Willan, 16 Ves. 81, 82, 85.
[2] 1 Ves. 126; Belt's Sup. 79. See Leonard *v.* Leonard, 2 B. & Beatt. 183.
[3] See Leonard *v.* Leonard, 2 B. & Beatt. 171, 180, 182.
[4] Mr. Belt, in his Supplement (p. 79), has given a more full account of the facts of the case, from the Register's book, which I have followed. As a family compromise, or a compromise with a stranger, claiming an adverse right under a mutual mistake, but in good faith, it is difficult to find any support for it in other authorities. See Stockley *v.* Stockley, 1 V. & B. 23; Cory *v.* Cory, 1 Ves. 19; Gordon *v.* Gordon, 3 Swanston, R. 463, 467, 471, 474, 477; Cann *v.* Cann, 1 P. Will. 723; 1 Ves. & B. 30; Naylor *v.* Winch, 1 Sim. & Stu. 564, 565; Leonard *v.* Leonard, 2 B. & Beatt. 171, 180, 182. The case of Corking *v.* Pratt (1 Ves. 400, and Belt's Supplement, 176) seems to have turned upon

125. The case of Lansdowne *v.* Lansdowne [1] was to the following effect: The plaintiff, who was heir at law and son of the eldest brother, had a controversy with his uncle (who was the youngest brother), whether he or his uncle was heir to the estate of another deceased brother of his uncle; and they consulted one Hughes, who was a schoolmaster and their neighbor, and he gave it as his opinion, upon examining the Clerk's Remembrancer, that the uncle had the right, because lands could not ascend; upon which the plaintiff and his uncle agreed to divide the lands between them, and in pursuance of this agreement they executed first a bond, and then conveyances of the shares fixed on for each. The plaintiff sought to be relieved against these instruments, alleging in his bill that he had been surprised and imposed upon by Hughes and his uncle. The uncle being dead, his son and Hughes were made defendants to the bill; and Hughes in his answer admitted that he had given the opinion, being misled by the book, and that he had recommended the parties to take further advice; but that the plaintiff had afterwards told him that if his uncle would, he would agree to share the land between them, let it be whose right it would, and thereby prevent all disputes and lawsuits. Upon which Hughes prepared the papers, and they were executed accordingly. Lord Chancellor King

a mistake, not of law, but of fact. But then it does not appear that at the time either party knew what the personal estate would ultimately amount to, and it might have been a matter of great doubt, and a compromise accordingly made. If so, could it be afterwards set aside? (See Burt *v.* Barlow, 3 Bro. Ch. R. 451; Leonard *v.* Leonard, 2 B. & Beatt. 171, 180.) If the case turned upon the ground of a suppression of facts, known to the mother and not to the daughter, or upon undue influence or imposition, there could be little difficulty in supporting it. The case of Ramsden *v.* Hylton (2 Ves. 304; Belt's Supplement, 350) turned upon other considerations. How can the case of Bingham *v.* Bingham, as a case standing upon general principles, be reconciled with Mildmay *v.* Hungerford (2 Vern. 243) and Pullen *v.* Ready (2 Atk. 587, 591)? Lord Cottenham, in Stewart *v.* Stewart, 6 Clark & Finell. R. 968, said: 'Bingham *v.* Bingham was not a case of compromise, but of a sale by the defendant to the plaintiff of an estate which was already his; and a return of the purchase-money was decreed at the Rolls upon the ground of mistake. That case therefore does not bear directly upon the present. If it were necessary to consider the principle of that decree, it might not be easy to distinguish that case from any other purchase in which the vendor turns out to have had no title. In both there is a mistake, and the effect of it in both is, that the vendor receives and the purchaser pays money without the intended equivalent.' See also Evans *v.* Llewellyn, 2 Bro. Ch. R. 150.

[1] Moseley, R. 364; s. c. 2 Jac. & Walk. 205.

decreed that it appeared that the bond and conveyances 'were obtained by mistake and misrepresentation of the law,' and ordered them to be given up to be cancelled. It was upon this occasion that his Lordship is reported to have used the language already quoted, that the maxim that ignorance of the law was no excuse, did not apply to civil cases; but if his judgment proceeded upon that ground, it was (as has been already stated) manifestly erroneous. This case has been questioned on several occasions, and is certainly open to much criticism. It appears to have been a case of a family dispute and compromise made by parties equally innocent, and upon a doubted question of title under a mutual mistake of the law. Under such circumstances there is great difficulty in sustaining it in point of principle or authority. It was most probably decided by Lord King on the untenable ground already suggested. If indeed it proceeded upon the ground of undue confidence in Hughes's opinion, or was induced by his undue persuasions and influence, such a misrepresentation of the law by him might, under such circumstances, furnish a reason for relief.[1] But that does not appear in any report of the case.[2]

[1] See Fitzgerald *v.* Peck, 4 Littell, 127.

[2] The case of Lansdowne *v.* Lansdowne has been doubted on several occasions. The report in 2 Jac. & Walk. 205 is more full than that in Moseley, though to the same effect. The decree was that the agreement 'was obtained by a mistake and misrepresentation of the law,' which under certain circumstances might furnish a ground for relief. The case was closely criticised and doubted by the Supreme Court of the United States, in Hunt *v.* Rousmaniere, 8 Wheat. R. 214, 215, and 1 Peters, Sup. C. R. 15, 16. The court seemed to think it might be explicable upon the ground that the plaintiff was ignorant of the fact that he was the eldest son; or, if he mistook his legal rights, that he was imposed upon by some unfair representations of his better-informed opponent; or that his ignorance of the law of primogeniture demonstrated such mental imbecility as would entitle him to relief. There is an apparent error in the suggestion of the Supreme Court that there was an award in the case. Hughes did not act as an arbitrator, but was merely consulted as a friend. If there had been a plain mistake of the law by an arbitrator, that would of itself in many cases have been a ground of relief. Corneforth *v.* Geer, 2 Vern. 705; Ridout *v.* Pain, 3 Atk. 494. Mr. Powell (on Contracts, vol. 2, p. 196) puts the case of Lansdowne *v.* Lansdowne as an illustration of a mistake of a fact, that is, of heirship. In Stewart *v.* Stewart, 6 Clark & Finnell. R. 966, Lord Cottenham made the following remarks: 'Lansdowne *v.* Lansdowne is a very strong case of setting aside a compromise, and a conveyance in pursuance of it; but it is impossible to ascertain the facts. It appears that fraud was alleged against the younger brother; and Hughes, who had advised upon the rights of the two, was made a defendant, which could only have been done upon

126. The distinction between cases of mistake of a plain and settled principle of law and cases of mistake of a principle of law not plain to persons generally, but which is yet constructively certain as a foundation of title, is not of itself very intelligible, or practically speaking very easy of application considered as an independent element of decision. In contemplation of law all its rules and principles are deemed certain, although they have not as yet been recognized by public adjudications. This doctrine proceeds upon the theoretical ground that ' Id certum est quod certum reddi potest; ' and that decisions do not make the law but only promulgate it. Besides, what are to be deemed plain and settled principles? Are they such as have been long and uniformly established by adjudications only, or is a single decision sufficient? What degree of clearness constitutes the line of demarcation? If there have been decisions different ways at different times, which is to prevail?[1] If a majority of the profession hold one doctrine and a minority another, is the rule to be deemed doubtful, or is it to be deemed certain?

---

an imputation of fraud, and in Moseley's Report it is said that the Lord Chancellor's decree proceeded upon the ground of mistake and misrepresentation. But Mr. Jacob's extract from the Registrar's book is no doubt correct in stating the ground to be "misrepresentation of the law." It is however to be observed that in Moseley the eldest son is reported to have said that he would rather divide the estate than go to law, though he had the right; and that the court is represented to have said that the maxim "ignorantia juris non excusat" did not hold in civil cases, which, it will be seen, has not been a doctrine recognized in modern cases.' He afterwards added: ' Bilbie v. Lumley is directly opposed to the doctrine upon which Lansdowne v. Lansdowne is stated in Moseley to have been decided; for it was held that "money paid by one with full knowledge (or the means of such knowledge in his hands) of all the circumstances cannot be recovered back again on account of such payment having been made under an ignorance of the law."' Stewart v. Stewart, 6 Clark & Finnell. 969.(a)

[1] There is much masculine force in the reasoning of Mr. Chancellor Kent on this subject, in Lyon v. Richmond, 2 John. Ch. R. 60. ' The court,' says he, ' do not undertake to relieve parties from their acts and deeds fairly done, though under a mistake of the law. Every man is to be charged, at his peril, with a knowledge of the law. There is no other principle which is safe and practicable in the common intercourse of mankind. And to suffer a subsequent judicial decision in any one given case on a point of law to open or annul everything that has been done in other cases of the like kind for years before under a different understanding of the law, would lead to the most mischievous consequences.'

(a) See note to § 111, at p. 118.

127. Take the case commonly put on this head of the construction of a will. Every person is presumed to know the law; and though opinions may differ upon the construction of the will before an adjudication is made, yet when it is made it is supposed always to have been certain. It may have been a question at the bar whether a devise was an estate for life, or in tail, or in fee simple. But when the court has once decided it to be the one or the other, the title is always supposed to have been fixed and certain in the party from the beginning. It will furnish a sufficient title to maintain a bill for the specific performance of a contract of sale of that title.

128. Where there is a plain and established doctrine on the subject so generally known and of such constant occurrence as to be understood by the community at large as a rule of property, such as the common canons of descent, there a mistake in ignorance of the law, and of title founded on it, may well give rise to a presumption that there has been some undue influence, imposition, mental imbecility, surprise, or confidence abused. But in such cases the mistake of the law is not the foundation of the relief, but it is the medium of proof to establish some other proper ground of relief.

129. Lord Eldon, in a case of a family agreement, seems to have thought that there might be a distinction between cases where there is a doubt raised between the parties as to their rights, and a compromise is made upon the footing of that doubt, and cases where the parties act upon a supposition of right in one of the parties, without a doubt upon it, under a mistake of law. The former might be held obligatory, when the latter ought not to be.[1] But his Lordship admitted that the doctrine attributed to Lord Macclesfield was otherwise, denying the distinction, and giving equal validity to agreements entered into upon a supposition of a right, and of a doubtful right.[2] It may be gathered

---

[1] Stockley v. Stockley, 1 V. & Beames, 31.

[2] Ibid. Cann v. Cann, 1 P. Will. 727; Stapilton v. Stapilton, 1 Atk. 10. Lord Eldon was here speaking in the case of a family agreement, and not between strangers; but it is by no means certain that he meant to limit his observations to such cases. In Dunnage v. White, 1 Swanst. R. 137, 151, Sir Thomas Plumer said: ' It is then insisted that the deed may be supported as a family arrangement, according to the doctrine of Stapilton v. Stapilton and Cann v. Cann. Undoubtedly parties entitled in different events may, while the uncertainty exists, each taking his chance, effect a valid compromise. In

however from these remarks that Lord Eldon's own opinion was that an agreement made or act done not upon a doubt of title, but upon ignorance of any title in the party, ought not to be obligatory upon him, although arising solely from a mistake of law.

130. There may be a solid ground for a distinction between cases where a party acts or agrees in ignorance of any title in him, or upon the supposition of a clear title in another, and cases where there is a doubt or controversy or litigation between parties as to their respective rights.[1] In the former cases (as has

---

Stapilton v. Stapilton, the legitimacy of the eldest son was doubtful. That was a question proper to be so settled; and the settlement was a consideration which gave effect to the deed.' In Stewart v. Stewart, 6 Clark & Finnell. R. 967, Lord Cottenham used the following language: 'In Stapilton v. Stapilton, Henry, the eldest son, being illegitimate, Philip, the second son, received no consideration for the arrangement by which the estates of which Philip was tenant in tail, subject to his father's life, were divided between them; but Lord Hardwicke, approving the doctrine of Lord Macclesfield in Cann v. Cann, said, " that an agreement entered into upon a supposition of a right, or of a doubtful right, though it after comes out that the right was on the other side, shall be binding, and the right shall not prevail against the agreement of parties; for the right must always be on the one side or the other, and therefore the compromise of a doubtful right is a sufficient foundation for an agreement;" and he therefore maintained the arrangement, and decreed a performance of what remained to be done to carry it into effect.'

[1] In Evans v. Llewellyn (2 Bro. Ch. R. 150; s. c. 1 Cox, R. 333), the Master of the Rolls (Lord Kenyon) did not seem to recognize any such distinction. The decree in that case seems to have been put upon the mere ground of surprise. But from Mr. Cox's Report it would seem that the party was not ignorant of the facts, or even of the law of his title. Mr. Brown represents the case a little differently. In Lang v. The Bank of the United States, Mr. Chief Justice Shippen, speaking of the effect of a mistake of right of a party, and that he was not barred by it, said: 'The case of Penn v. Lord Baltimore is decisive to this point. I was present at the argument half a century ago, and heard Lord Hardwicke say, though it is not mentioned in the Report, that if Lord Baltimore had made the agreement in question, under a mistake of his right to another degree of latitude, he ought to be relieved; but that he was not mistaken.' The cases of Ramsden v. Hylton, 2 Ves. 304, and Farewell v. Coker, cited 2 Meriv. R. 269, were upon mistakes of fact, not of law; or rather attempts were there made to extend the releases to property never intended by the parties. In Neale v. Neale, 1 Keen, R. 672, 683, A and B having an apparent title to copyhold lands as tenants in common in fee under the will of their father, entered into a parol agreement to make partition of the devised lands, and divided them accordingly, A, the elder brother, taking the larger share, a doubt being entertained whether their father had a right to devise the lands. A was in fact at the time of the agreement tenant in tail under the limitation, under a surrender made by his

been already suggested) the party seems to labor in some sort under a mistake of fact as well as of law.[1] He supposes as a matter of fact that he has no title, and that the other party has a title to the property. He does not intend to release or surrender his title, but the act or agreement proceeds upon the supposition that he has none. Lord Macclesfield, in the very case in which the language already cited[2] is attributed to him, is reported to have said that if the party releasing is ignorant of his right to the estate, or if his right is concealed from him by the person to whom the release is made, there would be good reasons for setting aside the release.[3] But (he added) the mere fact that the party making the release had the right and was controverting it with the other party can furnish no ground to set aside the release; for by the same reason there could be no such thing as compromising a suit, nor room for any accommodation. Every release supposes the party making it to have a right.[4]

131. The whole doctrine of the validity of compromises of doubtful rights rests on this foundation.[5] If such compromises are otherwise unobjectionable they will be binding, and the right will not prevail against the agreement of the parties; for the right must always be on one side or the other, and there

grandfather. After A's death, B, having discovered his own title as tenant in tail, repudiated the agreement, and brought an ejectment to recover the whole estate. On a bill filed by the devisee of A, the court, upon the ground on which it supports family arrangements, supported the partition, and decreed B to do all necessary acts to bar the entail.

[1] Ante, § 129. And see 2 Powell on Contracts, p. 196; Dunnage v. White, 1 Swanst. 137, 151; Harvey v. Cooke, 4 Russell, R. 34.

[2] Ante, § 122.

[3] Cann v. Cann, 1 P. Will. 727; Ramsden v. Hylton, 2 Ves. 304.

[4] 1 P. Will. 727. In Leonard v. Leonard (2 B. & Beatt. 180), Lord Manners takes notice of a distinction between a mere release and a deed of compromise. The former supposes that the parties know their rights, and that one surrenders his rights to the other; in the latter, that both parties are ignorant of their rights, and the agreement is founded in that ignorance, and that the party surrendering may in truth have nothing to surrender. But is it true in all cases that a release presupposes a right? Lord Redesdale has said that the accepting of a release is in no case an acknowledgment that a right existed in the releasor. It amounts only to this, — I give you so much for not seeking to disturb me. Underwood v. Lord Courtown, 2 Sch. & Lefr. 67.

[5] See the dictum of Lord Hardwicke in Brown v. Pring, 1 Ves. 407, 408, as to compromises made by parties with their eyes open and rightly informed.

would be an end of compromises if they might be overthrown upon any subsequent ascertainment of rights contrary thereto.[1](a) If therefore a compromise of a doubtful right is fairly made between parties, its validity cannot depend upon any future adjudication of that right.[2] And where compromises of this sort are fairly entered into, whether the uncertainty rests upon a doubt of fact or a doubt in point of law, if both parties are in the same ignorance the compromise is equally binding, and cannot be affected by any subsequent investigation and result.[3] But if the parties are not mutually ignorant, the case admits of a very different consideration, whether the ignorance be of a matter of fact or of law.[4] It has been emphatically said that no man can doubt

[1] Cann v. Cann, 1 P. Will. 727; Stapilton v. Stapilton, 1 Atk. 10; Stockley v. Stockley, 1 V. & B. 29, 31; Naylor v. Winch, 1 Sim. & Stu. 555; Goodman v. Sayers, 2 Jac. & Walk. 263; Pickering v. Pickering, 2 Beavan, R. 31, 56.

[2] Leonard v. Leonard, 2 Ball & Beatt. 179, 180; Shotwell v. Murray, 1 John. Ch. R. 516; Lyon v. Lyon, 2 John. Ch. R. 51; Dunnage v. White, 1 Swanst. 151, 152; Harvey v. Cooke, 4 Russell, 34; Stewart v. Stewart, 6 Clark & Finnell. 969.

[3] Leonard v. Leonard, 2 Ball & Beatt. 179, 180. See Gordon v. Gordon, 3 Swanst. 470; Pickering v. Pickering, 2 Beavan, R. 31, 56; Gossmour v. Pigge, The (English) Jurist, June 22, 1844, p. 526.

[4] Id. 180, 182; Gordon v. Gordon, 3 Swanst. R. 400, 467, 470, 473, 476; Stewart v. Stewart, 6 Clark & Finnell. 969. See also a case cited by Lord Thurlow in Mortimer v. Capper, 1 Bro. Ch. R. 158. In respect to compromises, it is often laid down that they must be reasonable. (Stapilton v. Stapilton, 1 Atk. 10.) By this we are not to understand that the consideration is adequate and there is no great inequality, but that the circumstances are such as to demonstrate that no undue advantage was taken by either party of the other. Thus in a case of compromise of doubtful rights under a will, the Master of the Rolls (Sir R. P. Arden) said: ' It (the agreement) must be reasonable. No man can doubt that this court will never hold parties acting upon their rights, doubts arising as to those rights, to be bound, unless they act with a full knowledge of all the doubts and difficulties that arise. But if parties will, with full knowledge of them, act upon them, though it turns out that one gains a great advantage, if the agreement was fair and reasonable at the time it shall be binding. There was a case before the Lord Chancellor, who spoke to me upon it, in which it was held that the court will enforce such an agreement, though it turns out that the parties were mistaken in point of law, *even supposing counsel's opinion was wrong.* Gibbons v. Caunt, 4 Ves. 849. See Stapilton v. Stapilton, 2 Atk. 10; Naylor v. Winch, 1 Sim. & Stu. 555; Neale v. Neale, 1 Keen, R. 672, 683; Stewart v. Stewart, 6 Clark & Finnell. 969.

(a) Stover v. Mitchell, 45 Ill. 213; Morris v. Munroe, 30 Ga. 630; Ex parte Lucy, 4 DeG. M. & G. 356; Stewart v. Stewart, 6 Clark & F. 911, 967.

that the Court of Chancery will never hold parties acting upon their rights to be bound unless they act with full knowledge of all the doubts and difficulties that do arise. But if parties will with full knowledge act upon them, though it turns out that one gains an advantage from a mistake in point of law, yet if the agreement was reasonable and fair at the time it shall be binding.[1] And transactions are not in the eye of a Court of Equity to be treated as binding even as family arrangements, where the doubts existing as to the rights alleged to be compromised are not presented to the mind of the party interested.[2]

132. There are cases of family compromises where upon principles of policy, for the honor or peace of families, the doctrine sustaining compromises has been carried further. And it has been truly remarked that in such family arrangements the Court of Chancery has administered an equity which is not applied to agreements generally.[3] (a) Such compromises fairly and reasonably made, (b) to save the honor of a family, as in case of suspected illegitimacy, to prevent family disputes and family forfeitures, are upheld with a strong hand, and are binding when in cases between mere strangers the like agreements would not

---

[1] Gibbons v. Caunt, 4 Ves. R. 849. See also Dunnage v. White, 1 Swanst. R. 137. See Stewart v. Stewart, 6 Clark & Finnell. 969; Pickering v. Pickering, 2 Beavan, R. 31, 56. In this case Lord Langdale said: 'When parties whose rights are questionable have equal knowledge of facts and equal means of ascertaining what their rights really are, and they fairly endeavor to settle their respective claims among themselves, every court must feel disposed to support the conclusions or agreements to which they may fairly come at the time, and that notwithstanding the subsequent discovery of some common error; and if in this case the parties had been on equal terms, the agreement might have been supported. But the parties were not on equal terms; and moreover I am of opinion that under the circumstances it was the duty of the defendant to see that the nature of the transaction was fully explained to his mother, and to see that she was placed in a situation to have the question properly considered on her behalf; and whatever may have been his intention in this respect (for I do not think it necessary to impute to him an intentional fraud throughout the transaction), I am of opinion that he did not perform this duty: and on the whole it appears to me that he is not entitled to the benefit of the settled account, and that the agreement must be set aside.'

[2] Henley v. Cooke, 4 Russell, R. 34.

[3] Stockley v. Stockley, 1 V. & Beames, 29.

(a) See Hurlbut v. Phelps, 30 Conn. 42, 50; Williams v. Sand, 3 Cold. 533.

(b) On full disclosure of material facts by each party to the other.

Smith v. Pincombe, 16 Jur. 205; s. c. 10 Eng. L. & E. 50. See Groves v. Perkins, 6 Sim. 576.

be enforced.[1] Thus it has been said that if on the death of a person seised in fee a dispute arises who is heir, and there is room for a rational doubt as to that fact, and the parties deal with each other openly and fairly, investigating the subject for themselves, and each communicating to the other all that he knows and is informed of, and at length they agree to distribute the property, under the notion that the elder claimant is illegitimate, although it turns out afterwards that he is legitimate, there the court will not disturb such an arrangement merely because the fact of legitimacy is subsequently established.[2] Yet in such a case the party acts under a mistake of fact. In cases of ignorance of title upon a plain mistake of the law there seems little room to distinguish between family compromises and others.

132 a. Thus where a father, being heir presumptive to A B, who was then supposed to be a lunatic, and being under an apprehension that unfair means might be resorted to, in the then state of mind of A B, to deprive the family of the succession to the estate, agreed with his eldest son that the son should sue out a commission of lunacy against A B, and carry on such other suits and law proceedings as should be necessary in the name of the father, at the expense of the son, in consideration of which agreement and natural love and affection the father covenanted that after the death of A B the estates which should thereupon descend to him should be conveyed to himself for life, remainder to his son for life, with remainder to his first and other sons in tail male. The son at his own expense and in the name of his father sued out the commission under which A B was found a lunatic, who soon afterwards died; whereupon the father succeeded as heir to the lunatic's estate. Upon a bill filed by the son to carry into effect this agreement, a specific performance was decreed; and it was held that the agreement was not volun-

[1] Stapilton *v.* Stapilton, 1 Atk. 210; Cann *v.* Cann, 1 P. Will. 727; Stockley *v.* Stockley, 1 V. & Beames, 30, 31; Persse *v.* Persse, 1 West, R. in House of Lords, 110; Cory *v.* Cory, 1 Ves. 19; Leonard *v.* Leonard, 2 B. & Beatt. 171, 180; 1 Fonbl. Eq. B. 1, ch. 2, § 7, note (*r*); Gordon *v.* Gordon, 3 Swanst. 463, 470, 473, 476; Dunnage *v.* White, 1 Swanst. 137, 151; Harvey *v.* Cooke, 4 Russell, R. 34. Frank *v.* Frank (1 Ch. Cas. 84) is generally supposed to have been decided upon this head. But it was apparently a case of misrepresentation; and Lord Manners has doubted its authority. Leonard *v.* Leonard, 2 B. & Beatt. R. 182, 183. Cory *v.* Cory, 1 Ves. 19, is very difficult to maintain; for the party was drunk at the time of the agreement.

[2] Gordon *v.* Gordon, 3 Swanst. R. 476; Id. 463.

tary, void for champerty or maintenance, or illegal either for want of mutuality or as being a fraud upon the great seal in lunacy; and considering the ages and situations of the parties, the father being sixty-two and the lunatic forty, and the objects to be gained by the prosecution of the commission of lunacy, that the consideration for the deed was not inadequate, but that deeds for carrying into effect family arrangements are exempt from the rules which affect other deeds, the consideration being composed partly of value and partly of love and affection.[1]

133. And where there is a mixture of mistake of title, gross personal ignorance, liability to imposition, habitual intoxication, and want of professional advice, there has been manifested a strong disinclination of Courts of Equity to sustain even family settlements. It was upon this sort of mixed ground that it was held in a recent case that a deed executed by the members of a family to determine their interests under the will and partial intestacy of an ancestor ought not to be enforced. It appeared on the face of the deed that the parties did not understand their rights or the nature of the transaction, and that the heir surrendered an unimpeachable title without consideration. Evidence was also given of his gross ignorance, habitual intoxication, and want of professional advice. But there was no sufficient proof of fraud or undue influence, and there had been an acquiescence of five years.[2]

134. Cases of surprise, mixed up with a mistake of law, stand upon a ground peculiar to themselves and independent of the general doctrine. In such cases the agreements or acts are unadvised and improvident, and without due deliberation; and therefore they are held invalid upon the common principle adopted by Courts of Equity to protect those who are unable to protect themselves, and of whom an undue advantage is taken.[3] Where the surprise is mutual there is of course a still stronger ground to interfere; for neither party has intended what has

---

[1] Persse v. Persse, 1 West, Rep. in H. of Lords, p. 110; s. c. 7 Clark & Finnell. R. 279.
[2] Dunnage v. White, 1 Swanst. R. 137.
[3] See Evans v. Llewellyn, 1 Cox, R. 333; s. c. 2 Bro. Ch. 150; Marquis of Townshend v. Stangroom, 6 Ves. 333, 338; Chesterfield v. Janssen, 2 Ves. 155, 156; Ormond v. Hutchinson, 13 Ves. 51.

been done. They have misunderstood the effect of their own agreements or acts, or have presupposed some facts or rights existing as the basis of their proceedings which in truth did not exist. Contracts made in mutual error, under circumstances material to their character and consequences, seem upon general principles invalid.[1] 'Non videntur, qui errant, consentire,' is a rule of the civil law;[2] and it is founded in common sense and common justice. But in its application it is material to distinguish between error in circumstances which do not influence the contract, and error in circumstances which induce the contract.[3]

135. There are also cases of peculiar trust and confidence, and relation between the parties, which give rise to a qualification of the general doctrine. Thus where a mortgagor had mortgaged an estate to a mortgagee who was his attorney, and in settling an account with the latter he had allowed him a poundage for having received the rents of the estate in ignorance of the law that a mortgagee was not entitled to such an allowance, which was professionally known to the attorney, it was held that the allowance should be set aside. But the Master of the Rolls upon that occasion put the case upon the peculiar relation between the parties, and the duty of the attorney to have made known the law to his client, the mortgagor. He said that he did not enter into the distinction between allowances in accounts from ignorance of law and allowances from ignorance of fact; that he did not mean to say that ignorance of law will generally open an account; but that, the parties standing in this relation to each other, he would not hold the mortgagor, acting in ignorance of his rights, to have given a binding assent.[4]

136. There are also some other cases in which relief has been granted in equity apparently upon the ground of mistake of law. But they will be found upon examination rather to be cases of

---

[1] Willan v. Willan, 16 Ves. 72, 81; Cowes v. Higginson, 1 Ves. & Beames, 524, 527; Ramsden v. Hylton, 2 Ves. 304; Farewell v. Coker, 2 Meriv. R. 269.

[2] Dig. Lib. 50, tit. 17, l. 116, § 2.

[3] 1 Fonbl. Eq. B. 1, ch. 2, § 7, note (*t*); Id. note (*x*). Mr. Fonblanque has remarked that the effect of error in contracts is very well treated by Pothier, in his Treatise on Obligations, Pt. 1, ch. 1, art. 3, §§ 1, 16. See also 1 Domat, Civil Law, B. 1, tit. 1, § 5, n. 10; Id. tit. 18, § 2; and ante, § 111, note 2.

[4] Langstaffe v. Fenwick, 10 Ves. R. 405, 406.

CHAP. V.] MISTAKE. 145

defective execution of the intent of the parties from ignorance of law as to the proper mode of framing the instrument. Thus where a husband upon his marriage entered into a bond to his wife, without the intervention of trustees, to leave her a sum of money if she should survive him; the bond, although released at law by the marriage, was held good as an agreement in equity, entitling the wife to satisfaction out of the husband's assets.[1] And so, e contra, where a wife before marriage executed a bond to her husband, to convey all her lands to him in fee, it was upheld in favor of the husband after the marriage as an agreement defectively executed, to secure to the husband the land as her portion.[2]

137. We have thus gone over the principal cases which are supposed to contain contradictions of or exceptions to the general rule, that ignorance of the law with a full knowledge of the facts furnishes no ground to rescind agreements or to set aside solemn acts of the parties. Without undertaking to assert that there are none of these cases which are inconsistent with the rule, it may be affirmed that the real exceptions to it are very few, and generally stand upon some very urgent pressure of circumstances.[3] The rule prevails in England in all cases of compromises of doubtful and perhaps in all cases of doubted rights, and especially in all cases of family arrangements.[4] It is relaxed in cases where there is a total ignorance of title founded in the mistake of a plain and settled principle of law, and in cases of imposition, misrepresentation, undue influence, misplaced confidence, and surprise.[5]

[1] Acton v. Pearce, 2 Vern. R. 480; s. c. Prec. Ch. 237.
[2] Cannel v. Buckle, 2 P. Will. 243; Newl. on Contr. ch. 19, pp. 315, 346; 1 Fonbl. Eq. B. 1, ch. 1, § 7.
[3] See Eden on Injunct. ch. 2, pp. 8, 9, 10, and note (b).
[4] Stewart v. Stewart, 6 Clark & Finnell. R. 911, 966 to 971; Pickering v. Pickering, 2 Beavan, R. 31, 56.
[5] Stewart v. Stewart, 6 Clark & Finnell. R. 911, 966 to 971. The English Elementary writers on this subject treat it in a very loose and unsatisfactory manner, laying down no distinct rules when mistakes of the law are or are not relievable in equity, but contenting themselves for the most part with mere statements of the cases. Thus Mr. Maddock, after saying that a mistake of parties as to the law is not a ground for reforming a deed founded on such mistake, and that it has been doubted whether ignorance of law will entitle a party to open an account, proceeds to add that there are several cases in which a party has been relieved from the consequences of acts founded on ignorance of the law. He afterwards states that in general agreements relating to real or personal estate, if founded on mistake (not saying whether of

In America the general rule has been recognized as founded in sound wisdom and policy, and fit to be upheld with a steady confidence. And hitherto the exceptions to it (if any) will be found not to rest upon the mere foundation of a naked mistake of law, however plain and settled the principle may be, nor upon mere ignorance of title founded upon such mistake.[1]

law or fact), will for that reason be set aside. 1 Madd. Ch. Pr. 60, 61, 62. Mr. Jeremy says: 'That Ignorantia juris non excusat, ignorance of the law will not excuse, is a maxim respected in equity as well as at law.' 'A knowledge of the law is consequently presumed, and therefore no mutual explanation of it is prima facie required between the parties to a compact. If one of them should in truth be ignorant of a matter of law involved in the transaction, and the other should know him to be so, and should take advantage of the circumstance, he would, it is conceived, be guilty of a fraud; (a) and although, if both should be ignorant thereof, it would be what is technically called a case of surprise, it does not appear that this court will in any other case interfere upon a mistake of law.' Jeremy on Eq. Jurisd. 366. Mr. Fonblanque has collected many of the cases in his valuable notes; but he has not attempted to expound the true principles on which they turn or the reason of the differences. 1 Fonbl. Eq. B. 1, ch. 2, § 7, note (v). Mr. Cooper (Eq. Plead. p. 140) disposes of the whole subject with the single remark: 'On the ground of mistake, or misconception of parties, Courts of Equity have also frequently interfered in a variety of cases.' Lord Redesdale leaves it in the same unsatisfactory manner. Mitford, Eq. Pl. by Jeremy, p. 129 (edit. 1827). Mr. Newland (on Contracts in Equity, ch. 28, p. 432) says: 'Cases of plain mistake or misapprehension, though not the effect of fraud or contrivance, are entitled to the interference of the court,' without making any distinction as to law or fact, and he cites Turner v. Turner, 2 Ch. R. 81, Bingham v. Bingham, 1 Ves. 126, and Lansdowne v. Lansdowne, Moseley, 364. He then adds that it is different in compromises of doubtful rights. Lord Hardwicke is reported to have said in Langley v. Brown, 2 Atk. 202, 'that [if] a person puts a groundless and unguarded confidence in another, [it] is not a foundation in a Court of Equity to set aside a deed.' This is true in the abstract. But groundless and unguarded confidence often constitutes, with other circumstances, a most material ingredient for relief.

[1] The general rule is affirmed in Shotwell v. Murray, 1 John. Ch. R. 512, 515, and Lyon v. Richmond, 2 John. Ch. R. 51, 60, and Storrs v. Barker, 6 John. Ch. R. 169, 170. In Hunt v. Rousmaniere, 8 Wheat. R. 211, 214, 215, the court said: 'Although we do not find the naked principle that relief may be granted on account of ignorance of the law asserted in the books, we find no case in which it has been decided that a plain and acknowledged mistake in law is beyond the reach of equity.' But when the case came again before the court upon appeal, in 1 Peters, Sup. C. R. 1, 15, the court (as has been already stated in the text) said: 'We hold the general rule to be that a mistake of this character (that is, a mistake arising from ignorance of the law), is not a ground for reforming a deed founded on such mistake. And whatever excep-

(a) See Cooke v. Nathan, 16 Barb. 342, 346; editor's note to § 191, post.

138. It is matter of regret that in the present state of the law it is not practicable to present in any more definite form the

tions there may be to this rule, they are not only few in number, but they will be found to have something peculiar in their characters.' (Ante, § 116.) But the court added that it was not their intention to lay it down that there may not be cases in which a Court of Equity will relieve against a plain mistake arising from ignorance of law. Id. p. 17. In the case of Marshall *v.* Collet, 1 Younge & Coll. 238, Lord Ch. Baron Abinger said, that for mistake of law equity would not set aside a contract. See also Cockerill *v.* Cholmeley, 1 Russ. & Mylne, 418, and McCarthy *v.* Decaix, 2 Russ. & Mylne, R. 614. The question again came under the review of the Supreme Court of the United States in the case of the Bank of the United States *v.* Daniel, 12 Peters, R. 32, 55, 56, where the main question was whether a mistake of law was relievable in equity, it being stripped of all other circumstances; and the court held that it was not. On that occasion the court said: 'The main question on which relief was sought by the bill, that on which the decree below proceeded, and on which the appellees relied in this court for its affirmance, is, Can a Court of Chancery relieve against a mistake of law? In its examination we will take it for granted that the parties who took up the bill for ten thousand dollars included the damages of a thousand dollars in the eight thousand dollar note; and did so, believing the statute of Kentucky secured the penalty to the bank, and that in the construction of the statute the appellees were mistaken. Vexed as the question formerly was, and delicate as it now is from the confusion in which numerous and conflicting decisions have involved it, no discussion of cases can be gone into without hazarding the introduction of exceptions that will be likely to sap the direct principle we intend to apply. Indeed the remedial power claimed by Courts of Chancery to relieve against mistakes of law is a doctrine rather grounded upon exceptions than upon established rules. To this course of adjudication we are unwilling to yield. That mere mistakes of law are not remediable is well established, as was declared by this court in Hunt *v.* Rousmaniere, 1 Peters, 15; and we can only repeat what was there said, "that whatever exceptions there may be to the rule, they will be found few in number, and to have something peculiar in their character," and to involve other elements of decision. (1 Story's Eq. Jurisp. § 116.) What is this case, and does it turn upon any peculiarity? Griffing sold a bill to the United States Bank at Lexington for ten thousand dollars, indorsed by three of the complainants and accepted by the other, payable at New Orleans; the acceptor, J. D., was present in Kentucky when the bill was made, and there accepted it; at maturity it was protested for non-payment and returned. The debtors applied to take it up, when the creditors claimed ten per cent damages by force of the statute of Kentucky. All the parties bound to pay the bill were perfectly aware of the facts; at least, the principals, who transacted the business, had the statute before them, or were familiar with it, as we must presume, they and the bank earnestly believing (as in all probability most others believed at the time) that the ten per cent damages were due by force of the statute, and, influenced by this opinion of the law, the eight thousand dollar note was executed, including the one thousand dollars claimed for damages. Such is the case stated and supposed to exist by the complainants, stripped of all other considerations standing in the way of relief. Testing the case by the principle "that a mistake or ignorance of the law forms no ground

doctrine respecting the effect of mistakes of law, or to clear the subject from some obscurities and uncertainties which still surround it. But it may be safely affirmed upon the highest authority as a well-established doctrine, that a mere naked mistake of law, unattended with any such special circumstances as have been above suggested, will furnish no ground for the interposition of a Court of Equity; and the present disposition of Courts of Equity is to narrow rather than to enlarge the operation of exceptions.[1] It may however be added that where a judgment is fairly obtained at law upon a contract, and afterwards upon more solemn consideration of the subject the point of law upon which the cause was adjudged is otherwise decided, no relief will be granted in equity against the judgment upon the ground of mistake of the law; for that would be to open perpetual sources for renewed litigation.[2]

139. Where a bona fide purchaser for a valuable consideration without notice is concerned, equity will not interfere to grant relief in favor of a party, although he has acted in ignorance of his title upon a mistake of law; for in such a case the purchaser has at least an equal right to protection with the party laboring under the mistake.[3] And where the equities are equal, the court withholds itself from any interference between the parties.[4]

of relief from contracts fairly entered into with a full knowledge of the facts," and under circumstances repelling all presumptions of fraud, imposition, or undue advantage having been taken of the party, none of which are chargeable upon the appellants in this case, the question then is, Were the complainants entitled to relief? To which we respond decidedly in the negative.' So far then as the Courts of the United States are concerned, the question may be deemed finally at rest.

[1] Lord Cottenham, in his elaborate judgment in Stewart v. Stewart, 6 Clark & Finnell. 964 to 971, critically examined all the leading authorities upon this subject, and arrived at the same conclusion; and his opinion was confirmed by the House of Lords. Mr. Burge shows, in his learned Commentaries on Colonial and Foreign Law (vol. 3, p. 742, &c.), that the like rule prevails in the Civil Law, and in foreign countries on the Continent of Europe where the Civil Law prevails. Kelly v. Solari, 9 Mees. & Wels. R. 54, 57, 58, contains a like recognition of the doctrine by Lord Abinger.

[2] Mitf. Pl. Eq. by Jeremy, 131, 132; Lyon v. Richmond, 2 John. Ch. R. 51.

[3] Ante, § 64 c, § 108; Post, §§ 154, 165, 381, 409, 434, 436.

[4] See Malden v. Merrill, 2 Atk. 8; Storrs v. Barker, 6 John. Ch. R. 166, 169, 170. In the Civil Law there is much discussion as to the effect of error of law; and no inconsiderable embarrassment exists in stating in what cases of error in law the party is relievable and in what not. It is certain that a

140. In regard to the other class of mistakes, that is, mistakes of fact, there is not so much difficulty.(*a*) The general rule is,

wide distinction was made between the operation of errors of law and errors of fact. 'In omni parte error in jure non eodem loco, quo facti ignorantia, haberi debebit; cum jus finitum et possit esse, et debeat; facti interpretatio plerumque etiam prudentissimos fallat.' Dig. Lib. 22, tit. 6, l. 2. Hence in many cases error of law will prejudice a party in regard to his rights; but not error of fact unless in cases of gross negligence. Dig. Lib. 22, tit. 6, l. 7. The general rule of the Civil Law seems to be, that error of law shall not profit those who are desirous of acquiring an advantage or right, nor shall it prejudice those who are seeking their own right. 'Juris ignorantia non prodest adquirere volentibus; suum vero petentibus non nocet.' Dig. Lib. 22, tit. 6, l. 7; Pothier, Pand. Lib. 22, tit. 6, § 2, n. 2, 3. But then this text is differently interpreted by different civilians. See 2 Evans's Pothier on Oblig. Appendix, No. xviii. pp. 408 to 447; Ayliffe, Pand. B. 2, tit. 15, p. 116; 1 Domat, B. 1, tit. 8, § 1, art. 13 to 16. Domat, after saying that error of law is not sufficient as an error in fact is to annul contracts, says, that error or ignorance of law hath different effects in contracts; and then he lays down the following rules: (1) If error or ignorance of law be such that it is the only cause of a contract in which one obliges himself to a thing to which he is otherwise not bound, and there be no other cause for the contract, the cause proving false, the contract is null. (2) This rule applies not only in preserving the person from suffering loss, but also in hindering him from being deprived of a right which he did not know belonged to him. (3) But if by an error or ignorance of the law one has done himself a prejudice which cannot be repaired without breaking in upon the right of another, the error shall not be corrected to the prejudice of the latter. (4) If the error or ignorance of the law has not been the only cause of the contract, but another motive has intervened, the error will not annul the contract. And he proceeds to illustrate these rules. 1 Domat, B. 1, tit. 18, § 1, art. 13 to 17. See also Ayliffe, Pand. B 2, tit. 15; Id. tit. 17; 2 Evans's Pothier on Oblig. Appendix, No. xviii. p. 408; Id. 437; Pothier, Pand. Lib. 22, tit. 6, per tot. Ante, § 111, and note.

(*a*) *Mistake of Fact.* — In the note on Mistake of Law appended to § 111 it is stated that relief from the consequences of mistake touching contracts is based on the consideration that the mistake relates to matter of the agreement as distinguished from inducements thereto, or to some condition precedent to the agreement; that is, on the ground that the minds of the parties have not met. It is not enough that there has been a mistake, however serious, in regard to an external matter not made a subject of the agreement or not a condition precedent thereto. See Dambmann *v.* Schulting, 75 N. Y. 55; Whittemore *v.* Farrington, 76 N. Y. 452; Laidlaw *v.* Organ, 2 Wheat. 178; post § 210.

It is there stated accordingly that the courts will interfere (*a*) where the minds of the parties did not meet at all, or (*b*) where they met on terms differing from those stated in the written embodiment of their contract. The first of these cases, (*a*), is a case for injunction and cancellation of the written instrument, and requires no proof of mistake or fault on the part of the defendant, if damages are not sought. Redgrave *v.* Hurd, 20 Ch. D. 1; Arkwright *v.* Newbold, 17 Ch. D. 301,

that an act done or contract made under a mistake or ignorance of a material fact is voidable and relievable in equity. The 320; Reese Silver Mining Co. *v.* Smith, L. R. 4 H. L. 64; Rawlins *v.* Wickham, 3 DeG. & J. 304; Paget *v.* Marshall, 28 Ch. D. 255. See Rider *v.* Powell, 28 N. Y. 310; Kilmer *v.* Smith, 77 N. Y. 226; Bridges *v.* McClendon, 56 Ala. 327, 333; Price *v.* Ley, 4 Giff. 235.

The second case, (*b*), is the case commonly spoken of as mutual mistake; so spoken of because usually the case is in fact one of mistake on both sides, if there is any mistake at all. This circumstance has often led courts to say that there must be mutual mistake to authorize the reformation of a contract, when it was only necessary to say that the *intention* with regard e. g. to a term sought to be imported into the writing must be mutual; that is, that that term must have been part of the contract actually made. It is clear that it need not be shown as necessary to this result either that the *defendant* was mistaken concerning the written instrument, or that he was guilty of fraud in putting it or having it put into the improper form. He merely may have seen that it was not in conformity with the agreement and kept silent; but this will not prevent rectification on satisfactory evidence of what was agreed. Rider *v.* Powell, 28 N. Y. 310. Comp. Cundy *v.* Lindsay, 3 App. Cas. 459. Upon the general proposition that the intention of the parties in regard to the term to be inserted or substituted should be one, see also Kilmer *v.* Smith, 77 N. Y. 226; Diman *v.* Providence R. Co., 5 R. I. 130; Thompsonville Co. *v.* Osgood, 26 Conn. 16; Ramsey *v.* Smith, 32 N. J. Eq. 28; Boyce *v.* Lorillard Ins. Co., 55 N. Y. 366; Dulany *v.* Rogers, 50 Md. 524; Young *v.* McGown, 62 Maine, 56; Schoonover *v.* Dougherty, 65 Ind. 463; Wright *v.* Goff, 22 Beav. 207; Metropolitan Soc. *v.* Brown, 26 Beav. 455; Paget *v.* Marshall, 28 Ch. D. 255. Of course a term in excess of the agreement, that is, not assented to by one side, may be struck out, though nothing is to be put into its place.

Equity will sometimes annex to a decree for the reformation of a contract a term or a condition not in the contemplation of the parties when they executed the contract, where this appears to be necessary to justice in the now altered situation. Thus where by mistake in drawing a lease the rent was put at a lower rate than that agreed and the lessee had entered, the court on a bill to set the matter right gave the lessee an election to continue the tenancy at the higher rate, or abandon and pay for use and occupation during occupancy at the higher rate, receiving in turn compensation for repairs of a permanent nature, but not for the expense of taking possession and getting established in business on the premises. Garrard *v.* Frankel, 30 Beav. 445; s. c. 8 Jur. N. S. 985. For another example see Mining Co. *v.* Coal Co., 8 W. Va. 406, infra. And see Burr *v.* Hutchinson, 61 Maine, 514, concerning protection in the decree of the interests of third persons, — a point considered infra.

But this right of reforming a written contract supposes that the situation has remained substantially unchanged. If on the contrary the parties cannot be put in statu quo substantially, equity will generally refuse relief. Crosier *v.* Acer, 7 Paige, 137, 143 (mistake of law); Eastman *v.* St. Anthony Falls Co., 24 Minn. 437. So if the fact about which the mutual mistake occurred was in its nature doubtful. Eastman *v.* St. Anthony Falls Co., supra.

Laches in the sense only of delay, though considerable, will not be a fatal objection to relief, especially in the

ground of this distinction between ignorance of law and ignorance of fact seems to be, that as every man of reasonable under-

case of a grantor who has remained in possession, and no change of position by the defendant has taken place. Hutson *v.* Furness, 31 Iowa, 154; Farmers' Bank *v.* Detroit, 12 Mich. 445; McIntosh *v.* Saunders, 68 Ill. 128. The second and third of these cases show that the rule holds against a grantee in possession.

Even change of position by the defendant since the mistake may not always be a fatal obstacle to rectification, for the change itself may be a result, easily rectified, of the same mistake. Thus notwithstanding the fact that a lot of land conveyed by mistake, instead of an adjoining lot supposed to have been conveyed, has since been mortgaged back to the grantor under the same mistake, equity may, it seems, correct the first conveyance at the suit of the grantee, on his offering to transfer the mortgage to the lot intended. See Weston *v.* Wilson, 31 N. J. Eq. 51; Burr *v.* Hutchinson, 61 Maine, 514. It is also to be inferred from Grymes *v.* Sanders, 93 U. S. 55, that equity may sometimes, in the clearest and strongest cases, grant relief, though the parties cannot be put in statu quo. And see Beauchamp *v.* Winn, L. R. 6 H. L. 223, that *difficulty* in restoring the parties to their former position is not an objection to relief.

If the rights of innocent third persons would be (materially?) affected by reforming a written instrument, equity will, generally speaking, refuse its aid. Malony *v.* Rourke, 100 Mass. 190; Burr *v.* Hutchinson, 61 Maine, 514; Trustees of Schools *v.* Otis, 85 Ill. 179; Tabor *v.* Cilley, 53 Vt. 487; Mining Co. *v.* Coal Co., 8 W. Va. 406; Gray *v.* Robinson, 90 Ind. 527. Indeed the rule may probably be stated in broader terms, — that mistake, whether arising upon a written or a verbal contract, will not be corrected against an innocent third person who has acquired a title or a right in reliance upon the outward aspect of the contract; such right or title arising out of the same as though there were no mistake.

Some difficult questions however grow out of this rule. Does this put mistake on a footing with fraud or misrepresentation? That is, is there a contract notwithstanding the mistake, — a contract voidable between the parties, but valid towards innocent purchasers? Has the rule referred to a broad application, or may it be limited to cases in which the action of the third person has been induced by the action of the party aggrieved by the mistake?

To consider the last question first: Suppose A has purchased a horse from B, the title to which, by reason of mistake in regard to the identity of the animal on a sale by C to B, did not in the ordinary sense pass, cannot C recover the horse or its value from A? See Burr *v.* Hutchinson, 61 Maine, 514, a case of land. But if in any case he can, it is not broadly true that mistake cannot be set up against the rights of innocent third persons, and here is then a case where mistake does not stand on the same footing with fraud or misrepresentation, which in their ordinary aspect make a contract voidable only, not void. There is however a settled principle of equity that where the equities of the parties are equal there can be no interference, and the equity of the innocent purchaser for value in general at least is considered equal to that of the party injured by the mistake. Infra, § 165. But that principle too must be limited if the case put would in any phase stand in equity as well as at law, as it probably would. Compare Burr *v.*

standing is presumed to know the law, and to act upon the rights which it confers or supports, when he knows all the facts, it is

Hutchinson, supra. The only limitation upon the principle which can be admitted and still leave the principle good, appears to be this: that it cannot apply to the case of a mistake not due in any way to the mistaken plaintiff. E. g. suppose in the case above put the horse had without fault jumped fence into the field supposed to be occupied by the horse intended, and that the latter had also without fault of the owner escaped his enclosure. Now if (still without fault of the owner) the horse not intended to be sold or bought should be led away and sold before the mistake could be made known to the purchaser, it would seem clear that the owner could recover his property; the rule concerning the equality of equities either would not apply, or it would be considered that the equities were not equal, the plaintiff's equity being the greater.

It seems then that it is because of some act of the mistaken party, innocent and proper it may be, such as subscribing a contract containing a mistake unknown to the party at the time, by which the third person has been induced to change his position materially, that relief is refused, if refused at all (see Burr *v.* Hutchinson, 61 Maine, 514, where relief was granted on terms, without prejudice to third persons), and that where such an act is absent from the particular case, nothing but mistake remaining, relief will be granted. It follows that mistake pure and simple differs from (ordinary) fraud or misrepresentation in that it prevents the very existence of a contract, not simply making the contract voidable. And then it may well be considered between the original parties to the mistake, if that should become material, that the supposed contract had never come into being, the inducing 'act' in the case of the third person not coming into play. See Cundy *v.* Lindsay, 3 App. Cas. 459.

The answer to the third question appears therefore to answer the other two. There is no contract in the case of mistake under consideration; there is only towards third persons an act which has the effect of precluding the mistaken plaintiff from alleging his mistake.

'Ordinary' fraud or misrepresentation has been spoken of here; for there is clearly a kind of fraud or misrepresentation which will be equivalent to mistake, so far as the present consideration is concerned. Thus if a person in obtaining insurance on risk A should represent it to be risk B, it would be clear that the minds of the parties had not met; there would be no contract, not merely a voidable contract. Goddard *v.* Monitor Ins. Co., 108 Mass. 56; Carpenter *v.* American Ins. Co., 1 Story, 57; Holmes, Common Law, 311. But fraud or misrepresentation which touches only the inducements to a contract is by the authorities deemed consistent with the existence of such contract; the contract however being voidable at the election of the injured party if that election is made before the rights of innocent persons have intervened.

Mistake will of course be corrected, where possible, against subsequent purchasers without value or with notice actual or constructive. Willcox *v.* Foster, 132 Mass. 320; Young *v.* Cason, 48 Mo. 259; Rhodes *v.* Outcalt, Ib. 367; Farmers' Bank *v.* Detroit, 12 Mich. 445; Adams *v.* Stevens, 49 Me. 362; Ruhling *v.* Hackett, 1 Nev. 360; infra, §§ 165, 176. Thus it has lately been decided that where a mortgage of land after being assigned has been discharged by the mortgagee by mistake, the assignee, though he has

culpable negligence in him to do an act or to make a contract, and then to set up his ignorance of law as a defence. The gen-

not recorded his assignment, is entitled in equity to have the discharge cancelled against a person claiming under a subsequent mortgage, which was in terms subject to the prior mortgage and was executed before that mortgage was discharged. Willcox v. Foster, 132 Mass. 320. And the same rule was held to apply against a person claiming under a mortgage made after the discharge, who knew of the mistake (see Childs v. Stoddard, 130 Mass. 110), though he was advised by counsel before taking his mortgage that the prior incumbrance would not be reinstated; and also against an assignee of the mortgage last executed, who took the assignment after the note secured by the mortgage assigned had passed its maturity, though in ignorance of the mistake. Willcox v. Foster, supra. And one who seeks to avoid a conveyance for mistake, against a subsequent grantee, must allege that the grantee was a volunteer or that he purchased with notice. Malony v. Rourke, 100 Mass. 190.

A deed may also be reformed against an attaching or a judgment creditor. Berry v. Sowell, 72 Ala. 14; Milmine v. Burnham, 76 Ill. 362; Lowe v. Allen, 68 Ga. 225. In the first case cited a creditor had attached the land conveyed by the deed as the property of the grantor, the deed being apparently a voluntary conveyance, — it purported to have been made on the ground only of love and affection, — but evidence was received that there was also a valuable consideration from the grantee to the grantor, and that this fact was omitted by mistake from the recitals.

Mere mistake of title on the part of a tenant in taking a lease of land and receiving possession from the lessor will not justify him in disputing the title of his lessor without surrendering the possession, unless the tenant has been evicted by or attorned to a title paramount. The tenant cannot set up an outstanding title against his landlord, from whom he received possession. Bigelow, Estoppel, 398 (3d ed.). The reason is that the landlord has parted with his possession in reliance upon the tenant's (implied) acknowledgment of his title.

But if the tenant did not receive possession from his landlord or from one under whom the landlord derives title, he may show that his acknowledgment of tenancy or attornment was made under mistake of fact as to the title. Ib. 399 et seq. So too the tenant may, at least on offering to surrender possession to his lessor, show a mutual mistake of the parties with regard to the title. Mays v. Dwight, 82 Penn. St. 462.

To justify the reformation of a written instrument for mistake, the mistake must be shown by evidence full, clear, and decisive, and the real intention of the parties must be clearly established. German Ins. Co. v. Davis, 131 Mass. 316; Alexander v. Coldwell, 55 Ala. 517, 522; Campbell v. Hatchett, Ib. 548; Harter v. Christolph, 32 Wis. 245; Peck v. Arehart, 95 Ill. 113; Ivinson v. Hutton, 98 U. S. 79, 82; Howland v. Blake, 97 U. S. 624. The mistake indeed, according to the current of authority, must be established beyond reasonable doubt. Hervey v. Savery, 48 Iowa, 313; Muller v. Rhuman, 62 Ga. 332; Fuchs v. Treat, 41 Wis. 404; Hinton v. Citizens Ins. Co., 63 Ala. 488; Tufts v. Larned, 27 Iowa, 330; Edmond's Appeal, 59 Penn. St. 220; Hudson Iron Co. v. Stockbridge Iron Co., 107 Mass. 290; Shattuck v. Gay, 45 Vt. 87; Miner v. Hess, 47 Ill. 170; Ruffner v. McConnell, 17 Ill. 212; Douglas v. Grant, 12 Ill. App. 273; Tucker v.

eral maxim here is, as in other cases, that the law aids those who are vigilant, and not those who slumber over their rights.

Madden, 44 Maine, 206; Hileman v. Wright, 9 Ind. 126; Linn v. Barkey, 7 Ind. 69; Davidson v. Greer, 3 Sneed, 384; Lake v. Meacham, 13 Wis. 355; Fowler v. Adams, Ib. 458. See Coale v. Merryman, 35 Md. 382; Bunse v. Agee, 47 Miss. 270; Hamlon v. Sullivant, 11 Ill. App. 423.

But equity may still reform the deed on parol evidence though the defendant denies the alleged mistake, if the court is fully satisfied on the evidence that there was a mistake. See § 156, infra; Stines v. Hays, 36 N. J. Eq. 364; Allen v. Yeater, 17 W. Va. 128. And if the mistake and the true intention are satisfactorily made out, equity will, as follows from what is said earlier in this note, interfere and change the most important terms of the contract. Ivinson v. Hutton, 98 U. S. 79; Snell v. Ins. Co., Ib. 85. In a case not deemed within the Statute of Frauds, the contract may then, and in the same suit, be specifically enforced if the subject be one for such a measure. Monroe v. Skelton, 36 Ind. 302 (under the Code). But see Mills v. Evansville Seminary, 47 Wis. 354. And see infra, p. 155.

Not only may a contract be reformed for mistake on parol evidence apart from statute; it may be reformed on the evidence of the plaintiff alone, if other evidence cannot be had. Hanley v. Pearson, 13 Ch. D. 545. But it is said that it must be an extreme case that will justify relief on such evidence. Harter v. Christolph, 32 Wis. 245; Kent v. Lasley, 24 Wis. 654; McClellan v. Sanford, 26 Wis. 595. On the other hand it is held that a deed may be reformed for mistake apparent on its face, such as the omission of a seal or a granting clause, without resort to parol evidence, if the true intention can be supplied from the deed itself. Michel v. Finsley, 69 Mo. 442; Huss v. Morris, 63 Penn. St. 367.

It is settled by a constant line of authorities in England that relief based on mistake of fact, or, it seems, on mistake of law (Beauchamp v. Winn, L. R. 6 H. L. 223, 233), is not to be refused either in equity or at law on the ground that the plaintiff had the means of knowledge at the time of the mistake; the doctrine of laches as to that point does not apply to such a case. Willmott v. Barber, 15 Ch. D. 96; Townsend v. Crowdy, 8 C. B. N. s. 477; Dails v. Lloyd, 12 Q. B. 531; Bell v. Gardiner, 4 M. & G. 11; Kelly v. Solari, 9 Mees. & W. 54. The cases in this country, without sufficient discrimination concerning the meaning of the text, infra, § 146, are not so clear; though a recent decision of the Court of Appeals of New York appears to be in accord with the English authorities. Kilmer v. Smith, 77 N. Y. 226. See Monroe v. Skelton, 36 Ind. 302. And see Webb v. Parker, 41 Ga. 478, where it is held that failing to inquire, in the case of one put on inquiry, where a fact stated on the other side has led to such failure, is not fatal to relief. That proposition would be universally accepted. See Hitchins v. Pettingill, 58 N. H. 3. But see as to the simpler case of means of knowledge not availed of, Brown v. Fagan, 71 Mo. 563; Grymes v. Sanders, 93 U. S. 55. And it is generally held in this country that where the mistake or ignorance was the result of gross negligence no relief will be granted. Conner v. Welch, 51 Wis. 431; Troops v. Snyder, 70 Ind. 554; Wood v. Patterson, 4 Md. Ch. 335; Voorhis v. Murphy, 11 C. E. Green, 434; Kearney v. Sascer, 37 Md. 264, where the plaintiff shut his eyes to the facts.

It is conceived that the English

CHAP. V.] MISTAKE. 155

And this reason is recognized as the foundation of the distinction, as well in the civil law as in the common law.[1] But no

[1] See Pothier, Pand. Lib. 22, tit. 6, § 3, n. 4, 5, 6, 7; § 4, n. 10, 11; Ayliffe's Pand. B. 2, tit. 15, p. 116; 1 Domat, B. 1, tit. 18, § 1; Doct. & Stud. Dial. 2, ch. 47; 1 Fonbl. Eq. B. 1, ch. 2, § 7, note (v); Pooley v. Ray, 1 P. Will. 355; Corking v. Pratt, 1 Ves. 406; Hitchcock v. Giddings, 4 Price, R. 135; Leonard v. Leonard, 2 Ball & Beatt. 171, 180 to 184; Pearson v. Lord, 6 Mass. R. 81; Garland v. Salem Bank, 9 Mass. R. 408; 1 Madd. Ch. Pr. 60 to 64; Daniell v. Mitchell, 1 Story, R. 172.

rule is the correct one, so far as the mere question of failing to inquire is concerned; for how can a man be entitled to property by an unintended gift simply on the ground that the 'giver' was negligent? There are no doubt cases where neglect of the means of safety at hand is and should be fatal. The administration of justice requires such a rule, — 'interest reipublicæ ut litium finis sit;' and what the author chiefly alluded to in this connection was probably the case of negligence in the trial of an action. He gives, it will be seen, as an example of his rather too general proposition, a case of that kind, which, it may be presumed, was the foundation of the proposition itself. 'If,' says the text, 'a party has lost his cause at law from the want of proof of a fact which by ordinary diligence he could have obtained, he is not relievable in equity.' § 146. Compare the editor's note on Accident, ante, § 78.

Concerning the old controversy on the operation of the Statute of Frauds when reformation is sought of a deed which by mistake conveys less than was agreed and paid for, it has lately been held that the case should not stand, with reference to the statute, as if there was no deed. The position is accordingly reaffirmed that the error may be corrected without proof of such part performance as would be necessary for a decree of specific performance of a contract for the sale of the whole tract when no part of it was conveyed. Hitchins v. Pettingill, 58 N. H. 386, citing a cloud of cases. But see contra Glass v. Hulbert, 102 Mass. 24, and cases there reviewed; the court holding that there must be part performance, or the defendant must in some way, other than by reason of mistake or even of fraud, be estopped to avail himself of the statute. See Stockbridge Iron Co. v. Hudson Iron Co., 107 Mass. 290, 321.

It should be noticed that the mistake which equity takes cognizance of is not mistake of judgment. Where one who has an election between two courses of action makes choice of one with full knowledge of the facts, he cannot afterwards have relief in equity on the ground that he made a mistake in his calculation. Childs v. Stoddard, 130 Mass. 110; Thomas v. Bartow, 48 N. Y. 193. See Durant v. Bacot, 2 Beasl. 201. Compare the note on Mistake of Law, ante, § 111. Nor is the case different where the mistake of judgment is the mistake of (the plaintiff's) legal counsel. Winchester v. Grosvenor, 48 Ill. 517; Hunt v. Rousmaniere, 8 Wheat. 174; s. c. 1 Peters, 1. If an agent of the defendant advises and induces the mistake, however innocently, the defendant will not be permitted to take advantage of it to the injury of the plaintiff. Snell v. Insurance Co., 98 U. S. 85, a case of mistake of law. See also Woodbury Bank v. Charter Oak Ins. Co., 31 Conn. 517.

Before the recent enabling acts concerning married women, it was held that mistake in a deed by a married

person can be presumed to be acquainted with all matters of fact; neither is it possible, by any degree of diligence, in all

woman conveying her own property could not be corrected against her. Martin v. Dwelly, 6 Wend. 9; Carr v. Williams, 10 Ohio, 105; Grapengether v. Fejervary, 9 Iowa, 163, 173. That may still be the rule in many States. Holland v. Moon, 39 Ark. 120; Leonis v. Lazzarovich, 55 Cal. 52. But see Carper v. Munger, 62 Ind. 481; Wedel v. Herman, 59 Cal. 507 (as to defective certificate of acknowledgment). Infra, § 177.

Concerning the right to relief against a minor who has received the purchase price for land, see Segee v. Thomas, 3 Blatchf. 11. But see Dickey v. Beatty, 14 Ohio St. 389.

Equity will not reform a voluntary deed for mistake, at the suit of the donee. Mulock v. Mulock, 31 N. J. Eq. 594; Conaway v. Gore, 24 Kans. 389; Wait v. Smith, 92 Ill. 385; Brown v. Kenney, 9 Jur. N. S. 1163; s. c. 33 Beav. 133; Eaton v. Eaton, 15 Iowa, 259; Hunt v. Frazier, 6 Jones, Eq. 290; Henderson v. Dickey, 35 Mo. 120; Hout v. Hout, 20 Ohio St. 119. See Morse v. Martin, 34 Beav. 500; post, § 176. Secus at suit of the grantor, when he can show that the deed does not in a material respect conform to his intention, or that he executed it under a total misapprehension of its effect. Mulock v. Mulock, supra. Secus too of defective execution of powers in favor of wives and children. Infra, § 170. But equity will take jurisdiction between different volunteers, even in favor of grandchildren of a grantor. Huss v. Morris, 63 Penn. St. 367.

It is also held that equity will not insert a condition subsequent omitted from a written instrument by mistake, and then declare a forfeiture for breach thereof. Mills v. Evansville Seminary, 47 Wis. 354. But compare Monroe v. Skelton, 36 Ind. 302, infra; § 161, infra.

It is held that demand and refusal of correction are necessary before equity will interfere, unless satisfactory excuse is offered for failing to show those facts, such e. g. as the death of the vendor of land and the infancy of his heir. Harold v. Weaver, 72 Ala. 373. See Axtel v. Chase, 83 Ind. 546.

The following cases may be enumerated from late decisions in which equity has granted relief for mistake or ignorance of fact: —

Mistake in the description of land in a deed. Dozier v. Mitchell, 65 Ala. 511; Mills v. Lockwood, 42 Ill. 111; Wilcox v. Lucas, 121 Mass. 21; Jones v. Clifford, 3 Ch. D. 779, 792; Dwight v. Tyler, 49 Mich. 614; Fuchs v. Treat, 41 Wis. 404; Turner v. Kelly, 70 Ala. 85. So of gross error in the amount conveyed when not conveyed by name of lot or by clear and understood bounds. Ladd v. Pleasants, 39 Tex. 415; Noble v. Googins, 99 Mass. 231; Winston v. Browning, 61 Ala. 80. Mistake in the vendor's interest. Irick v. Fulton, 3 Gratt. 193; Okill v. Whittaker, 1 DeG. & S. 83. See Colyer v. Clay, 7 Beav. 188, infra, p. 157. The use of the term 'more or less' in describing the quantity conveyed is not a fatal objection to interference except where the discrepancy is slight. If it is considerable, such as to imply fraud or to show gross mistake, equity will relieve. Paine v. Upton, 87 N. Y. 327; Belknap v. Sealey, 14 N. Y. 143; s. c. 2 Duer, 579; Noble v. Googins, 99 Mass. 231. See however Ketchum v. Stout, 20 Ohio St. 455; Stall v. Hart, 9 Gill, 446. The same is true of the terms 'about' or 'probably' so much. Yost v. Mallicote, 77 Va. 610. But it is held that a tax deed will not be corrected for error of description. Keepfer v. Force, 86 Ind. 81. The vendor, and not merely the purchaser, may

cases to acquire that knowledge; and therefore an ignorance of facts does not import culpable negligence. The rule applies not have relief for mistake in description operating against him. Fuchs *v.* Treat, 41 Wis. 404; Mining Co. *v.* Coal Co., 8 W. Va. 406. And if the purchaser will not pay for the excess conveyed by mistake on the basis of the purchase price, equity will rescind the whole contract of sale. Mining Co. *v.* Coal Co., supra. The purchaser has the option to rescind or pay for excess. Ib. Compare the converse cases of Hill *v.* Buckley, 17 Ves. 394; Paine *v.* Upton, 87 N. Y. 327. And the right to relief exists as well after the deed has been executed as before, if the facts were not then known. Paine *v.* Upton, supra, showing that there is no distinction between executed and executory contracts in regard to relief for mistake. See Noble *v.* Googins, 99 Mass. 231, 233.

A mortgage of land which by mistake does not cover all that was intended may be rectified even against the wife who released dower. Chapman *v.* Field, 70 Ala. 403. It is held in this case that such rectification may be made, though the wife (afterwards widow claiming dower) is not a party to the suit, the correction taking effect against her only from the time of the decree. Sed qu.

Of course there may be rescission if it turn out that the vendor of land had no title at all (Quivey *v.* Baker, 37 Cal. 465), and this though he honestly supposed he had title; fraud is not necessary to relief. Baptiste *v.* Peters, 51 Ala. 158; Lanier *v.* Hill, 25 Ala. 554; Diman *v.* Providence R. Co., 5 R. I. 130; Fane *v.* Fane, L. R. 20 Eq. 698.

Mistake in the location of land wholly or in part. Spurr *v.* Benedict, 99 Mass. 463; Watts *v.* Cummins, 59 Penn. 84; Best *v.* Stow, 2 Sandf. Ch. 298; McKelway *v.* Armour, 2 Stockt. 115; Quivey *v.* Baker, 37 Cal. 465; Fuchs *v.* Treat, 41 Wis. 404; Allen *v.* Yeater, 17 W. Va. 128. As where the conveyance includes a warehouse or a storehouse and lot. Fuchs *v.* Treat, supra; Allen *v.* Yeater, supra. Misdescription in a mortgage of the mortgage note. Prior *v.* Williams, 2 Keyes, 530. Omission of a granting clause in a deed. Michel *v.* Tinsley, 69 Mo. 442. Or of a reservation. Wells *v.* Yates, 44 N. Y. 525; Wilcox *v.* Lucas, 121 Mass. 21. Or of a limitation of the use of the property, as that it was conveyed for use as a road. Stines *v.* Hays, 36 N. J. Eq. 364. Mistake in the existence or duration of a leasehold interest, as in the sale of a reversionary interest which has already fallen in by the death of the prior owner without the knowledge of the parties. Colyer *v.* Clay, 7 Beav. 188; Okill *v.* Whittaker, 1 DeG & S. 83. Defective execution of a deed. Stark *v.* Starr, 94 U. S. 477, 491; Love *v.* Sierra Nev. Mining Co., 32 Cal. 639; Remington *v.* Higgins, 54 Cal. 620. Thus where the seal of a party, necessary to make an instrument valid and effectual, has been omitted by mistake, equity will treat the instrument, in favor of those entitled to its benefits, as sealed. It will either compel the affixing a seal or enjoin a defence based on the want of one. Bernards *v.* Stebbins, 109 U. S. 341, 349. See Draper *v.* Springport, 104 U. S. 501; Neal *v.* Gregory, 19 Fla. 356 ; Michel *v.* Tinsley, 69 Mo. 442; Probate Court *v.* May, 52 Vt. 182.

But where by statute the use of a seal is mandatory — 'an essential part of the transaction' — it is suggested that the case may be different. Bernards *v.* Stebbins and Draper *v.* Springport, supra. See infra, § 177. These cases were cases of town bonds, and relief was granted on the principle

only to cases where there has been a studied suppression or concealment of the facts by the other side which would amount to fraud, but also to many cases of innocent ignorance and mistake on both sides.[1] So if a party has bona fide entirely forgotten

---

[1] Ignorance of facts and mistake of facts are not precisely equivalent expressions. Mistake of facts always supposes some error of opinion as to the real facts; but ignorance of facts may be without any error, but result in mere want of knowledge or opinion. Thus a man knowing that he has some interest in a parcel of land may suppose it to be a life estate, when it is a fee.

---

upon which equity has relieved against the want of livery or of enrolment or other ceremony of the common law or statute, not positively essential. Nor will equity affix a seal to a voluntary instrument, though necessary and agreed upon. Eaton v. Eaton, 15 Iowa, 259.

On the other hand attaching a seal to a partnership note by mistake will be corrected. Lyman v. Califer, 64 N. Car. 572. Discharge of a mortgage or lien. Bruce v. Bonney, 12 Gray, 107; French v. DeBow, 38 Mich. 708. Allowing judgment to go by default on a mistaken cause of action. Young v. Morgan, 9 Neb. 169. Satisfaction of an execution. National Bank v. Rogers, 22 Minn. 224. Mistake in the date of a policy of insurance. Mercantile Ins. Co. v. Jaynes, 87 Ill. 199. And in the name of the person intended to be insured. Keith v. Globe Ins. Co., 52 Ill. 518. Misdescription of premises in a policy of insurance. Home Ins. Co. v. Meyer, 93 Ill. 271. Misdescription of property in a bill of sale of personalty. Menominee Co. v. Langworthy, 18 Wis. 444. Omission of interest clause from a promissory note. Gump's Appeal, 65 Penn St. 476. Omission of a necessary indorsement of a note. Hughes v. Nelson, 29 N. J. Eq. 547, treating the title in such a case as having passed in equity. Giving a guardian bond to a judge out of office. Hall v. Hall, 43 Ala. 488. Mistake of an executor, administrator, or other person bound to account, in charging too much against himself in making up his accounts. Brandon v. Brown, 106 Ill. 519. Omission of the name of a trustee in a trust deed may be supplied, especially where a blank was left with authority to fill. Burnside v. Wayman, 49 Miss. 356; Exchange Bank v. Russell, 50 Mo. 551. So of the character in which by mistake a magistrate has taken an acknowledgment of an instrument. Simpson v. Montgomery, 25 Ark. 365. Mistake of a magistrate in failing to mark the name of counsel to the defence of a suit resulting in judgment against him. Brewer v. Jones, 44 Ga. 71. Mistake of a trivial nature in the time for making a tender to save a forfeiture. Atkins v. Chilson, 11 Met. 112. Generally mistake of a scrivener will be corrected. Huss v. Morris, 63 Penn. St. 367; Van Douge v. Van Douge, 23 Mich. 321; Hartford Ore Co. v. Miller, 41 Conn. 112; Drury v. Hayden, 111 U. S. 223; Elliott v. Sackett, 108 U. S. 133; Clemens v. Drew, 2 Jones, Eq. 314; Stone v. Hale, 17 Ala. 557; Wilcox v. Lucas, 121 Mass. 21; Allen v. Brown, 6 R. I. 386; Sowler v. Day, 58 Iowa, 252.

But if a term or condition was omitted purposely, then it matters not that there was an oral understanding that the term or condition should be complied with; equity will not grant relief. Andrew v. Spurr, 8 Allen, 412; Betts v. Gunn, 31 Ala. 219.

the facts he will be entitled to relief, because under such circumstances he acts under the like mistake of the facts as if he had never known them.[1] Ignorance of foreign law is deemed to be ignorance of fact; because no person is presumed to know the foreign law, and it must be proved as a fact.[2] (a)

141. The rule as to ignorance or mistake of facts entitling the party to relief has this important qualification, that the fact must be material to the act or contract; that is, that it must be essential to its character, and an efficient cause of its concoction. For though there may be an accidental ignorance or mistake of a fact, yet if the act or contract is not materially affected by it, the party claiming relief will be denied it. This distinction may be easily illustrated by a familiar case. A buys an estate of B, to which the latter is supposed to have an unquestionable title. It turns out upon due investigation of the facts, unknown at the time to both parties, that B has no title (as if there be a nearer heir than B, who was supposed to be dead, but is in fact living); in such a case equity would relieve the purchaser and rescind the contract.[3] But suppose A were to sell an estate to B, whose location was well known to each, and they mutually believed it to contain twenty acres, and in point of fact it contained only nineteen acres and three fourths of an acre, and the difference would not have varied the purchase in the view of either party, in such a case the mistake would not be a ground to rescind the contract.[4]

142. In cases of mutual mistake going to the essence of the contract it is by no means necessary that there should be any

That is an error or mistake. But if he is ignorant that there exists any such land, and that he had any title to it, that very ignorance may lead him to form no opinion whatever on the subject. It may be a case of sheer negation of thought. The phrases are however commonly used as equivalent in legal discussions. Canal Bank *v.* Bank of Albany, 1 Hill, N. Y. R. 287.

[1] Kelly *v.* Solari, 9 Mees. & Wels. 54, 58.
[2] Leslie *v.* Bailie, 2 Younge & Coll. N. R. 91, 96; Haven *v.* Foster, 9 Pick. R. 113, 130; Raynham *v.* Canton, 3 Pick. R. 293; Kenny *v.* Clarkson, 1 Johns. R. 385; Trith *v.* Sprague, 14 Mass. R. 455; Consequa *v.* Willings, 1 Peters, Circ. R. 229.
[3] See 1 Evans, Pothier on Oblig. Pt. 1, ch. 1, art. 9, n. 17, 18; Bingham *v.* Bingham, 1 Ves. 126; 1 Fonbl. Eq. B. 1, ch. 2, § 7. See also Calverley *v.* Williams, 1 Ves. jr. 210, 211.
[4] See Smith *v.* Evans, 6 Binn. 102; Mason *v.* Pearson, 2 John. R. 37.

(a) McCormick *v.* Garnett, 5 De G. 112; King *v.* Doolittle, 1 Head, M. & G. 278; Haven *v.* Foster, 9 Pick. 77, 84.

presumption of fraud. On the contrary equity will often relieve, however innocent the parties may be. Thus if one person should sell a messuage to another, which was at the time swept away by a flood or destroyed by an earthquake without any knowledge of the fact by either party, a Court of Equity would relieve the purchaser upon the ground that both parties intended the purchase and sale of a subsisting thing, and implied its existence as the basis of their contract. It constituted therefore the very essence and condition of the obligation of their contract.[1](a) So if a person should execute a release to another party upon the supposition founded in a mistake that a certain debt or annuity had been discharged, although both parties were innocent, the release would be set aside upon the ground of the mistake.[2](b) The civil law holds the same principle. 'Domum emi, cum eam et ego et venditor combustam ignoraremus. Nerva, Sabinus, Cassius, nihil venisse, quamvis area maneat, pecuniamque solutam condici posse, aiunt.'[3]

143. The same principle will apply to all other cases where the parties mutually bargain for and upon the supposition of an existing right. Thus if a purchaser should buy the interest of the vendor in a remainder in fee, expectant upon an estate tail and the tenant in tail had at the time, unknown to both parties, actually suffered a recovery, and thus barred the estate in remainder, a Court of Equity would relieve the purchaser in regard to the contract purely upon the ground of mistake.[4]

143 a. It will make no difference in the application of the principle, that the subject-matter of the contract be known to

---

[1] Hitchcock v. Giddings, 4 Price, R. 135, 141; s. c. Daniel's R. 1; 2 Kent, Comm. Lect. 39, p. 469 (2d edit.). But see Sugden on Vendors, p. 237, and note 1, 7th edition; Stent v. Bailis, 2 P. Will. 220.

[2] Hone v. Brether, 12 Simons, R. 465.

[3] Dig. Lib. 18, tit. 1, l. 57; 2 Kent, Comm. Lect. 39, pp. 468, 469 (2d edit.); Grotius De Jure Belli, B. 2, ch. 11, § 7. If the house were partially burnt, the civilians seemed to have entertained different opinions, whether the vendor was bound by the contract, having an abatement of the price or allowance for the injury, or had an election to proceed or not with the contract, with such an abatement or allowance. See 2 Kent, Comm. Lect. 39, p. 469 (4th edit.); Pothier De Vente, n. 4. Grotius has made some sensible remarks upon the subject of error in contracts, Grotius De Jure Belli, B. 2, ch. 11, § 6.

[4] Hitchcock v. Giddings, 4 Price, R. 135; s. c. Daniel's R. 1.

(a) Colyer v. Clay, 7 Beav. 188.   (b) Fane v. Fane, L. R. 20 Eq. 698.

both parties to be liable to a contingency which may destroy it immediately; for if the contingency has, unknown to the parties, already happened, the contract will be void, as founded upon a mutual mistake of a matter constituting the basis of the contract. Thus if a life estate should be sold, and at the time of the sale the estate is terminated by the death of the party in whom the estate is vested, and that fact is unknown to both parties, a Court of Equity would rescind the contract upon the ground of a mutual mistake of the fact which constituted the basis of the contract.[1] So if a horse should be purchased, which is by both parties believed to be alive, but is at the time of the purchase in fact dead, the purchaser would upon the same ground be relieved by rescinding the contract if the money was not paid, and if paid, by decreeing the money to be paid back.[2]

143 *b*. The same principle has been applied to the case of a contract between two persons whereby one contracted for a large sum as a contingent compensation for his services in prosecuting a claim of the other against a foreign government for an illegal capture if it should be successful, and at the time of the contract the claim had, unknown to both parties, been allowed by the foreign government with a stipulation for a due payment thereof; for the very basis of the contract was future services to be rendered in prosecuting the claim, and unless such services were rendered there was no consideration to support it.[3]

144. The same principle will apply to cases of purchases where the parties have been innocently misled under a mutual mistake as to the extent of the thing sold. Thus if one party thought that he had bona fide purchased a piece of land as parcel of an estate, and the other thought he had not sold it under a mutual mistake of the bargain, that would furnish a ground to set aside the contract; because (as has been said) it is impossible to say that one shall be forced to give that price for part only which he intended to give for the whole, or that the other shall be obliged to sell the whole for what he intended to be the price of part only.[4]

144 *a*. But here the nature of the purchase often constitutes a material ingredient. Thus if a purchase is made of a thing in

---

[1] Allen *v.* Hammond, 11 Peters, R. 71.   [2] Ibid.
[3] Allen *v.* Hammond, 11 Peters, R. 63, 71 to 73.
[4] Calverley *v.* Williams, 1 Ves. jr. 210, 211.

gross, as for example of a farm, as containing in gross by estimation a certain number of acres (such a sale is called in the Roman law a sale per aversionem) by certain boundaries; then if the transaction be bona fide, and both parties be equally under a mistake as to the quantity but not as to the boundaries, the sale will be binding on both parties, whether the farm contain more or fewer acres.[1] (*a*)

145. It is upon the same ground that a Court of Equity proceeds where an instrument is so general in its terms as to release the rights of the party to property to which he was wholly ignorant that he had any title, and which was not within the contemplation of the bargain at the time when it was made. In such cases the court restrains the instrument to the purposes of the bargain, and confines the release to the right intended to be released or extinguished.[2]

146. It is not however sufficient in all cases to give the party relief that the fact is material, but it must be such as he could not by reasonable diligence get knowledge of when he was put upon inquiry. For if by such reasonable diligence he could have obtained knowledge of the fact, equity will not relieve him, since that would be to encourage culpable negligence. Thus if a party has lost his cause at law from the want of proof of a fact which by ordinary diligence he could have obtained, he is not relievable in equity; for the general rule is that if the party becomes remediless at law by his own negligence, equity will leave him to bear the consequence.[3] (*b*)

---

[1] Morris Canal Co. *v.* Emmatt, 9 Paige, R. 168; Stebbins *v.* Eddy, 4 Mason, R. 414; Post, § 195. See Dig. Lib. 18, tit. 6, 1. 35, § 5.

[2] Farewell *v.* Coker, cited 2 Meriv. 352; Ramsden *v.* Hylton, 4 Ves. 304.

[3] 1 Fonbl. Eq. B. 1, ch. 3, § 3; Penny *v.* Martin, 4 John. Ch. R. 566. The rule of the civil law is the same. 'Sed facti ignorantia ita demum cuique non nocet, si non ei summa negligentia objiciatur. Quod, enim si omnes in civitate sciant, quod ille solus ignorat? Et recte Labeo definit, scientiam neque curiosissimi neque negligentissimi hominis accipiendam; verum ejus, qui eam rem diligenter inquirendo notam habere possit.' Dig. Lib. 22, tit. 6, 1. 9, § 2; Pothier, Pand. Lib. 22, tit. 6, § 4, n. 11. In the late case of Bell *v.* Gardiner, 4 Mann. & Granger, 11, 24, it was held that at law a promise to pay a note under ignorance of facts, but where the party had the *means* of knowledge, and might have made inquiry, did not bind him. The same point was decided in Kelly *v.* Solari, 9 Mees. & Welsb. 54, and Lucas *v.* Worswick, 1 Mood. & Rob.

(*a*) See Noble *v.* Googins, 99 Mass. 231; note to § 140, at pp. 156, 157.

(*b*) See note to § 140, at p. 154.

147. Nor is it in every case where even a material fact is mistaken or unknown without any default of the parties that a Court of Equity will interpose. The fact may be unknown to both parties, or it may be known to one party and unknown to the other. If it is known to one party and unknown to the other, that will in some cases afford a solid ground for relief, as for instance where it operates as a surprise or a fraud upon the ignorant party.[1] But in all such cases the ground of relief is not the mistake or ignorance of material facts alone, but the unconscientious advantage taken of the party by the concealment of them.[2] For if the parties act fairly, and it is not a case where one is bound to communicate the facts to the other upon the ground of confidence or otherwise, there the court will not interfere. Thus if A, knowing that there is a mine in the land of B of which he knows that B is ignorant, should buy the land without disclosing the fact to B, for a price in which the mine is not taken into consideration, B would not be entitled to relief from the contract, because A, as the buyer, is not obliged from the nature of the contract to make the discovery.[3]

293. All these cases at law proceed upon the ground that a mistake of material facts will avoid a promise made on the foundation of that mistake, even when he had the means of knowledge within his reach. But Courts of Equity proceed upon a somewhat differently modified doctrine. If relief can be given at law, then there is no ground for any application to a Court of Equity for relief. But if a Court of Equity is asked to give relief in a case not fully remediable at law, or not remediable at all at law, then it grants it upon its own terms and according to its own doctrines. It gives relief only to the vigilant and not to the negligent; to those who have not been put upon their diligence to make inquiry, and not to those who, being put upon inquiry, have chosen to omit all inquiry which would have enabled them at once to correct the mistake or to obviate all ill effects therefrom. In short it refuses all its aid to those who by their own negligence, and by that alone, have incurred the loss or may suffer the inconvenience. It is one thing to act under a mistake of fact, having the means of inquiry but without being aware of the necessity of ascertaining the facts, and quite a different thing to omit all inquiry in due season, when the party is aware of the necessity, and the mode of the inquiry is pointed out to him or is within his reach. See post, §§ 400, 400 a.

[1] Jeremy on Eq. Jurisd. B. 3, ch. 2, pp. 366, 367; Id. ch. 3, p. 387; Leonard v. Leonard, 2 Ball & Beatt. 179, 180, and the case cited in Mortimer v. Capper by the Lord Chancellor, 4 Brown, Ch. R. 158; 6 Ves. 24; Gordon v. Gordon, 3 Swanst. 462, 467, 471, 473, 476, 477.

[2] See East India Company v. Donald, 9 Ves. 275; Earl of Bath and Montague's Case, 3 Ch. Cases, 56, 74, 103, 114.

[3] Post, § 207, note.

148. And it is essential, in order to set aside such a transaction, not only that an advantage should be taken, but it must arise from some obligation in the party to make the discovery; not from an obligation in point of morals only, but of legal duty. In such a case the court will not correct the contract merely because a man of nice morals and honor would not have entered into it. It must fall within some definition of fraud or surprise.[1] For the rules of law must be so drawn as not to affect the general transactions of mankind, or to require that all persons should in all respects be upon the same level as to information, diligence, and means of judgment. Equity as a practical system, although it will not aid immorality, does not affect to enforce mere moral duties; but its policy is to administer relief to the vigilant and to put all parties upon the exercise of a searching diligence.[2] Where confidence is reposed or the party is intentionally misled, relief may be granted; but in such a case there is the ingredient of what the law deems a fraud. Cases falling under this predicament will more properly come in review in a subsequent part of this work.[3]

149. A like principle applies to cases where the means of information are open to both parties, and where each is presumed to exercise his own skill, diligence, and judgment in regard to all extrinsic circumstances. In such cases equity will not relieve. Thus if the vendee is in possession of facts which will materially enhance the price of the commodity, and of which he knows the vendor to be ignorant, he is not bound to communicate those facts to the vendor, and the contract will be held valid.[4] It has been justly observed that it would be difficult to circumscribe the contrary doctrine within proper limits, where the intelligence is equally accessible to both parties.[5] And where it is not, the

---

[1] Fox v. Mackreth, 2 Bro. Ch. R. 420; 1 Madd. Eq. Pl. 63, 64; 1 Fonbl. Eq. B. 1, ch. 3, § 4, note (n); Earl of Bath and Montague's Case, 3 Ch. Cases, 56, 74, 103, 114.

[2] 1 Fonbl. Eq. B. 1, ch. 5, § 8, note (h).

[3] See Leonard v. Leonard, 2 Ball and Beatt. R. 179, 180; Gordon v. Gordon, 3 Swanst. 463, 467, 470, 473, 476, 477. See, on this subject, 1 Fonbl. Eq. B. 1, ch. 3, § 4, note (n); Jeremy on Eq. Jurisd. 383, &c.; 1 Madd. Eq. Pr. 204, &c.; Laidlaw v. Organ, 2 Wheat. R. 178; Pothier De Vente, n. 233 to 241; 2 Wheat. R. 185, note; Smith v. Bank of Scotland, 1 Dow Parl. R. 294; Pidcock v. Bishop, 3 B. & Cressw. 605; Etting v. Bank of U. S. 11 Wheat. R. 59, and cases there cited; post, § 260 to § 273, § 308 to § 328.

[4] Laidlaw v. Organ, 2 Wheat. R. 178, 195.   [5] 2 Ibid.

same remark applies with the same force if it is not a case of mutual confidence or of a designed misleading of the vendor.[1] Thus if a vendee has private knowledge of a declaration of war or of a treaty of peace or of other political arrangements (in respect to which men speculate for themselves) which materially affect the price of commodities, he is not bound to disclose the fact to the vendor at the time of his purchase; but, at least in a legal and equitable sense, he may innocently be silent. For there is no pretence to say that upon such matters men repose confidence in each other any more than they do in regard to other matters affecting the rise and fall of markets.[2] (a) The like principle applies to all other cases where the parties act upon their own judgment in matters mutually open to them. Thus if an agreement for the composition of a cause is fairly made between parties with their eyes open and rightly informed, a Court of Equity will not overhaul it, although there has been a great mistake in the exercise of their judgment.[3]

150. In like manner where the fact is equally unknown to both parties, or where each has equal and adequate means of information, or where the fact is doubtful from its own nature; in every such case if the parties have acted with entire good faith, a Court of Equity will not interpose.[4] For in such cases the equity is deemed equal between the parties; and when it is so, a Court of Equity is generally passive and rarely exerts an active jurisdiction. Thus where there was a contract by A to sell to B for £20 such an allotment as the commissioners under an

---

[1] Pothier, in his Treatise on the subject of Sales, has treated this subject with great ability, and has cited the doctrines of the civil law and the discussions of civilians and writers upon natural law on this subject. While he contends strenuously for the doctrine of good faith and full discovery in all cases, he is compelled to admit that the doctrines in foro conscientiæ have had little support in judicial tribunals, and indeed are not easily applicable to the common business of life. Indeed he admits that though concealment of material facts by the vendee, which may enhance the price, is wrong in foro conscientiæ, yet that it would too much restrict the freedom of commerce to apply such a rule in civil transactions. See Pothier, Traité de Vente, Pt. 2, ch. 2, n. 233 to 242; Id. Pt. 3, § 2, n. 294 to 298; 2 Wheat. R. 185, note (c).

[2] Ibid.

[3] Brown v. Pring, 1 Ves. 408.

[4] 1 Fonbl. Eq. B. 1, ch. 2, § 7, note (v); 1 Powell on Contr. 200; 1 Madd. Ch. Pr. 62 to 64.

(a) See Abbott v. Dermott, 34 Ga. 227.

enclosure act should make for him, and neither party at the time knew what the allotment would be, and were equally in the dark as to the value, the contract was held obligatory, although it turned out upon the allotment to be worth £200.[1] The like rule will apply to all cases of sale of real estate or personal estate made in good faith, where material circumstances affecting the value are equally unknown to both parties.

151. The general ground upon which all these distinctions proceed is, that mistake or ignorance of facts in parties is a proper subject of relief only when it constitutes a material ingredient in the contract of the parties and disappoints their intention by a mutual error, or where it is inconsistent with good faith and proceeds from a violation of the obligations which are imposed by law upon the conscience of either party. But where each party is equally innocent, and there is no concealment of facts which the other party has a right to know, and no surprise or imposition exists, the mistake or ignorance, whether mutual or unilateral, is treated as laying no foundation for equitable interference. It is strictly damnum absque injuria.[2]

152. One of the most common classes of cases in which relief is sought in equity on account of a mistake of facts is that of written agreements either executory or executed. Sometimes by mistake the written agreement contains less than the parties intended, sometimes it contains more, and sometimes it simply varies from their intent by expressing something different in substance from the truth of that intent.[3] In all such cases if the mistake is clearly made out by proofs entirely satisfactory, equity will reform the contract so as to make it conformable to the precise intent of the parties. But if the proofs are doubtful and unsatisfactory, and the mistake is not made entirely plain, equity will withhold relief, upon the ground that the written paper ought to be treated as a full and correct expression of the intent until the contrary is established beyond reasonable controversy.[4]

---

[1] Cited in Mortimer v. Capper, 2 Bro. Ch. R. 158; 6 Ves. 24; 1 Madd. Eq. Pr. 63; 1 Fonbl. Eq. B. 1, ch. 2, § 7, note (v). See also Pullen v. Ready, 2 Atk. R. 592; Gordon v. Gordon, 3 Swanst. 463, 467, 470, 471, 473, 476, 477; Ainslie v. Medlycott, 9 Ves. 13.

[2] See Jeremy on Eq. Jurisd. B. 3, Pt. 2, p. 358.

[3] See Durant v. Durant, 1 Cox, R. 58; Calverley v. Williams, 1 Ves. jr. 210.

[4] Shelburne v. Inchiquin, 1 Bro. Ch. R. 338, 341; Henkle v. Royal Assur.

153. It has indeed been said that where there is a written agreement the whole sense of the parties is presumed to be comprised therein; that it would be dangerous to make any addition to it in cases where there does not appear to be any fraud in leaving out anything; and that it is against the policy of the common law to allow parol evidence to add to, or vary the terms of, such an agreement.[1] As a general rule there is certainly much to recommend this doctrine. But however correct it may be as a general rule, it is very certain that Courts of Equity will grant relief upon clear proof of a mistake, notwithstanding that mistake is to be made out by parol evidence.[2] Lord Hardwicke upon an occasion of this sort said: 'No doubt but this court has jurisdiction to relieve in respect of a plain mistake in contracts in writing as well as against frauds in contracts; so that if reduced into writing contrary to the intent of the parties, on proper proof that would be rectified.'[3] And this doctrine has been recognized upon many other occasions.[4] (a)

Company, 1 Ves. 317; Davis v. Symonds, 1 Cox, R. 404; Townshend v. Stangroom, 6 Ves. 332 to 338; Woolam v. Hearn, 7 Ves. 217, 218; Gillespie v. Moon, 2 John. Ch. R. 585; Lyman v. United Ins. Co., 2 John. Ch. R. 630; Graves v. Boston Marine Insur. Co., 2 Cranch, 442, 444.

[1] 1 Fonbl. Eq. B. 1, ch. 3, § 11, and note (o); Irnham v. Child, 1 Bro. Ch. 92, 93; Woolam v. Hearn, 7 Ves. 211; Rich v. Jackson, 4 Bro. Parl. R. 514; s. c. 6 Ves. 334, note; Jeremy on Eq. Jurisd. B. 3, Pt. 2, ch. 4, § 1, p. 432; Davis v. Symonds, 1 Cox, R. 402, 404.

[2] Marquis of Townshend v. Stangroom, 6 Ves. 332, 333; 1 Fonbl. Eq. B. 1, ch. 3, § 11; Shelburne v. Inchiquin, 1 Bro. Ch. R. 338, 350; Simpson v. Vaughan, 2 Atk. 31; Langley v. Brown, 2 Atk. 203.

[3] Henkle v. Royal Assur. Co., 1 Ves. 314. See Townshend v. Stangroom, 6 Ves. 332 to 339; Shelburne v. Inchiquin, 1 Bro. Ch. R. 338, 350; Sugden on Vendors, pp. 146 to 159 (7th edit.); Hunt v. Rousmaniere, 8 Wheat. R. 211; s. c. 1 Peters, Sup. C. R. 13.

[4] Ibid.; Motteux v. London Assur. Co., 1 Atk. R. 545; Gillespie v. Moon, 2 John. Ch. R. 585; Lyman v. United Insur. Co., 2 John. Ch. R. 630; Simpson v. Vaughan, 2 Atk. 33; Langley v. Brown, 2 Atk. 203; Bust v. Barlow, 3 Bro. Ch. R. 454; 5 Ves. 595; Irnham v. Child, 1 Bro. Ch. R. 94; Baker v. Paine, 1 Ves. 457; Crosby v. Middleton, Pr. Ch. 309; Wiser v. Blachley, 1 John. Ch. R. 607; South Sea Co. v. D'Oliffe, cited 1 Ves. 317; 2 Ves. 377; 5 Ves. 601; Pitcairne v. Ogbourne, 2 Ves. 375; 1 Fonbl. Eq. B. 1, ch. 3, § 11, and note (o); Mitf. Pl. 127, 128; Clowes v. Higginson, 1 Ves. & Beames, 524; Ball v. Storie, 1 Sim. & Stu. R. 210; Marshall on Insurance, B. 1, ch. 8, § 4;

(a) Chapman v. Hurd, 67 Ill. 234; Parsons v. Bignold, 13 Sim. 518; Murray v. Dake, 46 Cal. 644; Rider v. Powell, 4 Abb. Dec. 63; New v. Wamback, 42 Ind. 456; and see note on Mistake of Law, ante, p. 154.

154. It is difficult to reconcile this doctrine with that rule of evidence at the common law which studiously excludes the admission of parol evidence to vary or control written contracts. The same principle lies at the foundation of each class of decisions, that is to say, the desire to suppress frauds and to promote general good faith and confidence in the formation of contracts. The danger of setting aside the solemn engagements of parties when reduced to writing, by the introduction of parol evidence substituting other material terms and stipulations, is sufficiently obvious.[1] But what shall be said where those terms and stipulations are suppressed or omitted by fraud or imposition? Shall the guilty party be allowed to avail himself of such a triumph over innocence and credulity to accomplish his own base designs? That would be to allow a rule introduced to suppress fraud to be the most effectual promotion and encouragement of it. And hence Courts of Equity have not hesitated to entertain jurisdiction to reform all contracts where a fraudulent suppression, omission, or insertion of a material stipulation exists, notwithstanding to some extent it breaks in upon the uniformity of the rule as to the exclusion of parol evidence to vary or control contracts; wisely deeming such cases to be a proper exception to the rule, and proving its general soundness.[2]

155. It is upon the same ground that equity interferes in cases of written agreements where there has been an innocent omission or insertion of a material stipulation contrary to the intention of both parties and under a mutual mistake. To allow it to prevail

Clinan v. Cooke, 1 Sch. & Lefr. 32, &c. See Sugden on Vendors, pp. 146 to 159 (7th edit.); Andrews v. Essex F. & M. Insur. Co., 3 Mason, R. 10.

[1] See Woolam v. Hearn, 7 Ves. 219.

[2] Newl. Eq. Contr. ch. 19; 1 Eq. Abridg. 20, pl. 5; Filmer v. Gott, 4 Bro. Parl. Cas. 230; 1 Fonbl. Eq. B. 1, ch. 2, § 8; Id. ch. 3, § 4, and note (n); Irnham v. Child, 1 Bro. Ch. R. 92; Portmore v. Morris, 2 Bro. Ch. R. 219; 1 Eq. Abridg. 19; Id. 20, Agreements, B.; Hunt v. Rousmaniere, 8 Wheat. R. 211; s. c. 1 Peters, Sup. C. R. 13. In cases of this sort it is often said, that the admission of the parol evidence to establish fraud or circumvention is not so much to vary the contract as to establish something collateral to it, which shows that it ought not to be enforced. Davis v. Symonds, 1 Cox, R. 402, 404, 405. But in cases of mistake the party often seeks to enforce the contract after insisting upon its being reformed. See 3 Starkie on Evid. Pt. 4, pp. 1015, 1016, 1018; Pitcairne v. Ogbourne, 2 Ves. 375, 376; Baker v. Paine, 1 Ves. 456. See also Attorney-Gen. v. Sitwell, Younge & Coll. 559, 582, and the remarks of Mr. Baron Alderson against the admission of parol evidence in such cases. Post, § 161, p. 173, note 4.

in such a case would be to work a surprise, or fraud, upon both parties; and certainly upon the one who is the sufferer. As much injustice would to the full be done under such circumstances as would be done by a positive fraud or an inevitable accident.[1] A Court of Equity would be of little value if it could suppress only positive frauds, and leave mutual mistakes, innocently made, to work intolerable mischiefs contrary to the intention of parties. It would be to allow an act originating in innocence to operate ultimately as a fraud, by enabling the party who receives the benefit of the mistake to resist the claims of justice under the shelter of a rule framed to promote it.[2] In a practical view there would be as much mischief done by refusing relief in such cases as there would be introduced by allowing parol evidence in all cases to vary written contracts.

156. We must therefore treat the cases in which equity affords relief, and allows parol evidence to vary and reform written contracts and instruments upon the ground of accident and mistake, as properly forming, like cases of fraud, exceptions to the general rule which excludes parol evidence and as standing upon the same policy as the rule itself.[3] If the mistake should be admitted by the other side, the court would certainly not overturn any rule of equity by varying the deed; but it would be an equity dehors the instrument.[4] And if it should be proved by other evidence entirely satisfactory and equivalent to an admission, the reasons for relief would seem to be equally cogent and conclusive.[5] It would be a great defect in the moral jurisdiction of the court if under such circumstances it were incapable of administering relief.[6]

---

[1] Joynes v. Statham, 3 Atk. 388; Ramsbottom v. Colden, 1 Ves. & Beames, R. 168; 1 Fonbl. Eq. B. 1, ch. 2, § 8, note (z); Id. § 7, note (v).

[2] Townshend v. Stangroom, 6 Ves. 336, 337; Gillespie v. Moon, 2 John. Ch. R. 596; Joynes v. Statham, 3 Atk. 385; 3 Starkie, Evid. Pt. 4, pp. 1018, 1019; Pitcairne v. Ogbourne, 2 Ves. R. 377, and South Sea Company v. D'Oliffe, there cited.

[3] Joynes v. Statham, 3 Atk. 388; Ramsbottom v. Golden, 1 Ves. & Beam. R. 168; 1 Fonbl. Eq. B. 1, ch. 2, § 11, note (o); Mitf. Eq. Pl. by Jeremy, 129; Clowes v. Higginson, 1 Ves. & Beam. R. 526, 527; Ball v. Storie, 1 Sim. & Stu. 210.

[4] Davis v. Symonds, 1 Cox, R. 404, 405.

[5] Irnham v. Child, 1 Bro. Ch. R. 92, 93.

[6] See Townshend v. Stangroom, 6 Ves. 336, 337; Gillespie v. Moon, 2 John. Ch. R. 596.

157. And this remark naturally conducts us back again to the qualification of the doctrine (already stated) which is insisted upon by Courts of Equity. Relief will be granted in cases of written instruments only where there is a plain mistake clearly made out by satisfactory proofs.[1] It is true that this in one sense leaves the rule somewhat loose, as every court is still left free to say what is a plain mistake, and what are proper and satisfactory proofs. But this is an infirmity belonging to the administration of justice generally; for in many cases different judges will differ as to the result and weight of evidence, and consequently they may make different decisions upon the same evidence.[2] But the qualification is most material, since it cannot fail to operate as a weighty caution upon the minds of all judges; (a) and it forbids relief whenever the evidence is loose, equivocal, or contradictory, or it is in its texture open to doubt or to opposing presumptions.[3]

158. Many of the cases included under this head have arisen under circumstances which brought them within the reach of the Statute of Frauds (as it is commonly called), which requires certain contracts to be in writing. But the rule as to rejecting parol evidence to contradict written agreements is by no means confined to such cases. It stands as a general rule of law independent of that statute.[4] It is founded upon the ground that the written instrument furnishes better evidence of the delib-

---

[1] Gillespie v. Moon, 2 John. Ch. R. 595 to 597; Lyman v. United Insurance Company, 2 John. Ch. R. 630; Henkle v. Royal Assurance Company, 1 Ves. 317; Jeremy on Eq. Jurisd. Pt. 2, ch. 2, p. 368; Id. ch. 4, p. 490, 491; Townshend v. Stangroom, 6 Ves. 328, 339.

[2] See Lord Eldon's Remarks in Townshend v. Stangroom, 6 Ves. 333, 334.

[3] Lord Thurlow in one case said that the final evidence must be strong irrefragable evidence. Shelburne v. Inchiquin, 1 Bro. Ch. R. 347. If by this language his Lordship only meant that the mistake should be made out by evidence clear of all reasonable doubt, its accuracy need not be questioned. But if he meant that it should be in its nature or degree incapable of refutation, so as to be beyond any doubt and beyond controversy, the language is too general. See Attorney-General v. Sitwell, 1 Younge & Coll. 583.

[4] Woolam v. Hearn, 7 Ves. 218; 1 Fonbl. Eq. B. 1, ch. 2, § 11, note (v); Clowes v. Higginson, 1 Ves. & Beames, R. 526; Pitcairne v. Ogbourne, 2 Ves. 375; Sugden on Vendors, ch. 3, § 3; Parteriche v. Powlet, 2 Atk. 383, 384; 3 Starkie on Evid. Pt. 4, tit. Parol Evid. pp. 995 to 1020; Davis v. Symonds, 1 Cox, R. 402, 404, 405.

(a) See Hall v. Claggett, 2 Md. Ch. 151, 153.

erate intention of the parties than any parol proof can supply.[1] And the exceptions to the rule originating in accident and mistake have been equally applied to written instruments within and without the Statute of Frauds. (a) Thus for instance relief has been granted or refused according to circumstances in cases of asserted mistakes in policies of insurance (b) even after a loss has taken place.[2] And in the same manner equity has interfered in other cases of contract, not only of a commercial nature but of any other nature.[3]

159. The relief granted by Courts of Equity in cases of this character is not confined to mere executory contracts by altering and conforming them to the real intent of the parties, but it is extended to solemn instruments which are made by the parties in pursuance of such executory or preliminary contracts. And indeed if the court acted otherwise there would be a great defect of justice, and the main evils of the mistake would remain irremediable. Hence in preliminary contracts for conveyances, settlements, and other solemn instruments the court acts efficiently by reforming the preliminary contract itself, and decreeing a due execution of it as reformed, if no conveyance or other solemn instrument in pursuance of it has been executed. And if such conveyance or instrument has been executed, it reforms the latter also by making it such as the parties originally intended.[4]

---

[1] Ibid.

[2] Motteux v. London Assur. Co., 1 Atk. 545; Henkle v. Royal Ex. Assur. Co., 1 Ves. 317; Lyman v. United Insur. Co., 2 John. Ch. R. 630; Head v. Boston Mar. Ins. Co., 2 Cranch, 419, 444; Marsh. Insur. B. 1, ch. 8, § 4; Id. Andrews v. Essex Fire and Mar. Ins. Co., 3 Mason, R. 10; Delaware Ins. Co. v. Hogan, 2 Wash. Cir. R. 5.

[3] Baker v. Paine, 1 Ves. 456; Getman's Executors v. Beardsley, 2 John. Ch. R. 274; Simpson v. Vaughan, 2 Atk. 30; Bishop v. Church, 2 Ves. 100, 371; Thomas v. Frazer, 3 Ves. 399; Finley v. Lynn, 6 Cranch, 238; Mitf. Pl. Eq. by Jeremy, 129, 130; Pitcairne v. Ogbourne, 2 Ves. 375, and South Sea Company v. D'Oliffe, there cited, p. 377; 3 Starkie, Evid. Pt. 4, p. 1019; Underhill v. Harwood, 10 Ves. 225, 226; Edwin v. East India Company, 2 Vern. 210; Edwards v. Child, 2 Vern. 727.

[4] See Newland on Contr. ch. 19, pp. 338 to 347; Mitf. Eq. Pl. by Jeremy,

---

(a) As to cases of land where the intention was to convey more than the deed covers, see Glass v. Hulbert, 102 Mass. 24. But see contra Hitchins v. Pettingill, 58 N. H. 386; ante, note to § 140, at p. 155.

(b) National Ins. Co. v. Crane, 16 Md. 260; Keith v. Globe Ins. Co., 52 Ill. 518; Oliver v. Mutual Ins. Co., 2 Curt. 277. See Mackenzie v. Coulson, L. R. 8 Eq. 368; Parker v. Benjamin, 53 Ill. 255.

160. There is less difficulty in reforming written instruments where the mistake is mainly or wholly made out by other preliminary written instruments or memoranda of the agreement. The danger of public mischief or private inconvenience is far less in such cases than it is in cases where parol evidence is admitted. And accordingly Courts of Equity interfere with far less scruple to correct mistakes in the former than mistakes in the latter.[1] Thus marriage settlements are often reformed and varied so as to conform to the previous articles; and conveyances of real estate are in like manner controllable by the terms of the prior written contract.[2] Memoranda of a less formal character are also admissible for the same purpose.[3] But in all such cases it must be plainly made out that the parties meant in their final instruments merely to carry into effect the arrangements designated in the prior contract or articles. For as the parties are at liberty to vary the original agreement if the circumstances of the

128, 129, 130; Sugden on Vendors, pp. 146 to 159 (7th edit.); South Sea Company *v.* D'Oliffe, cited 2 Ves. 377; 2 Atk. 525; Henkle *v.* Royal Ex. Assurance Comp., 1 Ves. 417, 318; Baker *v.* Paine, 1 Ves. 456. But see Attorney-Gen. *v.* Sitwell, 1 Younge & Coll. 559, 582; Post, § 161.

[1] Jeremy on Eq. Jurisd. Pt. 2, ch. 2, pp. 368, 369; ch. 4, § 5, pp. 490, 491; Durant *v.* Durant, 1 Cox, R. 58; Grounds and Rudim. of the Law, M. 113, p. 81 (edit. 1751); Toth. 229 [131].

[2] The cases on this head are exceedingly numerous. Many of them will be found collected in Newland on Contr. ch. 19, p. 337; Com. Dig. Chancery, 3 Z. 11, 12; 1 Fonbl. Eq. B. 1, ch. 3, § 11, note (*p*); Id. ch. 6, § 7, and notes; 2 Bridg. Dig. Marriage, ii. p. 300; 1 Fonbl. Eq. B. 1, ch. 2, § 7, note (*r*); Chitty, Eq. Dig. Settlement on Marriage, ix.; Randall *v.* Randall, 2 P. Will. 464; Randall *v.* Willis, 5 Ves. 275; West *v.* Erissey, 2 P. Will. 349, and Mr. Cox's note (1), p. 355; Jeremy, Eq. Jurisd. Pt. 2, ch. 2, p. 378 to 382; 3 Starkie, Evid. tit. Parol Evid. 10, 19; Barstow *v.* Kilvington, 5 Ves. 592. In cases of marriage articles the court will frequently give a construction to the words more favorable to the presumed intent of the parties than it does in some other cases. Thus in marriage articles, if there be a limitation to the parents for life, with remainder to the heirs of their bodies, the latter words are in equity generally construed to be words of purchase; and accordingly the court will carry such articles into effect by way of a strict settlement. Newland on Contr. ch. 19, p. 337; Fearne on Conting. Rem. pp. 90 to 113 (7th edit. by Butler); 1 Fonbl. Eq. B. 1, ch. 3, § 11, note (*p*); Id. ch. 6, § 7, and notes, § 16, note (*e*); Randall *v.* Willis, 5 Ves. 275; West *v.* Erissey, 2 P. Will. 349; and Mr. Cox's note, ibid. (1); Heneage *v.* Hunloke, 2 Atk. 455, and Sanders's note, Id. 457 (1); Jeremy on Eq. Jurisd. Pt. 2, ch. 2, pp. 378 to 382; Taggart *v.* Taggart, 1 Sch. & Lef. 84; Blackburn *v.* Staples, 2 V. & Beam. 368, 369; Jeremy on Eq. Jurisd. B. 3, Pt. 2, ch. 2, p. 377, 378, 379.

[3] Motteux *v.* London Assurance Company, 1 Atk. R. 545; Baker *v.* Paine, 1 Ves. 456.

case lead to the supposition that a new intent has supervened, there can be no just claim for relief upon the ground of mistake.[1] The very circumstance that the final instrument of conveyance or settlement differs from the preliminary contract affords of itself some presumption of an intentional change of purpose or agreement, unless there is some recital in it or some other attendant circumstance which demonstrates that it was merely in pursuance of the original contract.[2] It is upon a similar ground that Courts of Equity as well as Courts of Law act, in holding that where there is a written contract all antecedent propositions, negotiations, and parol interlocutions on the same subject are to be deemed merged in such contract.[3]

161. In cases of asserted mistake in written contracts where the mistake is to be established by parol evidence, the question has often been mooted how far a Court of Equity ought to be active in granting relief by a specific performance in favor of the party seeking to reform the contract upon such parol evidence, and to obtain performance of it when it shall stand reformed. It is admitted that a defendant against whom a specific performance of a written agreement is sought may insist by way of answer upon the mistake as a bar to such a bill; because he may insist upon any matter which shows it to be inequitable to grant such relief. A Court of Equity is not, like a Court of Law, bound to enforce a written contract; but it may exercise its discretion when a specific performance is sought, and may leave the party to his remedy at law.[4] It will not therefore interfere

---

[1] 1 Fonbl. Eq. B. 1, ch. 3, § 11, note (*p*); Id. ch. 6, §§ 1, 13; Legg *v.* Goldwire, Cas. Temp. Talb. 20; West *v.* Erissey, 2 P. Will. 349, and Mr. Cox's note (1), 355; Beaumont *v.* Bromley, 1 Turn. & Russ. R. 41; Jeremy on Eq. Jurisd. Pt. 2, ch. 2, pp. 379, 380; Id. 50, 51, 52, 53; ch. 4, § 5, pp. 490, 491; Id. 1 Madd. Eq. Pr. 85 (3d ed.).

[2] Ibid.

[3] Rich *v.* Jackson, 4 Bro. Ch. R. 513; s. c. 6 Ves. 334, note; Pickering *v.* Dawson, 4 Taunt. 786; Kain *v.* Old, 2 B. & Cressw. 634; Parkhurst *v.* Van Cortlandt, 1 John. Ch. R. 273; s. c. 14 John. R. 15; 1 Fonbl. Eq. B. 1, ch. 3, §§ 8, 11; Davis *v.* Symonds, 1 Cox, R. 402, 404; Vandervoort *v.* Smith, 2 Cain. R. 155.

[4] Com. Dig. Chancery, 2 C. 16; Joynes *v.* Statham, 3 Atk. 388; Garrard *v.* Grinling, 2 Swanst. R. 257; Pitcairne *v.* Ogbourne, 2 Ves. 375; Legal *v.* Miller, 2 Ves. 299; Mason *v.* Armitage, 13 Ves. 25; Clark *v.* Grant, 14 Ves. 519; Hepburn *v.* Dunlop, 1 Wheat. 197; Clowes *v.* Higginson, 1 Ves. & B. 524; Winch *v.* Winchester, 1 Ves. & B. R. 375; Ramsbottom *v.* Golden, 1 Ves. & B. 165; Flood *v.* Finley, 2 Ball & B. 53; Clark *v.* Grant, 14 Ves. 519; Gil-

to sustain a bill for a specific performance when it would be against conscience and justice so to do. On the other hand it seems equally clear that a party may as plaintiff have relief against a written contract by having the same set aside and cancelled or modified, whenever it is founded in a mistake of material facts, and it would be unconscientious and unjust for the other party to enforce it at law or in equity.[1] But the case intended to be put differs from each of these. It is where the party plaintiff seeks not to set aside the agreement, but to enforce it when it is reformed and varied by the parol evidence. A very strong inclination of opinion has been repeatedly expressed by the English courts not to decree a specific performance in this latter class of cases; that is to say, not to admit parol evidence to establish a mistake in a written agreement, and then to enforce it as varied and established by that evidence. On various occasions such relief has under such circumstances been denied.[2] But it is extremely difficult to perceive the principle upon which such decisions can be supported consistently with the acknowledged exercise of jurisdiction in the court to reform written contracts and to decree relief thereon.[3] In America

lespie v. Moon, 2 John. Ch. R. 585, 598; Townshend v. Stangroom, 6 Ves. 328; Price v. Dyer, 17 Ves. 357.

[1] See Ball v. Storie, 1 Sim. & Stu. R. and the cases there cited.

[2] See Woolam v. Hearn, 7 Ves. 211; Higginson v. Clowes, 15 Ves. 516; Clinan v. Cooke, 1 Sch. & Lef. 38, 39; Clowes v. Higginson, 1 Ves. & B. 524; Winch v. Winchester, 1 Ves. & B. 375; Clark v. Grant, 14 Ves. 519; Rich v. Jackson, 6 Ves. 335; 4 Bro. Ch. R. 514; Ogilvie v. Foljambe, 3 Meriv. R. 58, 63; Townshend v. Stangroom, 6 Ves. 328; Jeremy on Equity Jurisd. B. 3, Pt. 2, ch. 4, § 1, p. 432; Clark v. Grant, 14 Ves. 519; Baker v. Paine, 1 Ves. 457; Gordon v. Uxbridge, 2 Madd. R. 106; Attorney-Gen. v. Sitwell, 1 Younge & Coll. 559, 582.

[3] Mr. Baron Alderson, in Attorney-Gen. v. Sitwell (1 Younge & Coll. 559, 582, 583), expressed a strong opinion against the reforming of a contract and then decreeing the performance of it in equity. In that case the question was whether by a memorandum of agreement to sell a certain manor of the Crown 'with the appurtenances,' an advowson appurtenant or appendant thereto passed; the statute of 17 Edward 2, ch. 13, having distinctly provided that the king shall not convey an advowson without express words to that effect. Mr. Baron Alderson in delivering his judgment said: 'The second objection is upon the terms of the contract. The plaintiffs professed to sell the manor of Eckington " with the appurtenances;" and as the appurtenances of a manor ordinarily include an advowson appendant or appurtenant, the defendant contends that he is not bound to take the property unless there be a conveyance to him in the terms of the memorandum in which the plaintiffs executed the

Mr. Chancellor Kent, after a most elaborate consideration of the subject, has not hesitated to reject the distinction as unfounded in justice, and has decreed relief to a plaintiff standing in the precise predicament.[1] (a)

contract; and that the Crown must either give him the manor without excluding the advowson, or otherwise that the contract ought not to be performed. If the question was one between subject and subject, there would, I think, be great difficulty in decreeing the execution of the contract upon any other terms than those for which the defendant contends. It appears to me quite clear that the memorandum of agreement would carry this advowson under the general words "with the appurtenances." There are various authorities to that effect, and I may more particularly refer to Viner's Abridgment, tit. Prerog. (C. c.) 9. This would have been clear therefore as between subject and subject. And in that case the next question which would have arisen would have been, — whether or not, on the ground of mistake, one party not intending to sell, and the other not intending to purchase the advowson, I could have reformed the agreement and have directed the specific performance of it when so reformed. I confess I should have had great difficulty in holding that this could be done; because I cannot help feeling that in the case of an executory agreement, first to reform and then to decree an execution of it would be virtually to repeal the Statute of Frauds. The only ground on which I think the case could have been put would have been that the answer contained an admission of the agreement as stated in the bill; and the parties mutually agreeing that there was a mistake, the case might have fallen within the principle of those cases at law where there is a declaration on an agreement not within the statute, and no issue taken upon the agreement by the plea; because in such case it would seem as if, the agreement of the parties being admitted by the record, the case would no longer be within the statute. I should then have taken time to consider whether, according to the dicta of many venerable judges, I should not have been authorized to reform an executory agreement for the conveyance of an estate, where it was admitted to have been the intention of both parties that a portion of the estate was not to pass. But in my present view of the question it seems to me that the court ought not in any case, where the mistake is denied or not admitted by the answer, to admit parol evidence, and upon that evidence to reform an executory agreement.'

[1] Gillespie v. Moon, 2 John. Ch. R. 585; Keisselbrack v. Livingston, 4 John. Ch. R. 144. See also Baker v. Paine, 1 Ves. 456; Shelburne v. Inchiquin, 1 Bro. Ch. R. 339; Joynes v. Statham, 3 Atk. 388; 6 Ves. 337, 338; Ball v. Storie, 1 Sim. & Stu. 210; Burn v. Burn, 8 Ves. 573, 583; 1 Eq. Abridg. 20, Pl. 5; Sims v. Urrey, 2 Ch. Cas. 225; s. c. Freem. R. 16; Jalabert v. Chandos, 1 Eden, R. 372; Pember v. Matthews, 1 Bro. Ch. R. 52; Jones v. Sheriff, cited 9 Mod. 88; The Hiram, 1 Wheat. R. 444; Hunt v. Rousmaniere, 8 Wheat. R. 211; 1 Peters, Sup. C. R. 13; Hogan v. Dela-

(a) Hitchins v. Pettingill, 58 N. H. 386, and cases cited. See however Osborne v. Phelps, 19 Conn. 62; Elder v. Elder, 10 Maine, 80; Thomas v. McCormick, 9 Dana, 108; Climer v. Hovey, 15 Mich. 18; Glass v. Hulbert, 102 Mass. 24.

162. Courts of Equity will grant relief in cases of mistake in written contracts, not only when the fact of the mistake is expressly established, but also when it is fairly implied from the nature of the transaction. Thus in cases where there has been a joint loan of money to two or more obligors, and they are by the instrument made jointly liable, but not jointly and severally,

ware Insur. Co., 1 Wash. C. C. R. 422; Shelburne *v.* Inchiquin, 3 Bro. Ch. R. 338; Walker *v.* Walker, 2 Atk. 98. But see 1 Sch. & Lefr. 39; Kekewick, Dig. Ch. Equity, I. The distinction stated in the text is certainly of a very artificial character, and difficult to be reconciled with the general principles of Courts of Equity. It is in effect a declaration that parol evidence shall be admissible to correct a writing as *against* a plaintiff, but not in *favor* of a plaintiff, seeking a specific performance. There is therefore no mutuality or equality in the operation of the doctrine. The ground is very clear that a Court of Equity ought not to enforce a contract where there is a mistake against the defendant, insisting upon and establishing the mistake; for it would be inequitable and unconscientious. And if the mistake is vital to the contract there is a like clear ground why equity should interfere at the instance of the party as plaintiff and cancel it; and if the mistake is partial only, why at his instance it should reform it. In these cases the remedial justice is equal; and the parol evidence to establish it is equally open to both parties to use as proof. Why should not the party aggrieved by a mistake in an agreement have relief in all cases, where he is plaintiff as well as where he is defendant? Why should not parol evidence be equally admissible to establish a mistake, as the foundation of relief in each case? The rules of evidence ought certainly to work equally for the benefit of each party. Mr. Chancellor Kent has forcibly observed, 'That it cannot make any difference in the reasonableness and justice of the remedy whether the mistake was to the prejudice of one party or the other. If the court has a competent jurisdiction to correct such mistakes (and that is a point understood and settled), the agreement, when corrected and made to speak the real sense of the parties, ought to be enforced, as well as any other agreement perfect in the first instance. It ought to have the same efficacy and be entitled to the same protection when made accurate under the decree of the court as when made accurate by the act of the parties. "Res accendent lumina rebus."' Keisselbrack *v.* Livingston, 4 Johns. Ch. R. 148, 149. It may be added that if the doctrine be founded upon the impropriety of admitting parol evidence to contradict a written agreement, that rule is not more broken in upon by the admission of it for the plaintiff than it is by the admission of it for the defendant. If the doctrine had been confined to cases arising under the Statute of Frauds, it would, if not more intelligible, at least have been less inconvenient in practice. But it does not appear to have been thus restricted, although the cases in which it has been principally relied on have been of that description. It will often be quite as unconscientious for a defendant to shelter himself under a defence of this sort against a plaintiff seeking the specific performance of a contract and the correction of a mistake, as it will be to enforce a contract against a defendant, which embodies a mistake to his prejudice. See Comyns, Dig. Chancery, 2 C. 4; 2 X. 3; 4 L. 2; Attorney-Gen. *v.* Sitwell, 1 Younge & Coll. R. 583.

the court has reformed the bond and made it joint and several, upon the reasonable presumption from the nature of the transaction that it was so intended by the parties and was omitted by want of skill or by mistake.[1] The debt being joint, the natural if not the irresistible inference in such cases is, that it is intended by all the parties that in every event the responsibility should attach to each obligor and to all equally. This can be done only by making the bond several as well as joint; for otherwise, in case of the death of one of the obligors the survivor or survivors only would be liable at law for the debt.[2] Indeed it seems now well established as a general principle, that every contract for a joint loan is in equity to be deemed as to the parties borrowing a joint and several contract, whether the transaction be of a mercantile nature or not; for in every such case it may fairly be presumed to be the intention of the parties that the creditor should have the several as well as the joint security of all the borrowers for the repayment of the debt.[3] Hence if one of the borrowers should die, the creditor has a right to proceed for immediate relief out of the assets of the deceased party, without claiming any relief against the surviving joint contractors, and without showing that the latter are unable to pay by reason of their insolvency.[4]

163. But where the inference of a joint original debt or liability is repelled, a Court of Equity will not interfere; for in such a case there is no ground to presume any mistake.[5] This doctrine has been very clearly expounded by Sir William Grant.

---

[1] Simpson *v.* Vaughan, 2 Atk. 31, 33; Bishop *v.* Church, 2 Ves. 100, 371; Thomas *v.* Frazer, 3 Ves. 399; Devaynes *v.* Noble, Sleech's case, 1 Meriv. R. 538, 539; Sumner *v.* Powell, 2 Meriv. 30, 35; Howe *v.* Contencin, 1 Bro. Ch. R. 27, 29; Ex parte Kendall, 17 Ves. 519, 520; Underhill *v.* Howard, 10 Ves. 209, 227; Hunt *v.* Rousmaniere, 8 Wheat. R. 212, 213; s. c. 1 Peters, Sup. C. R. 16; Weaver *v.* Shryork, 6 Serg. & R. 262, 264; Ex parte Symonds, 1 Cox, R. 200; Burn *v.* Burn, 3 Ves. 573, 583; Ex parte Bates & Henckill, 3 Ves. R. 400, note; Gray *v.* Chiswell, 9 Ves. 118.

[2] Weaver *v.* Shryork, 6 Serg. & R. 262, 264; Gray *v.* Chiswell, 9 Ves. 118; Ex parte Kendall, 17 Ves. 525.

[3] Thorpe *v.* Jackson, 2 Younge & Coll. 553; Wilkinson *v.* Henderson, 1 Mylne & Keen, 582. But see Richardson *v.* Horton, 6 Beav. R. 185.

[4] Ibid. But in all such cases the surviving partners are properly to be made parties, as they have a right to contest the demand, and are interested in taking the account. Ibid.

[5] See Hunt *v.* Rousmaniere, 8 Wheat. R. 212, 213, 214; s. c. 1 Peters, 16. See Richardson *v.* Horton, 6 Beav. R. 185.

'When,' says he, 'the obligation exists only in virtue of the covenant, its extent can be measured only by the words in which it is conceived. A partnership debt has been treated in equity as the several debt of each partner, although at law it is only the joint debt of all.[1] But there all the partners have had a benefit from the money advanced or the credit given, and the obligation of all to pay exists independently of any instrument by which the debt may have been secured. So where a joint bond has in equity been considered as several, there has been a credit previously given to the different persons who have entered into the obligation. It is not the bond that first created the liability.'[2]

164. It is upon the same ground that a Court of Equity will not reform a joint bond against a mere surety, so as to make it several against him upon the presumption of a mistake from the nature of the transaction; but it will require positive proof of an express agreement by him that it should be several as well as joint.[3] (a) And in other cases where the obligation or covenant is purely matter of arbitrary convention, not growing out of any antecedent liability in all or any of the obligors or covenanters to do what they have undertaken (as for example a bond or covenant of indemnity for the acts or debts of third persons) a Court of Equity will not by implication extend the responsibility from that of a joint, to a joint and several undertaking.[4] But if there be an express agreement to the effect that

---

[1] Post, § 676.

[2] Sumner *v.* Powell, 2 Meriv. R. 35, 36. See also Underhill *v.* Harwood, 10 Ves. 227; Thorpe *v.* Jackson, 2 Younge & Coll. 553; Ex parte Kendall, 17 Ves. 525; Cowell *v.* Sykes, 2 Russ. R. 191.

[3] Ibid.; Weaver *v.* Shryork, 6 Serg. & R. 262, 264, 265.

[4] Sumner *v.* Powell, 2 Meriv. R. 30, 35, 36; Harrison *v.* Mirge, 2 Wash. R. 136; Ward *v.* Webber, 1 Wash. R. 274; Thomas *v.* Frazer, 3 Ves. 399, 402; Burn *v.* Burn, 3 Ves. 573, 582; Richardson *v.* Horton, 6 Beav. R. 186.

(a) So where an obligee of a joint and several bond elected to take a joint judgment against all the obligors, and thus at law lost his right to a several remedy, equity refused him a remedy against the personal assets of a deceased obligor, who was only a surety. United States *v.* Price, 9 How. 83, where the cases are reviewed. See Wright *v.* Russell, 3 Wils. 530; Waters *v.* Riley, 2 Har. & G. 310; Harrison *v.* Field, 2 Wash. 136; Weaver *v.* Shryork, 6 Serg. & R. 262; Kennedy *v.* Carpenter, 2 Whart. 361; United States *v.* Cushman, 2 Sum. 426; Higgens's Case, 6 Coke, 44; Lechmere *v.* Fletcher, 1 Cromp. & M. 623; Sheehy *v.* Mandeville, 6 Cranch, 253; Prior *v.* Williams, 3 Abb. Dec. 626.

an obligation or other contract shall be joint and **several**, or to any other effect, and it is omitted by mistake in the instrument, a Court of Equity will under such circumstances grant relief as fully against a surety or guarantee as against the principal party.[1] (*a*)

165. In all cases of mistake in written instruments Courts of Equity will interfere only as between the original parties, or those claiming under them in privity; such as personal representatives, heirs, devisees, legatees, assignees, voluntary grantees, or judgment creditors, or purchasers from them with notice of the facts.[2] (*b*) As against bona fide purchasers for a valuable consideration without notice, Courts of Equity will grant no relief, because they have at least an equal equity to the protection of the court.[3]

166. In like manner as equity will grant relief in cases of mistake in written instruments to prevent manifest injustice and

---

[1] Ibid.; Wiser *v.* Blachley, 1 John. Ch. R. 607; Crosby *v.* Middleton, Prec. Ch. 309; s. c. 2 Eq. Abridg. 188 F.; Berg *v.* Radcliffe, 6 John. Ch. R. 302, 307, &c.; Rawstone *v.* Parr, 3 Russell, R. 424; s. c. Id. 539.

[2] Warwick *v.* Warwick, 3 Atk. 293; Com. Dig. Chancery, 2 C. 2; 4 J. 4.

[3] 1 Fonbl. Eq. B. 1, ch. 1, § 7, and notes; Id. ch. 3, § 11, note; Newland on Contracts, 344, 345; Davis *v.* Thomas, Sugden on Vend. ch. 3, pp. 143, 159 (7th edit.); Warwick *v.* Warwick, 3 Atk. 290, 293; Malden *v.* Merrill, 2 Atk. 13; West *v.* Erissey, 2 P. Will. 349; Powell *v.* Price, 2 P Will. 535; Ante, §§ 64 *c*, 108, 139; Post, §§ 381, 409, 434, 436.

(*a*) Equity also will decree the surrender of a bond for cancellation where it has not been executed by all who were expected to become jointly bound as co-sureties. Thus where the creditor had prepared the deed so as to show on its face that it was intended to contain a joint and several covenant by two sureties, and had sent it in that form to be executed by one of such sureties, but had not procured the execution of it by the other, and had not informed the surety who had executed it of this fact, but on the contrary had afterwards written to him as 'one of the sureties,' the principal debtor having become insolvent, — in this state of things it was held that the surety who had executed the instrument was in equity entitled to relief from all liability upon it. Evans *v.* Bremridge, 2 Kay & J. 174. See Keith *v.* Goodwin, 31 Vt. 268. The relief is granted in such a case because a condition precedent, complete execution and delivery, never having been performed, the deed has not taken effect. See Black *v.* Lamb, 1 Beasl. 108.

(*b*) Whitehead *v.* Brown, 18 Ala. 682; Rhodes *v.* Outcalt, 48 Mo. 367; Baskins *v.* Calhoun, 45 Ala. 582; Simpson *v.* Montgomery, 25 Ark. 365; Wall *v.* Arvington, 13 Ga. 93; White *v.* Wilson, 6 Blackf. 448; Stone *v.* Hale, 17 Ala. 564; Burke *v.* Anderson, 40 Ga. 535; Young *v.* Cason, 48 Mo. 259; Adams *v.* Stevens, 49 Maine, 362.

wrong and to suppress fraud, it will also grant relief and supply defects where by mistake the parties have omitted any acts or circumstances necessary to give due validity and effect to written instruments. Thus equity will supply any defect of circumstances in conveyances occasioned by mistake; (*a*) as of livery of seisin in the passing of a freehold, or of a surrender in case of a copyhold or the like ; so also misprisions and omissions in deeds, awards, and other solemn instruments whereby they are defective at law.[1] It will also interfere in cases of mistake in judgments, and other matters of record injurious to the rights of the party.[2] (*b*)

167. The same principle applies to cases where an instrument has been delivered up or cancelled under a mistake of the party, and in ignorance of the facts material to the rights derived under it. A Court of Equity will in such cases grant relief, upon the ground that the party is conscientiously entitled to enforce such rights, and that he ought to have the same benefit as if the instrument were in his possession with its entire original validity.[3] (*c*)

168. And for the same reason equity will give effect to the real intentions of the parties as gathered from the objects of the instrument and the circumstances of the case, although the instrument may be drawn up in a very inartificial and untechnical

---

[1] 1 Fonbl. Eq. B. 1, ch. 1, § 7; Id. ch. 3, § 1, and the cases there cited; Id. ch. 2, § 7, and notes; Grounds and Rudim. of the Law, M. 112, p. 81 (edit. 1751); Com. Dig. Chancery, Z.; Kekewick, Dig. Ch. Equity, 1; Newland on Contracts, ch. 19, p. 342 to 350; Jeremy on Eq. Jurisd. B. 3, Pt. 2, ch. 2, pp. 367, 368, 369; Id. ch. 4, § 5, pp. 489, 490, 494, 495; Thorne *v.* Thorne, 1 Vern. R. 141; Com. Dig. Chancery, 2 T. 1, to 2 T. 7; 1 Madd. Ch. Pr. 42; Id. 55, 65; Fothergill *v.* Fothergill, 2 Freeman, R. 256, 257.

[2] Jeremy on Eq. Jurisd. B. 3, Pt. 2, ch. 4, § 5, p. 492; Barnsley *v.* Powell, 1 Ves. R. 119, 284, 289; Com. Dig. Chancery, 3 W.

[3] East India Co. *v.* Donald, 9 Ves. 275; East India Co. *v.* Neave, 5 Ves. 173.

(*a*) Commonwealth *v.* Reading Bank, 137 Mass. 431, 443; Batesville Institute *v.* Kauffman, 18 Wall. 151; Morris *v.* Bacon, 123 Mass. 58.

(*b*) See Quivey *v.* Baker, 37 Cal. 465; Gump's Appeal, 65 Penn. St. 476; Calwell *v.* Warner, 36 Conn. 224; Loss *v.* Obry, 7 C. E. Green, 52; Byrne *v.* Edmonds, 23 Gratt. 200; Bartlett *v.* Broderick, 34 Iowa, 517; Kearney *v.* Sacer, 37 Md. 264; Wheeler *v.* Kirtland, 23 N. J. Eq. 15; Palmer *v.* Bethard, 66 Ill. 529; Chapman *v.* Hurd, 67 Ill. 234; Wardlaw *v.* Wardlaw, 50 Ga. 544.

(*c*) See Lemon *v.* Phœnix Ins. Co., 38 Conn. 294; Scholefield *v.* Templer, Johns. (Eng. Ch.) 155.

manner. For however just in general the rule may be, 'Quoties in verbis nulla est ambiguitas, ibi nulla expositio contra verba expressa fienda est;'[1] yet that rule shall not prevail to defeat the manifest intent and object of the parties, where it is clearly discernible on the face of the instrument, and the ignorance or blunder or mistake of the parties has prevented them from expressing it in the appropriate language.[2] Thus if one in consideration of natural love should execute a feoffment, or a lease and release, or a bargain and sale, it would, notwithstanding the use of the technical words, be held to operate as a covenant to stand seised.[3] And the same rule would be applied if, under the like circumstances, instead of the words 'bargain and sell,' the words 'give and grant,' or 'enfeoff, alien, and confirm,' should be used in a deed.[4]

169. There is also another marked instance of the application of the remedial authority of Courts of Equity, and that is, in regard to the execution of powers. In no case will equity interfere where there has been a non-execution of a power as contradistinguished from a trust;[5] for if a trust be coupled with a power there (as we shall presently see)[6] the trust will be enforced, notwithstanding the force of the power does not execute it. But if there be a defective execution or attempt at execution of a mere power, there equity will interpose and supply the defect, not universally indeed, but in favor of parties for whom the person entrusted with the execution of the power is under a moral

---

[1] Co. Litt. 147 a.
[2] Jeremy on Eq. Jurisd. B. 3, Pt. 2, ch. 2, pp. 367, 368; Smith v. Packhurst, 3 Atk. 136; Stapilton v. Stapilton, 1 Atk. 8; 1 Fonbl. Eq. B. 1, ch. 6, §§ 11, 13, and note (d); Id. § 16, and note (e); Id. § 18, and note (n).
[3] Jeremy on Eq. Jurisd. B. 3, Pt. 2, ch. 3, pp. 367, 368; Thompson v. Attfield, 1 Vern. R. 40; Stapilton v. Stapilton, 1 Atk. 8; Thorne v. Thorne, 1 Vern. 141; Brown v. Jones, 1 Atk. 190, 191.
[4] Jeremy, ibid.; Harrison v. Austin, 3 Mod. R. 237. The same point was recognized in Doungsworth v. Blair, 1 Keen, R. 795, 801, where the Master of the Rolls said: 'An indenture, which is intended to be an indenture of release, but cannot operate as such, may for the purpose of carrying into effect the intention of the parties, and if there be a proper consideration, be construed as a covenant to stand seised.'
[5] See Brown v. Higgs, 8 Ves. 570; Holmes v. Coghill, 7 Ves. 499; s. c. 12 Ves. 206; Tollet v. Tollet, 2 P. Will. 489; 1 Fonbl. Eq. B. 1, ch. 1, § 7, note (v); Id. ch. 4, § 25, note (h) and (k); Jeremy on Eq. Jurisd. B. 3, Pt. 2, ch. 2, pp. 376, 377; Sugden on Powers, ch. 6, § 3; Post, § 176, note.
[6] Post, § 176, and note; Burrough v. Philcox, 5 Mylne & Craig, 73, 92.

or legal obligation to provide by an execution of the power. Thus such a defective execution will be aided in favor of persons standing upon a valuable or a meritorious consideration; such as a bona fide purchaser for a valuable consideration, a creditor, a wife, and a legitimate child,[1] unless indeed such aid of the defective execution would under all the circumstances be inequitable to other persons, or it is repelled by some counter equity.[2] Indeed if a general power to raise money for any purposes be given so that the donee of the power may if he choose execute it in his own favor, and he should execute it in favor of mere volunteers, there a Court of Equity will in favor of creditors deem the money assets against the volunteers, upon the ground that the donee of the power has an absolute dominion over the power and the property.[3]

170. The reason for this distinction between the non-execution of a power and the defective execution of it has been stated with great clearness and precision by a learned judge. 'The difference,' he said, ' is betwixt a non-execution and a defective execution of a power. The latter will always be aided in equity under the circumstances mentioned, it being the duty of every man to pay his debts, and of a husband or father to provide for his wife or child. But this court will not help the non-execution of a power which is left to the free will and election of the party whether to execute or not; for which reason equity will not say he shall execute it, or do that for him which he does not think fit to do for himself.'[4] Indeed a Court of Equity by

[1] 1 Fonbl. Eq. B. 1, ch. 1, § 7, note (v); Id. ch. 4, § 25, and note (h), (i), (m); Id. ch. 5, § 2, and notes; Fothergill v. Fothergill, 2 Freem. R. 256, 257; Com. Dig. Chan. 4 H. 1, to 4 H. 4; 4 H. 6; Gilbert, Lex Pretoria, pp. 300 to 306; Jeremy on Eq. Jurisd. B. 3, Pt. 2, ch. 2, p. 372.

[2] 1 Fonbl. Eq. B. 1, ch. 1, § 7, and note (v).

[3] Post, § 176, and note.

[4] The Master of the Rolls, in Tollet v. Tollet, 2 P. Will. 490. See also Lassells v. Cornwallis, 2 Vern. 465; Crossling v. Crossling, 2 Cox, R. 396; 1 Fonbl. Eq. B. 1, ch. 4, § 25, and notes; Id. ch. 1, § 7, and notes; Sugden on Powers, ch. 6, § 3, p. 315. Sir William Grant, in Holmes v. Coghill (7 Ves. 506), and Lord Erskine in the same case on appeal (12 Ves. 212), have expressed dissatisfaction with this distinction, as not quite consistent with the principles of law or equity, though fully established by authority. The former, in reasoning on the case of a power to charge an estate with £2000 by deed or will, which had not been executed, and of which creditors sought the benefit, as if executed, said: ' To say that, without a deed or will, this sum shall be raised, is to subject the owner of the estate to a charge in a case in which he

acting otherwise in the case of a non-execution of a power would in effect deprive the party of all discretion as to the exercise of it, and would thus overthrow the very intention manifested by never consented to bear it. The chance that it may never be executed, or that it may not be executed in the manner prescribed, is an advantage he secures to himself by the agreement, and which no one has a right to take from him. In this respect there is no difference between a non-execution and a defective execution of a power. By the compact the estate ought not to be charged in either case. It is difficult therefore to discover a sound principle for the authority, this court assumes, for aiding a defective execution in certain cases. If the intention of the party possessing the power is to be regarded, and not the interest of the party to be affected by the execution, that intention ought to be executed wherever it is manifested; for the owner of the estate has nothing to do with the purpose. To him it is indifferent whether it is to be exercised for a creditor or a volunteer. But if the interest of the party to be affected by the execution is to be regarded, why in any case exercise the power, except in the form and manner prescribed? He is an absolute stranger to the equity between the possessor of the power and the party in whose favor it is intended to be executed. As against the debtor, it is right that he should pay. But what equity is there for the creditor to have the money raised out of the estate of a third person, in a case in which it was never agreed that it should be raised? The owner is not heard to say it will be a grievous burthen, and of no merit or utility. He is told the case provided for exists; it is formally right; he has nothing to do with the purpose. But upon a defect which this court is called upon to supply, he is not permitted to retort this argument, and to say it is not formally right: the case provided for does not exist; and he has nothing to do with the purpose. In the sort of equity upon this subject there is some want of equality. But the rule is perfectly settled; and though perhaps with some violation of principle, with no practical inconvenience.'

There is much strength in this reasoning; but after all it is open to some question. The party possessing the power intends to execute it; he proceeds to do an act which he supposes to be a perfect act of execution. He possesses the right to do it in a formal manner; he has failed, by mistake, against his intention. But the objects in whose favor it is to be executed possess a high moral and equitable claim for its execution. Under such circumstances why should a mere mistake, contrary to the intention, defeat the bounty or the justice of the possessor of the power? If the case were one of an absolute property in the party, a Court of Equity would not fail to correct the mistake in favor of persons having such merits. Why should it hesitate when the possessor of the power has done an act intended to reduce it to the case of absolute property? There is no countervailing equity in such a case in favor of the other side. The case stands dryly upon a mere point of strict law. The difficulty in the argument is, that it deals with the power as a mere naked authority to act, without considering that when the party elects to act, an interest attaches to him in the execution of the power; and that the election thus made is defeated, and the interest thus created fails, by mere mistake, from the defective execution, against parties, standing on a strong equity, and in favor of others having none. See 1 Fonbl. Eq. B. 1, ch. 4, § 25.

the parties in the creation of the power. On the contrary when the party undertakes to execute a power, but by mistake does it imperfectly, equity will interpose to carry his very intention into effect, and that too in aid of those who are peculiarly within its protective favor; that is, creditors, purchasers, wives, and children.[1] (*a*)

171. What shall constitute an execution or preparatory steps or attempts towards the execution of a power entitling the party to relief in equity on the ground of a defective execution, has been largely and liberally interpreted. It is clear that it is not sufficient that there should be a mere floating and indefinite intention to execute the power, (*b*) without some steps taken to give it a legal effect.[2] Some steps must be taken or some acts done with this sole and definite intention, and be such as are properly referable to the power.[3] (*c*) Lord Mansfield at one time contended that whatever is an equitable ought to be deemed a legal execution of a power, because there should be a uniform rule of property; and that if Courts of Equity would presume that a strict adherence to the precise form pointed out in the creation of the power was not intended, and therefore not necessary, the same rule should prevail at law.[4] But this doctrine has been overruled. And indeed Courts of Equity do not deem the power well executed unless the form is adhered to; but in cases of a meritorious consideration they supply the defect.[5]

---

[1] Moody *v*. Reid, 1 Madd. R. 516; Jeremy on Eq. Jurisd. B. 3, Pt. 2, ch. 3, pp. 369, 370, 371, 372, 375; Darlington *v*. Pulteney, Cowp. 266, 267; Ellis *v*. Nimmo, Lloyd & Gould's Rep. 348. There seems a distinction in this respect between cases of the defective execution of powers and cases of voluntary contracts, covenants and settlements, of which specific performance is sought. See Jefferys *v*. Jefferys, 1 Craig & Phillips, 138, 141; Post, § 433, note; §§ 706, 706 *a*, 787, 793 *b*, 973, 987, 1040 *b*.

[2] See 2 Chance on Powers, ch. 23, § 3, art. 3005, 3011.

[3] See Sugden on Powers, ch. 6, § 2.

[4] Darlington *v*. Pulteney, Cowp R. 267.

[5] Sugden on Powers, ch. 6, § 1, p. 344; Id. § 359; Id. 361 to 370.

(*a*) Equity reformed the execution of a power by inserting a hotchpot clause, in Wilkinson *v*. Nelson, 7 Jur. N. s. 480. Concerning volunteers under deeds, see note to § 140, at p. 152.

(*b*) The intention to execute the power must be distinct. Garth *v*. Townsend, L. R. 7 Eq. 220.

(*c*) See Mitchell *v*. Denson, 29 Ala. 327. A contract to sell is sufficient to indicate an intention to execute a power of sale. In re Dyke's Estate, L. R. 7 Eq. 337.

172. And relief will be granted not only when the defect arises from an informal instrument not within the scope of the power, but also when the defect arises from the improper execution of the appropriate instrument. All that is necessary is, that the intention to execute the power should clearly appear in writing. Thus if the donee of a power merely covenant to execute it, or by his will desire the remainder-man to create the estate, or enter into a contract not under seal to execute the power, or by letters promise to grant an estate which he can execute only by the instrumentality of the power, — in all these and the like cases equity will supply the defect.[1] And even an answer to a bill in equity stating that the party does appoint and intends by a writing in due form to appoint the fund, will be an execution of the power for this purpose.[2]

173. The like rule prevails where the instrument selected is not that prescribed by the power, provided it is not in its own nature repugnant to the true object of the creation of the power. Thus if the power ought to be executed by a deed, but it is executed by a will, the defective execution will be aided.[3] But if the power ought to be executed by a will, and the donee of the power should execute a conveyance of the estate by an absolute deed, it will be invalid; because such a conveyance, if it avail to any purpose, must avail to the immediate destruction of the power, since it would no longer be revocable as a will would be. The intention of the power in its creation was to reserve an entire control over its execution until the moment of the death of the donee; and this intention would be defeated by any other instrument than a will.[4] An act done not strictly according to the terms of the power, but consistent with its intent, may be upheld in equity; but an act which violates the very purpose for which the power was created, and the very control over it which it meant to vest in the donee, is repugnant to it, and cannot be deemed in any just sense to be an execution of it.[5]

---

[1] Ibid.
[2] Carter v. Carter, Moseley, R. 365.
[3] Smith v. Ashton, 1 Freeman, R. 308; s. c. 1 Ch. Cas. 269; Sugden on Powers, ch. 6 (4th edit.), pp. 362 to 367; Follett v. Follett, 2 P. Will. 489; 2 Chance on Powers, ch. 23, § 1, pp. 507, 508; Id. 513 to 516; Com. Dig. Chancery, 4 H. 6.
[4] Reid v. Shergold, 10 Ves. R. 378, 380.
[5] See Bainbridge v. Smith, 8 Sim. R. 86; Ante, § 97.

174. But in other respects there is no difference between a defective execution of a power by a will and by a deed, for in each case the remedial interposition of equity will be applied. Thus if a power is required to be executed in the presence of three witnesses, and it is executed in the presence of two only, equity will interfere in such a case. So if the instrument, whether it be a deed or a will, is required to be signed and sealed, and it is without seal or signature, equity will relieve.[1] (*a*) And where a power is required to be executed by a will by way of appointment, there the appointment will be aided, although the will is not duly executed according to the Statute of Frauds; for it takes effect not under the will, but under the instrument creating the power.[2] Equity will also in many cases grant relief where by mistake a different kind of estate or interest is given from that which is authorized by the power, or where there is an excess of the power.[3] (*b*)

---

[1] Sugden on Powers, ch. 6 (4th edit.), pp. 369, 370; 2 Chance on Powers, ch. 23, pp. 507 to 510; Wade *v.* Paget, 1 Bro. Ch. R. 363.

[2] Wilkes *v.* Holmes, 9 Mod. 487, 488; Shannon *v.* Bradstreet, 1 Sch. & Lefr. 60; Sugden on Powers, ch. 6 (4th edit.), pp. 362 to 367; 2 Chance on Powers, ch. 23, § 1, pp. 507, 508. But see Gilb. Lex Pretoria, p. 301; Duff *v.* Dalzell, 1 Bro. Ch. R. 147; Wagstaff *v.* Wagstaff, 2 P. Will. 259, 260; Longford *v.* Eyre, 1 P. Will. 741; Com Dig. Chancery, 4 H. 7. Where an attempt is made to execute a power by a will (the power authorizing an execution by will), and the will is left imperfect, the same reason does not seem to exist, as may in other cases, to carry it into effect; for it may have been thus left intentionally imperfect, from a change of purpose. Lord Eldon, in remarking upon the difficulties of some of the cases, has said: ' If, in the instance of a want of a surrender of copyhold estate, the circumstance of the devise being to a child is considered, the more natural conclusion is, that the testator, whatever his purpose was, going only so far towards it, and not proceeding to make it effectual, had dropped it. So the attempt to execute a power is no more than an intimation that the party means to execute it. But if all the requisite ceremonies have not been complied with, it cannot be supposed that the intention continued until his death.' Finch *v.* Finch, 15 Ves. 51.

[3] Sugden on Powers, ch. 6, § 1, art. 2; Id. ch. 9, § 8, art. 2; 2 Chance on Powers, ch. 23, § 7, pp. 610, 613; Jeremy on Equity Jurisd. B. 3, Pt. 2, ch. 2, pp. 373, 374.

(*a*) See Bernards *v.* Stebbins, 109 U. S. 341, 349; ante, note, p. 157. But equity will not relieve in the case of a deed given by an attorney who has no power under seal. That is a case of a defective power, not of a defective execution of a power. Piatt *v.* McCullough, 1 McLean, 69.

(*b*) Where one had a power to appoint ' by his will or any writing in the nature of or purporting to be his will, or any codicil thereto,' and on

175. In all these cases it is to be understood that the intention and objects of the power are not defeated or put aside, but that they are only attempted by the party to be carried informally into effect. But where there is a defect of substance in the execution of the power, such as the want of co-operation of all the proper parties in the act, there equity will not aid the defect.[1] (*a*)

176. But in all these cases of relief by aiding and correcting defects or mistakes in the execution of instruments and powers, the party asking relief must stand upon some equity superior to that of the party against whom he asks it. If the equities are equal, a Court of Equity is silent and passive.[2] (*b*) Thus equity will not relieve one person claiming under a voluntary defective conveyance against another claiming also under a voluntary conveyance, but will leave the parties to their rights at law.[3] (*c*)

---

[1] See 2 Chance on Powers, ch. 23, § 2, pp. 540 to 543; Com. Dig. Chancery, 4 H. 7.

[2] See Sugden on Powers, ch. 6 (4th edit.), pp. 353, 358; 2 Chance on Powers, ch. 23, § 1, pp. 502, 504, 507.

[3] 1 Fonbl. Eq. B. 1, ch. 1, § 7, and notes; Id. ch. 4, § 25, and notes; Id. ch. 5, § 2, and notes; Goodwin *v.* Goodwin, 1 Rep. Chan. 92 [173]; Mitf. Eq. Pl. by Jeremy, 274; Moody *v.* Reid, 1 Madd. R. 516; 1 Madd. Eq. Pr. 45, 46,

his death the third and fourth sheets of a will were alone discovered, these being in his hand and signed by him with the attestation of two witnesses, and one of the sheets contained a perfect appointment, it was held in equity, after refusal of probate, that this could not be regarded as a valid execution of the power. Gullan *v.* Grove, 26 Beav. 64. See Pomfret *v.* Perring, 5 DeG. M. & G. 775. In another case it appeared that the testator had in the will given his wife several powers of appointment; one by deed or will, and others by 'deed or deeds, instrument or instruments, in writing, sealed and delivered.' The donee executed a deed of appointment reciting only the power by 'deed or deeds,' &c., which included only that particular estate; and it was held that this estate was well appointed, but that the appointment did not extend to any others. And the same person having afterwards by will appointed the same estate, it was held not to revoke the first appointment by deed, but to be wholly inoperative. Cooper *v.* Martin, 12 Jur. N. S. 887; S. C. L. R. 3 Ch. 47.

(*a*) See however Thorp *v.* McCallum, 1 Gilman, 614. So where the power is improperly exercised. Buckley *v.* Howell, 29 Beav. 546. As where the time for exercising it, being of the essence of the power, has elapsed. Cooper *v.* Martin, L. R. 3 Ch. 47. Ceremonials intended for the protection of a married woman are essential. Thackwell *v.* Gardiner, 5 DeG. & S. 58.

(*b*) Anderson *v.* Tydings, 8 Md. 427; Smith *v.* Turrentine, 2 Jones, Eq. 253.

(*c*) Hunt *v.* Hunt, 20 Ohio St. 119; ante, pp. 151-153, note.

For regularly equity is remedial to those only who come in upon an actual consideration; and therefore there should be some consideration, equitable or otherwise, express or implied.[1] (a) But there are excepted cases even from this rule, for a defective execution has been aided in favor of a volunteer where a strict compliance with the power has been impossible from circumstances beyond the control of the party; as where the prescribed witnesses could not be found, or where an interested party

47; Sugden on Powers, ch. 6 (4th edit.), pp. 353 to 358; 2 Chance on Powers, ch. 23, § 1, pp. 502, 504, 507; Com. Dig. Chancery, 4 H. 7, 4 H. 9, 2 T. 9, 2 T. 10, 2 C. 8, 4 O. 7; Post, §§ 433, 706 *a*, 787, 793 *a*, 793 *b*, 973, 987. There is one peculiarity as to the execution of powers which may be here taken notice of, although for obvious reasons this is not the place to discuss the nature and effects of powers generally. It is this. If a party possesses a general power to raise money for any purposes, so that, if he pleases, he may execute it in his own favor, and he executes it in favor of mere volunteers, in such a case it will be deemed assets in favor of creditors, upon the ground of his absolute dominion over the power. But if he does not execute the power at all, there equity will not deem it assets. 1 Fonbl. Eq. B. 1, ch. 4, § 12, note (*c*); Id. § 25, note (*n*); Harrington *v.* Harte, 1 Cox, R. 131; Townsend *v.* Windham, 2 Ves. 1; Troughton *v.* Troughton, 3 Atk. 656; Lassels *v.* Cornwallis, 2 Vern. 465; George *v.* Milbank, 9 Ves. 189; Holloway *v.* Millard, 1 Madd. R. 414, 419, 420; Jeremy on Eq. Jurisd. B. 3, Pt. 2, ch. 2, pp. 376, 377.(*b*) The distinction is a nice one, and not very satisfactory. Why, when the party executes a power in favor of others, and not of himself, a Court of Equity should defeat his intention, although within the scope of the power, and should execute something beside that intention, and contrary to it, is not very intelligible. If it be said that he ought to be just before he is generous, that addresses itself merely to his sense of morals. The power enabled him to give, either to himself, or to his creditors, or to mere voluntary donees. Why should a Court of Equity restrict this right of election, if bona fide exercised? Is not this to create rights, not given by law, rather than to enforce rights secured by law? If the power was bona fide created, why should a Court of Equity interpose to change its objects or its operations? See Sugden on Powers, ch. 6, § 3.

[1] 1 Fonbl. Eq. B. 1, ch. 5, § 2, and the cases there cited, note (*h*); 1 Madd. Eq. Pr. 44, 45; Sugden on Powers, ch. 6, § 1. See Ellis *v.* Nimmo, Lloyd & Gould's Rep. 333; Fortescue *v.* Barnett, 3 Mylne & Keen, 36, 42, 43; Post, § 372.

(*a*) In Morse *v.* Morse, 34 Beav. 500, defective execution in favor of a sister was aided against brothers otherwise provided for. See also Huss *v.* Morris, 63 Penn. St. 367.

(*b*) Clapp *v.* Ingraham, 126 Mass. 200; Commonwealth *v.* Duffield, 12 Penn. St. 277; Johnson *v.* Cushing, 15 N. H. 298; Fleming *v.* Buchanan, 3 DeG. M. & G. 976. The bona fide execution of such a power by a married woman does not in England fall within the rule. Clapp *v.* Ingraham, supra; Vaughan *v.* Vandersteegen, 2 Drew. 165, 363; Shattock *v.* Shattock, L. R. 2 Eq. 182; s. c. 35 Beav. 489.

having possession of the deed creating the power, has kept it from the sight of the party executing the power, so that he could not ascertain the formalities required.[1]

177. For the same reason equity will not supply a surrender or aid the defective execution of a power to the disinheritance of the heir at law. Neither will it supply such a surrender in favor of creditors where there are otherwise assets sufficient to pay their debts,[2] nor against a purchaser for a valuable consideration without notice.[3] And there are other cases of the defective execution of powers where equity will not interfere; as for instance in regard to powers which are in their own nature statutable, where equity must follow the law, be the consideration ever so meritorious. Thus the power of a tenant in tail to make leases under a statute, if not executed in the requisite form prescribed by the statute, will not be made available in equity, however meritorious the consideration may be.[4] And indeed it may be stated as generally although not universally true, that the remedial power of Courts of Equity does not extend to the supplying of any circumstance for the want of which the Legislature has declared the instrument void; for otherwise equity would in effect defeat the very policy of the legislative enactments.[5]

178. Upon one or both of these grounds, to wit, that there is no superior equity, or that it is against the policy of the law, the remedial power of Courts of Equity does not extend to the case of a defective fine as against the issue, or of a defective recovery

---

[1] 1 Fonbl. Eq. B. 1, ch 5, § 2, and note (*h*); Gilbert, Lex Pretoria, pp. 305, 306.

[2] 1 Fonbl. Eq. B. 1, ch. 1, § 7, note (*v*); Id. ch. 4, § 25, note (*c*); Jeremy on Eq. Jurisd. B. 3, Pt. 2, ch. 2, pp. 369, 370, 371.

[3] 1 Fonbl. Eq. B. 1, ch. 1, § 7; note (*r*); Id. ch. 4, § 25, and note (*f*); Id. B. 6, ch. 3, § 3. But see Id. B. 1, ch. 1, § 7, note (*t*).

[4] Darlington *v.* Pulteney, Cowp. R. 267; 1 Fonbl. Eq. B. 1, ch. 4, § 25, and note (*l*). But see 2 Chance on Powers, ch. 23, § 2, pp. 541 to 545. See Gilbert, Lex Pretoria, pp. 304, 305, the difference of a power created by the parties. See also 1 Fonbl. Eq. B. 1, ch. 4, § 25, and note (*l*).

[5] Ante, § 96; 1 Fonbl. Eq. B. 1, ch. 1, § 7, note (*t*); Hibbert *v.* Rolleston, 3 Bro. Ch. R. 571, and Mr. Belt's note, ibid.; Ex parte Bulteel, 2 Cox, R. 243; Duke of Bolton *v.* Williams, 2 Ves. jr. 138; Curtis *v.* Perry, 6 Ves. R. 739, 745, 746, 747; Mestaer *v.* Gillespie, 11 Ves. 621, 624, 625; Dixon *v.* Ewart, 3 Meriv. R. 321, 332; Thompson *v.* Leake, 1 Madd. R. 39; Thomson *v.* Smith, 1 Madd. R. 395; Bright *v.* Boyd, 1 Story, R. 478. Quære, how it would be, where a due execution was prevented by fraud, accident, or mistake. See 11 Ves. 625; 1 Madd. 39; Id. 395.

as against a remainder-man,[1] unless indeed there is something in the transaction to affect the conscience of the issue or the remainder-man.[2]

179. In regard to mistakes in wills there is no doubt that Courts of Equity have jurisdiction to correct them when they are apparent upon the face of the will, or may be made out by a due construction of its terms; for in cases of wills the intention will prevail over the words. But then the mistake must be apparent on the face of the will, otherwise there can be no relief; for at least since the Statute of Frauds, which requires wills to be in writing (whatever may have been the case before the statute),[3] parol evidence, or evidence dehors the will, is not admissible to vary or control the terms of the will, although it is admissible to remove a latent ambiguity.[4] (a)

---

[1] 1 Fonbl. Eq. B. 1, ch. 1, § 7, note (u); Id. ch. 5, § 2, and note (h).

[2] 1 Fonbl. Eq. B. 1, ch. 4, § 25, note (k); Id. 15; Com. Dig. Chancery, 2 T. 4, and 2 T. 8, 2 T. 10, 3 N. 2.

[3] Lord Hardwicke, in Milner v. Milner (1 Ves. R. 106), remarked that in the early ecclesiastical law, in accordance with the civil law, it was held that errors in legacies might be corrected by the intention of the testator, contrary to his words; and he cited Swinburne on Wills, p. 7, ch. 5, § 13, and Godolphin, pp. 3, 477, and the text of the civil law, and the commentary of Cujacius on the Digest, Lib. 30, tit. 1, l. 15; Cujacii Opera (edit. 1758), tom. 7. Comment. ad. id. Leg. pp. 993, 994. He then added: 'Indeed at the time some of these books were written, the Statute of Frauds had not taken place; and as the law [was] then held, parol evidence might be given in all courts to explain a will. And perhaps some contrariety of opinions may have been on this subject, where the intention appears on the face of the will, and where not; almost all the authorities in the civil law agreeing in the first case that the intention shall prevail against the words. But some have thought otherwise in the latter case, where the intention appeared, not on the face of the will, but only by matter dehors; although the better opinion even there is, that the intention shall prevail. However that difficulty cannot be here, as the intention appears on the face of the will.'

[4] Milner v. Milner, 1 Ves. R. 106; Ulrich v. Litchfield, 2 Atk. 373; Hampshire v. Peirce, 2 Ves. R. 216; Bradwin v. Harper, Ambler, R. 374; Stebbing v. Walkey, 2 Bro. Ch. R. 85; s. c. 1 Cox, R. 250; Danvers v. Manning, 2 Bro. Ch. R. 18; s. c. 1 Cox, R. 203; Campbell v. French, 3 Ves. 321; 1 Fonbl. Eq. B. 1, ch. 11, § 7, note (v); 1 Madd. Ch. Pr. 66, 67.

(a) Equity will not interfere, at least in this country, to correct alleged mistakes in the execution of wills as to the statutory requisites thereto. Nutt v. Nutt, 1 Freem. Ch. 128; Erwin v. Hanmer, 27 Ala. 296; Alter's Appeal, 67 Penn. St. 341. Nor to correct mistakes in the writing, as by inserting the name of another legatee in lieu of one which had been written by the mistake of the scrivener. Yates v. Cole, 1 Jones, Eq. 110. Nor in a

180. But the mistake, in order to lead to relief, must be a clear mistake or a clear omission, demonstrable from the structure and scope of the will.[1] Thus if in a will there is a mistake in the computation of a legacy, it will be rectified in equity.[2] So if there is a mistake in the name or description or number of the legatees intended to take,[3] or in the property intended to be bequeathed,[4] equity will correct it. (*a*)

181. But in each of these cases the mistake must be clearly made out, for if it is left doubtful, equity will not interfere.[5] And so if the words of the bequest are plain, evidence of a different intention is inadmissible to establish a mistake.[6] Neither

---

[1] Mellish *v.* Mellish, 4 Ves. 49; Phillips *v.* Chamberlain, Id. 51, 57; Del Mare *v.* Rebello, 3 Bro. Ch. R. 446; Purse *v.* Snaplin, 1 Atk. R. 415; Holmes *v.* Custance, 12 Ves. 279.

[2] Milner *v.* Milner, 1 Ves. R. 106; Danvers *v.* Manning, 2 Bro. Ch. R. 18; Door *v.* Geary, 1 Ves. R. 255, 256; Giles *v.* Giles, 1 Keen, 692.

[3] Stebbing *v.* Walkley, 2 Bro. Ch. R. 85; River's Case, 1 Atk. R. 410; Parsons *v.* Parsons, 1 Ves. jr. R. 266; Beemont *v.* Fell, 2 P. Will. 141; Hampshire *v.* Peirce, 2 Ves. 216; Bradwin *v.* Harper, Ambler, R. 374.

[4] Selwood *v.* Mildmay, 3 Ves. 306; Door *v.* Geary, 1 Ves. 250.

[5] Holmes *v.* Custance, 12 Ves. 279.

[6] Chambers *v.* Minchin, 4 Ves. R. 676. But see **Tonnereau *v.* Poyntz,** 1 case not one of ambiguity is evidence admissible that, where a society made the subject of a bequest is named as being in L, when there is no society of that name there, the testator meant a society of the same name elsewhere. In re Clergy Society, 2 Kay & J. 615.

In Box *v.* Barrett, L. R. 3 Eq. 244, a testator showed an intention in his will of giving his property equally among his four daughters, but recited that two of them, A and B, would become entitled to settled estates after his death, and that he had taken that into account in making his will, and had not given them as large a share as he otherwise would have done. He devised much more to the other two than to A and B, when in fact all his daughters were equally entitled to share in the settled estates, and in consequence of this mistake of the testator A and B would receive in the whole much less than the other two. But the will did not attempt to disturb the settled estates, and the court held that relief could not be granted. 'Because the testator,' said Romilly, M. R. 'has made a mistake, you cannot afterwards remodel the will, and make it that which you suppose he intended, and as he would have drawn it if he had known the incorrectness of his supposition.' See further as to the want of jurisdiction in equity to reform a will, Chambers *v.* Watson, 56 Iowa, 676; Sherwood *v.* Sherwood, 45 Wis. 351; infra, p. 198, note (*a*).

(*a*) A mistake in the date of the will may be shown by parol. Reffell *v.* Reffell, L. R. 1 P. & M. 139. But words will not be struck out on evidence that the scrivener inserted them inadvertently, where the testator, being a capable person, had the will read over to him. Guardhouse *v.* Blackburn, L. R. 1 P. & M. 109.

will equity rectify a mistake if it does not appear what the testator would have done in the case if there had been no mistake.[1] (*a*)

182. The same principle applies where a legacy is revoked or is given upon a manifest mistake of facts. Thus if a testator revokes legacies to A and B, giving as a reason that they are dead, and they are in fact living, equity will hold the revocation invalid and decree the legacies.[2] So if a woman gives a legacy to a man, describing him as her husband and in point of fact the marriage is void, he having a former wife then living, the bequest will in equity be decreed void.[3]

182 *a*. But though it is clear that a legacy given to a person in a character which the legatee does not fill, and by the fraudulent assumption of which character the testator has been deceived, will not take effect, yet if the testator is not deceived although a false character is in fact assumed, the legacy will be good. A fortiori it will be good if both parties not only know the actual facts, but are designedly parties to the assumption of the false character. Thus where the testator and the legatee A. G. were married, both knowing at the time that the legatee had a prior husband alive, and afterwards the testator gave all the residue of his estate to the legatee, describing her as his wife A. G., it was held that the legacy was good; for as both parties had a guilty knowledge of the facts, no fraud was committed on the testator. And it was then said, that however criminal the conduct of the parties might be, it was no part of the duty of Courts of Equity to punish parties for immoral conduct by depriving them of their civil rights.[4]

183. But a false reason given for a legacy or for the revocation of a legacy is not always a sufficient ground to avoid the act or bequest in equity. To have such an effect, it must be clear that no other motive mingled in the legacy, and that it constituted

Bro. Ch. R. 472, 480; Powell *v.* Mouchett, 6 Madd. R. 216; Smith *v.* Streatfield, 1 Meriv. R. 358.

[1] See Smith *v.* Maitland, 1 Ves. 363.
[2] Campbell *v.* French, 3 Ves. 321.
[3] Kennell *v.* Abbott, 4 Ves. R. 808.
[4] Giles *v.* Giles, 1 Keen, R. 685, 692, 693.

(*a*) Box *v.* Barrett, L. R. 3 Eq. 244; supra, p. 191, note.

the substantial ground of the act or bequest.[1] (a) The civil law seems to have proceeded upon the same ground. The Digest[2] says: 'Falsam causam legato non obesse, verius est; quia ratio legandi legato non cohaeret. Sed plerumque doli exceptio locum habebit, si probetur, alias legaturus non fuisse.' The meaning of this passage is, that a false reason given for the legacy is not of itself sufficient to destroy it. But there must be an exception of any fraud (b) practised, from which it may be presumed that the person giving the legacy would not, if that fraud had been known to him, have given it.[3] And the same reasoning applies to a case of clear mistake.

[1] Kennell v. Abbott, 4 Ves. R. 802.
[2] Dig. Lib. 35, tit. 1, l. 72, § 6. See also Swinburne on Wills, Pt. 7, § 22, p. 557.
[3] Kennell v. Abbott, 4 Ves. 808.

(a) See Wilkinson v. Joughin, 12 Jur. N. s. 330; In re Pitts's Will, 5 Jur. N. s. 1235.

(b) The term 'doli exceptio' merely means a plea of fraud; and the passage means that such a plea will be proper where the gift would not have been made had the truth been known.

CHAPTER VI.

ACTUAL OR POSITIVE FRAUD.

184. Let us now pass to another great head of concurrent jurisdiction in equity, that of Fraud. And here it may be laid down as a general rule subject to few exceptions, that Courts of Equity exercise a general jurisdiction in cases of fraud, sometimes concurrent with and sometimes exclusive of other courts.[1]

---

[1] Barker v. Ray, 2 Russ. R. 63; Post, §§ 238, 252, 264, 410. Mr. Fonblanque in his note (B. 1, ch. 2, § 3, note u) says: 'Whether Courts of Equity could interpose and relieve against fraud practised in the obtaining of a will, appears to have been formerly a point of considerable doubt. In some cases we find the Court of Chancery distinctly asserting its jurisdiction; as in Maundy v. Maundy, 1 Ch. Rep. 66; Well v. Thornagh, Pre. Ch. 123; Goss v. Tracy, 1 P. Wms. 287; 2 Vern. 700; in other cases disclaiming such jurisdiction, though the fraud was gross and palpable; as in Roberts v. Wynne, 1 Ch. Rep. 125; Archer v. Moss, 2 Vern. 8; Herbert v. Lownes, 1 Ch. Rep. 13; Thynn v. Thynn, 1 Vern. 296; Devenish v. Barnes, Pre. Ch. 3; Barnesly v. Powel, 1 Ves. 287; Marriott v. Marriott, Str. 666. That an action at law will lie upon a promise that if the devisor would not charge the land with a rent-charge, the devisee would pay a certain sum to the intended legatee of the rent. See Rockwood v. Rockwood, 1 Leon. 192; Cro. Eliz. 163. See also Dutton v. Poole, 1 Vent. 318, 332; Beringer v. Beringer, 16 June, 26 Car. II.; Chamberlain v. Chamberlain, 2 Freem. 34; Leicester v. Foxcroft, cited Gilb. Rep. 11; Reech v. Kenningall, 26 October, 1748. But since the cases of Kerrich v. Bransby, 3 Brown's P. C. 358, and Webb v. Cleverden, 2 Atk. 424, it appears to have been settled that a will cannot be set aside in equity for fraud and imposition, because a will of personal estate may be set aside for fraud in the Ecclesiastical Court and a will of real estate may be set aside at law; for in such cases, as the animus testandi is wanting, it cannot be considered as a will. Bennet v. Vade, 2 Atk. 324; Anon. 3 Atk. 17. Though equity will not set aside a will for fraud nor restrain the probate of it in the proper court, yet if the fraud be proved it will not assist the party practising it, but will leave him to make what advantage he can of it. Nelson v. Oldfield, 2 Vern. 76. But if the validity of the will has been already determined and acted upon, equity will restrain proceedings in the Prerogative Court to controvert its validity. Sheffield v. Duchess of Buckingham, 1 Atk. 628. Lord Hardwicke, having admitted that a Court of Equity cannot

It has been already stated that in a great variety of cases fraud is remediable, and effectually remediable, at law.[1] (*a*) Nay, set aside a will for fraud, observes, in the above case of Sheffield *v.* Duchess of Buckingham, that "the admission of a fact by a party concerned, and who is most likely to know it, is stronger than if determined by a jury; and facts are as properly concluded by an admission as by a trial." That the party prejudiced by the fraud may file a bill for a discovery of all its circumstances is unquestionable. Supposing then the defendant to admit the fraud, if the admission is to have the effect ascribed to it by Lord Hardwicke, it still remains to be determined how a Court of Equity ought to proceed. If it could not relieve, it would follow, as a consequence, that so much of the bill as seeks relief would be demurrable; but the invariable practice in such cases is to seek relief, and the issue directed is to furnish the ground upon which the court is to proceed in giving such relief.' But the question whether a Court of Equity will interpose and grant relief in cases of wills obtained or suppressed by fraud has been much litigated since the note of Mr. Fonblanque was written, and it is now well settled that a Court of Equity will not entertain jurisdiction to set aside a will obtained by fraud, or establish a will suppressed by fraud, whatever relief it may otherwise grant under special circumstances. See Allen *v.* Macpherson, 5 Beav. R. 469; s. c. on appeal, 1 Phillips, Ch. R. 133. In this case, upon the appeal Lord Cottenham discussed the authorities at large and said, 'The testator in this case had bequeathed a considerable property to the plaintiff by his will and subsequent codicils. He afterwards by a further codicil (the ninth) revoked these bequests, and in lieu of them made a small pecuniary provision in his favor. It was alleged by the bill that this alteration was procured by false and fraudulent representations made by an illegitimate son of the testator, and by the defendant Susannah Evans, his daughter, as to the character and conduct of the plaintiff, Susannah Evans being the residuary legatee. To this bill the defendants demurred. The Master of the Rolls overruled the demurrer, and from this judgment the defendants have appealed. The question is one of considerable importance. The same objection of fraud, founded upon the same facts, was made in the Ecclesiastical Court upon the application for probate. It did not however prevail. This then is in substance an attempt to review the proceedings in that court; for a sufficient case of imposition and fraud practised on the testator would have been a ground for refusing the probate. There are undoubtedly cases where, fraud being proved, this court has declared the party committing the fraud a trustee for the person against whom the fraud was practised; but none of these cases appear to me to go so far as the present. The case of Seagrave *v.* Kirwan has no very close application to the question now before the court. The Chancellor of Ireland, Sir Anthony Hart, declared the executor a trustee as to the residue for the next of kin. But in that case the testator never intended that the executor should take any benefit under the will. The rule which then prevailed, that the executor

---

[1] Ante, §§ 59, 60; 3 Black. Comm. 431; 1 Fonbl. Eq. B. 1, ch. 2, § 3, note (*r*); 4 Inst. 84; Bright *v.* Eynor, 1 Burr. R. 396; Jackson *v.* Burgott, 10 John. R. 457, 462.

(*a*) See editor's note to § 33, ante.

in certain cases, such as fraud in obtaining a will, whether of personal estate or real estate, the proper remedy is exclusively

was entitled to the residue unless otherwise disposed of, except where a legacy was bequeathed to him by the will, was a rule of interpretation or construction. The learned judge considered that it was the duty of the executor who prepared the will, and who was a gentleman of the bar, to have informed the testator that such was the rule. He was not allowed to profit from this omission, and was therefore decreed to be a trustee for the next of kin. The Ecclesiastical Court had no authority to order this. They had no power to do what the justice of the case required. So in Kennell v. Abbott (4 Ves. 802). There a fraud had been practised, and the question was one of intention. The testatrix intended the legacy for her husband. The legatee had fraudulently assumed that character. The Master of the Rolls, Sir Pepper Arden, came to the conclusion that the character he had so assumed was the only motive for the gift. The law therefore, he said, would not permit him to avail himself of the testatrix's bounty. In the case of Marriot v. Marriot, which is mentioned in Strange (p. 666), and also in Chief Baron Gilbert's Reports (p. 203; see p. 209), it does not appear what was the nature of the imputed fraud. The cause was compromised, and the judgment, according to the report in Gilbert, was written by the learned judge, but not delivered. He says that a Court of Equity may, according to the real intention of the testator, declare a trust upon a will, although it be not contained in the will itself, in these three cases. First, in the case of a notorious fraud upon a legatee; as if the drawer of a will should insert his own name instead of the name of the legatee, no doubt he would be a trustee for the real legatee. Secondly, where the words imply a trust for the relations, as in the case of a specific devise to the executors, and no disposition of the residue. Thirdly, in the case of a legatee promising the testator to stand as a trustee for another. And nobody, he adds, has thought that declaring a trust in these cases is an infringement upon the ecclesiastical jurisdiction. These are the only positions laid down in the intended judgment which are applicable to the present question. They do not admit of dispute, but are very distinguishable from the case now under consideration. It is sufficient to observe that in none of these instances would the Ecclesiastical Court be competent to afford relief. The same remarks will apply to the case also of Kennell v. Abbott, which I have already mentioned. But in Plume v. Beale (1 P. Wms. 188), where a legacy was introduced by forgery, Lord Chancellor Cowper refused to interfere, saying it might have been proved in the Ecclesiastical Court with a particular reservation as to that legacy. There the interference of the Court of Equity was unnecessary. The question might have been settled by the Ecclesiastical Court. In the case of Barnesly v. Powel (1 Ves. sen., p. 284), Lord Hardwicke says that fraud in making or obtaining a will must be inquired into and determined by the Ecclesiastical Court, but that fraud in procuring a will to be established in that court — fraud, not upon the testator, but upon the person disinherited thereby — might be the subject of inquiry in this court. Fraud, he says, in obtaining the will infects the whole, but the case of a will in which the probate has been obtained by fraud upon the next of kin is of another consideration; and Lord Apsley, in the case of Meadows v. The Duchess of Kingston (Amb. 762), recognizes this distinction. But the case which has the closest resemblance to this is Kerrich v. Bransby, decided in

vested in other courts; in wills of personal estate, in the Ecclesiastical Courts, and in wills of real estate, in the Courts of

the House of Lords (7 Bro. P. C. 457). It was alleged in that case that the will had been obtained by fraud and imposition practised on the testator; and the chancellor, Lord Macclesfield, was of that opinion, and pronounced a decree the effect of which was to deprive the legatee of all benefit under it. It is true that the prayer of the bill was that the will might be cancelled; but the decree did not do more than direct the legatee to account for the testator's personal estate, and that what should appear to be in his hands should be paid over to the plaintiff, and that if necessary the plaintiff should be at liberty to use the legatee's name to get in the debts or other personal estate of the testator; in substance declaring him a trustee for the plaintiff. But this judgment was reversed on appeal in the House of Lords. It was suggested at the bar upon the argument in the present case that the decree might perhaps have been reversed on the merits. That however has not been the understanding of the profession, and Lord Hardwicke, who probably was acquainted with the history of the case, expressly states in Barnesly v. Powel that it was decided on the question of jurisdiction. Lord Eldon also, in Ex parte Fearon (5 Ves. 633; see p. 617), observes that it was determined in Kerrich v. Bransby that this court could not take any cognizance of wills of personal estate as to matters of fraud. I am of opinion therefore, as well on authority as on principle, that the demurrer was proper, and ought to have been sustained.' Again in Price v. Dewhurst, 4 Mylne & Craig, R. 76, 80, 81, Lord Cottenham said: 'The first question which occurs is, How can this court in administering a testator's property take any notice of a will of which no probate has been obtained from the Ecclesiastical Court of this country? This court knows nothing of any will of personalty except such as the Ecclesiastical Court has by the probate adjudged to be the last will.' The same question occurred before the Supreme Court of the U. S. in the case of Gaines and wife v. Chew and others, 2 Howard, S. Ct. R. 619, 645, 646. In that case Mr. Justice McLean, in delivering the opinion of the court, said: 'In cases of fraud, equity has a concurrent jurisdiction with a court of law, but in regard to a will charged to have been obtained through fraud, this rule does not hold. It may be difficult to assign any very satisfactory reason for this exception. That exclusive jurisdiction over the probate of wills is vested in another tribunal is the only one that can be given. By art. 1637 of the Civil Code it is declared that "no testament can have effect unless it has been presented to the judge," &c. And in Clappier et al v. Banks, 11 Louis. Rep. 593, it is held that a will alleged to be lost or destroyed, and which has never been proved, cannot be set up as evidence of title in an action of revendication. In Armstrong v. Administrators of Kosciusko, 12 Wheat. 169, this court held that an action for a legacy could not be sustained under a will which had not been proved in this country before a Court of Probate, though it may have been effective as a will in the foreign country where it was made. In Tarver v. Tarver et al., 9 Peters, 180, one of the objects of the bill being to set aside the probate of a will, the court said, "The bill cannot be sustained for the purpose of avoiding the probate. That should have been done, if at all, by an appeal from the Court of Probate, according to the provisions of the law of Alabama." The American decisions on this subject have followed the English authorities. And a deliberate consideration of the question leads

Common Law.[1] (a) But there are many cases in which fraud is utterly irremediable at law; and Courts of Equity in relieving

us to say that both the general and local law require the will of 1813 to be proved before any title can be set up under it. But this result does not authorize a negative answer to the second point. We think, under the circumstances, that the complainants are entitled to full and explicit answers from the defendants in regard to the above wills. These answers being obtained may be used as evidence before the Court of Probate to establish the will of 1813 and revoke that of 1811. In order that the complainants may have the means of making, if they shall see fit, a formal application to the Probate Court for the proof of the last will and the revocation of the first, having the answers of the executors, jurisdiction as to this matter may be sustained. And indeed circumstances may arise on this part of the case which shall require a more definite and efficient action by the Circuit Court. For if the Probate Court shall refuse to take jurisdiction, from a defect of power to bring the parties before it, lapse of time, or on any other ground, and there shall be no remedy in the higher courts of the State, it may become the duty of the Circuit Court, having the parties before it, to require them to go before the Court of Probates and consent to the proof of the will of 1813 and the revocation of that of 1811. And should this procedure fail to procure the requisite action on both wills, it will be a matter for grave consideration whether the inherent powers of a Court of Chancery may not afford a remedy where the right is clear, by establishing the will of 1813. In the case of Barnesly v. Powel, 1 Ves. sen. 119, 284, 287, above cited, Lord Hardwicke decreed that the defendant should consent in the Ecclesiastical Court to the revocation of the will in controversy and the granting of administration, &c. If the emergencies of the case shall require such a course as above indicated, it will not be without the sanction of Louisiana law. The twenty-first article of the Civil Code declares that "in civil matters, where there is no express law, the judge is bound to proceed and decide according to equity. To decide equitably, an appeal is to be made to natural law and reason, or received usages where positive law is silent." This view seemed to be necessary to show on what ground and for what purpose jurisdiction may be exercised in reference to the will of 1813, though it has not been admitted to probate.' See also Gengell v. Horne, 9 Simons, R. 539, 548; Smith v. Spencer, 1 Younge & Coll. N. R. 75; Tucker v. Phipps, 3 Atk. R. 360; Tremblestown v. Lloyd, 1 Bligh (N. S.), R. 429; Cann v. Cann, 1 P. Will. 723; Dalston v. Coatsworth, 1 P.

---

[1] 1 Fonbl. Eq. B. 1, ch. 2, § 3, note (u); 3 Black. Comm. 431; Webb v. Cleverden, 2 Atk. 424; Kerrich v. Bransby, 3 Bro. Parl. Cas. 358; s. c. 7 Bro. Parl. Cas. by Tomlins, p. 437; Bennet v. Vade, 2 Atk. 324; Andrews v. Pavis, 2 Bro. Parl. Cas. 476; Jeremy Eq. Jurisd. B. 3, Pt. 2, ch. 4, § 5, pp. 488, 489; Pemberton v. Pemberton, 13 Ves. 297; 1 Hovenden on Frauds, Introd. 17; Cooper, Eq. Pl. 125.

(a) See Ellis v. Davis, 109 U. S. 485, 494; Broderick's Will, 21 Wall. 503; Trexler v. Miller, 6 Ired. Eq. 248; Allen v. McPherson, 1 H. L. Cas. 191. Secus as to a will which has been suppressed or fraudulently destroyed. Buchanan v. Matlock, 8 Humph. 390 ; Tucker v. Phipps, 3 Atk. 360; post, § 254. But see Myers v. O'Hanlon, 13 Rich. 196.

against it often go not only beyond but even contrary to the rules of law.[1] And with the exception of wills, as above stated, Courts of Equity may be said to possess a general and perhaps a universal concurrent jurisdiction with Courts of Law in cases of fraud cognizable in the latter; and exclusive jurisdiction in cases of fraud beyond the reach of the Courts of Law.[2] (a)

185. The jurisdiction in matters of fraud is probably coeval with the existence of the Court of Chancery; and it is equally probable that in the early history of that court it was principally exercised in matters of fraud not remediable at law.[3] Its present

Will. 733; Hampden v. Hampden, cited 1 P. Will. 733; s. c. 1 Bro. Parl. Cas. 250; Jones v. Jones, 3 Meriv. R. 161; s. c. 7 Price, R. 663; Bennet v. Vade, 2 Atk. R. 264; Webb v. Claverden, 2 Atk. 424; Mitf. Eq. Pl. by Jeremy, 257; Belt's Supplt. to Vesey, 74, 143. I use the qualified language of the text, though broader language is often used by elementary writers, who assert that Courts of Equity have jurisdiction to relieve against all frauds except in cases of wills. (See Cooper on Eq. Pl. 125; 1 Hovenden on Frauds, Introd. p. 17.) Lord Hardwicke, in Chesterfield v. Janssen, 2 Ves. 155, said: 'This court has an undoubted jurisdiction to relieve against every species of fraud.' Yet there are some cases of fraud in which equity does not ordinarily grant relief, as in warranties, misrepresentations, and frauds, on the sale of personal property, but leaves the parties to their remedy at law. So also in cases of deceitful letters of credit. See Russell v. Clark's Ex'ors, 7 Cranch, 89. But Lord Eldon has intimated that in such cases relief might also be had in equity; Evans v. Bicknell, 6 Ves. 182; and Mr. Chancellor Kent has affirmed the same doctrine; Bacon v. Bronson, 7 John. Ch. 201. In Hardwick v. Forbes's Adm's. (1 Bibb, Ky. R. 212) the court said: 'It is a well-settled rule of law, that wherever a matter respects personal chattels, and lies merely in damages, the remedy is at law only, and for these reasons: 1st. because courts of law are as adequate as a Court of Chancery to grant complete and effectual reparation to the party injured; 2d. because the ascertainment of damages is peculiarly the province of a jury.' And the court farther suggested that the same principle applied to a ratable deduction for fraud in like cases, but that a Court of Equity might properly interfere in such cases to set aside and vacate the *whole* contract at the instance of a party injured in a case of suppressio veri, or suggestio falsi, not entering into the point of damages. See Waters v. Mattinglay, 1 Bibb, R. 244.

[1] Garth v. Cotton, 3 Atk. 755; Man v. Ward, 2 Atk. 229; Trenchard v. Wanley, 2 P. Will. 167.

[2] Colt v. Wollaston, 2 P. Will. 156; Stent v. Bailis, 2 P. Will. 220; Bright v. Eynor, 1 Burr. 396; Chesterfield v. Janssen, 2 Ves. 155; Evans v. Bicknell, 6 Ves. 132.

[3] 4 Inst. 84.

(a) See Ramshire v. Bolton, L. R. 8 Eq. 294; Hill v. Lane, L. R. 11 Eq. 215; Hoare v. Bremridge, L.R. 14 Eq. 522; s. c. L. R. 8 Ch. 22; Jones v. Bolles, 9 Wall. 364.

active jurisdiction took its rise in a great measure from the abolition of the Court of Star Chamber, in the reign of Charles the First;[1] in which court the plaintiff was not only relieved, but the defendant was punished for his fraudulent conduct. So that the interposition of chancery before that period was generally unnecessary.[2]

186. It is not easy to give a definition of Fraud in the extensive signification in which that term is used in Courts of Equity; and it has been said that these courts have, very wisely, never laid down as a general proposition what shall constitute fraud,[3] or any general rule beyond which they will not go upon the ground of fraud, lest other means of avoiding the equity of the courts should be found out.[4] Fraud is even more odious than force; and Cicero has well remarked: 'Cum autem duobus modis, id est, aut vi, aut fraude, fiat injuria; fraus, quasi vulpeculæ, vis, leonis videtur. Utrumque homine alienissimum; sed fraus odio digna majore.'[5] Pothier says that the term 'fraud' is applied to every artifice made use of by one person for the purpose of deceiving another.[6] 'On appelle Dol toute espèce d'artifice, dont quelqu'un se sert pour en tromper un autre.'[7] Servius, in the Roman law, defined it thus: 'Dolum malum machinationem quandam alterius decipienda causa, cum aliud simulatur, et aliud agitur.' To this definition Labeo justly took exception, because a party might be circumvented by a thing done without simulation; and on the other hand without fraud one thing might be done and another thing be pretended. And therefore he defined 'fraud' to be any cunning, deception, or artifice used to circumvent, cheat, or deceive another. 'Dolum malum esse

---

[1] Stat. 16 Car. 1, ch. 10.
[2] 1 Fonbl. Eq. B. 1, ch. 2, § 12; 1 Madd. Ch. Pr. 89.
[3] Mortlock v. Buller, 10 Ves. 306.
[4] Lawley v. Hooper, 3 Atk. 279. Lord Hardwicke, in his letter to Lord Kaimes, of the 30th of June, 1759 (Parke's Hist. of Chan. p. 508), says: 'As to relief against frauds, no invariable rules can be established. Fraud is infinite; and were a Court of Equity once to lay down rules how far they would go, and no farther, in extending their relief against it or to define strictly the species or evidence of it, the jurisdiction would be cramped and perpetually eluded by new schemes, which the fertility of man's invention would contrive.' See also 1 Domat, Civil Law, B. 1, tit. 18, § 3, art. 1.
[5] Cic. de Offic. Lib. 1, ch. 13.
[6] 1 Pothier on Oblig. by Evans, Pt. 1, ch. 1, § 1, art. 3, n. 28, p. 19.
[7] Pothier, Traité des Oblig. Pt. 1, ch. 1, n. 28.

omnem calliditatem, fallaciam, machinationem ad circumveniendum, fallendum, decipiendum alterum, adhibitam.' And this is pronounced in the Digest to be the true definition. 'Labeonis definitio vera est.'[1]

187. This definition is beyond doubt sufficiently descriptive of what may be called positive, actual fraud, where there is an intention to commit a cheat or deceit upon another to his injury.[2] But it can hardly be said to include the large class of implied or constructive frauds which are within the remedial jurisdiction of a Court of Equity. Fraud indeed, in the sense of a Court of Equity, properly includes all acts, omissions, and concealments which involve a breach of legal or equitable duty, trust, or confidence, justly reposed, and are injurious to another, or by which an undue and unconscientious advantage is taken of another.[3] (a) And Courts of Equity will not only interfere in cases of fraud to set aside acts done, but they will also, if acts have by fraud been prevented from being done by the parties, interfere and treat the case exactly as if the acts had been done.[4]

188. Lord Hardwicke, in a celebrated case,[5] after remarking that a Court of Equity has an undoubted jurisdiction to relieve against every species of fraud, proceeded to give the following enumeration of the different kinds of fraud: First. Fraud which is dolus malus may be actual, arising from facts and circumstances of imposition, which is the plainest case. Secondly. It may be apparent from the intrinsic nature and subject of the bargain itself, such as no man in his senses and not under delusion would make on the one hand, and as no honest and fair man would accept on the other; which are inequitable and un-

---

[1] Dig. Lib. 4, tit. 3, l. 1, § 2; Id. Lib. 2, tit. 14, l. 7, § 9. See also 1 Domat, Civ. Law, B. 1, tit. 18, § 3, n. 1. See also 1 Bell, Comm. B. 2, ch. 7, § 2, art. 173; Le Neve v. Le Neve, 3 Atk. 654; s. c. 1 Ves. 64; Ambler, 446.

[2] Mr. Jeremy has defined fraud to be a device by means of which one party has taken an unconscientious advantage of the other. Jeremy on Eq. Jurisd. B. 3, Pt. 2, p. 358.

[3] See 1 Fonbl. Eq. B. 1, ch. 2, § 3, note (r); Chesterfield v. Janssen, 2 Ves. 155, 156.

[4] Middleton v. Middleton, 1 Jac. & Walk. 96; Lord Waltham's case, cited 11 Ves. 638.

[5] Chesterfield v. Janssen, 2 Ves. 155.

(a) Taylor v. Atwood, 47 Conn. 251; Smith v. Richards, 13 Peters, 26, 498, 503; Gale v. Gale, 19 Barb. 249, 36; Dailey v. Kastell, 56 Wis. 444, 452.

conscientious bargains, and of such even the common law has taken notice.[1] Thirdly. Fraud which may be presumed from the circumstances and condition of the parties contracting; and this goes farther than the rule of law, which is that it must be proved, not presumed. But it is wisely established in the Court of Chancery to prevent taking surreptitious advantage of the weakness or necessity of another, which knowingly to do is equally against conscience as to take advantage of his ignorance. Fourthly. Fraud which may be collected and inferred in the consideration of a Court of Equity, from the nature and circumstances of the transaction, as being an imposition and deceit on other persons, not parties to the fraudulent agreement. Fifthly. Fraud in what are called catching bargains with heirs, reversioners, or expectants in the life of the parents, which indeed seems to fall under one or more of the preceding heads.

189. Fraud then being so various in its nature and so extensive in its application to human concerns, it would be difficult to enumerate all the instances in which Courts of Equity will grant relief under this head. It will be sufficient if we here collect some of the more marked classes of cases in which the principles which regulate the action of Courts of Equity are fully developed, and from which analogies may be drawn to guide us in the investigation of other and novel circumstances.

190. Before however proceeding to these subjects, it may be proper to observe that Courts of Equity do not restrict themselves by the same rigid rules as Courts of Law do in the investigation of fraud, and in the evidence and proofs required to establish it. It is equally a rule in Courts of Law and Courts of Equity, that fraud is not to be presumed, but it must be established by proofs.[2] Circumstances of mere suspicion leading to no certain results will not in either of these courts be deemed a sufficient ground to establish fraud.[3] On the other hand neither

[1] See James *v.* Morgan, 1 Lev. 111.

[2] In 10 Coke, R. 56, it is laid down that covin shall never be intended or presumed at law, if it be not expressly averred: 'Quia odiosa et inhonesta non sunt in lege præsumenda, et, in facto, quod se habit ad bonum et malum, magis de bono, quam de malo, præsumendum est.' And this is in conformity to the rule of the civil law. 'Dolum ex indiciis perspicuis probari convenit.' Cod. Lib. 2, tit. 21, l. 6.

[3] Trenchard *v.* Wanley, 2 P. Will. 166; Townsend *v.* Lowfield, 1 Ves. 35; 3 Atk. 534; Walker *v.* Symonds, 3 Swanst. R. 61; Bath and Montague's Case, 3 Ch. Cas. 85; 1 Madd. Ch. Pr. 208; 1 Fonbl. Eq. B. 1, ch. 11, § 8.

of these courts insists upon positive and express proofs of fraud; but each deduces them from circumstances affording strong presumptions. But Courts of Equity will act upon circumstances as presumptions of fraud, where Courts of Law would not deem them satisfactory proofs. In other words Courts of Equity will grant relief upon the ground of fraud established by presumptive evidence, which evidence Courts of Law would not always deem sufficient proof to justify a verdict at law. It is in this sense that the remark of Lord Hardwicke is to be understood, when he said that 'fraud may be presumed from the circumstances and condition of the parties contracting; and this goes farther than the rule of law, which is that fraud must be proved, not presumed.'[1] (a) And Lord Eldon has illustrated the same proposition by remarking that a Court of Equity will, as it ought, in many cases order an instrument to be delivered up as unduly obtained, which a jury would not be justified in impeaching by the rules of law, which require fraud to be proved, and are not satisfied though it may be strongly presumed.[2]

191. One of the largest classes of cases in which Courts of Equity are accustomed to grant relief is where there has been a misrepresentation or suggestio falsi.[3] It is said indeed to be a

[1] Chesterfield v. Janssen, 2 Ves. 155, 156.
[2] Fullager v. Clark, 18 Ves. 483.
[3] Broderick v. Broderick, 1 P. Will. 240; Jarvis v. Duke, 1 Vern. 20; Evans v. Bicknell, 6 Ves. 173, 182.

(a) King v. Moon, 42 Mo. 551; Jackson v. King, 4 Cowen, 207; Smith v. Harrison, 2 Heisk. 230. Compare Kline v. Baker, 106 Mass. 61; Reed v. Noxon, 48 Ill. 323; Bullock v. Narrott, 49 Ill. 62; Waddingham v. Loker, 44 Mo. 132; In re Vanderveer, 5 C. E. Green, 463; Mahony v. Hunter, 30 Ind. 246; Parker v. Phetteplace, 2 Cliff. 70. The doctrine of the text has been directly challenged. Marksbury v. Taylor, 10 Bush, 519. The true rule, it is apprehended, is (not that a chancellor may find fraud on less evidence than a jury could in the same case, but) that such evidence should be required by all courts as to overcome the presumption of innocence. Ib. In cases of constructive fraud equity will be more easily satisfied than could a jury of *actual* fraud; but that is another thing. Equity itself would be more easily satisfied in the one case than in the other. A Law Court cannot presume (it may *infer*) fraud, because such a court has not jurisdiction of constructive frauds. See Bigelow, Fraud, 472; Jackson v. King, 4 Cowen, 207, 220. In all cases not between persons in relations of confidence or the like, the evidence of fraud should be clear and convincing. Lavassar v. Washburne, 50 Wis. 200; Martyn v. Westbrook, 7 Law T. N. S. 449; Bryan v. Hitchcock, 43 Mo. 527. See also Torrance v. Bolton, L. R. 8 Ch. 118.

very old head of equity, that if a representation is made to another person going to deal in a matter of interest upon the faith of that representation, the former shall make that representation good if he knows it to be false.[1] To justify however an interposition in such cases, it is not only necessary to establish the fact of misrepresentation, but that it is in a matter of substance, or important to the interests of the other party, and that it actually does mislead him.[2] For if the misrepresentation was of a trifling or immaterial thing, or if the other party did not trust to it or was not misled by it, or if it was vague and inconclusive in its own nature, or if it was upon a matter of opinion or fact equally open to the inquiries of both parties, and in regard to which neither could be presumed to trust the other, — in these and the like cases there is no reason for a Court of Equity to interfere to grant relief upon the ground of fraud.[3] (a)

---

[1] Evans v. Bicknell, 6 Ves. 173, 182.

[2] Neville v. Wilkinson, 1 Bro. Ch. R. 546; Turner v. Harvey, Jacob, Rep. 178; 1 Fonbl. Eq. B. 1, ch. 2, § 8; Small v. Atwood, 1 Younge, R. 407, 461; s. c. in Appeal, 6 Clark & Finnell. 232, 395.

[3] See 1 Domat, B. 1, tit. 18, § 3, art. 2; Trower v. Newcome, 3 Meriv. R. 704; 2 Kent, Comm. Lect. 39, p. 484 (2d edit.); Atwood v. Small, 6 Clark & Finell. 232, 233; s. c. Small v. Atwood, in Court of Exchequer, 1 Younge, R. 407.

(a) *Relievable Misrepresentation.* — Speaking in reference to a claim for damages based on deceit, it is commonly laid down that to entitle the plaintiff to recover, he must be prepared to show (1) that the defendant has made a false representation, (2) that he made it with knowledge of its falsity, (3) that the plaintiff believed the representation made to be true, (4) that it was made with intent that it should be acted upon, (5) that it was acted upon to the plaintiff's damage. Pasley v. Freeman, 3 T. R. 51.

The second, third, and fourth of these elements of liability, whether at law or in equity, are true only with important qualifications; the first and fifth are true as they stand. Each of them will now be taken into consideration, And first, of the representation itself.

The representation, generally speaking, must be of such a nature, or at least made under such circumstances, as to carry conviction to a man of average intelligence. It may be in acts or conduct as well as in words; it may be in a newspaper advertisement even. Richardson v. Silvester, L. R. 9 Q. B. 34; Bradbury v. Barding, 35 Conn. 577. But in whatever way it is conveyed, it must be sufficient to produce effect. If uncertain, indefinite, or vague, it cannot be made the basis of a demand or a defence. Wakeman v. Dalley, 51 N. Y. 27, 30; Smith v. Chadwick, 20 Ch. D. 27; Dimmock v. Hallett, L. R. 2 Ch. 21, 30; Arnold v. Bright, 41 Mich. 207.

But language or conduct which taken alone is vague and indecisive may be made certain by evidence from attending circumstances. Thus of

192. Where the party intentionally or by design misrepresents a material fact or produces a false impression [1] in order to mislead

[1] See Laidlaw v. Organ, 2 Wheat. R. 178, 195; Pidlock v. Bishop, 3 B. & Cressw. 605; Smith v. The Bank of Scotland, 1 Dow, Parl. R. 272; Evans v. Bicknell, 6 Ves. 173, 182.

doubtful language in the prospectus of a company the fact that the defendant has used language to others which would tend to show that the scheme in question was fraudulent, as e. g. that he has said that he was 'rigging the market,' will have a tendency to show that the language of the prospectus was used in a sense to make it false. Moore v. Burke, 4 Fost. & F. 258.

Whether conduct or particular acts amount to a representation that may be translated into a statement of fact which is false and actionable is to be determined by the natural import of the conduct or acts under the particular circumstances. In a recent case it was urged that a direction to a bank to honor the checks of a company 'signed by two of the directors, and countersigned by the secretary,' was equivalent to a representation by those who gave the direction that checks so signed were duly authorized by the company. But the court declined to adopt this view, and held that the direction was simply an indication in regard to the particular form in which drafts would be drawn by the company. Beattie v. Ebury, L. R. 7 H. L. 102. It was also laid down in this case (p. 126) that the mere fact of an agent's drawing a check on behalf of his principal does not amount to a representation on the part of the drawer that his principal has assets in hand or available sufficient to answer the draft, so as to make the agent liable for a false representation in case that is not the fact. Cases of actionable concealment of part, on a partial statement of the truth, as in Brewer v. Brown, 28 Ch. D. 309, are closely related to this subject. See infra, p. 208.

On the other hand the mere fact that A assumes to act for B is of itself a representation, or rather a warranty, that he has such authority. May v. Western Union Tel. Co., 112 Mass. 90; Richardson v. Williamson, L. R. 6 Q. B. 276; Collen v. Wright, 8 El. & B. 647; Randell v. Trimen, 18 C. B. 786; White v. Madison, 26 N. Y. 117, 124; Mahurin v. Harding, 28 N. H. 128; Noyes v. Loring, 55 Maine, 408; Indiana R. Co. v. Tyng, 63 N. Y. 653. Indeed in Massachusetts this rule has been applied to the case of a telegraph company delivering a particular message to the plaintiff never authorized by the supposed sender. This was deemed a false representation by the telegraph company of its authority to deliver the message. May v. Western Union Tel. Co., supra. But this would not be so in England. Playford v. United Kingdom Tel. Co., L. R. 4 Q. B. 706.

There are many other examples of acts amounting to implied warranties of the existence of facts. Thus the acceptance of a bill of exchange is a binding assertion of the genuineness of the drawer's signature, within certain limits. Price v. Neal, 3 Burr. 1354; Ellis v. Ohio Life Ins. Co., 4 Ohio St. 628; National Bank v. Bangs, 106 Mass. 441. So acceptance asserts the drawer's capacity to draw and the payee's capacity to indorse. Smith v. Marsack, 6 C. B. 486; Hallifax v. Lyle, 3 Ex. 446. And indorsement asserts the genuineness of prior signatures and the capacity of the prior parties. State Bank v. Fearing, 16 Pick. 533; Erwin v. Down, 15 N. Y. 575. But the mere failure of an indorser of a note to disclose to his

another, or to entrap or cheat him, or to obtain an undue advantage of him, — in every such case there is a positive fraud in the indorsee the fact that the maker is an infant is not a fraud. People's Bank's Appeal, 93 Penn. St. 107.

Again though there may be a clear and certain representation in language, it may still be wanting in its very nature of strength to carry conviction. Opinion is a familiar example. But opinion may be of several kinds. It may be expressed of a fact not capable of being known, in which case it matters not that it is expressed in the form of a positive statement, as that ' the centre of the earth is a molten mass;' or it may be expressed of a fact capable of being known, in which case it is opinion only when it is stated in the way of opinion and not as a fact. In the first of these two cases it is clear that no liability can attach, though every other element of liability were present, unless possibly some weak-minded person were made the victim of a meditated fraud. In the second case, where the opinion relates to a fact capable of being known, there can be no liability, provided no fact is known to the speaker to make the opinion false. If a fact of the kind is known to him, the ' opinion ' is no opinion at all, but a fraudulent disguise intended to prevent liability. If still there is clear indication that it was intended to be acted upon, acting upon it will, it seems, create liability, at least if it was of a nature to induce belief and action in the average man. Where this is true however, it is true, not because opinion amounts to a representation within the rule of liability, but because the opinion implies — that is, states by inference — the non-existence of the fact which makes the statement false. In other words the liability rests as in other cases on misrepresentation of fact, — of something capable of carrying conviction. Thus if a person, intending to deceive, should state that in his opinion a certain piece of land was a good dairy tract, that would by clear inference imply — as much so as if he had said it in words — that he knew of nothing to make the statement false; and if at the time he knew that something poisonous to cattle grew with the grass there, he has made a false representation and incurred liability. It seems to be enough, notwithstanding the fact that the statement is put in the form of an opinion, that with the scienter there was an actual intent that it should take effect. Birdsey v. Butterfield, 34 Wis. 52; Pike v. Fay, 101 Mass. 134, 137; Picard v. McCormick, 11 Mich. 68; Kost v. Bender, 25 Mich. 515. See also Haygarth v. Wearing, L. R. 12 Eq. 320; Hubbell v. Meigs, 50 N. Y. 480; Wakeman v. Dalley, 51 N. Y. 27; Martin v. Jordan, 60 Maine, 531; Holbrook v. Connor, Ib. 578; infra, § 198.

Besides while a falsely expressed opinion may not always be attended with liability in *damages*, it does not follow that a contract entered into upon the basis of an opinion can be enforced, at least in equity, when it is shown that the opinion was falsely, especially if it was also fraudulently, expressed. That would be to make fraud successful by the aid of the courts. The courts may decline to give the injured party damages because of his want of prudence; but they ought not on the other hand to aid a flagrant wrong-doer. Compare Redgrave v. Hurd, 20 Ch. D. 1; Arkwright v. Newbold, 17 Ch. D. 301, 320, on representations of fact. Indeed the wrong-doer might well be enjoined from attempting to enforce his contract. All this however is delicate ground.

Representations of the law, like statements of opinion, may also be definite and clear, and, though false to the knowledge of the party who makes

truest sense of the terms.[1] There is an evil act with an evil intent, — dolum malum ad circumveniendum. And the misrepre-

[1] Atwood *v.* Small, 6 Clark & Finnell. R. 232, 233; s. c. in Court of Exchequer, 1 Younge, R. 407; Taylor *v.* Ashton, 11 Mees. & Welsb. 401.

them and in other respects like actionable statements of fact, possibly not attended with any legal consequences. This if true proceeds upon the ground that all men are presumed to know the law; the plaintiff knew or ought to have known what the law was. But the proposition must be taken with much qualification. Even if it be quite true in any case between laymen on equal footing that a false and fraudulent statement of the law is not actionable (see Cooke *v.* Nathan, 16 Barb. 342, which implies the contrary), it is not true that such a representation would not be actionable, or a ground of defence or of relief in equity, according to circumstances, if made to a person standing on an inferior footing to that of him who makes it; as where it is made by an attorney to his client, by a trustee to his cestui que trust with regard to the trust property, by a person of average intelligence to a weak-minded person, by a citizen to a foreigner, or perhaps by any one whose advice is sought because of his supposed knowledge on the particular point. In any such case if the statement concerning the law is false and fraudulent, there should be redress. And the same should probably be true of most cases of the statement of opinion; if such were falsely and fraudulently made to a person in one of the situations named, liability should follow though no fact were known by the wrong-doer to make his opinion false; that is, though he had made it recklessly, without knowing whether it had any foundation or not. In the case of trustee and cestui que trust far less than this would suffice to justify relief to the latter. Indeed it will probably be found, when a particular misrepresentation has been dismissed, with discrimination, as a misrepresentation of law, that the case is one where the representation, had it been a representation of fact, as of authority to act for another, would have been actionable without proof of any scienter; when in such a case the representation has been declared to be a mere statement of law, the meaning is, or may be, that the representation is not actionable because it was not fraudulent. Compare Beattie *v.* Ebury, L. R. 7 Ch. 777, 800; s. c. L. R. 7 H. L. 102; Rashdall *v.* Ford, L. R. 2 Eq. 750; Eaglesfield *v.* Londonderry, L. R. 4 Ch. 693, 702.

Representations of value stand upon a special footing; 'simplex commendatio non obligat.' The vendor of property may indeed know that the property is not worth what he says it is worth; but the very fact that the representation is made by the owner is enough to put any person of average intelligence on his guard. But there may be cases where a statement of value may be attended with legal consequences. It might be worth inquiring if this would not be the case where a stranger has been asked his advice with regard to property of some peculiar kind the value of which he knows better than others; and where the value of property is falsely and fraudulently overstated, by the vendor even, to a person of weak mind, or by a trustee to his cestui que trust, it is probable that the law would take cognizance of the fraud. See Wise *v.* Fuller, 29 N. J. Eq. 262; Suessenguth *v.* Bingenheimer, 40 Wis. 370; infra, § 197. It is clear that where a false statement of value, such e. g. as the value of an invention, is connected with a misrepresentation of some clear mat-

sentation may be as well by deeds or acts, as by words; by artifices to mislead, as well as by positive assertions.[1] The civil law

[1] 3 Black. Comm. 165; 2 Kent, Comm. Lect. 39, p. 484 (2d edit.); Laidlaw v. Organ, 2 Wheat. 195; 1 Dow, Parl. R. 272.

ter of fact calculated to impose upon the plaintiff, to put him off his guard and to cause him to credit the statement of value, the law will give him all needed relief. Miller v. Barber, 66 N. Y. 558, 567.

Another class of representations commonly unattended with legal consequences is that of promissory statements. Because they look to the future for their fulfilment, it is considered that men of prudence will not confide in them. See Maddison v. Alderson, 8 App. Cas. 467, 473. If however a representation that a particular fact shall be true is fraudulently made, that is, with intent that it shall not be so, or with knowledge of facts that make it impossible that it shall be so, there is a case for the courts. Kimball v. Ætna Ins. Co., 9 Allen, 540. This probably proceeds, as in the case of opinion supra, on the ground that the representation is of a nature to imply a statement of fact, to wit, the existence of a present intent to have the result transpire, or that no fact is known to prevent the result expected.

But a plain statement of fact, in terms true, may be false and actionable; enough that it was likely under the circumstances to produce a false impression of the actual state of things. Clarke v. Dickson, 6 C. B. N. S. 453; Tapp v. Lee, 3 Bos. & P. 367; Moore v. Burke, 4 Fost. & F. 258; Peek v. Gurney, L. R. 6 H. L. 377; Corbett v. Brown, 8 Bing. 33; Arkwright v. Newbold, 17 Ch. D. 301; Brewer v. Brown, 28 Ch. D. 309. If a man e. g. while professing to answer a question as to the pecuniary standing of another were to select those facts only which would be likely to result in producing a favorable impression of the individual's credit, keeping back facts which would if known change the complexion of those stated, he might well be called a more artful knave than the man who tells a direct falsehood. Tapp v. Lee, supra, at p. 371; Peek v. Gurney, supra; New Brunswick Ry. Co. v. Muggeridge, 1 Dru. & S. 381; Central Ry. v. Kisch, L. R. 2 H. L. 99, 113. A good example of the rule is also found in Corbett v. Brown, supra. The plaintiff, being about to furnish the defendant's son with goods on credit, inquired of the defendant if the son, as the latter had asserted, had property of £300 value. The defendant answered in the affirmative, stating that he had advanced that sum to his son, but failed to state the fact that the son had given his promissory note for the amount. It was held that this was a false representation though it was true in a literal sense, and though money lent in this way by a parent was often intended as a gift.

Indeed the obvious meaning of the plainest language may be enlarged or modified by the situation or circumstances in which it was used. Thus a representation that a vessel is seaworthy may be shown, in connection with the very purpose for which it was sold, to mean seaworthy for the purpose of a specially hazardous voyage. Milne v. Morwood, 15 C. B. 778. In a word whatever the character of the language, all the facts of every kind bearing upon its sensible meaning in the particular case should be taken into account. See e. g. Cleveland Iron Co. v. Stephenson, 4 Fost. & F. 428; New Brunswick Ry. Co. v. Conybeare, 9 H. L. Cas. 711.

The meaning of the representation

has well expressed this when it says, 'Dolo malo pactum fit, quotiens circumscribendi alterius causa, aliud agitur, et aliud agi

is to be taken of course from the representation itself, that is, from the language or act interpreted by the light of attending facts, and not from the purpose of the party making it when that purpose would if received defeat the relief sought. Phelps *v.* White, 7 L. R. Ir. 160. In Arkwright *v.* Newbold, 17 Ch. D. 301, 322, Cotten, L. J., said that a person who issued a statement was answerable not only for what he actually intended to represent, but also for what any one might reasonably suppose to be the meaning of his language. Quoted with approval in Smith *v.* Chadwick, 20 Ch. D. 27, 79. See also Match *v.* Hunt, 38 Mich. 1. It will be observed that what the party actually intended may be accepted as distinguished from what the statement in itself imported.

The truth of the statement further is to be judged of as of the time when it is acted upon, if the party to whom it was made is still reasonably, or to the knowledge of him who made it, laboring under the impression created by it. Thus it is the duty of a person who knows that another is contracting with him upon the faith of a statement made by him which, though true when it was made, has become untrue at the time of executing the contract, to disclose to such person the change of fact. Arkwright *v.* Newbold, 17 Ch. D. 301, 310, Fry, J.; Reynell *v.* Sprye, 1 DeG. M. & G. 591; Henderson *v.* Lacon, L. R. 5 Eq. 249.

But in any case, speaking in reference to the result, the representation must have been adequate to produce it; that is, if towards the result it was not material, the courts will not take cognizance of it on behalf of the person to whom it was made. Smith *v.* Chadwick, 20 Ch. D. 27; Slaughter *v.* Genson, 13 Wall. 379; McAleer *v.* Horsey, 35 Md. 439 ; Bowman *v.* Carruthers, 40 Ind. 90; supra, § 190.

Verbal representations are not merged in written ones so as to be excluded from consideration in questions of fraud. Match *v.* Hunt, 38 Mich. 1.

Knowledge of defendant. — To enable one who complains of misrepresentation by another to recover damages for any loss he may have sustained thereby, it is necessary for him to show, whether his demand is preferred at law or in equity, what is or virtually amounts to moral fraud, — that the supposed wrong-doer made the representation either (1) with actual knowledge of its falsity, or (2) under circumstances showing that he ought to have had such knowledge, or (3) recklessly without knowing whether it was true or false. Joliffe *v.* Baker, 11 Q. B. D. 255; Arkwright *v.* Newbold, 17 Ch. D. 301, 320; Reese Silver Mining Co. *v.* Smith, L. R. 4 H. L. 64; Redgrave *v.* Hurd, 20 Ch. D. 1; Rawlins *v.* Wickham, 3 DeG. & J. 304; Collins *v.* Evans, 5 Q. B. 820, 826; Ormrod *v.* Huth, 14 Mees. & W. 651, 664; Behn *v.* Kemble, 7 C. B. N. s. 260; Barley *v.* Walford, 9 Q. B. 197, 208; Childers *v.* Wooler, 2 El. & E. 287; Mahurin *v.* Harding, 28 N. H. 128; Evertson *v.* Miles, 6 Johns. 138; Case *v.* Boughton, 11 Wend. 106, 108; Carley *v.* Wilkins, 6 Barb. 557; Edick *v.* Crim, 10 Barb. 445; Lobdell *v.* Baker, 1 Met. 193, 201; Bennett *v.* Judson, 21 N. Y. 138.

Of these three forms of the scienter only the second and third call for remark. Indeed the third is but a special form of the first; to make a positive statement of fact, without knowledge whether it is true or false, in fact implies what is false to the party's own knowledge, to wit, that he *has* information on the subject. It is well settled that such a representa-

simulatur.'[1] And again, 'Dolum malum à se abesse præstare venditor debet, qui non tantum in eo est, qui fallendi causa

[1] Dig. Lib. 2, tit. 14, 1. 7, § 9.

tion is actionable. Evans *v.* Edmonds, 13 C. B. 777, 786; Phelps *v.* White, 7 L. R. Ir. 160, 170; Morse *v.* Dearborn, 109 Mass. 593, 595; Twitchell *v.* Bridge, 42 Vt. 68; Beebe *r.* Knapp, 28 Mich. 53; Stone *v.* Covell, 29 Mich. 359; infra, § 193.

What circumstances are such as to show, under the second form of the scienter, that a man making a representation ought to know that it is false cannot be exactly defined. It is commonly said, and perhaps that is all that can be said in the way of a general proposition, that a man is bound to know the state of facts within his special means of knowledge. Jarrett *v.* Kennedy, 6 C. B. 319, 322; Doyle *v.* Hort, 4 L. R. Ir. Ex. D. 661; Morse *v.* Dearborn, 109 Mass. 593.

This lacks precision, and just what it means must in the nature of things be left to particular cases, or at most to particular classes of cases.

The implied assertion and warranty of one's authority to act for another for whom he assumes to act appears to be an example of the proposition. Collen *v.* Wright, 8 El. & B. 647; May *v.* Western Union Tel. Co., 112 Mass. 90; Mahurin *v.* Harding, 28 N. H. 128; Indiana R. Co. *v.* Tyng, 63 N. Y. 653; supra, p. 205. So probably of all other implied warranties.

Again under ordinary circumstances, that is, excluding cases of sudden or general commercial disturbances, a man not engaged in speculation or trade must know whether he is worth for example $10,000 or nothing. See Morse *v.* Dearborn, 109 Mass. 593. But probably one could not be presumed to know whether he was worth $10,000 or $9,000. That is, it would not be wrongful for a man to say that he was worth $10,000 when he was worth within a thousand or two of that sum, unless he actually knew that he was telling a falsehood, or made the statement recklessly without knowing anything about the facts. And the discrepancy would have to be material to make him liable in any case.

Indeed what a person in making a statement is bound to know must have regard to his particular means of knowledge and to the nature of the representation, and then be subject to the test of the knowledge which a man paying that attention which every man owes to his neighbor in making a representation would have acquired in the particular case by the use of such means. Doyle *v.* Hort, 4 L. R. Ir. Ex. D. 661, 670, Palles, C. B.

When however the party who has suffered from misrepresentation seeks, not damages, but the protection of the courts against the other party, to prevent him from deriving advantage from the misrepresentation he has made, as in obtaining a contract, it matters not whether such act was with knowledge of any sort or was done in perfect good faith and innocence, with full and just belief in its truth; the courts will grant the protection sought. To refuse to do so would virtually be to lend their aid to what now on the allegation that the representation was false, would be a known wrong; for the party complained of is now at all events apprised of the untruth of his representation, and he cannot press his advantage any longer without being guilty of fraud. Arkwright *v.* Newbold, 17 Ch. D. 301, 320 (C. A.); Redgrave *v.* Hurd, 20 Ch. D. 1 (C. A.); Reese Silver Mining Co. *v.* Smith, L. R. 4 H. L. 64 Rawlins *v.* Wickham, 3 DeG. & J. 304 ; Smith *v.* Land Corporation, 49 Law Times,

ACTUAL FRAUD.

obscure loquitur, sed etiam, qui insidiose obscure dissimulat.'[1]
The case here put falls directly within one of the species of frauds

[1] Dig. Lib. 18, tit. 1, l. 43, § 2; Pothier De Vente, n. 234, 237, 238.

532; Carpenter *v.* American Ins. Co., 1 Story, 57.

This rule though always distinctly maintained in equity (infra, § 193) has not been so fully recognized at law, and cases could be found in which Courts of Law have enforced contracts founded on misrepresentation where the misrepresentation was innocent when made. Cornfoote *v.* Fowke, 6 Mees. & W. 358. This has been the result in some cases perhaps of a confusion; the tests of a right of action for *damages* on account of misrepresentation have been applied to the case of a defence against the enforcement of a contract. But this is clearly wrong; the contract cannot be enforced, after the falsity of the representation has been brought to the knowledge of the plaintiff, without allowing, as we have seen, the perpetration upon the defendant of what is now at all events a fraud. But if a distinction between the views of Courts of Law and Courts of Equity on this question has become fixed in a particular State, as was at one time the case in England, — if at law a contract can be enforced notwithstanding a material misrepresentation by the plaintiff, where that misrepresentation was innocent, — then at all events the distinction must be deemed to have been done away in those States in which equitable pleas are fully allowed at law. Redgrave *v.* Hurd, 20 Ch. D. 1, 12.

Under what circumstances in the case of a claim for damages will the knowledge of an agent affect an innocent principal? The question of agency is of course immaterial in a case in which the principal is seeking to enforce a contract or is resisting an effort to have the contract annulled or an action upon it enjoined. In such a case the contract will be repudiated by the courts, agency or no agency (Houldsworth *v.* Glasgow Bank, 5 App. Cas. 317); assuming that the rights of innocent persons have not intervened. See e. g. Mullens *v.* Miller, 22 Ch. D. 194 (a suit for specific performance); Bell's Case, 22 Beav. 35 (defrauded party held not liable as a contributory to a company for stock in which he had subscribed); Ayre's Case, 25 Beav. 513 (the same sort of case); Scholefield *v.* Templer, Johns. (Eng.) 155; Fitzsimmons *v.* Joslin, 21 Vt. 129; Carpenter *v.* American Ins. Co., 1 Story, 57. If however others have in good faith acquired rights in reliance upon the contract, especially if it has been acted upon by the defrauded party, and benefits received under it, the courts will, for *their* protection, uphold it. Thus where a party has been induced by the fraudulent representations of the agents of a company to subscribe to the same, and he has received dividends thereon, and his subscription has been followed by that of innocent persons, it is obvious that to excuse him from liability to contribute to the payment of claims against the company according to his contract would be to cast a burden on the later subscribers which they did not undertake to carry. Their rights must be protected, and his contract must therefore be held binding, — this however entirely irrespective of the innocence of the company in respect of the fraud. See Mixer's Case, 4 DeG. & J. 575 (overruling Brockwell's Case, 4 Drew. 205); Dodgson's Case, 3 DeG. & S. 85; Bernard's Case, 5 DeG. & S. 289. But if there be no one whose rights would be unjustly affected by

enumerated by Lord Hardwicke, to wit, fraud arising from facts and circumstances of imposition.[1]

[1] Chesterfield v. Janssen, 2 Ves. 155. In Neville v. Wilkinson, 1 Bro. Ch. R. 546, the Lord Chancellor (Thurlow) said: 'It has been said, here is no evidence of actual fraud on R.; but only a combination to defraud him. A court of justice would make itself ridiculous if it permitted such a distinction. Misrepresentation of circumstances is admitted, and there is positively a deception.' And he added: 'If a man upon a treaty for any contract will make a false representation by means of which he puts the party bargaining under a mistake upon the terms of the bargain, it is a fraud. It misleads the parties contracting, on the subject of the contract.'

releasing such party from liability to contribute, his demand for relief will be granted. Parbury's Case, 3 DeG. & S. 43; Bell's Case, 22 Beav. 35; Ayre's Case, 25 Beav. 513. Unless he purchased his shares not from the company but from a third person. Bell's Case, supra.

Indeed it seems sufficient in principle to disentitle the defrauded party to rescission that innocent persons have since his subscription become creditors of the company or subscribed to its stock, without any showing that the defrauded party had recognized his engagement, as by receiving benefits under it; for his engagement is valid until repudiated. See Oakes v. Turquand, L. R. 2 H. L. 325, 348. When as in Houldsworth v. Glasgow Bank, 5 App. Cas. 317, 322, 330, rescission of the contract is stated to be the proper course in the case of a 'going' company, where fraud has been practised upon the plaintiff, the limitation here stated must doubtless be understood.

But the question whether the innocent principal is liable in damages for the fraudulent representations of the agent not as such authorized by the principal, but within the scope of the agent's authority, is not so easily answered. The English courts have had frequent occasion to consider the question in recent times, and have found great difficulty in answering it. It appears to be agreed however that where the principal has derived a benefit from his agent's act, he will be liable in damages for the agent's fraud in the transaction. Barwick v. English Joint-Stock Bank, L. R. 2 Ex. 259 (Ex. Ch.); Mackay v. Commercial Bank, L. R. 5 P. C. 394; Udell v. Atherton, 7 Hurl. & N. 172; National Exchange Co. v. Drew, 2 Macq. 103; Ranger v. Great Western Ry. Co., 5 H. L. Cas. 72; Fuller v. Wilson, 3 Q. B. 58; Swift v. Winterbotham, L. R. 8 Q. B. 244; s. c. sub nom. Swift v. Jewsbury, L. R. 9 Q. B. 301, reversing L. R. 8 Q. B. 244; Swire v. Francis, 3 App. Cas. 106; Weir v. Bell, 3 Ex. D. 238; Houldsworth v. Glasgow Bank, 5 App. Cas. 317.

Indeed in the first two of these cases it is thought to be enough to make the principal liable that the act of the agent within the general scope of his authority was *done* for the principal's benefit; though in fact the principal had there received the benefit. It was considered in those cases that there was no distinction in respect of the liability of the employer between cases of fraud and other cases of wrong. See also Houldsworth v. Glasgow Bank, at p. 327. Swift v. Winterbotham, supra, appears to have gone still further in the Queen's Bench, and to have held the principal liable irrespective of benefit derived or sought; though the court said that the representations in question 'were, and were intended to be, communications between the' principals. But on this point the case was reversed.

198. Whether the party thus misrepresenting a material fact knew it to be false, or made the assertion without knowing

L. R. 9 Q. B. 301. In the Exchequer Chamber, Lord Coleridge, who delivered the principal opinion, now said: 'There can be no doubt that a different set of principles altogether applies where an agent of a corporation or a joint-stock company, at any rate in carrying on its business, does something of which the company takes advantage, or by which it profits or may profit, and it turns out that the act of the agent is fraudulent.' (See Houldsworth v. Glasgow Bank, 5 App. Cas. 317, 324, 329.) And the case was considered to be in accord with Barwick v. English Joint-Stock Bank, supra. See Mackay v. Commercial Bank, L. R. 5 P. C. 394, 412.

The House of Lords had held in Western Bank v. Addie, L. R. 1 H. L. Scotch, 145, in a suit to rescind a contract for the purchase of shares and for restitution in integrum or in the alternative for damages, that in the absence of evidence of fraud on the part of the defendants, the action could not be maintained, though the defendants' agent had been guilty of fraud in securing the contract. The Lord Chancellor (Chelmsford) declared that an action for deceit could not be maintained against the company in such a case; the remedy was against him who committed the fraud. And Lord Cranworth said that an attentive consideration of the cases had convinced him that the true principle was that corporate bodies could be made responsible for the frauds of their agents to the extent to which the principals had profited from the fraud, but that they could not be sued as wrong-doers by imputing to them the misconduct of those whom they had employed.

Later in Swire v. Francis, 3 App. Cas. 106, another question arose in the Privy Council, of the defendants' liability for their agent's fraud committed in the course of his business, that is, in the course of a transaction within his authority as an agent. The defendants were innocent, and derived no actual benefit from the transaction, though the agent's act was professedly and ostensibly for their benefit; but they were held liable on the principle of Barwick v. English Joint-Stock Bank and Mackay v. Commercial Bank, supra. About the same time the Court of Appeal reached a contrary conclusion on a similar case. Weir v. Bell, 3 Ex. D. 238, Cotten, L. J., dissenting. And this — the non-liability to damages, of an innocent principal who had derived no benefit from his agent's fraud — is now the prevailing doctrine in England with regard to the one case of buying into a company by the purchase of shares from it. Houldsworth v. Glasgow Bank, 5 App. Cas. 317 (House of Lords, A. D. 1880), where the law is well explained. See especially pp. 329, 330, Lord Selborne. Whether the broader dicta in Barwick v. English Joint-Stock Bank, and in some of the other cases, are to prevail, making the principal liable in damages in other cases, though he was innocent and received no benefit from the agent's fraud in the course of his employment, is expressly left an open question in Houldsworth v. Glasgow Bank. See pp. 339-341, Lord Blackburn. (In this connection may be noticed the decision in Miles v. McIlwraith, 8 App. Cas. 120, in the Privy Council, where an innocent principal was held not liable to certain penalties of statute incurred if at all by the fraud of his agents. But the court held that there had been no transaction on behalf of the principal.)

It is thought however by a learned writer that, with the exception of the

214   EQUITY JURISPRUDENCE.   [CHAP. VI.

whether it were true or false, is wholly immaterial; for the affirmation of what one does not know or believe to be true is

one case of buying into a company (supra, Houldsworth v. Glasgow Bank), the prevailing rule in England is that laid down in Barwick v. English Joint-Stock Bank, denying any distinction, in cases of agency, between fraud and trespass, and holding the principal liable regardless of benefit received. F. Pollock in April No., 1885, of Law Quarterly Review, p. 218. But see Weir v. Bell, 3 Ex. D. 238, 244, Lord Bramwell, where however the old but unfortunate distinction in regard to *wilful* wrongs of a servant is repeated.

It is equally clear in this country, that the principal is liable in damages where he has derived a benefit from his agent's fraud. Jeffrey v. Bigelow, 13 Wend. 518 ; Bennett v. Judson, 21 N. Y. 238; Allerton v. Allerton, 50 N. Y. 670; Craig v. Ward, 3 Keyes, 393; Elwell v. Chamberlin, 31 N. Y. 619; Chester v. Dickerson, 52 Barb. 349; Davis v. Bemis, 40 N. Y. 453, note; Durst v. Burton, 47 N. Y. 167; s. c. 2 Lans. 137; Sandford v. Handy, 23 Wend. 260 ; Locke v. Stearns, 1 Met. 560; Cook v. Castner, 9 Cush. 266; White v. Sawyer, 16 Gray, 586. Nor according to several of these cases is the principal's liability limited to the benefit received, but extends to the amount of damage done. Jeffrey v. Bigelow; White v. Sawyer. These cases are therefore inconsistent with the view sometimes suggested, that the action against the principal when innocent may be treated as an action for money had and received. Barwick v. English Joint-Stock Bank, L. R. 2 Ex. 259 ; Mackay v. Commercial Bank, L. R. 5 P. C. 394, 414.

It would seem to follow that the principal would be held liable for the fraud of his agent in the course of his employment though he had derived no benefit whatever from the transaction; and this view is strengthened by the fact that our courts, adopting language of Lord Holt in the nisi prius case of Hern v. Nichols, 1 Salk. 289, commonly rest the liability of the principal on the ground that he has held the agent out as a person entitled to confidence. Sandford v. Handy, 23 Wend. 260 ; Davis v. Bemis, 40 N. Y. 453, note; Locke v. Stearns, 1 Met. 560. But see Kennedy v. McKay, 43 N. J. 288. This view however appears to have lost ground in recent times in England, otherwise there could not have been that hesitancy and refusal to hold an innocent principal liable which the cases above cited show. But in Weir v. Bell, 3 Ex. D. 238, 245, supra, Bramwell, L. J., reasserts, or rather restates, apparently in stronger terms, the old doctrine of Hern v. Nichols, supra. The learned Lord Justice there says that the true ground is that every person who authorizes another to act for him in making a contract undertakes for the absence of fraud in that person in the execution of his authority; though he holds to the doctrine that liability for damages in deceit broadly is based on moral fraud. He considered the defendant, a director, as not the true principal of the agent.

While however it appears to be a just interpretation of the situation to say that one who holds another out as having authority to act for him holds that person out as an honest man, it is probably contrary to the fact in nearly every case to say that he has intended to *warrant* the honesty of his agent. If inquired of in advance, the principal would in most cases probably say that he intended nothing of the kind, though he would doubtless say that he *believed* his agent an honest man. If this is the true interpreta-

equally in morals and law as unjustifiable as the affirmation of what is known to be positively false.[1] And even if the party

[1] Ainslie v. Medlycott, 9 Ves. 21; Graves v. White, Freem. R. 57. See also Pearson v. Morgan, 2 Bro. Ch. R. 389; Foster v. Charles, 6 Bing. R. 396; s. c. 7 Bing. R. 105; Taylor v. Ashton, 11 Mees. & Welsb. 401.

tion, the principal ought not to be liable in damages, apart from advantage derived, unless he was himself guilty of fraud or of negligence in holding out his agent as honest, — in the absence of strong public policy to the contrary. To go further is virtually to say that when a man's business is such as to demand the employment of help, he ought to be held to a stricter accountability than he would be held to if he could do the business alone. Nothing short of urgent public policy should be sufficient to extend a doctrine of this kind beyond its recognized bounds; to extend to new cases the rule that one man may be held liable for another man's wrongs can be justified only by the strongest reasons. It may not yet be too late to urge the point.

The directors of a company — to pass on — are not agents of each other so as to bind each other by fraudulent acts not authorized or participated in by those whom it is sought to bind. Thus a director is not liable merely because he is a director, for the fraudulent issuance of a prospectus by his co-directors, or by any other agent of the company. Cargill v. Bower, 10 Ch. D. 502.

Knowledge of Plaintiff. — But the plaintiff's right to relief, or the defendant's right of defence, based on misrepresentation depends upon his ignorance of the true state of facts and his belief in the representation made. In other words, if such party knew or under the circumstances ought to have known that the representation was false, his case or defence will fail. Pasley v. Freeman, 3 T. R. 51; s. c. Bigelow's L. C. Torts, 1; Salem Rubber Co. v. Adams, 23 Pick. 256; Ely v. Stewart, 2 Md. 408; Camberwell Building Soc. v. Holloway, 13 Ch. D. 754; Delaine Co. v. James, 94 U. S. 207.

The only difficulty in the situation is to determine when the plaintiff ought to have known the facts. The rule cannot here be always applied that applies to the converse case of knowledge on the part of the one who made the misrepresentation, to wit, that he is supposed to know all facts within his special means of knowledge, for the plaintiff notwithstanding his means of knowledge may well have been prevented from availing himself of the same by the very misrepresentation in question; it is well settled that the plaintiff need not inquire in the face of a plain representation of fact, though the truth thereof might easily be ascertained. Negligence is no bar to relief. Redgrave v. Hurd, 20 Ch. D. 1, 13, Jessel, M. R.; David v. Park, 103 Mass. 501; Keller v. Equitable Ins. Co., 28 Ind. 170; Parham v. Randolph, 4 How. (Miss.) 435; Kiefer v. Rogers, 19 Minn. 32; Holland v. Anderson, 38 Mo. 55; Mead v. Bunn, 32 N. Y. 275, 280; McClellan v. Scott, 24 Wis. 81, 87; Webster v. Bailey, 31 Mich. 36; Matlock v. Todd, 19 Ind. 130; Phelps v. White, 7 L. R. Ir. 160; Stanley v. McGauran, 11 L. R. Ir. 314.

Doubtless when the means of ascertaining the truth were directly before the plaintiff's eyes, it may require strong evidence to convince the court that he relied upon the defendant's statements or acts and refrained from making inspection. See e. g. Salem Rubber Co. v. Adams, 23 Pick. 256,

innocently misrepresents a material fact by mistake, it is equally conclusive; for it operates as a surprise and imposition upon the other party.[1]

[1] See Pearson *v.* Morgan, 2 Bro. Ch. R. 389; Burrows *v.* Locke, 10 Ves. 475; De Manville *v.* Compton, 1 Ves. & B. 355; Ex parte Carr, 3 Ves. & B. 111; 1 Marsh. on Insur. B. ch. 10, § 1; Carpenter *v.* American Ins. Co., 1 Story, R. 57. In Pearson *v.* Morgan, 2 Bro. Ch. R. 385, 388, the case was that A, being interested in an estate in fee, which was charged with £8000 in favor of B, was applied to by C, who was about to lend money to B, to know if the £8000 was still a subsisting charge on the estate. A stated that it was, and C lent his money to B accordingly; it appearing afterwards that the charge had been satisfied, it was nevertheless held that the money lent was a charge on the lands in the hands of A's heirs, because he either knew or ought to have known the fact of satisfaction, and his representation was a fraud on C.

the language in which appears however to be rather too strong against the plaintiff, in the light of the later cases. It seems clear that the plaintiff may rest satisfied with the defendant's representations however easily he might have tested their truth.

Where however the opposite party has said or done nothing having a tendency to prevent inquiry, as where he has remained silent, the failure to inquire will be fatal to relief in ordinary cases. Thus the fact that a married woman did not read a mortgage executed by her upon her separate estate to secure a debt of her husband will not entitle her to relief against the instrument in the absence of fraud. Thacher *v.* Churchill, 118 Mass. 108. See also on the failure to read an instrument, Hardy *v.* Brier, 91 Ind. 91; Watts *v.* Burnett, 56 Ala. 341; Rogers *v.* Place, 35 Ind. 577; Bacon *v.* Markley, 46 Ind. 116; Hawkins *v.* Hawkins, 50 Cal. 558; Craig *v.* Hobbs, 44 Ind. 363; Watson *v.* Planters' Bank, 22 La. An. 14; Miller *v.* Sawbridge, 29 Minn. 442. So too it is no defence to a bill to set aside for fraud a conveyance made on exchange for other property that the plaintiff's property was encumbered, if the plaintiff did nothing to conceal the fact of the incumbrance, and was under no duty to disclose the same. Knowlton *v.* Amy, 47 Mich. 204.

But there are cases in which a man cannot justify himself in being silent, as where he stands in a relation of confidence towards the party dealing with him. Infra, §§ 308 et seq.

In cases of the sale of personalty, the rule of caveat emptor requires the buyer to investigate all questions about which no actual representation has been made by the vendor, unless indeed there is an implied warranty in the case, such as that of the title of a vendor in possession, or that an article is suitable for the purpose for which it is expressly sold.

There is no implied warranty of title in the sale of realty, or of the fitness of the estate for the purpose for which it is sold or leased. Keats *v.* Cadogan, 10 C. B. 591. There must either be a warranty or an actual misrepresentation to justify relief to the vendor, unless there has been a prior written contract of sale. See In re Gloag, 23 Ch. D. 320, infra; Camberwell Building Soc. *v.* Holloway, 13 Ch. D. 754. And even where there has been the one or the other in a previous contract for the sale of the land, with an agreement that error or misstatement by the vendor shall entitle the purchaser to compensation,

194. These principles are so consonant to the dictates of natural justice that it requires no argument to enforce or sup-

there has been considerable doubt whether the law requires the purchaser to make all investigation before the completion of the contract by conveyance, or permits him to claim compensation on discovering error or misstatement afterwards. Vice-Chancellor Malius has more than once insisted, against decisions by Jessel, M. R., and other judges, that the investigation of title must be made before conveyance. Manson *v.* Thacker, 7 Ch. D. 620; Besley *v.* Besley, 9 Ch. D. 103; Allen *v.* Richardson, 13 Ch. D. 524. But this cuts short the natural import of the agreement, and the contrary view has prevailed. In re Turner, 13 Ch. D. 132; Palmer *v.* Johnson, 13 Q. B. D. 351; s. c. 12 Q. B. D. 32; Cann *v.* Cann, 3 Sim. 447; Bos *v.* Helsham, L. R. 2 Ex. 72; Phelps *v.* White, 7 L. R. Ir. 160, 165.

Indeed in the case last cited it is held that taking a conveyance with knowledge of error in the description of the land is not evidence of substituted performance of the prior contract of sale where there is a clause providing for compensation. See In re Gloag, 23 Ch. D. 320, to the same effect. On the other hand it is laid down that if the prior contract of sale, providing for a good title, contains no stipulation in regard to possession, and the purchaser takes possession before completion of the contract, with knowledge of defects which the vendor cannot remove, the taking possession is a waiver of the right to require the removal of the defects or to repudiate the contract. If the defects are removable by the vendor, taking possession is no waiver. In re Gloag, 23 Ch. D. 320. And if the prior contract for sale is silent concerning the title to be made, then, though the presumption is that a good title is to be made, this presumption may be rebutted by evidence that the purchaser had notice, before such contract was executed, of defects in the vendor's title. Ib. But compare Camberwell Building Soc. *v.* Holloway, 13 Ch. D. 754, Jessel, M. R., denying Madeley *v.* Booth, 2 DeG. & S. 718, 722. These were cases in which the contract itself, being silent as to the title to be made, showed on its face, in the particulars and conditions of sale, the defect.

In like manner if in a contract of sale it has been declared that the purchaser 'shall assume and admit that everything (if anything were necessary) was done and performed,' he cannot afterwards maintain an action against the vendor based on a discovery that the vendor's title was defective. Such a clause does not merely mean that the purchaser shall not require the vendor to prove that everything has been done; the purchaser cannot avail himself of facts which he himself has discovered. Best *v.* Hamand, 12 Ch. D. 1 (C. A.). Baggalay, L. J., here alluded to the settled distinction between cases in which the vendor is not bound to produce evidence of a fact, — there of course the purchaser might do so, — and cases in which the fact is to be accepted without question. Hume *v.* Bentley, 5 DeG. & S. 520; Waddell *v.* Wolfe, L. R. 9 Q B. 515.

It is however laid down by the same court that a condition of sale is bad as misleading, first if it requires the purchaser to assume what the vendor knows is false, or secondly if it declares that the state of the title is not accurately known, when in fact it *is* known to the vendor. In re Banister, 12 Ch. D. 131 (C. A.).

Again mere knowledge that fraud is being perpetrated on one will not bar relief if one were unable to prevent the result. Where e. g. a corpo-

port them. The principles of natural justice and sound morals do indeed go further, and require the most scrupulous good faith,

ration is in the hands of unfaithful directors, the mere fact that stockholders are aware of wrong-doing by them will not prevent the corporation afterwards, when such directors have been retired, from proceeding to obtain relief from their acts. The corporation cannot be concluded by the failure of any number of its stockholders to act unless a case is shown of such acquiescence, assent, or ratification as would make it inequitable to permit what has been done to be set aside, or unless the rights of innocent purchasers have so intervened as to create an equitable bar to relief. Pacific R. Co. *v.* Missouri Pacific Ry., 111 U. S. 505, 520.

It is not to be supposed however that stockholders are entirely at the mercy of the directors during their term of office. Even while wrongdoing is going on and before it has been fully consummated, stockholders, though a minority of the whole, in a proper case may proceed on behalf of themselves and others, or alone, against the corporation and its officers, and those participating in the fraud, for relief. Brewer *v.* Boston Theatre, 104 Mass. 378; Peabody *v.* Flint, 6 Allen, 52. See Dousman *v.* Wisconsin Mining Co., 40 Wis. 418. The bill however should show that the plaintiffs are powerless of redress through the corporation. Brewer *v.* Boston Theatre.

A word may be added concerning notice to the plaintiff. Probably in no case of fraud is an injured party to be deemed affected with notice thereof, so as to be considered as having consented to the same, merely because some very prudent and cautious person, on having his attention called to a particular fact, would be apt to seek an explanation of it. Thus it has been said of a question of notice of a defective title that 'there must be some neglect to inquire after actual notice that the title is in some way defective, or some fraudulent and wilful blindness as distinguished from mere caution.' Briggs *v.* Rice, 130 Mass. 50; Jones *v.* Smith, 1 Hare, 43, 55; Ware *v.* Egmont, 4 DeG. M. & G. 460. But this is not to say that a man is not affected with notice by facts which would cause a man of fair average prudence to inquire; such would be a case of notice clearly, and equivalent, as a bar, to knowledge. Warren *v.* Swett, 31 N. H. 332; Cambridge Bank *v.* Delano, 48 N. Y. 326; Willis *v.* Vallette, 4 Met. (Ky.) 186; Kennedy *v.* Green, 3 Mylne & K. 718. See further, post, § 400, and notes.

Intention that the Representation should be acted upon. — This may always be shown by the outward manifestation of the case. It matters not what the party's actual intention may have been; if the representation in connection with the circumstances attending it reasonably indicate that the party who made it made it with a view to its being acted upon, that is enough so far as intention is concerned. See e. g. among many cases, Collins *v.* Denison, 12 Met. 549; Bigelow, Torts, 31 (Student's Series). And the implication of intention from the outward aspect, if on the whole to arise, is conclusive; the defendant cannot then say that he in fact had no such intention in his mind. See Holmes, Common Law, 134.

Any actual intention however, as by declarations at the time or by admissions, may be shown, it seems, without relying upon the nature and circumstances of the transaction. Indeed it is probable that evidence of actual intention that the representation should be acted upon would be admissible where the language and cir-

candor, and truth in all dealings whatsoever. But courts of justice generally find themselves compelled to assign limits to the exercise of their jurisdiction far short of the principles deducible ex æquo et bono; and with reference to the concerns of human life they endeavor to aim at mere practical good and general convenience. Hence many things may be reproved in sound morals which are left without any remedy except by an appeal in foro conscientiæ to the party himself.[1] Pothier has expounded this subject with his usual force and sterling sense. 'As a matter of conscience,' says he, 'any deviation from the most exact and scrupulous sincerity is repugnant to the good faith that ought to prevail in contracts. Any dissimulation concerning the object of the contract, and what the opposite party has an interest in knowing, is contrary to that good faith; for since we are commanded to love our neighbor as ourselves, we are not permitted to conceal from him anything which we should be unwilling to have had concealed from ourselves under similar circumstances. But in civil tribunals a person cannot be allowed to complain of trifling deviations from good faith in the party with whom he has contracted. Nothing but what is plainly injurious to good faith ought to be there considered as a fraud sufficient to impeach a

[1] Pothier De Vente, n. 234, 235, 239.

cumstances were such as to leave the question of intention, as judged from the external aspect, in doubt; assuming that the representation was such as to justify one in acting upon it.

It is hardly necessary to add that the injured party is not required in any case to prove a motive of personal benefit to himself on the part of the defendant. Pasley v. Freeman, 3 T. R. 51; s. c. Bigelow's L. C. Torts, 1; Foster v. Charles, 6 Bing. 396; s. c. 7 Bing. 1051. Nor an intention to harm. Leddell v. McDougal, 29 Week. R. 403 (C. A.).

Acting on the Representation. — Unless the representation has been acted upon, no case for relief can arise; and unless it has been acted upon to one's loss, no damages can be awarded, though if a contract was executed under the influence of misrepresentation, the contract may be set aside, or its enforcement enjoined or successfully resisted, as we have seen.

With regard to proof that the representation was acted upon, it is laid down of cases of contract that if the representation was of a nature to induce or tend to induce a person to enter into a contract, the inference from entering into the contract is that he acted on the inducement so held out; no direct evidence that he did so act is in the first instance necessary. The defendant however may, to overturn this inference, show that the plaintiff knew the truth before he entered into the contract, and hence could not have relied upon the representation, or he may show that the plaintiff avowedly did not rely upon it whether he knew the facts or not. Smith v. Chadwick, 20 Ch. D. 27, 44 (C. A.), Jessel, M. R.

contract, such as the criminal manœuvres and artifices employed by one party to induce the other to enter into the contract. And these should be fully substantiated by proof. "Dolum non nisi perspicuis indiciis probari convenit." [1]

195. The doctrine of law as to misrepresentation being in a practical view such as has been already stated, it may not be without use to illustrate it by some few examples. In the first place the misrepresentation must be of something material, constituting an inducement or motive to the act or omission of the other party and by which he is actually misled to his injury.[2] Thus if a person owning an estate should sell it to another, representing that it contained a valuable mine, which constituted an inducement to the other side to purchase, and the representation were utterly false, the contract for the sale and the sale itself, if completed, might be avoided for fraud; for the representation would go to the essence of the contract.[3] But if he should represent that it contained twenty acres of wood-land or meadow, and the actual quantity was only nineteen acres and three quarters, there, if the difference in quantity would have made no difference to the purchaser in price, value, or otherwise, it would not on account of its immateriality have avoided the contract.[4] So if a person should sell a ship to another, representing her to be five years old, of a certain tonnage, coppered and copper-fastened, and fully equipped, and found with new sails and rigging, either of these representations, if materially untrue so as to affect the essence or value of the purchase, would avoid it. But a trifling difference in either of these ingredients in no way impairing the fair value or price, or not material to the purchaser, would have no such effect. Thus for instance if the ship was a half ton less in size, was a week more than five years old, was not copper-fastened in some unimportant place, and was deficient in some trifling rope, or had some sails which were in a very slight degree worn, — these differences would not avoid the contract; for under such circumstances the differences must be treated as wholly

---

[1] 1 Pothier on Oblig. by Evans, p. 19, n. 30; Cod. Lib. 2, tit. 21, l. 6.
[2] Phillips v. Duke of Bucks, 1 Vern. 227; 1 Fonbl. Eq. B. 1, ch. 2, § 8.
[3] See Lowndes v. Lane, 2 Cox, R. 363.
[4] See the Morris Canal Co. v. Emmett, 9 Paige, R. 168; Stebbins v. Eddy, 4 Mason, R. 414; 2 Freem. R. 107; Twypont v. Warcup, Finch, R. 310; Winch v. Winchester, 1 Ves. & Beam. 375.

inconsequential.[1] The rule of the civil law would here apply, 'Res bona fide vendita, propter minimam causam inempta fieri non debet.'[2] Indeed it may be laid down as a general rule that when the sale is fair and the parties are equally innocent, and the thing is sold in gross, by the quantity, by estimation and not by measurement, a deficiency will not ordinarily entitle a party to relief either by an allowance for the deficiency or by a rescission of the contract.[3] Thus for example the sale of a farm by known boundaries, containing by estimation a certain number of acres, will bind both parties whether the farm contains more or less.[4] (a)

196. So if an executor of a will should obtain a release from a legatee upon a representation that he had no legacy left him by the will, which was false,[5] or if a devisee should obtain a release from the heir at law upon a representation that the will was duly executed[6] when it was not, in each of these cases the release might be set aside for fraud. But if in point of fact in the first case the legacy though given in the will had been revoked by a codicil, or in the second case if the will had been duly executed, although not at the time or in the manner or under the circumstances stated by the devisee, the misrepresentation would not avoid the release because it is immaterial to the rights of either party.

197. In the next place the misrepresentation must not only be in something material, but it must be in something in regard to which the one party places a known trust and confidence in the other.[7] It must not be a mere matter of opinion equally open to both parties for examination and inquiry where neither party is presumed to trust to the other, but to rely on his own judgment. Not but that misrepresentation even in a matter of opinion may

[1] See 1 Domat, B. 1, tit. 2, § 11, art. 12.
[2] Dig. Lib. 18, tit. 1, l. 54; 1 Domat, B. 1, tit. 2, § 11, art. 3.
[3] Stebbins v. Eddy, 4 Mason, R. 414; Morris Canal Co. v. Emmett, 9 Paige, R. 168.
[4] Ibid.; ante, § 144 a.
[5] Jarvis v. Duke, 1 Vern. 19.
[6] Broderick v. Broderick, 1 P. Will. 239, 240; Pusey v. Desbouvrie, 3 P. Will. 318, 320.
[7] See Smith v. The Bank of Scotland, 1 Dow, Parl. R. 272; Laidlaw v. Organ, 2 Wheat. R. 178, 195; Evans v. Bicknell, 6 Ves. 173, 182 to 192.

(a) See ante, pp. 156, 157, note.

be relieved against as a contrivance of fraud in cases of peculiar relationship or confidence, or where the other party has justly reposed upon it and has been misled by it. But ordinarily matters of opinion between parties dealing upon equal terms, though falsely stated, are not relieved against, because they are not presumed to mislead or influence the other party when each has equal means of information. Thus a false opinion, expressed intentionally by the buyer to the seller, of the value of the property offered for sale, where there is no special confidence or relation or influence between the parties, and each meets the other on equal grounds, relying on his own judgment, is not sufficient to avoid a contract of sale.[1] In such a case the maxim seems to apply, — ' Scientia, utrinque par, pares contrahentes facit.' [2]

[1] But see Wall *v.* Stubbs, 1 Madd. R. 80; Cadman *v.* Homer, 18 Ves. 10; 2 Kent, Comm. Lect. 39, p. 485 (4th edit.). A mistaken opinion of the value of property, if honestly entertained, and stated as opinion merely, unaccompanied by any assertion or statement untrue in fact, can never be considered as a fraudulent misrepresentation. Hepburn *v.* Dunlop, 1 Wheat. R. 189.

[2] 1 Marshall on Insur. B. 1, ch. 11, § 3, p. 473; 1 Domat, B. 1, tit. 2, § 11, art. 3, 11, 12. Mr. Chancellor Kent has expounded the doctrine on this subject with admirable clearness and strength in the following passage of his Commentaries. (Vol. 2, Lect. 39, pp. 484, 485, 4th edit.) ' When however the means of information relative to facts and circumstances affecting the value of the commodity are equally accessible to both parties, and neither of them does or says anything tending to impose upon the other, the disclosure of any superior knowledge which one party may have over the other as to those facts and circumstances is not requisite to the validity of a contract. There is no breach of any implied confidence that one party will not profit by his superior knowledge as to facts and circumstances open to the observation of both parties, or equally within the reach of their ordinary diligence; because neither party reposes in any such confidence unless it be specially tendered or required. Each one in ordinary cases judges for himself, and relies confidently and perhaps presumptuously upon the sufficiency of his own knowledge, skill, and diligence. The common law affords to every one reasonable protection against fraud in dealing; but it does not go to the romantic length of giving indemnity against the consequences of indolence and folly, or a careless indifference to the ordinary and accessible means of information. It reconciles the claims of convenience with the duties of good faith to every extent compatible with the interests of commerce. This it does by requiring the purchaser to apply his attention to those particulars which may be supposed within the reach of his observation and judgment, and the vendor to communicate those particulars and defects which cannot be supposed to be immediately within the reach of such attention. If the purchaser be wanting of attention to these points where attention would have been sufficient to protect him from surprise or imposition, the maxim " caveat emptor " ought to apply. Even against this maxim he may provide by requiring the vendor to warrant that which the law would not imply to be warranted; and if the

198. But it would be otherwise where a party knowingly places confidence in another and acts upon his opinion, believing it to be honestly expressed. Thus if a man of known skill and judgment in paintings should sell a picture to another, representing it to have been painted by some eminent master, as for instance by Rubens, Titian, or Correggio, and it should be false, there can be no doubt that it would be a misrepresentation for which the sale might be avoided.[1] And the same principle would apply in a like case if he should falsely state his opinion to be that it was a genuine painting of a great master, with an intent to influence the buyer in the purchase, and the latter, placing confidence in the skill and judgment and assertion of the seller, should complete the purchase on the faith thereof. But if the seller should truly represent the painting to be of such a master, and add that it once belonged to a nobleman, or was fixed in a church (which circumstances he knew to be untrue), in such a case, if the representation of these collateral circumstances had no real tendency in the mind of the buyer to enhance or influence the purchase, it would not avoid the contract.[2]

199. Nor is it every wilful misrepresentation, even of a fact, which will avoid a contract upon the ground of fraud, if it be of such a nature that the other party had no right to place reliance on it, and it was his own folly to give credence to it; for Courts of Equity, like Courts of Law, do not aid parties who will not use their own sense and discretion upon matters of this sort.[3] This may be illustrated by a case at law, where a party upon making a purchase for himself and his partners falsely stated to the seller, to induce him to the sale, that his partners would not give more for the property than a certain price. It was held that no action would lie at law for a deceitful representation of

vendor be wanting in good faith, "fides servanda" is a rule equally enforced at law and in equity.' See also 1 Domat, B. 1, tit. 2, § 11.

[1] See 1 Pothier on Oblig. n. 17 to 20, and note (a); Atwood v. Small, 6 Clark & Finnell. 232, 233; s. c. 1 Younge, R. 407.

[2] See 2 Kent, Comm. Lect. 39, pp. 482, 483 (4th edit.); Hill v. Gray, 1 Starkie, R. 352.

[3] See Trower v. Newcome, 3 Meriv. R. 704; Scott v. Hanson, 1 Simons, R. 13; Fenton v. Browne, 16 Ves. 144; 2 Kent, Comm. Lect. 39, pp. 484, 485 (4th edit.); Id. 486, 487, note (b); Davis v. Meeker, 5 John. R. 354; Hervey v. Young, Yelv. R. 21, and Metcalf's note; 1 Domat, B. 1, tit. 2, § 11, art. 11, 12; Sherwood v. Salmon, Day, R. 128.

this sort. Lord Ellenborough on this occasion expressed himself in the following language, which presents many suggestions applicable to the subject now under consideration. 'If,' said he, 'an action be maintainable for such a false representation of the will and purpose of another with reference to the purposed sale, should not an action be also at least equally maintainable for a false representation of the party's own purpose? But can it be contended that an action might be maintained against a man for representing that he would not give, upon a treaty of purchase, beyond a certain sum, when it could be proved that he had said he would give much more than that sum? And supposing also that he had upon such treaty added, as a reason for his resolving not to give beyond a certain sum, that the property was in his judgment damaged in any particular respect; and supposing further that it could be proved he had, just before the giving such reason, said he was satisfied it was not so damaged; would an action be maintainable for this untrue representation of his own purpose, backed and enforced by this false reason given for it? And in the case before us, does the false representation made by the defendant of the determination of his partners amount to anything more than a falsely alleged reason for the limited amount of his own offer? And if it amount to no more than this, it should be shown, before we can deem this to be the subject of an action, that in respect of some consideration or other existing between the parties to the treaty, or upon some general rule or principle of law, the party treating for a purchase is bound to allege truly, if he state at all, the motives which operate with him for treating or for making the offer he in fact makes. A seller is unquestionably liable to an action of deceit if he fraudulently represent the quality of the thing sold to be other than it is in some particulars which the buyer has not equal means with himself of knowing, or if he do so in such a manner as to induce the buyer to forbear making the inquiries which for his own security and advantage he would otherwise have made. But is a buyer liable to an action of deceit for misrepresenting the seller's chance of sale, or the probability of his getting a better price for his commodity than the price which such proposed buyer offers? I am not aware of any case or recognized principle of law upon which such a duty can be considered as incumbent upon a party bargaining for a purchase.

It appears to be a false representation in a matter merely gratis dictum by the bidder, in respect to which the bidder was under no legal pledge or obligation to the seller for the precise accuracy and correctness of his statement, and upon which therefore it was the seller's own indiscretion to rely; and for the consequences of which reliance therefore he can maintain no action.'[1]

200. A Court of Equity would, under the like circumstances, probably hold a somewhat more rigorous doctrine, at least if the party appeared to have been materially influenced by the representation to his disadvantage; and if it did not avoid the contract, it would refuse a specific performance of it.[2] If the seller of a farm should falsely affirm at the sale that it had been valued by two persons at the price, and the assertion had induced the buyer to purchase it, the contract would certainly not be enforced in equity, and upon principle it would seem to be void. So if a vendor on a treaty for the sale of property should make representations which he knows to be false, the falsehood of which however the purchaser has no means of knowing, but he relies on them, a Court of Equity will rescind the contract entered into upon such treaty, although the contract may not contain the misrepresentations.[3] But then in all such cases the court will not rescind the contract without the clearest proof of the fraudulent misrepresentations, and that they were made under such circumstances as show that the contract was founded upon them.[4]

200 a. On the other hand if the purchaser, choosing to judge for himself, does not avail himself of the knowledge or means of knowledge open to him or his agents, he cannot be heard to say that he was deceived by the vendor's misrepresentations; for the rule is 'Caveat emptor,' and the knowledge of his agents is as binding on him as his own knowledge.[5] It is his own folly and laches not to use the means of knowledge within his reach, and he may properly impute any loss or injury in such a case to his

---

[1] Vernon v. Keys, 12 East, 637, 638; Sugden on Vendors (7th edit.), p. 6. See also Davis v. Meeker, 5 John. R. 354; 2 Kent, Comm. Lect. 39, p. 486, and note (b); Id. 487 (4th edit.).

[2] 2 Kent, Comm. Lect. 39, pp. 486, 487, and note (b), (4th edit.); Buxton v. Lister, 3 Atk. 386.

[3] Atwood v. Small, 6 Clark & Finnell. 232, 233.

[4] Ibid.

[5] Atwood v. Small, 6 Clark & Finnell. 232, 233.

own negligence and indiscretion. Courts of Equity do not sit for the purpose of relieving parties, under ordinary circumstances, who refuse to exercise a reasonable diligence or discretion.

201. To the same ground of unreasonable indiscretion and confidence may be referred the common language of puffing and commendation of commodities, which, however reprehensible in morals as gross exaggerations or departures from truth, are nevertheless not treated as frauds which will avoid contracts. In such cases the other party is bound, and indeed is understood, to exercise his own judgment if the matter is equally open to the observation, examination, and skill of both. To such cases the maxim applies, — 'Simplex commendatio non obligat.' The seller represents the qualities or value of the commodity, and leaves them to the judgment of the buyer.[1] The Roman law adopted the same doctrine. 'Ea quæ commendandi causa in venditionibus dicuntur, si palam appareant, venditorem non obligant; veluti si dicat servum speciosum, domum bene ædificatam.'[2] But if the means of knowledge are not equally open, the same law pronounced a different doctrine. 'At si dixerit, hominem literatum, vel artificem, præstare debet; nam hoc ipso pluris vendidit.'[3] The misrepresentation enhances the price. The same rule will apply if any artifice is used to disguise the character or quality of the commodity,[4] or to mislead the buyer at the sale; such as using puffers and underbidders at an auction or other sale, (*a*) or holding out false colors and thereby taking the buyer by surprise.[5]

202. In the next place the party must be misled by the misrepresentation; for if he knows it to be false when made, it cannot be said to influence his conduct, and it is his own indiscretion,

---

[1] 2 Kent, Comm. Lect. 39, p. 485 (4th edit.).

[2] Dig. Lib. 18, tit. 1, l. 43.

[3] Dig. Lib. 18, tit. 1, l. 43.

[4] 2 Kent, Comm. Lect. 39, pp. 482, 483, 484 (4th edit.); Turner *v.* Harvey, Jacob, R. 178.

[5] Bromley *v.* Alt, 3 Ves. 624; Smith *v.* Clarke, 12 Ves. 483; Twining *v.* Morrice, 2 Bro. Ch. R. 330; Marquis of Townshend *v.* Stangroom, 6 Ves. 338; Bexwell *v.* Christie, Cowper, R. 385; 1 Fonbl. Eq. B. 1, ch. 4, § 4, note (*x*); Pickering *v.* Dawson, 4 Taunt, R. 785.

(*a*) See Tomlinson *v.* Savage, 6 B. Mon. 630; Veazie *v.* Williams, Ired. Eq. 430; Latham *v.* Morrow, 6 3 Story, 610, 623.

and not any fraud or surprise, of which he has any just complaint to make under such circumstances.[1]

203. And in the next place the party must have been misled to his prejudice or injury; for Courts of Equity do not, any more than Courts of Law, sit for the purpose of enforcing moral obligations or correcting unconscientious acts, which are followed by no loss or damage. It has been very justly remarked, that to support an action at law for a misrepresentation there must be a fraud committed by the defendant, and a damage resulting from such fraud to the plaintiff.[2] And it has been observed with equal truth by a very learned judge in equity, that fraud and damage coupled together will entitle the injured party to relief in any court of justice.[3]

203 a. In the next place the defrauded party may, by his subsequent acts with full knowledge of the fraud, deprive himself of all right to relief as well in equity as at law. (a) Thus for example, if with full knowledge of the fraud he should settle the matter in relation to which the fraud was committed, and give a release to the party who has defrauded him, he would lose all title to legal and equitable relief.[4] The like rule would apply if he knew all the facts, and with such full information continued to deal with the party.[5] (b)

204. Another class of cases for relief in equity is where there is an undue concealment, or suppressio veri, to the injury or prejudice of another.[6] It is not every concealment, even of facts material to the interest of a party, which will entitle him to the interposition of a Court of Equity. The case must amount to the suppression of facts which one party under the circumstances

[1] See Pothier De Vente, n. 210.
[2] Vernon v. Keys, 12 East, 637, 638.
[3] Bacon v. Bronson, 7 John. Chan. R. 201; Fellows v. Lord Gwydyr, 1 Simons, R. 63.
[4] Parsons v. Hughes, 9 Paige, R. 591.
[5] Vigers v. Pike, 3 Clark & Finnell. R. 545, 630.
[6] 1 Fonbl. Eq. B. 1, ch. 2, § 8, and note (z); Id. ch. 3, § 4, and notes; Jarvis v. Duke, 1 Vern. R. 19; Evans v. Bicknell, 6 Ves. 173, 182. Sometimes, as in the case of Broderick v. Broderick (1 P. Will. 239, 240), there may occur both a suppressio veri and a suggestio falsi.

(a) See Ex parte Briggs, L. R. 1 Eq. 483.
(b) But the party wronged is allowed a reasonable time after the discovery of the fraud before taking action. Neblett v. Macfarland, 92 U. S. 101, 105; Gatling v. Newell, 9 Ind. 572.

is bound in conscience and duty to disclose to the other party, and in respect to which he cannot innocently be silent. It has been said by Cicero, ' Aliud est celare, aliud tacere. Neque enim id est celare, quidquid reticeas; sed cum, quod tu scias, id ignorare emolumenti tui causa velis eos, quorum intersit id scire.' [1] It has been remarked by a learned author that this definition of concealment, restrained to the efficient motives and precise subject of any contract, will generally hold to make it void in favor of either party who is misled by his ignorance of the thing concealed.[2] And Cicero proceeds to denounce such concealment in terms of vehement indignation. ' Hoc autem celandi genus quale sit, et cujus hominis, quis non videt? Certe non aperti, non simplicis, non ingenui, non justi, non viri boni; versuti potius, obscuri, astuti, fallacis, malitiosi, collidi, veteratoris, vafri.' [3]

205. But this statement is not borne out by the acknowledged doctrines either of Courts of Law or of Courts of Equity in a great variety of cases. However correct Cicero's view may be of the duty of every man in point of morals to disclose all facts to another with whom he is dealing, which are material to his interest,[4] yet it is by no means true that courts of justice generally, or at least in England and America, undertake the exercise of such a wide and difficult jurisdiction.[5] Thus it has been held by Lord Thurlow (and the case falls precisely within the defini-

---

[1] Cic. de Offic. Lib. 3, ch. 12, 13. See also Pothier De Vente, n. 242, 243.
[2] Marshall on Insur. B. 1, ch. 11, § 3, p. 473.
[3] Cic. de Offic. Lib. 3, cap. 13.
[4] Dr. Paley adopts Cicero's doctrine in its full extent as a duty of moral and religious obligation. 'To advance,' says he, ' a direct falsehood in recommendation of our wares by ascribing to them some quality which we know they have not, is dishonest. Now compare with this the designed concealment of some fault which we know they have. The motives and the effects of actions are the only points of comparison in which their moral quality can differ. But the motives in these two cases are the same, namely, to produce a higher price than we expect otherwise to obtain; the effect, that is, the prejudice to the buyer, is the same.' Paley, Moral Philos. B. 3, ch. 7, p. 116. The question, What degree of concealment is unjust in a legal or moral sense? has been often mooted by distinguished jurists, as well upon the cases put by Cicero as in other cases. See Grotius, B. 2, ch. 12, § 9; Puffendorf, Law of Nature, B. 5, ch. 3, § 4; Pothier De Vente, n. 233 to 242; Id. n. 297, 298; 2 Kent, Comm. Lect. 39, pp. 485 to 491 (4th edit.), and notes; 1 Ruth. Inst. B. 1, ch. 13, §§ 11 to 19.
[5] See Pothier, Contract. de Vente, n. 234, 239, 242, 243; 1 Domat, B. 1, tit. 2, § 11; 2 Kent, Comm. Lect. 39, pp. 484, 485, 490, 491, and note (c) (4th edit.).

nition by Cicero of undue concealment), that if A, knowing there is a mine in the land of B of which he knows B to be ignorant, should, concealing the fact, enter into a contract to purchase the estate of B for a price which the estate would be worth without considering the mine, the contract would be good; because A, as the buyer, is not obliged, from the nature of the contract, to make the discovery. In such cases the question is not whether an advantage has been taken which in point of morals is wrong, or which a man of delicacy would not have taken. But it is essentially necessary, in order to set aside the transaction, not only that a great advantage should be taken, but also that there should be some obligation on the party to make the discovery. A Court of Equity will not correct or avoid a contract merely because a man of nice honor would not have entered into it. The case must fall within some definition of fraud, and the rule must be drawn so as not to affect the general transactions of mankind.[1] And this in effect is the conclusion to which Pothier arrived, after a good deal of struggle, in adjusting the duties arising from moral obligation with the necessary freedom and convenience of the common business of human life.[2]

206. Mr. Chancellor Kent, in his learned Commentaries, after admitting the doctrine and authority of Lord Thurlow in the case above stated, concludes with the following acute and practical reflections; 'From this and other cases it would appear that human laws are not so perfect as the dictates of conscience, and the sphere of morality is more enlarged than the limits of civil jurisdiction. There are many duties that belong to the class of imperfect obligations, which are binding on conscience, but which human laws do not and cannot undertake directly to enforce. But when the aid of a Court of Equity is sought to carry into execution such a contract, then the principles of ethics have a more extensive sway; and a purchase made with such a reservation of superior knowledge would be of too sharp a character to be aided and forwarded in its execution by the powers of the Court of Chancery. It is a rule in equity that all the material facts must be known to both parties, to render the agreement fair and just in all its parts; and it is against all the prin-

[1] Fox *v.* Mackreth, 2 Bro. Ch. R. 420; Turner *v.* Harvey, 1 Jacob, Rep. 178.

[2] Pothier De Vente, n. 234 to 242; Id. n. 295 to 299; ante, § 194.

ciples of equity, that one party, knowing a material ingredient in an agreement, should be permitted to suppress it and still call for a specific performance.'[1] The importance and value of the distinction here pointed out will be made more apparent when we come to the consideration of the cases in which Courts of Equity refuse to decree a specific performance of contracts which yet they will not undertake to set aside.[2]

207. The true definition then of undue concealment which amounts to a fraud in the sense of a Court of Equity, and for which it will grant relief, is the non-disclosure of those facts and circumstances which one party is under some legal or equitable obligation to communicate to the other; and which the latter has a right, not merely in foro conscientiæ, but juris et de jure, to know.[3] Mr. Chancellor Kent has avowed a broader doctrine. 'As a general rule,' says he, 'each party is bound in every case to communicate to the other his knowledge of material facts provided he knows the other to be ignorant of them, and they be not open and naked, or equally within the reach of his observation.'[4] This doctrine in this latitude of expression may perhaps be thought not strictly maintainable, or in conformity with that which is promulgated by Courts of Law or Equity. For many most material facts may be unknown to one party and known to the other and not equally accessible, or at the moment within the reach of both; and yet contracts founded upon such ignorance on one side and knowledge on the other, may be completely obligatory.[5] Thus if one party has actual knowledge of

---

[1] 2 Kent, Comm. Lect. 39, pp. 490, 491 (4th edit.); Parker *v.* Grant, 1 John. Ch. R. 630; Ellard *v.* Llandaff, 1 B. & Beatt. 250, 251.

[2] See 2 Story on Eq. Jurisp. §§ 693, 769, 770.

[3] Fox *v.* Mackreth, 2 Bro. Ch. R. 420; 1 Fonbl. Eq. B. 1, ch. 3, § 4, note (*n*). Mr. Justice Buller, in Pearson *v.* Morgan, 2 Bro. Ch. 390, said: 'In cases where it [fraud] is a question of fact, it is always considered as a constructive fraud where the party knows the truth and conceals it; and such constructive fraud always makes the party liable.' But in that case the party when applied to misrepresented the fact and concealed the truth; and the language must be limited to such circumstances. See Fox *v.* Mackreth, 2 Bro. Ch. R. 420; Turner *v.* Harvey, Jacob, R. 178.

[4] 2 Kent, Comm. Lect. 39, p. 482 (4th edit.), and note, ibid., where it is now qualified.

[5] The case of the unknown mine, already put, in the case of Fox *v.* Mackreth, 2 Bro. Ch. R. 420, seems to fall within this predicament; and in Turner *v.* Harvey, Jacob, R. 178, Lord Eldon said: 'The court in many cases has been in the habit of saying that where parties deal for an estate they may

an event or fact from private sources not then known to the other party from whom he purchases goods, and which knowledge would materially enhance the price of the goods, or change the intention of the party as to the sale, the contract of sale of the goods will nevertheless be valid.[1]

208. Even Pothier himself, strongly as he inclines in all cases of this sort to the principles of sound morals, declares that the buyer cannot be heard to complain that the seller has not informed him of circumstances extrinsic of the thing sold, whatever may be the interest which he has to know them.[2] So that the doctrine of Mr. Chancellor Kent would seem to require some qualification by limiting it to cases where one party is under some obligation to communicate the facts, or where there is a peculiar known relation, trust, or confidence between them, which authorizes the other party to act upon the presumption that there is no concealment of any material fact. Thus if a vendor should sell an estate knowing that he had no title to it, or knowing that there were incumbrances on it of which the vendee was ignorant, the suppression of such a material fact, in respect to which the vendor must know that the very purchase implied a trust and confidence on the part of the vendee that no such defect existed, would clearly avoid the sale on the ground of fraud.[3]

put each other at arm's length; the purchaser may use his own knowledge, and is not bound to give the vendor information of the value of the property. As in the case that has been mentioned, if an estate is offered for sale, and I treat for it, knowing that there is a mine under it, and the other party makes no inquiry, I am not bound to give him any information of it. He acts for himself, and exercises his own sense and knowledge. But a very little is sufficient to affect the application of the principle. If a single word is dropped which tends to mislead the vendor, that principle will not be allowed to operate.' See also ante, §§ 147 and 148.

[1] See Laidlaw v. Organ, 2 Wheat. 178; Fox v. Mackreth, 2 Bro. Ch. R. 20. In Laidlaw v. Organ, 2 Wheat. 195, the question was put in this general form: 'Whether the intelligence of extrinsic circumstances which might influence the price of the commodity, and which was exclusively within the knowledge of the vendee, ought to have been communicated by him to the vendor?' And on this question, so put, the court expressed an opinion, 'that he was not bound to communicate it,' without adding any qualification. But the court added: 'It would be difficult to circumscribe the contrary doctrine within proper limits, where the means of intelligence are equally accessible to both parties.' Ante, § 149.   [2] Pothier De Vente, n. 242, 298, 299.

[3] Arnott v. Biscoe, 1 Ves. 95, 96; Pothier De Vente, n. 240; Pillage v. Armitage, 12 Ves. 78; ante, §§ 142, 143.

209. The like reason would apply to a case where the vendor should sell a house, situate in a distant town, which he knew at the time to be burnt down, and of which fact the vendee was ignorant; for it is impossible to suppose that the actual existence of the house should not be understood by the vendee, as implied on the part of the vendor, at the time of the bargain.[1] The same doctrine prevails in the civil law. 'Sin autem venditor quidem sciebat domum esse exustam, emptor autem ignorabat, nullam venditionem stare.'[2]

210. These latter cases are founded upon circumstances intrinsic in the contract, and constituting its essence. And there is often a material distinction between circumstances which are intrinsic and form the very ingredients of the contract, and circumstances which are extrinsic and form no part of it, although they may create inducements to enter into it, or affect the value or price of the thing sold.[3] Intrinsic circumstances are properly those which belong to the nature, character, condition, title, safety, use, or enjoyment, &c., of the subject-matter of the contract, such as natural or artificial defects in the subject-matter. Extrinsic circumstances are properly those which are accidentally connected with it, or rather bear upon it at the time of the contract, and may enhance or diminish its value or price, or operate as a motive to make or decline the contract; such as facts respecting the occurrence of peace or war, the rise or fall of markets, the character of the neighborhood,[4] the increase or diminution of duties, or the like circumstances.

211. In regard to extrinsic as well as to intrinsic circumstances the Roman law seems to have adopted a very liberal doctrine, carrying out to a considerable extent the clear dictates of sound morals. It required the utmost good faith in all cases of contracts involving mutual interests; and it therefore not only prohibited the assertion of any falsehood, but also the suppression of any facts touching the subject-matter of the contract of which the other party was ignorant, and which he had an interest in knowing. In an especial manner it applied this doctrine to

---

[1] See Pothier De Vente, n. 4; ante, § 142.
[2] Dig. Lib. 18, tit. 1, l. 57, § 1; ante, § 142.
[3] 2 Kent, Comm. Lect. 39, p. 482 (4th edit.); Pothier, n. 242, 243; Id. n. 203 to 210; 1 Domat, B. 1, tit. 2, § 8, art. 11; Id. § 11, art. 2, 3, 5, 15.
[4] Pothier De Vente, n. 236.

cases of sales, and required that the vendor and vendee should disclose, each to the other, every circumstance within his knowledge touching the thing sold, which either had an interest in knowing. The declaration in regard to the vendor (as we have seen) is, 'Dolum malum a se abesse præstare venditor debet; qui non tantum in eo est, qui fallendi causa obscure loquitur; sed etiam, qui insidiose, obscure dissimulat;' and the same rule was applied to the vendee.[1] According to these principles the vendor was by the Roman law required not only not to conceal any defects of the thing sold, which were within his knowledge, and of which the other party was ignorant, whenever those defects might, as vices upon the implied warranty created by the sale, entitle him to a redhibition or a rescission of the contract, but also all other defects which the other party was interested in knowing.[2]

212. In regard to intrinsic circumstances the common law however has in many cases adopted a rule very different from that of the civil law, and especially in cases of sales of goods. In such cases the maxim 'caveat emptor' is applied; and unless there be some misrepresentation or artifice to disguise the thing sold, or some warranty as to its character or quality, the vendee is understood to be bound by the sale, notwithstanding there may be intrinsic defects and vices in it, known to the vendor and unknown to the vendee, materially affecting its value. However questionable such a doctrine may be in its origin, in point of morals or general convenience (upon which many learned doubts have at various times been expressed), it is too firmly established to be now open to legal controversy;[3] and Courts of Equity as well as Courts of Law abstain from any interference with it.

213. In regard to intrinsic circumstances generally Courts of Equity as well as Courts of Law seem to adopt the same maxim to a large extent, and relax its application only when there are circumstances of peculiar trust or confidence or relation between the parties.[4]

[1] Dig. Lib. 18, tit. 1, 1: 43, § 2; Pothier De Vente, n. 233 to 241; Id. n. 296; ante, § 192; Laidlaw v. Organ, 2 Wheat. R. 178; Pothier De Vente, cited in note c, p. 185.
[2] Pothier De Vente, n. 235.
[3] See 2 Kent, Comm. Lect. 39, pp. 478, 479 (4th edit.); 2 Black. Comm. 451.
[4] The case of Martin v. Morgan, 1 Brod. & Bing. R. 289, is a strong application of the doctrine of concealment, avoiding a payment. In that case there

214. But there are cases of intrinsic circumstances in which Courts of Law and Courts of Equity both proceed upon a doctrine strictly analogous to that of the Roman law, and treat the concealment of them as a breach of trust and confidence justly reposed. Indeed in most cases of this sort the very silence of the party must import as much as a direct affirmation, and be deemed equivalent to it.[1]

215. Thus if a party taking a guaranty from a surety conceals from him facts which go to increase his risk and suffers him to enter into the contract under false impressions as to the real state of the facts, such a concealment will amount to a fraud, because the party is bound to make the disclosure; and the omission to make it under such circumstances is equivalent to an affirmation that the facts do not exist.[2] (*a*) So if a party knowing himself to be cheated by his clerk, and concealing the fact, applies for security in such a manner and under such circumstances as holds the clerk out to others as one whom he considers as a trustworthy person, and another person becomes his security, acting under the impression that the clerk is so considered by his employer, the contract of suretyship will be void;[3] for the very silence under such circumstances becomes expressive of a trust and confidence held out to the public equivalent to an affirmation. (*b*)

216. Cases of insurance afford a ready illustration of the same

was no special confidence between the parties; but a post-dated check being paid to the holder by a banker, at a time when the latter had no funds of the drawer, and the holder knew that the drawer had become insolvent, of which the banker was ignorant, the amount was allowed to be recovered back on account of the concealment.

[1] See Martin *v.* Morgan, 1 Brod. & Bing. 289; Pidlock *v.* Bishop, 3 B. & Cressw. 605; 2 Kent, Comm. Lect. 39, p. 483; Id. 488, note (4th edit.); Smith *v.* Bank of Scotland, 1 Dow, Parl. R. 292, 294; Etting *v.* Bank of United States. 11 Wheat. R. 59.

[2] Pidlock *v.* Bishop, 3 B. & Cressw. 605; post, § 383.

[3] Maltby's Case, cited 1 Dow, Parl. Cas. 294; 11 Wheat. R. 68, note (*d*); Smith *v.* Bank of Scotland, 1 Dow, Parl. Cas. 272. See Etting *v.* Bank of United States, 11 Wheat. R. 59.

(*a*) See Carew's Case, 7 DeG. M. & G. 43. If a surety has by his conduct reasonably led a co-surety to believe that he is a principal, equity will not give him relief against the co-surety. Coleman *v.* Norman, 10 Heisk. 590.

(*b*) It is held that there is no such duty of disclosure towards a surety as there is towards one in a relation of confidence, though very little said or done may vitiate the surety's contract. Davies *v.* London Ins. Co., 8 Ch. D. 469. See post, § 324, and note.

doctrine. In such cases the underwriter necessarily reposes a trust and confidence in the insured as to all facts and circumstances affecting the risk which are peculiarly within his knowledge, and which are not of a public and general nature, or which the underwriter either knows or is bound to know.[1] Indeed most of the facts and circumstances which may affect the risk are generally within the knowledge of the insured only, and therefore the underwriter may be said emphatically to place trust and confidence in him as to all such matters. And hence the general principle is, that in all cases of insurance the insured is bound to communicate to the underwriter all facts and circumstances material to the risk, within his knowledge; and if they are withheld, whether the concealment be by design or by accident, it is equally fatal to the contract.[2].

217. The same principle applies in all cases where the party is under an obligation to make a disclosure and conceals material facts. Therefore if a release is obtained from a party in ignorance of material facts which it is the duty of the other side to disclose, the release will be held invalid.[3] (a) So in cases of family agreements and compromises, if there is any concealment of material facts, the compromise will be held invalid upon the ground of mutual trust and confidence reposed between the parties.[4] And in like manner if a devisee, by concealing from the heir the fact that the will has not been duly executed, procures from the latter a release of his title, pretending that it will facilitate the raising of money to pay the testator's debts, the release will be void on account of the fraudulent concealment.[5]

218. But by far the most comprehensive class of cases of undue concealment arises from some peculiar relation or fidu-

---

[1] Marshall on Insur. B. 1, ch. 11, § 3.

[2] Ibid.; Lindenau v. Desborough, 8 B. & Cressw. 586, 592; 2 Kent, Comm. Lect. 39, p. 488, note (4th edit.). It has been remarked by Lord Eldon, that concealment is of different natures; an intentional concealment, and an actual concealment, where there may be an obligation not to conceal, even if a disclosure is not required. Walker v. Symonds, 3 Swanst. R. 62.

[3] Bowles v. Stewart, 1 Sch. & Lefr. 209, 224; Broderick v. Broderick, 1 P. Will. 240; ante, §§ 147, 148, 196, 197.

[4] Gordon v. Gordon, 3 Swanst. R. 399, 463, 467, 470, 473, 476, 477; Leonard v. Leonard, 2 B. & Beatt. R. 171, 180, 181, 182.

[5] Broderick v. Broderick, 1 P. Will. 239, 249.

(a) Lee v. Pearce, 68 N. Car. 76.

ciary character between the parties. Among this class of cases are to be found those which arise from the relation of client and attorney, principal and agent, principal and surety, landlord and tenant, parent and child, guardian and ward, ancestor and heir, husband and wife, trustee and cestui que trust, executors or administrators and creditors, legatees, or distributees, appointor and appointee under powers, and partners, and part-owners. In these and the like cases the law, in order to prevent undue advantage from the unlimited confidence, affection, or sense of duty which the relation naturally creates, requires the utmost degree of good faith (uberrima fides) in all transactions between the parties. If there is any misrepresentation, or any concealment of a material fact, or any just suspicion of artifice or undue influence, Courts of Equity will interpose and pronounce the transaction void, and as far as possible restore the parties to their original rights.[1]

219. This subject will naturally come in review in a subsequent page, when we come to consider what may be deemed the peculiar equities between parties in these predicaments, and the guards which are interposed by the law by way of prohibition upon their transactions.[2] It may suffice here, merely by way of illustration, to suggest a few applications of the doctrine. Thus for instance if an attorney employed by the party should designedly conceal from his client a material fact or principle of law by which he should gain an interest not intended by the client, it will be held a positive fraud, and he will be treated as a mere trustee for the benefit of his client and his representatives. And in a case of this sort it will not be permitted to the attorney to set up his ignorance of law, or his negligence, as a defence or an excuse. It has been justly remarked that it would be too dangerous to the interests of mankind to allow those who are bound to advise, and who ought to be able to give good and sound advice, to take advantage of their own professional ignorance to the prejudice of others.[3] Attorneys must, from the nature of the relation, be held bound to give all the information which they ought to give, and not be permitted to plead ignorance of that which they ought to know.[4]

[1] See Ormond v. Hutchinson, 13 Ves. 51; Beaumont v. Boultbee, 5 Ves. 485; Gartside v. Isherwood, 1 Bro. Ch. R. App. 558, 560, 561.
[2] Post, §§ 308 to 328.
[3] See Lord Eldon's Judgment in the House of Lords, in Bulkley v. Wilford, 2 Clark & Finnell. R. 102, 177 to 181, 183; post, § 311. [4] Ibid.

220. In like manner a trustee cannot by the suppression of a fact entitle himself to a benefit to the prejudice of his cestui que trust. Thus a creditor of the husband concealing the fact cannot, by procuring himself by such concealment to be appointed the trustee of the wife, entitle himself to deduct his debt from the trust fund against the wife or her representatives, or even against the person in whose favor and at whose instance he has made the suppression.[1] So if a partner who exclusively superintends the business and accounts of the concern should by concealment of the true state of the accounts and business purchase the share of the other partner for an inadequate price by means of such concealment, the purchase will be held void.[2]

221. Having taken this general notice of cases of fraud arising from the misrepresentation or concealment of material facts, we may now pass to the consideration of some others which in a moral as well as in a legal view seem to fall under the same predicament, — that of being deemed cases of actual intentional fraud as contradistinguished from constructive or legal fraud. In this class may properly be included all cases of unconscientious advantages in bargains obtained by imposition, circumvention, surprise, and undue influence over persons in general, and in an especial manner all unconscientious advantages, or bargains obtained over persons disabled by weakness, infirmity, age, lunacy, idiocy, drunkenness, coverture, or other incapacity, from taking due care of or protecting their own rights and interests.[3] (a)

222. The general theory of the law in regard to acts done and contracts made by parties affecting their rights and interests is, that in all such cases there must be a free and full consent to bind the parties. Consent is an act of reason accompanied with deliberation, the mind weighing as in a balance the good and evil on each side.[4] And therefore it has been well remarked by an

---

[1] Dalbiac v. Dalbiac, 16 Ves. 115, 124; Neville v. Wilkinson, 1 Bro. Ch. R. 543; post, § 321.

[2] Maddeford v. Austwick, 1 Sim. R. 89. See Smith in re Hay, 6 Madd. R. 2.

[3] See Gartside v. Isherwood, 1 Brown, Ch. R. 358, 360, 361.

[4] 1 Fonbl. Eq. B. 1, ch. 2, § 3; Grotius De Jure Belli, Lib. 2, ch. 11, § 5.

(a) See Connelly v. Fisher, 3 Tenn. Ch. 382; Simonton v. Bacon, 49 Miss. 582; Cadwallader v. West, 48 Mo. 483; Joest v. Williams, 42 Ind. 565; Musselman v. Cravens, 47 Ind. 1; Reinskoff v. Rogge, 37 Ind. 207; Killian v. Badgett, 27 Ark. 166; Phelan v. Gardner, 43 Cal. 306.

able commentator upon the law of nature and nations, that every true consent supposes three things: first a physical power, secondly a moral power, and thirdly a serious and free use of them.[1] And Grotius has added that what is not done with a deliberate mind does not come under the class of perfect obligations.[2] And hence it is that if consent is obtained by meditated imposition, circumvention, surprise, or undue influence, it is to be treated as a delusion, and not as a deliberate and free act of the mind. For although the law will not generally examine into the wisdom or prudence of men in disposing of their property or in binding themselves by contracts or by other acts, yet it will not suffer them to be entrapped by the fraudulent contrivances, or cunning or deceitful management, of those who purposely mislead them.[3]

223. It is upon this general ground, that there is a want of rational and deliberate consent, that the contracts and other acts of idiots, lunatics, and other persons non compotes mentis, are generally deemed to be invalid in Courts of Equity.(b) Grotius has with great propriety insisted that it is a part of the law of nature; for, says he, the use of reason is the first requisite to constitute the obligation of a promise, which idiots, madmen, and infants are consequently incapable of making. 'Primum requiritur usus rationis; ideo, et furiosi, et amentis, et infantis nulla est promissio.'[4] The civil law has emphatically adopted the same principle. 'Furiosus,' say the Institutes, 'nullum negotium gerere potest, quia non intelligit quod agit.'[5] And afterwards in the same work, distinguishing infants from pupils (technically so called), the civil law proceeds to declare that infants are in the

---

[1] Puffendorf, Law of Nat. and Nations, Barbeyrac's note, 1, B. 3, ch. 6, § 3, cited 1 Fonbl. Eq. B. 1, ch. 2, § 1, note (a).
[2] Grotius De Jure Belli et Pacis, Lib. 2, ch. 11, § 4.
[3] See Fonbl. Eq. B. 1, ch. 2, § 3, notes (r), (u); Id. § 8.
[4] De Jure Belli, Grotius, B. 2, ch. 11, § 5.
[5] Inst. Lib. 3, tit. 20, § 8; Dig. Lib. 50, tit. 17, l. 5, l. 40.

(a) See Waring v. Waring, 12 Jur. 947; s. c. 6 Moore, P. C. 341; Creagh v. Blood, 2 Jones & L. 509; Davis Machine Co. v. Barnard, 43 Mich. 379; Rogers v. Blackwell, 49 Mich. 192. The last case declares that the deed of an insane person is void, and not merely voidable. But as to that see Carrier v. Sears, 4 Allen, 336; Allis v. Billings, 6 Met. 415; Arnold v. Richmond Iron Works, 1 Gray, 434; 2 Kent, 451; Ashcraft v. De Armond, 44 Iowa, 229; Riggan v. Green, 80 N. Car. 236.

like situation as madmen: 'Nam infans, et qui infantiæ proximus est, non multum a furioso distant; quia hujusmodi ætatis pupilli nullum habent intellectum.'[1]

224. The doctrine laid down in the older writers upon the common law is not materially different. Bracton says: 'Furiosus autem stipulari non potest, nec aliquod negotium agere, quia non intelligit quid agit. Eodem modo nec infans, vel qui infanti proximus est, et qui multum a furioso non distat, nisi hoc fiat ad commodum suum et cum tutoris auctoritate.'[2] And Fleta repeatedly uses language to the same effect.[3]

225. Yet clear as this doctrine appears in common sense and common justice, it has met with a sturdy opposition from the common lawyers, who have insisted (as has been justly remarked), in defiance of natural justice and the universal practice of all the civilized nations in the world,[4] that according to a known maxim of the common law no man of full age should be admitted to disable or stultify himself; and that a Court of Equity could not relieve against a maxim of the common law.[5] And a distinction has been taken between the party himself and his privies in blood (heirs) and privies in representation (executors and administrators). For it has not been doubted that privies in blood and privies in representation might after the death of the insane party avoid his contract or other acts upon the ground that he was non compos mentis.[6] How so absurd and mischievous a maxim could have found its way into any system of jurisprudence professing to act upon civilized beings, is a

[1] Inst. Lib. 3, tit. 20, § 10; Dig. Lib. 50, tit. 17, l. 5, l. 40; 1 Domat, B. 1, tit. 2, § 1, art. 11, 12. See Ersk. Inst. B. 1, tit. 7, § 51, p. 160; B. 3, tit. 1, § 15, p. 485.

[2] Bracton, Lib. 3, ch. 2, § 8, p. 100.

[3] Fleta, Lib. 2, ch. 56, § 19; Id. Lib. 3, ch. 3, § 10; Beverley's Case, 4 Co. R. 126.

[4] 1 Fonbl. Eq. B. 1, ch. 2, § 1.

[5] See Sugden on Powers, ch. 7, § 1. The best defence of the maxim which I have seen is in 3 Bac. Abridg. Idiots and Lunatics, F., where it is put upon the ground of public policy to favor alienations. Yet it seems wholly unsatisfactory in principle. Mr. Evans has exposed the absurdity of the maxim in a few striking remarks, in his note to Pothier on Oblig. vol. 2, App. No. 3, p. 28.

[6] Co. Litt. 247, a. b.; Beverley's Case, 4 Co. R. 123, 124; 2 Black. Comm. 291, 292; 1 Fonbl. Eq. B. 1, ch. 2, § 1, and note (*h*); Shelford on Lunatics, ch. 6, § 2, pp. 255, 263; Newland on Contracts, ch. 1, p. 19; Sugden on Powers, ch. 7, § 1.

matter of wonder and humiliation.[1] There have been many struggles against it by eminent lawyers in all ages of the common law; but it is perhaps somewhat difficult to resist the authorities which assert its establishment in the fundamentals of the common law,[2] a circumstance which may well abate the boast, so often and so rashly made, that the common law is the perfection of human reason. Even the Courts of Equity in England have been so far regardful of the maxim that they have hesitated to retain a bill to examine the point of lunacy,[3] although when a party has been found a lunatic under an inquisition they will entertain a bill by his committee or guardian to avoid all his acts from the time at which he has been found non compos.[4] And formerly they were so scrupulous in adhering to the maxim, that cases have occurred in which a lunatic was not allowed to be a party to a bill to be relieved against an act done during

---

[1] See Evans's note, 2 Pothier on Oblig. App. No. 3, p. 28.

[2] 3 Black. Comm. 291, 292; 1 Fonbl. Eq. B. 1, ch. 2, § 1, and note (d); Co. Litt. 247; Beverley's Case, 4 Co. R. 123; Yates v. Boen, 2 Str. R. 1104. See Shelford on Lunatics, ch. 6, § 2, p. 263; ch. 9, § 2, p. 407, &c.; Baxter v. Portsmouth, 7 Dowl. & Ryl. 618; s. c. 5 Barn. & Cressw. 170; Brown v. Joddrell, 3 Carr. & Payne, 30; Newland on Contracts, ch. 1, pp. 15 to 21. The subject is a good deal discussed by Mr. Justice Blackstone in his Commentaries, who does not attempt to disguise its gross injustice. (2 Black. Comm. 291, 292.) It is also fully discussed by Mr. Fonblanque, in his learned notes (1 Fonbl. Eq. B. 1, ch. 2, § 1, and notes (a) to (k); and by Lord Coke in his Commentary on Littleton (Co. Litt. 247, a. and b.), who adheres firmly to it (as we should expect) as a maxim of the Common Law. See also Beverley's Case (4 Co. R. 123, and Shelford on Lunatics, ch. 6, §§ 1, 2, pp. 242, 255; ch. 9, § 2, p. 407, &c.). In America this maxim has not been of universal adoption in the State Courts, if indeed it has ever been recognized as binding in any of the Courts of Common Law. See Somes v. Skinner, 16 Mass. R. 348; Webster v. Woodford, 3 Day, R. 90, 100; Mitchell v. Kingman, 5 Pick. R. 431. In modern times the English Courts of Law seem to be disposed, as far as possible, to escape from the maxim. Baxter v. Earl of Portsmouth, 5 Barn. & Cressw. 170; s. c. 7 Dowl. & Ryl. 614; Ball v. Mannin, 3 Bligh, R. (new series) 1. And even in England, although the party himself could not set aside his own act, yet the king, as having the general custody of idiots and lunatics, might, by his attorney-general, on a bill, set aside the same acts. See 1 Fonbl. Eq. B. 1, ch. 2, § 2; Co. Litt. 247; Newland on Contracts, ch. 1, pp. 15 to 21; Buller, N. Prius, 172.

[3] 1 Fonbl. Eq. B. 1, ch. 2, § 1, note (e); cites Tothill, R. 130. See also 1 Eq Abridg. 278, B. 1.

[4] 1 Fonbl. Eq. B. 1, ch. 2, § 1, note (e); 1 Eq. Abridg. 278, B. 2; Addison v Dawson, 2 Vern. 678; s. c. 1 Eq. Abridg. B. 4; Newland on Contracts, ch. 1, pp. 17 to 21.

CHAP. VI.] ACTUAL FRAUD. 241

his lunacy.[1] But this rule is now with great propriety abandoned.[2]

226. The true and only rational exposition of the maxim (which has been adopted by Courts of Equity) is, that the maxim is to be understood of acts done by the lunatic in prejudice of others, as to which he shall not be permitted to excuse himself from civil responsibility on pretence of lunacy; and it is not to be understood of acts done to the prejudice of himself, for this can have no foundation in reason and natural justice.[3]

227. The ground upon which Courts of Equity now interfere to set aside the contracts and other acts, however solemn, of persons who are idiots, lunatics, and otherwise non compotes mentis, is fraud. Such persons being incapable in point of capacity to enter into any valid contract or to do any valid act, every person dealing with them, knowing their incapacity, is deemed to perpetrate a meditated fraud upon them and their rights. And surely if there be a single case in which all the ingredients proper

---

[1] Attorney-General v. Parkhurst, 1 Cas. Ch, 112. See also Attorney-General v. Woolrich, 1 Cas. Ch. 153. Some acts of a lunatic are, by the Common Law, deemed voidable, and some void. Where the estate passes by his own hand, as by livery of seisin, there it is voidable; where by a deed, and the conveyance does not pass by his own hand, it is void. For example a surrender by deed of a non compos tenant for life will not bar a contingent remainder. 1 Fonbl. Eq. B. 1, ch. 2, § 1; 1 Eq. Abridg. 278, B. 3; Thompson v. Leach, 3 Mod. R. 301; 1 Ld. Ray. 313; 2 Salk. 427; Shower, Parl. Cas. 150; 3 Lev. R. 284. See Shelford on Lunatics, ch. 6, § 2, p. 255, &c.

[2] See Ridler v. Ridler, 1 Eq. Abridg. 278, 279, B. 5; Addison v. Dawson, 2 Vern. R. 678; Clerk v. Clerk, 2 Vern. R. 412; Shelford on Lunatics, ch. 10, § 2, p. 415, &c.; Newland on Contracts, ch. 1, p. 17 to 19; 1 Fonbl. Eq. B. 1, ch. 2, § 2, and note (n).

[3] 1 Fonbl. Eq. B. 1, ch. 2, § 2; Ridler v. Ridler, 1 Eq. Abridg. 279, B. 5; 3 Bac. Abridg. Idiots and Lunatics, C. F. In discussing the subject of idiots and lunatics and persons non compotes mentis in this place it is important to state that it is not intended to examine the nature and history of the jurisdiction of the Court of Chancery, or rather of the Chancellor personally, as the special delegate of the Crown over idiots, lunatics, and other persons non compotes generally. That is a subject of a widely different character from the one now before us; for here the Court of Chancery acts upon its general principles in setting aside the contracts and acts of such persons upon the ground of fraud, circumvention, imposition, and undue advantage taken of them. The jurisdiction of the Crown, as parens patriæ, to take care of idiots, lunatics, and other persons non compotes, is given at considerable length in Jeremy on Equity Jurisd. B. 1, ch. 4, p. 210; 2 Madd. Ch. Pr. ch. 4, p. 565; 2 Fonbl. Eq. Pt. 2, ch. 2, § 1, and note (a); 1 Fonbl. Eq. B. 1, ch. 2, § 2, and note (e). See also Beverley's case, 4 Co. R. 124; 2 Story on Equity Jurisp. §§ 1362 to 1365.

to constitute a genuine fraud are to be found, it must be a case where these unfortunate persons are the victims of the cunning, the avarice, and corrupt influence of those who would make an inhuman profit from their calamities. Even Courts of Law now lend an indulgent ear to cases of defence against contracts of this nature, and if the fraud is made out will declare them invalid.[1]

228. But Courts of Equity deal with the subject upon the most enlightened principles, and watch with the most jealous care every attempt to deal with persons non compotes mentis. Whereever from the nature of the transaction there is not evidence of entire good faith (uberrimæ fidei), or the contract or other act is not seen to be just in itself or for the benefit of these persons, Courts of Equity will set it aside or make it subservient to their just rights and interests. Where indeed a contract is entered into with good faith and is for the benefit of such persons, such as for necessaries, there Courts of Equity will uphold it as well as Courts of Law.[2] And so if a purchase is made in good faith without any knowledge of the incapacity, and no advantage has been taken of the party, Courts of Equity will not interfere to set aside the contract if injustice will thereby be done to the other side, and the parties cannot be placed in statu quo, or in the state in which they were before the purchase.[3] (*a*)

229. And not only may contracts and deeds of a person non compos be thus set aside for fraud, but other instruments and acts of the most solemn nature, even of record, such as fines levied and recoveries suffered by such a person, may in effect be overthrown in equity, although held binding at law.[4] For

---

[1] Yates *v.* Boen, 2 Str. R. 1104; Baxter *v.* Earl of Portsmouth, 5 B. & Cressw. 170; s. c. 7 Dowl. & Ryland, 618; Faulder *v.* Silk, 3 Camp. R. 126; Brown *v.* Joddrell, 1 Mood. & Malk. 105; s. c. 3 Carr. & Payne, 30; Levy *v.* Barker, 1 Mood. & Malk. 106, and note (*b*).

[2] Baxter *v.* Earl of Portsmouth, 5 B. & Cressw. 170; s. c. 7 Dow. & Ryl. R. 614, 618. See also ex parte Hall, 7 Ves. 264.

[3] Niell *v.* Morley, 9 Ves. 478, 482; Sergeson *v.* Sealy, 2 Atk. 412.

[4] See Mansfield's case, 12 Co. R. 123, 124. But at law the king might avoid the fine or recovery by a scire facias during the lifetime of the idiot.

(*a*) Riggan *v.* Green, 80 N. Car. 236; Ashcraft *v.* De Armond, 44 Iowa, 229, and cases cited in note to § 223, to the effect that the contracts of insane persons are only voidable at most. But see Rogers *v.* Blackwell, 49 Mich. 192. As to the effect of lapse of time see Stedman *v.* Hart, Kay, 607; Edson *v.* Munsell, 10 Allen, 557; Allore *v.* Jewell, 94 U. S. 506.

CHAP. VI.] ACTUAL FRAUD. 243

although Courts of Equity will not venture to declare such fines and recoveries utterly void and vacate them, yet they will decree a reconveyance of the estate to the party prejudiced, and hold the conusee of the fine, and the demandant in the recovery, to be a trustee for the same party.[1]

230. Lord Coke has enumerated four different classes of persons who are deemed in law to be non compotes mentis. The first is an idiot or fool natural; the second is he who was of good and sound memory, and by the visitation of God has lost it; the third is a lunatic, 'lunaticus, qui gaudet lucidis intervallis,' and sometimes is of good and sound memory, and sometimes non compos mentis; and the fourth is a non compos mentis by his own act, as a drunkard.[2] In respect to the last class of persons, although it is regularly true that drunkenness doth not extenuate any act or offence committed by any person against the laws, but it rather aggravates it, and he shall gain no privilege thereby,[3] and although in strictness of law the drunkard has less ground to avoid his own acts and contracts than any other non compos mentis,[4] yet Courts of Equity will relieve against acts done and contracts made by him while under this temporary insanity, where they are procured by the fraud or imposition of the other party.[5] (a) For whatever may be the demerit of the drunkard himself, the other party has not the slightest ground to

---

[1] Fonbl. Eq. B. 1, ch. 2, § 2; Beverley's case, 4 Co. R. 124, 126 b; Tourson's case, 8 Co. R. 338; 3 Bac. Abridg. Idiots and Lunatics, C. and F.

[1] See Addison v. Dawson, 2 Vern. 678; Welby v. Welby, Tothill, R. 164; Wright v. Booth, Tothill, R. 166; Shelford on Lunatics, ch. 6, § 1, p. 252; 1 Fonbl. Eq. B. 1, ch. 2, § 2, and note (k); Wilkinson v. Brayfield, 2 Vern. 307. See Clark v. Ward, Preced. Chan. 150; Ferres v. Ferres, 2 Eq. Abridg. 695; 3 Bac. Abridg. Idiots and Lunatics, F. What circumstances afford proofs or presumptions of insanity are not fit topics for discussion in this place, but more properly belong to a treatise on Medical Jurisprudence. There are many reported cases in which the subject is discussed with great ability and acuteness. See Shelford on Lunatics, ch. 2, pp. 35 to 74; Attorney-Gen. v. Paruther, 3 Bro. Ch. R. 441; 1 Fonbl. Eq. B. 1, ch. 2, § 3, note (x). See also Mr. Evans's note to 2 Pothier on Oblig. No. 3, p. 25.

[2] Beverley's case, 4 Co. R. 124; Co. Litt. 247, a.

[3] Ibid.; 4 Black. Comm. 25; 3 Bac. Abridg. Idiots and Lunatics, A.

[4] 3 Bac. Abridg. Idiots and Lunatics, A.

[5] 1 Fonbl. Eq. B. 1, ch. 2, § 3; Johnson v. Medlicott, cited 3 P. Will. 130, note (A).

(a) O'Conner v. Rempt, 29 N. J. Eq. 156; Storrs v. Scongale, 48 Mich. 387; Lavette v. Sage, 29 Conn. 577.

claim the protection of Courts of Equity against his own grossly immoral and fraudulent conduct.[1]

231. But to set aside any act or contract on account of drunkenness, it is not sufficient that the party is under undue excitement from liquor. It must rise to that degree which may be called excessive drunkenness, where the party is utterly deprived of the use of his reason and understanding; for in such a case there can in no just sense be said to be a serious and deliberate consent on his part, and without this no contract or other act can or ought to be binding by the law of nature.[2] If there be not that degree of excessive drunkenness, then Courts of Equity will not interfere at all unless there has been some contrivance or management to draw the party into drink, (*a*) or some unfair advantage taken of his intoxication to obtain an unreasonable bargain or benefit from him.[3] For in general Courts of Equity, as a matter of public policy, do not incline on the one hand to

---

[1] See Cook *v.* Clayworth, 18 Ves. 12. The maxim has sometimes been laid down, 'Qui peccat ebrius, luat sobrius.' Hendricks *v.* Hopkins, Cary, R. 93. But even at law drunkenness is a good defence against a deed executed by a party when so drunk that he does not know what he is doing. Cole *v.* Robins, Bull. N. P. 172. See 2 Shelford on Lunatics, ch. 7, p. 276; Id. 304.

[2] 1 Fonbl. Eq. B. 1, ch. 2, § 3; Cook *v.* Clayworth, 18 Ves. 12; Reynolds *v.* Waller, 1 Wash. R. 207; Rutherford *v.* Ruff, 4 Desaus. R. 350; Wade *v.* Colvert, 2 Rep. Const. Ct. 27; Peyton *v.* Rawlins, 1 Hayw. 77. Sir Joseph Jekyll is said to have intimated an opinion that the having been in drink is not any reason to relieve a man against any deed or agreement gained from him to encourage drunkenness. Secus, if through the management or contrivance of him who gained the deed, &c., the party from whom the deed has been gained was drawn in to drink. Johnson *v.* Medlicott, 1734, cited 3 P. Will. 130, note A. But this distinction seems wholly unsatisfactory; for in each case it is the fraud of the party who obtained the deed or agreement which constitutes the ground of declaring it invalid; and the fraud is in morals and common sense the same, whether the drunken party has been enticed into the drunkenness, or becomes the victim of the cunning of another, who takes advantage of his mental incapacity. The case of Cook *v.* Clayworth (18 Ves. 12,) requires no such distinction, where the circumstances indicate fraud. In this last case Sir William Grant said: 'As to that extreme state of intoxication that deprives a man of his reason, I apprehend that even at law it would invalidate a deed obtained from him while in that condition.' See also Cole *v.* Robins, Buller, N. P. 172; Wigglesworth *v.* Steers, 1 Hen. & Munf. 70.

[3] Cook *v.* Clayworth, 18 Ves. 12; Say *v.* Barwick, 1 Ves. & Beames, 195; Campbell *v.* Ketcham, 1 Bibb, R. 406; White *v.* Cox, 3 Hayw. R. 82; Wigglesworth *v.* Steers, 1 Hen. & Munf. 70; Taylor *v.* Patrick, 1 Bibb. R. 168.

(*a*) O'Conner *v.* Rempt, 29 N. J. Eq. 156.

CHAP. VI.] ACTUAL FRAUD. 245

lend their assistance to a person who has obtained an agreement or deed from another in a state of intoxication; and on the other hand they are equally unwilling to assist the intoxicated party to get rid of his agreement or deed merely on the ground of his intoxication at the time. They will leave the parties to their ordinary remedies at law, unless there is some fraudulent contrivance or some imposition practised.[1]

232. It is upon this special ground that Courts of Equity have acted in cases where a broader principle has sometimes been supposed to have been upheld. They have indeed indirectly, by refusing relief, sustained agreements which have been fairly entered into although the party was intoxicated at the time.[2] And especially they have refused relief where the agreement was to settle a family dispute and was in itself reasonable.[3] But they have not gone the length of giving a positive sanction to such agreements, so entered into, by enforcing them against the party, or in any other manner than by refusing to interfere in his favor against them.[4]

233. In regard to drunkenness the writers upon natural and public law adopt it as a general principle, that contracts made by persons in liquor, even though their drunkenness be voluntary, are utterly void, because they are incapable of any deliberate consent in like manner as persons who are insane or non compotes mentis. The rule is so laid down by Heineccius[5] and Puffendorf.[6] It is adopted by Pothier, one of the purest of jurists, as an axiom which requires no illustration.[7] Heineccius, in discussing the subject, has made some sensible observations. 'Either,' says he, 'the drunkenness of the party entering into a contract is excessive or moderate. If moderate, and it did not quite so much obscure his understanding as that he was ignorant with whom or for what he had contracted, the contract ought to bind him. But if his

[1] Cook v. Clayworth, 18 Ves. 12; Newland on Contracts, ch. 22, p. 365; Rich v. Sydenham, 1 Ch. Cas. 202.

[2] Cook v. Clayworth, 18 Ves. 12. See also 5 Barn. & Cressw. 170.

[3] Cory v. Cory, 1 Ves. R. 19. See Stockley v. Stockley, 18 Ves. R. 30; Dunnage v. White, 1 Swanst. R. 137, 150.

[4] See Cragg v. Holme, cited 18 Ves. 14, and note (C) at the Rolls, 1811.

[5] Heinecc. Elem. Jur. Natur. Lib. 1, ch. 14, § 392, and note ibid.

[6] Puffend. Law of Nat. and Nat. B. 1, ch. 4, § 8.

[7] Pothier, Traité des Oblig. n. 49. See also 2 Evans, Pothier on Oblig. No. 3, p. 28.

drunkenness was excessive, that could not fail to be perceived; and therefore the party dealing with him must have been engaged in a manifest fraud; or at least he ought to impute it to his own fault that he had dealt with a person in such a situation.[1] The Scottish law seems to have adopted this distinction, for by that law persons in a state of absolute drunkenness and consequently deprived of reason cannot bind themselves by any contracts. But a lesser degree of drunkenness which only darkens reason has not the effect of annulling contracts.'[2]

234. Closely allied to the foregoing are cases where a person, although not positively non compos or insane, is yet of such great weakness of mind as to be unable to guard himself against imposition or to resist importunity or undue influence. And it is quite immaterial from what cause such weakness arises; whether it arises from temporary illness, general mental imbecility, the natural incapacity of early infancy, the infirmity of extreme old age, or those accidental depressions which result from sudden fear or constitutional despondency or overwhelming calamities. For it has been well remarked that although there is no direct proof that a man is non compos or delirious, yet if he is a man of weak understanding, and is harassed and uneasy at the time, or if the deed is executed by him in extremis or when he is a paralytic, it cannot be supposed that he had a mind adequate to the business which he was about, and he might be very easily imposed upon.[3]

235. It has indeed been said by a learned judge, that if a weak man give a bond, and there be no fraud or breach of trust in the obtaining of it, equity will not set aside the bond only for the weakness of the obligor, if he be compos mentis; neither will a Court of Equity measure the size of people's understandings or capacities, there being no such thing as an equitable incapacity where there is a legal capacity.[4] But whatever weight there may be in this remark in a general sense, it is obvious that weakness of understanding must constitute a most material ingredient

[1] Heinecc. Juris. Nat. Lib. 1, ch. 14, § 392, note.
[2] Erskine, Inst. B. 1, tit. 1, § 15, p. 485; 1 Madd. Ch. Pr. 239; 1 Stair, Inst. B. 1, tit. 10, § 13; 2 Stair, Inst. B. 4, tit. 20, § 49.
[3] 1 Fonbl. Eq. B. 1, ch. 2, § 3.
[4] Sir Joseph Jekyll, in Osmond v. Fitzroy, 3 P. Will. 129, 130. See also Ex parte Allen, 15 Mass. R. 58.

in examining whether a bond or other contract has been obtained by fraud or imposition or undue influence; for although a contract made by a man of sound mind and fair understanding may not be set aside merely from its being a rash, improvident, or hard bargain, yet if the same contract be made with a person of weak understanding, there does arise a natural inference that it was obtained by fraud or circumvention or undue influence.[1]

236. It has been asserted by another eminent judge, that it is not sufficient to set aside an agreement in a Court of Equity, to suggest weakness and indiscretion in one of the parties who has engaged in it; for supposing it to be in fact a very hard and unconscionable bargain, if a person will enter into it with his eyes open, equity will not relieve him upon this footing only, unless he can show fraud in the party contracting with him, or some undue means made use of to draw him into such an agreement.[2] But this language, if maintainable at all, requires many qualifications; for if a person is of a feeble understanding and the bargain is unconscionable, what better proof can one wish of its being obtained by fraud or imposition or undue influence, or by the power of the strong over the weak?[3] (a)

---

[1] 1 Fonbl. Eq. B. 1, ch. 2, § 3, note (r); Blackford v. Christian, 1 Knapp, R. 73, 77; Clarkson v. Hanway, 2 P. Will. 203; Gartside v. Isherwood, 1 Bro. Ch R. Appendix, 559, 560, 561. Lord Thurlow is said to have remarked, in Griffin v. De Veulle (3 Wooddes. Lect. App. 16), that he admitted, 'That this court would not set aside the voluntary deed of a weak man who is not absolutely non compos, nor any deed of improvidence or profuseness, for these reasons merely, where no fraud appears, as was laid down by Sir Joseph Jekyll, in Osmond v. Fitzroy, 3 P. Will. 130. But he said that Sir Joseph Jekyll might have been pleased to add, that from these ingredients there might be made out and evidenced a collection of facts, that there was fraud and misrepresentation used. The case of Osmond v. Fitzroy cannot be supported but upon the mixed ground of Lord Southampton's extreme weakness of understanding, as well as the situation of Osmond.' And in Mr. Cox's note to 3 P. Will. 131, he is represented to have stated, ' That in almost every case upon this subject a principal ingredient was a degree of weakness short of a legal incapacity.' Mr. Maddock seems to think that Osmond v. Fitzroy went principally upon the ground of the relation between the parties (servant and master); and he holds the doctrine of Sir Joseph Jekyll the most conformable to the authorities. 1 Madd. Ch. Pr. 224, 225. See Stock on Lunacy.

[2] Lord Hardwicke in Willis v. Jernegan, 2 Atk. R. 251.

[3] See Malin v. Malin, 2 John. Ch. R. 238; Shelford on Lunatics, ch. 6, § 3, pp. 258, 267, 268, 272; White v. Small, 2 Ch. Cas. 103; Bridgman v.

(a) To influence a weak-minded person to do what is just and lawful cannot be termed undue influence. Dailey v. Kastell, 56 Wis. 444.

237. The language of another eminent judge in a very recent case is far more satisfactory and comprehensive, and applies a mode of reasoning to the subject compatible at once with the dictates of common sense and legal exactness and propriety. 'The law,' said Lord Wynford, 'will not assist a man who is capable of taking care of his own interest, except in cases where he has been imposed upon by deceit, against which ordinary prudence could not protect him. If a person of ordinary understanding, on whom no fraud has been practised, makes an imprudent bargain, no court of justice can release him from it. Inadequacy of consideration is not a substantial ground for setting aside a conveyance of property. Indeed from the fluctuation of prices, owing principally to the gambling spirit of speculation that now unhappily prevails, it would be difficult to determine what is an adequate price for anything sold. At the time of the sale the buyer properly calculates on a rise in the value of the article bought, of which he would have the advantage. He must not therefore complain if his speculations are disappointed, and he becomes a loser instead of a gainer by his bargain. But those who from imbecility of mind are incapable of taking care of themselves are under the special protection of the law. The strongest mind cannot always contend with deceit and falsehood. A bargain therefore into which a weak one is drawn under the influence of either of these ought not to be

---

Green, 2 Ves. 627; Clarkson *v.* Hanway, 2 P. Will. 203; Bennet *v.* Vade, 2 Atk. 325, 529; Nantes *v.* Corrick, 9 Ves. 181, 182; Willan *v.* Willan, 16 Ves. 72; Blackford *v.* Christian, 1 Knapp, R. 73 to 87; Griffith *v.* Robins, 3 Madd. R. 191; Ball *v.* Mannin, 3 Bligh, R. 1 (new series); s. c. 1 Dow, R. 392 (new series); 1 Fonbl. Eq. B. 1, ch. 2, § 3, note (*r*); Filmer *v.* Gott, 7 Bro. Par. R. 70; Dodds *v.* Wilson, 1 Rep. Const. Ct. of S. Car. 448; Newland on Contracts, ch. 22, p. 362; Gartside *v.* Isherwood, 1 Bro. Ch. R. 558, 560, 561. In truth there was not the slightest proof of any weakness of understanding of the party in the case of Willis *v.* Jernegan, 2 Atk. 251, but merely of a sanguine and ardent temper and imagination, speculating with rashness upon the hope of imaginary profits. And indeed it appears that the speculation might have been profitable, but for the party's insisting upon an exorbitant premium for the lottery tickets until the market had fallen. The weakness alluded to in this case by Lord Hardwicke was probably not so much incapacity of mind as credulity or want of judgment; for he expressly negatives any fraud or imposition. See Lord Eldon's Remarks in Huguenin *v.* Basley, 14 Ves. 290; Fox *v.* Mackreth, 2 Bro. Ch. R. 420; 2 Hovend. Suppt. 113, note to 9 Ves. 182; Shelford on Lunatics, Introd. § 2, p. 36, &c.; Id. ch. 6, § 3, pp. 265, 267, 268, 272. See also Lewis *v.* Pead, 1 Ves. jr. 19; 1 Fonbl. Eq. B. 1, ch. 2, § 3, and note (*r*).

held valid; for the law requires that good faith should be observed in all transactions between man and man.' (a) And, addressing himself to the case before him, he added: 'If this conveyance could be impeached on the ground of the imbecility of F only, a sufficient case has not been made out to render it invalid; for the imbecility must be such as would justify a jury under a commission of lunacy in putting his property and person under the protection of the chancellor. But a degree of weakness of intellect far below that which would justify such a proceeding, coupled with other circumstances to show that the weakness such as it was had been taken advantage of, will be sufficient to set aside any important deed.'[1]

238. The doctrine therefore may be laid down as generally true, that the acts and contracts of persons who are of weak understandings, and who are thereby liable to imposition, will be held void in Courts of Equity if the nature of the act or contract justify the conclusion that the party has not exercised a deliberate judgment, but that he has been imposed upon, circumvented, or overcome by cunning, or artifice, or undue influence.[2] (b) The rule of the common law seems to have gone further in cases

---

[1] Blackford v. Christian, 1 Knapp, R. 77. See Gartside v. Isherwood, 1 Bro. Ch. R. App. 560, 561.

[2] See Gartside v. Isherwood, 1 Bro. Ch. R. App. 560, 561. In the treatise on Equity (1 Fonbl. Eq. B. 1, ch. 2, § 3) it is laid down that the protection of Courts of Equity 'is not to be extended to every person of a weak understanding, unless there be some fraud or surprise; for Courts of Equity would have enough to do if they were to examine into the wisdom and prudence of men in disposing of their estates. Let a man be wise therefore, or unwise, if he be legally compos mentis he is a disposer of his property, and his will stands instead of a reason. S. P. Bath and Montague's case, 3 Ch. Cas. 107.

(a) See Allore v. Jewell, 94 U. S. 506, 511; Wooley v. Drew, 49 Mich. 290; Connelly v. Fisher, 3 Tenn. Ch. 382; Dalton v. Dalton, 14 Nev. 419; Mann v. Betterly, 21 Vt. 326; Aiman v. Stout, 42 Penn. St. 114; Darnell v. Rowland, 30 Ind. 342; Cain v. Warford, 33 Md. 23; Beverley v. Walden, 20 Gratt. 147; Gass v. Mason, 4 Sneed, 497; Hunt v. Hunt, 2 Beasl. 161.

(b) Nor will lapse of time, even for six years, bar a weak-minded grantor from the right to have his grant set aside where the same was obtained from him by imposition, unless during the time, from the death of witnesses or other cause, a full presentation of the case by the defendant has become impossible. And this too though valuable improvements, not exceeding a reasonable rent of the property, have meantime been put upon the land to the knowledge all along of the plaintiff. Allore v. Jewell, 94 U. S. 506, three judges dissenting.

of wills (for it is said that perhaps it can hardly be extended to deeds without circumstances of fraud or imposition), since the common law requires that a person, to dispose of his property by will, should be of sound and disposing memory, (*a*) which imports that the testator should have understanding to dispose of his estate with judgment and discretion; and this is to be collected from his words, actions, and behavior at the time, and not merely from his being able to give a plain answer to a common question.[1] But as fraud in regard to the making of wills of real estate belongs in a peculiar manner to Courts of Law, and fraud in regard to personal estate to the Ecclesiastical Courts, although sometimes relievable in equity, that part of the subject seems more proper to be discussed in a different treatise.[2]

239. Cases of an analogous nature may easily be put where the party is subjected to undue influence, although in other respects of competent understanding.[3] As where he does an act or makes a contract when he is under duress or the influence of extreme terror or of threats, or of apprehensions short of duress. For in cases of this sort he has no free will, but stands in vinculis. And the constant rule in equity is, that where a party is not a free agent and is not equal to protecting himself, the court will protect him.[4] The maxim of the common law is, ' Quod alias bonum et justum est, si per vim vel fraudem petatur, malum et injustum efficitur.'[5] On this account Courts of Equity watch with extreme jealousy all contracts made by a party while under imprisonment, and if there is the slightest ground to suspect oppression or imposition, in such cases they will set the contracts aside.[6] Circum-

---

[1] 1 Fonbl. Eq. B. 1, ch. 2, § 3, and notes (*u*) and (*x*); Donegal's case, 2 Ves. R. 407, 408; Attorney-Gen. *v.* Parmenter, 3 Brown, Ch. R. 441; Id. 1 Fonbl. Eq. B. 1, ch. 2, § 3, note (*x*).

[2] 1 Fonbl. Eq. B. 1, ch. 2, § 3, and notes (*u*) and (*x*); ante, § 184; Allen *v.* Macpherson, 5 Beav. R. 469; s. c. on appeal, 1 Phillips, Ch. R. 133.

[3] See Debenham *v.* Ox, 1 Ves. 276; Cory *v.* Cory, 1 Ves. 19; Young *v.* Peachey, 2 Atk. 254; 1 Madd. Ch. Pr. 245, 246.

[4] Evans *v.* Llewellyn, 1 Cox, R. 340; Crome *v.* Ballard, 1 Ves. jr. 215, 220; Hawes *v.* Wyatt, 3 Bro. Ch. R. 158; Jeremy on Equity Jurisd. B. 3, Pt. 2, ch. 3, § 1; 2 Eq. Abridg. 183, pl. 2; Gilb. Eq. R. 9; 3 P. Will. 294, note *E*; Attorney-Gen. *v.* Sothen, 2 Vern. R. 497.

[5] 3 Co. R. 78.

[6] Roy *v.* Duke of Beaufort, 2 Atk. 190; Nichols *v.* Nichols, 1 Atk. 409; Hinton *v.* Hinton, 2 Ves. 634, 635; Falkner *v.* O'Brien, 2 B. & Beatt. 214;

(*a*) See Waring *v.* Waring, 6 Moore, P. C. 341.

stances also of extreme necessity and distress of the party, although not accompanied by any direct restraint or duress, may in like manner so entirely overcome his free agency as to justify the court in setting aside a contract made by him on account of some oppression or fraudulent advantage or imposition attendant upon it.[1]

Griffith *v.* Spratley, 1 Cox, R. 333; Underhill *v.* Harwood, 10 Ves. 219; Attorney-Gen. *v.* Sothen, 2 Vern. R 497.

[1] See Gould *v.* Okeden, 3 Bro. Parl. R. 560; Bosanquet *v.* Dashwood, Cas. Temp. Talbot, 37; Proof *v.* Hines, Cas. T. Talb. 111; Hawes *v.* Wyatt, 3 Bro. Ch. R. 156; Picket *v.* Loggon, 14 Ves. 215; Beasley *v.* Maggreth, 2 Sch. & Lefr. 31, 35; Carpenter *v.* Elliot, cited 2 Ves. jr. 494; Wood *v.* Abrey, 3 Madd. R. 417; Ramsbottom *v.* Parker, 6 Madd. R. 6; Fitzgerald *v.* Rainsford, 1 B. & Beatt. R. 37, note (*d*); Underhill *v.* Harwood, 10 Ves. 219; 1 Fonbl. Eq. B. 1, ch. 2, § 9, note (*e*); Crowe *v.* Ballard, 1 Ves. jr. 215, 220; Huguenin *v.* Baseley, 14 Ves. 273; Newland on Contracts, ch. 22, p. 362, &c.; Ib. p. 365, &c. The doctrine of the common law upon the subject of avoiding contracts upon the ground of mental weakness, or force, or undue influence, does not seem in any essential manner to differ from that adopted in the Roman law, or in the law of modern continental Europe. Thus we find in the Roman law that contracts may be avoided, not only for incapacity, but for mental imbecility, the use of force, or the want of liberty in regard to the party contracting. 'Ait prætor, Quod metus causa gestum erit, ratum non habebo.' Dig. Lib. 4. tit. 2, l. 1. But then the force or fear must be of such a nature as may well overcome a firm man. 'Metum accipiendum, Labeo dicit, non quemlibet timorem, sed majoris malitatis.' Dig. Lib. 4, tit. 2, l. 5. The party must be intimidated by the apprehension of some serious evil of a present and pressing nature. 'Metum non vani hominis, sed qui merito et in hominem constantissimum cadat.' Dig. Lib. 4, tit. 2, l. 6. He must act, 'Metu majoris malitatis;' and feel that it is immediate, — 'Metum presentum accipere debemus, non suspicionem inferendi ejus.' See Dig. Lib. 4, tit. 2, l. 9; 1 Domat, Civil Law, B. 1, tit. 18, § 2, art. 1 to 10. Pothier gives his assent to this general doctrine; but he deems the civil law too rigid in requiring the menace or force to be such as might intimidate a constant or firm man, and very properly thinks that regard should be had to the age, sex, and condition of the parties. Pothier on Oblig. n. 25. Mr. Evans thinks that any contract produced by the actual intimidation of another ought to be held void, whether it were the result of personal infirmity merely, or of such circumstances as might ordinarily produce the like effect upon others. 1 Evans, Pothier on Oblig. n. 25, note (*a*), p 18. The Scottish law seems to have followed out the line of reasoning of the Roman law with a scrupulous deference and closeness. Ersk. Instit. B. 4, tit. 1, § 26. The Scottish law also puts the case of imposition from weakness upon a clear ground. 'Let one be ever so subject to imposition, yet if he has understanding enough to save himself from a sentence of idiocy, the law makes him capable of managing his own affairs; and consequently his deeds, however hurtful they may be to himself, must be effectual, unless evidence be brought that they have been drawn or extorted from him by unfair practices. Yet where lesion (injury) in the deed and facility in the grantor concur, the most slender circumstances of fraud or circumvention are sufficient to set it

240. The acts and contracts of infants, that is, of all persons under twenty-one years of age (who are by the common law deemed infants), are a fortiori treated as falling within the like predicament. For infants are by law generally treated as having no capacity to bind themselves, from the want of sufficient reason and discernment of understanding, and therefore their grants and those of lunatics are in many respects treated as parallel both in law and reason.[1] There are indeed certain excepted cases in which infants are permitted by law to bind themselves by their acts and contracts. But these are all of a special nature ; as for instance infants may bind themselves by a contract for necessaries suitable to their degree and quality,[2] or by a contract of hiring and services for wages,[3] or by some act which the law requires them to do. And generally infants are favored by the law as well as by equity in all things which are for their benefit, and are saved from being prejudiced by anything to their disadvantage.[4] But this rule is designed as a shield for their own protection; it is not allowed to operate as a fraud or injustice to others, at least not where a Court of Equity has authority to reach it in cases of meditated fraud.[5] (a)

241. In regard to the acts of infants some are voidable and

aside.' Ersk. Inst. B. 4, tit. 1, § 27. Mr. Bell has also stated the same principle in the Scottish law with great clearness. There may be in one of perfect age a degree of weakness, puerility, or prodigality, which, although not such as to justify a verdict of insanity, and place him under guardianship as insane, may yet demand some protection for him against unequal or gratuitous alienation. 1 Bell, Comm. 139.

[1] 1 Fonbl. Eq. B. 1, ch. 2, § 4.
[2] Zouch v. Parsons, 3 Burr. 1801; 1 Fonbl. Eq. B. 1, ch. 2, § 4, and notes (y) and (a); Co. Litt. 172 a.
[3] Woode v. Fenwick, 10 Mees. & Welsb. 195.
[4] 1 Fonbl. Eq. B. 1, ch. 2, § 4, and notes (y) and (a).
[5] See 1 Fonbl. Eq. B. 1, ch. 2, § 4, note (z); Zouch v. Parsons, 3 Burr. 1802.

(a) It is well settled that no liability in damages can be fixed upon an infant by reason of a false representation that he is of age, whereby a credit has been given him. Johnson v. Pye, 1 Sid. 258; s. c. 1 Keb. 913; Bartlett v. Wells, 1 Best & S. 836; Merriam v. Cunningham, 11 Cush. 40; Burley v. Russell, 10 N. H. 184. But this is not saying that an infant may always retain the fruits of a contract obtained by him through a false representation of that kind. A lease e. g. obtained in that way by an infant may be declared void and possession ordered given up. Lamprière v. Lange, 12 Ch. D. 675, Jessel, M. R.

some are void; and so also in regard to their contracts, some are voidable and some are void. Where they are utterly void, they are from the beginning mere nullities and incapable of any operation. But where they are voidable, it is in the election of the infant to avoid them or not, which he may do when he arrives at full age. In this respect he is by law differently placed from idiots and lunatics; for the latter, as we have seen, are not, or at least may not, at law be allowed to stultify themselves. But an infant may at his coming of age avoid or confirm any voidable act or contract at his pleasure. In general where a contract may be for the benefit or to the prejudice of an infant, he may avoid it as well at law as in equity. Where it can never be for his benefit, it is utterly void.[1] And in respect to the acts of infants of a more solemn nature, such as deeds, gifts, and grants, this distinction has been insisted on, that such as do take effect by delivery of his hand are voidable; but such as do not so take effect are void.[2]

242. But independently of these general grounds it is clear that contracts made and acts done by infants in favor of persons knowing their imbecility and want of discretion, and intending to take advantage of them, ought upon general principles to be held void, and set aside on account of fraud, circumvention, imposition, or undue influence. And it is upon this ground of an inability to give a deliberate and binding consent, that the nullity of such acts and contracts is constantly put by publicists and civilians.[3] 'Infans non multum a furioso distat.'

243. In regard to femes covert the case is still stronger; for, generally speaking, at law they have no capacity to do any acts or to enter into any contracts, and such acts and contracts are treated as mere nullities. And in this respect equity generally follows the law.[4] This disability of married women proceeds, it is said, upon the consideration that if they were allowed to bind themselves, the law having vested their property in their husbands, they would be liable on their engagements without the

---

[1] 1 Fonbl. Eq. B. 1, ch. 2, § 4, notes (*y*), (*z*), (*b*); Zouch *v.* Parsons, 3 Burr. 1801, 1807.

[2] Zouch *v.* Parsons, 3 Burr. R. 1794; Perkins, § 12. See 8 American Jurist, 327 to 330.

[3] See ante, §§ 222, 223; Ayliffe, Pand. B. 2, tit. 38, pp. 216, 217.

[4] 1 Fonbl. Eq. B. 1, ch. 2, § 6.

means of answering them. And if they were allowed to bind their husbands, they might, by the abuse of such a power, involve their husbands and families in ruin.[1] But perhaps the more exact statement would be, that it is a fundamental policy of the common law to allow no diversity of interests between husband and wife; and for this purpose it is necessary to take from the wife all power to act for herself without his consent, and to disable her, even with his consent (for her own protection against his influence), from becoming personally bound by any act or contract whatsoever done in pais.[2] Courts of Equity have indeed broken in upon this doctrine, and have in many respects treated the wife as capable of disposing of her own separate property and of doing other acts, as if she were a feme sole.[3] In cases of this sort the same principles will apply to the acts and contracts of a feme covert as would apply to her as a feme sole, unless the circumstances give rise to the presumption of fraud, imposition, unconscionable advantage, or undue influence.[4]

244. Of a kindred nature to the cases already considered are cases of bargains of such an unconscionable nature and of such gross inequality as naturally lead to the presumption of fraud, imposition, or undue influence. This is the sort of fraud to which Lord Hardwicke alluded in the passage already cited,[5] when he said that they were such bargains as no man in his senses and not under delusion would make on the one hand, and as no honest and fair man would accept on the other, being inequitable and unconscientious bargains.[6] Mere inadequacy of price or any other inequality in the bargain is not however to be understood as constituting, per se, a ground to avoid a bargain in equity.[7] For Courts of Equity as well as Courts of Law act

[1] 1 Fonbl. Eq. B. 1, ch. 2, § 6, note (h).

[2] See Comyns, Dig. Baron and Feme, D. 1, E. 1 to 3, H. N. O. P. Q.; Id Chancery, 2 M. 1 to 16.

[3] See on this subject the learned notes of Mr. Fonblanque in 1 Fonbl. Eq. B. 1, ch. 2, § 6, notes (h) to (s); Chancy on Rights, &c. of Husband and Wife; and Roper on Husband and Wife; Com. Dig. Chancery, 2 M. 1 to 16.

[4] See 1 Fonbl. Eq. B. 1, ch. 2, § 8; Dalbiac v. Dalbiac, 16 Ves. 115.

[5] Ante, § 188; Mitf. Pl. Eq. by Jeremy, 132, 133, 134; Roosevelt v. Fulton, 2 Cowen, R. 129; M'Donald v. Neilson, 2 Cowen, R. 139.

[6] Chesterfield v. Janssen, 2 Ves. 155; 1 Fonbl. Eq. B. 1, ch. 2, § 9, note (e).

[7] Griffith v. Spratley, 1 Cox, R. 383; Copis v. Middleton, 2 Madd. R. 409; Collier v. Brown, 1 Cox, R. 428; Low v. Barchard, 8 Ves. 133; Western v. Russel, 3 Ves. & Beam. R. 180; Naylor v. Winch, 1 Sim. & Stu. R. 565;

upon the ground that every person who is not from his peculiar condition or circumstances under disability is entitled to dispose of his property in such manner and upon such terms as he chooses; and whether his bargains are wise and discreet, or profitable or unprofitable or otherwise, are considerations not for courts of justice but for the party himself to deliberate upon.

245. Inadequacy of consideration is not then of itself a distinct principle of relief in equity. The common law knows no such principle. The consideration, be it more or less, supports the contract. Common sense knows no such principle. The value of a thing is what it will produce; and it admits of no precise standard. It must be in its nature fluctuating and will depend upon ten thousand different circumstances. One man, in the disposal of his property, may sell it for less than another would. He may sell it under a pressure of circumstances which may induce him to part with it at a particular time. If Courts of Equity were to unravel all these transactions, they would throw everything into confusion and set afloat the contracts of mankind.[1] Such a consequence would of itself be sufficient to show the inconvenience and impracticability if not the injustice of

[1] Fonbl. Eq. B. 1, ch. 2, § 9, note (d); Osgood v. Franklin, 2 John. Ch. R, 1; Borell v. Dann, 2 Hare, R. 440, 450. In this case Mr. Vice-Chancellor Wigram said: 'Now with respect to the adequacy of the consideration alone, considered apart from the alleged improvidence in the manner of selling, I certainly understand the rule of the court to be that, even in ordinary cases, and a fortiori in cases of sales by public auction, mere inadequacy of consideration is not a ground even for refusing a decree for specific performance of an unexecuted contract (White v. Damon, Ex parte Latham), and still less can it be a ground for rescinding an executed contract. The only exception which I believe can be stated is, where the inadequacy of consideration is so gross as of itself to prove fraud or imposition on the part of the purchaser. Fraud in the purchaser is of the essence of the objection to the contract in such a case. The case must however be strong indeed in which a court of justice shall say that a purchaser at a public auction between whom and the vendors there has been no previous communication affecting the fairness of the sale, is chargeable with fraud or imposition only because his bidding did not greatly exceed the amount of the vendor's reserved bidding. I am perfectly satisfied that the plaintiff's case cannot be sustained upon the ground of mere inadequacy. Another principle must be introduced. It must be made out that the assignees were guilty of a breach of trust in fixing so low a reserved bidding as £900, and (as I have already observed) that the purchaser was bound to have ascertained that a breach of trust had not been committed in that respect before he accepted the conveyance.'

[1] Per Lord Ch. Baron Eyre in Griffith v. Spratley, 1 Cox, R. 383; 1 Madd. Ch. Pr. 213, 214.

adopting the doctrine that mere inadequacy of consideration should form a distinct ground for relief.

246. Still however there may be such an unconscionableness or inadequacy in a bargain as to demonstrate some gross imposition or some undue influence, and in such cases Courts of Equity ought to interfere, upon the satisfactory ground of fraud.[1] But then such unconscionableness or such inadequacy should be made out as would (to use an expressive phrase) shock the conscience and amount in itself to conclusive and decisive evidence of fraud.[2] (a) And where there are other ingredients in the case of a suspicious nature or peculiar relations between the parties, gross inadequacy of price must necessarily furnish the most vehement presumption of fraud.[3] (b)

247. The difficulty of adopting any other rule which would not in the common intercourse and business of human life be found productive of serious inconvenience and endless litigation is conceded by civilians and publicists; and for the most part they seem silently to abandon cases of inadequacy in bargains where there is no fraud to the forum of conscience and morals and religion. Thus Domat, after remarking that the law of nature obliges us not to take advantage of the necessities of the seller to buy at too low a price, adds: 'But because of the difficulties in fixing the just price of things, and of the inconveniences which would be too many and too great if all sales were annulled in which the things were not sold at their just value, the laws connive at the injustice of buyers, except in the sale of lands where the price given for them is less than half of their

---

[1] Ibid.; Gartside v. Isherwood, 1 Bro. Ch. R. App. 558, 560, 561.

[2] Coles v. Trecothick, 9 Ves. 246; Underhill v. Harwood, 10 Ves. 219; Copis v. Middleton, 2 Madd. R. 409; Stillwell v. Wilkinson, Jacob, R. 280; Peacock v. Evans, 16 Ves. 512; Gwynne v. Heaton, 1 Bro. Ch. R. 9; Osgood v. Franklin, 2 John. Ch. R. 1, 23; s. c. 14 John. R. 527.

[3] Ibid.; 1 Fonbl. Eq. B. 1, ch. 2, § 9, note (e); Id. § 10, and notes (g) and (h); Id. § 11; Id. ch. 4, § 26; 1 Madd. Ch. Pr. 212, 213, 214; Howe v. Wheldon, 2 Ves. 516, 518; Com. Dig. Chancery, 3 M. 1; Huguenin v. Basley, 14 Ves. 273.

(a) See Ray v. Womble, 56 Ala. 32; Irwin v. Parham, 12 How. 197 (dissenting opinion of Nelson, J.); Wright v. Wilson, 2 Yerg. 294; Deaderick v. Watkins, 8 Humph. 520; Howard v. Edgell, 17 Vt. 9; Mayo v. Carrington, 19 Gratt. 74; Weld v. Rees, 48 Ill. 428.

(b) See Wooley v. Drew, 49 Mich. 290; Allore v. Jewell, 94 U. S. 506, 511; Holliway v. Holliway, 77 Mo. 392; Butler v. Haskell, 4 Desaus. 651.

value.'[1] So that in the civil law sales of personal property are usually without redress, and even sales of immovable property are in the same predicament, unless the inadequacy of price amounts to one half the value; a rule purely artificial, and which must leave behind it many cases of gross hardship and unconscionable advantage. The civil law therefore in fixing a moiety and confining it to immovable property admits in the most clear manner the impracticability of providing for all cases of this nature. 'Rem majoris pretii,' says the Code, 'si tu vel pater tuus minoris distraxerit; humanum est ut vel pretium te restituente emptoribus fundum venundatum recipias, auctoritate judicis intercedente; vel si emptor elegerit, quod deest justo pretio, recipias;'[2] thus laying down the broadest rule of equity and morals adapted to all cases. But the lawgiver, struck with the unlimited nature of the proposition, immediately adds in the same law that the party shall not be deemed to have sold at an undervalue, unless it amounts to one half: 'Minus autem pretium esse videtur, si nec dimidia pars veri pretii soluta sit;'[3] a logic not very clear or indisputable.[4] And yet the civil law was explicit enough in denouncing fraudulent bargains. 'Si pater tuus per vim coactus domum vendidit, ratum non habebitur, quod non bona fide gestum est. Malæ fidei emptio irrita est.[5] Ad rescindendam venditionem, et malæ fidei probationem, hoc solum non sufficit, quod, magno pretio fundum comparatum, minoris distractum esse, commemoras.'[6] So that we see in this last passage the very elements of the doctrine of equity on this subject.

---

[1] 1 Domat, Civil Law, B. 1, tit. 2, §§ 3, 9, art. 1. See also Heineccius, Elem. I. N. et G. § 352; Id. § 340.

[2] Cod. Lib. 4, tit. 44, l. 2; Id. l. 9; Heinecc. Elem. J. N. and N. § 340, 352. Post, § 248.

[3] Cod. Lib. 4, tit. 44, l. 2; Id. l. 9; 1 Domat, Civil Law, B. 1, tit. 2, § 9; 1 Fonbl. Eq. B. 1, ch. 2, § 10, note (*f*).

[4] In another place the civil law, in relation to sales, seems plainly to wink out of sight the immorality of inadequate bargains. 'Quemadmodum in emendo et vendendo naturaliter concessum est, quod pluris sit, minoris emere, quod minoris sit, pluris vendere. Et ita invicem se circumscribere, ita in locationibus quoque et conditionibus juris est.' Dig. Lib. 19, tit. 2, l. 22, § 3; 1 Domat, Civil Law, B. 1, tit. 18, p. 247.

[5] Cod. Lib. 4, tit. 44, l. 1, 4, 8.

[6] Cod. Lib. 4, tit. 44, l. 4; Id. l. 8, 10. See 1 Domat, B. 1, tit. 18, Vices of Covenants, p. 247.

248. Pothier too, of whom it has been remarked that he is generally swayed by the purest morality, says: 'Equity ought to preside in all agreements. Hence it follows that in contracts of mutual interest where one of the contracting parties gives or does something for the purpose of receiving something else as a price and compensation for it, an injury suffered by one of the contracting parties, even when the other has not had recourse to any artifice to deceive him, is alone sufficient to render such contracts vicious. For as equity in matters of commerce consists in equality, when that equity is violated, as when one of the parties gives more than he receives, the contract is vicious for want of the equity which ought to preside in it.' He immediately adds: 'Although any injury whatever renders contracts inequitable and consequently vicious, and the principle of moral duty (le for interieur) induces the obligation of supplying the just price, yet persons of full age are not allowed in point of law to object to their agreements as being injurious unless the injury be excessive; a rule wisely established for the security and liberty of commerce, which requires that a person shall not be easily permitted to defeat his agreements, otherwise we should not venture upon making any contract for fear that the other party, imagining himself to be injured by the terms of it, would oblige us to follow it by a lawsuit. That injury is commonly deemed excessive which amounts to more than a moiety of the just price. And the person who has suffered such an injury may within ten years obtain letters of rescission for annulling the contract.'[1]

249. After such concessions we may well rest satisfied with the practical convenience of the rule of the common law, which does not make the inequality of the bargain depend solely upon the price, but upon the other attendant circumstances which demonstrate imposition or some undue influence.[2] The Scottish law has adopted the same practical doctrine.[3]

250. This part of the subject may be concluded by the remark that Courts of Equity will not relieve in all cases even of very gross inadequacy, attended with circumstances which might otherwise induce them to act, if the parties cannot be placed in

[1] Pothier on Oblig. n. 33, 34, by Evans; ante, § 247.
[2] 1 Fonbl. Eq. B. 1, ch. 2, § 10.
[3] Erskine, Inst. B. 4, tit. 1, § 27.

statu quo; as for instance in cases of marriage settlements, for the court cannot unmarry the parties.[1]

251. Cases of surprise and sudden action without due deliberation may properly be referred to the same head of fraud or imposition.[2] An undue advantage is taken of the party under circumstances which mislead, confuse, or disturb the just result of his judgment, and thus expose him to be the victim of the artful, the importunate, and the cunning. It has been very justly remarked by an eminent writer that it is not every surprise which will avoid a deed duly made. Nor is it fitting; for

---

[1] 1 Madd. Ch. Pr. 215; North *v.* Ansall, 2 P. Will. 619.

[2] See ante, § 120, note 2; Howe *v.* Wheldon, 2 Ves. 516. Mr. Baron Powel, in the Earl of Bath and Montague's Case (3 Ch. Cas. 56), used the following language : ' It is said that this is a deed that was obtained by surprise and circumvention. Now I perceive this word "surprise" is of a very large and general extent. They say that if the deed be not read to or by the party, that is a surprise; nay, the mistake of a counsel that draws the deed either in his recitals or other things, that is a surprise of a counsel, and the surprise of counsel must be interpreted the surprise of the client, &c. If these things be sufficient to let in a Court of Equity, to set aside deeds found by the verdict to be good in law, then no man's property can be safe. I hardly know any surprise that should be sufficient to set aside a deed after a verdict, unless it be mixed up with fraud, and that expressly proved.' Lord Chief Justice Treby in the same case (p. 74) said: ' As to the first point of surprise, &c., I confess I am still at a loss for the very notion of surprise, for I take it to be either falsehood or forgery, that is, — though I take it they would not use the word in this case, — fraud; if that be not the meaning of it, to be something done unawares, nor with all the precaution and deliberation, as possibly a deed may be done. Here was a case cited not long ago, &c., out of the Civil Law about surprise, &c. A man was informed by his kinsman that his son was dead, and so got him to settle his estate upon him. This is called, in the Civil Law, surreptio, &c. Now the civilians define that thus: "Surreptio est cum per falsam rei narrationem aliquid extorquetur," when a man will by false suggestion prevail upon another to do that which otherwise he would not have done. And I make no doubt that equity ought to set aside that; but then this is probably called a fraud.' See Lord Holt's opinion in the same case (p. 103). The Lord Keeper (Lord Somers) in the same case said (p. 114): ' Now for this word "surprise," it is a word of a general signification, so general and so uncertain that it is impossible to fix it. A man is surprised in every rash and indiscreet action, or whatsoever is not done with so much judgment as it ought to be. But I suppose the gentlemen who use that word in this case mean such surprise as is attended and accompanied with fraud and circumvention. Such a surprise may indeed be a good ground to set aside a deed so obtained in equity, and hath been so in all times. But any other surprise never was, and I hope never will be, because it will introduce such a wild uncertainty in the decrees and judgments of the court as will be of greater consequence than the relief in any case will answer for.' See ante, § 120, note 2.

it would occasion great uncertainty, and it would be impossible to fix what is meant by surprise; for a man may be said to be surprised in every action which is not done with so much discretion as it ought to be.[1] The surprise here intended must be accompanied with fraud and circumvention,[2] or at least by such circumstances as demonstrate that the party had no opportunity to use suitable deliberation, or that there was some influence or management to mislead him. If proper time is not allowed to the party and he acts improvidently, if he is importunately pressed, if those in whom he places confidence make use of strong persuasions, if he is not fully aware of the consequences but is suddenly drawn in to act, if he is not permitted to consult disinterested friends or counsel before he is called upon to act in circumstances of sudden emergency or unexpected right or acquisition, — in these and many like cases, if there has been great inequality in the bargain, Courts of Equity will assist the party upon the ground of fraud, imposition, or unconscionable advantage.[3]

252. Many other cases might be put, illustrative of what is denominated actual or positive fraud.[4] Among these are cases of the fraudulent suppression or destruction of deeds and other instruments in violation of or injury to the rights of others,[5] fraudulent awards with an intent to do injustice,[6] fraudulent and illusory appointments and revocations under powers,[7] fraudulent prevention of acts to be done for the benefit of others under false statements or false promises,[8] frauds in relation to trusts of a

---

[1] 1 Fonbl. Eq. B. 1, ch. 2, § 8.

[2] Ibid.; 1 Madd. Ch. Prac. 212, 213, 214.

[3] Evans v. Llewellyn, 1 Cox, R. 439, 440; s. c. 1 Bro. Ch. R. 150; Irnham v. Child, 1 Bro. Ch. R. 92; Townshend v. Stangroom, 6 Ves. 338; Picket v. Loggon, 14 Ves. 215.

[4] See Com. Dig. Chancery, 3 M. 1, &c.

[5] 1 Madd. Ch. Pr. 255 to 260; Bowles v. Stewart, 1 Sch. & Lefr. 222, 225; Dormer v. Fortescue, 3 Atk. 124; Eyton v. Eyton, 2 Vern. 280; Dalton v. Coatsworth, 1 P. Will. 733.

[6] 1 Madd. Ch. Pr. 233, 234; Brown v. Brown, 1 Vern. 157, and Mr. Raithby's note (1), 159; Com. Dig. Chancery, 2 K. 6; Champion v. Wenham, Ambl. R. 245.

[7] 1 Madd. Ch. Pr. 246 to 252.

[8] 1 Madd. Ch. Pr. 252, 253; Luttrell v. Lord Waltham, 14 Ves. 290; Jones v. Martin, 6 Bro. Parl. Cas. 437; 5 Ves. 266, note; 1 Fonbl. Eq. B. 1, ch. 2, § 13, note (*q*); Id. B. 1, ch. 4, § 25, and notes; 2 Chance on Powers, ch. 23, § 3, art. 3015 to 3025; Sugden on Powers, ch. 6, § 2, pp. 377, 387 (3d edit.).

secret or special nature,[1] frauds in verdicts, judgments, decrees, and other judicial proceedings,[2] (*a*) frauds in the confusion of boundaries of estates and matters of partition and dower,[3] frauds in the administration of charities,[4] and frauds upon creditors and other persons standing upon a like equity.[5]

253. Some of the cases falling under each of these heads belong to that large class of frauds commonly called constructive frauds, which will naturally find a place in our future pages. But as it is the object of these commentaries not merely to treat of questions of relief, but also of principles of jurisdiction, a few instances will be here adduced as examples of both species of fraud.

254. In the first place as to the suppression and destruction of deeds and wills and other instruments. If an heir should suppress them in order to prevent another party as a grantee or a devisee from obtaining the estate vested in him thereby, Courts of Equity upon due proof by other evidence would grant relief, and perpetuate the possession and enjoyment of the estate in such grantee or devisee.[6] For cases for relief against spoliation

---

[1] 2 Madd. Ch. Pr. 97, 98; 1 Hovenden on Frauds, ch. 13, p. 468, &c.; Dalbiac *v.* Dalbiac, 16 Ves. 124.

[2] 1 Madd. Ch. Pr. 236, 237; Com. Dig. Chancery, 3 M. 1, 3 N. 1, 3 W.

[3] 1 Madd. Ch. Pr. 237; Mitf. Eq. Pl. 117; 1 Hovenden on Frauds, ch. 8, p. 239; Id. ch. 9, p. 244.

[4] 2 Hovenden on Frauds, ch. 28, p. 288.

[5] Jeremy on Eq. Jurisd. B. 3, Pt. 2, ch. 3, § 4, p. 411, &c.; 1 Fonbl. Eq. B. 1, ch. 4, §§ 12, 13, 14, and notes; Com. Dig. Chancery, 3 M. 4; Jones *v.* Martin, 6 Bro. Parl. Cas. 437; 5 Ves. 266, note.

[6] See ante, § 184, and note; post, § 440; 1 Fonbl. Eq. B. 1, ch. 2, § 3, note (*u*); Hunt *v.* Matthews, 1 Vern. R. 408; Wardour *v.* Binsford, 1 Vern. R. 452; 2 P. Will. 748, 749; Dalton *v.* Coatsworth, 1 P. Will. 731; Woodreff *v.* Barton, 1 P. Will. 734; Finch *v.* Newnham, 2 Vern. 216; Hampden *v.* Hampden, 1 Bro. Parl. Cas. 250; s. c. cited, 1 P. Will. 733; Barnesly *v.* Powel, 1 Ves. R. 119, 284, 289; Tucker *v.* Phipps, 3 Atk. R. 360. In this last case Lord Hardwicke said: 'In this court the rule is not to allow a suit against an executor for a legacy before a probate of the will; but in the present case the plaintiff ought not to be put to the difficulty of going into the spiritual court to cite the defendant, because that would be giving the defendant a great advantage from his own bad acts in destroying or suppress-

(*a*) Actual as distinguished from constructive fraud is necessary to sustain a bill to set aside a judgment or decree. Patch *v.* Ward, L. R. 3 Ch. 203. It must be shown that there was a good defence to an action resulting in a judgment alleged to have been obtained by fraud. White *v.* Crow, 110 U. S. 183.

come in a favorable light before Courts of Equity, 'in odium spoliatoris'; and where the contents of a suppressed or destroyed instrument are proved, the party (as he ought) will receive the same benefit as if the instrument were produced.[1] (a)

ing the will; for here the spoliation is, I think, proved so sufficiently as to entitle the plaintiff to come here in the first instance for a decree. As to the spoliation, consider it generally as a personal legacy where the will is destroyed or concealed by the executor, and I think in such a case if the spoliation is proved plainly (though the general rule is to cite the executor into the Ecclesiastical Court), the legatee may properly come here for a decree upon the head of spoliation and suppression. There are several cases where if spoliation or suppression is proved it will change the jurisdiction and give this court a jurisdiction which it had not originally; as in the case of Lord Hunsdon, Hob. 109, where the title was a title merely at law, yet there being a suppression of the deeds under which that title accrued, the plaintiff had a decree here for possession and quiet enjoyment. As the jurisdiction may be changed with regard to a court of law, why may it not with regard to the Spiritual Court; and I think the case of Weeks v. Weeks, which came before me some time ago, an authority that it may; here the spoliation or suppression is certainly fraudulent, voluntary, and malicious, and therefore differs from the case of Pascall v. Pickering, where the spoliation did by no means appear to be fraudulent or malicious, but rather inadvertently done, and without any bad design. I think in such cases of malicious and fraudulent spoliations the court will not put the plaintiff under the difficulty of going into the Ecclesiastical Court, where he must meet with much more difficulty than proving the contents of a deed at law which has been lost or secreted. For in the Spiritual Court the plaintiff must prove it a will in writing, and must likewise prove the contents in the very words, which will be a difficulty almost insuperable, and which Courts of Law do not put a person upon doing; the plaintiff must also prove the whole will, though the remainder of it does not at all belong to or regard his legacy. I think if this had been a mere personal legacy, the court under the circumstances of this case ought to interpose; and the rather, because in bringing suits against an executor this court goes further in requiring a probate than courts at law. But here the case is stronger to entitle the plaintiff to a decree, because the legacy is out of real and personal estate both; and as to the real estate there is no occasion to prove the will in the Spiritual Court to entitle the legatee to recover his legacy out of the real estate. This would be clearly the case where the charge is only upon the real estate; and though the heir is entitled to have the personal estate to exonerate his real, yet if he is made executor, and has, by a voluntary and fraudulent act, put the legatee under such difficulties as make it almost impossible for him to prove the will, it is reasonable to let in the legatee to have his legacy, and leave the executor to pay himself out of the personal estate.'

[1] Saltern v. Melhuish, Ambler, R. 247; Cowper v. Cowper, 2 P. Will. 748, &c.; Rex v. Arundel, Hob. R. 109; Hampden v. Hampden, 1 P. Will. 733; 1 Bro. Parl. Cas. 250; Bowles v. Stewart, 1 Sch. & Lefr. 225.

(a) But laches may bar relief in such cases. Chatham v. Hoare, L. R. 9 Eq. 571.

255. In the next place, frauds in regard to powers of appointment. A person having a power of appointment for the benefit of others shall not by any contrivance use it for his own benefit. Thus if a parent has a power to appoint to such of his children as he may choose, he shall not by exercising it in favor of a child in a consumption gain the benefit of it himself, (*a*) or by a secret agreement with a child in whose favor he makes it derive a beneficial interest from the execution of it.[1] The same rule applies to cases where a parent, having a power to appoint among his children, makes an illusory appointment by giving to one child a nominal and not a substantial share; for in such a case Courts of Equity will treat the execution as a fraud upon the power.[2]

256. In the next place the fraudulent prevention of acts to be done for the benefit of third persons. Courts of Equity hold themselves entirely competent to take from third persons, and a fortiori from the party himself, the benefit which he may have derived from his own fraud, imposition, or undue influence in procuring the suppression of such acts.[3] Thus where a person had fraudulently prevented another upon his death-bed from suffering a recovery at law with a view that the estate might devolve upon another person with whom he was connected, it

[1] McQueen *v.* Farquhar, 11 Ves. 479; Meyn *v.* Belcher, 1 Eden, R. 138; Palmer *v.* Wheeler, 2 Ball & Beatt. 18; Sugden on Powers, ch. 7, § 2; Morris *v.* Clarkson, 1 Jac. & Walk. 111.

[2] Sugden on Powers, ch. 7, § 2; ch. 9, § 4; Butcher *v.* Butcher, 9 Ves. 382; 2 Hovenden on Frauds, ch. 23, p. 220, &c.; 1 Madd. Ch. Pr. 246 to 252; Campbell *v.* Horne, 1 Younge & Coll. N. R. Ch. 664.

[3] Bridgman *v.* Green, 2 Ves. R. 627; Huguenin *v.* Baseley, 14 Ves. 289; ante, § 252; post, § 768.

(*a*) Topham *v.* Portland, 11 H. L. Cas. 32; s. c. L. R. 5 Ch. 40; Williams's Appeal, 73 Penn. 249, 284; Hinchinbrooke *v.* Seymour, 1 Bro. C. C. 395, — a case explained and denied in Henty *v.* Wrey, 21 Ch. D. 332, 343, 344, so far as it may be thought to decide that a power for children shall not be raised until wanted. See also Wellesley *v.* Mornington, 2 Kay & J. 143; Keily *v.* Keily, 4 Dru. & W. 38; s. c. 2 Con. & L. 334. In Henty *v.* Wrey, supra, Lindley, L. J., says, at p. 359, that appointments vesting portions charged on land in children of tender age who die soon afterwards are looked upon with suspicion, and that very little additional evidence of improper motive will induce the courts to set aside the appointment or treat it as invalid; but that without some additional evidence this will not be done. Nor will the mere fact that the appointor may derive some benefit with the appointees be fatal necessarily to the exercise of the power. In re Huish, L. R. 10 Eq. 5; Cooper *v.* Cooper, L. R. 5 Ch. 203.

was adjudged that the estate ought to be held as if the recovery had been perfected, and that it was against conscience to suffer it to remain where it was.[1] So if a testator should communicate his intention to a devisee of charging a legacy on his estate, and the devisee should tell him that it is unnecessary and he will pay it; the legacy being thus prevented, the devisee will be charged with the payment.[2] And where a party procures a testator to make a new will, appointing him as executor, and agrees to hold the property in trust for the use of an intended legatee, he will be held a trustee for the latter upon the like ground of fraud.[3]

257. We may close this head of positive or actual fraud by referring to another class of frauds of a very peculiar and distinct character. Gifts and legacies are often bestowed upon persons upon condition that they shall not marry without the consent of parents, guardians, or other confidential persons. And the question has sometimes occurred how far Courts of Equity can or ought to interfere where such consent is fraudulently withheld by the proper party for the express purpose of defeating the gift or legacy, or of insisting upon some private and selfish advantage, or from motives of a corrupt, unreasonable, or vicious nature. The doctrine now firmly established upon this subject is that Courts of Equity will not suffer the manifest object of the condition to be defeated by the fraud, or dishonest, corrupt, or unreasonable refusal of the party whose consent is required to the marriage.[4] It is indeed a very delicate and difficult duty to be performed by such courts. But to permit a different rule to prevail would be to encourage frauds and to enable a party to withhold consent upon grounds utterly wrong or upon motives grossly corrupt and unreasonable.

[1] Luttrell v. Lord Waltham, cited 14 Ves. 290; s. c. 11 Ves. 638.
[2] Cited in Mestaer v. Gillespie, 11 Ves. 638. See Goss v. Tracey, 1 P. Will. 288; 2 Vern. 700; Thynn v. Thynn, 1 Vern. 296; Reach v. Kennigate, Ambler, R. 67; Chamberlain v. Agar, 2 Ves. & B. 259; Drakeford v. Walker, 3 Atk. 539.
[3] Thynn v. Thynn, 1 Vern. 296; Reach v. Kennigate, Ambler, R. 67; Devenish v. Barnes, Prec. Ch. 3; Oldham v. Litchfield, 2 Vern. R. 504; Barrow v. Greenough, 3 Ves. 152; Chamberlain v. Agar, 2 Ves. & B. 262; Whitton v. Russell, 1 Atk. R. 448. See also cases in note (a) to 3 Ves. 39.
[4] Peyton v. Bury, 2 P. Will. 625, 628; Eastladd v. Reynolds, 1 Dick. R. 317; Goldsmid v. Goldsmid, 19 Ves. 368; Strange v. Smith, Ambler, R. 263; Clarke v. Parkins, 19 Ves. 1, 12; Mesgrett v. Mesgrett, 2 Vern. R. 580; Merry v. Ryves, 1 Eden, R. 1, 4.

Printed in the United States
42593LVS00001B/6